PERSISTERS AND DESISTERS IN CRIME FROM ADOLESCENCE INTO ADULTHOOD

Persisters and Desisters in Crime from Adolescence into Adulthood

Explanation, Prevention and Punishment

Edited by

ROLF LOEBER,
University of Pittsburgh, USA

MACHTELD HOEVE,
University of Amsterdam, The Netherlands

N. WIM SLOT
VU University Amsterdam, The Netherlands

PETER H. VAN DER LAAN
Netherlands Institute for the Study of Crime and Law Enforcement and VU University Amsterdam, The Netherlands

Routledge
Taylor & Francis Group
LONDON AND NEW YORK

First published 2012 by Ashgate Publishing

Published 2016 by Routledge
2 Park Square, Milton Park, Abingdon, Oxfordshire OX14 4RN
711 Third Avenue, New York, NY 10017, USA

First issued in paperback 2016

Routledge is an imprint of the Taylor & Francis Group, an informa business

British Library Cataloguing in Publication Data
Persisters and desisters in crime from adolescent into
adulthood : explanation, prevention and punishment.
1. Juvenile delinquency. 2. Criminal psychology.
3. Recidivists. 4. Juvenile delinquents--Rehabilitation.
5. Crime prevention. 6. Crime and age.
I. Loeber, Rolf.
364.3-dc23

Library of Congress Cataloging-in-Publication Data
Persisters and desisters in crime from adolescence into adulthood :
explanation, prevention, and punishment/by Rolf Loeber ... [et al.].
p. cm.
Includes bibliographical references and index.
ISBN 978-1-4094-3192-3 (hardback)
1. Crime and age. 2. Juvenile delinquency--Age factors. 3.
Juvenile delinquency--Prevention. I. Loeber, Rolf.
HV6163.P47 2012
364.36--dc23

2011052210

ISBN 13: 978-1-138-27445-7 (pbk)
ISBN 13: 978-1-4094-3192-3 (hbk)

Contents

List of Figures, Tables and Boxes

Tables

Boxes

List of Contributors

Jessica J. Asscher is Assistant Professor at the Department of Forensic Child and Youth Care Sciences at the University of Amsterdam, The Netherlands. She graduated in Developmental Psychology. Her main research interests are effectiveness of prevention and intervention programmes, the development of problem behaviour, and psychopathy.

Margit Averdijk is Research Associate at the Swiss Federal Institute of Technology Zurich (ETH; Zurich Project for the Social Development of Children and Youths) and at the University of Zurich (Criminological Institute), Switzerland. Her research interests include the study of victimization, social contexts of crime, and individuals' development of violent behaviour.

Catrien C.J.H. Bijleveld is Professor of Research Methods in Criminology at the VU University Amsterdam, The Netherlands, and is a senior researcher at the Netherlands Institute for the Study of Crime and Law Enforcement (NSCR), Amsterdam. Her research interests include criminal careers, sex offending, experimental criminological research, and international crime.

Arjan A.J. Blokland is Professor of Criminology and Criminal Justice at the Department of Criminology at Leiden University, The Netherlands, and is a Senior Researcher at the Netherlands Institute for the Study of Crime and Law Enforcement (NSCR), Amsterdam. His research mainly focuses on developmental and life-course criminology. He is the principle investigator of the Transition to Adulthood in Amsterdam Study and, with Patrick Lussier, is editing the book *Sex Offenders: A Criminal Career Approach.*

Martine Blom is Researcher at the WODC (Research and Documentation Centre) of the Dutch ministry of Security and Justice, The Hague, The Netherlands. She studied social psychology and methodology at Leiden University. Her research interests are in life-course criminology and trends in (juvenile) crime rates. Furthermore she is associated with several studies in which (interventions concerning) traffic offenders are central.

Leonieke Boendermaker is Professor of the Implementation in Youth Care at the Hogeschool van Amsterdam, University of Applied Sciences (HvA), and Senior Researcher at the Department of Special Needs Education and Youth Care, Faculty of Behavioural and Social Sciences, University of Groningen, The Netherlands. Her research interests include the development, implementation, fidelity and effectiveness of interventions with a special focus on residential care and antisocial and delinquent behaviour.

Erik Bulten is Psychologist, Head of Assessment, Research and Professional Development at the Pompe Foundation, Nijmegen, and Senior Researcher at the ACSW, Radboud University, Nijmegen, The Netherlands. His expertise is in forensic psychiatry.

Maja Deković is Professor at Utrecht University, The Netherlands, and leader of the research programme 'Development and Treatment of Psychosocial Problems'. Her research interests include development of problem behaviour, parent–child relationships, family interaction, and effects of family-based interventions.

Andrea G. Donker is Professor at the University of Applied Sciences, Leiden, and Senior Researcher at the University of Applied Sciences, Utrecht, The Netherlands. Her expertise is in developmental criminology and biopsychocriminology, and recently she started working on the dual role relationship in probation work.

Henk Elffers is Professor of Empirical Research into Criminal Law Enforcement at the VU University Amsterdam, The Netherlands, and is Senior Researcher at The Netherlands Institute for the Study of Crime and Law Enforcement (NSCR), Amsterdam. He graduated in mathematical statistics at the University of Amsterdam, and received his Ph.D. in Psychology of Law at Erasmus University Rotterdam on a thesis on income tax evasion. He held various research appointments in Amsterdam (mathematics), Utrecht (geography), Rotterdam and Antwerp (Belgium, law and psychology). His research interests are spatial aspects of crime, rational choice theory of rule compliance, relationship between judges and the general public, and measurement in criminology.

David P. Farrington, O.B.E., is Professor of Psychological Criminology at the Institute of Criminology, Cambridge University and Adjunct Professor of Psychiatry at Western Psychiatric Institute and Clinic, University of Pittsburgh, USA. He is Director of the Cambridge Study in Delinquent Development, which is a prospective longitudinal survey of over 400 London males from age 8 to age 48. His major research interest is in developmental criminology. In addition to over 500 published journal articles and book chapters on criminological and psychological topics, he has published over 75 books, monographs and government reports.

Kristine Amlund Hagen is Research Director at the Center for Child and Adolescent Mental Health, Eastern and Southern Norway (RBUP, Oslo, Norway). In recent years, she has conducted intervention research on families with children and adolescents with conduct problems. She received her Ph.D. in Developmental

Psychology from Virginia Commonwealth University in 2004. Her doctoral research focused on risk and resilience in children and youth, specifically children who experienced parental incarceration. She has published on social competence, antisocial behaviour, effects of family and community interventions, and risk and protective factors.

Jan Hendriks studied pedagogics and psychology at Leiden University, The Netherlands. His Ph.D. focused on subtypes and recidivism of juvenile sex offenders. He is working as a clinical psychologist at De Waag in The Hague, a forensic psychiatric outpatient treatment centre. He is Professor of Forensic Psychiatry and Psychology at the VU University Amsterdam, and Professor of Forensic Pedagogics at the University of Amsterdam. His research interests include (juvenile) sex offenders, (young) female offenders and forensic interventions.

Machteld Hoeve is Assistant Professor of Forensic Child and Youth Care Sciences at the Research Institute Child Development and Education of the University of Amsterdam, The Netherlands. Currently, she is a Marie Curie visiting research fellow at the Division of Child and Adolescent Psychiatry of Columbia University (2011–2012). Her research interests include the development of delinquency, and specifically, environmental influences such as family processes, psychopathology, and gender differences in relation to development of criminal behaviour.

Martin Killias is Professor of Criminology and Criminal Law at the University of Zurich, Switzerland. He has been involved in international crime victimization and self-reported delinquency surveys as well as in comparative research in the field of criminal justice. From 1993–2010, he chaired the European Sourcebook of Crime and Criminal Justice Statistics project. He has also directed several randomized trials on the effects of different sanctions.

Willemijn H. Lame is a Ph.D. student at the Netherlands Institute for the Study of Crime and Law Enforcement (NSCR) in Amsterdam. Her research interests include probation supervision, the effects of sanctions, and victimization.

Ton Liefaard is Assistant Law Professor and Researcher at the Willem Pompe Institute of Criminal Law and Criminology, Utrecht University, and Professor of Children's Rights (UNICEF-chair), Leiden University, The Netherlands. In addition, he is a deputy juvenile judge at the District Court of Amsterdam and a member of the independent supervisory committee of a closed youth institution for boys in Amsterdam. His research focuses primarily on the interpretation and implementation of international human rights law affecting children and the law at the domestic level. He has a special interest in youth justice and children in detention. He has published various academic articles and a number of books and research reports.

Rolf Loeber is Distinguished University Professor of Psychiatry, and Professor of Psychology and Epidemiology at the University of Pittsburgh, USA, and Professor of Juvenile Delinquency and Social Development at the Free University, Amsterdam, The Netherlands. He is Co-director of the Life History Program and is principal investigator of two longitudinal studies, the Pittsburgh Youth Study and the Pittsburgh Girls Study. He has published widely in the fields of juvenile antisocial behaviour and delinquency, substance use, and mental health problems.

Mauri Matsuda is a Ph.D. student in the Department of Criminology and Criminal Justice at the University of Maryland, College Park, USA. Her research interests include neighbourhood dynamics, the life course, macrostructural perspectives, and the role of race, gender and class inequality in crime and justice.

Terje Ogden is Professor at the Institute of Psychology, University of Oslo, Norway, and Research Director at the Norwegian Center for Child Behavioral Development, Unirand (from 2003). The aim of the Center is to integrate research and practice in order to increase multidisciplinary knowledge and enhance clinical competence in the prevention and treatment of serious behaviour problems among children and youth. He has been the director of the research programme on the national implementation and evaluation of empirically supported programmes for the prevention and treatment of serious behaviour problems in children and youth in Norway. He is also the project leader of a longitudinal prospective study of the social development of children in which the development of approximately 1,200 children is followed from 6 months to 4 years (The Behavior Outlook Norwegian Developmental Study – BONDS).

Hanneke Palmen has been since July 2009 a post-doctoral researcher on the TransAM project at the Netherlands Institute for the Study of Crime and Law Enforcement (NSCR) in Amsterdam. She obtained her M.A. degree in Developmental Psychology at Utrecht University, The Netherlands, in 2002, after which she entered a Ph.D. programme at the Research Centre Psychosocial Development in Context at Utrecht University in 2005. From 2005–2009 she worked on her Ph.D. project about peer relations and aggression.

Santiago Redondo is Professor of Criminology at the University of Barcelona, Spain. He is Principal Researcher of the group Advanced Studies in Violence (http://www.ub.edu/geav) at this same university. His former positions were as prison psychologist, prison governor, and director of prison rehabilitation services at the Justice Department of the Region of Catalonia, Spain. His current research is in the fields of treatment programmes for offenders, risk assessment, developmental criminology and criminological theory. He has published numerous papers, book chapters and books on such topics as offender rehabilitation, juvenile delinquency, sex and partner violence, social control, and general criminology.

Stijn Ruiter is Senior Researcher at the Netherlands Institute for the Study of Crime and Law Enforcement (NSCR), Amsterdam. He studied Sociology at the University of Nijmegen, and received his Ph.D. in Social Sciences from the Radboud University Nijmegen, The Netherlands. His research interests include spatio-temporal aspects of crime, life-course criminology, simulation in criminology, and public opinions about sentencing.

Jerzy Sarnecki is Professor of General Criminology at Stockholm University, Sweden. He has worked as a researcher at the Swedish National Council for Crime Prevention, where he was between 1986 and 1993 head of the inquiry division. The main focus of his research is criminal networks and life course studies. He has published a number of reports, articles, chapters, books and textbooks in criminology, bureaucratic systems, police efficiency, and leisure-time activities among young people. He is co-chairman of the jury for the Stockholm Prize in Criminology. He has received numerous research grants and has led a large number of major research projects.

Meike I. Slagt is Junior Researcher at Utrecht University, The Netherlands. Her research interests include child-rearing processes and how these shape child development, children's differential susceptibility to parenting, and prevention of problem behaviour.

N. Wim Slot is Professor of Developmental Othopedagogy at the VU University Amsterdam, The Netherlands. His research interests are child protection, antisocial behaviour and youth care.

Han J.M. Spanjaard is Psychologist and Researcher at Peadologisch Institute (PI) Research in Duivendrecht, The Netherlands, and develops methods and programmes for youth care. He has written manuals and books and developed and conducted various training programmes for professionals who work with children and families. He is interested in cognitive and social skill training, family treatment, residential treatment, juvenile delinquency, juvenile sex offenders, prevention, and assessment instruments.

Geert Jan J.M. Stams is Professor of Forensic Child and Youth Care Sciences at the University of Amsterdam, The Netherlands. He has conducted meta-analyses, longitudinal research and intervention studies in the area of socio-emotional and moral development. His interests include parent–child relationship quality, juvenile delinquency, developmental psychopathology, and effectiveness of youth care.

Terence P. Thornberry is Distinguished University Professor in the Department of Criminology and Criminal Justice at the University of Maryland, USA, and the Principal Investigator of the Rochester Youth Development Study, a three-generation panel study begun in 1986 to examine the causes and consequences of delinquency and other forms of antisocial behaviours. In 2008 he was the recipient of the American Society of Criminology's Edwin H. Sutherland Award. He is the author of a number of books including *Gangs and Delinquency in Developmental Perspective*, which received the American Society of Criminology's Michael J. Hindelang Award in 2004.

Victor van der Geest is Assistant Professor of Criminology at the VU University Amsterdam, The Netherlands, and researcher at the Netherlands Institute for the Study of Crime and Law Enforcement (NSCR), Amsterdam. His research interests include criminal careers, and more specifically, mutual influences between employment and crime, and the role of substance abuse.

Leontien M. van der Knaap is Associate Professor at the International Victimology Institute Tilburg (INTERVICT) at Tilburg University, The Netherlands. Previously, she has worked as a senior researcher at the Research and Documentation Centre of the Dutch Ministry of Justice. She is a developmental psychologist and received her Ph.D. from the VU University Amsterdam. Her main research interests are risk assessment, domestic violence, and child and adolescent development.

André M. van der Laan is Senior Researcher at the WODC (Research and Documentation Centre) of the Dutch Ministry of Security and Justice, The Hague, Netherlands. He studied developmental psychology at the University of Leiden, The Netherlands, and received his Ph.D. from the University of Groningen, The Netherlands, on the topic of 'Defiance and Delinquency'. His research interests are in developmental and life-course criminology and explanations of trends in juvenile crime rates, the effects of juvenile sanctions, and juvenile experiences of judicial sanctions.

Peter H. van der Laan is Professor of Probation and Parole at the VU University Amsterdam, The Netherlands, and is Senior Researcher at the Netherlands Institute for the Study of Crime and Law enforcement (NSCR), Amsterdam. His research interests include juvenile delinquency, criminal justice issues, and the effectiveness of criminal justice interventions.

Claudia E. van der Put is Postdoctoral Research Fellow at the Department of Forensic Child and Youth Care Sciences, University of Amsterdam, The Netherlands. She is an advisor for the Dutch Ministry of Justice on developing and implementing risk assessment instruments used in juvenile justice.

Preface

Paul Schnabel

Four years ago, on 7 January 2008, the cover of the German weekly *Der Spiegel* pronounced in big letters: 'Junge Männer: die gefährlichste Spezies der Welt' ('Young men: The world's most dangerous species'). In more than ten pages, the article expounded the extent to which crime, and violent crime in particular, is the pursuit of young men between the ages of 15 and 25. They are the most dangerous 'species', no less, not even defined as a group or an age phase, and clearly very different from the rest of society. Obviously, this is exaggerated, yet the German figures alone show us how deviant the picture of adolescent young males is. Two per cent of the young men aged between 16 and 20 are suspected of one or more violent crimes; the same goes for more than one per cent of the boys between the ages of 14 and 15 and also for more than one per cent of the men aged between 21 and 24. Above that age, the figure rapidly drops to less than 0.1 per cent. On occasion, girls and young women also become physically aggressive, but even during their most violent age phase (ages 18–20) this involves no more than one girl against eight boys. Moreover, there is also an overrepresentation of migrants among the boys.

What is true for Germany also roughly applies to the Netherlands and all other Western countries. Violent crime is chiefly committed by adolescent men, often against other young men. It is frequently thought that this phenomenon is on the rise, yet rather the opposite is true. Nowadays we pay much more public attention to it, and as a result we also worry more about young people's aggressive behaviour. The sensitivity to the violence that is actually committed has continually increased as well. This is by no means contrary to the fascination with the portrayal of violence in films, cartoons, games or pop music. The kind of behaviour that is now increasingly becoming taboo in everyday life gets free rein in the realm of fantasy. That this in turn might serve as a source of unwanted examples is still the subject of debate.

It is rather the exception than the rule that research provides a definitive answer to urgent social issues. Usually, such issues are more encompassing than can be answered in research, let alone in one study. More often than not, the answers are not unambiguous either. Correlations are not yet causalities. Even when, for instance, the risk factors have been soundly mapped out, the predictive value is generally small in specific cases. This makes it necessary to exercise caution with preventive or early interventions on the one hand, and makes it inevitable to continue taking into account unexpected violent behaviour on the other.

A lot of research has been done on the causes and backgrounds of criminal behaviour. Meanwhile, it has become clear that monocausal argumentations make no sense in this context. It always involves a complicated, combined interaction of biological, psychological and social factors in a particular historical, social, political and economic context.

In due course, the attention shifts from one type of factor to the other – from biological to sociological or psychological factors and back again – but it never returns exactly to its original focus. In the meantime, the various disciplines also continue to develop and constantly offer new theoretical, methodological and statistical approaches. Brain activity can now be observed *in vivo*, while researchers in psychology have continuously improved and standardized measuring instruments at their disposal and researchers in sociology have improved not only their statistical descriptions but their explanatory abilities as well.

The present, extensive study by Loeber et al. try to find an answer to the question about the chances and the nature of the shift from the delinquent behaviour of young people to the criminal behaviour of adults. Most adolescents or young men do not stick to delinquent, criminal or violent behaviour. Precisely on or just past the threshold of adulthood, the criminal activity rapidly diminishes, to finally come to an end completely. This does not apply to all, however, and exactly those who remain active often cause society the greatest harm.

Now, who stays criminally active and who does not? Why do some young men remain criminally active while most do not? In brief, these are the questions on which this book focuses, step by step and very systematically, in a summarizing presentation and critical discussion of the scientific research literature. This deals with a lot of material, which often provides very different and sometimes even completely contradictory outcomes with regard to the same subject. Nonetheless, with regard to outcomes, a dominant one often emerges, while some studies are also clearly superior to others because of their set-up and scale.

Due to its structure, this study is something in between a thesaurus (what research has been done?) and a meta-analysis (which research material can be included in the new analysis?). Because of the strict approach, during which the authors also continually examine possible alternative or competing explanations and connections, each chapter generates the further growth of a decision tree with branches of varying strength and a roof of foliage of variable density. The enormous volume of the discussed research material and the continuous branching off of the research questions carry with them the danger that readers will be unable to see the wood for the trees. Yet luckily, the summarizing accounts and the closing chapter will come to their aid time and again. These also contain a number of recommendations for research and policy.

Young men remain a dangerous species. Loeber et al. do not offer a solution to that problem, but they have carefully mapped out the risk factors at play and also give advice about the best or at least better methods to deal with this problem. After all, the ultimate goal is to stop young men from inflicting serious and all too often irreparable damage to their own lives or the lives of others as the result of their behaviour.

Paul Schnabel
The Netherlands Institute for Social Research/SCP
The Hague, The Netherlands

Preface

Friedrich Lösel

During the twentieth century the situation of young people changed dramatically. There is not only a much earlier onset of puberty and a strong physical acceleration, but also in many countries a change of lifestyles due to less authoritarian parenting, mass media, and other modern influences. Therefore, typical youth behaviours are now exhibited at younger ages, for example, going out at night, drinking alcohol, smoking, having sexual relations, and hanging around in cliques. However, the physical and social acceleration has not led to an earlier maturation into adulthood. In contrast, important developmental tasks are now mastered later than in former times (for example, completing education, regular work, socioeconomic independence, marriage, and foundation of own family).

As the offending of young people is often related to developmental transitions and coping problems (Moffitt, 1993), such epochal changes are also relevant for criminology. And indeed, young adulthood is a particularly important period for criminological research and practice. Traditionally, the 'iron law' of the age–crime curve shows that offending strongly increases during adolescence and then decreases at around age 18. However, the peak of prevalence in the age–crime curve does not only vary for different types of crime, but is partially shifting towards young adulthood. In England and Wales or Germany, for example, the prevalence of official crime per 100,000 of the respective age group is already higher at ages 18–20 than at 14–17 years (Lösel, 2012). Similar trends have been observed in the Netherlands (this volume). In contrast to such observations, criminological research and the justice systems focus on either juvenile delinquency or adult offending in general. It seems as if the most common legal definition of 'adulthood' at age 18 functions as too sharp a cutoff, although various countries have more differentiated approaches in criminal law. Such a dichotomy may conceal that the transition from late adolescence to young adulthood is a very important period for late onset, continuity, and aggravation of or desistance from offending. Of course, most offenders desist over time and many beyond age 30 (Laub and Sampson, 2003); however, the turning points in criminal careers often coincide with stable employment and marriage in young adulthood. For the latter reason, this age period is also relevant for not transferring behavioural and social problems to the next generation (Farrington, Coid and Murray, 2009).

Although prospective longitudinal studies have substantially increased our knowledge on the origins and long-term development of criminal behaviour across the lifespan, the highly dynamic period of young adulthood has rarely been addressed. Only recently there is more awareness of the issue that young adult offenders are somehow lost in transition. Therefore, the present volume is highly welcome. It contains thorough analyses and new findings on both continuity and change in the development of offending from adolescence to adulthood. The authors describe different patterns of criminal 'careers' and investigate risk and protective factors as well as causal explanations of various trajectories. In doing this, the focus is not only on the individual but also on micro-level and wider social contexts. In addition to these developmental analyses, the book contains very rich material on practical issues such as risk assessment, early developmental prevention, punishment, correctional intervention, and an organization of criminal justice that meets the specific needs and challenges of offenders in the transition from adolescence into adulthood. From my British and German background I see it as a particular strength of this book that it not only addresses North American data and structures (as it is most often the case in criminology), but takes a broad international perspective.

The working group of experts who have produced this impressive volume have done an excellent job with regard to both the quality of individual chapters and their integration. In my view, this is the richest and deepest empirical and conceptual investigation that has yet been carried out on the transition from adolescent to young adult offending. The book complements and extends similarly valuable reports of previous working groups on child delinquency and youth offending that have also been coordinated by Rolf Loeber (Loeber and Farrington, 1998, 2001). Together with these volumes on earlier ages, the present book suggests that it is never too early and never too late for evidence-based interventions into antisocial development.

The volume is a milestone of developmental criminology and extremely useful for research, teaching, practice, and policy making. An effective transfer of its evidence-based recommendations into practice will not only help to reduce (re-)offending and its related harm, but also save money for society. As many countries have to cope with the current financial crisis, this message is very timely and highly welcome.

Friedrich Lösel
Institute of Criminology, Cambridge University
England

References

Farrington, D.P., Coid, J.W., and Murray, J. (2009). Family factors in the intergenerational transmission of offending. *Criminal Behaviour and Mental Health*, 19, 109–24.

Laub, J.H. and Sampson, R.J. (2003). *Shared Beginnings, Divergent Lives: Delinquent Boys to Age 70*. Cambridge, MA: Harvard University Press.

Loeber, R. and Farrington, D.P. (eds) (1998). *Serious & Violent Juvenile Offenders: Risk Factors and Successful Interventions*. Thousand Oaks, CA: Sage.

Loeber, R. and Farrington, D.P. (eds) (2001). *Child Delinquents: Development, Intervention and Service Needs*. Thousand Oaks, CA: Sage.

Lösel, F. (2012). What works in correctional treatment and rehabilitation for young adults? In F. Lösel, A.E. Bottoms and D.P. Farrington (eds), *Young Adult Offenders: Lost in Transition?* Milton Park: Routledge.

Moffitt, T. (1993). Adolescence-limited and life-course-persistent antisocial behavior: A developmental taxonomy. *Psychological Review*, 100, 674–701.

Acknowledgements

This volume would not have appeared without the strong support from the Netherlands Institute for the Study of Crime and Law Enforcement (NSCR), particularly its Director, Gerben Bruinsma. We are much indebted for the administrative support provided by Ariena van Poppel and Peter van der Voort in Amsterdam and Jennifer Wilson in Pittsburgh, who have assisted greatly with the references. Anne Mullin Burnham assisted in a wonderful way with the checking of the English language and the readability of the chapters.

We are very grateful for the advice and support from our advisory board, including Gerben Bruinsma (NSCR), Martin Dirksen (Jeugdzorg Overijssel), Theo Doreleijers (VU), Shadik Harchaoui (Voorzitter Raad van Bestuur Forum), Frans Leeuw (WODC), Peter Nijkamp (VU), Paul Schnabel (NISR/SCP), Dieneke ten Hoorn Boer (Directeur-Generaal Preventie, Jeugd en Sancties), Monique de Groot (plaatsvervangend Directeur Directie Jeugd en Sancties) and Ineke van der Zande (Veiligheidsregio Kennemerland).

We benefited also from a focus group convened in Amsterdam with the expert advice from Rosaly Brandon, Mette van Duin (Amsterdam, Openbare Orde en Veiligheid), Marjan Koopman (Spirit), Herman Budde (Bureau Jeugdzorg, reclassering), Ron Goudsmit (Openbaar Ministerie), Rob Schuddemat (Schrikkerstichting), Ronnie van de Water (Judge), Natasja Los (police of the City of Amsterdam), Martin Wiznertzer (Dutch Institute for Forensic Psychiatry and Psychology) and Marije Stoter (Probation Service). In addition, we are grateful for Arne Popma's advice.

Throughout the years members of the study group had contact with many of the members of the US study group on the same topic (chaired by Rolf Loeber and David P. Farrington), resulting in frequent sharing of ideas and information relevant to North America and Europe. We are particularly grateful to David P. Farrington for his hard work and advice in advancing the work of the two study groups.

We would like also to thank our partners (Herman van den Berg, Magda Stouthamer-Loeber, Monika Smit and René Peeters) for their patience and support during the formative period of the study group and the time that we needed to write and edit this volume. The senior editor is also much indebted to Lucille Stark for her kind hospitality in her house in the country over many weekends of work on this volume.

Rolf Loeber, Machteld Hoeve, N. Wim Slot, and Peter H. van der Laan
Former Penal Colony, Veenhuizen, Netherlands, March/June 2011

Editors' Summary

Rolf Loeber, Machteld Hoeve, N. Wim Slot and
Peter H. van der Laan

All adolescents eventually become adults, but they differ in the speed at which and the degree to which they reach adulthood, adopt adult roles, and stop irresponsible and impulsive behaviours that are often characteristic of adolescence and early adulthood. We are particularly concerned with the transition between juvenile delinquency and adult crime for three categories of individuals: young people who persist in offending from adolescence to early adulthood; youth who desist from offending, particularly between adolescence and early adulthood; and those individuals who start offending during early adulthood (Figure 1.1). These offenders inflict harm on a large proportion of the population, which is costly for the victims, the justice system and society alike.

Although lawmakers, justice personnel and the general public tend to have strong opinions about the transition from juvenile delinquency to adult crime and what causes individual differences in persistence, desistance and onset of offending, the debates usually do not include the empirical evidence from hundreds of relevant studies. This volume attempts to rectify this situation by presenting the current state of empirical evidence for the course of offending between adolescence and early adulthood, causal factors influencing that course, and optimal interventions inside and outside of the justice system to reduce offending at the interface between adolescence and adulthood.

To gather and interpret the empirical evidence, we brought together and sought the advice of a study group of 33 scholars from the Netherlands and other parts of Europe, and invited them to contribute to the present international report. The study group members were asked to address a series of questions about which offenders tend to persist in offending between adolescence and early adulthood, which juvenile offenders tend to desist from offending, and which individuals tend to have early adult onset of offending. In addition, they were asked to report on explanations of persistence in and desistance from offending, special categories of high-risk offenders, and how effectively juvenile and adult justice systems deal with offenders in the adolescent to early adulthood period. The main focus was on findings from Dutch research and relating these findings to research in other European countries and in the US. Our study group findings were reinforced by the findings of a US study group of 32 scholars, chaired by Rolf Loeber and David P. Farrington. The findings from the US study group report can be found in the Conclusions (Chapter 12) to this volume.

The relationship between offending and age is bell-shaped: the *prevalence* of offending (the percentage of offenders in a population) tends to increase from late childhood, peaks in the teenage years (around ages 15–19), and then declines in the early 20s (Figure 1.2). This bell-shaped age trend is called the *age–crime curve*, which is universal in all Western populations.

Research shows that, irrespective of the age of onset of offending, most desistance from juvenile delinquency takes place in the right-hand down-slope tail of the age–crime curve. This down-slope varies between different populations of young people but often extends from adolescence to adulthood. Unexpectedly, Dutch research shows that officially registered offending is more prevalent during early adulthood than during the juvenile years.

Persistence, Desistance and Onset

The key questions addressed in this volume concerning criminal careers are: *How common is persistence in and desistance from offending between adolescence and early adulthood, and how common is the onset of offending during early adulthood?*

There is strong continuity in offending from adolescence to adulthood, with estimates ranging from 40–60 per cent. Studies show large variations in persistence, which has much to do with the type of data (official records or self-reported delinquency) and the population of youth studied (general populations vs offender populations). Continuity of offending from the juvenile into the early adult years is higher for those youth who start offending at a young age, for chronic juvenile delinquents, and for violent compared to nonviolent offenders. Therefore, knowledge about different offence characteristics and about the residual length of criminal careers is relevant for justice personnel making decisions about length and types of sentences, treatment, parole, and incarceration.

Studies agree that a certain proportion of juvenile delinquents desists from offending between adolescence and early adulthood (typically about 40–60 per cent). However, the period between late adolescence and early adulthood is characterized by an increasing severity of offending (including violence) by a minority of delinquents, and a decreasing severity of offending by others. This process of escalation for some young males and de-escalation for others is usually not complete for all juvenile delinquents by age 18, which is the most widely accepted distinction between adolescence and adulthood and between the operation of the juvenile and the adult criminal justice system, but extends into early adulthood. Studies also agree that a proportion of individuals starts offending during early adulthood. This figure is typically about 10–30 per cent of offenders, but the estimates vary greatly.

In summary, developmental studies of the persistence in and the desistance from offending between adolescence and early adulthood do not support the notion that there is any kind of naturally occurring break in the prevalence of offending at age 18. Persistence in offending is not immutable: interventions outside of the justice system (discussed below) can improve a young person's desistance from offending between adolescence and early adulthood.

Explanations for Persistence in and Desistance from Offending, and Adult Onset Offending

We identified ten explanatory processes:

1. Early individual differences in self-control (discussed in Chapters 4 and 12).
2. Brain maturation (Chapters 4 and 12).
3. Cognitive changes (for example, decision making to change behaviour; Chapters 4 and 12).
4. Behavioural risk factors (disruptive behaviour and delinquency) and behavioural protective factors (nervousness and social isolation) (Chapters 4 and 12).
5. Social risk and protective factors (family, peers, school; Chapters 4 and 12).
6. Mental illnesses and substance use/abuse (Chapter 12).
7. Life circumstances (for example, getting married, becoming employed; Chapters 3, 5 and 12).
8. Situational context of specific criminal events, including crime places and routine activities (Chapters 3 and 12).
9. Neighbourhood (for example, living in a disadvantaged neighbourhood, and the concentration of impulsive and delinquent individuals in disadvantaged neighbourhoods; Chapters 3 and 12).
10. Justice responses (for example, transfer to adult court, longer sentences; Chapters 3, 7, 8 and 12).

The Study Group posed three questions: (a) *Does each process explain persistence in offending from adolescence to adulthood?* (b) *Does each process also explain desistance during that period?* and (c) *Does each process explain the onset of offending during early adulthood?*

We found that there are multiple explanatory ('causal') processes of offending from early childhood to early adulthood. Persistence in offending from adolescence to adulthood is explained by several of these, including early individual differences, behavioural risk factors, individuals' exposure to social risk factors, delayed brain maturation, and justice systems responses.

Only some processes are implicated in desistance from offending, for example favourable individual differences and exposure to few behavioural risk factors. In addition, early brain maturation and the presence of cognitive changes encourage desistance. There is strong evidence that, for males, getting married and holding a stable job foster desistance, whereas unstructured activities with peers are associated with persistence. While risk factors tend to predict a lower probability of desistance during the period between adolescence and early adulthood, the evidence for protective factors encouraging desistance is far from clear.

Unfortunately, the sparse research on adult-onset offending provides little guidance on which factors explain why some individuals who were not delinquent during adolescence become adult offenders. However, there is some evidence that, while nervousness inhibits offending during adolescence, this is not the case during adulthood.

The explanatory frameworks reviewed tend to take place at different age periods from childhood to early adulthood and, consequently, may influence different but interrelated outcomes (Figure 1.3). For example, early individual differences become manifest after birth and evolve subsequently, exposure to new risk factors increases from childhood through adolescence, while changes in desirable life circumstances – such as marriage and employment – typically accelerate from late adolescence to early adulthood.

None of the published longitudinal studies has ascertained the relative contribution to offending of each of these processes from childhood through early adulthood. In those instances in which the explanatory processes are malleable (for example, good supervision by parents, self-control, employment of young people), we do not know which explanatory processes, once changed, will be most effective in lowering the persistence of juveniles' offending to adulthood. We shall return to this when reviewing the effectiveness of preventive and remedial interventions.

Importantly, *none* of the aforementioned processes that operate during the transition between adolescence and early adulthood clearly maps onto the age 18 dividing line. Instead, such an arbitrary age distinction is irrelevant with respect to most of the above processes that are ongoing around that age, including brain maturation and moving from external to internal behaviour control.

Vulnerable Groups and Special Categories of Offenders

There are major individual timing differences among youth in their speed and extent of maturation. For that reason, the Study Group addressed the question: *Which categories of youth are likely to mature more slowly in their cognitive ability to control their behaviour and take longer than others to desist from delinquency?* Research findings show that youth formerly in juvenile institutions, compared to youth in the general population, have longer criminal careers and are convicted more often. The same applies to youth of low intelligence, who require special attention in the justice system, not just because they often are less competent to understand court proceedings, but also because, compared to more intelligent youth, they tend to have higher cognitive impulsivity and are more often charged for delinquent offences.

Life transitions in these groups were also found to differ from the general population. Men and women who were placed in residential care in their childhood are, on average, less successful in making the transition to adulthood. However, compared to non-vulnerable youth, vulnerable females tend to make several life transitions, including motherhood and marriage, at an atypically early age.

Combined with the vulnerable females' typical exposure to other risk factors, this may result in their offspring's poor adjustment later.

In addition to several vulnerable groups, the Study Group investigated sex offenders as a special category of offenders. Sex offenders who victimize peers usually have an earlier age of onset than those who victimize children. Sex offenders against children, compared to sex offenders against peers, however, tend to persist more in their offending from adolescence to early adulthood. The US Study Group considered several additional categories of young offenders, including drug dealers, gang members, and homicide offenders. Research shows differences in the criminal careers for some, but not all, types of special offenders. Drug use is common among nearly all, but drug dealers are uncommon. Of all categories of offences, drug dealing and gun carrying had the highest persistence from adolescence to adulthood. Joining a gang tends to take place in early adolescence and peak in mid-adolescence, and often precedes the onset of other criminal activities. It increases the rate of offending, but gang involvement is often a transient experience. Homicide differs from other types of offences in that it is usually a one-time event, and it tends to occur in late adolescence and early adulthood. However, gang killings mostly take place during adolescence.

Risk and Needs Assessments

Risk assessments are often carried out to aid juvenile judges in making decisions about young offenders. This is consistent with the more individualized, rehabilitative approach of the juvenile court. Risk assessment instruments are also used with juveniles and adults in institutional settings (including mental health settings) to inform release decisions. Consequently, the main objective of many instruments is to predict the probability of recidivism. However, to our knowledge, no instruments have been designed to predict persistence in offending in the transition from the juvenile to the early adult years. In most screening studies, the follow-up period of offenders has been very short (often one year). Risk assessment is rarely used to inform sentencing in the adult criminal court because of its more punitive retributive approach. Yet risk assessment for young adult offenders would be useful because for some offenders the probability of recidivism is low due to the natural decrease in offending that is part of the down-slope of the age–crime curve.

Well-researched screening instruments are available to assess juveniles' criminogenic risks and needs, but relatively little is known about which are the most optimal screening instruments for young adults. The Study Group addressed the importance of risk factors that vary with age for the optimal design of risk assessment instruments. While the impact of criminogenic factors seems to decrease among juveniles as they grow older, the impact of a number of them tends to increase among young adults. In particular, the impact on recidivism of problems with regard to school and work and the use of alcohol and drugs tends to be highest in older young adults.

Risk assessments are often administered in conjunction with needs assessments to measure to what extent offenders can be held responsible for the committed crime. Among the needs assessments are the assessment of intelligence and mental health problems. The basic notion is that vulnerable youth often have special needs, should be treated individually in court, and should receive more specialized services such as, for example, treatment for mental disorders. Reliable and valid assessment instruments to assess young people's cognitive (and brain) maturation still need to be developed.

Preventive Interventions and Interventions with Known Delinquents

A crucial issue for this volume is whether programmes outside of the various justice systems reduce the probability of delinquency and particularly the persistence of offending between adolescence and early adulthood. The study group approached it by posing the following questions:

a. *How effective are family-based programmes during toddlerhood in reducing offending during the young adult years?* There is good evidence that early interventions in childhood (for example, nurse home visiting, preschool intellectual enrichment programmes and parent management training) are effective in preventing delinquency. However, it is not always clear whether children who received early interventions committed fewer offences during their adult years.
b. *How effective are individually based programmes during childhood in reducing offending during the young adult years?* The best evaluations of early child intervention programmes with no-treatment controls show that they yielded reductions in offending that extended to adulthood.
c. *How effective are community and school-based interventions in reducing young adult offending?* Some but not all of the school-based interventions have led to a reduction in offending even during the transition between adolescence and early adulthood. More research on the best programmes (for example, Communities That Care, mentoring) is much needed. Employment initiatives, such as the U.S. Job Corps programme, are effective in reducing offending by young adults.
d. *How effective are intervention programmes in improving self-control in young children*? Importantly, a meta-analysis of 34 programmes focusing on improving self-control in children up to age 10 reported enhanced self-control and reductions in offending. Thus, self-control is malleable and improved self-control has long-term benefits. It is less clear, however, to what extent improved self-control is associated with accelerated brain maturation, a faster outgrowing of impulsive and sensation-seeking behaviours during adolescence, a

lowering of the age–crime curve for individuals, and a curtailing of the age–crime curve into early adulthood.

e. *How effective are interventions with older juvenile delinquents (ages 14–17) in preventing continuation into young adult offending?* Multisystemic Therapy (MST), Multidimensional Treatment Foster Care (MTFC) and Functional Family Therapy (FFT) have been shown to reduce recidivism into early adulthood.
f. *Do early interventions lower the age–crime curve?* One of the limitations of evaluation studies is the absence of yearly follow-ups of treated and non-treated individuals during adolescence and early adulthood. For that reason, published evaluation studies have not been able to show the degree to which interventions lowered the age–crime curve.

In summary, there are many intervention programmes available outside justice systems that reduce recidivism and prevent persistence of offending from adolescence to early adulthood. Preliminary results indicate that such interventions may lower the age–crime curve.

What is Known about the Financial Benefits and Costs of Different Interventions that Might Reduce Offending in the Young Adult Years?

In Europe the financial benefits and costs of interventions are hardly investigated, but a review of cost–benefit studies in the US concluded that the benefits of programmes often outweigh their costs. This was true, for example, of MTFC ($8 saved per $1 expended), FFT ($10 saved per $1 expended), MST ($3 saved per $1 expended), vocational education in prison ($12 saved per $1 expended), cognitive-behavioural therapy in prison ($22 saved per $1 expended), drug treatment in prison ($6 saved per $1 expended), and employment training in the community ($12 saved per $1 expended). Thus it is clear that many programmes not only reduce offending in the young adult years but also save taxpayers a lot of money in the long run.

Research and Policy Recommendations

Research Priorities

We conclude that there are significant gaps in knowledge about the development of offending careers between ages 15 and 29. Little is known (especially from self-reports) about prevalence, frequency, types of crimes, co-offending, motives for offending, specialization, escalation, persistence as opposed to desistance, intermittency and adult-onset offending. Surprisingly little is known about even the most basic questions of how many juvenile offenders (ages 15–17) persist to adult offending (at age 18 or later), and what factors in the juvenile years predict persistence into the adult years. Little is known about processes that may influence offending between ages 15 and 29, especially individual factors (including those that tend to develop with age, such as psychosocial maturity, impulse control, cognitive decision-making, executive functioning, risk-taking, emotion regulation, as well as other factors that tend to emerge with age such as mental health problems). More needs to be known about how life circumstances (such as education, employment, romantic relationships and cohabitation, substance use, and peer relationships) influence the development of offending. In addition, there is a need to better understand how individuals' routine activities and their neighbourhood and situational contexts influence offending.

We recommend two ways to advance knowledge about the development of offending careers and influencing factors. First, undertake secondary data analyses on existing longitudinal datasets and/or investigate to what extent *within-individual* changes in influencing factors are followed by *within-individual* changes in offending. Few studies have carried out within-individual analyses, which require repeated assessments. Not all secondary data analyses, however, can address all of the key questions posed in this volume and deal with the full range of putative processes from psychosocial maturity to neighbourhood and situational influences. Therefore, our second recommendation is to start *two longitudinal studies*, one of a community sample and the other of a sample of offenders (this dual method has previously been used by Marc Le Blanc in Quebec). Two such studies would have complementary advantages and disadvantages. The community study makes it possible to generalize results to the whole population but may have a low yield of serious offenders. The offender study provides a lot of information about existing offenders, but it is not clear to what extent the results can be generalized to the whole population or what the characteristics of adult-onset offenders are over the age range. By carrying out both studies in the same location during the same time period with similarly aged youth, valid conclusions can be drawn about both juvenile offenders and the whole population. This research could be modelled on the Pittsburgh Youth Study, which is a community study with a high-risk sample, and the Pathways to Desistance Study, which is the most important longitudinal study of juvenile offenders to date.

We propose that for optimal results the two studies be carried out in several European countries simultaneously, but we shall outline both more ambitious as well as perhaps more financially realistic projects. Ideally, large numbers of males and females and persons from different racial/ethnic backgrounds would be followed up, but – more realistically perhaps – about 500 males would be followed up in each study (at least initially). There would be oversampling of high-risk youth in the community study (to increase the yield of offenders while still permitting generalization to the population), and the offender study would begin with persons petitioned to or adjudicated in the juvenile court. Ideally, youth would be followed up in annual face-to-face interviews from age 15–29, but more realistically interviews would be carried out every two years from age 15–24, making a total of six. Repeated

Box ES.1 Aims of the proposed longitudinal studies focusing on the transition between juvenile offending and adult crime

1. To study the development of offending careers between ages 15 and 24: prevalence, frequency, types of crimes, co-offending, motives for offending, specialization, escalation, persistence as opposed to desistance, intermittency and adult-onset offending.
2. To compare self-report and official record information about offending careers.
3. To obtain information about key predictive relationships in offending careers, such as how the probability of persistence or desistance at each age and the residual length of criminal careers varies according to previous criminal career features (for example, age of onset, time since the last offence) and especially the extent to which future adult criminal careers can be predicted at age 17.
4. To study the relationship between offending and individual factors such as executive functioning, neurobiological and brain development, cognitive factors, decision making, impulsiveness, self control, psychosocial maturity, emotion regulation, and adjudicative competence.
5. To assess the strength of relationships between risk factors (individual, family, peers, school, neighbourhood and community), life events and life transitions (for example, employment, marriage, drug selling and gang membership) and later criminal career features.
6. To assess development in different communities and neighbourhoods.
7. To assess situational factors, routine activities, and opportunities that influence whether a person with a certain degree of antisocial potential commits a crime in a particular time and place.
8. To study what factors influence successful transitions to adult roles such as employment, good accommodation, marriage or cohabitation, and parenthood.
9. To assess the effects of different types of official processing (for example, juvenile vs criminal court, different disposals) at different ages, using quasi-experimental comparisons and propensity score matching to deal with selection effects.
10. To assess the accuracy of risk/needs as sessment instruments in predicting persistence versus desistance.
11. To assess the effectiveness of different types of interventions inside and outside of the juvenile and adult justice system at different ages.
12. To assess the financial benefits and costs of different types of interventions and court processing.
13. To study how offending careers and other results vary according to race/ethnicity and (if possible) gender.

self-reports and official records of offending would be collected, so the cooperation of official agencies in the various cities would be crucial.

The main aims of these studies are summarized in Box ES.1. Some of these aims can be addressed more effectively in the community sample, and some in the offender sample.

Policy Recommendations

Several of the following recommendations are relevant for reducing prison populations, particularly by curtailing the flow of juveniles from the juvenile justice system into the adult prison system.

There are many good reasons why juvenile offenders are treated differently from adult offenders in courts and correctional facilities. In comparing youths to adults, Box ES.2 summarizes some distinguishing juvenile features, which leads to the conclusion that young adult offenders aged 18 to about 24 are more similar to juveniles than to adults. Therefore, we make the following policy recommendations, including alternatives:

1. Changes in legislation in most countries are warranted to deal with juvenile offenders being handled as adult criminals. We recommend raising the minimum age for referral of young people to the adult court to age 24 so that fewer young offenders are dealt with in the adult criminal justice system. There are several advantages: fewer young offenders will be incarcerated, fewer of them will be exposed to the criminogenic influences of incarceration, and more of them will receive alternative, non-custodial sanctions. We expect that, consequently, the number of adult prisoners will be decreased and considerable savings for taxpayers will accrue. To prompt legislative change, we recommend cost–benefit analyses in several European countries to quantify the benefits of legally raising the age of juvenile jurisdiction to age 21, 23, or even 24. Such cost–benefit analyses have been conducted in the UK but need to be done in other European countries as well.
2. Alternatively, special courts for young adult offenders aged 18–24 could be established on an experimental basis in a small number of areas (building on the experience of the UK Transition to Adulthood initiative: see www.t2a.org.uk). Three reasons support creating special courts for young adult offenders: (i) preventing excessive punishment of young people who land in the adult justice system; (ii) youthfulness as a mitigating factor; and (iii) the developmental needs of young people. Along that line, several European countries (for example, Sweden, Germany and Austria) have long had separate young adult sentencing options and separate institutions for ages 18–21. The focus should be on rehabilitation rather than retribution. Since juveniles who are transferred to adult courts tend to receive more severe sentences and tend to have higher recidivism rates than those in juvenile courts, we expect that these special courts would decrease recidivism and

Box ES.2 Some juvenile attributes that are relevant for judicial evaluations

1. Less mature judgement.
2. Poorer decision making in offending opportunities.
3. Poorer executive functioning, reasoning, abstract thinking, planning.
4. More influenced by immediate gratification than longer-term possible undesirable consequences.
5. Poorer impulse control, more likely to take risks and commit crimes for excitement rather than according to a rational choice.
6. Less set in their offending habits, more malleable, more redeemable.
7. Less culpable or blameworthy, diminished responsibility, less deserving of punishment.
8. Poorer emotion regulation and self-regulation.
9. Less sense of avoidance of self-harm.
10. Lower adjudicative competence to communicate with lawyers, make legal decisions, understand and participate in legal procedures, stand trial.
11. More susceptible to peer influences.

decrease incarceration, and consequently save taxpayer money. In addition, they should be designed to have fewer ongoing stigmatizing effects than adult criminal courts.

3. A third option is to set up special correctional facilities for young adult offenders and include programmes such as cognitive-behavioural therapy, drug treatment, restorative justice, mentoring, education and vocational training, and work release. Special facilities for young adults already exist in some states of the US (for example, Pennsylvania). The Netherlands used to have such special facilities, but these were abolished some time ago. Most research shows that there is no evidence that either longer sentences or lengthening the period of incarceration provides practical benefits in terms of reducing the recidivism of serious offenders.
4. There should be an 'immaturity discount' for young adult offenders: a decrease in the severity of penalties that takes into account young persons' lesser culpability and diminished responsibility.
5. There should be risk/needs assessments and screening of young adult offenders to guide the selection of appropriate disposals and interventions. This screening should assess the topics listed in Box ES.2 (1–11) in addition to risk factors, such as low intelligence. Young adult offenders with substance use problems should be diverted to drug treatment, and those with mental health problems should be dealt with by mental health professionals.
6. There should be evidence-based programmes for young adult offenders (including females and minorities) in the community after release, including Multisystemic Therapy, cognitive-behavioural therapy, drug treatment,

> restorative justice, mentoring, and educational and vocational training programmes. Employment and relationship programmes should be offered to encourage desistance, as well as other programmes aimed at reducing disorderly transitions, such as not graduating from high school and teenage single parenthood. Other useful programmes are those aiming to reduce opportunities for offending, such as 'hot spots policing' and situational crime prevention, and reducing drug dealing (especially targeted at high-crime neighbourhoods). In addition, in light of the long-term positive effects of early nurse-home visiting, parent training and family-based programmes, these also should be more widely implemented and followed up to assess their effects on young adult offending.

All of these initiatives should be rigorously evaluated by sound experimental studies and cost–benefit analyses should be carried out. Age, gender and racial/ethnic differences in the effectiveness of programmes should be studied.

We urge governments to develop action plans to implement the key recommendations of this report to assist local governments in changing their statutes and practices so that justice is applied more fairly and with more knowledge of how youth develop into mature adults. We believe that in order to improve the safety of citizens and communities our recommendations offer more hope of crime reduction and less burden on the taxpayer than the implementation of longer prison sentences of young adults or the referral of more juvenile offenders to the adult criminal justice system.

Chapter 1

Introduction

Rolf Loeber, Machteld Hoeve, N. Wim Slot and Peter H. van der Laan

Juvenile delinquency is a vexing problem across countries in Europe (ESB, 2010), and is one of the major causes of physical harm and property loss inflicted on victims. Countries differ in major ways in the manner in which they deal with juvenile delinquents inside and outside the juvenile court and, sometimes, the adult court systems. Countries also differ in their legal definitions of the age of criminal responsibility (ranging from 8 to 18) or the youngest age at which adult criminal law can be applied to juveniles (ranging from 15–18) (see Killias, Redondo and Sarnecki, this volume).

Scholars, professionals and lay people regularly debate what causes young people to commit crimes. Some argue that there are 'bad' individuals who from childhood are already out of control, many of whom become life-course-persistent delinquents. Others argue that juvenile delinquents are to a high degree a product of their environment: the worse the environment, the worse their behaviour over time. In this volume we present evidence that both positions are tenable, but we also provide proof that many juvenile delinquents tend to stop offending in late adolescence and early adulthood.

Since in most countries in Europe as well as in the US the legal transition between adolescence and adulthood takes place at age 18, another point of discussion is whether young people by age 18 have full control over their behaviour and whether their brain maturation is complete at that age. If so, does this mean that from age 18 onwards we can attribute the causes of offending and culpability to persisting individual difference factors rather than mental immaturity and disadvantages in families, schools, and social environment?

This volume focuses on the age period between mid-adolescence and early adulthood (roughly ages 15–29)[1] and it addresses what we know about individual differences among offenders in their persistence compared to desistance from offending. The volume draws on studies in North America and Europe (see Killias

1 There are no empirical boundaries for the age range encompassing adolescence and early adulthood. Note that the Transition to Adulthood (T2A) initiative defines early adulthood between ages 'approximately 18 and 24', but acknowledges that this age range is 'blurry at the edges' (Helyar-Cardwell, 2009, p. 12). Our choice of setting the upper age limit at 29 is governed by the evidence that the majority of young people outgrow offending by that age.

Figure 1.1 Offending in the juvenile and early adult years

	Adult Non-Offender	Adult Offender
Juvenile Non-Offender	Non-Offender	Adult-onset Offender
Juvenile Offender	Adult Desister	Juvenile/Adult Persister

et al., this volume). Figure 1.1 summarizes the four key groups we are interested in: juvenile/adult persisters whose offending continues from adolescence to early adulthood (and perhaps later); early adult desisters who were juvenile offenders who desist during adolescence and do not continue to offend into early adulthood; adult-onset offenders who did not offend during adolescence but who become offenders during early adulthood; and, lastly, non-offenders, who do not offend either in adolescence or early adulthood. We shall examine the four groups in general population samples, but we shall also focus on sex offenders (see Bijleveld, Van der Geest and Hendriks, this volume).

Maturation

In general, childhood is seen as a period in which children have not yet fully developed self-control, and impulsivity tends to lead to misbehaviour and acts of delinquency (Jolliffe and Farrington, 2009; Moffitt, 1993). This is why during the period from childhood into adolescence parents, teachers and other adults help to modulate children's poor internal controls, teach them skills to navigate problems in life, and help them avoid inflicting harm on others. Thus the years across childhood and adolescence are seen as a pivotal period in which to bring about in young people a shift from external to internal controls. However, the appearance of physical maturity in late adolescence and early adulthood does not necessarily mean that mental maturity has been fully achieved and that internal controls are completely formed and are regularly exercised by the young person (see, for example, Steinberg et al., 2009; but see critique by Fischer, Stein and Heikkinen, 2009).[2]

The presence of internal controls can be expressed in a number of complementary ways:

- Improved decision making vs letting things happen.
- Improved perception of the future consequences of actions.
- Avoidance of self-harm.
- Increased self-regulation.
- Decreased sensation seeking.
- Decreased impulsiveness.

2 In fact, physical growth (bone weight) continues to increase until about age 23 (Doreleijers and Fokkens, 2010).

- Decreased risk taking.
- Improved emotional control.
- Decreased susceptibility to peer influences.

Control in one area does not mean necessarily that control in another area is also in place. However, there is a lack of agreement among scholars regarding the age at which psychosocial maturity and general cognitive capacity reach their maximum values (Steinberg et al., 2009; Fischer, Stein and Heikkinen, 2009). There are major individual differences in the gradual mastering of internal controls, with some youth maturing early in this respect, and others in more vulnerable populations (see Bijleveld et al., Chapter 5, this volume, and also Overview, this volume) taking a much longer time (see below). Contrary to legal assumptions, age 18 is not a fixed date of completion of this process for all young people.

While all young persons go through the transition between adolescence and adulthood, scholars disagree about whether an in-between stage of 'emerging adulthood' is a separate stage of development, prompted in part by demographic delays in industrial societies over the past decades in the timing of marriage and parenthood (Arnett, 2000). There is some agreement that in recent years 'the transition to adulthood has become increasingly prolonged with more youth staying in education longer, marrying later, and having their first child later than in the past' (Hendry and Kloep, 2007, p. 74) and that this applies to a number of industrialized countries (see Blokland and Palmen, this volume; Fussell and Furstenberg, 2005). Masten et al. (2004) characterized the transition period between adolescence and early adulthood as a window of opportunity to change the life course in terms of individuals having second-chance opportunities and turning points in their lives. Other scholars, however, see the transition period as an instance of delayed adulthood accompanied by delayed outgrowing of adolescent behaviours.

The Age–Crime Curve

Research findings agree that the prevalence of offending increases from late childhood to adolescence, peaks in late adolescence, and decreases subsequently to adulthood. This is generally known as the *age–crime curve* (Farrington, 1986; Tremblay and Nagin, 2005; Laub and Sampson, 2003). An example of such a curve is shown in Figure 1.2. The curve can be observed in all populations of youth. Less well known is the fact that, although an early – compared to a later – age of onset of offending is associated with a longer criminal career, the highest concentration of desistance takes place during late adolescence and early adulthood *irrespective* of age of onset, which corresponds with the down-slope of the age–crime curve (see Overview, this volume). In fact the decrease in prevalence in the down-slope of the age–crime curve is very substantial, in some datasets from about 50 per cent to about 10 per cent of all persons (for example, Loeber et al., 2008).

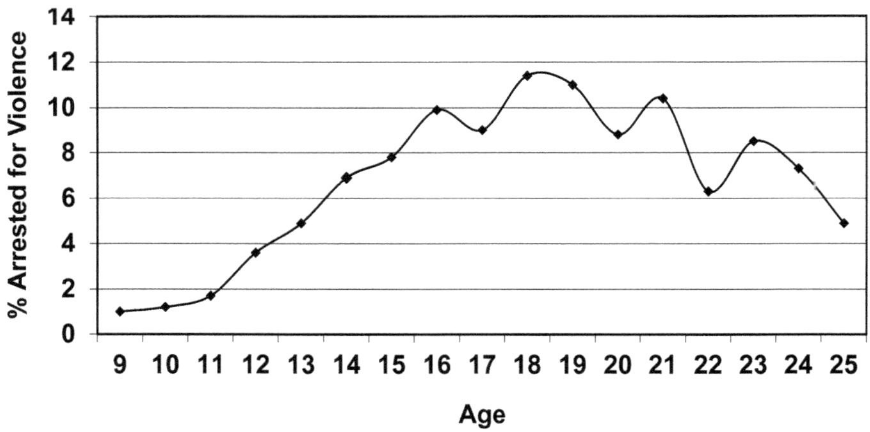

Figure 1.2 An example of an age–crime curve (Loeber and Stallings, 2011)

All available research on age–crime curves shows that the legal age of adulthood at 18 has no significant relevance and is not accompanied by a sharp change (or decrease) in offending at exactly that age. Serious offences (such as rape, robbery, homicide and fraud) tend to occur after the emergence of less serious offences in the late adolescence/early adulthood window. Even for serious offences, however, there is no clear dividing line at age 18. Steinberg et al. (2009) conclude, 'The notion that a single line can be drawn between adolescence and adulthood for different purposes under the law is at odds with developmental science' (p. 583).

Offending Careers

This volume addresses what we know about individuals' persistence in contrast to desistance from offending (see Figure 1.1). The main focus is on serious offending careers (for example, violence, drug dealing and sexual crimes), which for a substantial number of offenders extend beyond age 18 into adulthood and for other offenders cease after adolescence (see Blokland and Palmen, Chapter 2, this volume; Piquero, Hawkins and Kazemian, 2012). Blokland and Palmen address the following key questions about delinquency careers: *How common is persistence in and desistance from offending between adolescence and early adulthood? How common is the onset of offending during early adulthood?* The criminal career parameters that are reviewed in Chapter 2 are prevalence and frequency, continuity, escalation and specialization, types of crimes and criminal careers, co-offending, prediction of offending into adulthood, and prediction of onset of offending in the young adult years. In addition, we focus on certain categories of offenders (drug dealers, gang members, homicide offenders and sex offenders) and ask whether – compared to other offenders – they are more likely to persist in offending into adulthood (see Overview, Chapter 12, this volume).

The Search for Causes

As mentioned, the down-slope of the age–crime curve represents a very substantial decrease in the number of offenders from the peak of the curve in middle to late adolescence.[3]

Causes (here called explanations) of persistence in and desistance from offending are reviewed in Chapters 3, 4, 5, 11 and 12. These chapters also focus on explanations for the shape of the age–crime curves in different populations. We consider the following ten explanatory processes:

1. Early individual differences in self-control.
2. Brain maturation.
3. Cognitive changes (for example, decision making to change behaviour).
4. Behavioural risk factors (disruptive behaviour and delinquency) and behavioural protective factors (nervousness and social isolation).
5. Social risk and protective factors (family, peers, school).
6. Mental illnesses and substance use/abuse.
7. Life circumstances, such as getting married, becoming employed, moving to another neighbourhood.
8. Situational context of specific criminal events, including crime places and routine activities.
9. Neighbourhood (for example, living in a disadvantaged neighbourhood, and the concentration of impulsive and delinquent individuals in disadvantaged neighbourhoods).
10. Justice response (for example, transfer to adult court, longer sentences).

We address the following questions: (a) *Does each process explain persistence in offending from adolescence to early adulthood?* (b) *Does each process also explain desistance during that period?* (c) *Does each process explain the onset of offending during early adulthood?* The explanatory processes tend to operate at different ages of juveniles, some early and some later in offending careers, which is shown in Figure 1.3

Justice Response

Justice response to law breaking by young people is specified in part in countries' criminal codes but partly depends on how that code is interpreted and how much

---

3 The decrease in the prevalence of offending from about 50 per cent in the teens to about 10 per cent in the 20s translates into a very large standardized mean difference effect size of about 1.0. The reason that we emphasize this effect size is because we identify explanations that separately or collectively explain most of the down-slope of the age–crime curve.

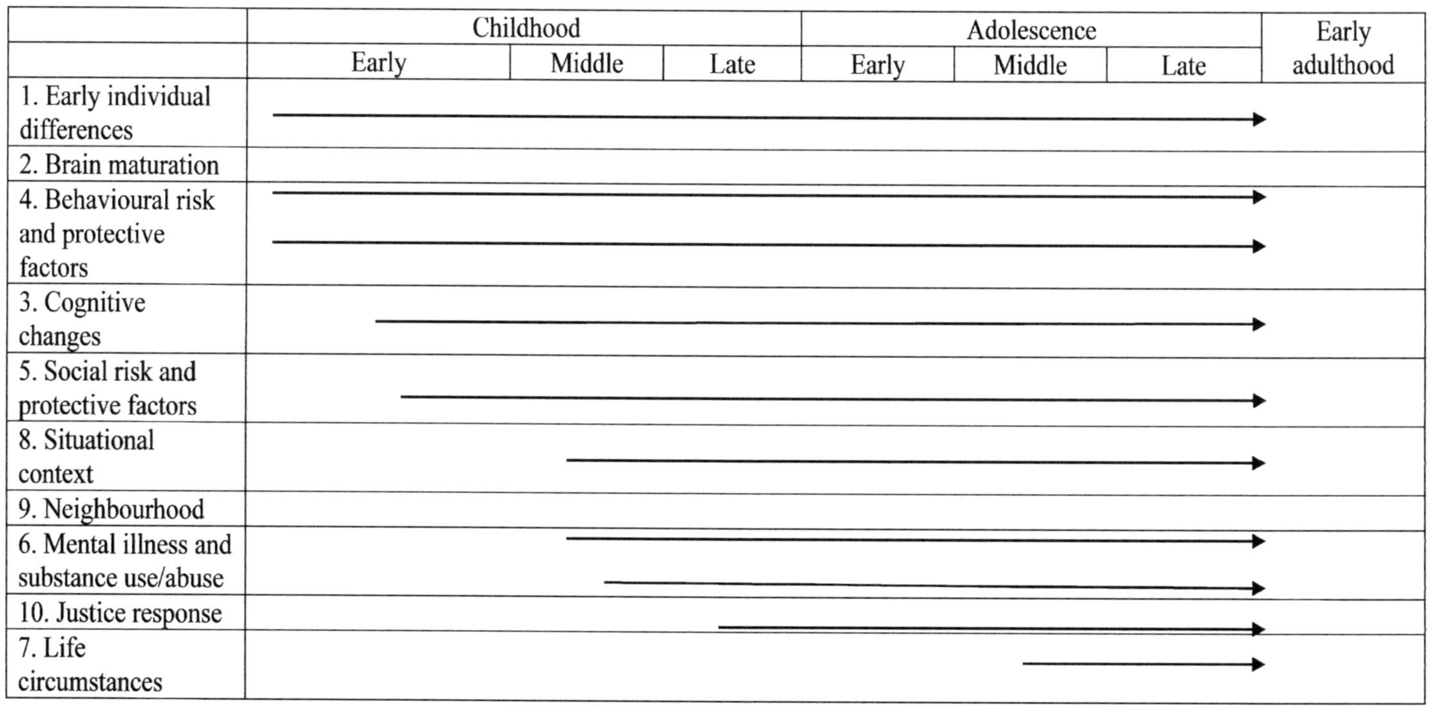

Figure 1.3 Approximate temporal ordering of explanatory processes investigated for persistence in, desistance from, and adult-onset of offending

discretion is given to the police, judges, prosecutors, and other justice personnel. The justice response is also much influenced by legislators at the local and national government level who, rightly or wrongly, call for harsher and longer sentences to be applied to young offenders, in particular for those older than 15.

Over recent decades, discussions in the Netherlands have focused on whether or not to adjust lower and upper age limits for penal procedures. From a variety of perspectives it has been proposed to implement separate or amended sanctions and procedures for young adults. In this regard, the main question here addressed by Liefaard (Chapter 7, this volume), Van der Laan et al. (Chapter 8, this volume), and in the Overview (Chapter 12, this volume) is: *How well does persistence in and desistance from offending during the transition between adolescence and adulthood map onto the minimum legal age of adulthood (i.e., age 18 in most countries)?*

As mentioned, there are many explanations for persistence in and desistance from offending between adolescence and early adulthood, and for young adult onset of offending. These explanations are relevant to legislation and to the administration of juvenile and adult justice. In Chapters 7 and 8 we address the following points: *What are the legal implications of knowledge of explanatory processes from adolescence to adulthood? Are legal boundaries related to young people's maturation and development of cognitive control (or lowered impulsivity)? Does the legal system improve young people's cognitive control or are the juvenile and adult justice systems impervious to young people's cognitive development?*

Several other key questions are relevant for legislative consideration: *What is the usefulness of legislation stipulating minimum or longer sentences for offences for young offenders? Would lowering the age of adulthood, for example to age 16, decrease young people's offending and lower the crime rate of young individuals? Would increasing the age of adulthood, for example from age 16–18, or from age 18–21 or higher, decrease young people's offending and lower the crime rate of young individuals?* In Chapters 7, 8 and 12 we review advantages and disadvantages of several legal and practical options pertaining to young offenders: (a) lowering the legal age at which the adult justice system becomes applicable; (b) raising the legal age at which the adult justice system becomes applicable; (c) increasing sanctions, particularly by means of legislative offence exclusion, minimum length of sentences, and longer incarceration; and (d) the creation of special courts for young adult offenders.

In the current era of evidence-based decision making and legislation, we find the following questions to be critical: *What is known about the relative effectiveness of the juvenile and criminal justice systems in reducing recidivism? What is the justification for special treatment of young persons (and especially young adults) compared to older adult persons?*

In Chapters 5 and 12 we also address several questions that pertain to categories of vulnerable youth who come into contact with the law, such as youth who have been in juvenile institutions (Chapter 5) and youth of low intelligence (Chapter

12). Questions relevant to these youth are: *Which categories of youth are likely to mature more slowly in their cognitive ability to control their behaviour and take longer than others to desist from offending? Do vulnerable groups experience more atypical life transitions (for example, dropping out of school, teenage parenthood) between adolescence and early adulthood? Are vulnerable youth competent enough to understand judicial and court proceedings that affect their future?*

Screening

Increasingly, intake officers, probation officers and youth workers in the justice system use risk assessment screening instruments (reviewed by Spanjaard et al., Chapter 6, this volume; see also Hoge, Vincent and Guy, 2012) to inform the sentencing of juveniles. Risk assessment instruments are also used with juveniles and adults in institutional settings (including mental health settings) to inform release decisions. We are particularly interested in risk assessment instruments at ages 15–17 that predict persistence or desistance in the young adult years. Furthermore, we compare the impact of risk factors on recidivism in adolescents and young adults (Donker et al., Chapter 4, this volume). In addition, in the Overview (Chapter 12), we review three other types of assessments relevant to young offenders: assessments for mental competence to understand court proceedings, assessments of mental health and the presence of psychiatric disorder(s), and assessments of mental maturity.

Although screening to identify vulnerable youth (i.e., those who are not competent to understand court proceedings) has improved (Hoge et al., 2012), screening for youth who are cognitively immature is still under development. While screening for the risk of recidivism has advanced considerably, there are no screening instruments for the identification of juveniles at risk for adult crime, and for adult onset of offending.

Interventions Outside the Justice System

Over recent decades a range of proven interventions outside the justice system has become available to reduce and/or prevent conduct problems that often precede delinquency. Deković et al. (Chapter 9, this volume) review long-term effects of prevention programmes in early and middle childhood on criminal behaviour in early adulthood. Moreover, Boendermaker, Deković and Asscher (Chapter 10, this volume) provide an overview of interventions aimed at late adolescents and young adults. They raise the following questions about extra-judicial interventions for different age ranges and targeted youth populations: *How effective are family-based programmes during toddlerhood in reducing offending during the young adult years? How effective are individually based programmes during childhood in reducing offending during the young adult years? How effective are school-based interventions in reducing young adult offending? How effective are interventions with older juvenile delinquents (ages 14–17) in preventing continuation into young adult offending? How effective are labour market interventions in reducing young adult offending?* (See Deković et al., and Boendermaker et al. in Chapters 9 and 10 respectively, and Overview, Chapter 12, all in this volume).

Not all intervention programmes are equally effective and not all have a similar effect when applied more broadly that is beyond the demonstration phase. For that reason we address the following: *What is known about the financial benefits and costs of different interventions that might reduce offending in the young adult years? What is known about the success of implementing demonstration programmes on a large scale?* (see Overview, Chapter 12, this volume).

Gender Issues

There is increasing knowledge that results obtained with males may not apply to females and that what may be good for one gender may not necessarily be good for the other (see Overview, Chapter 12, this volume). Consequently, we ask: *How do criminal career features vary with gender? Are different theories of offending needed for each gender? Are genetic and biological influences the same for each gender? Do life events, life transitions, situational factors and neighbourhood factors have different effects for each gender?*

We do know that there are major gender differences in the experience of handicaps and the need for screening to identify these handicaps and so we pose the following: *Are psychiatric disorders (for example, depression, borderline personality disorder) more common among young female than male offenders? How does the predictive accuracy of risk factors, needs and protective factors vary with gender? How effective is juvenile versus adult court treatment for each gender? Are interventions outside of the justice system differentially effective with each gender?*

Ethnicity

In the Netherlands, young people with a Turkish, Moroccan or Surinamese background are among the largest non-indigenous groups. These ethnic groups are overrepresented in official delinquency records of arrest and conviction. However, self-reported delinquency studies have found no or very few differences between Dutch indigenous and non-indigenous groups (Junger-Tas and Slot, 2001; Wissink, 2006). One important question to ask is to what extent the age–crime curve and persistence of offending from adolescence to early adulthood is different for various ethnic groups (addressed by Blokland and Palmen, Chapter 2, this volume; Van der Laan et al., Chapter 8, this volume).

Headline Conclusions

This volume is largely based on evidence from a wide range of empirical studies conducted all over the world but particularly in the Netherlands and in Europe. It also refers to North American research, which is more extensively reviewed in the volume edited by Loeber and Farrington (2012). In addition, several new data analyses have been executed especially for this volume. These aspects present new insights into the interface between offending and the justice system during adolescence and early adulthood.

Section III of Overview (Chapter 12) summarizes the headline findings and arguments about the minimum legal age of adulthood and how it does not relate closely to the age–crime curve or to adolescents' mental maturation process that leads to less impulsive behaviour and more self-control. The findings point to an unplanned and unrecognized overreach of the justice system, particularly when meting out long sentences for young offenders or transferring juveniles from the jurisdiction of the juvenile to the adult court. We consider these matters especially important for categories of vulnerable offenders, such as those with low intelligence or mental health problems. The Overview (Chapter 12) contains major recommendations for the more effective screening of young people in the justice system and the establishment of Young Adult Offender Courts, specifically geared to the transition period from adolescence to young adulthood, that can provide rehabilitation rather than retribution only, as is common in the adult justice system.

Clearly, the justice system plays a major role in dealing with known offenders, but the system should not be the first – and often the most expensive – resort for dealing with young law breakers in the crucial period between adolescence and young adulthood. We point to major evidence that impulsive behaviours are malleable and that there are programmes for juveniles with demonstrated effectiveness in reducing impulsivity *and* later offending, even into early adulthood.

We posit that the findings reported in this volume are vital and 'need to know information' relevant for legislators, judges, prosecutors and other personnel in the juvenile and adult justice systems, as well as educators and individuals working in child and adolescent programmes to reduce conduct problems and delinquency, to ensure that today's juvenile delinquents do not become tomorrow's persistent adult criminals.

Acknowledgements

We are much indebted to comments by David P. Farrington and James C. Howell on an earlier draft of this chapter.

References

Arnett, J.J. (2000). Emerging adulthood: A theory of development from the late teens through the twenties. *American Psychologist*, 55, 469–80.

Doreleijers, T. and Fokkens, J.W. (2010). Minderjarigen en jongvolwassenen: Pleidooi voor een evidence based strafrecht. *Rechtsreeks*, 2, 1–47.

ESB (2010). *European Sourcebook of Crime and Criminal Justice Statistics* (4th edn). The Hague: Boom Juridische Uitgevers. At www.europeansourcebook.org, accessed 20 February 2012.

Farrington, D.P. (1986). Age and crime. In M. Tonry and N. Morris (eds), *Crime and Justice: An Annual Review of Research* (vol. 7). Chicago, IL: Chicago University Press, 189–250.

Fischer, K.W., Stein, Z., and Heikkinen, K. (2009). Narrow assessments misrepresent development and misguide policy: Comment on Steinberg, Cauffman, Woolard, Graham, and Banich (2009). *American Psychologist*, 64, 595–600.

Fussell, E. and Furstenberg, F.F. (2005). The transition to adulthood during the twentieth century: Race, nativity, and gender. In R.A. Settersten, F.F. Furstenberg and R.G. Rumbaut (eds), *On the Frontier of Adulthood: Theory, Research, and Public Policy*. Chicago, IL: University of Chicago Press, 29–75.

Helyar-Cardwell, V. (2009). *A New Start: Young Adults in the Criminal Justice System*. London: Transition to Adulthood Alliance.

Hendry, L.B. and Kloep, M. (2007). Conceptualizing emerging adulthood: Inspecting the emperor's new clothes? *Child Development Perspectives*, 1, 74–9.

Hoge, R.D., Vincent, G. and Guy, L. (2012). Prediction and risk/needs assessments. In R. Loeber and D.P. Farrington (eds), *From Juvenile Delinquency to Adult Crime: Criminal Careers, Justice Policy and Prevention*. New York: Oxford University Press.

Jolliffe, D. and Farrington, D.P. (2009). A systematic review of the relationship between childhood impulsiveness and later violence. In M. McMurran and R. Howard (eds), *Personality, Personality Disorder, and Violence*. New York: John Wiley & Sons, 41–61.

Junger-Tas, J. and Slot, N.W. (2001). Preventie van ernstig delinquent en gewelddadig gedrag [Prevention of serious delinquent and violent behavior]. In R. Loeber, N.W. Slot and J.A. Sergeant (eds), *Ernstige en gewelddadige jeugdcriminaliteit: Omvang, oorzaken, en interventies*. Houten/Diegem: Bohn Stafleu Van Loghem, 265–89.

Laub, J.H. and Sampson, R.J. (2003). *Shared Beginnings, Divergent Lives: Delinquent Boys to Age 70*. Cambridge, MA: Harvard University Press.

Loeber, R., Farrington, D.P., Stouthamer-Loeber, M., and White, H.R. (2008). *Violence and Serious Theft: Development and Prediction from Childhood to Adulthood*. Mahwah, NJ: Lawrence Erlbaum.

Loeber, R. and Farrington, D.P. (eds) (2012). *From Juvenile Delinquency to Adult Crime: Criminal Careers, Justice Policy and Prevention*. New York: Oxford University Press.

Masten, A.S., Burt, K.B., Roisman, G.I., Obradović, J., Long, J.D., and Tellegen, A. (2004). Resources and resilience in the transition to adulthood: Continuity and change. *Development and Psychopathology*, 16, 1071–94.

Moffitt, T.E. (1993). Adolescence-limited and life-course-persistent antisocial behavior: A developmental taxonomy. *Psychological Review*, 100, 674–701.

Piquero, A.R., Hawkins, J.D., and Kazemian, L. (2012). Criminal career patterns. In R. Loeber and D.P. Farrington (eds), *From Juvenile Delinquency to Adult Crime: Criminal Careers, Justice Policy and Prevention*. New York: Oxford University Press.

Steinberg, L., Cauffman, E., Woolard, J., Graham, S., and Banich, M. (2009). Are adolescents less mature than adults?: Minors' access to abortion, the juvenile death penalty, and the alleged APA 'flip-flop'. *American Psychologist*, 64, 583–94.

Tremblay, R.E. and Nagin, D.S. (2005). The developmental origins of physical aggression in humans. In R.E. Tremblay, W.H. Hartup and J. Archer (eds), *Developmental Origins of Aggression*. New York: Guilford Press, 83–106.

Wissink, I.B. (2006). *Parenting, Friendship Relations and Adolescent Functioning in Different Ethnic Groups*. Unpublished doctoral dissertation, University of Amsterdam, Amsterdam.

Chapter 2

Criminal Career Patterns

Arjan A.J. Blokland and Hanneke Palmen

A popular way of depicting the life course in Dutch sixteenth- and seventeenth-century folk art was by means of a metaphorical staircase. These 'steps of life' started at birth, with each step representing a succeeding decade in the lifespan. In these popular images it took five steps to reach the upper plateau, the prime of life, from which another five steps descended towards old age and ultimately death. Even more than the biological maturation of the individual, these steps of life signified the perils and pitfalls associated with each life phase and the way, in accordance with the Christian ethics at that time, these could best be avoided. Learning a reputable trade, getting married, starting a family and making a career were all perceived as vital to reaching a fulfilled and happy life. Today, this sixteenth-century folk wisdom re-echoes in many developmental and life-course criminological theories as they seek to explain criminal desistance.

Almost without exception, developmental and life-course criminological theories have stressed the importance of conventional adult roles in the process of desistance from crime. Sampson and Laub's (1993; Laub and Sampson, 2003) age-graded theory, for example, assumes that social ties embedded in adult transitions foster desistance. Transitions to adult roles, like work and marriage, provide new situations and new sources of social control, lead to a restructuring of routine activities, and provide the opportunity for identity transformation. According to the age-graded theory, these transitions elicit desistance and act as turning points to which many offenders choose to respond by refraining from future crime. Similarly, Moffitt's (1993) developmental taxonomy pinpoints the involvement in adult social roles as pivotal for desistance from crime. As delinquent adolescents transition to adulthood, formal and informal sanctions associated with continued criminal behaviour increasingly incur commitment costs as past accomplishments and future goals are perceived to be jeopardized. The bulk of delinquent adolescents respond to these shifting reinforcement contingencies by committing to these newly available adult roles and giving up delinquent behaviour. Other theorists, though sometimes stressing different causal mechanisms, have also pointed to transitions to adult roles as being crucial in understanding the process of criminal desistance (for example, Giordano, Cernkovich and Rudolph, 2002).

If the life course resembles a sequence of small steps, then early adulthood might best be considered 'one giant leap'. According to data from Statistics Netherlands (Huishoudstatistiek, 2008), at age 18, 80 per cent of Dutch youths live at home with their parents, only one per cent is married, and 1.3 per cent

Figure 2.1 Population by place in the household by age

has children. At age 28 these numbers have changed dramatically: over 90 per cent have left the parental home, 70 per cent live with a partner, and about 40 per cent have had their first child. Furthermore, the sum of youths employed almost quadruples from 22 per cent between ages 15–20 to 84 per cent between ages 25 and 30. The full extent of these changes is shown vividly in the graphical representation given in Figure 2.1. It illustrates that within a period of roughly ten years the vast majority of Dutch young people exits the relatively role-less period of adolescence and increasingly starts taking on adult obligations. With these striking demographic changes come similarly impressive offending. In 2008 the total number of arrests per capita shows a 37.5 per cent drop from age 18–28. This change is even more pronounced when we consider particular types of offences such as public order offences, for which the per capita rate declines a full 75 per cent across early adulthood. Thus, early adulthood is a period of profound change in demographics and offending.

What these population-level data do not show, however, is that – while abundant – change during early adulthood is anything but uniform. That is, while many young adults experience changes in their residential, occupational or marital status, as well as in the nature and level of their offending, not all young adults necessarily make the same transitions nor follow the same developmental pathway. Instead, individual-level pathways may differ substantially from those surfacing from population-level cross-sectional data. As a result, individuals aged 28 are not only vastly different from those aged 18, but they are also more different from each other than individuals are at age 18. Demographers, for instance, find family-life trajectories of young adults to have become increasingly dissimilar and show more variance (Elzinga and Liefbroer, 2007). Alternative living arrangements like cohabitation, postponement of marriage, unmarried parenthood, and higher divorce rates have broadened the options for individual shaping of the transition to adulthood. Criminologists in turn, using longitudinal data on offending, are finding individual-level criminal trajectories that are shaped very differently from the population-level age–crime curve (Piquero, 2008). Some trajectories show a steep decrease in crime after a peak in adolescence, whereas in others desistance is far more gradual. Despite overall levels of offending going down, some individuals follow trajectories that show an almost flat rate of offending for much of their adult life. So while change is common during early adulthood, it is far from universal across individuals.

Finally, life stages are not immutable and the perils and pitfalls associated with them may apply differently to diverse groups of individuals. Structural variables such as gender or ethnicity may influence the timing and the way young people experience the transition to young adulthood (Arnett, 2004). Economic or cultural factors may further structure or limit the extent to which young adults are able to postpone adult obligations or try out alternative living arrangements and take the 'long and leisurely route' towards adulthood (Arnett, 2007). Given that different societal groups may each experience early adulthood in their own way, patterns of continuity and change in offending may also be expected to vary substantially across groups.

Piquero, Hawkins and Kazemian (2012) recently reviewed the international literature on criminal careers during early adulthood. They concluded that participation in crime usually peaks during adolescence: in early adolescence when considering self-reports, and in late adolescence when considering official records. The empirical evidence of the overall pattern and stability of the frequency of offending during this period is far less clear. More so than participation, observed patterns in individual offending frequency vary across different samples, different measures of offending, and different age periods observed. The available evidence further reveals strong continuity in criminal behaviour from adolescence to adulthood. About one third of officially registered juvenile delinquents are also arrested as adults, and frequent offenders show the strongest and longest continuity in offending. Yet it also shows that nearly half of adult offenders did not have a juvenile record. These adult-onset offenders seemed less likely to reoffend than offenders who started offending during adolescence, or to develop a chronic criminal career.

Available research suggests that males participate in crime at higher rates than females, and that girls' and women's developmental patterns may differ from those of men (for a recent review see also Block et al., 2010). In the US, the limited set of studies that compare individuals from different cultural backgrounds tend to show that among African–Americans participation in crime is more prevalent and peaks at an earlier age that it does among Caucasians (Piquero et al., 2012). The criminal careers of African–American males also tend to show more continuity across early adulthood (for example, Tracy and Kempf-Leonard, 1996). Information about females, especially minority females, and cultural groups other than African–Americans (for example, Hispanics, Asians), constitutes an important gap in the available criminal career literature.

It is against this backdrop of change and divergence and the results of prior international studies, that this chapter will sketch a picture of the development of criminal behaviour during the transition to adulthood in the Netherlands. Based on a review of available Dutch research and on new analyses of both population-level and individual-level data on the criminal careers of Dutch young adults, we examine the level and nature of crime during the third decade of life and review what is known on various criminal career dimensions during this age period. When examining the criminal career development among Dutch young adults our analysis will take as point of departure the conceptual tools provided by the criminal career paradigm (Piquero, Farrington and Blumstein, 2003). A special focus will be on patterns of continuity and change, both in offending frequency as well as in the seriousness and diversity of offending. As far as the data available to us allow, we shall examine and compare these criminal career dimensions for both male and female offenders and for offenders of Dutch and non-Dutch descent.

Population-level Patterns of Offending from Adolescence to Early Adulthood: Evidence from Cross-sectional Studies

Over 200,000 suspects are apprehended by the police every year in the Netherlands, of whom one third are young adults aged 18–28 (Goudriaan and Eggen, 2009). Young adults are clearly overrepresented in police data, given that their share of the total population eligible for police registration is 15 per cent. The age distribution of suspects apprehended in the Netherlands follows the general age–crime curve – familiar to criminologists from many prior studies – with a peak in the late teens followed by a steady decline (for example, Farrington, 1986). To illustrate, Figure 2.2 provides the cross-sectional age–crime curves for property offences, violence, and public order offences based on the number of court cases registered in 2008 controlled for the age composition of the Dutch population (Statistics Netherlands, 2008). All three curves mirror the shape of the total age–crime curve and show that adolescence and early adulthood are the periods of greatest change. For example, the number of registered property offenders per 1,000 residents peaked at age 16 at 14.9, and decreased by half (7.2) at age 28. Similarly, the number of violent offenders decreased by almost half between ages 17 and 28 (from 10.8 to 5.8). The decline was steepest for public order offenders, which decreased by almost three quarters during this age period (12.5 to 3.30).

This drop in the prevalence of offending with age is also observed in self-reported delinquency data based on the 1996 NSCR self-report survey, which contains delinquency data from a cross-sectional sample representative of the Dutch population aged 15 and older (Wittebrood and Ter Voert, 1997). Respondents reported on property offences (theft, shoplifting, switching price

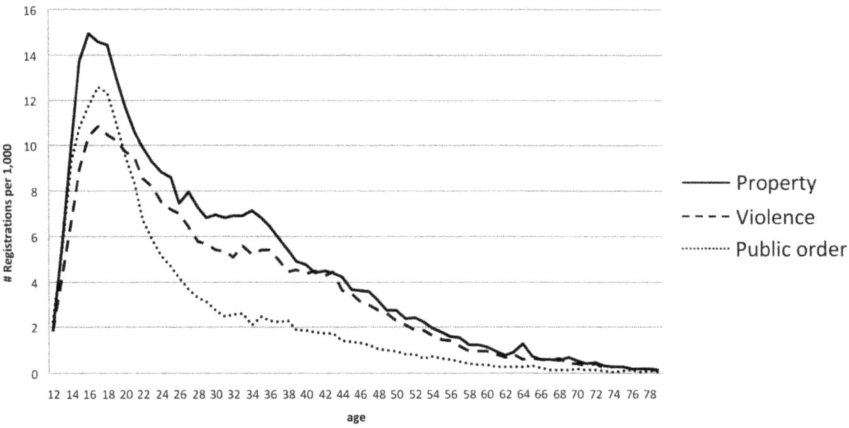

Figure 2.2 Age–crime curve based on number of registered court cases for property, violent and public order offences (Statistics Netherlands, 2008)

tags, fencing and fraud), violent offences (threatening, assault and aggravated assault), and public order offences (damaging public goods and damaging private goods). Figure 2.3 shows the mean standardized variety scores for all three offence types across three-year age periods. Standardized variety scores range from '0' denoting no offence, to '1' denoting the maximum number of different offences in that particular category. The variety of self-reported delinquent acts decreased considerably between adolescence and early adulthood.

It has been suggested that the transition to adulthood may progress differently for men and women. If so, crime during early adulthood may also be expected to develop differently for men and women. Dutch crime statistics show that over 80 per cent of all apprehended suspects are male (Goudriaan and Eggen, 2009). Despite crime being far more prevalent in males, the shape of the age–crime curve is remarkably similar for males and females (Goudriaan and Eggen, 2009), but differs slightly in an important way. The age–crime curve for females tends to peak about three years earlier than for males, which may indicate that desistance processes may be set in motion earlier for women. As shown in the age–crime curve (Figure 2.4), the change in the prevalence of offending during early adulthood was just as great for women as for men. Likewise, self-report data also show a similar decline in offending variety for men and women (1996 NSCR self-report survey). Besides gender, offending varies for different ethnic groups between adolescence and early adulthood. Dutch-registered crime statistics have only just begun to incorporate information on the ethnic (cultural) background of those involved. However, the court registration data used in this chapter to illustrate the age–crime

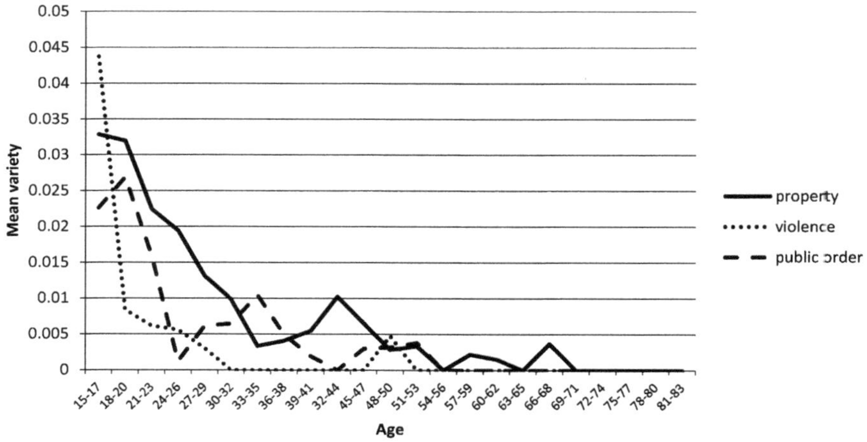

Figure 2.3 **Mean standardized variety score across three-year age periods for self-reported property, violent and public order offences (NSCR-survey 1996)**

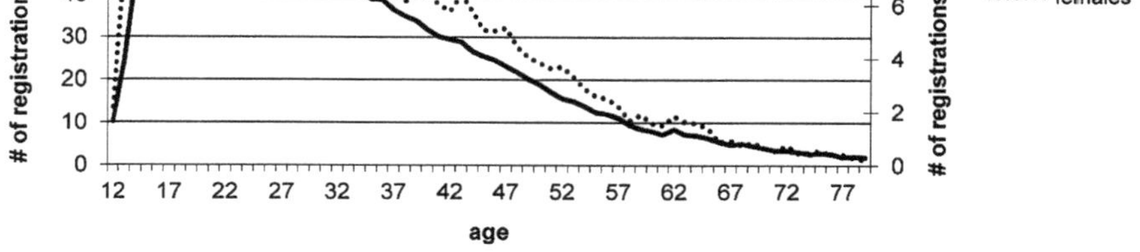

Figure 2.4 **Age–crime curve based on number of registered court cases by gender (Statistics Netherlands, 2008)**

curve do not contain information on ethnicity. Instead, a recent series of reports issued by the Ministry of Justice examine the prevalence of offending among Dutch citizens from different cultural backgrounds (Blom et al., 2005; Jennissen and Blom, 2007; Jennissen, 2009). These reports typically find an overrepresentation of minority groups in registered crime.[1] Individuals from Dutch Antillean, Moroccan and Surinamese descent especially account for a much larger share of registered crime than would be expected based on their proportion of the total population. In addition, the age–crime curve for Moroccans and Dutch Antilleans diverges substantially from that of the native Dutch population (Jennissen, 2009). The age–crime curve for Moroccans rises steeply to a peak during the late teens, much higher than for the native Dutch population, but then shows a steep decline through the 20s and 30s much like the curve for the Dutch population. As a result, the overrepresentation of Moroccans in registered crime is largest for adolescents and declines steadily with age. On the other hand, the age–crime curve for Dutch Antilleans does not show a continued decline beyond age 20 but instead seems to reach a plateau that lasts well into the 40s. As a result, the overrepresentation of Dutch Antilleans – relative to native Dutch – is especially large during the 20s, 30s and 40s. Differences in the nature of the offences typically attributed to these minorities do not entirely explain these deviating age–crime curves.

In summary, cross-sectional studies suggest that there is significant change in offending accompanying the transition to adulthood. Between ages 18 and 28 increasingly fewer individuals are registered for or report having committed an offence, which may mean that desistance increases during this age period or that the individual offending frequency decreases. Furthermore, this change in offending seems similar for males and females. Cross-sectional data suggest that the development of offending during early adulthood might be different for different cultural groups. However, it must be kept in mind that cross-sectional data do not address individual-level patterns of continuity and change in offending. Thus, one must be very cautious in drawing conclusions about the development of individual criminal careers from these kinds of data (Jennissen, 2009). To clarify individual-level patterns of continuity and change in offending, we have to turn to longitudinal studies.

Individual-level Patterns of Offending from Adolescence to Early Adulthood: Evidence from Longitudinal Studies

While developmental and life-course criminology has become an important subfield of Dutch criminology in recent years (Donker, Kleemans, Van der Laan and Nieuwbeerta, 2004), initially the criminal career approach was not as warmly

1 Some studies find minorities of Western European, Indonesian or Asian descent to be somewhat underrepresented (Blom et al., 2005), but others find overrepresentation across all groups (Van Wijk and Blokland, 2008).

welcomed in the Netherlands as it was in the US (Van de Bunt, 1988; Kommer, 1988). As a result, most longitudinal studies available in the Netherlands today were not specifically designed to measure the development of offending, but instead had a broader outlook, including a focus on problem behaviour as part of a wide range of undesirable outcomes. Many of these studies, although longitudinal, do not report on specific criminal career dimensions and, for example, do not distinguish offending participation from frequency. Furthermore, Dutch longitudinal studies often combine a relatively short-term follow-up, with a focus on childhood and adolescence. As a result few longitudinal studies cover criminal development beyond age 18. In a recent overview of Dutch longitudinal research on delinquency and crime, Blokland and Nieuwbeerta (2006) found that only four out of 13 studies actually had multiple years of data beyond age 18.

The first Dutch panel study to incorporate data on antisocial behaviour and delinquency is the South Holland study (Verhulst, Akkerhuis and Althaus, 1985). The South Holland study started in 1983 following a representative sample of boys and girls aged four to 16. The study consists of five biennial waves and a sixth wave in 1997. The Achenbach Checklists (CBCL, TRF and YSR) were used to measure antisocial behaviour during the first five waves. Only the sixth wave – when respondents were aged 18–32 – included a self-reported delinquency measure. The study found that 23.9 per cent of the sample reported having committed a delinquent act (excluding fare dodging) in the previous year. Receiving (buying and selling stolen goods) was most often reported (8.5 per cent), followed by (petty) theft from the workplace (8.1 per cent). Violence (6.5 per cent) and selling drugs (1.4 per cent) were less prevalent. Men reported having committed significantly more offences during the past year than did women. Women were also more likely to be one-time offenders (Donker, 2004). Given that delinquency and crime were only measured during the final wave of the study, the South Holland study does not provide information about patterns on continuity and change in offending.[2]

A second longitudinal study that includes self-reported delinquency is the Child Rearing and Family in the Netherlands Study (CRFNS) (Gerris et al., 1993). The CRFNS consists of three measurement waves spanning a period of ten years with self-report measures of delinquency and crime available for the second and third wave. At ages 19–27 the respondents were asked about their criminal behaviour during the past 12 months, and 18 per cent of respondents reported having committed at least one moderate to serious offence (Hoeve et al., 2007).

2 Analyses using information on problem behaviour measured during earlier waves showed, however, that overt problem behaviour measured at ages 6–11 better predicted overt behavioural problems at ages 20–25 than it did problem behaviour at ages 12–17 (Donker et al., 2003). These results were interpreted as supporting Moffitt's (1993) taxonomy.

Self-reported delinquency data are also available in the Utrecht Study on Adolescent Development (USAD). The USAD is a three-wave study that started in 1991. Participants were over 3,000 males and females between ages 12 and 24. Unlike data from the other self-report studies, the USAD data have been previously used to examine delinquency trajectories up to age 18 (Landsheer and Van Dijkum, 2005). The authors found distinct trajectories based on the level of delinquency in early adolescence (ages 12–14), middle adolescence (ages 15–17), and late adolescence/early adulthood (ages 18–20), but the findings show far less continuity in offending by females than by males. However, one category of females, although small in number, engaged in a persistent pattern of delinquency and was as criminally active during late adolescence/early adulthood as its male counterpart.

The fourth Dutch longitudinal study is the Criminal Career and Life-course Study (CCLS) (Nieuwbeerta and Blokland, 2003). The CCLS was set up specifically to measure development in offending as evident from official data. The CCLS is based on a large sample of individuals who had a criminal justice contact in 1977. The criminal careers of these individuals were retrospectively reconstructed from age 12 and prospectively followed up until 2003. Criminal trajectories were estimated from ages 12–72 (Blokland, Nagin and Nieuwbeerta, 2005). While the majority of offenders followed a criminal trajectory that resembled the age–crime curve as found in cross-sectional data, a small percentage of offenders followed a more persistent criminal pathway involving substantial offending rates into their 40s and 50s. The CCLS has data on over 400 female offenders, which has allowed for the comparison and separate analysis of male and female criminal careers (Blokland and Van Os, 2010; Block et al., 2009).

A fifth study, not included in the Blokland and Nieuwbeerta (2006) review, is the 1984 birth cohort study. This study makes use of national police data on the criminal careers of all individuals born in the Netherlands in 1984 (Blokland et al., 2010). A unique feature of the 1984 birth cohort dataset is that it has information on the cultural background of each of the respondents, allowing for detailed comparisons between criminal career features across cultural groups.

In summary, in the Netherlands there are only a few longitudinal studies on the continuity and change in offending during early adulthood. Prior studies indicate that, while not as prevalent as during late adolescence, offending beyond age 18 is common, especially up to the early 20s. Research also suggests that, while most offenders desist from crime somewhere during the third decade of life, a minority goes on to develop a much more persistent pattern of offending. However, we shall present the results of two secondary longitudinal data analyses to provide insights into the patterns of continuity and change in offending from adolescence to early adulthood.

Criminal Careers up to Age 23: Continuity and Change in the 1984 Birth Cohort

The 1984 birth cohort study uses police data on all individuals born in the Netherlands in 1984 (Blokland et al., 2010). Police data in the Netherlands are registered in the Police Record System (PRS), which has been operational since 1986 but which can only be reliably used for scientific analyses from 1996 onwards (Bijleveld, 2006). Since the minimum age of legal responsibility in the Netherlands is 12, the 1984 birth cohort is the first cohort for which complete data on the entire criminal career are available.

The total number of individuals in the 1984 birth cohort is 170,891 (87,528 men and 83,363 women) – excluding individuals who either died or emigrated prior to the end of the follow-up period, which currently is 2007. Following the example of Statistics Netherlands, we define a person's cultural background on the basis of the country of birth of one of his or her parents: a person is native Dutch when both parents were born in the Netherlands, whereas if a person has at least one parent who was born outside of the Netherlands, that person is classified as ethnically non-Dutch. Based first on the country of birth of the mother, and second, in case the mother was born in the Netherlands, the country of birth of the father, we distinguished between five large categories of minorities: Surinamese (n = 4,484), Turks (n = 4,067), Moroccans (n = 3,674), Dutch Antilleans (n = 1,032), and a remainder category of all other ethnically non-Dutch (n = 12,835) (compared to total Dutch = 144,799). The male–female ratio is approximately 50–50 for all groups. Ethnically non-Dutch individuals in the 1984-birth cohort are by definition second-generation immigrants as they themselves were born in the Netherlands but at least one of their parents was not. The PRS contains information on every suspect detained by the police and the indictable offence(s) the person was accused of. Indictable offences, which in a later stage result in an acquittal or discharge from further prosecution, are removed from the PRS. The same applies to prosecutorial dismissals due to illegally obtained evidence, unlawful use of force, or wrongful accusations. Individuals who accept an out-of-court settlement remained in the PRS, as did some prosecutorial dismissals due to technical reasons other than those already mentioned. Furthermore, the removal of acquittals and discharges from prosecution was not always 100 per cent accurate. While cognisant of these differences in legal status, to adhere to the parlance of the criminal career paradigm we refer to individuals registered in the PRS as 'offenders' and not as 'suspects'.

Prevalence and Frequency of Offending between Adolescence (Ages 12–17) to Early Adulthood (Ages 18–23)

Of all 170,891 individuals in the study, 8.8 per cent (n = 7,680) of the men and 2.1 per cent (n = 1,719) of the women were registered as a suspect of a crime at least once as an adolescent (ages 12–17). The average age of onset for male juvenile offenders in the 1984 birth cohort was 15.5 years compared to 15.3 for that of female juvenile offenders. Of those juveniles registered at least once, 45.8 per cent of the boys were under age 16 at the time of first registration and 10.4 per cent were under age 14. Girls registered as juveniles were under age 16 in 52.3 per cent of the cases and under age 14 in 12.1 per cent of the cases. When we consider the average offending frequency only for those who have at least one registration in the PRS – or lambda – we found that the average male juvenile offender accounted for 2.6 registrations prior to age 18 compared to an average of 1.6 for female juvenile offenders. Most registrations of juvenile offenders pertained to property offences (respectively 42.0 and 43.9 per cent for boys and girls). Unexpectedly, violent offences were more common among female juvenile offenders (43.9 per cent) compared to male juvenile offenders (24.4 per cent). However, vandalism and public order offences were more common among boys than girls (respectively 25.5 vs 16.4 per cent). Of all juvenile offenders, relatively more girls (41.1 per cent) than boys (38.9 per cent) were registered at least once for a violent offence prior to age 18.

Participation in offending in early adulthood was higher than during adolescence. Of all individuals in the 1984 birth cohort, 21.4 per cent (n = 18,698) of the males and 4.5 per cent (n = 3,783) of the females were registered at least once between ages 18 and 23. Figure 2.5 shows that the cumulative age of onset curve for offenders in the 1984 birth cohort across the entire age period 12–23 for both men and women was very similar. For each gender, the linear increase in the cumulative percentage during early adulthood (ages 18–23) indicates that a considerable portion of those eventually registered did not have any registrations prior to age 18. In fact, new offenders entered the offender population at almost similar rates during both adolescence and early adulthood.

The frequency of offending was also higher during early adulthood than during adolescence, but during early adulthood it was lower for females than males (2.7 and 1.7 offences, respectively). As in adolescence, registrations in early adulthood pertained mostly to property offences. Violence was less common during early adulthood, especially among female offenders: registrations for violent offences made up 23.3 per cent of all registrations during this period for males and 20.7 per cent of all registrations for females. While more common among females than males during adolescence, violence is more common among males during early adulthood. Of all young adult offenders 35.4 per cent of the males and 25.6 per cent of the females were registered for a violent offence at least once.

Continuity and Change in Offending from Adolescence (Ages 12–17) to Adulthood (Ages 18–23)

To examine patterns of continuity and change in offending we categorized offenders as one-time offenders, recidivists, and chronics, based on the number of registrations they accumulated in each of the six-year age periods. Prior research has often categorized offenders as 'chronic' based on the relatively arbitrary number of five or more offences (Wolfgang, Figlio and Sellin, 1972).

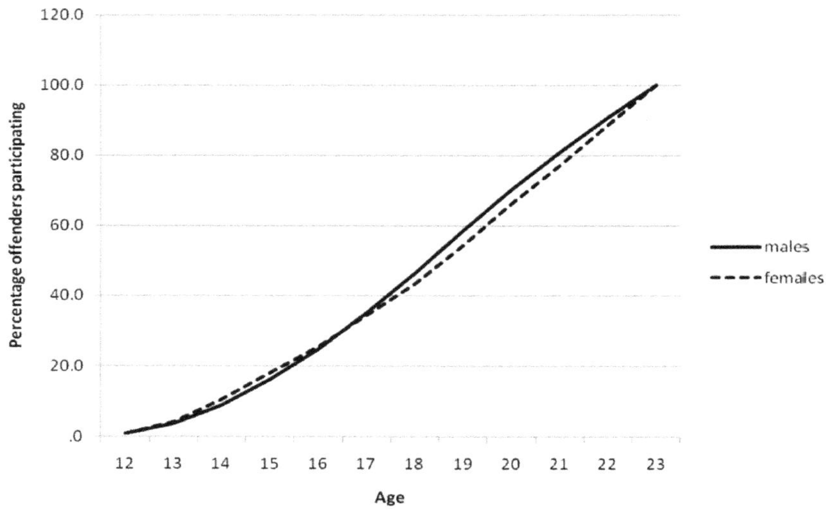

Figure 2.5 Per cent of offenders participating (cumulative) by age (1984 cohort)

Another, less arbitrary, approach is to calculate recidivism probabilities after each offence (Piquero, Farrington and Blumstein, 2007). It is often thought that, since the recidivism probability after a certain number of offences becomes relatively stable, this indicates that the remaining offenders constitute a relatively homogeneous group. Recidivism probabilities usually increase substantially after the second offence as a result of many one-time offenders desisting after their first offence. In the 1984 birth cohort data the recidivism probability after the first juvenile offence was 0.47 for males and 0.29 for females. As an example, Figure 2.6 shows that for male offenders the probability of recidivism increased from 0.60 to 0.73 after the second to fifth registration respectively. From the sixth registration onwards the recidivism probability stabilized at values close to 0.80. For male offenders, recidivism probabilities during early adulthood showed a similar trend, jumping from 0.48 to 0.60 after the second offence and then stabilizing at an average of 0.80 from the sixth registration onwards. For female offenders recidivism probabilities also showed a steep increase from the first to fifth registration (0.29 to 0.46 and 0.30 to 0.46 for adolescence and early adulthood, respectively). After the fifth registration the mean recidivism probability for female offenders was 0.63 during adolescence and 0.71 during early adulthood. However, the pattern for females became more variable due to small numbers of female offenders accumulating more than six registrations. Based on these outcomes during adolescence and early adulthood, we chose to define the following offender categories: non-offenders (no registration in this particular age period), one-time offenders (one registration in this particular age period), recidivists (two to five registrations in this particular age period), and

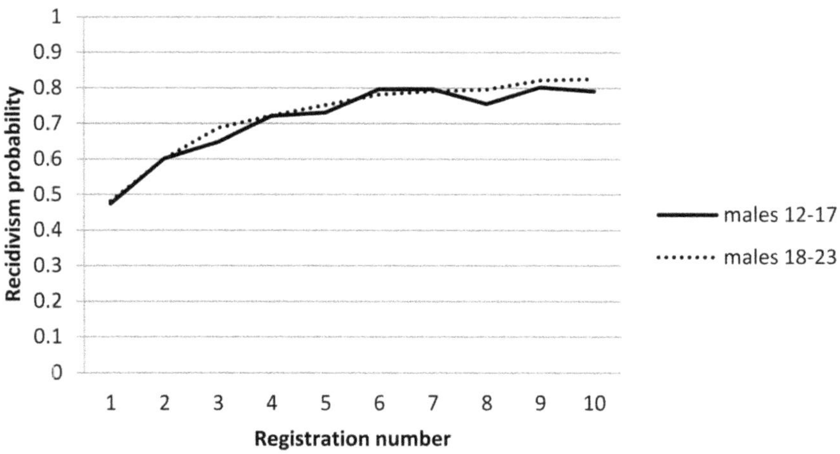

Figure 2.6 Recidivism probabilities for ages 12–17 and 18–23 by several numbers of registrations (1984 cohort)

chronic offenders (six or more registrations in this particular age period). Figures 2.7a and 2.7b show a schematic overview of continuity and change in offending from adolescence to early adulthood for males and females, respectively. Given their large share, 'stable non-offenders' – those individuals who did not accumulate any police registrations in either adolescence or early adulthood – are omitted from these figures. Of the males, 75 per cent did not have any police registrations up to age 23; for females, the percentage of stable non-offenders was 94. The figures thus pertain only to the 25 per cent of males and six per cent of the females who had at least one registration during early adulthood. Of those males registered at least once, 65 per cent were registered only as adults. Thus, these individuals did not have any police registrations prior to age 18. In contrast, 14.5 per cent of offenders had registrations prior to age 18 (of which the majority had only one), and thus remained registration free for at least five subsequent years prior to the end of the follow-up. A period of five years of non-offending is argued to be indicative of desistance rather than merely a temporary lull in offending (Blokland, 2005, pp. 34–5).

We also investigated changes and stability in the frequency of offending with age. Nearly three quarters (73.1 per cent) of male offenders showed an increase in the frequency of offending from adolescence to early adulthood – 8.9 per cent of all male offenders when we only considered those who started offending during adolescence and increased their level of offending during early adulthood. Moreover, 4.1 per cent of all male offenders showed a stable pattern of multiple registrations in both adolescence and early adulthood, and 1.7 per cent of all male offenders had six or more registrations in both age periods.

We next examined the relationship between the age of onset and chronicity of offending. Adolescent chronic offenders had the highest likelihood of becoming

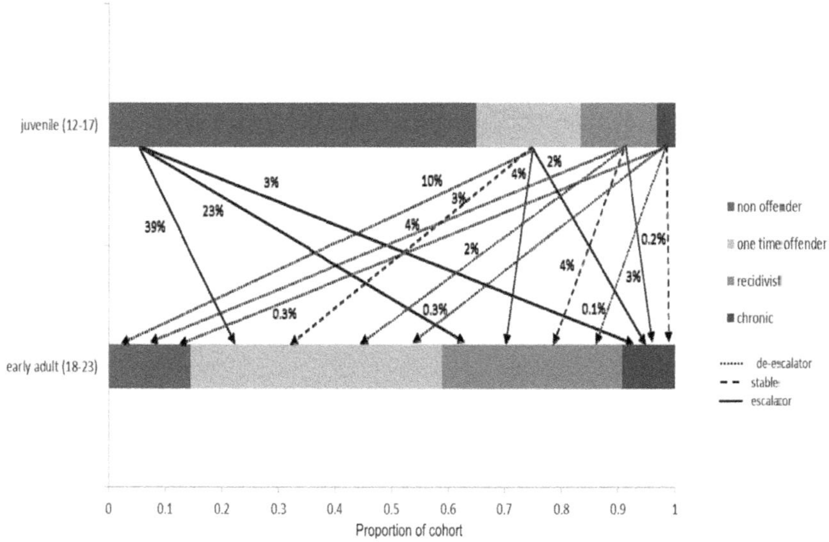

Figure 2.7a Continuity and discontinuity of offending between juvenile (12–17) and early adult (18–23) offending, male offenders only

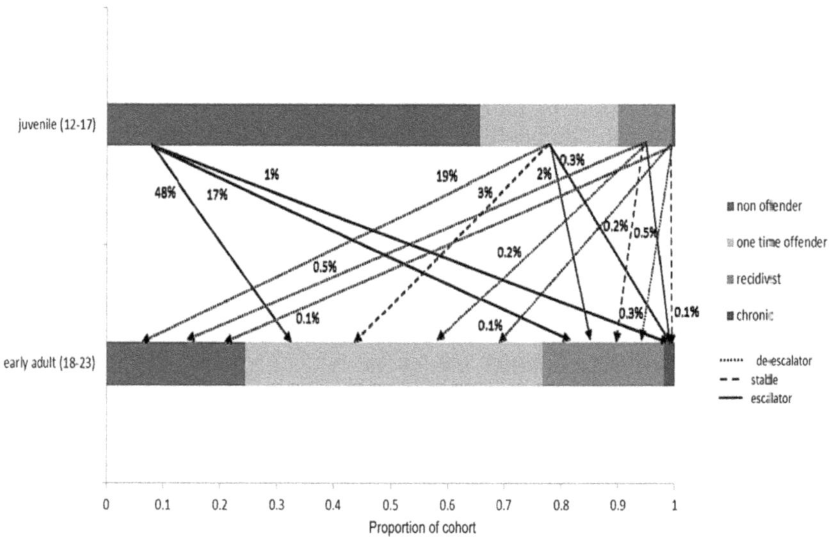

Figure 2.7b Continuity and discontinuity of offending between juvenile (12–17) and early adult (18–23) offending, female offenders only

adult chronic offenders. Male juvenile chronic offenders had a 3.9 greater probability of becoming adult chronic offenders than did juvenile non-chronic offenders.[3] For males, onset age was associated with offender type, with stable chronics having on average the earliest onset (age 14.2). The frequency of juvenile offending also predicted adult offending, with chronic juvenile offenders having the highest likelihood of becoming adult chronic offenders.

We investigated gender differences in offending between adolescence and early adulthood. Of all female offenders in the 1984 cohort, two thirds (66 per cent) were registered only during early adulthood. About one quarter (24 per cent) of female offenders were registered only during adolescence, compared to 14.5 per cent for males. Thus, there was more discontinuity in offending between adolescence and early adulthood for females than males. There were also gender differences in the frequency of offending: 68.4 per cent of female offenders – 2.8 per cent when we consider only those who started offending during adolescence and increased their level of offending during early adulthood – showed an accelerating pattern of offending between adolescence and early adulthood. Stable chronic offenders were rare among female compared to male offenders, with only 72 female offenders (0.1 per cent) following this developmental pattern, compared to 1.7 per cent of male offenders.

Similar to the findings on males, the age of onset of offending in females was related to offending frequency, with chronic female juvenile offenders having the earliest onset of offending. Chronic juvenile offending in females also strongly predicted chronic adult offending. In females, the probability of juvenile chronic offenders becoming adult chronic offenders was 8.07 higher than for juvenile non-chronic offenders.

Table 2.1 shows the percentage of offenders with at least one registration for a particular type of offence during early adulthood for males and females. The prevalence of violence was highest among stable chronic offenders, with almost all male stable chronic offenders and all female stable chronic offenders (96.0 and 100 per cent, respectively) having at least one registration for a violent offence up to age 23. Table 2.1 does not show any clear signs of specialization in offending, other than that female offenders were less likely than male offenders to be registered for vandalism and public order offences.

Ethnicity

The prevalence of offending during adolescence differed greatly for individuals from different cultural backgrounds. Figures 2.8a and 2.8b show the prevalence of offending during adolescence and early adulthood by cultural background for males and females. For all groups participation was higher during early adulthood

3 Relative risk = (number of juvenile chronic offenders becoming adult chronic offenders/total number of juvenile chronic offenders)/(number of juvenile non-chronic offenders becoming adult chronic offenders/total number of juvenile non-chronic offenders).

Table 2.1 Percentage of offenders registered at least once between ages 12 and 23 for different offender types

		Males			Females		
		% violence	% property	% vandalism	% violence	% property	% vandalism
Juvenile only	One time	23.5	30.6	31.7	31.0	46.8	15.8
	Recidivist	45.3	51.1	55.8	49.4	58.0	33.5
	Chronic	50.0	90.8	80.3	100.0	50.0	50.0
De-escalator	Recidivist – one time	59.3	64.7	62.0	79.2	68.8	37.7
	Chronic – one time	70.4	93.0	73.2	100.0	75.0	75.0
	Chronic – recidivist	86.3	94.7	86.3	76.5	82.4	76.5
Adult-onset	One time	18.8	16.0	24.1	16.9	37.7	10.3
	Recidivist	41.3	30.6	48.9	38.9	55.6	29.1
	Chronic	73.0	69.0	73.0	54.7	86.8	62.3
Escalator	One time – recidivst	61.7	56.1	61.1	63.4	69.3	47.5
	One time – chronic	81.2	80.6	77.8	85.7	92.9	64.3
	Recidivist – chronic	90.4	89.0	86.6	91.7	95.8	79.2
Stable	One time	40.5	39.7	46.4	54.6	60.5	21.1
	Recidivist	74.4	73.9	73.5	75.7	78.6	58.3
	Chronic	96.0	98.7	91.7	100.0	100.0	83.3

Source: 1984 cohort.

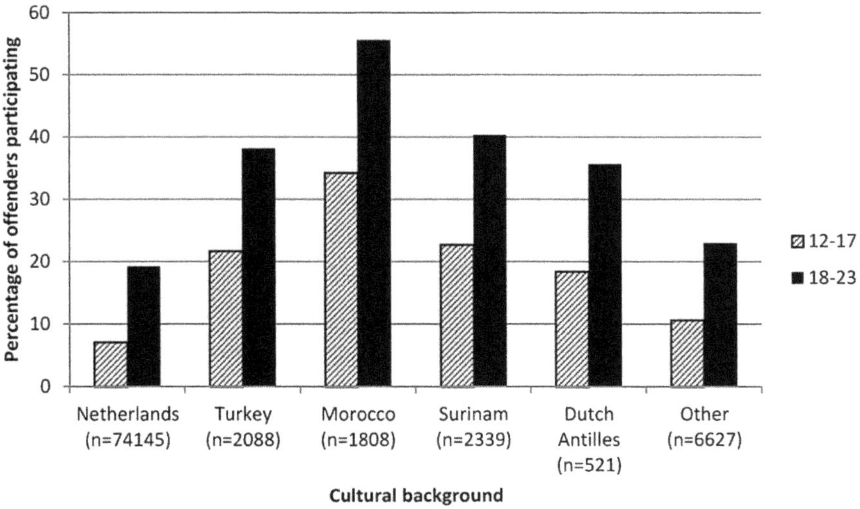

Figure 2.8a Criminal participation in the juvenile (ages 12–17) and early adult (ages 18–23) period across cultural background – males (1984 cohort)

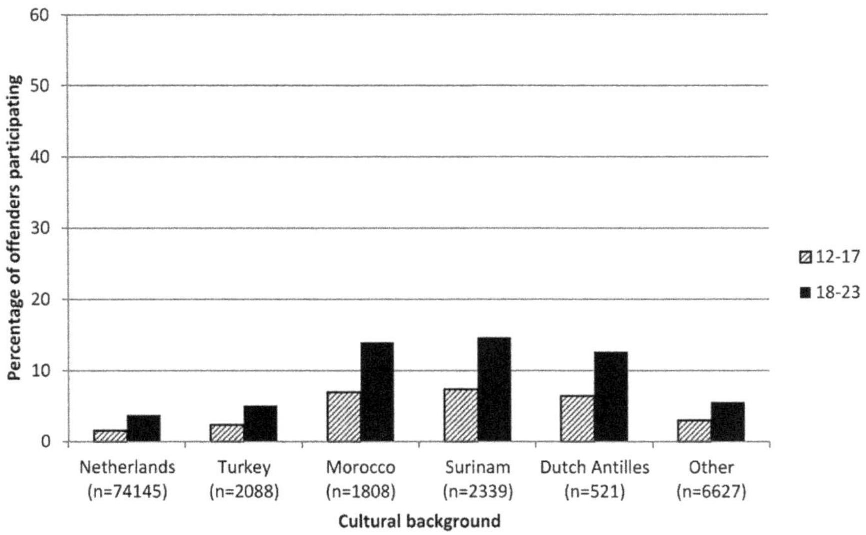

Figure 2.8b Criminal participation in the juvenile (ages 12–17) and early adult (ages 18–23) period across cultural background – females (1984 cohort)

Table 2.2 The prevalence of offender type for each cultural group by gender for ages 12–23

Offender pattern		Males						
		% Dutch	% Turkish	% Moroccan	% Surinamese	% Antillian	% Other	% Total
Non-offenders		77.6	54.5	37.1	52.2	57.8	72.3	75.0
Offenders		22.4	45.5	62.9	47.8	42.2	27.7	25.0
Juvenile only	One time	9.9	10.6	7.2	9.8	9.5	11.3	9.9
	Recidivist	4.0	5.1	4.0	5.3	5.9	5.4	4.3
	Chronic	0.3	0.5	0.4	0.6	–	0.5	0.3
De-escalator	Recidivist – one time	2.1	2.7	2.9	2.6	2.3	2.3	2.2
	Chronic – one time	0.3	0.3	0.5	0.4	–	0.3	0.3
	Chronic – recidivist	0.8	1.4	3.7	1.8	2.3	1.1	1.0
Adult-onset	One time	41.8	27.4	19.2	26.2	30.9	38.5	38.8
	Recidivist	23.1	21.9	20.5	22.6	21.4	20.2	22.6
	Chronic	3.3	3.0	5.7	3.6	4.1	3.2	3.4
Escalator	One time – recidivist	3.8	5.8	6.1	5.6	5.0	3.9	4.1
	One time – chronic	1.2	2.7	3.2	1.8	2.3	1.6	1.5
	Recidivist – chronic	2.0	4.2	7.6	4.7	5.5	2.7	2.6
Stable	One time	2.9	5.1	2.7	4.0	2.7	3.0	3.0
	Recidivist	3.4	6.7	8.4	8.1	5.5	4.3	4.1
	Chronic	1.2	2.5	7.8	2.7	2.7	1.6	1.7

Offending pattern		Females						
		% Dutch	% Turkish	% Moroccan	% Surinamese	% Antillian	% Other	% Total
Non-offenders		95.0	93.1	82.0	80.8	83.8	92.4	94.0
Offenders		5.0	6.9	18.0	19.2	16.2	7.6	6.0
Juvenile only	One time	19.3	19.7	16.4	15.8	14.5	20.8	18.9
	Recidivist	4.9	7.3	5.7	7.8	7.2	5.5	5.4
	Chronic	0.1	–	0.3	–	–	0.4	0.1
De-escalator	Recidivist – one time	1.3	2.9	3.0	1.2	3.6	1.9	1.5
	Chronic – one time	0.1	–	–	–	–	0.2	0.1
	Chronic – recidivist	0.1	–	1.5	1.2	1.2	0.2	0.3
Adult-onset	One time	50.0	45.3	34.8	43.2	42.2	45.0	47.7
	Recidivist	16.2	19.0	25.6	17.0	16.9	15.3	16.9
	Chronic	1.1	0.7	0.9	1.2	1.2	0.6	1.1
Escalator	One time – recidivist	1.8	1.5	3.9	2.2	4.8	1.7	2.0
	One time – chronic	0.2	–	0.9	0.2	1.2	0.2	0.3
	Recidivist – chronic	0.4	–	0.9	0.7	-	0.4	0.5
Stable	One time	2.5	2.2	3.3	6.1	2.4	4.5	3.0
	Recidivist	1.7	1.5	3.0	3.4	4.8	2.8	2.1
	Chronic	0.1	–	–	–	–	0.4	0.1

Source: 1984 cohort.

compared to adolescence. Overall, the prevalence in offending was higher in males compared to females. Participation was highest among Moroccan males, and girls from a Surinamese, Moroccan or Dutch Antillean background.

We addressed next to what extent ethnic differences in the prevalence of offending agreed with ethnic differences in the frequency of offending. The results for the frequency of offending were very similar to the results for the prevalence of offending, although the non-Dutch/Dutch ratios were much smaller. Thus, although many more individuals from non-Dutch backgrounds participated in crime, those who did had an offending rate that was similar to that of their Dutch counterparts (see also Blokland et al., 2010).

We also investigated ethnic difference in offending for males and females in the 1984 cohort during adolescence and early adulthood. Table 2.2 shows the percentages of offenders in each offender category for native Dutch and minority males and females. Percentages for each offender category are calculated as a percentage of the active offenders. For example, of all Dutch males, 22.4 per cent were registered at least once between ages 12 and 23. Of that group, 9.9 per cent were only registered once during adolescence and did not accumulate any other registrations during early adulthood. Table 2.2 shows that adult onset of male offending was most prevalent among Dutch youths (68.2 per cent of those registered) and was least prevalent (45.4 per cent) among Moroccans, indicating that more than half of those Moroccan boys who were registered in the PRS were registered prior to age 18. In addition, the juvenile-only pattern was least prevalent among Moroccan males, indicating that Moroccan boys who had police contacts were more likely than other minority boys to continue their criminal careers through early adulthood. As a result, escalating and stable offending patterns were most prevalent in Moroccan young males, with 7.8 per cent of Moroccan young adult offenders characterized as stable chronics, compared to 2.5–2.7 per cent of other minorities and 1.2 per cent of Dutch young adult males. Based on police registrations, Moroccan boys – even more so than boys of other minorities – showed a pattern of early-onset offending and frequent and persistent offending during adolescence, which placed them at risk to become adult chronic offenders.

For minority females, the adult-onset pattern was least common among Antillean, Moroccan and Surinamese girls, respectively 60.2, 61.3 and 61.4 per cent, compared to 67.3 per cent in Dutch girls. The juvenile-only pattern of offending was least common among Dutch Antillean girls. Both Moroccan and Dutch Antillean female offenders were at the highest risk of developing an escalating pattern of offending and of increasing frequency of offending from adolescence to early adulthood.

Criminal Careers up to Ages 24–29 and Beyond: Continuity and Change in the Criminal Career and Life-course Study

The second data set analysed here is the Criminal Career and Life-course Study (CCLS), a large-scale research project conducted by the Netherlands Institute for the Study of Crime and Law Enforcement (NSCR), which has been previously used to describe lifespan offending trajectories and the effects of life circumstances on these trajectories (Blokland, Nagin and Nieuwbeerta, 2005; Blokland and Nieuwbeerta, 2005). Court information and life-course data were collected on 4,612 randomly selected individuals, all convicted of a crime in the Netherlands in 1977. The respondents consisted of a representative sample of four per cent of all the criminal cases conclusively resolved in the Netherlands; they were either cases where a judge pronounced a sentence or cases dismissed by the public prosecutor for reasons of policy or due to insufficient evidence.[4] Ninety per cent of the CCLS sample were male, 10 per cent female; 13 per cent were born outside the Netherlands. Reflecting the historical period in which the CCLS sample was drawn, those born outside the Netherlands originated primarily from Surinam. Currently – unlike the 1984 birth cohort data – the CCLS holds no information on ethnic background for those born in the Netherlands. A more detailed description of the CCLS can be found in Blokland (2005).

Using extracts from the General Documentation Registry of the Ministry of Justice Court Documentation Service, a complete list of the criminal convictions of the individuals was drawn at the beginning of 2003. The Documentation Registry contains information on all the criminal cases registered by public prosecutors (not including crimes prosecuted abroad either before or after 1977). The regular extracts are supplemented by information on court cases not referred to in the extracts because of the period of limitation. This chapter only addresses registered crimes that led to conviction and charges that were dismissed by the public prosecutor for reasons of policy, concisely referred to here as 'convictions'. Acquittals and prosecurial dismissals for technical reasons, such as insufficient evidence, are not considered convictions under this definition.

Since the CCLS data is based on a conviction cohort, the data pose different restrictions on the analyses of continuity and change in offending compared to the 1984 birth cohort. The principal difference between a birth cohort and a conviction cohort is that in the latter all individuals have to have at least one criminal justice contact to be included in the sample. In the CCLS this is the 1977 index offence. Similar to the analysis of the 1984 birth cohort data, we distinguished between adolescence (ages 12–17), early adulthood (ages 18–23) and adulthood (ages 24–29). Of the total of 4,180 men in the CCLS sample, 637 (15 per cent) had their index offence between ages 12 and 17; 1,384 (33 per cent) between ages 18 and

4 In constructing the original sample serious crimes were oversampled while traffic crimes were undersampled. In the current analyses a weight factor is used to let the offenders again be representative of the Dutch offender population in 1977.

23; 865 (21 per cent) between ages 24 and 29; and the remaining 1,294 (31 per cent) were aged 30 or older in 1977. We selected the 1,384 men and 89 women convicted between ages 18 and 23 as our starting point. Given that our focus is in continuity and change in offending during early adulthood, we excluded all individuals who died prior to age 30 (n males = 26, n females = 3). We also excluded individuals whose 1977 index offence did not result in a 'conviction' and had no other convictions during early adulthood (n males = 51; n females = 25), leaving a sample of 1,297 men and 71 women available for the analyses. Given the small number of women in the remaining sample, the majority of the analyses apply to men only.

Prevalence and Frequency of Offending During Early Adulthood

Figure 2.9 shows the prevalence of offending and the frequency of offending among active offenders (lambda) by age, based on the longitudinal data of those aged 18 –23 at the time of their 1977 index offence. Participation in this sample resembled the familiar age–crime curve, with a slight overrepresentation of participation during early adulthood as a result of the nature of the sample. After reaching a peak during the late teens, participation in the early 20s gradually decreased as age increased. The frequency of offending, on the other hand, increased to about an average of two convictions per year at age 26 and remained stable from that age onwards. Fluctuations in lambda at later ages result from the

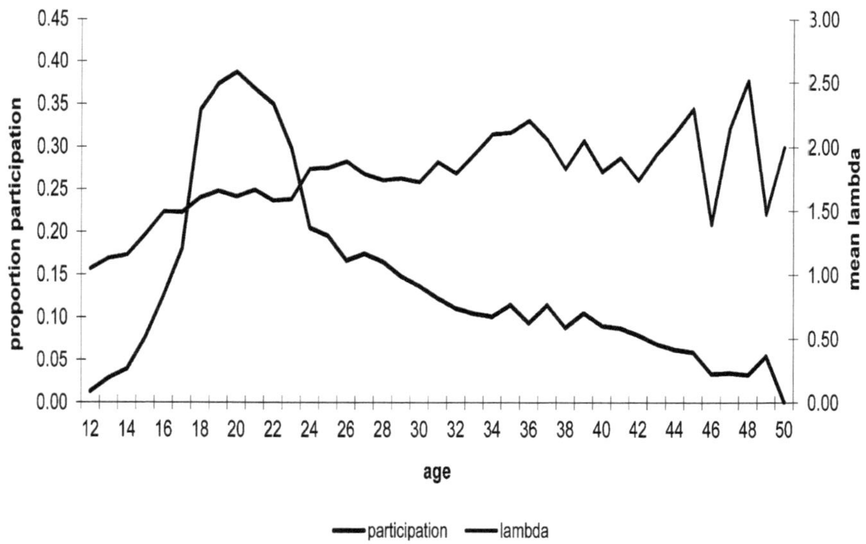

Figure 2.9 Participation and lambda by age (two-year periods) for men convicted between ages 18 and 23 (CCLS)

decreasing number of available active offenders. Figure 2.10 shows that, with age, fewer individuals were convicted, and those who were convicted committed crimes at a fairly stable average rate of around two convictions per year.

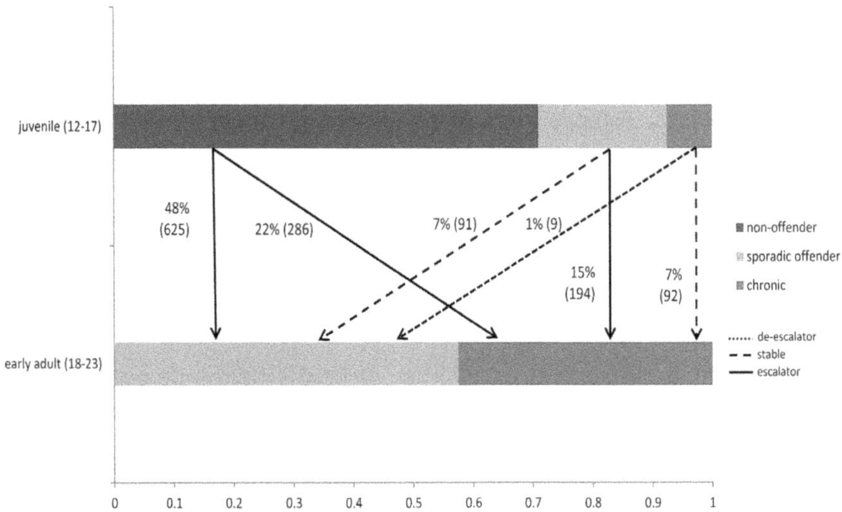

Figure 2.10 Graphical portrayal of the (dis)continuity between juvenile and early adult offending in males (CCLS)

Continuity and Change from Adolescence to Adulthood

Similar to our analyses of the 1984 birth cohort data, we calculated recidivism probabilities to distinguish offender categories within each age period. In the CCLS data, recidivism probabilities level off at the third offence at about 80 per cent. Because there was no clear difference in the probability of recidivism after the first and second offence, we distinguished for adolescence and early adulthood separately between 'non-offenders' with no convictions, 'sporadic offenders with one or two convictions, and 'chronics' with three or more convictions.

Figure 2.10 shows the continuity and change in offending for the sample. Notice that, unlike Figure 2.7 that was based on the 1984 birth cohort, Figure 2.10 does not have a category 'early adult non-offender'; the reason was that we had taken those between ages 18 and 23 at the time of their index offence as the starting point, and as a consequence there were no 'non-offenders' during this age period.[5]

5 When we analysed continuity and change among those aged 12–17 at the time of their index offence, we found that 61 per cent of men convicted between ages 12 and 17 were reconvicted in the age period 18–23. These percentages, however, do not readily

Some of those convicted in early adulthood did not have prior convictions, so we do have a 'non-offender' category during adolescence.

Focusing on those criminally active between ages in early adulthood, a striking 70 per cent were categorized as adult onsetters, who did not show any convictions prior to age 18. One in seven offenders in early adulthood could be characterized as escalators showing an increase in the frequency of offending from adolescence to early adulthood. Another seven per cent showed a stable pattern of chronic offending and had at least three convictions in either period. Few young adult offenders with prior juvenile convictions showed a pattern of stable sporadic offending (seven per cent) or de-escalation (less than one per cent).[6] Chronic young adult offenders (three or more convictions during early adulthood) had a 13.0 higher probability of having a history of chronic offending than did sporadic young adult offenders (OR = 14.7, $df = 1$, $p < 0.001$).

The Prevalence of Violence

Not surprisingly, the prevalence of violence differed significantly between non-offenders, sporadic offenders and chronic offenders (OR = 4.8, $df = 1$, $p < 0.001$), and was highest among chronic offenders in early adulthood, with 44.2 per cent of the chronic offenders having at least one conviction for violence by age 23. Overall, violence was slightly more common during ages early adulthood than during adolescence. Of those convicted during adolescence, 19.4 per cent were convicted for at least one violent offence compared to 24.8 per cent of those convicted in early adulthood. The frequency of violent convictions ranged from one to five during adolescence and from one to nine during early adulthood. The average proportion of violence within the criminal career was higher during early adulthood across all groups, except for the stable sporadic offender group. While stable sporadic offenders were more violent in early adulthood than adult-onset sporadic offenders ($t = -2.575$, $df = 105$, $p = 0.011$), chronic offenders showed no such difference ($t = -1.848$, $df = 376$, $p = 0.065$). Compared to adult sporadic offenders, adult chronic offenders had a three times higher likelihood of being convicted for a violent offence prior to age 18 (OR = 3.4, $df = 1$, $p < 0.001$).

---

translate to those aged 18–23 at the time of their index offence because individuals from different birth cohorts might show different developmental patterns.

6 Given that the sampling frame is based on being convicted in 1977 and that those showing a de-escalating pattern by definition have few convictions between ages 18 and 23, de-escalators are less likely to be included in the sample. To the extent that more active offenders have a higher chance of being sampled in 1977, the prevalence of the de-escalating pattern is underestimated in these data.

Continuity and Change Between Ages 12–23 and 24–29

Given that the follow-up period of the CCLS currently is 25 years, we could extend the analysis of continuity and change for this sample to the age period 24–29 (called adulthood). Figure 2.11 shows both continuity and change from ages 12–29. Desistence was common during adulthood, with over half of former offenders not showing any additional convictions during this period.[7] Unsurprisingly,

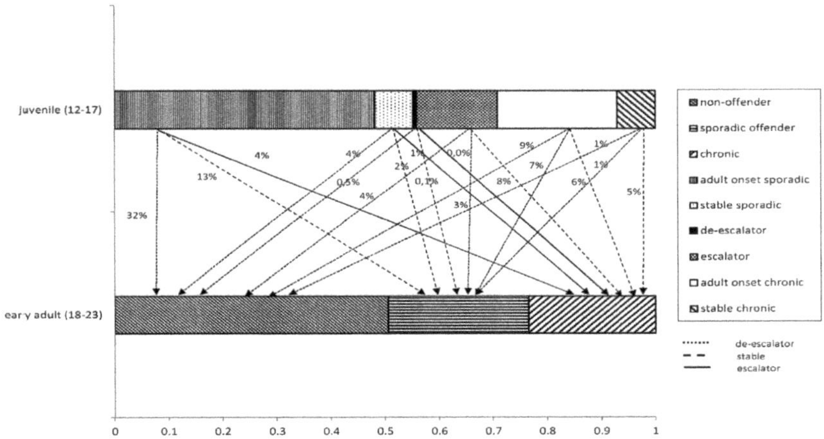

Figure 2.11 Graphical portrayal of the (dis)continuity between early adult and adult offending in males (CCLS)

desistance was most prominent among those offenders who did not show chronic offending during early adulthood: with about half to two thirds of stable sporadic offenders, de-escalators and adult-onset sporadic offenders (55, 66 and 66 per cent, respectively) not incurring a conviction during adulthood. Chronic offenders in early adulthood had a significantly greater probability of developing a persistent criminal career (OR = 8.6, $df = 1, p < 0.001$). Almost half of the chronic offenders (43.0 per cent) during early adulthood continued offending at a chronic level during adulthood compared to 8.0 per cent for those only sporadically convicted during early adulthood. Thus, among early adult offenders, a history of juvenile chronic offending was strongly predictive of chronicity during adulthood (OR = 6.7, $df = 1, p < 0.001$).

7 Again, given the selection of those convicted between ages 18 and 23 as our starting point, we did not have a category of onsetters at ages 24–29 in Figure 2.12. However, analysing the criminal careers of those aged 24–29 at the time of their index offence tells us that 49 per cent did not have any prior convictions.

Violent Offending from Ages 12–29

Figure 2.12 shows that the stable chronic offenders had the highest likelihood of being convicted for at least one violent offence. Both at the overall level as well as on the level of the individual criminal career – as shown in Figure 2.13 – the CCLS data did not show any clear sign of escalation beyond age 23. In fact only for the least active offender categories, slightly more offenders were convicted for violence between ages 24 and 29 than was the case during early adulthood, while for the more active categories this trend was reversed. When we consider the proportion of violence convictions relative to the entire number of convictions

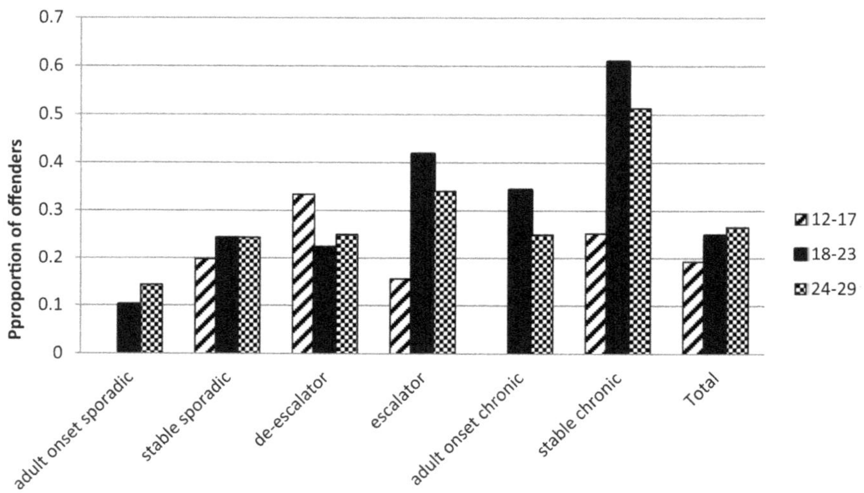

Figure 2.12 Proportion of male offenders with at least one conviction for a violent offence at different age periods for those convicted in that age period by offender type (CCLS)

during adolescence, early adulthood and adulthood, violence was either as prominent or less prominent in the criminal careers of high frequency offenders (ages 12–17: F = 2.030, $df = 3$, $p = 0.074$; ages 18–23: F = 5.068, $df = 5$, $p < 0.01$; ages 24–29: F = 1.586, $df = 5$, $p = 0.162$). Violent offending during adolescence predicted chronic offending during adulthood (OR = 2.9, $df = 1$, $p < 0.01$).

Residual Career Length and Residual Number of Offences

The long-term follow-up of the CCLS allowed for yet another perspective on continuity and change in offending. Given that we selected offenders aged 18–23 at the time of their 1977 index offence and that we had available criminal career data up to 2003, we could analyse the residual career length of those offenders

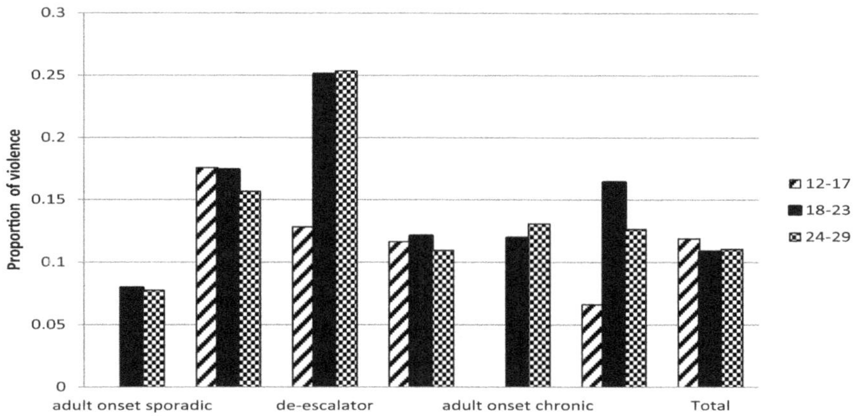

Figure 2.13 Average proportion of violence at different age periods for males convicted in that age period by offender type (CCLS)

all the way up to ages 43–48. Residual career length (RCL) is defined as the remaining number of years until the last offence. We also calculated the residual number of offences (RNO) defined as the number of offences still remaining in the criminal career. For instance, imagine a stable sporadic offender convicted once at age 16, 22 and 28. His or her respective RCL at each age would be 12, 6 and 0, and his or her RNO respectively 2, 1 and 0. Since very few datasets have long-term prospective information on criminal careers, the distribution of RCL and RNO is an understudied topic in criminal career research (Kazemian and Farrington, 2006). We calculated the residual career length up to age 40 for those offenders with at least one conviction during early adulthood and at least one conviction beyond that period leaving 797 male offenders in the analyses. Since the data are right censored at age 43–48 depending on the offender's age at the time of the index offence, this comes down to a period of three to eight years of non-offending being counted as desistance, which seems reasonable given the prior literature and the overall low prevalence of offending after age 40 in the CCLS data set (Blokland, Nagin and Nieuwbeerta, 2005).

Figure 2.14 depicts the average RCL and RNO for the total of 797 selected offenders at each age from 18–40, controlled for attrition due to early deaths. For those convicted at age 18, the average number of years until their last officially recorded conviction was 19.1 (with a maximum possible RCL of 25 years), while those convicted at age 24 could also be expected to remain criminally active until age 37. As shown in Figure 2.14, both RCL and RNO showed a linear decline with age and were significantly correlated. Prior to age 26, the average RCL was higher than the average RNO, indicating intermittency in offending. After age 30, RNO exceeds RCL indicating a higher conviction rate among those offenders still active during these later ages.

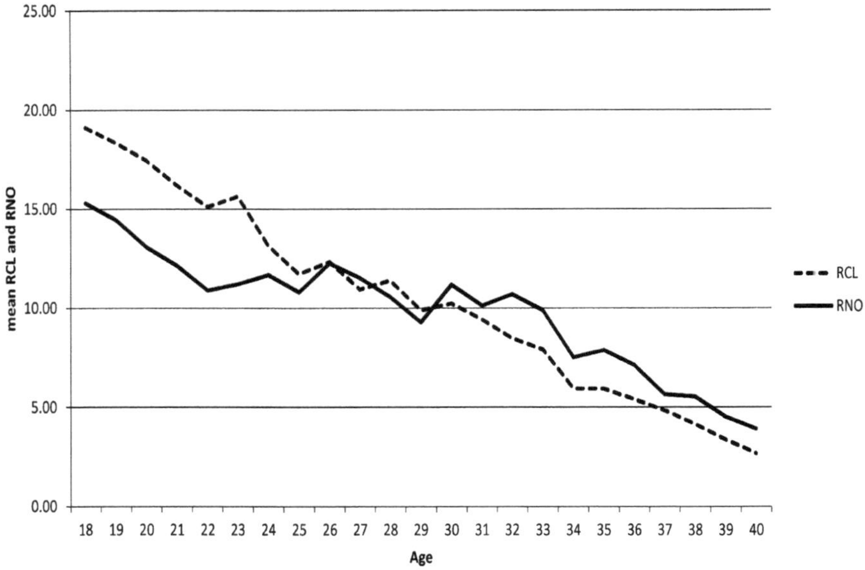

Figure 2.14 Residual career length (RCL) and residual number of offences (RNO) by age in males (CCLS)

Table 2.3 compares the distribution of RCL and RNO according to age on offence and offender type as shown in Figure 2.11. Offender type was significantly related to both RCL and RNO (F = 44.058, *df* = 5, $p < 0.01$; F = 104.207, *df* = 5, $p < 0.01$). The residual career length was highest for offenders showing an escalating pattern of offending from adolescence to early adulthood. After offending during early adulthood, the average escalating offender could be expected to be criminally active for another 18.8 years compared to another 13.7 years for offenders whose criminal behaviour during early adulthood showed a declining trend. Of all offenders, stable chronic offenders had the highest RNO. The average number of additional offences for offenders in this category was 21.9, 18, and 9.5 at ages 18–23, 24–29, and 30 and higher, respectively. RCL and RNO diverged most between offender groups in the age period 30 and higher, suggesting that the effect of age 12–23 offender type was greatest in that age period compared to early adulthood (the interaction between ages 12–23 offender type and age was statistically significant for both RCL: F = 4.175, *df* = 10, $p < 0.01$, and RNO: F = 9.567, *df* = 10, $p < 0.01$). If those de-escalating between ages 12–23 showed any criminal activity beyond age 30, this seemed sporadic and short lived, while escalators and chronics active beyond age 30 committed crimes at a continuously high rate.

Table 2.3 Average residual career length (RCL) and residual number of offences (RNO) according to age on offence and offender typology at ages 12–23

	Age on offence							
	18–23		24–29		30 plus		Total	
Offender type at ages 12–23	RCL	N	RCL	N	RCL	n	RCL	n
Adult-onset sporadic	13.8	352	8.3	309	3.1	403	8.1	1,063
Stable sporadic	16.5	81	10.3	57	5.0	97	10.3	235
De-escalator	13.7	7	5.6	6	.6	4	7.8	18
Escalator	18.8	622	13.8	411	5.6	628	12.6	1,660
Adult-onset chronic	16.2	640	11.6	330	5.2	492	11.5	1,462
Stable chronic	18.4	312	13.0	214	6.1	348	12.2	874
Total	**16.9**	**2,013**	**11.7**	**1,327**	**5.0**	**1972**	**11.2**	**5,312**
	RNO	N	RNO	N	RNO	n	RNO	n
Adult-onset sporadic	3.9	352	4.5	309	3.3	403	3.8	1,063
Stable sporadic	4.3	81	3.8	57	1.9	97	3.2	235
De-escalator	2.8	7	1.1	6	2	4	1.6	18
Escalator	16.9	622	14.3	411	7.5	628	12.7	1,660
Adult-onset chronic	10.5	640	10.1	330	5.8	492	8.8	1,462
Stable chronic	21.9	312	18.0	214	9.5	348	16.0	874
Total	**12.8**	**2,013**	**11.1**	**1,327**	**6.3**	**1,972**	**9.9**	**5,312**

Source: CCLS.

Criminal Careers of Males and Females

While the CCLS data set has information on over 400 women, due to the age limitations applied in the current analysis (at least one conviction during early adulthood) only 71 women remained in the dataset. Together these 71 women accounted for 230 convictions. The prevalence of offending by females was always lower than that of males during adolescence and early adulthood. The average offending frequency of active female offenders was also lower than that for males, but the offence frequency of female offenders was as stable with age as for male offenders. With regard to continuity from adolescence to early adulthood, we found that 84 per cent of female offenders fell into the adult onset category. Nine per cent showed a pattern of stable sporadic offending and three per cent a de-escalating criminal career. For four per cent of female offenders the number of convictions escalated from less than three during adolescence to more than three during early adulthood. None of the female offenders fell into the category of stable chronics. Extending the analysis to include adulthood, we found that 66 per cent of female offenders convicted between during early adulthood desisted from crime in the subsequent six-year period. Fifteen per cent showed an escalating pattern and had more convictions during adulthood than during early adulthood. RCL for female offenders decreased linearly with age, as with male offenders. RNO started out lower and decreased less steeply for females. In summary, women's criminal behaviour tended to start later and was shorter than that of men. However, the results should be interpreted with caution because the number of women in each of the offender categories was small.

Conclusions and Discussion

Prevalence and Frequency

Officially registered offending was more prevalent during early adulthood than it was during adolescence. However, the average offending frequency for active offenders was only slightly higher during early adulthood. Therefore, the shape of the age–crime curve for populations seemed to be predominantly driven by age-graded differences in participation.

Patterns of Continuity and Change

Contrary to common opinion in the criminological literature (for example, Farrington, 2003), but in line with a growing number of other studies (Piquero et al., 2012), we found a large proportion of offenders with an onset of offending during adulthood. In fact, the offender population increased almost linearly from adolescence to early adulthood. Change from offending to non-offending was common during early adulthood too, as many offenders desisted from crime, especially during their late 20s. Besides change, we also found continuity in offending. Chronic juvenile offending predicted persistence in offending in early adulthood. A stable pattern of frequent offending from ages 12–23 was associated with prolonged and frequent criminal involvement.

Crime Mix

While fewer juveniles than young adults engaged in violence, we found no evidence for criminal careers becoming increasingly violent with age. Even more so than the criminal careers of temporary and sporadic offenders, chronic young adult offenders' careers were dominated by property offences.

Gender Differences

Crime was both more prevalent and frequent among male than among female young adults. Female criminal careers, while showing comparable patterns of onset across adolescence and early adulthood, were relatively short lived, with females showing less continuity in offending from adolescence to early adulthood.

Minorities

Young adults from minority backgrounds were overrepresented in officially registered crime. Boys of Moroccan descent stood out especially in terms of the early onset, frequency and persistence of their offending. Police registrations were also more common among Surinamese, Moroccan and Dutch Antillean girls compared to Dutch girls. However, it is important to bear in mind that minority youths were overrepresented in crime only relative to their share of the total population. These findings do not indicate that the majority of juvenile or young adult offenders in the Netherlands are of a minority background. Given that non-Western minorities in the Netherlands constitute only around 10 per cent of the population, in absolute numbers native Dutch offenders account for the lion's share of all crime.

Caveats

The current analyses have certain limitations in that they made use only of official records. Official data are potentially biased – to some unknown extent – because they measure not only respondents' behaviour, but also the behaviour of the criminal justice system. In contrast, self-reported delinquency also includes delinquent acts that have not come to the attention of the police. Longitudinal studies should gather both official and self-report data on the same population in an effort to triangulate information on patterns of continuity and change in criminal behaviour over age. Having their roots in research into juvenile delinquency, current self-report studies tend to focus mainly on less serious crime. As original samples age, and research attention is broadened to young adults, self-report studies will have to adapt their measurement instrument to encompass different types of offences. When studying criminal development during early adulthood, self-report studies can be especially valuable to gain insight into crimes that are notoriously less visible to the criminal justice system, such as delinquency in the workplace and family violence.

A second limitation lies in the time frame of the available studies. By necessity, studies with longer follow-up periods are based on older cohorts. Although not completely separated from individuals' biological maturation, different life stages originate primarily from a society's larger socioeconomic structure. As structural conditions change, so will the conceptual segmentation of the lifespan. Since the 1970s the social timetable of the life course has undergone dramatic changes and 'emerging adulthood' might even be considered a fairly recent phenomenon. Given the importance life course criminological theories attribute to the commitment to adult social roles in desistance from crime, the increased postponement of adult obligations and the resulting evolution of early adulthood might have important repercussions for the development of criminal careers, which in turn limits the extent to which results obtained from older samples will be replicated for criminal development in younger cohorts.

Implications for Theory

Our findings reflect both continuity and change and are in line with ontogenetic theories (for example, Gottfredson and Hirschi, 1990) and developmental theories (for example, Moffitt, 1993). We found that chronic offending during early adulthood is associated with a history of many juvenile convictions, and to a lesser extent juvenile violence. In turn, a stable pattern of frequent offending during adolescence and early adulthood predicted persistence in crime, a long residual career length, and especially a high number of convictions.

Our results also show substantial variability in the criminal career patterns of young adults. This variability complicates the notion of rank-order stability in criminal behaviour hypothesized by ontogenetic theories (for example, Gottfredson and Hirschi, 1990). Every category of juvenile offenders had individuals showing escalating as well as de-escalating criminal career patterns as they aged into young early adulthood. This finding makes it hazardous to predict criminal career progression based solely on juvenile criminal career characteristics. At the same time, the observed diversity in offending patterns is difficult to reconcile with the notion that individual offenders' frequency of offending follows the age–crime curve. Finally, our analyses showed that many offenders started offending only past age 18. These offenders developed a more than 'sporadic' criminal career, which does not seem to fit well within the theoretical framework of Moffitt's (1993) taxonomy.

Early adulthood is the decade of life in which the majority of adolescents increasingly immerse themselves in adult social roles and obligations. Criminological theories have stressed the potential dampening effects of these transitions on offending due to the changing incentive structures that are inherent in these transitions (Laub and Sampson, 2001; Averdijk, Elffers and Ruiter, Chapter 3, this volume). Increased conventional bonding provides young adults with a growing stake in conformity, rendering them less likely to engage in behaviour that might jeopardize their newly acquired position. Prior research underlines the effect life-course transitions can have on criminal development (see the review by Blokland and Nieuwbeerta, 2010). In the present data many offenders appeared to desist from crime during early adulthood. Yet the criminal careers of a considerable number of offenders showed just the opposite development. For these offenders delinquency started or became increasingly frequent as they made the transition to adulthood. This pattern is more difficult to reconcile with the idea of increased conventional social bonding.

At least three processes may underlie divergent developmental patterns of offending during early adulthood. First, as suggested by interactional theory (Thornberry and Krohn, 2005) the escalating pattern of offending during early adulthood may reflect individual characteristics whose negative outcomes had thus far been buffered by a supportive social environment. When social support starts to wane as young people age and when young adults are increasingly left to their own devices, deficits in human capital – especially low academic competence – can quickly become deficits in social capital. As these young adults start to lag behind their same-aged peers and increasingly fail to make the expected transitions to adulthood, they become increasingly vulnerable to crime as a way to cope with the accumulation of life stressors they experience. According to Thornberry and Krohn (2005), individual characteristics, such as low intelligence, do not directly make an individual more prone to crime; it is only in interaction with shifting contextual demands that these vulnerabilities cause young adults to embark on a criminal trajectory.

Second, the linkage between adult roles and crime is not a one-way street. Adult social roles can affect subsequent criminal development. However, prior criminal behaviour may also affect individuals' success and completion of transitions to conventional roles. Although some rule breaking is condoned or even considered normative during adolescence, some teenagers experience negative labelling as a result of their delinquent behaviour. When society's reaction is disapproving and isolating, crime has the two-pronged effect of both weakening restraints and strengthening incentives for future criminal behaviour. This negative labelling may alter individuals' self-image, foreclose avenues of conventional development, or increase associations with deviant subgroups. Sampson and Laub's (1997) age-graded theory mentions cumulative continuity as a major force in bringing about persistence in crime during early adulthood. Criminal behaviour has an attenuating effect on an individual's social and institutional bonds, disconnecting adolescents from conventional developmental trajectories. Attenuated bonds in turn make future criminal behaviour more likely, thus setting in motion a downward spiral of cumulative disadvantage that leads to prolonged criminal involvement throughout adulthood. Moffitt (1997) mentioned that adolescent delinquents can become ensnared by the detrimental consequences of their delinquent involvement, making desistance from crime more difficult.

Third, transitions to adult roles also bring along new opportunities and motivations for crime. For example, a new job can provide unsupervised access to valuable goods. In the same manner, a new relationship can provide the context for intimate partner violence. Extant developmental theories, such as Moffitt's taxonomy, have primarily addressed these opportunities and the new types of criminal behaviour that result from them in terms of the continuation of an antisocial lifestyle (Moffitt, 1997). However, transitions to adult roles may not only provide for new criminal opportunities but also carry with them new obligations and expectations that, when young adults experience trouble meeting these expectations, can also provide new and strong incentives for criminal behaviour.

The transition to parenthood, for example, has been shown to elevate criminal behaviour in those who highly value parenthood but at the same time feel that they themselves are failing at being a good parent (Liu and Kaplan, 2001; see also Bijleveld, Van der Geest and Hendriks, Chapter 5, this volume). In their efforts to explain criminal career patterns during early adulthood, developmental and life course criminological theories should pay equal heed to the opportunities and impetus for crime that are as inherent in adult transitions as are its impediments.

While crime – especially officially registered crime – was less prevalent among women than among men, patterns of continuity and change show important differences between the sexes. The existing empirical focus on the criminal behaviour of boys has left the generalisability of current developmental theories questionable. Future longitudinal studies should focus on both men and women. For the same reason, studies should also make an effort of including individuals from different cultural backgrounds, especially in the European context, where minorities often are residents of former colonies or migrant workers from non-Western countries. These groups may adhere to different cultural codes regarding the social timing and sequencing of important life course transitions or even the age at which crime is deemed exceedingly inappropriate. General risk factors, like low socioeconomic status, may to a large extent suffice to explain differences in criminal participation between different cultural groups. However, differences in what is considered the appropriate timing of transitions or the obligations and expectations associated with different adult roles might help to explain the way crime develops when adolescents transition to adulthood in these different minority populations.

Policy Implications

From a policy perspective our results support a focus on delinquent youths. A history of juvenile delinquency increases adolescents' risk for persistent offending in adulthood. However, at the same time our results warrant caution: most juvenile delinquents, including those with a substantial number of criminal justice contacts, showed a slowing down or a termination of offending as they made the transition to adulthood. On the other hand, a significant number of adolescents showed an offending trajectory starting in early adulthood and escalating in severity with age. Predictions of future criminal development based solely on juvenile delinquent history are therefore bound to produce a considerable amount of errors.

Adult onset was common in our data. This suggests that intervention programmes aimed at preventing young people from commencing on a criminal trajectory should therefore not stop when youths formally reach the 'adult' age of 18, or even age 21. The third decade in life has increasingly become characterized by independence, role explorations, and opportunities. However, some youths have few capacities for independence and lack the skills needed to steer clear of the negative consequences some of these explorations can have.

For these youths who are unable to take full advantage of opportunities when they arise, this newly demarcated period of freedom and 'role-lessness' can trigger a downward spiral leading to prolonged criminal involvement. Official labelling as a delinquent may add to this accumulation of disadvantage. For that reason, criminal justice interventions should be organized in ways to prevent blocking juveniles from conventional avenues of development as much as possible.

Finally, efforts should be made to better understand the specific difficulties encountered by adolescents from immigrant backgrounds. While it is clear that these youths experience an elevated risk of continued criminal justice contacts during adolescence and early adulthood, far less is known about whether this results from these youths experiencing higher levels of risk factors similar to those experienced by the majority population. It is also possible that other barriers, like cultural conflict or dissonance, or discrimination on the labour and marriage market, make it more difficult for minority youths to successfully make the transition to adulthood.

This chapter is best viewed as a first 'sketch' of patterns of continuity and change in offending during early adulthood. Criminal career research in the Netherlands, while not in its infancy anymore, has yet to reach its full growth. Currently, only a limited number of population-based studies can provide information on the development of crime in young adults. Notwithstanding the need for more longitudinal studies that encompass the period between ages 18 and 28, the analyses presented in this chapter convey important information on criminal careers patterns among Dutch young adults and provide the foundation for more in-depth analysis.

In the introduction to this chapter we referred to the 'steps of life' in a metaphorical staircase of life development, a concept that was popular in the Netherlands in the sixteenth and seventeenth centuries. For many Dutch adolescents the transition from adolescence to adulthood, while not as clear cut as ascending a next step on a flight of stairs, seems to materialize sometime during the third decade of life. Given the interdependency of conventional and criminal trajectories, this decade constitutes a key period in our efforts to understand the processes of continuity and change in criminal career development.

References

Arnett, J.J. (2004). *Young Adulthood: The Winding Road from Late Teens through the Twenties*. New York: Oxford University Press.

Arnett, J.J. (2007). The long and leisurely route: Coming of age in Europe today. *Current History*, March, 130–6.

Bijleveld, C.C.J.H. (2006). *Methoden en technieken van onderzoek in de criminologie*, 2nd revised edition. The Hague: Boom Juridische Uitgevers.

Block, R., Blokland, A., Van der Werff, N., Van Os, R., and Nieuwbeerta, P. (2010). Long-term patterns of offending in women. *Feminist Criminology*, 5, 73–107.

Blokland, A. and Nieuwbeerta, P. (2005). The effects of life circumstances on longitudinal trajectories of offending. *Criminology*, 43(4), 1203–40.

Blokland, A. and Nieuwbeerta, P. (2006). *Developmental and Life Course Studies in Delinquency and Crime: A Review of Contemporary Dutch Research*. The Hague: Boom Legal Publishers.

Blokland, A. and Nieuwbeerta, N. (2010). Life course criminology. In S.G. Shoham and P. Knepper (eds), *International Handbook of Criminology*. Boca Raton, FL: CRC Press/Taylor and Francis, pp. 51–94.

Blokland, A. and Van Os, R. (2010). Life span offending trajectories of convicted Dutch women. *International Criminal Justice Review*, 20, 169–87.

Blokland, A., Grimbergen, K., Bernasco, W., and Nieuwbeerta, P. (2010). Criminaliteit en etniciteit; Criminele carrières van autochtone en allochtone jongeren uit het geboorte cohort 1984. *Tijdschrift voor Criminologie*, 52, 122–52.

Blokland, A.A.J. (2005). *Crime over the Lifespan: Trajectories of Criminal Behavior in Dutch Offenders*. Leiden: NSCR.

Blokland, A.A.J., Nagin, D.S., and Nieuwbeerta, P. (2005). Life span offending trajectories of a Dutch conviction cohort. *Criminology*, 43, 19–54.

Blom, M., Oudhof, J., Bijl, R.V., and Bakker, B.F.M. (eds) (2005). *Verdacht van criminaliteit. Allochtonen en autochtonen nader bekeken*. The Hague: WODC.

Donker, A. (2004). *Precursors and Prevalence of Young-adult and Adult Delinquency*. Leiden: University of Leiden (Ph.D. dissertation).

Donker, A., Kleemans, E., Van der Laan, P.H., and Nieuwbeerta, P. (2004). Ontwikkelings- en levensloop criminologie in vogelvlucht. *Tijdschrift voor Criminologie*, 46(4), 322–9.

Donker, A., Smeenk, W., Van der Laan, P.H., and Verhulst, F. (2003). Individual stability of antisocial behavior from childhood to adulthood: Testing the stability postulate of Moffitt's developmental theory. *Criminology*, 41, 593–609.

Elzinga, C.H. and Liefbroer, A.C. (2007). De-standarization of family-life trajectories of young adults: A cross-national comparison using sequence analysis. *European Journal of Population*, 23, 225–50.

Farrington, D.P. (1986). Age and crime. In M. Tonry and N. Morris (eds), *Crime and Justice, Annual Review of Research* (vol. 7). Chicago, IL: University of Chicago Press, pp. 189–250.

Farrington, D.P. (2003). Developmental and life-course criminology: Key theoretical and empirical issues – The 2002 Sutherland Award address. *Criminology*, 41, 221–56.

Gerris, J.R.M., Vermulst, A.A., Van Boxtel, D.A.A.M., Jansens, J.M.A.M., Van Zutphen, R.A.H., and Felling, A.J.A. (1993). *Parenting in Dutch Families: A Representative Description of Dutch Family Life in terms of Validated Concepts Representing Characteristics of Parents, Children, The Family as a System and Parental Socio-cultural Value Orientations*. Nijmegen: Institute of Family Studies, University of Nijmegen.

Giordano, P.C., Cernkovich, S.A., and Rudolph, J.L. (2002). Gender, crime, and desistance: Toward a theory of cognitive transformation. *American Journal of Sociology*, 107, 990–1064.
Gottfredson, M.R. and Hirschi, T. (1990). *A General Theory of Crime*. Palo Alto, CA: Stanford University Press.
Goudriaan, H. and Eggen, A.Th.J. (2009). Verdachten van criminaliteit. In S.N. Kalidien and A.Th.J. Eggen (eds), *Criminaliteit en rechtshandhaving 2008; ontwikkelingen en samenhangen*. The Hague, NL: WODC/CBS, pp. 101–36.
Hoeve, M., Smeenk, W., Loeber, R., Southamer-Loeber, M., Van der Laan, P.H., Gerris, J.R.M., and Dubas, J.S. (2007). Long-term effects of parenting and family characteristics on delinquency of male young adults. *European Journal of Criminology*, 4, 161–94.
Huishoudstatistiek (2008). At www.cbs.nl, accessed 16 February 2012.
Jennissen, R. (2009). *Criminaliteit, leeftijd en etniciteit: over de afwijkende leeftijdsspecifieke criminaliteitscijfers van Antillianen en Marokkanen*. The Hague: WODC.
Jennissen, R.P.W. and Blom, M. (2007). *Allochtone en autochtone verdachten van verschillende delicttypen nader bekeken*. The Hague: WODC.
Kazemian, L. and Farrington, D.P. (2006). Exploring residual career length and residual number of offenses for two generations of repeat offenders. *Journal of Research in Crime and Delinquency*, 43, 89–113.
Kommer, M.M. (1988). Criminele carrières; van inhoudelijk concept tot analytisch instrument. *Justitiële Verkenningen*, 14, 7–36.
Landsheer, J.A. and Van Dijkum, C. (2005). Male and female delinquency trajectories from pre through middle adolescence and their continuation in late adolescence. *Adolescence*, 40, 729–48.
Laub, J.H. and Sampson, R.J. (2001). Understanding desistance from crime. *Crime and Justice: A Review of Research*, 28, 1–69.
Laub, J.H. and Sampson, R.J. (2003). *Shared Beginnings, Divergent Lives: Delinquent Boys to Age 70*. Cambridge, MA: Harvard University Press.
Liu, X. and H.B. Kaplan (2001). Role strain and illicit drug use: The moderating influence of commitment to conventional values. *Journal of Drug Issues*, 31, 833–56.
Moffitt, T.E. (1993). Adolescence-limited and life-course-persistent antisocial behavior: A developmental taxonomy. *Psychological Review*, 100, 674–701.
Moffitt, T.E. (1997). Adolescence-limited and life-course-persistent offending: A complementary pair of developmental theories. In T.P. Thornberry (ed.), *Developmental Theories of Crime and Delinquency* (vol. 7). New Brunswick, NJ: Transaction Publishers, pp. 11–54.
Nieuwbeerta, P. and Blokland, A.A.J. (2003). *Criminal Careers of Adult Dutch Offenders (Codebook and Documentation)*. Leiden: NSCR.
Piquero, A.R. (2008). Taking stock of developmental trajectories of criminal activity over the life course. In A.M. Liberman (ed.), *The Long View of Crime: A Synthesis of Longitudinal Research*. New York: Springer, pp. 23–78.

Piquero, A.R., Farrington, D.P., and Blumstein, A. (2003). The criminal career paradigm. In M. Tonry (ed.), *Crime and Justice* (vol. 30). Chicago, IL: Chicago University Press, pp. 359–506.

Piquero, A.R., Farrington, D.P. and Blumstein, A. (2007). *Key Issues in Criminal Career Research: New Analyses of the Cambridge Study in Delinquent Development*. Cambridge: Cambridge University Press.

Piquero, A.R., Hawkins, J.D. and Kazemian, L. (2012). Criminal career patterns between adolescence and young adulthood. In R. Loeber and D. Farrington (eds), *From Juvenile Delinquency to Adult Crime: Criminal Careers, Justice Policy and Prevention*. New York: Oxford University Press.

Sampson, R.J. and Laub, J.H. (1993). *Crime in the Making: Pathways and Turning Points through Life*. Cambridge, MA: Harvard University Press.

Sampson, R.J. and Laub, J.H. (1997). A life course theory of cumulative disadvantage and the stability of delinquency. In T.P. Thornberry (ed.), *Developmental Theories of Crime and Delinquency*. New Brunswick, NJ: Transaction Publishers, pp. 133–61.

Statistics Netherlands (2008). At www.cbs.nl, accessed 16 February 2012.

Thornberry, T.P. and Krohn, M.D. (2005). Applying interactional theory to the explanation of continuity and change in antisocial behavior. In D.P. Farrington (ed.), *Integrated Developmental and Life-course Theories of Offending*. New Brunswick, NJ: Transaction Publishers, pp. 183–209.

Tracy, P.E. and Kempf-Leonard, K. (1996). *Continuity and Discontinuity in Criminal Careers*. New York: Plenum.

Van de Bunt, H.G. (1988). Criminele carrières en selectieve onschadelijkmaking. *Justitiële Verkenningen*, 14, 78–99.

Van Wijk, A. and Blokland, A. (2008). Zedendelinquentie en etniciteit. Een exploratief onderzoek op basis van politiegegevens. *Mens en Maatschappij*, 83, 109–27.

Verhulst, F.C., Akkerhuis, G.W., and Althaus, M. (1985). Mental health in Dutch children: (1) A cross cultural comparison. *Acta Psychiatrica Scandinavica*, 323, 1–108.

Wittebrood, K. and Ter Voert, M.J. (1997). *Netherlands Survey on Criminality and Law Enforcement: Documentation of the Survey*. Leiden: NSCR.

Wolfgang, M.E., Figlio, R.M., and Sellin, T. (1972). *Delinquency in a Birth Cohort*. Chicago, IL: University of Chicago Press.

Chapter 3

Disentangling Context Effects on Criminal Careers

Margit Averdijk, Henk Elffers and Stijn Ruiter

Several scholars have noted that offending often depends on the context in which the delinquent acts take place (Horney, Tolan and Weisburd, 2012; Wortley and Mazerolle, 2008). Delinquents tend to aggregate in certain neighbourhoods or hang out at certain locations within neighbourhoods. This chapter addresses the key question whether individuals' rate of offending changes when they move from one neighbourhood to another. It also deals with other types of context changes in the direct social context such as those associated with 'leaving home' during adolescence and early adulthood due to marriage or employment opportunities. We argue that neither of the two types of context can be understood adequately without controlling for the effects of the other.

Different Meanings of 'Context' and their Interrelatedness

'Context' can be conceptualized in at least two different ways. In criminal career research it usually refers to the context of the immediate social environment, such as an individual's relationship to his or her parents, partner, children, friends and colleagues. In this usage, 'context' has a clear sociopsychological content, and 'context change' refers to major changes in the *direct social context*. Such changes include leaving the parental home, marriage, divorce, parenthood, as well as closely associated changes in the social environment such as starting and completing education, and getting or losing a job. This chapter reviews current knowledge of the effect of changes in the direct social context on the persistence in and desistance from offending between adolescence and early adulthood.

A second conceptualization of 'context' is derived from environmental criminology (Wortley and Mazerolle, 2008), where 'context' is often referred to as *neighbourhood context*. Environmental criminologists hypothesize that what happens to a certain individual at a given point in time and space depends on the characteristics of that individual him- or herself (personality, history, social circumstances), and the characteristics of events within his/her direct geographical environment. A well-known example is Shaw and McKay's (1969 [1942]) claim that the level of neighbourhood social organization influences whether or not inhabitants become offenders, and a high level of social organization helps a neighbourhood to deter crime through intensive guardianship. The present chapter reviews the empirical knowledge about the extent to which offending between adolescence and early adulthood is influenced by individuals' moves from one neighbourhood to another.[1]

We argue that, in the study of the effects of either of the two types of context changes on criminal careers, it is essential to simultaneously take into account changes in other contexts as well. When an individual moves from one neighbourhood to another, other life changes usually also occur, such as the composition of his or her household, changing friendships, changes in employment, or with respect to his or her level of education or wealth. Likewise, changes in the direct social context often lead individuals to move to another neighbourhood. For example, individuals who start university education often leave their parental homes, move to a different city, meet new friends, and start a job to cater for their financial needs. Clearly, in these cases many context changes co-occur. To take another example, divorce often means that one of the partners leaves the common dwelling and moves to a different neighbourhood. The contingent links between these different context changes pose a challenge for researchers interested in identifying the confounded influences of each context change on the development of individuals' offending. We found, however, that most research has not taken into account changes in neighbourhood context, which often co-occur with changes in the direct social context.

In line with the aims of this book, this chapter focuses on a specific period of life: the transition from late adolescence to early adulthood. This period is typically characterized by a host of context changes, which take place both in the direct social environment – family, education, work – and in the neighbourhood context. Once juveniles become young adults, individuals typically leave the parental home, start or complete their education, get their first job, marry, and start a family. Some or all of these changes come with moving to a different neighbourhood. Thus, it is argued that, for the study of the effects of context changes in the transition from adolescence to early adulthood, it is especially important to simultaneously control for a range of potentially confounding changes in the direct social environment and neighbourhood context.

The chapter consists of two parts. We first review the literature on the impact on offending of changes in the direct social context and changes in neighbourhood context. Second, we demonstrate how to disentangle both types of context changes. Since we did not identify literature addressing this point, we present a short empirical analysis, by way of example, on how to disentangle context changes. We used a dataset assembled by us from Statistics Netherlands, which contains indicators of direct social context as well as neighbourhood context for

1 The neighbourhood context itself may also change within any given neighbourhood over time, but this usually happens at a relatively slow pace. The most marked changes in neighbourhood context for a specific individual usually occur when he or she moves to another neighbourhood.

criminal careers in the relevant age frame. This analysis extends prior research by the use of longitudinal data, by its focus on the transition from adolescence to early adulthood, and by simultaneously controlling for a range of potentially confounding factors in the direct social environment and neighbourhood context. Our work does not pretend to provide a fully exhaustive analysis of context change on criminal careers but is meant to explore the feasibility of disentangling the impact of neighbourhood and direct social context on individuals' offending.

Our literature review contains two parts: first, direct social context change; second, the influence of neighbourhood context. The review on direct social context change draws partly from the recent excellent overview by Horney et al. (2012), which we augmented with knowledge based on European studies. For the second part, there is currently not much literature available on the influence of neighbourhood context change on criminal careers, but there is more literature on the influence of neighbourhood context on the likelihood of offending. For the present chapter it is therefore useful not only to review the theory and literature on the effects of neighbourhood context changes, but also to take stock of the literature that considers the influence of the neighbourhood context as such (i.e., studies based on cross-sectional data), since this literature highlights the theoretical mechanisms involved in the relationship between neighbourhoods and offending. From this literature we can derive hypotheses on how neighbourhood context change may lead to a change in offending. While in theory it is possible that a neighbourhood context change in itself influences offending frequency regardless of the characteristics of the old and the new neighbourhood, it seems safe to assume that it is primarily the change in neighbourhood *characteristics* that drives changes in offending.

Changes in the Direct Social Context during the Transition from Adolescence to Early Adulthood

The transition from adolescence to adulthood is typically characterized by a range of changes in the direct social context (i.e. marriage or cohabitation, parenthood, employment, leisure activities), which often are accompanied by moving to another neighbourhood. We briefly describe several such social context changes that are likely to affect criminal careers. For a more comprehensive overview of the possible effects, we refer to Horney et al. (2012).

Marriage

Research shows that marriage may stimulate desistance from offending. Marriage may elicit responsible behaviour and typically leads to more settled lifestyles, thereby altering deviant routine activities. Spouses often provide social support (Cullen, 1994) and emotional attachment, and it is not uncommon that offenders, when continuing to offend, risk losing the partner's support and attachment.

Moreover, spouses may exert direct social control by taking charge of the household and monitoring their partners' activities. In doing so, spouses are capable of pulling offenders away from deviant friends and problematic social environments (Laub and Sampson, 2003; Warr, 1998). Marriage, especially with a partner who is better off financially, can also provide other benefits, such as employment, housing, and consumer power. The review by Horney et al. (2012) shows that marriage is associated with reduced offending, but that the effects for females are less strong and consistent than those for males. It should be noted that the effects of marriage may depend greatly on the offending history of the marriage partner. Simons et al. (2002) found that a romantic relationship with an antisocial partner and his or her peer affiliations was associated with offending. Offenders have been found to be relatively likely to marry a criminal partner (Van Schellen, Nieuwbeerta and Poortman, 2008). This was especially the case among female offenders, providing a potential explanation for why the negative effect of marriage on criminal careers is smaller among female than male offenders (Bersani, Laub and Nieuwbeerta 2009). Horney et al. (2012) showed that non-marital cohabitation, which in many Western societies has become common among young adults, has smaller benefits on offending than more formalized unions. They argued, in line with the literature they reviewed, that the underlying mechanism explaining such effect size differences may lie in the quality of the relationship, time spent with deviant peers, and the types of leisure activities employed. On the other hand, recent Finnish research found a stronger effect of cohabitation on offending compared to marriage (Savolainen, 2009). As a potential explanation, the author offered that, 'in a culture in which a typical marriage is preceded by several years of cohabitation, a relatively quick decision to marry a recidivistic offender may indicate greater tolerance for a criminal lifestyle' (p. 300), suggesting that a reluctance to enter into marriage with an offender may be more effective in encouraging him or her to desist

Parenthood

Becoming a parent may change individuals' *routine activities* because parenthood can stimulate settling down and engaging in family-oriented activities, with consequently less free time available for hanging out with deviant friends. In addition, parenthood may initiate a new sense of responsibility that can contribute to decisions to desist from crime (Laub and Sampson, 2003). In their review, Horney et al. (2012) found that the effects of parenthood on reduced offending are mixed. Results were stronger for females and for those who lived with (and not just had) children, and were more consistent for reductions in substance abuse than for other offending behaviours. Giordano et al. (2002) argued that it is not parenthood as such but the quality of it (attachment) that could make a difference, but they were not able to corroborate this hypothesis. In contrast to American findings, Savolainen (2009) using Finnish data found strong support for an association between parenthood and desistance. Savolainen stressed that Finnish public policy, by offering benefits to families with children, may contribute to this outcome. De Goede, Blokland and Nieuwbeerta (2011) found that Dutch male offenders were more likely to desist in offending after the birth of their first child (unless they were very young when this happened), over and above the effect for marriage, which often co-occurred. For women, however, they found no effect of the birth of a first child.

Employment

Another context change apparent in the transition from adolescence to early adulthood is starting a working life. Although the role of employment in changes in criminal careers remains somewhat unclear, stable work seems to facilitate desistance from offending (Laub and Sampson, 2003; Savolainen, 2009; Wadsworth, 2006). Not only do jobs provide financial stability, having a job also provides structured routine activities. In addition, employers and co-workers may exert social control, which prevents employees from displaying deviant behaviour. When offenders are willing to invest in a steady job, or when they are monitored by employers, they are likely to want to avoid putting their job at risk because of offending (Laub and Sampson, 2003). Jobs may thus function as motivators for desistance. Horney et al. (2012) pointed out that the empirical literature on this subject is age stratified, as the meaning and content of having work changes rapidly between adolescence and early adulthood, and that results seem to differ during these time periods. In early adult years, employment is associated with lower crime levels, while this is not the case for adolescents, although the latter findings have been attributed to selection effects. Various authors have pleaded for the use of longitudinal within-person studies to assess the effects of employment on offending (for example, Apel et al., 2008). Such analyses have shown either no effect or a beneficial effect of employment among adolescents. Horney et al. (2012) furthermore found that the empirical literature on the effects of job characteristics – such as job stability and job quality – on offending is somewhat mixed.

Further Education

Going to college may interrupt existing relationships with delinquent friends (Warr, 1998) and may increase conventional bonds to society, thereby acting as a potential crime reducing influence. On the other hand, going to college has also been associated with risky behaviours such as alcohol use (Raymore, Barber and Eccles, 2001). Empirical research is somewhat undecided about the effect of entering college on criminal careers. Although some researchers reported that entering college contributes slightly but significantly to desistance from offending (Warr, 1998), other researchers have not found significant effects (Blokland and Nieuwbeerta, 2005).

Leaving Home

At some point during adolescence or early adulthood, most youngsters leave the parental home. Such moves presumably lessen direct parental control over their behaviour. Most parents exercise control over their children in ways that counter offending. Consequently, leaving the parental home lessens such social control, thereby increasing opportunities to engage in risky activities since young people will start visiting different places at different times in new company involved in different activities. Horney et al.'s (2012) review highlighted that unstructured and unsupervised socializing with peers is associated with offending (Osgood et al., 1996). We note that the effect of leaving the parental household may not be the same for all young adults. Although in many cases parents will exercise social control over their children and thereby discourage criminal involvement, this may not be the case when parents themselves are involved in criminal activities. For example, Van de Rakt et al. (2010) showed that children who have a criminal father are also more likely to commit crime. However, the impact of crimes committed by the father was smaller when the parents were divorced. This suggests that, in some cases, not living with a parent may be related to less instead of more offending. Interestingly enough, we did not find much literature on the effects of leaving the parental household on crime involvement, perhaps because this event is so often confounded with other changes in the direct social context and in the neighbourhood context.

Many of the highlighted changes in the direct social context coincide with individuals moving to another neighbourhood. Therefore, analyses on the relationship between social context change and criminal careers in the transition to adulthood need to control for potentially confounding changes in the direct social context and changes in neighbourhood context.

Theoretical Overview of Neighbourhood Effects on Crime

The idea that neighbourhoods influence offending patterns of its residents has a long history in criminology. Three key mechanisms have been proposed explaining the direct effect of neighbourhood context on offending (Dahlbäck, 1996; Oberwittler, 2007a).[2] First, according to social disorganization and related theories, a lack of informal social control exerted by residents leads to decreased community

2 According to another mechanism, neighbourhood context has no direct effect on criminal behaviour and the relationship between neighbourhood and offending can be explained through the composition of the population in a neighbourhood. Residents from the same neighbourhood typically share similar demographic characteristics and lifestyles, which in turn are associated with criminal behaviour. As a result, the spatial concentration of crime-prone individuals leads to variation in offender rates on the neighbourhood level. Since this mechanism can explain spatial variation in offender rates across neighbourhoods,

resistance to offending, which in turn increases the likelihood that its residents will offend. Social disorganization theory was originally developed by researchers of the Chicago School who found that offending rates in certain neighbourhoods remained high, even when the composition of the neighbourhood changed. From this they concluded that neighbourhood context affected offending over and above neighbourhood composition (Shaw and McKay, 1969 [1942]; Shaw et al., 1929). According to Shaw and McKay, neighbourhood levels of economic deprivation are associated with residential mobility and ethnic heterogeneity, which in turn increases social disorganization. Residential mobility prevents the formation of social ties, collective identification and common values, and thus promotes social disorganization. Ethnically or culturally heterogeneous populations have different social norms and values or cannot communicate effectively due to language differences, which also promotes social disorganization (Müller, 2008). Recent work related to the social disorganization tradition has focused primarily on the relationship between crime and self-efficacy or guardianship of residents, that is, the extent to which residents are able and willing to intervene when confronted with crime (Reynald, 2010; Sampson, 2004; Sampson, Raudenbusch and Earls, 1997; Steenbeek and Hipp, 2011).

The second explanation views the relationship between offending and neighbourhood context through the social relationships and interactions between residents of a neighbourhood. Residents of disadvantaged neighbourhoods are relatively likely to come from a disadvantaged background themselves. Through learning processes among peers, social problems can spread from resident to resident. For example, delinquency has been theorized and shown to be in part a learned activity in which peers play a central role (see differential association theory by Sutherland, 1947; Akers, 1985; De Cuyper, Weerman and Ruiter, 2009; Weerman, 2011). Engagement in deviant peer cultures is more likely in environments where residents are susceptible to peer influences, which is the case in poor, minority neighbourhoods (Crane, 1991). In such neighbourhoods, the street forms a shared meeting space for residents (Van Gemert, 1998). Due to a lack of structured leisure activities, a lack of institutional connections, and poor parental monitoring, youth (especially boys) get the opportunity to participate in group life with peers on the streets. Peer groups provide them with social contacts and social recognition, and normative collective codes give structure and meaning to group behaviour. Successful criminals in the neighbourhood may provide a role model for youth who, as a result, may pursue a similar criminal career (Miedema, 2002).

The third explanation of what may affect offending focuses on opportunities and perceived disorder in neighbourhoods. Visible signs of physical and social disorder can lead to fear, stigmatization, and perceived lower social control (Müller, 2008), which in turn may increase offending. According to Wagers, Sousa and Kelling (2008), 'disorder left untended is a sign that nobody cares and leads to

but not intra-individual changes in offending as a consequence of moving to a different neighbourhood, we do not consider it here.

fear of crime, withdrawal from public spaces, a breakdown of community controls, and more serious crime' (p. 248). Recent evidence has shown that observing violations of social norms or rules by others causes individuals to violate norms and rules themselves (Keizer, Lindenberg and Steg, 2008). According to this line of thinking, residents of neighbourhoods high in disorder are more likely to violate rules themselves.

Based on these three mechanisms, we hypothesize that moving to a new neighbourhood that differs from one's old neighbourhood in the level of informal social control, in prevailing peer cultures, and in opportunity structures, affects an individual's criminal career. Such a move can provide a turning point in criminal careers, for example by cutting off ties with deviant peer groups in the old neighbourhood. In their qualitative research with former delinquents, Laub and Sampson (2003) identified neighbourhood change as one of four 'major self-described turning points in the desistance process' in adulthood (p. 148). The characteristics of the new neighbourhood are important for the direction of the effects. We expect that moving to a new neighbourhood that is less disadvantaged and has more informal social control than the old neighbourhood decreases the likelihood of offending. This should be the case because 'better' neighbourhoods are better capable of exerting social control on their own residents, thereby providing supervision and social support, which in turn provide an important motivation for desisting from crime (Laub and Sampson, 2003). At the same time, we expect that moving to a neighbourhood that is more disadvantaged and has less informal social control increases the likelihood of offending.

Review of Neighbourhood Effects in European Research

Little research has been conducted in Europe on the effects of neighbourhood context change on the development of offending. Therefore we shall first provide a short overview of existing European literature on this issue in general, but not on effects of neighbourhood change on criminal career development. Based on this literature, we formulate expectations on the relationship between effects of neighbourhood context change on criminal careers.

Although several European studies have found that particular neighbourhoods have disproportionally high concentrations of offenders (Bernasco, 2006; Eisner and Wikström, 1999; Hesseling, 1992; Pauwels, 2007; Rovers, 1999), studies have generally failed to find sizeable direct effects of neighbourhood context on delinquency. That is, when researchers investigated whether neighbourhood differences in crime rates could be explained by direct neighbourhood effects over and above compositional differences (often by conducting multilevel analyses), they found that only a very small share of individual variation in offending could be explained on the neighbourhood level. For example, Rovers (1999) conducted research on the impact of neighbourhood on juvenile delinquency in the city of Rotterdam, the Netherlands. He reported that variation in self-reported and official delinquency scores between neighbourhoods was very small and occurred primarily between individuals. For eight of ten dependent variables, the percentage variance that could be explained on the level of neighbourhoods was less than 3. Schneiders et al. (2003) similarly reported low neighbourhood variance in their study in Rotterdam. Pauwels (2007) conducted research among adolescents aged 12–14 in the city of Antwerp, Belgium. He reported that only about one per cent of individual variation in delinquency could be explained on the neighbourhood level. Moreover, when controlled for youth demographic characteristics, the variation on the neighbourhood level did not differ significantly from zero. Dahlbäck (1996) investigated the relationship between areas of residence and officially registered offending among ages 15–25 in the city of Stockholm, Sweden. He reported that the proportion of variance in criminality explained by area of residence did not exceed .03. In Dutch research among ages 12–17 in the city of Nijmegen, Weijters (2006) did not find evidence for neighbourhood-level variation in juvenile delinquency.

Likewise, neighbourhood characteristics have been found to have limited predictive power. For example, Weijters (2006) found that neighbourhood disadvantage and residential mobility did not have a direct influence on youth delinquency, but attachment to parents and school were a deterrent for youth from advantaged neighbourhoods and not for youth from disadvantaged neighbourhoods. Conversely, less favourable attitudes towards deviant behaviour were a better deterrent for youth from disadvantaged neighbourhoods than for youth from advantaged neighbourhoods. In follow-up research, Weijters (2008) found that, among several indicators for neighbourhood disadvantage, only the percentage of single-parent families affected youth delinquency. In Iceland, Thorlindsson and Bernburg (2004) investigated the link between community social order and adolescent delinquency. Results showed some but limited support for the hypothesis that community-level integration was related to lower delinquency. These effects were in part mediated by individual experiences of anomie and peer delinquency.

In contrast to the mentioned European studies that found very limited direct effects of neighbourhoods on delinquency, two European studies have reported sizeable neighbourhood effects. Reijneveld et al. (2005) examined the relationship between neighbourhood deprivation and child psychosocial problems (including delinquency and aggression) among a representative Dutch sample of children aged 4 to 16. They found that child psychosocial problems were about 80 per cent higher in the most compared to the least deprived third of the neighbourhoods. Only 20 per cent of the neighbourhood variation could be explained by individual-level variables. The other European study that has revealed strong support for neighbourhood effects was conducted in Germany by Oberwittler (2004, 2007a. 2007b), who investigated the relationship between ethnic and social segregation and serious delinquency among ages 13–16. He found strong support for the existence of neighbourhood effects on serious juvenile offending, although the effects were small compared to individual-level effects. Neighbourhood effects existed only for native adolescents, and only for those with local friendship circles. This is in line with differential association and learning theories. These results are at odds with other European studies in which small or no neighbourhood-level effects were found. Oberwittler (2007b) noted that related research had also found that social inequality and structural disadvantage had a stronger effect on behaviour in Germany compared to other European countries.

Notwithstanding these two exceptions, European studies have generally shown limited effects of neighbourhood context on delinquency. This suggests that moving to a different neighbourhood may have a limited impact on the development of an individual's criminal career. However, in order to test this, longitudinal data that follow the same individual over a longer period of time are needed. To our knowledge, only two European studies utilized a longitudinal design to investigate the relationship between criminal behaviour and neighbourhoods. Schneiders et al. (2003) investigated the link between neighbourhood socioeconomic disadvantage and externalizing behaviour (delinquency and aggression) from late childhood into early adolescence. They used two-wave longitudinal data from Rotterdam. Children were aged 10–12 at the first wave and 12–14 at the second. Neighbourhood disadvantage significantly increased the likelihood of externalizing behaviour at both ages, but effects were small and neighbourhood-level variance was low. However, Schneiders et al. (2003) did not study how *changes* in neighbourhood context affected delinquency development. In contrast, Dahlbäck (1996) investigated the effect on offending of moving to a different residential area in the city of Stockholm. This was done by calculating the difference in the crime rates of the residential areas individuals previously lived in and subsequently moved to, and by calculating the difference in an individual's criminality before and after moving. These two scores were then correlated. The author did not find a consistent relationship of notable strength.

In sum, these empirical results suggest that neighbourhoods exert only limited influence on delinquency, implying that a change in neighbourhood context might not predict changes in offending. It should be noted that European evidence is at odds with evidence from the US, which indicates larger effects of neighbourhoods on delinquency (although also in the US neighbourhood context effects are small compared to individual-level effects; Duncan and Raudenbush, 1999). Potential explanations for the differential neighbourhood effects found in both continents include the higher contrasts between neighbourhoods and larger neighbourhood physical, commercial and economic barriers in the US compared to Europe (Oberwittler, 2007c; Weijters, Scheepers and Gerris, 2007). In addition, European systems of social welfare, social housing policies, and urban renewal have prevented extensive processes of social and ethnic segregation and concentration (Body-Gendrot, 1999; De Haan, 1999). As a result, differences in neighbourhood contextual characteristics, such as social cohesion, are small in Europe compared to the US (Müller, 2008). These socioeconomic differences are especially high between the US and Western European countries, from which all European research discussed here stems.

Unresolved Issues in Research on Neighbourhood Effects

We have seen that in Europe there is still little research on the relationship between neighbourhood context and delinquency and offending. Most European studies on neighbourhood effects are cross-sectional and focus only on differences in delinquent behaviour between individuals. Little is known about changes in offending when individuals move from one to another neighborhood (Pauwels, 2007). Longitudinal data are needed to investigate this.

Another area that requires attention is an extension of research to different age ranges. Most prior studies on neighbourhood effects focus on adolescents. Relatively little is known about the influence of the neighbourhood context in the period from late adolescence to early adulthood. The only European study we are aware of that has considered this age range is the aforementioned study by Dahlbäck (1996). It is important to consider effects of neighbourhoods in early adulthood because this constitutes 'a critical time, as it typically involves leaving the parental home, completing education, beginning full-time employment, marriage, and the first years of parenthood. The extent to which people experience success or failure in these early tasks sets the stage for achievement and well-being later in life' (Amato, Loomis and Booth, 1995, p. 900).

Future research should not only employ a longitudinal design and a focus on additional age ranges: we argue that it needs to simultaneously take account of changes in the direct social context.

Defining the Transition from Adolescence to Early Adulthood

The central notion in this book is to explain why individuals persist in or desist from offending between adolescence and early adulthood. However, it is somewhat arbitrary to take age 18 as a dividing line between adolescence and adulthood. Many of the context changes treated above that are typical for the transition to adulthood do not happen at age 18. For example, leaving the parental household, which is arguably one of the first transitions in the direct social context, often occurs after age 20 (Bucx, 2008; Liefbroer, 2005). Indeed, we expect a prolonged period in which individuals undergo or make several context changes that together constitute the transition to adulthood. During recent decades, substantial delays have taken place in the timing of many of the social context changes that typically denote the transition from adolescence to adulthood. In Western countries, marriage and childbirth currently take place (if at all) at much later ages than before (Latten, 2004; Liefbroer, 2005). Likewise, researchers report delays in leaving full-time education and entry into employment as well as delays in leaving the parental home (Bucx, 2008; Liefbroer, 2005). Therefore, the transition from adolescence to adulthood comprises a relatively long period in which a series of context changes may take place. For example, a young male may start his university education at age 17, still live with his parents at this time, move to student housing when at age 19, graduate at 20, move home when he starts his first job, marry at 23, and may then move again. All of these changes take place in the transition between adolescence and early adulthood.

Controlling for Various Context Changes

Our review has identified several unresolved issues in the literature as well as a number of methodological issues that are important for the analyses of the effects of context changes on offending. First and foremost is the necessity to control for confounding factors since several context changes may co-occur during this period. We have not found an empirical study that controls for neighbourhood change when studying direct social context change, or vice versa. Thus, the question is whether it is feasible to disentangle the two, thereby enabling us to estimate direct effects of the one while controlling for the other. To answer this question, we executed secondary data analyses using longitudinal data in combination with a longitudinal modelling technique to analyse the effects of both types of context change on criminal careers in the transition from adolescence to adulthood. The analysis disentangles various changes in the direct social environment and in the neighbourhood context. We considered a prolonged period in which individuals make several context changes that together constitute the transition to adulthood.

Empirical Analysis

The analysis is based on data from Statistics Netherlands (CBS, 2011). In recent years, Statistics Netherlands has linked data from many different sources into the Social Statistical database (SSB: *Sociaal Statistisch Bestand*). The core of the SSB consists of information on demographic and socioeconomic characteristics for the entire Dutch population. The Dutch Population Administration (GBA: *Gemeentelijke Basisadministratie*) provides the kernel of these data. It registers the following events: date of birth, date of death, date of change in marital status, date of childbirth, and dates and details of changes in home addresses. Dutch residents are required by law to report these events to the Population Administration. Although registration discipline is not perfect, the registration is generally considered to be of very high quality. We reconstructed residential histories from the GBA and matched these with official contextual data at the neighbourhood level.

Because the SSB provides a link between GBA data and other datasets, we were able to combine the GBA data with annual police register data on offending and individual-level employment data. The police data were provided to Statistics Netherlands by the Dutch National Police Service (*Korps Landelijke Politie Diensten*).

We assembled a dataset from the SSB with special permission from Statistics Netherlands and with strict privacy regulations. Statistics Netherlands confidentiality rules required us to do the analyses at their premises.[3]

Dependent Variable

We analysed offence data of all Dutch residents who were born in or after 1984 and who had a police-recorded offence count larger than zero in the years 1996–2007. This time period was dictated by the present availability of police records at Statistics Netherlands. The selection of years of birth stemmed from our choice to study only individuals for whom we have complete criminal careers as recorded by Dutch police. Because the minimum age of criminal responsibility in the Netherlands is 12, individuals who were born before 1984 could have committed crimes that were not included in the police records available to us. Therefore, we excluded all years before the first registered offence, focusing on the relationship between context changes and *recidivism*. Thus, the youngest persons in our dataset are aged 13. We combined the following crime types: sexual violence (rape, sexual assault, and other sexual crimes), violence, robbery, property crime, vandalism, public order violations, drug crimes, and a category of 'other' crimes. Traffic offences were not included. Although the number of different offences is recorded for each person for each year, for reasons of parsimony we analyse a dichotomous dependent variable, which indicates whether (1) or not (0) a person committed at least one offence in a specific year.

Individual-level Predictors

Variables included in the analysis are described below. Note that for most variables, we considered the situation on the first day (1 January) of each given year. These variables thus temporally preceded the dependent variable, which indicates whether offences were committed during the remainder of each year.

The variable indicating whether an individual *moved to another neighbourhood* is central to this empirical analysis because many context changes often co-occur when an adolescent or young adult makes such a move. We did not classify moving to a new address within the same neighbourhood as change.

We included two variables to indicate family situation. The first indicates whether an individual *left the parental household*. Although Statistics Netherlands does not provide direct information on whether individuals leave their parental homes, we constructed the variable based on information about an individual's position in the household as recorded in the SSB. If at the start of a given year the household position changed from 'child' to something else, we coded the individual as having left the parental home. The second variable measures whether

3 This means that replication of our analyses by other researchers can only be done if they obtain permission from the CBS (see www.cbs.nl).

the individual was *married or widowed*.[4] The data did not indicate whether an individual cohabitated with a romantic partner without being married. Observing that many young adults currently prefer cohabitation over formal marriage (Latten, 2004), our marriage indicator underestimates the target primary context variable of having a stable romantic relationship. Thus, we use a conservative test for the link between romantic relationships and the likelihood of recidivism.

Employed indicates whether an individual had a paid job, either full time or part time, and either stable or temporary. This variable excludes self-employment because social control mechanisms are assumed to be less operative when individuals do not have colleagues or supervisors. Source data were obtained from the Dutch Institute of Employees Insurances (*Uitvoeringsinstituut Werknemersverzekeringen*, UWV) and the Dutch tax agency. Based on all start and end dates for all jobs, we constructed a measure that indicates the proportion of the year during which an individual had held a job. Because social control by colleagues operates throughout the entire year, we preferred this measure over a measure timed at 1 January.

We included two variables that relate to the role of time in the criminal career. First, *years since last crime* measures how many years have passed since an individual last committed a crime. This variable was included in order to determine whether the likelihood of recidivism changes as time passes. *Years without crime* measures the degree of continuity of offending. It counts the total number of years without crime that have passed since age 12. A lower score indicates a more continuous criminal career. We also included an interaction term between *years without crime* and *left the parental household* to assess whether the impact of leaving the parental household (arguably one of the most significant transitions from adolescence to adulthood) differs between those with a continuous criminal career and those whose criminal career ceased.

In addition, we controlled for potential effects of the opportunity to commit crime. We assessed whether a person resided *outside of the Netherlands* at 1 January, since individuals who do not reside in the Netherlands for part of the year are less likely to have opportunities to commit a crime within the Netherlands. In addition, the opportunity for committing a crime is reduced when individuals are incarcerated. Unfortunately, the data do not directly inform us about incarceration. We derived an *incarceration proxy* from the home address. When individuals are incarcerated, their registered address changes to the address of the prison. We constructed a proxy variable for the time incarcerated that indicates whether an individual moved to a neighbourhood in which a prison is located.[5]

---

4 Too few individuals were widowed at such young age to allow for a separate category in the analysis. Therefore, we combine them with the married because the widowed had also made the transition into marriage.

5 Note that other individuals who were not incarcerated, but just lived in a neighborhood in which a prison is located, are also classified as being incarcerated. However, given the limited number of cases that were incorrectly classified as moving to a prison because the

Finally, a variable for *age* (including squared and cubic transformations) was derived from date of birth and was included to account for the well-known bell shape of the age–crime curve.

Neighbourhood-level Predictors

We included a number of characteristics of the neighbourhood that people live in because several ecological theories of crime argue that such characteristics affect the likelihood of offending. Neighbourhood characteristics were obtained from official CBS data. *Population density* indicates the number of residents per square kilometer. *Residential mobility* captures the total neighbourhood in- and outflow per 1,000 residents. The *percentage non-Westerners* indicates the share of the total population that is made up of residents of non-Western descent. Statistics Netherlands calculates the *average housing value* for each neighbourhood based on the value of each house as determined for tax purposes. *Average income* is the average after-tax income for each neighbourhood resident. We also included the *percentage living on social benefits*, which indicates the share of all neighbourhood residents aged between 15 and 64 that claim social benefits. Our neighbourhood-level predictors were not available for each separate year but were derived from data for the years 2004–2008. Given that differences between neighbourhoods are relatively stable over time, we do not consider this to be very problematic. We used the geographical boundaries for neighbourhood regions as defined in 2008. This ensured that we did not run into problems associated with changes in administrative regions over the years.

Limitations

As mentioned, SSB data are generally considered to be of good quality. However, they are not perfect when it comes to adolescents' living locations. Not everyone reports address changes to the city authorities. Since young adults move relatively often, it might be the case that they are especially prone to not reporting this information to the authorities.

Although the SSB provides extensive data, the selection of predictors on the individual and neighbourhood level was limited because Statistics Netherlands is still in the process of linking data from different sources. Compared to our earlier inventory of possibly relevant changes in the primary context, variables for some relevant domains are unfortunately missing. On the individual level, information on whether an individual becomes a parent is not available. However, given the high average age at which Dutch females have their first child (Liefbroer, 2005), this might not be a major problem. Furthermore, data on education and income were not available. This means that our neighbourhood-level variables for

home address was in a neighbourhood in which a prison was located (< three per cent of person-years) we do not consider this to be very problematic.

socioeconomic status (*average income* and *average housing value*) are likely to pick up some of the individual income effects. We hope that the inclusion of the variable for employment somewhat ameliorates this issue. On the neighbourhood level, we have no information on the aggregated delinquency level of its residents. However, the analysis does contain several other important theoretically informed neighbourhood variables.

Notwithstanding these limitations, the SSB dataset is unique in its scope and size and in the longitudinal availability of information on primary and secondary context changes. After combining all data, the final dataset consists of 122,814 individuals and 375,246 person-years, including about 20 per cent females and 58 per cent individuals of Dutch ethnicity.[6]

Method

To make optimal use of the time structure of the data, we applied panel regression models. Consider a typical panel regression model of the form:

$$y_{it} = \beta x_{it} + y_i + \varepsilon_{it} \quad (1)$$

where the outcome variable y_{it} and predictors vary x_{it} across both individuals and time, and where i stands for a given individual and t for a given time period. The term γ_i represents time-invariant unobserved individual effects and ε_{it} denotes the error of the model. A fixed effects model is used here, which eliminates time-invariant heterogeneity (see Bjerk, 2009; Bushway, Brame and Paternoster, 1999; Halaby, 2004).

Given that the dependent variable is dichotomous, logit fixed effects models are used. Although our initial dataset contains 122,814 persons, all individuals with stable characteristics drop out of the fixed effects equation. Consequently, the results presented below are based on a smaller, but still very large, sample of 164,447 person-years, pertaining to 38,312 individuals.

Results

Table 3.1 provides descriptive statistics for the dependent and independent variables. Note that for 22 per cent of all person-years one or more crimes were recorded, that moving to a different neighbourhood occurred in 12 per cent of all person-years, and that only a very small minority of the individuals in the dataset is married or widowed. In 83 per cent of the person-years, individuals lived with their parents.

6 An individual is considered to be of Dutch ethnicity if neither of his parents was born outside the Netherlands.

Table 3.1 Summary statistics

Variable	N person-years	Mean	Std. Dev.	Min.	Max.
Dependent variable					
Crime in a specific year (yes=1)	375,246	.223	.416	0	1
Individual-level predictors					
Moved to another neighbourhood (yes=1)	375,246	.118	.322	0	1
Left parental household (yes=1)	375,246	.174	.379	0	1
Married or widowed (0 = no, 1 = yes)	375,246	.001	.023	0	1
Employed (0 = no, 1 = yes)	375,246	.449	.457	0	1
Years since last crime	375,246	2.646	1.715	1	15
Years without crime	375,246	2.036	1.583	0	10
Outside of the Netherlands (yes=1)	375,246	.007	.083	0	1
Incarceration proxy (yes=1)	375,246	.027	.161	0	1
Age (centred)	375,246	2.449	2.133	−2.794	6.206
Neighbourhood-level predictors					
Population density	375,246	6,316.337	4,690.561	6	25,725
Residential mobility	375,246	111.410	58.958	0	4,237
Percentage non-Westerners in neighbourhood	375,246	18.340	19.260	0	91
Average housing value	375,246	192.329	74.324	67	1,752
Average income	375,246	12.502	2.137	5.700	44.800
Percentage living on social benefits	375,246	18.587	7.171	3	92

Results of the fixed effects models for the likelihood of recidivism are shown in Table 3.2. Given that we used a logit fixed effects model, a positive beta-parameter (β) shows that an increase in the independent variable is associated with a higher likelihood of recidivism. The focus of this analysis is to estimate effects of context change while simultaneously taking into account confounding effects of other context changes. The results show that moving to a different neighbourhood is associated with a lower likelihood of recidivism, although the effect size is small. With regard to the neighbourhood characteristics, moving to a neighbourhood with higher residential mobility and higher housing values is associated with a lower likelihood of recidivism. However, moving to a neighbourhood with a higher

Table 3.2 Fixed effects logistic model for likelihood of recidivism

	Regression coefficient β	Standard error of β
Individual-level predictors		
Moved to another neighbourhood	−.050*	(.024)
Left parental household	−.838***	(.042)
Married or widowed	.803	(.471)
Employed	.088**	(.028)
Years since last crime	1.853***	(.042)
Years without crime	−3.285***	(.020)
Outside of the Netherlands	−.897***	(.149)
Incarceration proxy	−.500***	(.078)
Age (centred)	.140***	(.039)
Age (centred) squared	−.037***	(.004)
Age (centred) cubic	.002***	(.001)
Neighbourhood-level predictors		
Population density	.000	(.000)
Residential mobility	−.001***	(.000)
Percentage non-Westerners in neighbourhood	.005**	(.002)
Average housing value	−.002***	(.000)
Average income	.059***	(.011)
Percentage living on social benefits	−.002	(.003)
Left parental household * Years without crime	.426***	(.017)
Number of persons	38,312	
Number of person-years	164,447	

Note: a) *** $p<.001$; ** $p<.01$; * $p<.05$, b) Coefficients reported are unstandardized betas.

percentage of non-Western residents and a higher average income is associated with a higher likelihood of recidivism. Overall, effect sizes are small.

Regarding the direct social environment, we find that – controlled for neighbourhood change – leaving the parental household is an important predictor that reduces the likelihood of recidivism. Getting married or becoming widowed has no influence on recidivism, which is contrary to our expectation. Unexpectedly, getting a job is associated with a higher likelihood of recidivism.

The interpretation of time effects is complex, as they consist of ageing and crime history effects and they are of course controlled for one another. The more years have passed since the last crime, the higher the likelihood of recidivism. This indicates that, controlled for the increase of age (inherent in passing of time), the risk that an offender reoffends increases. At the same time, a higher number of years without crime (which indicates a less prolific criminal career) reduces the likelihood of recidivism. Thus, those adolescents who frequently come into contact with the police are relatively likely to continue their criminal careers. Or conversely, the more years individuals abstained from offending, the less the likelihood that they will reoffend. Note that the latter effect is, in absolute terms, almost twice as large as the former. This suggests that, when an individual refrained from crime in the previous year, with all things being equal, the effects can be combined and turn out to be negative. Reduced opportunities to commit crime have a strong impact on the likelihood of recidivism. Both moving abroad and incarceration reduce the likelihood of recidivism.

Finally, the interaction term shows that, for those individuals who had a less active criminal career, leaving the parental household is associated with a slightly higher likelihood of recidivism compared to those who had a more active criminal career.

Conclusions and Discussion

We reviewed theoretical notions to explain the relationship between context changes and criminal careers, provided an overview of European literature on the topic, and discussed how effects of changes in the direct social context are possibly linked to changes in neighbourhood context, and vice versa. We concluded that there is little research in Europe on the relationship between neighbourhood context and offending. This is especially the case for longitudinal research and for research on the transition from adolescence to early adulthood.

We presented a new analysis of context effects on criminal careers during the transition from adolescence to early adulthood. We argued that, in order to isolate direct effects on offending of change in neighbourhood context, it is important to control for the confounding of neighbourhood changes with changes in the direct social context, as well as vice versa. Given that changes in the neighbourhood context often co-occur with changes in the direct social context, a research design that can disentangle the two is needed. The current study is a first attempt to execute such a study and demonstrates the feasibility of the approach.

Our results showed that moving to a different neighbourhood was associated with a lower likelihood of recidivism. This research confirms that moving to a new neighbourhood can provide a turning point in a criminal career and contribute to desistance (Laub and Sampson, 2003). Thus, changes in the neighbourhood context matter for the continuation of the criminal career during the transition to adulthood. Given that the analysis investigated recidivism, i.e., the people concerned have already started a criminal career, an explanation for this result may be that such a move may cut off ties with deviant peers in the old neighbourhood.

We expected that the characteristics of the new neighbourhood were important in predicting recidivism. For example, it may be expected that moving to a new neighbourhood that is less disadvantaged and has more informal social control than the old neighbourhood decreases the likelihood of recidivism, and vice versa. Results were somewhat mixed. The model included indicators for economic deprivation (for example, average income, average housing value), residential mobility, and ethnic heterogeneity (percentage of non-Western residents), which in the literature have all been linked to a higher level of social disorganization and thereby should lead to an increase of the risk of recidivism. However, although high average housing value did indeed predict lower recidivism, and although a higher percentage of non-Western residents did indeed predict a higher risk of recidivism, other results were not as hypothesized. For example, residential mobility was associated with a lower risk of recidivism. It is unclear why this should be the case; note, however, that the coefficient was very small. Furthermore, higher average income was associated with a higher risk of recidivism. A potential explanation may be that moving to a neighbourhood with higher income increases the number of attractive targets for property crimes and may therefore promote recidivism.

Overall, it should be observed that the coefficients for moving to a new neighbourhood and for the neighbourhood-level predictors were small. This is in line with the majority of European research, which has shown very limited effects of neighbourhood context on offending.

We argued that age 18 is not a good marker for the transition from adolescence to early adulthood, but that changes in context are more important. For example, leaving the parental household is arguably an important life change but does not occur for all individuals at the same age. Our results showed that leaving the parental household reduces the likelihood of recidivism. However, this seems to be primarily the case for those who had an active criminal career. Several alternative mechanisms may be at work. On the one hand, when individuals commit a first crime and they still live with their parents, some parents increase social control over their children, which leads to a less active career. When these children leave the parental household, parental control decreases, which increases opportunities for committing offences. On the other hand, when adolescents are already active offenders and parental control is low, moving out of the parental household may lead to an impulse in which the now young adult feels increased responsibility for his own household, which leads to an increase in conventional activities and a reduced likelihood of recidivism.

The absence of a significant effect of marriage is not in line with prior research. Perhaps we see here the mitigating effect of controlling for neighbourhood change that almost certainly will be the case after marriage, though another explanation for this could be that our marriage indicator does not include cohabitation, which is currently much more common than marriage among Dutch young adults. Although prior research suggests that cohabitation may not have the same crime-reducing effect as marriage (see Horney et al., 2012), Finnish research has suggested that cohabitation actually has a stronger effect than marriage. In addition, it can be argued that although marriage may contribute to desistance for some, it also provides the opportunity for partner abuse and may therefore lead to recidivism for others (Horney et al., 2012).

Our results on employment were also surprising. Although we expected that employment would provide financial stability, structured routine activities, and social control by co-workers and thus would facilitate desistance, this did not appear to be the case. In contrast, employment seemed to contribute to recidivism. This effect may be explained through the absence of information on whether jobs were stable or temporary, and on the type of job. In addition, available data lacked information on educational activities so that we do not know whether those who are unemployed are still involved in school or other educational activities. Furthermore, it may be that youth who start working broke off their educational careers, thereby potentially removing attachment to families and conventional society and providing them with resources to pursue a risky lifestyle, although this has not been confirmed in recent research (Horney et al., 2012).

Finally, the results showed that an active prior criminal career is a strong predictor for continuation. In sum, these results suggest that prior behaviour is a strong predictor of future behaviour, but that changes in the neighbourhood context and in the direct social context may provide turning points in criminal careers.

Recommendations for Future Research

As noted, the data we used were limited in the number of variables that we could include, especially for the direct social context. For example, indicators for education, becoming a parent, individual income, and neighbourhood-level crime could not be included. We recommend that such indicators be included in future research to better estimate effects of context changes on criminal careers. In addition, our dependent variable was dichotomous and not a count variable. This may have led to a loss of information. We recommend that future research investigates the extent to which different measures of the dependent variable affect outcomes. Furthermore, the research design analysed relatively short-term effects of context changes on the continuation of criminal careers. It thereby allowed for transitory patterns and frequent changes in contexts (Horney et al., 2012). However, the longer-term effects of such context changes were not investigated. We recommend that such effects be studied in future research. Moreover, the results showed that context changes have a different impact on different types of criminal careers. That is, we found that, for those with a less active criminal career, leaving the parental household decreased the likelihood of recidivism to a much lesser extent. Future research should investigate whether the impact of moving to a different neighbourhood, getting married, and getting a job also differs for different types of criminal careers (less active versus more active). The extent to which such effects differ not only for different criminal careers but also across sexes and races, is another topic worthy of more investigation since prior research suggests that context changes may affect males and females differently (Horney et al., 2012). This is especially interesting since researchers have observed that different subpopulations within the same age cohort increasingly experience social context changes at different ages (Liefbroer, 2005). For example, Dutch research has found that the timing of leaving the parental household varies across subpopulations (De Graaf and Loozen, 2006). Extending the current research with studies on how neighbourhood and direct social context changes affect different subpopulations is needed.

We are aware that our analysis is only a first step towards more fully exploiting a unique nationwide dataset of offenders in the Netherlands that includes indicators on both the individual direct social context and the neighbourhood-level context, thereby enabling us to disentangle the two. We believe we have shown the feasibility of using complex datasets for disentangling both types of context effects on continuing criminal careers from adolescence to early adulthood. Controlling for other context change effects, we found that moving to a new neighbourhood contributes to desistance, albeit to a limited extent. Also, changes in the direct social context, notably leaving the parental household and getting a job, affected the criminal career. We conclude that a previously active criminal career promotes further offending, but that context changes in the transition from adolescence and adulthood provide opportunities for turning points in individuals' criminal careers.

References

Akers, R.L. (1985). *Deviant Behavior: A Social Learning Approach*. Belmont, CA: Wadsworth.

Amato, P.R., Loomis, L.S., and Booth, A. (1995). Parental divorce, marital conflict, and offspring well-being during early adulthood. *Social Forces*, 73, 895–915.

Apel, R., Bushway, S.D., Raymond, P., Brame, R., and Sweeton, G. (2008). Using state child labor laws to identify the causal effect of youth employment on deviant behavior and academic achievement. *Journal of Quantitative Criminology*, 24, 337–62.

Bernasco, W. (2006). *Demografie en misdaad in stadsbuurten: theoretische en empirische relaties*. Paper presented at the WODC/NIDI congres Veranderingen in bevolkingssamenstelling, levensloop en criminaliteit: gevolgen voor justitie, Ede.

Bersani, B.E., Laub, J.H., and Nieuwbeerta, P. (2009). Marriage and desistance from crime in the Netherlands: Do gender and socio-historical context matter? *Journal of Quantitative Criminology*, 25, 3–24.

Bjerk, D. (2009). How much can we trust causal interpretations of fixed-effects estimators in the context of criminality? *Journal of Quantitative Criminology*, 25, 391–417.

Blokland, A.A.J. and Nieuwbeerta, P. (2005). The effects of life circumstances on longitudinal trajectories of offending. *Criminology*, 43, 1203–40.

Body-Gendrot, S. (1999). Urban violence in France: The quest for new policies. In G.J.N. Bruinsma and C.D. Van de Vijver (eds), *Public Safety in Europe*. Enschede: International Police Institute Twente, 33–44.

Bucx, F. (2008). Nestverlaters. Patronen van uit huis gaan bij jongvolwassenen en de geografische afstand tussen ouders en jongvolwassen kinderen. *Demos*, 24, 2–4.

Bushway, S., Brame, R., and Paternoster, R. (1999). Assessing stability and change in criminal offending: A comparison of random effects, semiparametric, and fixed effects modeling strategies. *Journal of Quantitative Criminology*, 15, 23–61.

CBS (2011) Sociaal Statistisch Bestand (SSB). At www.cbs.nl/nl-NL/menu/methoden/dataverzameling/ssb-onderzoeksbeschrijving-art.htm, accessed 4 January 2011.

Crane, J. (1991). The epidemic theory of ghettos and neighborhood effects on dropping out and teenage childbearing. *American Journal of Sociology*, 96, 1226–59.

Cullen, F.T. (1994). Social support as an organizing concept for criminology: Presidential address to the academy of criminal justice sciences. *Justice Quarterly*, 11, 527–59.

Dahlbäck, O. (1996). Urban place of residence and individual criminality. *British Journal of Criminology*, 36, 529–45.

De Cuyper, R., Weerman, F., and Ruiter, S. (2009). De co-evolutie van vriendschapsrelaties en delinquent gedrag onder Nederlandse jongeren: Spelen kenmerken van de vriendschapsrelatie een rol? *Mens & Maatschappij*, 84, 300–28.

De Goede, S., Blokland, A., and Nieuwbeerta, P. (2011). Ouderschap en crimineel gedrag. Het effect van het krijgen van een eerste kind op de ontwikkeling van crimineel gedrag. *Tijdschrift voor Criminologie*, 53, 3–22.

De Graaf, A. and Loozen, S. (2006). Uit huis gaan van jongeren. *Bevolkingstrends*, 54, 34–40.

De Haan, W.J.M. (1999). Violence in troubled neighborhoods. In G.J.N. Bruinsma and C.D. van de Vijver (eds), *Public Safety in Europe*. Enschede: International Police Institute Twente, 75–91.

Duncan, G.J. and Raudenbush, S.W. (1999). Assessing the effects of context in studies of child and youth development. *Educational Psychologist*, 34, 29–41.

Eisner, M. and Wikström, P-O.H. (1999). Violent crime in the urban community: A comparison of Stockholm and Basel. *European Journal on Criminal Policy and Research*, 7, 427–42.

Giordano, P.C., Cerkovich, S.A., and Rudolph, J.L. (2002). Gender, crime, and desistance: Toward a theory of cognitive transformation. *American Journal of Sociology*, 107, 990–1064.

Halaby, C.N. (2004). Panel models in sociological research: Theory into practice. *Annual Review of Sociology*, 30, 507–44.

Hesseling, R.B.P. (1992). Using data on offender mobility in ecological research. *Journal of Quantitative Criminology*, 34, 95–112.
Horney, J., Tolan, P., and Weisburd, D. (2012). Contextual influences. In R. Loeber and D.P. Farrington (eds), *From Juvenile Delinquency to Adult Crime: Criminal Careers, Justice Policy and Prevention*. New York: Oxford University Press.
Keizer, K., Lindenberg, S., and Steg, L. (2008). The spreading of disorder. *Science*, 322, 1681–5.
Latten, J. (2004). Trends in samenwonen en trouwen. De schone schijn van burgerlijke staat. *Bevolkingstrends*, 52, 46–60.
Laub, J.H. and Sampson, R.J. (2003). *Shared Beginnings, Divergent Lives: Delinquent Boys to Age 70*. Cambridge, MA: Harvard University Press.
Liefbroer, A.C. (2005). *Changes in the Transition to Adulthood in Europe; An Empirical Analysis of Changes Among Cohorts born Between the 1950's and 1960's in Europe and Among Dutch Cohorts born between 1900 and 1982*. Report for the Robert Bosch Foundation, The Hague: NIDI.
Miedema, S. (2002). Onderzoek nader onderzocht. Een vergelijkende analyse van etnografisch onderzoek naar de relatie tussen etniciteit, groepsvorming en delinquentie bij jongens. *Tijdschrift voor Criminologie*, 44, 150–61.
Müller, B. (2008). *Soziale Kohäsion in der Nachbarschaft. Eine Empirische Analyse von Einflussfaktoren auf Quartier- und Individualebene*. Zürich: Zürcher Projekt zur Sozialen Entwicklung von Kindern.
Oberwittler, D. (2004). A multilevel analysis of neighbourhood contextual effects on serious juvenile offending. *European Journal of Criminology*, 1, 201–35.
Oberwittler, D. (2007a). *The Effects of Ethnic and Social Segregation on Children and Adolescents: Recent Research and Results from a German Multilevel Study*. Berlin: Wissenschaftszentrum Berlin für Sozialforschung.
Oberwittler, D. (2007b). The effects of neighbourhood poverty on adolescent problem behaviour: A multi-level analysis differentiated by gender and ethnicity. *Housing Studies*, 22, 781–803.
Oberwittler, D. (2007c). Social exclusion and youth crime in Europe – The spatial dimension. Do disadvantaged neighbourhoods cause adolescents to become more delinquent? In K. Aromaa (ed.), *Penal Policy, Justice Reform, and Social Exclusion. Plenary Presentations held at the Fifth Annual Conference of the European Society of Criminology, 31 August – 3 September 2005, Krakow, Poland*. Helsinki: European Institute for Crime Prevention and Control, pp. 27–44.
Osgood, D.W., Wilson, J.K., O'Malley, P.M., Bachman, J.G., and Johnston, L.D. (1996). Routine activities and individual deviant behavior. *American Sociological Review*, 61, 635–55.
Pauwels, L. (2007). *Buurtinvloeden en jeugddelinquentie. Een toets van de Sociale Desorganisatietheorie*. The Hague: Boom Juridische uitgevers.
Raymore, L.A., Barber, B.L., and Eccles, J.S. (2001). Leaving home, attending college, partnership and parenthood: The role of life transition events in leisure

pattern stability from adolescence to young adulthood. *Journal of Youth and Adolescence*, 30, 197–223.

Reijneveld, S.A., Brugman, E., Verhulst, F.C., and Verloove-Vanhorick, S.P. (2005). Area deprivation and child psychosocial problems. A national cross-sectional study among school-aged children. *Social Psychiatry and Psychiatric Epidemiology*, 40, 18–23.

Reynald, D. (2010). Guardians on guardianship: Factors affecting the willingness to supervise, the ability to detect potential offenders, and the willingness to intervene. *Journal of Research in Crime & Delinquency*, 47, 358–90.

Rovers, B. (1999). De invloed van buurtkenmerken op criminaliteit van jonge inwoners. In S. Mustard and A. Goethals (eds), *De invloed van de buurt* Amsterdam: SISWO, pp. 94–128.

Sampson, R.J. (2004). Neighbourhood and community: Collective efficacy and community safety. *New Economy*, 11, 106–13.

Sampson, R.J., Raudenbusch, S.W., and Earls, F. (1997). Neighborhoods and violent crime: A multilevel study of collective efficacy. *Science*, 277, 918–24.

Savolainen, J. (2009). Work, family and criminal desistance: Adult social bonds in a Nordic welfare state. *British Journal of Criminology*, 49, 285–304.

Schneiders, J., Drukker, M., Van der Ende, J., Verhulst, F.C., Van Os, J., and Nicolson, N.A. (2003). Neighbourhood socioeconomic disadvantage and behavioural problems from late childhood into early adolescence. *Journal of Epidemiology and Community Health*, 57, 699–703.

Shaw, C.R. and McKay, H.D. (1969 [1942]). *Juvenile Delinquency and Urban Areas: A Study of Rates of Delinquency in Relation to Differential Characteristics of Local Communities in American Cities* (2nd edn). Chicago, IL: University of Chicago.

Shaw, C.R., Zorbaugh, F.M., McKay, H.D., and Cottrell, L.S. (1929). *Delinquency Areas: A Study of the Geographic Distribution of School Truants, Juvenile Delinquents, and Adult Offenders in Chicago*. Chicago, IL: University of Chicago Press.

Simons, R.L., Stewart, E., Gordon, L.C., Conger, R.D., and Elder, G.H., Jr. (2002). A test of life- course explanations for stability and change in antisocial behavior from adolescence to young adulthood. *Criminology*, 40, 401–34.

Steenbeek, W. and Hipp, J. (2011). A longitudinal test of social disorganization theory: Feedback effects among cohesion, social control, and disorder. *Criminology*, 49, 833–71.

Sutherland, E.H. (1947). *Principles of Criminology*. Philadelphia, PA: J.B. Lippincott.

Thorlindsson, T. and Bernberg, J.G. (2004). Durkheim's theory of social order and deviance: A multi-level test. *European Sociological Review*, 20, 271–85.

Van de Rakt, M., Ruiter, S., De Graaf, N.D., and Nieuwbeerta, P. (2010). When does the apple fall from the tree? Static versus dynamic theories predicting intergenerational transmission of convictions. *Journal of Quantitative Criminology*, 26, 371–89.

Van Gemert, F. (1998). *Crips in drievoud. Een dossieronderzoek naar drie jeugdbendes*. Amsterdam: Regioplan.

Van Schellen, M., Nieuwbeerta, P., and Poortman, A.R. (2008). Partners in crime? De criminele carrières van veroordeelden en hun huwelijkspartners. *Tijdschrift voor Veiligheid*, 7, 3–21.

Wadsworth, T. (2006). The meaning of work: Conceptualizing the deterrent effect of employment on crime among young adults. *Sociological Perspectives*, 49, 343–68.

Wagers, M., Sousa, W., and Kelling, G. (2008). Broken windows. In R. Wortley and L. Mazerolle (eds), *Environmental Criminology and Crime Analysis*. Cullompton: Willan, 247–62.

Warr, M. (1998). Life-course transitions and desistance from crime. *Criminology*, 36, 183–216.

Weerman, F. (2011). Delinquent peers in context: A longitudinal network analysis of selection and influence effects. *Criminology*, 49, 253–86.

Weijters, G. (2006). Jeugddelinquentie: Wat is de invloed van de buurt? In J.R.M. Gerris (ed.), *Het belang van school, ouders, vrienden en buurt*. Assen: Van Gorcum, 75–88.

Weijters, G., Scheepers, P., and Gerris, J. (2007). Distinguishing the city, neighbourhood, and individual level in the explanation of youth delinquency: A multilevel approach. *European Journal of Criminology*, 4, 87–108.

Weijters, G.G.M. (2008). *Youth Delinquency in Dutch Cities and Schools: A Multilevel Approach*. Nijmegen: Radboud University (Ph.D. dissertation).

Wortley, R. and Mazerolle, L. (2008). *Environmental Criminology and Crime Analysis*. Cullompton: Willan.

Chapter 4
Explanations of Offending

Andrea G. Donker, Erik Bulten, Terence P. Thornberry
and Mauri Matsuda

In recent decades criminologists have mapped trajectories of criminal activity in ever-sharper detail. In this chapter we present major explanatory frameworks to account for individual variations in trajectories of offending during the transition from adolescence to adulthood. As explained in Chapter 1 of this volume, this transition is one of the most important stages in the life course. Rindfuss, Swicegood and Rosenfeld (1987) have referred to it as a 'demographically dense' period because it often involves multiple transitions: in education, work, residence, family formation and parenthood. The timing and success of these transitions have important consequences for the long-term development both of the individual and of his or her family (Elder, 1997). The transition from adolescence to adulthood has been described also as a window of opportunity when developmental and contextual changes converge to support positive turnarounds, including desistance from offending, and redirections of the life course (Masten et al., 2009; Masten, Obradović and Burt, 2006).

In this chapter we review several major theoretical explanatory frameworks for criminal offending during the transition years, as well as some of the empirical support associated with them. We begin by specifying the patterns of offending that seem to be the most salient to explain and identify key questions that explanatory frameworks should address with respect to these patterns.

Patterns of Offending

As described by Blokland and colleagues in Chapter 2 (this volume), age–crime curves reflect the prevalence of offending in the population. Crime rates organized by age indicate rapidly escalating rates of offending or arrests during the second decade of life, followed by a steep (but more gradual) decline in the third decade, often peaking around age 18 (ages 16–20 or so, depending on the type of crime). This overall pattern requires explanation. However, hidden within the age–crime curve are marked individual differences in crime and arrest rates, and several notable subgroups of trajectories. These trajectory subgroups include the following patterns: one that shows offending already before adolescence and persistence of high crime rates into adulthood; one characterized by persistently low rates of offending (never showing a rise); a group that shows the age–crime curve pattern of a rise and fall; and a group that shows a late rise relative to the age–crime curve, when overall crime rates are falling in the general population (Piquero, 2008). The age–crime curve is a compilation of individual patterns. Explanatory frameworks of offending must account for the overall pattern and for the subgroups that show such markedly different trajectories.

As individuals move from adolescence through emerging adulthood (Arnett, 2000) and on to the greater stability of the adult years, there are three patterns of offending that seem particularly important to understand. These are: persistent involvement in offending, desistance from offending, and adult-onset offending. For the general population, the modal age of onset of criminal offending is during mid-adolescence, that is, most individuals who become offenders have done so by age 16 or 17 (Krohn et al., 2001; see also Blokland and Palmen, Chapter 2, this volume). Persistence refers to the continuity in offending between adolescence and early adulthood and beyond. Explanatory frameworks ought to be able to explain why some juveniles persist in offending during the early adult years and to identify factors associated with continuity in offending at this particular developmental stage.

Desistance is the flip side of persistence. Following Bushway et al. (2001), we define desistance as the process of changing from active involvement in offending to a zero or a near-zero rate that persists over the life course. Three issues about the process of desistance are particularly salient to address: what causes offenders to desist; what factors maintain offending at a near-zero rate over time, or why former offenders maintain their abstinence from crime; and whether or not these processes vary developmentally. Some offenders desist relatively early – during late adolescence – while others desist later, during emerging adulthood, and it is important to know whether processes associated with desistance are the same at different developmental stages.

Adult-onset offending refers to the initiation of offending after the normative age of onset period (age 18 or later), beyond the modal age of onset and at or past the point where the age–crime curve begins downward inflection. Two theoretical questions are particularly important for understanding adult-onset cases: what are the assets and promotive factors that prevented or delayed involvement in delinquency earlier during childhood and adolescence, and what are the developmental processes that are associated with the onset of offending during the transition to adulthood, when the normative trend is towards declining rates?

Four Explanatory Frameworks

As it is beyond the scope of this chapter to review all work done in this field, we focus on four broad frameworks that currently inform the field's understanding of the patterns of offending. Two explanatory frameworks are one-dimensional, offering one model for all types of offenders. These two frameworks, however, stem from diametrically different points of view: the static versus the dynamic perspective. We refer to the third framework as the dual developmental perspective as it distinguishes two theoretical models explaining two distinct offending patterns. And, finally, the fourth explanatory framework is the biopsychosocial perspective, in our view extremely relevant though not yet fully developed. Within this perspective emphasis is on recognizing gradual, dimensional and interactional processes in order to explain in more detail the complexity of individuals' development in real life.

The first group, the static or population heterogeneity models, adopts an ontogenetic perspective to explain offending across the life course. There are two defining aspects to static explanatory frameworks of crime. First, the basic causes of criminal behaviour and changes in offending over time are to be found in individual endowments that are established relatively early in the life course. Second, these early endowments create inter-individual (or relative) stability in the behaviour, that is, across the life course individuals are generally expected to maintain their position relative to other individuals with respect to their levels of offending. There are several explanatory frameworks of criminal behaviour that adopt this approach, including the works of Glueck and Glueck (1950), Mednick (1977), Wilson and Hernstein (1985), but particularly the work of Gottfredson and Hirschi (1990) is seen as the exemplar of a static explanatory framework.

The next group of explanatory frameworks is often referred to as dynamic or life course developmental models. In contrast to the static framework, the dynamic models adopt a pure sociogenetic approach. In these models, human behaviour is never viewed as set or established or inevitably stemming from early endowments. Sociogenesis emphasizes 'the uniquely "open" or "unfinished" character of the human organism in relation to its environment' (Dannefer, 1984, p. 107), a plasticity that persists across the full life course. The tremendous variability in social experiences and environments combined with the variation among individuals of the same age interacting with those environments minimizes the chances of observing a universal pattern of inter-individual stability or intra-individual change.

There are several sociogenetic explanatory frameworks of delinquency, as found in the works of such theorists as Akers (1998), Catalano and Hawkins (1986), Elliott, Huizinga and Ageton (1985), Sampson and Laub (1993, 1997), and Thornberry and Krohn (2001, 2005). Sociogenetic frameworks with a focus on the emotional and cognitive processes accompanying social transitions are proposed by Giordano, Cernkovich and Rudolph (2002), Matsueda and Heimer (1997), and with regard to the relevance of identity and status by Warr (2002).

The third perspective is the dual developmental perspective. Models from this perspective distinguish two types of delinquent development. One rare type resembles the static ontogenetic model with its emphasis on factors early in life, creating population heterogeneity, whereas the etiology of the other more prevalent type has a more sociogenetic origin explaining the rise of delinquent behaviour among adolescents. Stability and change over the lifespan is explained from micro- (for example, neurological factors) to macro- (for example, sociological) level factors. Possibility of change continues throughout the lifespan, but the dynamics of change are more evident when negative developmental processes occur later in life, beyond childhood. Early experiences can have profound consequences, narrowing the options for change.

The explanatory frameworks of Moffitt (1993) and Patterson, Capaldi and Bank (1991) are dual developmental frameworks. The explanatory framework of Farrington (2003) resonates with this perspective. In his model, however, duality is not present along the lines of two types of delinquents but on the causal level. In Farrington's explanatory framework, long-term antisocial potential accounts for inter-individual differences whereas short-term antisocial potential explains intra-individual differences, in other words: 'Why does someone offend right there and then?'

The last perspective is the biopsychosocial perspective. With regard to the emphasis on developmental processes as well as on the possibility of concentrated windows of opportunity or vulnerability over the life course, this perspective bears resemblance to the dual developmental perspective. In this case, however, there is no fixed typology, rather the recognition of gradual, dimensional and interactional processes. This perspective integrates ideas from the sciences of human development, general systems theory, clinical psychology, psychiatry, sociology, paediatrics, neuroscience, behavioural genetics, and so on (Cicchetti, 2006; Masten, 2006; Sroufe, 2007).

We continue by discussing how each of the frameworks explains offending patterns during the transition years, with particular attention to issues of persistence, desistance, and adult-onset offending.

Static Explanatory Frameworks

The most prominent explanatory framework of crime with a static population heterogeneity perspective is Gottfredson and Hirschi's (1990) self-control framework. In this framework, the propensity to engage in crime is viewed as a product of the individual's level of self-control, which is established roughly by age 8 and from then on stays relatively stable through life (Hirschi and Gottfredson, 2001). In this line of thinking, youth who are exposed to effective parenting styles at early ages and who have positive relations with their parents are likely to have high levels of self-control and therefore low rates of offending at all ages. In contrast, youth who experience poor parenting styles and have harsh, brittle relationships with their parents are likely to have low levels of self-control and therefore high levels of offending at all ages. By and large, the factors involved in the level of self-control determine the onset of offending, which in turn determines the criminal trajectory. According to this explanatory framework, the overall shape of offending careers is universal, follows the general age–crime curve, and reflects the ontogenetic assumption of inter-individual stability (Gottfredson and Hirschi, 1990, p. 132).

There is substantial empirical support for the relevance of low self-control to the onset and persistence of crime. Gottfredson (2006) cites a considerable body of research, tested on diverse samples and utilizing various outcome measures in support of this framework. Further, a meta-analysis (Pratt and Cullen, 2000) shows support for the effect of low self-control on crime and analogous behaviours. In general, the prediction that low self-control is associated with higher rates of offending is borne out by the empirical literature, especially when attention focuses on explanations of onset and persistence. Even so, support for the self-control explanatory framework is weaker in studies that utilize a longitudinal design (Pratt and Cullen, 2000).

It could be argued that low self-control is a symptom of offending rather than a causal factor. Similar difficulties in establishing causal influence have been described for other factors as well (Farrington, 2007). Heavy drinking, for instance, can be seen as a symptom of an antisocial personality as well as a potential cause of disruptive behaviour. Similarly, childhood-onset offending cannot be considered an explanatory predictor, as it is heterotypically continuous with the offending behaviour that is predicted. A similar non-explanatory notion might apply to self-control, the core concept of Gottfredson and Hirschi's explanatory framework, particularly when it is measured using disruptive behaviour items. Apart from the wide variety of measures used to measure low self-control, there are also many constructs similarly referring to a poor ability to control behaviour, and equally related to measures of offending (for example, impulsiveness, hyperactivity, restlessness, clumsiness, sensation-seeking, risk-taking, etc.; Farrington, 2007).

According to Gottfredson and Hirschi's framework, persistence is associated with individuals with the lowest levels of self-control, which cause high levels of offending during adolescence, and the general stability of self-control over the life course increases the likelihood of continuity in offending into the adult years. Within this framework, desistance is entirely a function of maturational reform and 'maturational reform is just that, change in behaviour that comes with maturation … spontaneous desistance is just that, change in behaviour that cannot be explained and change that occurs regardless of what else happens' (Gottfredson and Hirschi, 1990, p. 136). Maturation accounts for intra-individual change across time but does not fundamentally disturb the inter-individual stability that can be traced back to early and middle childhood. A similar view was presented by Glueck and Glueck: 'the biological process of maturation is the chief factor in the behavior changes of criminals' (1940, p. 107). Developmental variables, such as association with delinquent peers, gang membership, and, at later ages, marriage and employment exert no causal impact on the likelihood or timing of desistance; relationships between these variables and desistance are entirely spurious (Gottfredson and Hirschi, 1990). The static explanatory framework of offending does not anticipate the presence of adult-onset cases as a meaningful portion of the population.

In contrast with the static explanatory framework of Gottfredson and Hirschi, there appears to be more to the explanation of patterns of offending than low self-control. In the Dunedin (New Zealand) study, for instance, multiple factors were found to be predictive for life-course persistent offending. Several of these constructs were associated with low self-control (under-controlled temperament, neurological abnormalities and delayed motor development – all measured at age 3 – hyperactivity and slow heart rate) but also with other individual factors (low intellectual ability, poor reading and memory), and with family-environmental factors (teenaged single parents, mothers with poor mental health, harsh and inconsistent discipline, neglect, much family conflict, many changes of primary caretaker, low family socioeconomic status, and rejection by peers in school; Moffitt, 2006, pp. 279–80).

Similarly contrasting with the static explanatory frameworks is the clear empirical support for the state dependence argument regarding prior offending, central to the dynamic explanatory frameworks, which we shall discuss later. In a three-wave panel study of juvenile delinquency, Nagin and Paternoster (1991) compare the evidence for population heterogeneity and state dependence arguments by examining the effect of unobserved and observed heterogeneity relative to prior participation in crime on later offending. They found that prior participation in offending had a positive and significant effect on later offending, controlling for persistent unobserved heterogeneity, thus providing greater evidence for the state dependence effect. Paternoster et al. (1997) find support for both population heterogeneity and state dependence arguments in their longitudinal examination of a sample of North Carolina juveniles released from training schools. Although the effect of prior arrests is reduced after individual differences are controlled, lending support to the population heterogeneity position, prior arrest maintained a positive, significant effect on future arrests, bolstering the state dependence position.

Dynamic Explanatory Frameworks

Frameworks that adopt a dynamic, life course perspective of crime do not deny that early established behaviours continue to influence behaviour over the life course (for example, Sampson and Laub, 1993; Thornberry, 2005). Nevertheless, the primary explanation for later offending is to be found in the changing social environment that individuals confront as they traverse the life course. For example, changing relationships with parents and peers, the timing and success of transitions along major life-course trajectories such as family, school and work, and the consequences of earlier involvement in delinquency and contact with the juvenile justice system are all expected to exert a strong influence on diverging patterns of offending such as persistence and desistance (Akers, 1998; Catalano and Hawkins, 1986; Laub and Sampson, 2003; Thornberry and Krohn, 2005).

In dynamic explanatory frameworks persistence is not primarily an outcome of early endowments, as it is in static explanatory frameworks, but to the contrary is primarily an outcome of more proximal developmental processes that were often set in motion by earlier developments, including earlier involvement in delinquent behaviour. A principal key to the explanation for persistence is the negative consequences of earlier involvement in delinquent behaviour, as is true of all state dependence models (Nagin and Paternoster, 1991). Thornberry's (1987) interactional explanatory theory views delinquency as embedded in mutually reinforcing causal relationships. Delinquency attenuates bonds to conventional people and institutions, increases subsequent involvement in delinquent peer networks and street gangs, and strengthens delinquent belief systems (see also Akers, 1998). Individuals with weakened prosocial bonds and who are enmeshed in delinquent behaviours and networks are likely to experience high levels of persistence in offending.

Successful completion of the developmental challenges of adolescence is distorted by delinquency, resulting in weakened prosocial bonds. Delinquents are likely to become alienated from parents and family, fail at school, and become entangled in delinquent peer groups. All of these factors – delinquency plus its consequences – were found to be related to disorderly and unsuccessful transitions to adult roles. For example, they are associated with increased levels of school dropout, teen parenthood, unstable employment records and marital instability (Krohn, Lizotte and Perez, 1997). Horney, Osgood and Marshall (1995) found that illegal drug use, heavy drinking and living with a girlfriend lead to increases in short-term offending, whereas living with a wife and attending school lead to reductions in short-term offending. In turn, failure to make timely and successful transitions from adolescent to adult roles reduces both human and social capital and increases the likelihood of persistent involvement in offending.

A parallel negative general process has to do with involvement in the juvenile justice system (Bernburg and Krohn, 2003; Paternoster and Iovanni, 1989; Sampson and Laub, 1997). Official records of arrest and incarceration have long-term consequences for the individual. Official labelling increases entanglement in criminal social networks, which increases persistence in offending (Bernburg, Krohn and Rivera, 2006). Similarly, official labels increase the likelihood of school dropout and unstable employment, both of which are also associated with increased persistence in offending (Bernburg and Krohn, 2003). Farrington et al. (1986) found that unemployment increased involvement in crimes that led to financial gain, but not to an increase in other types of crimes.

Dynamic life course explanatory frameworks thus point to at least three processes that are associated with persistence in offending: the stability of earlier deficits, the life-course consequences of delinquency attenuating bonds to conventional people and institutions, and the effects of official labelling.

In dynamic explanatory frameworks, desistance is largely explained by the re-establishment of bonds to conventional society (Sampson and Laub, 1993; Thornberry, 1987) and by concordant changes in the individual's social networks (Warr, 1998). Desistance is more likely to occur when the causal factors that created delinquency in the first place are less numerous, less extreme and less intertwined (Thornberry and Krohn, 2001, 2005). Offenders who increase attachment to conventional people and commitment to prosocial activities such as school and work are more likely to escape persistent involvement in criminal behaviour: 'a cascade of successful relationships and acceptance by conventional people can result in stronger social bonds, and this process can, in turn, lessen the propensity for crime' (Cohen and Vila, 1996, p. 139). The changing network constellation provides both new sources of control and new opportunity structures (Warr, 1998) that channel behaviour away from crime.

Sampson and Laub's social control theory (1993) emphasizes the importance of adult social bonds, such as marital attachments, in accounting for desistance during the transition years. Part of this effect is direct. A 'quality' marriage increases attachment to others thereby increasing social control and reducing offending. But part of this effect is indirect because marriage alters the nature of routine activities (Horney, Osgood and Marshall, 1995), for example, by reducing time spent on street corners, in bars and with delinquent peer networks (Warr, 1998, 2002). All of these changes reduce opportunities and reinforcements for criminal behaviour, thereby enhancing the likelihood of desistance.

Using data originally collected by Sheldon and Eleanor Glueck (1940), Sampson and Laub (1993) found that disruptive behaviour in childhood and in adolescence predicted arrest, military offences, and a range of negative family, school and work outcomes in adulthood. They also found that job stability, commitment and marital attachment in young- and middle adulthood reduced the likelihood of future offending for the 'Glueck men' (1993). The follow-up life history interviews of the sample showed that men who desisted were indeed more likely to have experienced positive turning points, such as marriage. Being married reduced the likelihood of offending by over 30 per cent, controlling for both between individual (for example, criminal propensity) and within individual (for example, age) factors (Laub and Sampson, 2003). Farrington and West (1995) found that getting married decreased involvement in crime while later separation increased involvement in crime.

The marriage effect has also been demonstrated in the Netherlands using the Criminal Career and Life Course Study (CCLS) data (Bersani, Laub and Nieuwbeerta, 2009), which revealed that the effect of marriage holds for previously convicted males and females. Data from the same study showed also that other life circumstances (work, parenthood) substantially influenced chances for desistance, except for the high-rate chronic offending group (Blokland and Nieuwbeerta, 2005).

Although marriage appears in time a proximal predictive factor for desistance, proximity on the conceptual level is more difficult to grasp, as the theoretical mechanism behind its effect is not yet understood. For disadvantaged women, the marriage effect was smaller than the effect from becoming a mother (Kreager, Matsueda and Erosheva, 2010).

The marriage effect does not equate with an intimate partner effect. Meeus, Branje and Overbeek (2004) found no effect of having an intimate partner on desistance among young adults. On the contrary, adolescents who consistently have a partner show more delinquent behaviour than those without a partner. For this latter group, continuing parental support appears to be related to a reduction in the level of delinquency.

Age may be an important condition that moderates the effects of social control variables such as work and marriage. For instance, Uggen (2000) found that assignment to an experimental work programme reduced recidivism for older offenders, although it had no significant effect on younger offenders.

Other primary sources of social bonding that have been linked to desistance during the transition years are commitment to conventional activities, such as military service (Bouffard and Laub, 2004), and work (Uggen, 2000). The hypothesized mechanisms linking these activities to cessation in crime include financial incentives, direct supervision or control, and a generalized stake in conformity (Toby, 1957).

Some explanatory frameworks with equal sociogenetic underpinnings focused particularly on the cognitive processes of desistance. Giordano, Cernkovich and Rudolph (2002) developed a 'theory of cognitive transformation', describing cognitive shifts that precede, accompany and follow desistance from crime, which emphasizes that individuals vary in their openness and receptivity to particular catalysts or 'hooks for change'. A variety of experiences can operate as successful hooks for change. These are important not only as a source of social control, but also because they foster new definitions of the situation (attitudes), a blueprint for how to succeed as a changed individual, and a satisfying and achievable replacement self (see also Maruna, 2001; Matsueda and Heimer, 1997).

Maruna (2001) focuses heavily on desisters' feelings of redemption, even beyond the specifically religious connotations of the term (see also McAdams et al., 1997). Persisters believe they are stuck in their current circumstances, while desisters have more positive, agentic worldviews, including feelings of pride that they have been able to put considerable distance between the old criminal self and the one they have crafted around the process of 'making good'.

Relatively little theoretical attention has been paid to adult-onset offending in these dynamic models. Thornberry and Krohn (2005) hypothesized that late-onset offenders are likely to have the multiple causal factors that are associated with early-onset offending, but at earlier ages they are buffered from the effects of these risk factors by strong social bonds. The hypothesis is that family structure creates a supportive environment by providing both social control and social support to constrain behaviour (Mannheim, 1967). During emerging adulthood, however, individuals begin to leave this protective environment. The resulting deficits in human capital become a serious impediment to acquiring meaningful employment and establishing stable partner relationships. The difficulties experienced during the transition years also make them more vulnerable to the influence of deviant friends and to the consequences of alcohol and drug use, which often escalate at these ages. The combination of a stressful transition to adult status and emerging substance use increases the probability of both adult-onset and further continuation of offending.

Dual Developmental Explanatory Frameworks

These emphasize the relevance of distinguishing two distinct trajectories of offending, differing in etiological background, in offending patterns and in prognosis. Models within this framework identify two major groups of offenders: a childhood-onset group called early starters (Patterson et al., 1991) or life-course persistent offenders (Moffitt, 1993), and an adolescence-onset group, called late starters (Patterson et al., 1991) or adolescence-limited offenders (Moffitt, 1993). The etiology of the childhood-onset group combines ontogenetic and sociogenetic processes, with an emphasis on the former. The adolescence-onset group's etiological process is mainly sociogenetic.

The childhood-onset group, which is relatively small, has a persistent pattern of offending. In Patterson et al.'s explanatory framework this is largely due to ineffective parenting styles and to the coercive exchanges that develop in distressed families. In Moffitt's explanatory framework early-onset offending is primarily due to the interplay between individual deficits, especially neuropsychological deficits, and ineffective parenting styles. The second group – late starters or adolescence-limited offenders – have an onset of serious offending during the adolescent years and delinquent careers that tend to be relatively short. For this group, both explanatory frameworks focus on challenges associated with adolescent development to explain involvement in delinquency. Association with delinquent peers, failure in school, and frustration associated with adjusting to the maturity gap identified by Moffitt are major factors accounting for delinquency.

According to these explanatory frameworks, persistence is primarily associated with the childhood-onset offender, illustrated by Moffitt's life-course-persistent offender for whom persistence is caused by two general developmental processes. The first, contemporary continuity, refers to the relatively strong continuity in the original disruptive behaviours 'such as high activity level, irritability, poor self-control, and low cognitive ability' (Moffitt, 1993, p. 683). Continuity in these behaviours adds negatively to the second process: cumulative consequences. This term refers to the continuous accumulation of the consequences of disruptive behaviour from an early age, such as isolation in delinquent peer groups, school failure, involvement in the juvenile justice system, and ultimately difficulty in the transition to adult roles, illustrated by failure to finish school, teen parenthood, and unemployment. These consequences of earlier offending make it difficult for the individual to escape involvement in delinquent behaviour, 'narrowing the options for change' and thus increasing the likelihood of persistence of delinquent careers.

The term life-course persistence does not mean that middle-aged or older people will offend at a pace similar to juveniles. Moffitt states that 'the taxonomy accepts that antisocial participation declines markedly in mid-life, but, nonetheless, it expects rank-order stability, particularly on age-relevant measures of antisocial activity' (2006, p. 294; see also Piquero, 2008, p. 51).

Robust empirical support has indeed been found for the relevance of the age of onset regarding persistent offending (see Blokland and Palmen, Chapter 2, this volume). In her seminal study, Robins (1978) found that childhood disruptive behaviours predict high levels of adult criminal behaviour in samples that vary by race, historical period, geographic area, and age at follow-up. According to these findings, childhood antisocial behaviour was a prerequisite of adult antisocial behaviour. This has been corroborated multiple times. Moffitt (1993, p. 695) consequently proposed the hypothesis: 'estimates of the individual stability of antisocial behaviour are expected to violate the longitudinal law, which states that relationships between variables become weaker as the time interval between them grows longer'. Empirical support for this hypothesis is found in a Swedish study (Stattin and Magnusson, 1991) and also in a Dutch study (Donker et al., 2003) using data from the South Holland study. In this study, stability from childhood to young adulthood exceeded the stability from adolescence to young adulthood with regard to overt delinquency (oppositional aggressive behaviours), not for covert delinquency (secretive behaviours such as property offences). Desistance from overt delinquency appears to occur prior to desistance from covert delinquency, at least for the adolescence-onset offenders (Donker et al., 2003).

Apart from early age of onset, other early characteristics also add to the prediction of levels of offending (several excellent reviews are available, such as Farrington, 2000; Hawkins et al., 1998; Lipsey and Derzon, 1998). Negative temperamental traits (irritability, impulsivity), ineffective parenting styles, poverty, school failure (poor executive functioning), and delinquent family members and peers are all linked to the onset and maintenance of delinquent careers (Catalano and Hawkins, 1996; Farrington, 2003; Thornberry and Krohn, 2005).

In the dual developmental explanatory frameworks, desistance is primarily associated with the other, numerically larger, adolescence-onset group of offenders referred to either as late starters by Patterson and colleagues (1991) or as adolescence-limited offenders by Moffitt (1993). In Moffitt's framework, adolescence-limited offending is largely a product of the gap between the onset of physical maturity (ability to reproduce) and the onset of social maturity or adult roles and privileges in advanced industrial societies. The subsequent frustration leads to imitation of the behaviours of the life-course-persistent offenders, as they appear to have access to more mature privileges (alcohol, sex, material goods). As individuals age, mature privileges come into reach, and frustration wanes and diminishes the motivating forces supporting delinquency. Consequently, desistance becomes an attractive option and also one that is within reach since these offenders have had a rather normal socialization process in their youth. Therefore, adolescence-limited offenders are apt to make successful transitions to adult roles such as partner, parent and employee.

The desistance process of the adolescence-onset group has clear resemblance to the aforementioned dynamic perspective of desistance. As Farrington describes it, desistance is related to 'changes in socialization influences (decreasing importance of peers, increasing importance of the female partners and children), and life events such as getting married, having children, moving home and getting a steady job' (2003, p. 235). Life-course-persistent offenders, on the contrary, suffer from contemporary continuity and cumulative consequences of criminogenic factors and processes, reducing their chances for positive transitions that could induce desistance.

Piquero (2008) presented a very thorough review of the trajectory literature based on recently developed mixture models that have become increasingly popular to differentiate patterns of offending trajectories across the life course (Nagin and Land, 1993; Nagin, 2005). One of his main conclusions is that there appears to be an adolescent-peaked pattern and a chronic offender pattern: 'These findings emerge across a range of studies around the world, with different follow-up lengths, sample depictions, and use of self-, parent-, and teacher-ratings as well as different sources of official records including police contacts, arrests, and convictions' (Piquero, 2008, p. 49).

Strong empirical support for a chronic pattern of serious offending has been found, for instance, in the Dunedin cohort sample. Respondents resembling the life-course-persistent model were involved in more serious and violent behaviour, had mental health and substance abuse problems, financial and employment problems, and committed domestic abuse of women and children (Moffitt, 2006; see also for a list of longitudinal studies with findings of a persistent chronic group of offenders). In the Cambridge Study on Delinquent Development, one third of those persistent offenders who had convictions before and after age 21 were still offending at age 48 and suffered other problems similar to the Dunedin group (Farrington et al., 2006). Likewise, after extending the Glueck data to include arrests through to age 70, Laub and Sampson (2003) found their high-rate chronic offenders peaked around age 35 and desisted at age 60.

In the Netherlands, strong support was also found in the Criminal Career and Life Course Study based on a Dutch conviction cohort (CCLS; Blokland, Nagin and Nieuwbeerta, 2005; see also Blokland and Palmen, Chapter 2, this volume). Four trajectory groups were identified, of which the high-rate persisters continued offending even through to age 72.

At age 26, desistance patterns of the males of the Dunedin study were analysed (Moffitt et al., 2002). Contrary to the original dual taxonomy model, males on the adolescence-limited path (approximately 25 per cent of all males) were still engaged in property offending and substance abuse, but they were not involved in more serious offending. Similar findings were reported using semi-parametric analytical methods (Moffitt, 2006).

The dual developmental perspective, as the name implies, does not incorporate a late-onset trajectory. However, a third chronic offending pattern has been consistently identified in the trajectory literature. This pattern continues into adulthood, but at a much lower rate compared to the other persistence trajectory (Piquero, 2008).

In fact, the Dunedin sample also appears to contain such a third group, once wrongfully labelled the recovery group (Moffitt, 2006). These children did show extremely disruptive behaviour, but in contrast to the life-course-persistent group, they refrained from extreme delinquency in adolescence. In (young) adulthood, however, they showed low-level chronic offending at least until age 26. The key to this group appears to be a tendency towards socially isolated lives, partly due to disorders such as depression and anxiety (Moffitt, 2006). This has been found as well for several other longitudinal studies of low-level chronic groups (Farrington et al., 2006; Wiesner and Capaldi, 2003).

The Biopsychosocial Perspective (BPS)

This perspective regards illness, including aggressive behaviour, the result of interacting mechanisms at biological, psychological, interpersonal and environmental levels. Determinants from all levels are regarded as dimensional, gradual and dynamic. As a multilevel approach, it insists on the notion that a single-level explanatory framework is probably insufficient. The empirical support for the biopsychosocial perspective has increased considerably over the years in all sorts of scientific domains. Studies have shown, for instance, the dynamics of the brain (so-called experience-independent, experience-dependent and experience-expectant plasticity), closely shaped by and physically changing due to life experiences (Draganski et al., 2004; Peters, 2010).

Plasticity and flexibility of the brain are also illustrated by the dynamic, massive neural developmental changes during early childhood, changes that support the development of mature regulation of emotion and behaviour. However, there are differences in the developmental trajectories across brain regions. Some changes are linear with age, while other changes show a more non-linear pattern. Some regions of the brain show more or less simple growth trajectories, while others have the most complex developmental trajectories (Shaw et al., 2008).

Developmental trajectories of the brain may be influenced by all sorts of factors: chronic exposure to stress (Lupien et al., 2009); childhood socioeconomic status (Hackman and Farah, 2009); early parental care (Rao et al., 2010); malnutrition (Rosales et al., 2009), etc., but also by gender, as shown by a significant interaction of gender and the volume of the anterior cingulate cortex (ACC) predicting aggressive and defiant behaviour. In a study of 117 non-referred children (ages 7–17), Boes et al. (2008) found a significant negative partial correlation between aggressive and defiant behaviours in boys and volume of the right ACC. These behaviours were associated with decreased right ACC volume in boys but not in girls. Another finding adding to a growing body of evidence of gender-specific development comes from a study on neural mechanisms underlying affective processing. A study of adolescent aggression during parent–child interactions found amygdala volume to be correlated positively with duration of aggressive behaviours, suggesting an inability to downregulate quickly, but again only for boys. There may also be gender differences in the neural mechanisms underlying affective and behavioural regulation during early adolescence (Wager et al., 2003, Whittle et al., 2008)

Age-related changes in brain activity accompany the anatomic shifts across development. Brain circuits involved in cognitive control, attention, and emotion regulation are actively developing throughout childhood and adolescence. The prefrontal cortex, for example, undergoes considerable maturation during childhood (Tsujimoto, 2008); however, the frontal regions involved in executive function and attention processes mature later than regions involved in more basic functions, such as motor or sensory cortices (Shaw et al., 2008). Remarkable evidence from clinical studies of adults and adolescents implicates altered function in the ACC-amygdala circuit in the pathophysiology of emotion and behavioural disregulation. And reduced activation of the ACC and increased reactivity of the amygdala in aggressive individuals suggests that in many of these individuals the regulatory function of the ACC is compromised.

These are examples of how the development of the brain is associated with aggression and externalizing behaviour and of the growing evidence on the (neuro) biological determinants for early-onset and persistent disruptive and delinquent behaviour. Kruesi et al. (2004) reported, for instance, that there are significant similarities between brain abnormalities of antisocial personality-disordered or aggressive adults and early-onset conduct-disordered children. Neurobiological findings and psychological insights also challenge more or less traditional explanatory frameworks to prove their validity with new insights. For instance, a recent study by Passamonti et al. (2010) indicates that Moffitt's explanatory framework probably needs to be revised because of studies showing that adolescence-onset conduct disorder is also associated with abnormal neurophysiological functioning, which in Moffitt's framework is restricted to early-onset conduct disorder.

Currently there is no comprehensive neurobiological explanatory framework explaining persistence, desistance and late-onset antisocial behaviour by combining genetic, hormonal, neurophysiological, neuropsychological and neuroimaging research findings and neurobiological risk factors (such as malnutrition). In such an explanatory framework the more or less normal neurobiological development during adolescence should also be integrated. Because of the lack of a comprehensive framework, we only can discuss some of the partial neurobiological explanatory frameworks. The focus of this section will be on biological and some psychological aspects, while acknowledging that neurobiological/psychological influences can only be understood properly if social factors are also taken into account, and that all these factors interact in a complex and an evident manner.

Socialization depends in part on the ability of the child to learn from reward and punishment (for example, fear conditioning) within proper conditions (social, economical, psychological bonding/attachment etc.). Neurobiologically based malfunctions of these learning faculties create conditions for failure in the process of (moral) socialization. For instance, Fairchild et al. (2009) observed fear conditioning deficits in participants with early- and adolescence-onset forms of conduct disorder. Compromised fear conditioning contributes to antisocial behaviour and probably to lack of conscience. This is illustrated by a longitudinal study by Gao et al. (2010), which demonstrated that poor fear conditioning at age 3 predisposes individuals to crime at age 23 because those who lack fear are less likely to avoid situations and events associated with future punishment. Several parts of the cortex and the amygdala-hippocampal complex are involved in this process of socialization and social learning, building up 'morality' and the sensitivity for reward and punishment (Van Overwalle and Baetens, 2009; Schug et al., 2010).

Early-onset conduct disorders persistent through adolescence to adulthood can be understood up to some level by brain impairments that result in a failing process of socialization, but only in combination with other factors such as the quality of parenting and peer pressure. When the engines of adolescence are turned on as a result of pubertal changes, in the context of poor parenting and deviant peers these young individuals are more likely to engage in risky or thrill-seeking behaviour, as well as early sexual activity and smoking, and alcohol and drug use (Obradović and Boyce, 2009).

One of the most salient characteristics of adolescence is a steady increase in executive functioning, which is thought to be central to human cognition; and, therefore, adolescence can be seen as a period of significant cognitive advancements. During this time children increasingly master the ability to control their thoughts and actions to make them consistent with internal goals, but, in general, the research points to adolescence as a time of intensification of emotional experience, to increases in sensation seeking, and to an immature capacity of affective regulation and self-control (Galvan, 2006).

Early in adolescence a dramatic remodelling of the brain's reward circuitry occurs as a result of puberty, resulting in 'go' systems that fuel sensation seeking and risky behaviour (Van Leijenhorst et al., 2009, 2010). A more gradual and lengthier maturation of brain systems involved in self-regulation has also been demonstrated (Steinberg, 2010) including 'stop and think' systems in the prefrontal cortex that, however, will not mature before early adulthood (Van Leijenhorst et al., 2009, 2010). These differences create a kind of maturity gap: reward seeking tends to increase between preadolescence and mid-adolescence and declines thereafter by a curvilinear pattern. Levels of impulsivity, on the other hand, follow a linear pattern, declining steadily from age 10 on. The combination of relatively higher tendencies to seek reward and still-maturing capacities for self-control may be responsible for the heightened vulnerability to risk taking in middle adolescence (Steinberg, 2010).

It seems plausible that improvement in self-control during adolescence partly underlies desistance from delinquent behaviour. Maturation of impulse control and suppression of aggression, however, is also associated with other brain systems involved in the maturation of personal responsibility, resistance to peer influence, and consideration of others. Maturation of these two brain systems (the 'cognitive-control' and the 'socio-emotional') may be differentially related to desistance from antisocial behaviour (Monahan et al., 2009).

Casey, Jones and Hare (2008) have shown that an imbalance between cognitive control and appetitive cues may be predictive for a greater risk for alcohol and substance dependence. As adolescence is a critical developmental period for the maturation of neurobiological processes, which can temporarily lead to such imbalances, substance abuse typically emerges during adolescence. Furthermore, substance abuse can negatively influence the brain's regulatory function. Diminished self-control not only increases the imbalance between the reward and regulatory functions in the brain but also decreases the threshold to criminal behaviour. As substance abuse is associated with the risk of criminal behaviour it might indirectly explain – to some extent – late-onset antisocial behaviour.

Psychophysiological features are also of interest in explaining behaviour during the transition from adolescence to adulthood since these features appear to be associated with aggression and criminal behaviour. Electrophysiological disruptions have been measured in adult psychopaths in Dutch studies (Brazil et al., 2009; Von Borries et al., 2010) and also in younger antisocial individuals (Gao et al., 2009). Low heart rate in childhood has been demonstrated to be predictive for aggression during adolescence, while, in contrast, high heart rate 'protected' against it (Ortiz and Raine, 2004). Antisocial adolescents who desisted from criminal offending showed higher heart rates. In a Dutch study, young delinquents in the age range 12–14 consistently had lower overall levels of arousal as measured by heart rate (Popma and Raine, 2006).

In general, a low heart rate (HR) and reduced skin conductance (SC) are considered to be factors associated with antisocial behaviour in children and adolescents (Ortiz and Raine, 2004). However, whether higher HR and normal SC can function as protective factors remains to be seen (Loeber et al., 2007).

Genetic research focuses on estimates of inheritable antisocial behaviour as well as on candidate genes for antisocial behaviour in interaction with the environment, the so-called gene–environment interaction. Twin studies provided substantial evidence for these genetic influences of aggressive and antisocial behaviour (Popma and Raine, 2006; Schug et al., 2010). Although early-onset persistent antisocial behaviour appears more heritable than later-onset conduct disorders, Silberg et al. (2007) found that genetic factors influenced antisocial behaviour through all phases of development. More precisely, some genes seem to influence antisocial behaviour across the entire lifespan, whereas others only appear to operate in adolescence or adulthood. There is some preliminary evidence that specific candidate genes are associated with adolescence-onset antisocial behaviour (Burt and Mikolajewski, 2008) and persistence is theoretically associated with genetic approaches also (Silberg et al., 2007). There appears to be a short-lived effect during puberty, a shared-environmental effect beginning in adolescence, and a specific genetic effect on young adult antisocial behaviour.

Undoubtedly, the expression of genes is embedded in complex gene–environment interactions and the initiation and maintenance of aggression is influenced by, for instance, the family environment. Within such a complex interaction the explanatory power of these biological pre-dispositional variables may be relatively greater in more or less 'healthy' family circumstances where the 'social push' towards antisocial behaviour is low (Schug et al., 2010; Popma and Raine, 2006). During adolescence, negative peer influences form an example of such a 'social push'.

Goozen et al. (2007) provide perhaps the most comprehensive framework, highlighting the interplay between neurobiological deficits and cognitive and emotional functioning as mediators of the link between early adversity and antisocial behaviour problems in childhood and adolescence. Stress-response systems have a mediating role between early social adversity and juvenile antisocial behaviour. Malfunctions in the stress-response system may contribute to the explanation of early-onset and persistent antisocial behaviour.

Central to this framework is the HPA-axis and the role of cortisol. The HPA-axis is a major part of the neuroendocrine system that controls reactions to stress and regulates many bodily processes. The results of a Dutch study on delinquent boys with a disruptive behaviour disorder illustrated the importance of altered activity in the HPA-axis (Popma et al., 2007). Cortisol is released as a reaction to stress and as a hormone pertaining to the HPA-axis. In general, a higher cortisol reactivity level is considered a risk for maladjustment (Boyce and Ellis, 2005). With regard to disruptive and delinquent behaviour, however, both high and low levels of cortisol have been found relevant. For instance, low cortisol in preadolescent boys aged 10–12 was associated with lower self-control and more aggressive behaviour later at ages 15–17 (Shoal et al., 2003). In children with low levels of callous–unemotional (CU) traits and HPA-axis hyperactivity, early adversity appears to be important to the development of antisocial behaviour, whereas for a particularly severe subgroup of children for whom antisocial behaviour develops somewhat independently of adversity, high levels of CU traits and HPA-axis hypoactivity appear to be characteristic (Hawes, Brennan and Dadds, 2009). Because coping with transitional stress is dependent on the quality and maturity of the brain's stress systems, the timing of puberty is seen as a critical moderator of antisocial behaviour (Susman et al., 2010). As such, biological (HPA-axis, timing of puberty), psychological (CU traits) and social (environmental adversity) factors are involved in the explanation of the development of antisocial behaviour. Two early-onset pathways to antisocial behaviour can be distinguished based on the presence or absence of CU traits combined with HPA-axis activity.

So far we have discussed some neurobiological explanations of early- and adult-onset desistance and persistence in offending. More or less, (neuro) psychological concepts can also contribute to understanding age–crime curves. For instance, the concept of 'hostile attributional bias' provides one example of a cognitive process that is theorized to result in life course persistence of aggressive behaviour. Aggressive children are more likely than their non-aggressive counterparts to have a tendency to over-attribute negative intentions in others, even in ambiguous situations (Dodge, 2006; Dodge et al., 1990).

Bloningen (2010) claims that, in general, the developmental literature on personality should provide a major psychological contribution in explaining age–crime curves. He opposes the misconception within some criminological literature that personality traits are stable, fixed attributes and therefore can solely account for the stability over time in the persistence of antisocial behaviour. Based on a large body of research, he concludes that personality traits are dynamic, not static, and that they can change from adolescence to early adulthood.

During adolescence, mean-level neuroticism and disagreeableness decline, while traits like self-control and conscientiousness increase. According to Bloningen, such developmental changes in personality traits mirror desistance in crime in early adulthood, although several other factors are also involved. For instance, the brain may be 'hijacked' by drug addiction; the culture of college may be conducive to binge drinking; a young person may be recruited by an antisocial or anti-society organization (these are dangerous 'mentors'), and discrimination may lead a young person away from mainstream goals. Some young people are cut off from societal opportunities because of lingering consequences of earlier missteps (for example, school dropout or a criminal record). And some young people may simply be unlucky in that the consequences of their behaviour alter their opportunities or potential (for example, a person becomes pregnant or is injured in an accident). A combination of these factors could increase the probability of persistent involvement in offending for some, or adult-onset offending for others, resulting in a variety of offending trajectories over the course of adolescence and early adulthood that do not follow the decline of criminal behaviour in the transition to adulthood observed in age–crime curves.

This claim that psychological factors should be integrated into explanatory frameworks explaining the age–crime curve is just one example of the challenges of integrating previous and more recent psychological and neurobiological findings. The biopsychosocial explanatory framework, with its dimensional approach, appears the most promising pathway to explore this process of integration.

Summary and Conclusions

To sum up our discussion of the four explanatory perspectives on persistence and desistance of offending (as few theoretical explanations are proposed for adult-onset offending, this pattern is omitted here):

1. The static perspective claims that people differ due to their experiences until around age 8 when their level of self-control is established. Extremely low levels of self-control will make individuals persist in offending for a long time; the others will desist while growing up, or hardly start at all.
2. The dynamic perspective strongly opposes the idea of stable inter-individual differences claimed by the static perspective. According to the dynamic perspective, people can always change, while inter-individual stability and uniform patterns of intra-individual change are not thought to exist. Causes of onset of offending are not specified in great detail, but the relevance of the early years is recognized as is the changing relationship with parents and peers. Persistence occurs when offenders are unable to make positive social transitions, often due to the social and more formal consequences following earlier offending (for instance, labelling). When social bonds are formed by marriage, work, military service, etc., these bonds may provide the necessary hooks for change leading to desistance.
3. According to the dual developmental perspective, two models are required to explain patterns of offending. The first small group suffers cumulative and contemporary consequences of disruptive behaviours from early

childhood on in combination with negative parenting practises. This results in a persistent pattern of offending, consistent negative feedback, social failure, and consequently, narrowing options for positive social transitions. The far more prevalent adolescence-onset group starts offending due to frustration (maturity gap) and association with delinquent peers. They desist when growing up offers new possibilities and social change.
4. The biopsychosocial perspective shows that on all causal levels all factors involved should be considered on their gradual, dimensional and interactional merits.

There is indeed remarkable empirical evidence for the relevance of early childhood factors on persistence of offending. This robust finding is primarily supportive of the dual developmental explanatory frameworks, and less so for the static or the dynamic life-course frameworks. However, differences between these frameworks may be somewhat inflated as studies from both perspectives have emphasized different research questions. Most studies based on dynamic explanatory frameworks have been done on desistance, whereas most studies on Moffitt's model have focused on persistence and the reduced chances for the life-course persisters to obtain the necessary social bonds or 'hooks for change'.

With regard to the mechanisms behind persistence in the transition phase to adulthood, only minor theoretical differences appear between the dynamic explanatory frameworks and the persistent offenders from the dual developmental perspective. Narrowing options for change caused by cumulative and contemporary consequences of early problem behaviours (Moffitt, 1993) resonates considerably with the notion that persistence should be attributed to the negative consequences of delinquent behaviour and official sanctioning by the justice system, as well as the maintenance of causal factors, or continuity in individual differences (Thornberry, 2005; Sampson and Laub, 1997).

With regard to desistance, the weight of the empirical evidence is consistent with the basic expectations of dynamic explanatory frameworks of crime. More proximal, dynamic factors are strongly related to patterns of offending, whereas age of onset and early endowments are less important during the transition years. In general, strong social bonds, movement away from deviant peer groups, and successful transitions to adulthood in such crucial areas as school, work and family are associated with desistance from crime. In contrast, failure to make successful and orderly transitions from adolescence to adulthood, and the related failure to establish strong prosocial bonds are associated with persistent offending across this stage of the life course.

Nagin and Paternoster (2000) summarize a decade of empirical research on both perspectives with two conclusions: first, individual differences (i.e. population heterogeneity arguments) do play a significant role in the propensity to offend; second, time-varying characteristics (i.e. state dependence arguments) are also implicated in criminal offending in the long run. These results suggest that both perspectives are important. Further studies should focus on disentangling high and low chronic etiology. The development of the biopsychosocial framework promises to lead to a more profound understanding of the chronic as well as the more temporary pathways traversing the transition from adolescence to adulthood.

Acknowledgements

The authors would like to thank Peggy C. Giordano, Christopher Uggen and Ann S. Masten of the National Institute of Justice Study Group on Transitions from Juvenile Delinquency to Adult Offending for letting us use their manuscript as a starting point for this chapter.

References

Akers, R.L. (1998). *Social Learning and Social Structure: A General Theory of Crime and Deviance*. Boston, MA: Northeastern University Press.

Arnett, J.J. (2000). Emerging adulthood: A theory of development from the late teens through the twenties. *American Psychologist*, 55, 469–80.

Bernburg, J.G. and Krohn, M.D. (2003). Labeling, life chances, and adult crime: The direct and indirect effects of official intervention in adolescence on crime in early adulthood. *Criminology*, 41, 1287–318.

Bernburg, J.G., Krohn, M.D., and Rivera, C.J. (2006). Official labeling, criminal embeddedness, and subsequent delinquency: A longitudinal test of labeling theory. *Journal of Research in Crime and Delinquency*, 43, 67–88.

Bersani, B., Laub, J.H., and Nieuwbeerta, P. (2009). Marriage and desistance from crime in the Netherlands: Do gender and socio-historical context matter? *Journal of Quantitative Criminology*, 25, 3–24.

Blokland, A.A.J. and Nieuwbeerta, P. (2005). The effects of life circumstances on longitudinal trajectories of offending. *Criminology*, 43, 1203–40.

Blokland, A.A.J., Nagin, D.S., and Nieuwbeerta, P. (2005). Life span offending trajectories of a Dutch conviction cohort. *Criminology*, 43, 919–54.

Blonigen, D.M. (2010). Explaining the relationship between age and crime: Contributions from the developmental literature on personality. *Clinical Psychology Review*, 30, 89–100.

Boes, A.D., Tranel, D., Anderson, S.W., and Nopoulos, P. (2008). Right anterior cingulate: A neuroanatomical correlate of aggression and defiance in boys. *Behavioral Neuroscience*, 122, 677–84.

Bouffard, L.A. and J.H. Laub. (2004). Jail or the army: Does military service facilitate desistance? In S. Maruna and R. Immarigeon (eds), *After Crime and Punishment: Pathways to Offender Reintegration.* Portland, OR: Willan, pp. 129–51.

Boyce, W.T. and Ellis, B.J. (2005). Biological sensitivity to context: I. An evolutionary developmental theory of the origins and functions of stress reactivity. *Development and Psychopathology*, 17, 217–301.

Brazil, I., Debruijn, E., Bulten, B., Vonborries, A., Vanlankveld, J., Buitelaar, J., and Verkes, R. (2009). Early and late components of error monitoring in violent offenders with psychopathy. *Biological Psychiatry*, 65, 137–43.

Burt, S.A. and Mikolajewski, A.J. (2008). Preliminary evidence that specific candidate genes are associated with adolescent-onset antisocial behavior. *Aggressive Behavior*, 34, 437–45.

Bushway, S.D., Piquero, A.R., Broidy, L. Cauffman, E., and Mazerolle, P. (2001). An empirical framework for studying desistance as a process. *Criminology*, 39, 491–516.

Casey, B., Jones, R.M., and Hare, T.A. (2008). The adolescent brain. *Annals of the New York Academy of Sciences*, 1124, 111–26.

Catalano, R.F. and Hawkins, J.D. (1986). The social development model: A theory of antisocial behavior. Paper presented at the Safeco Lectureship on Crime and Delinquency, School of Social Work, University of Washington, Seattle, WA.

Catalano, R.F. and Hawkins, J.D. (1996). The social development model: A theory of antisocial behavior. In J.D. Hawkins (ed.), *Delinquency and Crime: Current Theories*. New York: Cambridge University Press.

Cicchetti, D. (2006). Development and psychopathology. In D. Cicchetti and D. Cohen (eds), *Developmental Psychopathology: Vol. 1. Theory and Method* (2nd edn). Hoboken, NJ: Wiley, pp. 1–23.

Cohen, L.E. and Vila, B.J. (1996). Self-control and social control: An exposition of the Gottfredson–Hirschi/Sampson–Laub debate. *Studies on Crime and Crime Prevention*, 5, 125–50.

Dannefer, D. (1984). Adult development and social theory: A paradigmatic appraisal. *American Sociological Review*, 49, 100–16.

Dodge, K.A. (2006). Translational science in action: Hostile attributional style and the development of aggressive behavior problems. *Developmental Psychopathology*, 18, 791–814.

Dodge, K.A., Price, J.M., Bachorowski, J., and Newman, J.P. (1990). Hostile attributional biases in severely aggressive adolescents. *Journal of Abnormal Psychology*, 99, 385–92.

Donker, A.G., Smeenk, W.H., Van der Laan, P.H., and Verhulst, F.C. (2003). Individual stability of antisocial behavior from childhood to adulthood: Testing the stability postulate of Moffitt's developmental theory. *Criminology*, 41, 593–609.

Draganski, B., Gaser, C., Busch, V., Schuierer, G., Bogdahn, U., and May, A. (2004). Neuroplasticity: Changes in grey matter induced by training. *Nature*, 427, 311–12.

Elder, G.H., Jr. (1997). The life course and human development. In R.M. Lerner (ed.), *Handbook of Child Psychology, Vol. 1: Theoretical Models of Human Development*. New York: Wiley, pp. 939–91.

Elliott, D.S., Huizinga, D., and Ageton, S.S. (1985). *Explaining Delinquency and Drug Use*. Beverly Hills, CA: Sage Publications.

Fairchild, G., Van Goozen, S.H., Calder, A.J., Stollery, S.J., and Goodyer, I.M. (2009). Deficits in facial expression recognition in male adolescents with early-onset or adolescence-onset conduct disorder. *Journal of Child Psychology and Psychiatry*, 50, 627–36.

Farrington, D.P. (2000). Explaining and preventing crime: The globalization of knowledge – The American Society of Criminology 1999 Presidential Address. *Criminology*, 38, 1–24.

Farrington, D.P. (2003). Developmental and life-course criminology: Key theoretical and empirical issues – the 2002 Sutherland Address. *Criminology*, 41, 221–55.

Farrington, D.P. (2007). Childhood risk factors and risk-focussed prevention. In M. Maguire, R. Morgan and R. Reiner (eds), *The Oxford Handbook of Criminology* (4th edn). Oxford: Oxford University Press, pp. 602–40.

Farrington, D.P. and West, D.J. (1995). Effects of marriage, separation and children on offending by adult males. In J. Hagan (ed.), *Current Perspectives on Aging and the Life Cycle, Vol.4: Delinquency and Disrepute in the Life Course*. Greenwich, CT: JAI Press, pp. 249–81.

Farrington, D.P., Gallagher, B., Morley, L., St. Ledger, R.J., and West, D.J. (1986). Unemployment, school leaving, and crime. *British Journal of Criminology*, 26, 335–56.

Farrington, D.P., Coid, J.W., Harnett, L.M., Jolliffe, D., Soteriou, N., Turner, R.E., and West, D.J. (2006). *Criminal Careers up to Age 50 and Life Success up to Age 48: New Findings from the Cambridge Study in Delinquent Development* (No. 299). London: Home Office.

Galvan, A. (2006). Earlier development of the accumbens relative to orbitofrontal cortex might underlie risk-taking behavior in adolescents. *Journal of Neuroscience*, 26, 6885–92.

Gao, Y., Raine, A., Venables, P.H., Dawson, M.E., and Mednick, S.A. (2009). Association of poor childhood fear conditioning and adult crime. *American Journal of Psychiatry*, 167, 56–60.

Gao, Y., Raine, A., Venables, P.H., Dawson, M.E., and Mednick, S.A. (2010). Reduced electrodermal fear conditioning from ages 3 to 8 years is associated with aggressive behavior at age 8 years. *Journal of Child Psychology and Psychiatry*, 51, 550–8.

Giordano, P.C., Cernkovich, S.A., and Rudolph, J.L. (2002). Gender, crime, and desistance: Toward a theory of cognitive transformation. *American Journal of Sociology*, 107, 990–1064.

Glueck, S. and Glueck, E.T. (1940). *Juvenile Delinquents Grown Up*. New York: The Commonwealth Fund.

Glueck, S. and Glueck, E.T. (1950). *Unraveling Juvenile Delinquency*. Cambridge, MA: Harvard University Press.

Gottfredson, M.R. (2006). The empirical status of control theory in criminology. In F.T. Cullen, J.P. Wright and K.R. Blevin (eds), *Taking Stock: The Status of Criminological Theory*. New Brunswick, NJ: Transaction Publishers, pp. 77–100.

Gottfredson, M.R. and Hirschi, T. (1990). *A General Theory of Crime*. Palo Alto, CA: Stanford University Press.

Hackman, D.A. and Farah, M.J. (2009). Socioeconomic status and the developing brain. *Trends in Cognitive Sciences*, 13, 65–73.

Hawes, D.J., Brennan, J., and Dadds, M.R. (2009). Cortisol, callous-unemotional traits, and pathways to antisocial behavior. *Current Opinion in Psychiatry*, 22, 357–62.

Hawkins, J.D., Herrenkohl, T., Farrington, D.P., Brewer, D., Catalano, R.F., and Harachi, T.W. (1998). A review of predictors of youth violence. In R. Loeber and D.P. Farrington, *Serious and Violent Juvenile Offenders: Risk Factors and Successful Interventions*. Thousand Oaks, CA: Sage Publications, pp. 106–46.

Hirschi, T. and Gottfredson, M.R. (2001). Self-control theory. In R. Paternoster and R. Bachman (eds), *Explaining Criminals and Crime: Essays in Contemporary Criminological Theory*. Los Angeles, CA: Roxbury Publishers, pp. 81–96.

Horney, J., Osgood, D.W., and Marshall, I.H. (1995). Criminal careers in the short-term: Intra individual variability in crime and its relation to local life circumstances. *American Sociological Review*, 60, 655–73.

Kreager, D.A., Matsueda, R.L., and Erosheva, E.A. (2010). Motherhood and criminal desistance in disadvantaged neighborhoods. *Criminology*, 48, 221–57.

Krohn, M.D., Lizotte, A.J., and Perez, C.M. (1997). The interrelationship between substance use and precocious transitions to adult statuses. *Journal of Health and Social Behavior*, 38, 87–103.

Krohn, M.D., Thornberry, T.P., Rivera, C., and Le Blanc, M. (2001). Later delinquency careers. In R. Loeber and D.P. Farrington (eds), *Child Delinquents: Development, Intervention, and Service Needs*. Thousand Oaks, CA: Sage Publications, pp. 67–93.

Kruesi, M., Casanova, M., Mannheim, G., and Johnsonbilder, A. (2004). Reduced temporal lobe volume in early onset conduct disorder. *Psychiatry Research: Neuroimaging*, 132, 1–11.

Laub, J.H. and Sampson, R.J. (2003). *Shared Beginnings, Divergent Lives: Delinquent Boys to Age 70*. Cambridge, MA: Harvard University Press.

Lipsey, M.W. and Derzon, J.H. (1998). Predictors of violent or serious delinquency in adolescence and early adulthood: A synthesis of longitudinal research. In R. Loeber and D.P. Farrington (eds), *Serious and Violent Juvenile Offenders: Risk Factors and Successful Interventions*. Thousand Oaks, CA: Sage Publications, pp. 86–105.

Loeber, R., Pardini, D.A., Stouthamer-Loeber, M., and Raine, A. (2007). Do cognitive, physiological, and psychosocial risk and promotive factors predict desistance from delinquency in males? *Development and Psychopathology*, 19, 867–87.

Lupien, S.J., McEwen, B.S., Gunnar, M.R., and Heim, C. (2009). Effects of stress throughout the lifespan on the brain, behaviour and cognition. *Nature Reviews Neuroscience*, 10, 434–45.

Mannheim, H. (1967). *Comparative Criminology*. Boston, MA: Houghton Mifflin.

Maruna, S. (2001). *Making good: How Ex-convicts Reform and Rebuild their lives*. Washington, DC: American Psychological Association Books.

Masten, A. (2006). Developmental psychopathology: Pathways to the future. *International Journal of Behavioral Development*, 31, 46–53.

Masten, A.S., Obradović, J., and Burt, K. (2006). Resilience in emerging adulthood: Developmental perspectives on continuity and transformation. In J.J. Arnett and J.L. Tanner (eds), *Emerging Adults in America: Coming of Age in the 21st Century*. Washington, DC: American Psychological Association Press, pp. 173–90.

Masten, A.S., Long, J.D., Kuo, S.I-C., McCormick, C.M., and Desjardins, C.D. (2009). Developmental models of strategic intervention. *European Journal of Developmental Science*, 3, 282–91.

Matsueda, R.L. and Heimer, K. (1997). A symbolic interactionist theory of role-transitions, role commitments, and delinquency. In T.P. Thornberry (ed.), *Developmental Theories of Crime and Delinquency*. New Brunswick, NJ: Transaction Publishers, pp. 162–213.

McAdams, D.P., Diamond, A., De St. Aubin, E., and Mansfield, E.D. (1997). Stories of commitment: The psychosocial construction of generative lives. *Journal of Personality and Social Psychology*, 72, 678–94.

Mednick, S.A. (1977). A biosocial theory of the learning of law-abiding behavior. In S.A. Mednick and K.O. Christiansen (eds), *Biosocial Bases of Criminal Behavior*. New York: Gardner Press, pp. 1–8.

Meeus, W., Branje, S., and Overbeek, G.J. (2004). Parents and partners in crime: A six-year longitudinal study on changes in supportive relationships and delinquency in adolescence and young adulthood. *Journal of Child Psychology and Psychiatry*, 45, 1288–98.

Monahan, K.C., Steinberg, L., Cauffman, E., and Mulvey, E.P. (2009). Trajectories of antisocial behavior and psychosocial maturity from adolescence to young adulthood. *Developmental Psychology*, 45, 1654–68.

Moffitt, T.E. (1993). Adolescence-limited and life-course-persistent antisocial behavior: A developmental taxonomy. *Psychological Review*, 100, 674–701.

Moffitt, T.E. (2006). A review of research on the taxonomy of life-course-persistent versus adolescence-limited antisocial behavior. In F.T. Cullen, J.P. Wright and K.R. Blevin (eds), *Taking Stock: The Status of Criminological Theory*. New Brunswick, NJ: Transaction Publishers, pp. 277–312.

Moffitt, T.E., Caspi, A., Harrington, H., and Milne, B.J. (2002). Males on the life-course persistent and adolescence-limited antisocial pathways: Follow-up at age 26 years. *Development and Psychopathology*, 14, 179–207.

Nagin, D. and Land, K.C. (1993). Age, criminal careers, and population heterogeneity: Specification and estimation of a nonparametric, mixed Poisson model. *Criminology*, 31, 327–62.

Nagin, D.S. (2005). *Group-based Modeling of Development*. Cambridge, MA: Harvard University Press.

Nagin, D.S. and Paternoster, R. (1991). On the relationship of past and future participation in delinquency. *Criminology*, 29, 163–89.

Nagin, D.S. and Paternoster, R. (2000). Population heterogeneity and state dependence: State of the evidence and directions for future research. *Journal of Quantitative Criminology*, 16, 117–45.

Obradović, J. and Boyce, W.T. (2009). Individual differences in behavioral, physiological, and genetic sensitivities to contexts: Implications for development and adaptation. *Developmental Neuroscience*, 31, 300–8.

Ortiz, J. and Raine, A. (2004). Heart rate level and antisocial behavior in children and adolescents. *Journal of the American Academy of Child & Adolescent Psychiatry*, 43, 154–62.

Passamonti, L., Fairchild, G., Goodyer, I.M., Hurford, G., Hagan, C.C., Rowe, J.B., and Calder, A.J. (2010). Neural abnormalities in early-onset and adolescence-onset conduct disorder. *Archives of General Psychiatry*, 67, 729–38.

Paternoster, R. and Iovanni, L. (1989). The labeling perspective and delinquency: An elaboration of the theory and assessment of the evidence. *Justice Quarterly*, 6, 359–94.

Paternoster, R., Dean, C.W., Piquero, A.R., Mazzerolle, P., and Brame, R. (1997). Generality, continuity, and change in offending. *Journal of Quantitative Criminology*, 13, 231–66.

Patterson, G.R., Capaldi, D., and Bank, L. (1991). An early starter model for predicting delinquency. In D.J. Pepler and K.H. Rubin (eds), *The Development and Treatment of Childhood Aggression*. Hillsdale, NJ: Lawrence Erlbaum, 139–68.

Peters, D.C. (2010). Personality disorders and biosocial trait theories: The argument for radical legal reform. *Behavioral Sciences & the Law*, 28, 289–302,

Piquero, A.R. (2008). Taking stock of developmental trajectories of criminal activity over the life course. In A. Liberman (ed.), *The Long View of Crime: A Synthesis of Longitudinal Research*. New York: Springer, pp. 23–78.

Popma, A. and Raine, A. (2006). Will future forensic assessment be neurobiologic? *Child and Adolescent Psychiatric Clinics of North America*, 15, 429–44.

Popma, A., Vermeiren, R., Geluk, C., Rinne, T., Vandenbrink, W., Knol, D., Jansen, L., Van Engeland, H., and Doreleijers, T.A.H. (2007). Cortisol moderates the relationship between testosterone and aggression in delinquent male adolescents. *Biological Psychiatry*, 61, 405–11.

Pratt, T.C. and Cullen, F.T. (2000). The empirical status of Gottfredson and Hirschi's general theory of crime: A meta-analysis. *Criminology*, 38, 931–64.

Rao, H., Betancourt, L., Giannetta, J.M., Brodsky, N.L., Korczykowski, M., Avants, B.B., Gee, J.C., et al. (2010). Early parental care is important for hippocampal maturation: Evidence from brain morphology in humans. *NeuroImage*, 49, 1144–50.

Rindfuss, R.R., Swicegood, C.G., and Rosenfeld, R.A. (1987). Disorder in the life course: How common and does it matter? *American Sociological Review*, 52, 785–801.

Robins, L.N. (1978). Sturdy childhood predictors of adult antisocial behavior: Replications from longitudinal studies. *Psychological Medicine*, 8, 611–22.

Rosales, F.J., Reznick, J.S., and Zeisel, S.H. (2009). Understanding the role of nutrition in the brain & behavioral development of toddlers and preschool children: Identifying and overcoming methodological barriers. *Nutritional Neuroscience*, 12, 190–202.

Sampson, R.J. and Laub, J.H. (1993). *Crime in the Making: Pathways and Turning Points through Life*. Cambridge, MA: Harvard University Press.

Sampson, R.J. and Laub, J.H. (1997). A life-course theory of cumulative disadvantage and the stability of delinquency. In T.P. Thornberry (ed.), *Developmental Theories of Crime and Delinquency*. New Brunswick, NJ: Transaction Publishers, pp. 133–62.

Schug, R.A., Gao, Y., Glenn, A.L., Yang, Y., and Raine, A. (2010). The developmental evidence base: Neurobiological research and forensic applications. In G.L. Towl and D.A. Crighton (eds), *Forensic Psychology*. Crighton: Wiley-Blackwell, pp. 73–94.

Shaw, P., Kabani, N.J., Lerch, J.P., Eckstrand, K., Lenroot, R., Gogtay, N., Greenstein, D., et al. (2008). Neurodevelopmental trajectories of the human cerebral cortex. *Journal of Neuroscience*, 28, 3586–94.

Shoal, G.D., Giangola, P.R., and Kirillova, G.P. (2003). Salivary cortisol, personality,and aggressive behavior in adolescent boys: A 5-year longitudinal study. *Journal of American Academy of Child and Adolescent Psychiatry*, 42, 1101–7.

Silberg, J.L., Rutter, M., Tracy, K., Maes, H.H., and Eaves, L. (2007). Etiological heterogeneity in the development of antisocial behavior: The Virginia Twin Study of Adolescent Behavioral Development and the young adult follow-up. *Psychological Medicine*, 37, 1193–202.

Sroufe, L.A. (2007). The place of development in developmental psychopathology. In A.S. Masten (ed.), *Multilevel Dynamics in Developmental Psychopathology: Pathways to the Future. The Minnesota Symposia in Child Psychology* (vol. 34), Mahwah, NJ: Erlbaum, pp. 285–98.

Stattin, H. and Magnusson, D. (1991). Stability and change in criminal behaviour up to age 30: Findings from a prospective, longitudinal study in Sweden. *British Journal of Criminology*, 31, 327–46.

Steinberg, L. (2010). A dual systems model of adolescent risk-taking. *Developmental Psychobiology*, 52, 216–24.

Susman, E.J., Dockray, S., Granger, D.A., Blades, K.T., Randazzo, W., Heaton, J.A., and Dorn, L.D. (2010). Cortisol and alpha amylase reactivity and timing of puberty: Vulnerabilities for antisocial behaviour in young adolescents. *Psychoneuroendocrinology*, 35, 557–69.

Thornberry, T.P. (1987). Toward an interactional theory of delinquency. *Criminology*, 25, 863–91.

Thornberry, T.P. (2005). Explaining multiple patterns of offending across the life course and across generations. In R.J. Sampson and J.H. Laub (eds), *Developmental Criminology and its Discontents: Trajectories of Crime from Childhood to Old Age*. Thousand Oaks, CA: Sage Publications, pp. 156–95.

Thornberry, T.P. and Krohn, M.D. (2001). The development of delinquency: An interactional perspective. In S.O. White (ed.), *Handbook of Youth and Justice*. New York: Plenum, pp. 289–305.

Thornberry, T.P. and Krohn, M.D. (2005). Applying interactional theory to the explanation of continuity and change in antisocial behavior. In D.P. Farrington (ed.), *Integrated Developmental and Life-course Theories of Offending*. New Brunswick, NJ: Transaction Publishers.

Toby, J. (1957). Social disorganization and stake in conformity. *Journal of Criminal Law, Criminology, and Police Science*, 48, 12–17.

Uggen, C. (2000). Work as a turning point in the life course of criminals: A duration model of age, employment, and recidivism. *American Sociological Review*, 67, 529–46.

Van Goozen, S.H.M., Fairchild, G., Snoek, H., and Harold, G.T. (2007). The evidence for neurobiological model of childhood antisocial behavior. *Psychological Bulletin*, 133, 149–82.

Van Leijenhorst, L., Zanolie, K., Van Meel, C.S., Westenberg, P.M., Rombouts, S.A., and Crone, E.A. (2009). What motivates the adolescent? Brain regions mediating reward sensitivity across adolescence. *Cerebral Cortex*, 20, 61–9.

Van Leijenhorst, L., Moor, B.G., Op de Macks, Z.A., Rombouts, S.A., Westenberg, P.M., and Crone, E.A. (2010). Adolescent risky decision-making: Neurocognitive development of reward and control regions. *NeuroImage*, 51, 345–55.

Van Overwalle, F. and Baetens, K. (2009). Understanding others' actions and goals by mirror and mentalizing systems: A meta-analysis. *NeuroImage*, 48, 564–84.

Von Borries, A.K.L., Brazil, I.A., Bulten, B.H., Buitelaar, J.K., Verkes, R.J., and De Bruijn, E.R.A. (2010). Neural correlates of error-related learning deficits in individuals with psychopathy. *Psychological Medicine*, 40, 1559–68.

Wager, T.D., Phan, K.L., Liberzon, I., and Taylor, S.F. (2003). Valence, gender, and lateralization of functional brain anatomy in emotion: a meta-analysis of findings from neuroimaging. *NeuroImage*, 19, 513–31.

Warr, M. (1998). Life-course transitions and desistance from crime. *Criminology*, 36, 183–216.

Warr, M. (2002). *Companions in Crime*. New York: Cambridge University Press.

Whittle, S., Yap, M.B., Yücel, M., Fornito, A., Simmons, J.G., Barrett, A., Sheeber, L., and Allen, N.B. (2008). Prefrontal and amygdala volumes are related to adolescents' affective behaviors during parent–adolescent interactions. *Proceedings of the National Academy of Sciences*, 105, 3652–7.

Wiesner, M. and Capaldi, D.M. (2003). Relations of childhood and adolescent factors to offending trajectories of young men. *Journal of Research in Crime and Delinquency*, 40, 231–62.

Wilson, J.Q. and Hernstein, R.J. (1985). *Crime and Human Nature*. New York: Simon & Schuster.

Chapter 5
Vulnerable Youth in Pathways to Adulthood

Catrien C.J.H. Bijleveld, Victor van der Geest
and Jan Hendriks

As argued in the Introduction to this volume, the transition from adolescence to adulthood is a developmental phase in which opportunities emerge and during which profound and numerous life changes take place. These transitions are foremost physical, as the body matures and becomes fully grown, and intellectual, as the brain matures and intellectual functioning increases. Changes during this period are also contextual in the sense that young people tend to have their first romantic relationships, start having sex more regularly, and move away from the family home as they assume the responsibilities of a job or further vocational or academic education. Later on, most people become parents. This chapter focuses on these life transitions and investigates their relationship to changes in offending from adolescence to adulthood in several high-risk groups.

Two categories of youth are the focus of this chapter: young men and women who were placed in residential care in their childhood, and special offenders. They tend to share childhoods marred by trouble. These vulnerable and high-risk youths often had serious behavioural problems, including delinquency, when young. Many were raised in problematic and dysfunctional family environments and lived in disadvantaged neighbourhoods. The justice authorities had 'flagged' them and, for many, intervened in both their upbringing and education.

These youth are important to study because for some of them a problematic childhood was the start of a life as an adult with similar problems. Part of the increased risk for later problems may be due to the fact that – because of their backgrounds – they are unable to successfully make the transition to adult roles. An alternative explanation is that their problems persist (or accumulate) despite a successful transition into conventional roles (for example, because new social contexts provide new criminal opportunities).

Thus a first question to ask is whether these transitions to adulthood occur in a similar way for both vulnerable and normative youth. A second question is whether these transitions function in a similar manner for different vulnerable groups, as turning points away from delinquency and offending.

The first two groups we studied comprise men and women who were placed in residential care in their childhood and who are at high risk of offending. The third group – hands-on juvenile sex offenders (i.e. distinct from exhibitionists) – is at elevated risk of sexual recidivism. We chose to study known delinquents rather than a normative population because of their high offending rate and the associated higher possibility of detecting statistical effects. We considered studying other vulnerable groups, such as gang members or drugs abusers, but could not do so for lack of Dutch datasets with sufficiently rich information over a sufficiently long time span.

We asked, to what extent, and when, do individuals in each of the three groups transition to adult roles? Do young men who sexually offended against children find a romantic partner and have children later in life? And if they do, do they do this at normative ages, or earlier or later than what is average? Do residentially re-educated young men find romantic partners? Do their female counterparts find employment after discharge from the treatment institution?

The second question we address is whether the timing of these transitions to adult roles (i.e. employment, marriage and parenthood) at earlier or later than normative ages affects the criminal careers of these special groups of offenders as they are known to do in normative samples of men and women from the Dutch population.

Lastly, we investigate to what extent our findings differ for sample members from Western and non-Western backgrounds, and to what extent they differ for respondents functioning at a below normal intellectual level. For both non-Western youth and those with low IQs, we may expect that entry into the labour market can be harder, which might moderate the impact of the transition between offending in adolescence and adulthood. Similarly, we investigate the relevance of cultural differences in the function of marriage and parenthood for sample members from non-Western backgrounds, and whether persons with low IQs may also have more problems finding a romantic partner.

Literature

In the Netherlands very little is known about the transition of vulnerable groups to adulthood. We were unable to find studies that investigate the long-term societal reintegration of residentially treated youth, or studies on the association between offending and the transition to adulthood of young men and women after a placement in residential judicial care, or of juvenile sex offenders.[1] We found a number of studies that bear on our research questions in the sense that they investigate societal integration and offending of vulnerable juveniles, such as children placed in care homes or in foster care.

Two studies investigate the wellbeing of Dutch youth who had been placed in care, relatively shortly after that care situation had ended. Boendermaker (1998) studied youngsters who had been treated residentially for behavioural problems. She investigated their living situation 15 months after release, when they were on

1 Numerous studies have focused on recidivism as a measure of the impact or effectiveness of treatment. We shall not review these studies, as they do not bear on our research question.

average about age 18. Boendermaker found that attachment problems (insecure or avoiding attachment style) upon admission, as evidenced by screening psychologists and psychiatrists, for many juveniles made it difficult to enter into relationships after release. Many had trouble spending their free hours in a meaningful way. Many used drugs. Those who did not finish treatment were at a particularly high risk of finding themselves in unsatisfactory living arrangements: 55 per cent held jobs (of which 13 per cent were in an on-the-job training scheme), 28 per cent were unemployed, and 17 per cent were still in school. One third were problematic alcohol and/or drugs users; they used more drugs than other young people of their age. One fifth suffered from ongoing psychological or psychiatric problems. Many had financial problems.

Wouda (1987) interviewed juveniles from various care homes (not judicial justice institutions) at 7.5 and 16.5 months after leaving the care placement. At the second interview they were on average about age 19. Those who had left 'irregularly', or earlier than planned (for example, by running away), were particularly at higher risk of becoming what the researchers classified as 'very problematic'. Violence before the care situation ended was the strongest predictor of later adaptation problems.

A study carried out in the UK by Save the Children (1995; n = 77) showed that many young people who had been cared for in reform houses or foster families – at mostly ages 16–21 at follow-up – led highly uncertain and financially precarious lives. Less than half had some kind of low-income employment and most led (extremely) stressful lives. Half had health problems because they did not eat properly. One third had a partner; 20 per cent had children. The study shows how financial problems are for many the starting point of a negative spiral or chain reaction, with the unemployed particularly not having enough money to go out and meet suitable romantic partners.

A study carried out by Bullock et al. (1990) followed up youth who had been placed in secure accommodation; one third of the boys had been placed for offending, the remainder for misbehaviour. One in seven girls had been placed for offending. The follow-up period was two years. Within that period, 72 per cent of the males and 29 per cent of the females had been (re)convicted. One in four was dependent on welfare.

Vinnerljung et al. (2006) followed up 2,195 children born in Stockholm between 1968 and 1975 who had been placed in care in their youth. A group of over 8,500 children born in or around Stockholm at around the same time served as controls. The children were followed up until age 25. Offending was much elevated in the care group: 34 per cent of the men had offended against 14 per cent of control men; for women the figures were 15 per cent against two per cent in the control group. At age 25, 30 per cent of both men and women were dependent on welfare. In a separate study, Vinnerljung, Franzen and Danielsson (2007) showed that 16–19 per cent of women who had been placed in care became teenage parents.

Verhofstadt-Deneve (1980) followed up children who had been placed in foster care homes, with a maximum follow-up to age 24. Of the males, 42 per cent were unemployed. For women, having run away from the institution was a risk factor for unemployment. As a whole, the group had many social problems. Particularly men were less well integrated into society. Even so, 53 per cent of men were in a stable relationship, as were 83 per cent of females.

While these studies are not highly comparable, and while none of them gauges outcomes such as employment against normative samples, they illustrate several issues. First, employment tends to be low among youth who were (partly) raised in care, and many of them become dependent on welfare. Teenage parenthood occurs regularly in similarly raised females. Many youth, particularly men, find it difficult to enter and sustain a relationship with a romantic partner. Offending is elevated, and money problems are prominent. It appears that many youth carry with them into adulthood already existing problems, as evidenced by ongoing psychiatric and psychological problems. Those who left care prematurely had an increased risk for negative outcomes, as well as those who had committed violent offences prior to the care placement (See also Smit (1991), who presents an overview of these and a number of other studies on related topics).

Samples and Measurements

The first two samples featured in this chapter consist of men and women who in their childhood had been placed under (semi-)secure residential care in the Netherlands. The male sample consists of 270 males discharged from a judicial treatment institution for juveniles between January 1989 and June 1996 (Van der Geest and Bijleveld, 2008).[2] The men's average age by early 2009 (the end of the data collection period) was 34; ten (3.7 per cent) males had died prematurely; three had emigrated. The female sample consisted of 148 females discharged from the same institution between January 1992 and December 1995 (Megens and Day, 2007). Their average age by early 2009 (the end of the data collection period) was 32; five (3.4 per cent) females died prematurely, two had emigrated. All respondents had received treatment during their stay. Inclusion criteria for the sample were a minimum length of stay in the institution of two months, and a complete treatment dossier. Analyses showed that both males and females scored high on known risk factors for offending (Wong, Bijleveld and Slotboom, 2009).

2 In the Netherlands, juveniles can be treated in a secure judicial setting for serious behavioural problems (including delinquency) or because their family situation or their behaviour makes it impossible for them to remain at home. Treatment can be imposed as a civil law measure up to age 18. Figures for juveniles in institutions from age 12 up were slightly higher a few years ago, at 1.5 per cent in 1998. As absolute numbers are so low, the percentages, rounded to one digit, are unstable. Up to age 18 treatment can also be imposed as a criminal law measure, in which case the juvenile is (also) treated for offending. The risk profiles of the two groups are similar (Wijkman, Van der Geest and Bijleveld, 2006).

The sex offender sample (Hendriks, 2006) consists of 498 males who had committed at least one sex offence[3] while they were underage. Most of them had been convicted for these offences, and a few had been screened and/or treated under a civil law measure. Along the typology derived by Hendriks (2006), we distinguished between child abusers, peer abusers, and group abusers. A child abuser has sexually abused a prepubertal victim who is at least five years younger. A group abuser has committed the sexual offence with at least one co-offender (average group size is four). A peer abuser has acted alone in abusing a victim who is not more than four years younger. The sex offenders' average age by late 2009 (the end of the data collection period) was 29. Seven had died prematurely, 14 had emigrated.

For all groups, we investigated offending patterns (see details below), employment patterns, and marriage and parenthood. Respondents who died prematurely or who emigrated are included until they are lost to follow-up. For the male samples, we have a control group drawn randomly from the Dutch population, matched by date of birth to the high-risk males, thus constituting a randomly drawn matched-birth cohort. For the females we do not as yet have such a sample; when possible we gauge findings against those reported by Statistics Netherlands.

Offending

Offending information in all samples is based on convictions registered in the Judicial Documentation (JD) abstracts of the Netherlands Ministry of Justice (comparable to 'rap sheets' in the US). These abstracts contain information on every case that is registered at the Public Prosecutor's Office including the type of offence, the date of commission of the offence, and the ensuing verdict. These abstracts span both juvenile and adult offending, i.e. from age 12 up, 12 being the minimum age of criminal responsibility in the Netherlands. We investigated all types of offending, excluding traffic and technical violations, such as violations of business laws, as well as violations of municipal ordinances. Permission for extraction of these data was obtained from the Dutch Ministry of Justice.

3 In the Netherlands, around 0.6 per 1,000 juveniles aged 12–17 are arrested each year for a sex offence. Sex offences these days make up about one per cent of all arrests. Hands-on sex offences are included in the Dutch criminal code under articles 242–9. Sexual acts become an offence when they have been forced upon another person, or when they have been carried out on or with someone who is not (fully) able to freely consent, either because he or she is a child, or because he or she is in an unequal power relationship with the perpetrator, such as a pupil–teacher relationship. Sexual acts with children under age 12 are always an offence; acts with adolescents under age 16 are also always an offence but are prosecuted only after consultation with the minor victim. For details, see Bijleveld (2007).

Employment

Employment data were collected from the national database of the Ministry of Social Affairs and Employment (SZW) in Rotterdam, for the male sample in 2007, and for the female and sex offender samples in 2009. This database contains individual-level information about employment from 1992 onwards. We also accessed the trade register managed by the Netherlands Chamber of Commerce, which contains historical information about business ownership. We collected information on the day a person started a job and the day the position ended. Whether a position referred to full-time or part-time employment was unclear; the registers contain only information on the number of days a contract spanned. We distinguished between two types of work: 'regular' work (registered on the payroll of the employer) and 'temporary' employment via a temporary job agency. Employment in sheltered workshops, such as for the handicapped (which often is long term), was classified as regular employment. Social security information was also available to us for information on the type of social support (for example, a disability scheme, support for the homeless, etc.).

Since the number of days employed was based on the days a contract spanned, this overestimates the number of days of part-time employment. In principle, there can be wide variation in the number of days per week people work. In the Netherlands part-time employment does not have formal limits. In our samples, only a few received social security benefits to raise their incomes to the social minimum while being employed, indicating that most probably worked several days a week. Permission for extraction of these data was obtained from the Netherlands Ministry of Social Affairs and Employment (SOZAWE).

Marriage and Parenthood

Data on marriages and parenthood were extracted from the GBA (Gemeentelijke Basis Administratie), a computerized municipal registration system in operation since 1994. Any Dutch citizen alive in 1994 is registered in this system, which records data on parent(s), marriage and divorce, as well as legal parenthood. Marriages are indistinguishable from registered partnerships, which constitute a contract signed with a notary and are the legal equivalent of marriage. Only children acknowledged by their parents are registered. This means that for females we always know whether they had children; but if males have not legally acknowledged their biological children, their fatherhood does not appear in the system. Permission for extraction of these data was obtained from the Bureau Persoonsregistratie (BPR) at the Ministry of the Interior (BZK).

Personal and Background Variables

Personal and background characteristics were extracted from juveniles' screening and treatment files, to which we shall refer as dossiers. For the male and female sample the dossiers are held within the juvenile justice institution archive. For the sex offenders sample this varied: those who had been treated residentially had treatment files in their treatment institution; for those who had been screened non-residentially, reports were held by the De Waag outpatient treatment centre or its predecessors. Most files contained the results of psychological tests and psychiatric interviews, advisory notes on extensions, and treatment evaluations. Personality variables had been assessed by the institution's therapists or consulting psychologist or psychiatrist using validated instruments (for example, the Amsterdam Biographical Questionnaire for Children, the Adolescent Temperament List, and the Netherlands Personality Questionnaire-Youth), and prevailing guidelines were used to categorize the scores into norm values. Intelligence scores (mostly obtained through the Wechsler Intelligence Scale for Children – Revised for the Netherlands or the Raven Progressive Matrices) were also categorized according to prevailing norm values. Data extraction from the dossiers was done 'blind', in that all files were scored before information about any post-release offending or employment became known. Permission for extraction of these data was obtained from the Dienst Justitiële Inrichtingen (DJI, 2010).

Offending, Employment, Marriage and Parenthood

Changes in Offending from Adolescence to Adulthood

Figure 5.1 shows offending participation, defined as the proportion of individuals convicted for an offence per age, from ages 12–32 for all three samples as well as for the control males. For the high-risk males and females offending participation peaked at age 15, which is the average year at which they were admitted to the juvenile justice institution. After that age offending decreased, with similar declines for men and women. For the sex offenders, the peak offending age was 14, which is also the average age at which their sampling offence was committed. The pattern of offending for the sex offenders becomes unstable at older ages as fewer sample members are present at the end of the observation period and sample size dwindles.

Figure 5.1 also shows that relatively more high-risk males offended than sex offenders and females. High-risk males outgrew delinquency at a much lower rate and over a much longer period than the control group. For the women, participation in delinquency decreased step-wise at the end of adolescence and around age 28. Offending participation was substantially lower for the control men. In addition, it did not follow the classic age–crime curve.

Figure 5.2 presents, for each of the groups, the yearly frequency of offending by age, defined as the total number of offences divided by the total number of active offenders in a certain age group. While fewer high-risk men offended at older ages, those who did tended to offend more, making for a much slower decline of average frequency than of participation over time. The same happened for the women, but only in adolescence: in that period more women offended, but

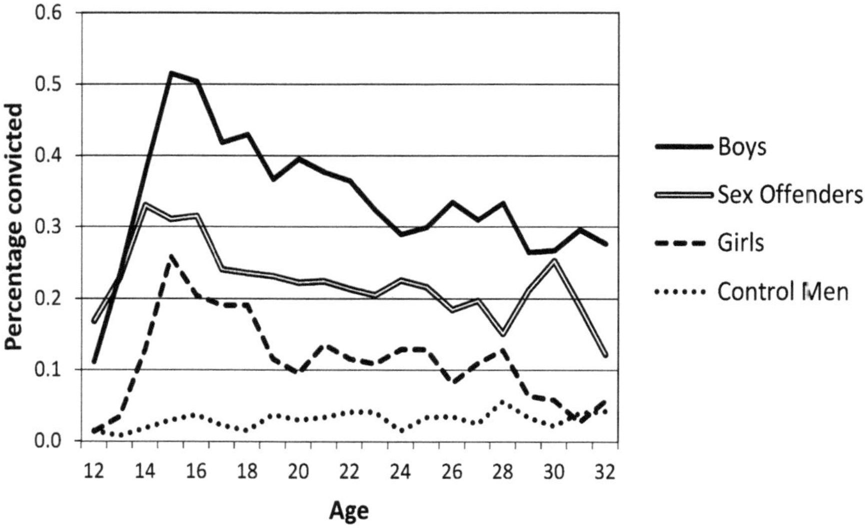

Figure 5.1 Development of offending participation (proportion convicted yes/no by age) for all three vulnerable samples, and one control sample of males

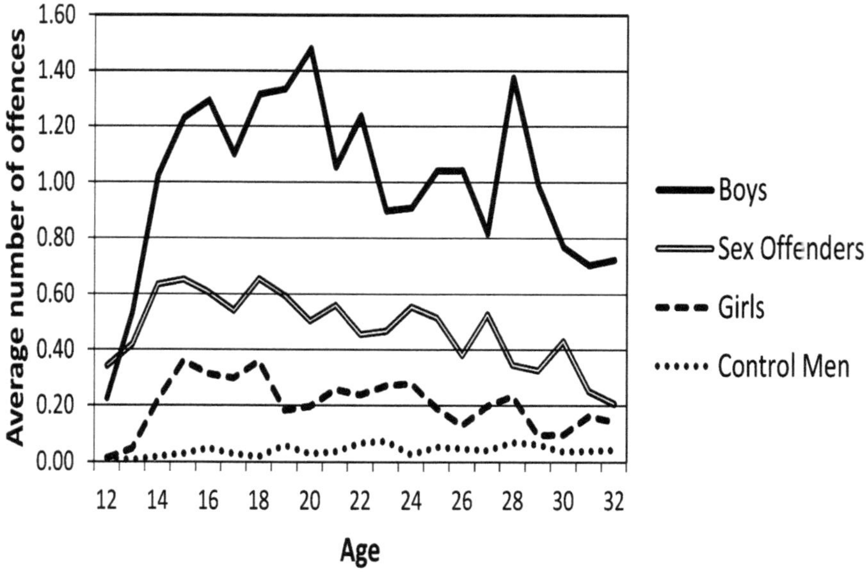

Figure 5.2 Development of offending frequency (average number of offences by age) for offenders in all four samples

more infrequently. The development of offending frequency for the sex offenders followed that of the in-care females, although at higher levels. As expected, offending frequency for the control men was almost level. The results show that the frequency of convictions for females and sex offenders converged to near normative offending levels as these groups reached their 30s.

We concluded that, for all three at-risk samples, offending prevalence and frequency decreased with age. Level differences were as we had expected, with high-risk men at the highest level, followed by the sex offenders and lastly the high-risk females. Offence frequency by offenders within the high-risk male sample in particular remained high with age and decreased much less steeply than was the case for offending for all the high-risk men. This means that a proportion of high-risk men remained highly active offenders.

Employment

Figure 5.3 depicts the prevalence of employment for high-risk males, high-risk females, and sex offenders ages 18–32. Prevalence is defined as the total number of persons participating in the official labour market at a certain age, divided by the total number of persons at that age.

Employment for the high-risk men rose steeply from ages 18–24. The employment level of the sex offenders developed similarly, although they started off at much higher levels. This may be due to the fact that a large proportion of the sex offenders were not treated residentially and perhaps therefore had fewer problems than the high-risk men entering the labour market directly out of school. It may also be as a result of the fact that these men entered the labour market in later years, when the SUWINET system had better coverage. Female levels started out a little lower and ended at much lower levels.

Comparison of these levels with normative levels in the Dutch population shows that all groups were employed at much lower levels than average Dutch men and women of comparable ages. This is not due to the generally low levels of education in these groups, as they still compare negatively to low-educated Dutch men and women. We also compared our groups with figures on employment for Dutch men and women (average population as well as low educated) at ages 20 and 30 (retrieved from Statline, the internet application from Statistics Netherlands). These comparisons show that both sex offenders and high-risk males over their life courses participated (much) less in the official labour market than average- and low-educated Dutch men did.

By age 30, all sample groups participated less than the norm for males and females in the official economy. This negative picture does not appear to be simply an issue of delayed entry: the levelling off of the curve for the men indicates that their very low labour market participation was probably permanent. For the females, there did appear to be an increase from age 28/29 onwards, although this might also be due to chance as sample size dwindles at later ages.

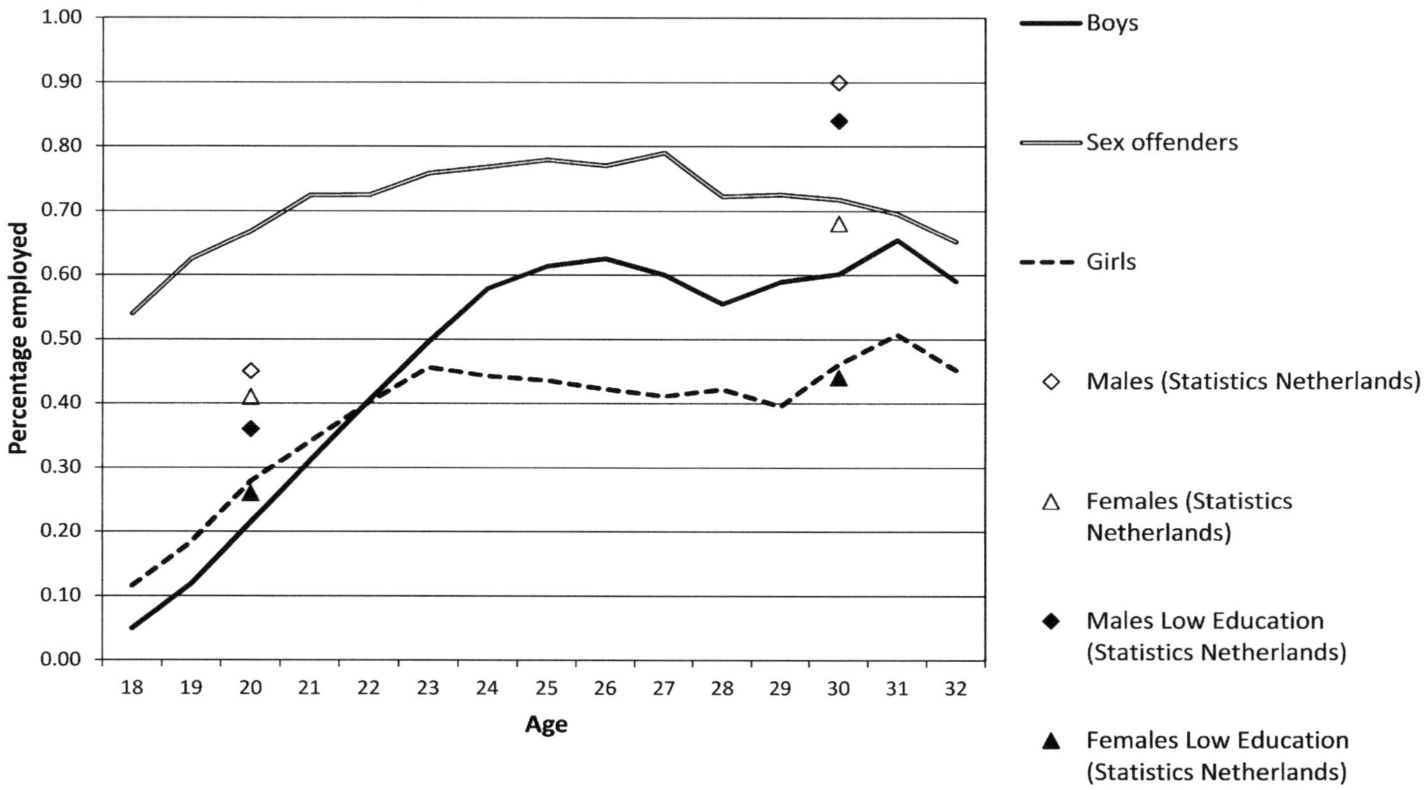

Figure 5.3 Development of employment participation for the three samples

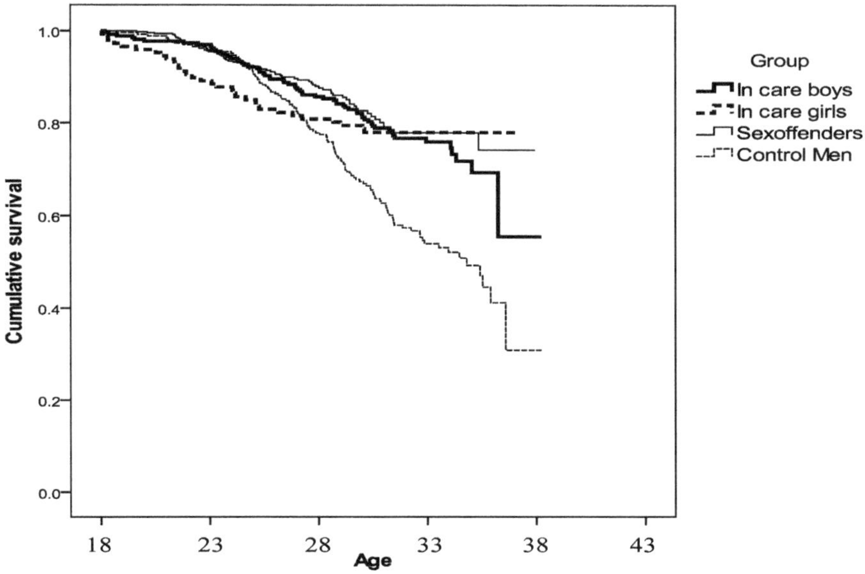

Figure 5.4 Survival functions marriage from age 18

Marriage

Figure 5.4 shows the survival curve for the three groups to the age of first marriage, starting from age 18, which is the legal age at which people may be wed in the Netherlands without permission from their parents.

Only a small proportion of the three problematic groups married. For the sex offenders, this figure could still increase as they were younger than the two other groups at the end of the observation period. However, if we look at the trend in the survival function, it is probable that a large proportion of all men and women in the three groups will stay unmarried. This does not mean that they were not in a romantic relationship or did not cohabit; it means that they did not formalize their situations in a marriage or partnership contract. High-risk women married earlier although not more than the sex offenders. High-risk men married most often, perhaps due to their higher average age. For all three groups, by age 30 about 20 per cent, and by age 33 about 25 per cent were married. By age 33, however, almost 50 per cent of the control men were married. The survival function was significantly different for the four groups (Breslow test=23.203, df=3, $p<.001$). This is mostly due to the different pattern for the control males. We concluded that fewer of the vulnerable groups married than average men in the Netherlands.

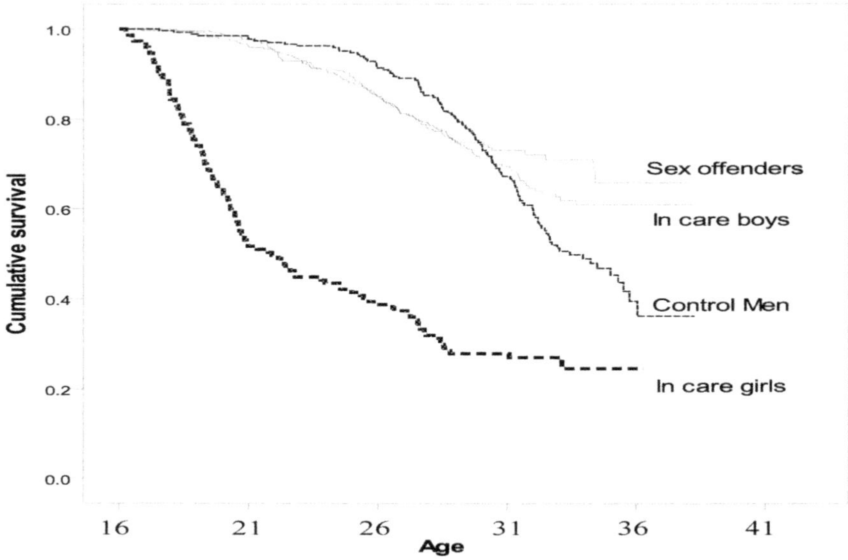

Figure 5.5 Survival functions parenthood from age 18 for the three samples and control males

Parenthood

Figure 5.5 presents the survival curve of the age at which members of the four groups became parents. The results show striking and significant differences (Breslow=314.690, df=3, p<.001) between the three groups, mainly due to the high-risk females who had children at very young ages. By age 21, 50 per cent of the high-risk females were already mothers. This figure is much elevated compared to what is normal in the Dutch population: for average Dutch women in this cohort, only six per cent are mothers by age 21, 30 per cent by age 28, and the 50 per cent mark is not reached until age 32.

The pattern for the at-risk men is quite different as they became parents at much later ages. It should be recalled that for the men we can count only those children they legally acknowledge – which would mean that they would have to pay child support, etc. It is likely that more men have fathered children, but this is not clear from the data.

The curve for the sex offenders and for the high-risk men is strikingly similar up to age 29. While the control men continued to become fathers, from age 32 new fatherhood levelled off for the high-risk males and the sex offenders. Thus the high-risk men were not only late in making the transition to fatherhood, but fewer made this transition at all.

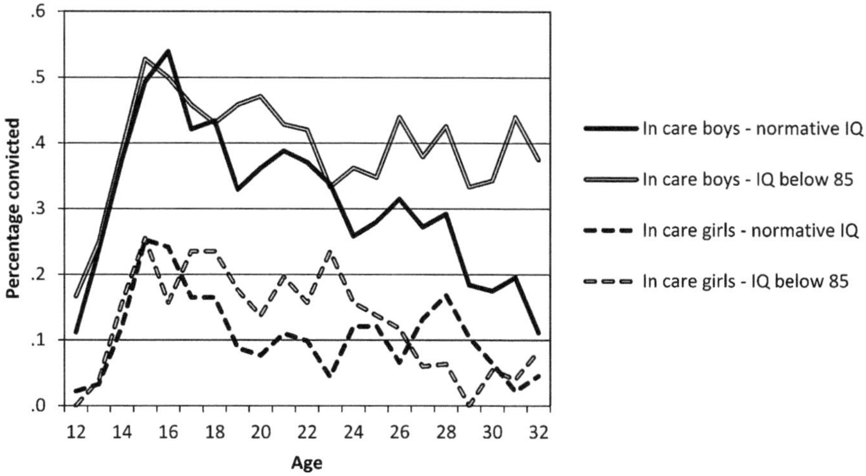

Figure 5.6 Conviction participation for males and females as a function of level of intelligence

Low Intelligence

Next, we investigated whether outcomes were different for those functioning at intellectually average levels and above, and those functioning at below normal levels (IQ < 85). In the male sample, 72 men had an IQ below 85. The IQ of 47 had not been reliably assessed and so they were omitted from the analyses. In the female sample, 51 women had an IQ below 85; the IQ of 4 had not been reliably assessed and as a result these were omitted from the analyses.

Figure 5.6 shows that those with low intellectual functioning continued to be convicted longer and at higher rates compared to those with average intellectual levels. This held most strongly for men, but also for women. While for women there appeared to be simply a level difference, the course of the graph for men appears different and perhaps does not in fact decrease from age 20–32.

Figure 5.7 shows that men as well as women functioning at low intellectual levels were employed less often. For men, the difference was minimal – though consistent – with IQ<85 men always less often employed. For the women, differences were greater: at age 26 it was largest with participation rates of 16 per cent among women at low intellectual levels, against 33 per cent among women of average intellectual levels. Overall the difference hovered around 10 per cent.

We also found that differences between the IQ groups regarding marriage – while only marginally significant (Breslow=3.578, df=1, p=.059 for the males; Breslow=1.834, df=1, p=.176 for the females) – nevertheless were revealing. Low IQ males tended to marry less often than intellectually normal males. Low IQ females on the other hand tended to marry sooner and more often than females with

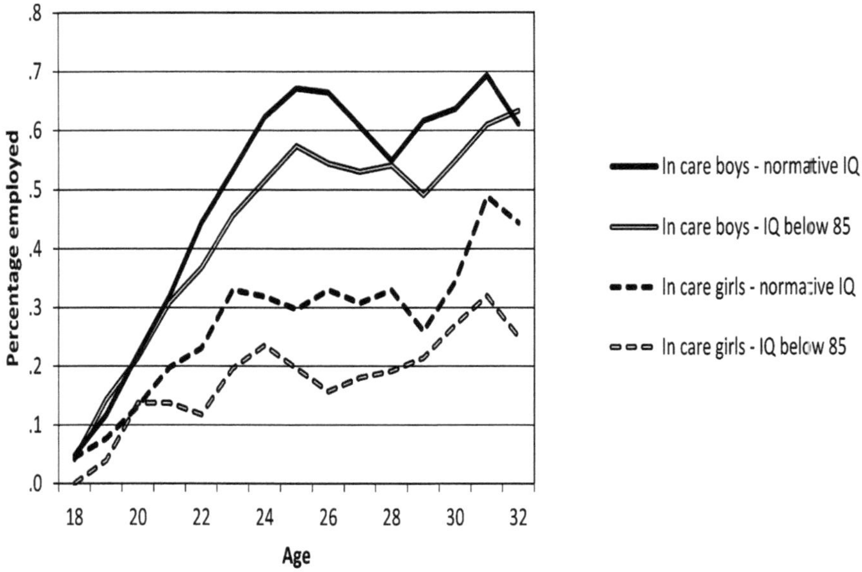

Figure 5.7 Per cent employed males and females as a function of intelligence

normal and above normal IQs. This finding is remarkable in that it shows that, while a low IQ apparently makes it harder for a high-risk man to find a marriage partner, it seems to make it easier for women. For parenthood we found only small and no significant differences between low IQ and normal IQ groups.

Ethnic Minorities and Ethnic Dutch

Next, we investigated whether outcomes were different for those who were ethnic Dutch and those who were not. In the male sample, 110 men were non-ethnic Dutch; for six men this information was missing, and we left them out of these analyses. In the female sample, 65 were non-ethnic Dutch, and for five this information was missing, so they also were left out.

Figure 5.8 shows that, for convictions, there is a small but consistent level difference between minorities and ethnic Dutch. Offending by minority men peaked at a slightly earlier age and they continued to offend more often than ethnically Dutch men. Differences were minimal from age 26 onwards. For the women of different ethnic groups differences were even smaller.

Men as well as women from ethnic minorities were employed consistently less than their ethnic Dutch counterparts. The differences were larger for the females, at a fairly stable 10 per cent (20 per cent against 30 per cent).

Non-ethnic Dutch females married much less than ethnic Dutch females (approx. 10 per cent at age 26 against approximately 30 per cent at age 26 for the ethnic Dutch: Log rank=6.826, df=1, p=.009). Part of this may be cultural: a sizeable proportion of

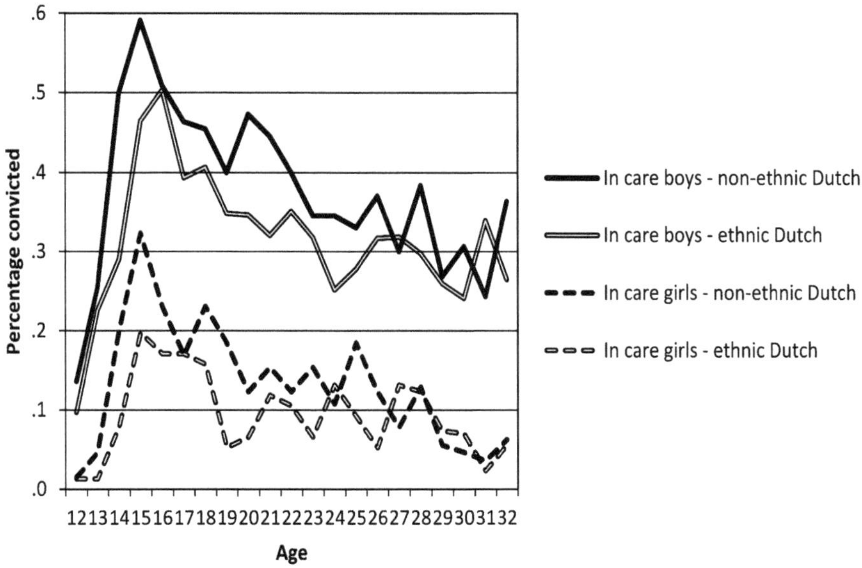

Figure 5.8 Conviction participation for ethnic and non-ethnic Dutch males and females

the non-ethnic Dutch females in our group are Surinamese and Antillean. For these groups it is known that fewer females (and males) tend to marry. For ethnic Dutch and non-ethnic Dutch we found no significant differences in parenthood.

Subgroups of Juvenile Sex Offenders

As mentioned previously, we distinguished among three subtypes of juvenile sexual offenders: group offenders, peer abusers and child abusers. The last two subtypes are solo offenders. Child abusers offended less frequently than the other two types of sex offenders. The group abusers were much more active in their teen years but pretty soon converged – apart from some instability – with the offending pattern of the peer abusers.

The development of employment was quite similar for the three groups of sex offenders. Marriage patterns were also fairly similar, although more of the child abusers tended to marry. There were clear level differences, however, as Figure 5.9 shows, among the three sex offender groups in the timing of parenthood (Log rank=11.670, df=2, p=.003). Fatherhood comes earliest for group offenders, followed by peer abusers, and lastly child abusers.

Within the group of sex offenders we found few differences between ethnic minorities and native Dutch, as well as between those who functioned at intellectually below average and at average or above levels.

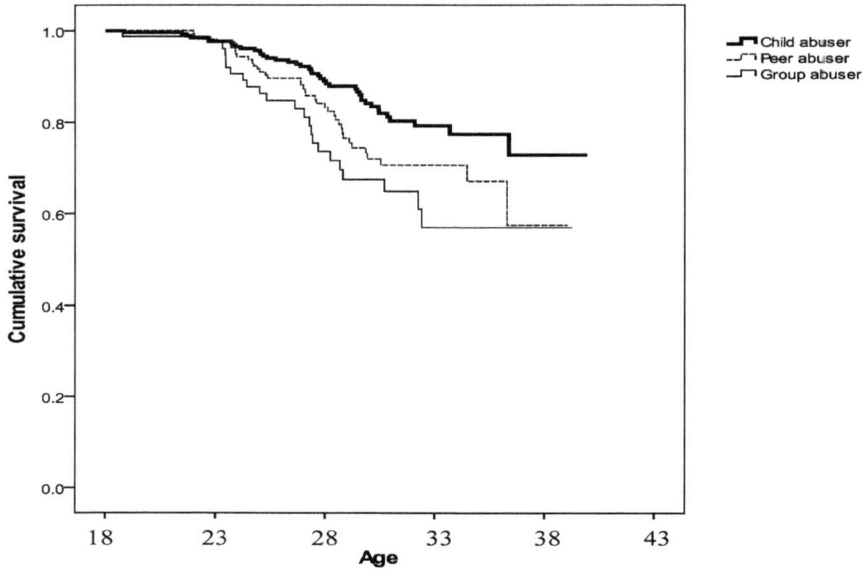

Figure 5.9 Survival functions parenthood from age 18 for three subtypes of juvenile sex offenders

Changes in Offending as a Function of Employment, Marriage and Parenthood

For each sample, we investigated whether offending frequency decreases when employed, married, or as parents. For marriage and parenthood we gauge any decrease against the change in those sample members who did not marry or did not become a parent. For employment, we do so only by means of within-person comparisons, i.e., we compare for each person whether his or her offending levels were lower in periods of employment than in periods of unemployment, corrected for incarceration.

High-risk Males

The average age at which high-risk males married was 26.9. The average age of fatherhood was 26.5. Men's offending lambda (defined as the number of offences per exposure year) was significantly lower while married (0.388) than while not married (.900) ($t=3.901$, $df=165$, $p<.001$). Men's offending lambda was also lower after fatherhood (0.671) than before (.999); this difference is (just) significant ($t=1.976$, $df=205$, $p<.050$). The lambda while employed was much lower (.023) than while unemployed (.526); the difference is significant ($t=-6.151$, $df=218$, $p<.001$). Thus, we see that in high-risk males marriage, parenthood, and employment all are associated with lower levels of offending.

High-risk Females

The average age at which high-risk females married was 23.2. The average age of motherhood was 21.2. Women's offending lambda was barely lower while married (0.257) than while not married (.261); this difference is far from significant ($t=.031$, $df=137$, $p=.975$). Women's offending lambda was higher after motherhood (0.378) than before (.214); this difference is not significant ($t=-1.035$, $df=138$, $p=.302$). The lambda while employed was much lower (.004) than while unemployed (.154); this difference for females, as for males, is highly significant ($t=-5.174$, $df=96$, $p<.001$ demonstrating that for high-risk females only employment is associated with a lower level of offending.

Juvenile Sex Offenders

The average age at which juvenile sex offenders married was 25.6. The average age of fatherhood was 24.8. As sex offenders were followed up to an average age of 28, this meant that, for the purpose of comparing married against never-married men, sample size dwindled, as quite a few were still under the average age for marriage or children and thus cannot serve as comparisons. The same holds true if we make within-person comparisons of periods of employment against periods of unemployment, for the reason that relatively more sex offenders than male and female sample members are either continuously unemployed or continuously employed over the observation period.

Sex offenders' offending lambda while married was substantially (but not significantly) lower (0.399) than while not married (.650) ($t=1.259$, $df=211$, $p=.209$). Sex offenders' offending lambda was higher (but not significantly) after fatherhood (1.025) than before (.763) ($t=-.762$, $df=81$, $p=.448$). However, the lambda while employed was significantly lower (.073) than while unemployed (.186) ($t=-3.403$, $df=289$, $p<.001$). Thus, only employment is associated with lower levels of offending in sex offenders.

Summary and Conclusions

In examining the effects of social changes, or life transitions, in relationship to changes in offending from adolescence to adulthood in several special groups, we found that, with only one exception, all three groups made the transitions into adult domains (employment, marriage, parenthood) later – and probably in the end less well – than the average Dutch man or woman.

The exceptions are high-risk women who start parenthood at exceptionally young ages. Other than that, it appears that these groups lag behind for all domains to the extent to which they make the transition to adulthood. Similarly, they take a longer time than normative samples in outgrowing delinquency. We found that all three groups of vulnerable youth – high-risk males, high-risk females and juvenile sex offenders – continued to offend well into adulthood. It appears that only as these men and women reach their 30s, is a reduction in prevalence and frequency of offending reached. Particularly for high-risk males, levels remained elevated for a long period. This shows that the high risk for offending identified in these group at an early age manifests itself later, and predominantly so for the high-risk males.

While a number of high-risk women marry early, overall high-risk men as well as high-risk women and juvenile sex offenders end up marrying less than the average Dutch man or woman. On average, Dutch men and women postpone marriage for a while, but at age 32, 50 per cent of Dutch men are married while for high-risk men the figure at that age is a little over 20 per cent. With regard to parenthood, the differences are less striking, but the pattern is the same: at age 32, 50 per cent of Dutch men are fathers, while for high-risk men the figure is about 35 per cent. It could be that high-risk men father more children but that these children are not acknowledged and as such do not appear in our data. Comparison of official records with self-reported data on a number of respondents from treatment and penitentiary files (Bijleveld, 2010) shows, however, that this is unlikely to account for all of the difference. Also, many men and women could have had stable romantic partners they did not marry that do not appear in our official data, and so we are bound to have undercounted the extent to which they are involved in (steady) romantic relationships. The same, however, applies to average Dutch men and women. Our groups may be less likely to legalize their romantic involvements or children. In that case, our undercounting is more serious and leads to bias.

All in all, while taking into account these issues, high-risk men and women as well as sex offenders clearly make the transition to adulthood differently than average men and women. They assume adult roles less well, and later, than average Dutch men and women. In their early 30s, they are much less settled. While this could still be a delay and they could recoup at later ages, we have argued that it is likely that part of the difference will turn out to be permanent. This shows that, as the literature we discussed in our introduction pointed out for similar groups, for many of these high-risk men and women their problems are not limited to childhood but extend well into adulthood.

All three groups perform (well) below norm on the labour market, while taking into account their low educational levels. Many hold positions only for a short time, being employed in short contracts or by temporary job agencies. At any adult age, some 40 per cent of at-risk males are unemployed. These men make the transition to employment at a far lower rate than the average Dutch male. Again, we have reason to assume that this is not entirely delayed entry, but likely to be partly permanent. For high-risk women the situation is slightly less striking, not in the sense that they are more successful in the labour market, but that low-educated average Dutch females also do not participate at high rates. Many low-educated Dutch females may have made the choice not to enter the official labour force, choosing instead be a housewife and/or a mother, which in many segments of Dutch society are regarded as respectable occupations.

Thus, to answer our first research question, it appears as if the special groups we investigated are indeed substantially less successful in finding (and keeping) employment, and in settling down. To what this is attributable is a matter for further research. It is possible that the offending records of some of the men and women have hampered their entry into the official labour market (the 'scarring' theory from labour economics). On the other hand, those without or with only very minimal criminal records keep mostly menial jobs, such as a handyman or a janitor, or run businesses of their own, such as keeping a store for ethnic clothing, for which a criminal record need not be an absolute impediment. In all likelihood, however, it is more probable that the personality, psychiatric and childhood problems of these youth have underequipped and scarred them socially to the extent that they are unable to sustain ties, whether to jobs or to partners. It is also reasonable to assume that those with particularly violent careers make less attractive marriage partners. This also explains why differences are smallest when we regard parenthood, a state that may be embarked upon with little effort, and that one never leaves. Such explanations are but a starting point and too simplistic as a final conclusion, as underlined by our analyses of, for example, differences between respondents with adequate and sub-adequate levels of intellectual functioning. More research is needed here, particularly in-depth qualitative research, to unravel the mechanisms and identify the stumbling blocks, the negative spirals, and the chain reactions and interactions with contextual issues.

While all three groups thus make less successful transitions to adulthood than average Dutch people, the three domains we investigated impact on offending more or less as we would expect on the basis of the literature (see introduction to this chapter, and Blokland and Palmen, Chapter 2, this volume). High-risk men's offending is reduced by marriage as well as by parenthood and by employment. Obviously, these domains may be collinear and further studies are needed to unravel whether each of them makes an independent contribution to the reduction of offending.

For females and sex offenders, the picture is less straightforward. For females, we see that motherhood is associated – although not significantly so – with increased offending. Many of the women we investigated may in fact have been single mothers, a condition that is tough even on women with exemplary resumes. The fact that marriage did not reduce offending levels may be the result of women 'marrying down'. According to this viewpoint, women (and perhaps particularly high-risk women) simply have fewer choices of 'good' partners and are thus more likely than men to marry a criminal partner and consequently be exposed to a mate's antisocial behaviour. Any positive effect of the marital state might then have been counterbalanced. Such explanations are mere guesses, and here also more qualitative research is needed. All in all, it does appear that vulnerability impacts men and women differently. We suggest that in the Netherlands it is still more acceptable for women to withdraw from the labour market and 'escape' into early motherhood. Females at additional disadvantage (for example, non-ethnic Dutch, of below normal intellectual functioning) were markedly lower in terms of labour participation than their male counterparts. While these women are either unwanted in the labour market or do not choose to enter it, their intellectual handicap appears to be an asset on the marriage market. They have children out of wedlock and at extremely young ages for the Netherlands. However, they continue offending at elevated rates.

Within the group of sex offenders, we found fewer differences than we had anticipated. Beyond that, we saw that, strikingly, more of the child abusers tend to marry but also tend to have fewer children. One explanation might be that some child abusers will become paedophiles and thus may not reproduce. Child abusers were also the most 'integrated' in that they continued offending at the lowest levels. Unfortunately, also due to the relatively short follow-up period as compared to the relatively late ages at which they married, we were unable to conduct more in-depth analyses, disaggregated by the sex offender subgroup.

Overall, we believe that our most important finding is the consistent effect of employment on offending. It is in a sense a 'lucky' finding as employment is an intervention that can to a certain extent be encouraged, while obviously this would be harder, if not impossible to do regarding marriage or parenthood. The effect of employment cannot be explained by selection effects, as we conducted our analyses within persons. In that sense it is a fairly robust finding. It is a striking finding too, as we also found that among the groups studied educational levels were low, few participated in the official labour force, and many held small jobs and switched jobs repeatedly.

What generates the effect is a matter for further scrutiny: is it the earnings, social capital, routine activities? These questions are extremely relevant from a theoretical perspective.

There are several recommendations that flow from our research findings. In order to reduce recidivism for high-risk groups as they transition from adolescence to adulthood, we recommend that: (a) all young offenders, and particularly offenders in high-risk groups, have access to education, both while in care and in after-care; (b) the offenders should receive job skills training and should have available employment programmes that continue after discharge from an institution.

References

Bijleveld, C.C.J.H. (2007). Sex offending and sex offenders. In M. Tonry and C.C.J.H. Bijleveld (eds), *Crime & Justice in the Netherlands: Crime & Justice, A Review of Research*, Vol. 35. Chicago, IL: University of Chicago Press, pp. 261–318.

Bijleveld, C.C.J.H. (2010). Het gebruik van registers voor criminologisch onderzoek. In Bart Bakker, Paul Bransz, Harry Ganzeboom, Leander Kuijvenhoven and Els Tettelaar (eds), *Registers in sociaalwetenschappelijk onderzoek, mogelijkheden en valkuilen*. The Hague: CBS, pp. 65–73.

Boendermaker, L. (1998). *Eind goed, al goed? De leefsituatie van jongeren een jaar na vertrek uit de justitiele behandelinrichting*. Onderzoek & Beleid, No. 167. The Hague: WODC.

Bullock, R., Hosie, K., Little, M., and Millham, S. (1990). Secure accommodation for very difficult adolescents: Some recent research findings. *Journal of Adolescence*, 13, 205–16.

DJI (2010). Feiten en cijfers. At http://www.dji.nl/Organisatie/Feiten-en-cijfers/Justitiele Jeugdinrichtingen/dji_capaciteit_bezetting.aspx#paragraph4, accessed 9 February 2010.

Hendriks, J. (2006). *Jeugdige zedendelinquenten – een studie naar subtypen en recidive*. Amsterdam: VU University (Ph.D. dissertation).

Megens, K. and Day, S. (2007). Delinquentie van meisjes. Over de relatie tussen risicofactoren en delinquent gedrag na behandeling in een JJI. *Tijdschrift voor Criminologie*, 49, 370–85.

Save the Children UK (1995). *You're on your Own: Young People's Research on Leaving Care*. London: Save the Children.

Smit, M. (1991). De situatie van jongeren na een tehuisverblijf. Resultaten uit een literatuuronderzoek. *Tijdschrift voor Orthopedagogiek*, 30, 476–92.

Van der Geest, V. and Bijleveld, C.C.J.H. (2008). Personal, background and treatment characteristics associated with offending after residential treatment: A 13-year follow up in adolescent males. *Psychology, Crime & Law*, 14, 159–76.

Verhofstadt-Deneve, L. (1980). *De ontwikkeling van sociaal onaangepaste jongens en meisjes tot jonge volwassenen. Een follow-up studie vanuit differentieel en./o ontwikkelingspsychologisch oogpunt*. Mededelingen & Werkdocumenten 10. Rijksuniversiteit Gent, Lab voor Psychologie.

Vinnerljung, B., Franzen, E., and Danielsson, M. (2007). Teenage parenthood among child welfare clients: A Swedish national cohort study of prevalence and odds. *Journal of Adolescence*, 30, 97–116.

Vinnerljung, B., Sundell, K., Lofhölm, C.A., and Humlesjö, E. (2006). Former Stockholm child protection cases as young adults: Do outcomes differ between those that received services and those that did not? *Children and Youth Services Review*, 28, 59–77.

Wijkman, M., Van der Geest, V., and Bijleveld, C.C.J.H. (2006). Problematiek en criminele carrière van op civielrechtelijke en strafrechtelijke titel behandelde jongeren. *Familie- en Jeugdrecht*, 28, 18–26.

Wong, T.M.L., Bijleveld, C.C.J.H., and Slotboom, A.M. (2009). Van probleemmeisje naar delinquente vrouw? Criminele carrières van residentieel behandelde meisjes, van 12 tot 32 jaar. *Tijdschrift voor Criminologie*, 51, 246–61.

Wouda, P.L. (1987). *Jongeren tussen wal en schip*. Leiden: University of Leiden (Ph.D. dissertation).

Chapter 6
Risk Assessment and the Impact of Risk and Protective Factors

Han J.M. Spanjaard, Leontien M. van der Knaap,
Claudia E. van der Put and Geert Jan J.M. Stams

Risk assessment forms a critical link between a person who commits a crime and an effective intervention to reduce the risk of recidivism (Schwalbe, 2007). The two main questions in risk assessment are: (1) what is the risk of recidivism (*risk* assessment), and (2) which dynamic risk factors, or criminogenic needs, contribute to this risk and should therefore be the target of intervention in order to prevent recidivism (*needs* assessment)?

The risk of recidivism to some extent can be predicted by static risk factors such as age and offence history, but these factors are not malleable. Criminogenic needs, in contrast, relate to dynamic risk factors such as antisocial attitudes and deviant peer associations that are potentially changeable (Andrews and Bonta, 1994; Bonta, 1996). Reductions in dynamic risk factors are associated with reduced recidivism (Bonta, 1996). Nearly all current risk assessment instruments make a distinction between 'static' and 'dynamic' risk factors. Static factors are used for assessing an offender's overall risk level, whereas assessment of dynamic factors is needed if we want to identify targets for intervention and assess changes in factors related to risk (for example, after treatment).

Knowledge of an offender's risk and needs levels enables probation officers and other professionals to make good decisions regarding supervision, intervention and prevention. Because of the developmental changes that occur between adolescence and early adulthood, different assessment instruments and different interventions have been developed for use with adolescents and (young) adults. During early adulthood many individuals desist from criminal behaviour, while some continue (see Blokland and Palmen, Chapter 2, this volume). From a developmental psychological perspective, it can be expected that the impact of different dynamic factors varies as juveniles and young adults grow older. In other words, at different ages risk factors probably have different impacts. As a result, in developing assessment instruments it is important to choose those domains, factors, items and item responses that are relevant to the developmental stages of the offender population with which the instrument will be used. For instance, if over time family factors become less important, and individual factors such as having skills of self-control and finding and keeping a job become more important, assessment instruments should be able to address these changes. The changes in the relative impact of different dynamic factors with development might furthermore aid in predicting which adolescents will continue their criminal careers into young adulthood and which will not. Our recent work on risk assessment instruments indicates a shift in the relative importance of different criminogenic needs in predicting recidivism from adolescence through young adulthood. Although cross-sectional in nature, these data may guide future research on long-term prediction of recidivism into adulthood. We shall present and discuss the results on predicting recidivism among different age groups ranging from adolescents to young adults.

In the first part of this chapter we discuss the use and quality requirements of structured risk assessment instruments. Next, we introduce the two instruments that have been used for data collection in our study on dynamic risk factors in adolescence and young adulthood. Finally, we present and discuss our findings regarding the different impact of dynamic risk factors at different ages.

Structured Risk Assessment

Structured risk assessment for juveniles and adults has become increasingly important in the field of justice and corrections. Andrews, Bonta and Wormith (2006) provide a detailed description of the recent history of structured risk assessment, a common characteristic of which is that the instrument(s) *predicted* the likelihood of a certain outcome. Structured assessment makes an inventory of risk and protective factors in the individual and his/her circumstances to predict his/her behaviour. However, a prediction can never be 100 per cent accurate. Even when an inventory of risk and protective factors is very extensive, uncertainty remains. The newest (fourth) generation of risk assessment instruments not only offers leads for setting appropriate goals for intervention but also enables better case management planning by offering the possibility of linking reassessments with the initial assessment, with service plans, and with service delivery (Andrews et al., 2006). As such, fourth-generation assessments integrate prediction, intervention planning, and reassessment. Most risk assessment instruments rely on gathering data from different sources, including police, justice system data, and information from parents, teachers and offenders.

However, the availability of a single general risk score often does not include sufficient information to conduct appropriate case management. Individuals with minor crimes (misdemeanours) have, on average, a higher risk of recidivism than those who commit serious crimes (see for example, Wartna, Tollenaar and Blom, 2005). For instance, boys who commit shoplifting of trivial items have – especially during adolescence – relatively high-risk scores for recidivism. To decide whether a delinquent poses a risk of harm to others and what kind of security, supervision and intervention is suitable, information is also needed about the seriousness of the predicted recidivism. Therefore it is desirable that risk assessment also provides information about the probability of certain types of future offences and their possible severity. Broadly speaking, there are two types of structured risk assessment: general and specific risk assessments.

General Structured Risk Assessment

General structured risk assessment instruments ascertain the probability of two aspects: (1) what are the chances that the individual will be in contact with the police and the justice system again because of a new crime; and (2) what are the risk and protective factors associated with this risk? Thus, general risk assessment instruments mostly give a broad picture of the individual and his/her environment. Some general risk assessment instruments use different steps in the assessment procedure. Typically, the assessments start with a global screening (pre-screen) in which information is collected that is rather easy to obtain and is predictive enough to draw first conclusions and decisions. The information can be objective information from files from police and/or justice departments but can also be collected in a short, structured interview with the offender. If there is moderate- or high risk, then the next step is a full screening (or a specific assessment). If the full screening reveals risk levels in certain domains (for example, high risk on drug and alcohol abuse, or negative attitude), further assessments or diagnostic research may be required.

Two widely disseminated instruments for juvenile offender assessment are the *Youth Level of Service/Case Management Inventory* (YLS/CMI; Hoge and Andrews, 2001) and the *Washington State Juvenile Court Assessment* (WSJCA; Barnoski, 2004a, 2004b). During dissemination the WSJCA received different titles, such as the *Case Management Assessment Protocol* (CMAP), the *Positive Achievement Change Tool* (PACT; Baglivio, 2007) and the *Youth Assessment and Screening Instrument* (YASI; Orbis Partners, 2007). All these instruments include a structured case planning protocol.

Often different instruments are used for adult offenders. Instruments used for assessing risk and needs in adult offenders include the American *Correctional Offender Management Profiling for Alternative Sanctions* (COMPAS; information available at www.northpointeinc.com), the Canadian *Level of Service/Case Management Inventory* (LS/CMI; Andrews, Bonta and Wormith, 2004), and the British *Offender Assessment System* (OASys; Howard, Clark and Garnham, 2003). The LS/CMI is the latest iteration in a long sequence of instruments that began with the scale that Andrews (1982) originally named the *Level of Supervision Inventory* (LSI).

Specific Risk Assessments

Specific risk assessment instruments investigate particular aspects of the person more deeply or investigate the risk of a particular type of offender, such as sex offenders. For example, there are specific risk assessment instruments for violent and sexual offenders, such as the *Historical, Clinical, Risk Management-20* (HCR-20, which estimates an individual's probability of violence); the *Sexual Violence Risk* (SVR-20) for adults; and the *Structured Assessment of Violence Risk in Youth* (SAVRY) and *Juvenile Sex Offender Assessment Protocol-II* (J-SOAP-II) for juveniles. In addition, there are specific instruments for assessing psychopathy or psychopathic personality traits including the *Pyschopathy Checklist Revised* (PCL-R), with a screening version (PCL-SV) and a youth version (PCL-YV). Some of these measured traits and behaviour characteristics are related to violence and recidivism in general. Although strictly speaking the PCL-R and PCL-YV are not risk assessment instruments, they can be used within risk assessment protocols.

Risk and Protective Factors

The domains of information included in risk assessment can vary. Whether personal history, school, family, peers, attitudes, social skills and mental health are included depends on the goals of the assessment instrument. Less information is needed to derive a risk score than to estimate criminogenic needs. The specific goals of risk assessment and the target group to be assessed determine the (number of) factors, the (number of) items, the weighting scheme for each item and each factor, and the wording used for each item and item response.

There has been extensive research and discussion on risk and protective factors associated with the onset, persistence, and desistance of criminal activity (Thornberry and Krohn, 2003; Stouthamer-Loeber et al., 2002; Lipsey and Derzon, 1998; Loeber and Stouthamer-Loeber, 1987). Factors that predict the onset of crime are not necessarily the same as factors that predict recidivism. Moreover, factors that predict the onset of crime and/or recidivism can change over time and can be different for subcategories of offenders (male/female, different ages, different cultural groups, etc.). Previous research has identified a wide range of contextual (for example, criminality in family of origin, high crime neighbourhood) and individual (for example, antisocial attitudes, skill deficits, negative peer associations) risk factors for offending. Similarly, studies have reported a large number of protective factors (for an overview, see for example, Stouthamer-Loeber et al., 2002; Stouthamer-Loeber et al., 2008; Van der Laan et al., 2009a). Some argue that risk and protective factors are opposite poles of a similar construct; others argue that this is sometimes but not always the case. In this discussion a useful distinction is made between promotive and protective factors. Promotive factors lower the probability of problem behaviour, regardless of the presence of risk factors, while protective factors, which can be seen as a subcategory of promotive factors, moderate the effects of risk factors on problem behaviour (Van der Laan et al., 2009b). The more promotive and the fewer risk factors, the lower the percentage of (serious) recidivism (Van der Laan et al., 2009b; Van der Laan and Blom, 2006; Stouthamer-Loeber et al., 2002).

Assessment instruments differ in the way they use risk and protective factors. Some instruments – specifically those that assess risk and needs in adults – include only risk items, whereas other instruments include both. Hoge, Vincent and Guy (2012) summarized the factors most commonly listed in the literature. While Hoge and his colleagues made the overview of instruments used in North America, the current authors did it for instruments used in the Netherlands (see Table 6.1).

Making this overview was somewhat difficult and arbitrary because the language used in the instruments varies and it was not always easy to determine equivalence in the terms used.

The Quality of Risk Assessment

When judging the quality of structured risk assessment instruments, the first necessary condition is *reliability*. A reliable instrument produces the same assessment results for the same subject when done by different assessors (also called inter-rater reliability). For an instrument to be reliable there must be clear definitions for the concepts that are assessed and clear instructions on how to gather the information (file searching, semi-structured interviews, etc.) and for scoring (giving interpretation to the raw information). For some instruments, extensive training precedes the use of the assessment. Only individuals who have completed the training and are certified are allowed to perform these assessments. Some instruments use implementation protocols that provide information on who can implement the tool, and require certification and quality assurance.

A second necessary condition for good risk assessment is the *validity* of the instruments: does the instrument accurately measure what it intends to measure? At least two types of validity are important: content validity and predictive validity. Content validity refers to the extent to which a measure represents all facets of a certain concept or construct, for example, a risk factor. In the case of risk assessment it means that the instrument adequately represents the factors related to recidivism. Content validity is related to face validity; that is, whether an instrument 'looks valid' to the professional who uses it. Unless the risk assessment is considered by the practitioner to be a useful tool for working with offenders, he or she will not consider the assessment valid. To enhance content and face validity, the development of most instruments starts with a thorough examination of the existing literature and field experience to guide the selection and development of major domains and items (Barnoski, 2004b).

Predictive validity is the extent to which the assessment score accurately predicts recidivism. In a study of predictive validity, the risk scores are computed first, then at some later time information on recidivism is collected. Measuring recidivism involves a minimum follow-up period of at least 18 months. Barnoski (2004a) proposed an extra year for the adjudication process because it takes time before a new crime is registered in the official records of the Ministry of Justice. The validity of a prediction instrument refers to the percentage of cases that are later correctly classified (as recidivists or non-recidivists) based on the instrument's assessment. This accuracy can be expressed by means of the area under the curve (AUC) statistic. An AUC of 1 represents a perfect instrument; an AUC of .50 is not better than chance. In general, an AUC value above .70 is good, and above .75 is considered to be high (Dolan and Doyle, 2000; Shapiro, 1999; Barnoski and Drake, 2007; Brennan, Dieterich and Ehret, 2009). In a meta-analysis of the

Table 6.1 Empirically based risk factors included in some risk assessment tools (factors based on Hoge et al., 2012)

	Youth Tools				Adult Tools	
Factors	**WSJCA**	**YLS/CMI**	**LIJ**	**SAVRY**	**RISc**	**HCR-20**
Personal Risk Factors – Static						
History of joblessness	X	X	X		X	X
History of school suspensions/expulsions	X		X	X		X
Early school leaving	X		X	X	X	
History of homelessness		X	X		X	
Early conduct problems			X		X	X
Early age of onset for offending	X		X		X	X
Early violence/aggression			X	X		X
Prior probation/custody	X	X	X	X		X
Exposure to violence (early)	X	X	X	X	X	X
Early caregiver disruption	X		X	X	X	X
History of violence	X		X	X		X
History of non-violent delinquency/offending	X	X	X	X	X	
History of abuse/maltreatment	X	X	X	X		X

Contextual Risk Factors – Static						
Antisocial attitudes, values, beliefs, family	X	X	X			
Criminality in family	X	X	X	X	X	
Mental illness in family	X	X	X			
Marital conflicts in family	X	X	X			
Joblessness in family	X	X	X			
Low family income	X	X	X		X	
Inadequate family housing		X				
Dysfunctional neighbourhood/ community disorganization				X	X	
High crime neighbourhood				X	X	X
Personal Risk Factors – Dynamic						
Antisocial attitudes, values, beliefs	X	X	X	X	X	X
Attention disorder	X	X	X	X		
Psychopathy (adult tools)						X
Low empathy/remorse		X	X	X	X	
Inflated self-worth	X	X	X		X	
Sensation seeking			X	X	X	
Impulsivity	X	X	X	X	X	X
Chronic lying						
Hostile, aggressive, violent	X	X	X	X		X
Anger management issues	X	X	X	X	X	

Table 6.1 continued

	Youth Tools				Adult Tools	
	WSJCA	YLS/CMI	LIJ	SAVRY	RISc	HCR-20
Lack of motivation		X	X	X	X	
Drug abuse	X	X	X	X	X	X
Alcohol abuse	X	X	X	X	X	X
Poor school adjustment	X	X	X	X		X
Poor school performance	X	X	X	X	X	
Poor coping ability	X	X	X	X	X	X
Mental illness/health	X		X		X	X
Contextual Risk Factors – Dynamic						
Dysfunctional family environment	X	X	X	X	X	
Ineffective parenting	X	X	X	X		
Parent–youth conflicts/attachment problem	X	X	X			X
Lack of family support	X		X	X		X
Poor maternal/paternal coping			X			
Negative peer associations	X	X	X	X	X	X
Personal Factors (Positive/Strengths)						
Emotional maturity					X	
Positive, prosocial attitude	X	X	X	X	X	
Good problem-solving skills	X		X		X	

Good social skills	X		X		X	
Motivation to addrcss personal issues/readiness			X	X	X	
Job stability	X	X	X		X	X
Educational commitment/achievement	X	X	X	X	X	
Positive hobby/sport involvement	X	X	X	X		
Intelligence			X			
Positive attitude towards authority/treatment	X		X	X	X	
Resilient personality traits				X	X	
Contextual Factors (Positive/Strengths)						
Stable and cohesive family unit	X	X	X			
Supportive parent	X	X	X	X		
Supportive other adult	X		X	X		
Stable marital/partner relationship	X				X	X
Positive peer associations	X	X	X	X	X	
Strong attachment and bonds	X		X	X		

predictive validity of risk assessment instruments for young people, Schwalbe (2007) found that the AUC value ranges from .53 to .78, with a mean AUC of .64.

Risk Assessment in the Netherlands

Most risk assessment instruments used in the Netherlands are translations and adaptations of foreign instruments. Two Dutch instruments for general risk assessment are the *Landelijk Instrumentarium Jeugdstrafrechtketen* (LIJ; *National Instrument Juvenile Justice*) for juveniles and the *Recidive Inschattingsschalen* (RISc; *Recidivism Risk Assessment Scales*) for adults, which is more than just a translation of non-Dutch instruments.

LIJ

The LIJ is mainly based on the WSJCA, but has some specific Dutch adaptations and supplements (Spanjaard et al., 2009; Van der Put et al., 2010). The LIJ is designed to answer the following questions:

- What is the general risk of recidivism?
- What is the risk of violence towards other persons?
- What are the criminogenic factors that constitute this risk?
- What is the responsivity: can the individual profit from a specific intervention?
- What is the risk of harm towards the individual him- or herself (suicide, self-harm)?
- What are the signals of mental problems or disorders?

Assessment of risk, needs and responsivity are necessary to choose the right interventions for preventing recidivism. Assessment of harm towards others helps to decide which level of security and supervision is needed to protect society. Assessment of self-harm and symptoms of mental problems and disorders can signal the need for treatment and special measures.

As mentioned, most items and domains of the LIJ are derived from the WSJCA, a comprehensive risk, need and protective factor assessment instrument designed for use in juvenile probation and other high-risk youth service settings. To assess signals of mental health problems and the need for care, some LIJ-items have been derived from the BARO, a semi-structured questionnaire completed by personnel of the Child Protection Board in cases where a juvenile (aged 12–17) is suspected of having committed a criminal offence (called Basisraadsonderzoek: Doreleijers et al., 1999; Spaander, 2003). Whereas the WSJCA consists of a pre-screen assessment and a full risk assessment, the LIJ uses a three-step assessment procedure: pre-screen (based on static factors and conducted by the police), quick-screen (assessment using a selection of items of static and dynamic factors and conducted by the Child Protection Board (CPB)), and full-screen (assessment of all items by CPB, probation or parole personnel). One of the aims of the LIJ is to apply a criminogenic and non-criminogenic risk and needs assessment in as brief a manner as possible and as comprehensively as needed. Decisions to move on to the next step in assessment are based upon the severity of the offence, the risk of recidivism, and the dynamic risk profile.

The LIJ full-screen includes the following ten major domains related to juvenile delinquency and continued criminal activity based on the research literature:

1. school,
2. employment,
3. family,
4. free time,
5. relationships,
6. alcohol, drugs and gambling,
7. mental health,
8. attitude,
9. aggression, and
10. skills.

Each domain consists of a number of items, varying from three to 24, adding up to a total of 118 items. For the quick- and full-screen, a structured interview is conducted with the youth and the youth's parents. The assessor uses the guidelines of the instrument and his or her professional judgement to interpret the interview information and complete the assessment. This analysis requires a thorough understanding of the assessment concepts and the ability to elicit and interpret information. The quick-screen provides a general score of the number of dynamic risk factors, called the 'dynamic risk profile'. As in the WSJCA, the method is empirically determined: adding together weighted scores on different items. The full screen leads to better risk and protective scores on different domains.

Compared to most other countries, the Netherlands has many more professionals in contact with a delinquent juvenile and his or her parents. The LIJ aims to provide not only a reliable and valid assessment instrument for all the professionals involved but also a framework in which different professionals can continue assessment and case planning with information already gathered by other assessors. The police assess the static factors such as offence history, current crime, age, and gender. After this pre-screen, an officer from the Child Protection Board conducts the quick-screen and if necessary the full-screen. Using the results of the assessment, the CPB officer then advises the prosecutor or court based on the criminogenic factors, signs of mental problems and disorders, and responsivity. The decisions of the prosecutor or the court are based on this advice, the severity of the committed crime, and the individual's criminal history. The prosecutor or court can take different actions. In cases where the juvenile is obliged to get supervision or probation, a probation officer is responsible for interventions and further (re-)assessment; in cases where the juvenile is sent to a youth prison for further treatment, the youth prison or parole service is responsible for further (re-) assessment.

Specific forensic organizations can do further psychological or psychiatric assessment when needed. The youth prison uses additional assessment instruments, such as the *Strengths and Difficulties Questionnaire* (SDQ), the *Massachusetts Youth Screening Instrument Version 2* (MAYSI-2) and the *Structured Assessment of Violence Risk in Youth* (SAVRY). The SDQ (Goodman, 1997) is a brief behavioural screening questionnaire for children and adolescents ages 4 through 18 and their parents, and assesses emotional symptoms, conduct problems, hyperactivity/inattention, peer relationship problems, and pro-social behaviour. The MAYSI-2 (Grisso and Barnum, 2006) is a brief screening tool designed to assist juvenile justice facilities in identifying youths at admission who might have special mental health needs. The SAVRY (Borum, Bartel and Forth, 2002; Lodewijks et al., 2003; Lodewijks, 2008) is a risk assessment tool of adolescents between ages 12 and 18 and can be used to make plans for intervention and supervision concerning the risk of violence in youth.

When a juvenile is sentenced to probation, the assessment becomes the first step in the rehabilitative process in which the probation officer lets the youth and family know the officer is interested in their strengths as well as their weaknesses. Based on the initial assessment, the youth and parents work with the juvenile probation officer to set rehabilitation goals and to match the youth with an intervention designed for the youth's particular risk profile.

The RISc

The RISc is based on the British *Offender Assessment System* (OASys; Howard, Clark and Garnham, 2003). In 2004, when the Dutch Ministry of Justice introduced the RISc, the goals were as follows:

- to assess an offender's likelihood of recidivism (defined as a new conviction),
- to identify and classify offending-related needs,
- to assess an offender's responsivity, and
- to indicate the need for further specialist assessment.

As with the LIJ, Dutch probation officers use the RISc to advise the prosecutor and the court as well as to formulate supervision and rehabilitation plans. RISc is completed by trained probation officers and provides an offending-related needs profile that identifies the most important factors contributing to the risk of recidivism. Accordingly, it identifies the criminogenic needs that should be addressed in order to reduce the likelihood of recidivism.

RISc consists of twelve scored sections, each corresponding to a criminogenic factor:

1. offending history,
2. current offence and pattern of offences,
3. accommodation,
4. education, work and training,
5. financial management and income,
6. relationships with partner, family and relatives,
7. relationships with friends and acquaintances,
8. drug misuse,
9. alcohol misuse,
10. emotional well-being,
11. thinking and behaviour, and
12. attitudes/orientation.

Each section consists of a number of items, varying from three to eight, adding up to a total of 61. Some RISc items use a dichotomous *yes/no* response scale, but the majority are scaled 0, 1 or 2, where 0 signifies *No problems*, 1 equals *Some problems*, and 2 equals *Significant problems*. The raw scores, the sum of the scores on individual items within each section, are then converted into weighted scores, recognizing that not all offending-related factors are expected to be equally correlated with the likelihood of reconviction. The weighting is based on a review of empirical studies of the relative contribution of criminogenic needs to the prediction of reconviction (Adviesbureau Van Montfoort and Reclassering Nederland, 2004). The item scores of Sections 1 and 2 are combined into one section score relating to information on offences (both recent and older offences). The likelihood of reconviction – the overall RISc score – is calculated by adding together the 11 weighted section scores, thus including information on both static and dynamic risk factors. Weighted section scores are grouped into three levels of criminogenic needs: *no criminogenic needs present*, *criminogenic needs present* and *serious criminogenic needs present*. The overall score is grouped into three categories of risk: *low risk*, *medium risk* and *high risk*.

RISc's internal consistency is adequate to good for most sections with alpha coefficients ranging from .70 for Section 8 (*drug misuse*) to .88 for Section 4 (*education, work and training*) (Van der Knaap, Leenarts and Nijssen, 2007). The internal consistency for Sections 6 (*relationships with partner, family and relatives*) and 9 (*alcohol misuse*) is less satisfactory, however, with an alpha coefficient of .61 for Section 6 and .65 for Section 9. RISc's overall score shows satisfactory internal consistency: alpha = .79. Inter-rater reliability is moderate to substantial for RISc's sections and overall score. The assessment of criminogenic needs and risk of reconviction thus appears to be relatively free of rater influences. In other words, probation officers independently reached more or less the same conclusions on the presence of criminogenic needs and on the risk of recidivism when rating the same offender (Van der Knaap, Leenarts and Nijssen, 2007). Validity for RISc's prediction of any new court case, as assessed by AUC, is equal to or exceeds similar instruments (Van der Knaap et al., 2012).

Furthermore, with an AUC of .70 RISc's predictive validity can be considered satisfactory. When recidivism is defined as any new court case for an offence that is liable to punishment with a prison sentence of at least four years, RISc's predictive validity increased slightly (AUC = .72), as is the case when defining recidivism as any new court case for an offence that is liable to punishment with a prison sentence of at least eight years (AUC = .73) (Van der Knaap and Alberda, 2009).

Changes in the Impact of Risk and Protective Factors during Adolescence and Young Adulthood

The development and implementation of reliable and valid assessment instruments in the Netherlands is still ongoing. The LIJ, the instrument for assessing juveniles (aged 12–18), was in a pilot phase in 2010 and 2011. It is therefore difficult at this time to draw any conclusions on the instrument's ability to predict which juvenile offenders will become adult offenders. Nevertheless, some interesting data are already available to examine the link between risk and needs assessment outcomes for different age groups.

We examined whether recidivism rates at different ages fit with the generally acknowledged age–crime curve. This curve describes declining rates of offending as youth grow older: criminal offending onset peaks between ages 8 to 14, prevalence peaks between ages 15–19, and desistance peaks between ages 20 and 29 (Farrington, 2003). Secondly, we are interested to learn whether the contribution or impact of different risk and protective factors changes over the years. For example, the influence of family factors on the risk of recidivism can be expected to decrease as juveniles grow older, and at the same time the influence of peers, attitude, and skills can be expected to increase. The literature suggests that starting work, being in a stable relationship and having appropriate living conditions become more important during adolescence and early adulthood.

To investigate these issues, we used Dutch data of risk assessment of juveniles and young adults from ages 12–30. There are some limitations to these data, which should be considered first:

- The assessment of risk factors for juveniles and young adults has been done with different instruments: the Dutch version of the WSJC*PA* (Washington State Juvenile Court *Pre-screen* Assessment) and the RISc. Although there is some overlap in the risk domains, the items and factors are not the same.
- For juveniles aged 12 through 17, not all the dynamic risk factors could be assessed because only the scores on a limited number of items were available for risk factors regarding behaviour, school, family and friends (no data were available for risk factors regarding attitudes and skills).

Nevertheless, we can present some interesting findings. As we shall show, changing recidivism rates and differences in dynamic risk factors reflect the age–crime curve.

Sample 1: Juveniles Aged 12–17

Van der Put et al. (2010) examined to what extent risk factors for recidivism changed between ages 12 and 17. Data were collected by council researchers using the BARO questionnaire (Basisraadsonderzoek). The BARO documents whether the committed offence signals underlying disorders or problems in the youngster's circumstances and advises judicial authorities what penalty to impose. The BARO contains questions about functioning in a number of areas including family, leisure activities, school, friends, external factors, development, case history, physical condition, behaviour, emotions, and substance abuse.

The information of the BARO reports of 1,396 juveniles aged 12–18 suspected of having committed an offence was used to score the items of the social section of the WSJC*PA*. The inter-rater reliability was high; the kappas showed a minimum of .85. The criminal section scores were based on information retrieved from the Research and Policy database Judicial Documentation (OBJD) of the Research and Documentation Centre of the Ministry of Justice (WODC). Of the 1,396 juveniles, 82 per cent are male: 41 per cent are native Dutch, 10 per cent Surinamese, seven per cent Turkish, six per cent Antillean, 22 per cent Moroccan and 14 per cent other. Recidivism is defined here as the reoccurrence of judicial contact(s) within two years. In order to measure recidivism, again data from the OBJD were used.

Recidivism Scores for Juveniles

The recidivism rate was 41 per cent for the juveniles who were aged 12–13 at the time the BARO was used (*n*=104); 54 per cent for juveniles aged 14–15 (*n*=284); and 48 per cent for juveniles aged 16–17 *n*=295). This means that the course of the relationship between recidivism and age (the age–recidivism curve) broadly concurs with the course of the age–crime curve: recidivism peaked for juveniles aged 14–15. National figures confirm that, of all juveniles with a criminal case

Table 6.2 Two-year recidivism for each age group

	2-year recidivism		
	N	N	%
Age 12–13	255	104	40.8
Age 14–15	527	284	53.9
Age 16–17	614	295	48.0

settled in 2003, recidivism was highest among adolescents aged 14 (Wartna and Tollenaar, 2006). Table 6.2 shows the two-year recidivism for each age group.

The accuracy of the prediction of recidivism on the basis of static and dynamic risk factors has been examined by means of Chaid analyses. Three separate prediction models were set up for the three different age groups: one model based on static risk factors, another one for dynamic risk factors (as far as available), and a third model in which the scores of the first two are combined. Separate

Table 6.3 Accuracy of prediction of recidivism; the area under the curve (AUC) per age group for prediction with static, dynamic, and both static and dynamic risk factors

	Age 12–13 (n=255)	*95% CI**	Age 14–15 (n=527)	*95% CI*	Age 16–17 (n=614)	*95% CI*
Static risk factors	.73	*.67 – .80*	.74	*.70 – .78*	.70	*.66 – .74*
Dynamic risk factors	.72	*.66 – .78*	.59	*.54 – .64*	.59	*.55 – .64*
Static and dynamic risk factors	.80	*.74 – .85*	.76	*.72 – .80*	.71	*.67 – .75*

Note: The Confidence Interval (CI) indicates the reliability of an estimate.

construction and validation survey samples were used when these models were constructed. Table 6.3 shows the AUC values for the three models.

Recidivism in each age group can be predicted rather well: the AUC value of the total was larger than .70 in each age group. Static risk factors measured at ages 14–15 and ages 16–17 also predicted recidivism well. Dynamic risk factors only when measured at ages 12–13 contributed significantly to an improvement in the prediction. No significant differences were found between age groups in the AUC values of the prediction models with only static risk factors. However, the AUC values of the prediction models that are based on only dynamic risk factors were significantly different when measured at different ages: the AUC value for ages 12–13 was significantly higher than the AUC values for ages 14–15 and ages 16–17. The AUC values of the models including both static and dynamic risk factors showed a significant decrease with age: recidivism could be predicted *very well* (AUC=.80) for the age group 12–13, *quite well* (AUC=.76) for the age group 14–15, and *acceptable* (AUC=.71) for the age group 16–17.

The prevalence of criminal history risk factors increased with age during adolescence: the older the juveniles, the more they had judicial contacts, the more they had committed violent offences or offences against property, and the more they had been ordered by the court to engage in community service (diversion programmes) or had been detained.

Van der Put et al. (2010) also found that the magnitude of the correlation between static risk factors and recidivism increased with age. Gender was not a significant predictor of recidivism for ages 12–13, but in middle- and late adolescence boys have a higher risk of recidivism than girls. The correlation between gender and recidivism was particularly high at ages 14–15; in fact, it is the most important predictor in this age group. Likewise, the type of the index offence is predictive only at a later stage: adolescents aged 16–18 who have committed a non-violent property offence ran a higher risk of recidivism, whereas the adolescents from this age group who committed a sexual offence reoffended relatively infrequently. Criminal history was predictive of recidivism in all age groups and, here also, the correlations increase with age (Van der Put et al., 2009).

Sample 2: Young Adults Aged 18–29

Data on young adults were gathered from a database containing all RISc assessments that had been conducted between November 2004 and September 2007 (Van der Knaap and Alberda, 2009). This database contained 36,345 unique records of completed RISc assessments. As a single offender can have several RISc assessments, and because we wished to avoid any dependency in the data, we chose to select the oldest RISc assessment for any offender who had been assessed more than once. After this selection 34,756 records relating to unique offenders remained. Information on their criminal history until 1 July 2008 was collected in official records of criminal cases using OBJD. By further limiting the analyses to all offenders who had been 'at risk' at least two years after the RISc assessment, the sample was reduced to 16,239 offenders. In doing so we corrected for any time spent in prison. Next, we identified three age groups: (1) a group aged 18 through 21 (N = 2,856); (2) a group aged 22 through 25 (N = 2,113); and (3) a group aged 26 through 29 (N = 1,591).[1] Of these offenders, 91 per cent were male and 58.4 per cent were native Dutch; 37.5 per cent had a non-Western cultural background; and 2.5 per cent had a Western cultural background (information on cultural background was missing for another 2.5 per cent of the sample). Recidivism was assessed using the same definitions and data collection method as for juveniles.

Recidivism Scores for Young Adults

Table 6.4 shows that the two-year recidivism rates for young adults decreased with increasing age: almost half of the youngest age group had at least one new court case within two years, whereas the two oldest groups showed a recidivism rate of approximately 40 per cent. Differences between the youngest age group and both other age groups were statistically significant (18–21 vs 22–25: $\chi^2(1)$ =

1 The remainder of the sample was either aged 30 or older (N = 9,727) or younger than 18 (N = 42).

Table 6.4 Two-year recidivism for young adults

	2-year recidivism		
	N	N	%
Age 18–21	2856	1391	48.7
Age 22–25	2113	881	41.7
Age 26–29	1591	616	38.7

23.96, p = .00, Cramer's V = .07; 18–21 vs 26–29: $\chi^2(1) = 41.44$, p = .00, Cramer's V = .10), but the two oldest age groups did not differ significantly ($\chi^2(1) = 3.45$, p = .07, Cramer's V = .03). Compared to older offenders, recidivism rates were higher for each of the young adult groups: 28.8 per cent of the offenders aged 30 or older recidivated within two years after the RISc assessment (comparing all age groups yields $\chi^2(3) = 452.02$, p = .00, Cramer's V=.17).

Predicting two-year recidivism based on RISc's overall scores proved to be more accurate as offenders became older (see Table 6.5). Compared to RISc's predictive validity as reported by Van der Knaap and Alberda (2009) for a sample of over 13,000 offenders aged 18 and older (AUC .70), AUC values were smaller for all age groups, whereas an ROC analysis for offenders aged 30 or older yields an AUC value of .72 (95% CI = .70–.73). Also, RISc's predictive validity for young adults fell short of meeting the criterion of .70 for satisfactory

Table 6.5 Accuracy of prediction of two-year re-offence with the RISc; the area under the curve (AUC) per age group for prediction with RISc overall scores (static and dynamic risk factors)

	AUC	*95% CI*
Age 18–21	.66	*.64–.68*
Age 22–25	.68	*.66–.71*
Age 26–29	.69	*.66–.72*

validity in every age group, although the 95 per cent confidence intervals for the two oldest groups include .70.

Recidivism and the Age–crime Curve

When we consider the data of the Dutch version of the WSCJ*PA* and the RISc together, a picture of the age–crime curve emerges (see Figure 6.1). This age–crime curve, however, does not depict the prevalence of criminal behaviour, but rather shows recidivism rates (a recidivism curve is not necessarily the same as an age–

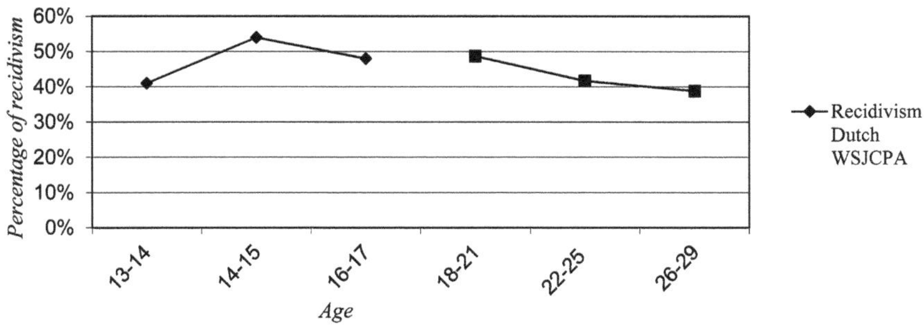

Figure 6.1 Recidivism in adolescence and young adulthood

crime curve). Nevertheless, the preceding results on recidivism are in line with the age–crime curve, although the peak in the recidivism rate is somewhat earlier and the decrease after adolescence is less impressive than researchers have found in data about the prevalence of delinquency.

Criminogenic Risk Factors for Juveniles

The pre-screen of the WSJCA (WSJC*P*A) is primarily an instrument to assess the risk of recidivism. Nevertheless some items also assess criminogenic needs because they seem to be of additional value compared to prediction based on static risk factors. Although the Dutch version of the WSJ*P*CA does not include all the relevant factors for assessing criminogenic needs, the results show some interesting trends. Table 6.6 and Figure 6.2 present the prevalence and impact of dynamic risk factors for different age groups up to age 18. The first three columns in Table 6.6 represent the percentage of juveniles for whom each particular risk factor was present. The last three columns show the correlations between risk factors and recidivism at different ages (impact).

Table 6.6 shows significant age differences in the prevalence of dynamic risk factors regarding friends, substance abuse, family (total), running away from home, and parental rule enforcement. The occurrence of all these problems is relatively low at ages 12–13. Problems with friends, family, and parental authority occurred more frequently at ages 14–15, whereas running away from home was most common between ages 16 and 18. On average, the fewest number of risk factors occurred between ages 12 and 13. More of the risk factors at those ages were predictive for future recidivism than at later ages. Thus, while in the older age groups dynamic risk factors occurred more often, they had a lower predictive power.

In summary, the impact of dynamic risk factors (as shown in correlations) decreased as adolescents became older. The 12–13 age group showed by far the highest number of risk factors that were significantly correlated with recidivism, and the correlations were considerably higher compared to those of the other age groups. On the other hand, the groups aged 14–15 and 16–17 did not differ greatly, but here

Table 6.6 Percentage of prevalence of dynamic risk factors and the correlation of these risk factors with recidivism, split up according to age group

	Prevalence (%)				Correlation with recidivism (r)					
Risk factors	**Age 12–13 (n=255)**	**Age 14–15 (n=527)**	**Age 16–17 (n=614)**		**Age 12–13 (n=255)**		**Age 14–15 (n=527)**		**Age 16–17 (n=614)**	
Problems related to										
School	49	55	53		.17	**	.11	**	.08	**
Friends	20	33	31	***	.21	***	.11	**	.10	***
Use of free time	31	35	32		.32	***	.09	**	.08	**
Mental health	20	22	24		.04		.05		.03	
Substance abuse	2	9	14	***	.00		.07		.02	
Family (total)	51	58	55	***	.28	***	.11	***	.04	
- Out-of-home placement	6	7	9		.11	*	-.01		.03	
- Runaway from home	5	8	10	**	.03		.13	**	.05	
- Victim of neglect	7	6	8		.10		.00		-.01	
- Victim of abuse	18	18	16		.26	***	-.01		-.01	
- Sibling with judicial contact	21	20	16		.15	**	.00		.01	

- Parent(s) with judicial contact	9	8	10		.22	***	-.04	.07
- Parent(s) in detention	3	2	2		.13	**	-.01	.07
- Substance abuse by parent(s)	9	6	6		.06		.07	-.01
- Parental rule enforcement	33	41	33	***	.14	**	.04	.06
Average number of risk factors home situation	1.9	2.0	2.0					
Average number of risk factors total	3.3	3.7	3.7	***				

Note: * P < .10, ** P < .05, *** P <.01.

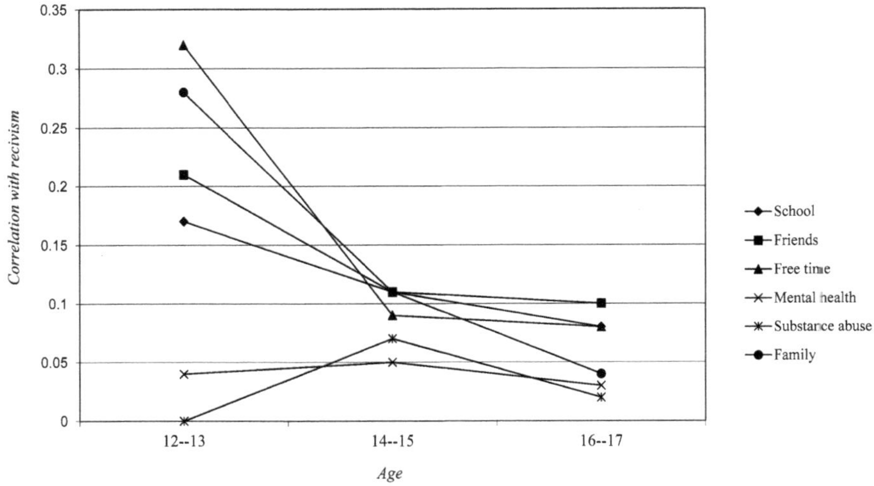

Figure 6.2 Correlation between criminogenic factors and recidivism in different ages during adolescence

Table 6.7 Correlations between RISc sections and two-year recidivism[a]

	Age 18–21			Age 22–25			Age 26–29		
	N	r		N	r		N	r	
1&2 Offending history and current offence	2,444	.24	**	1,812	.31	**	1,316	.27	**
3 Accommodation	2,301	.15	**	1,663	.20	**	1,239	.19	**
4 Education, work and training	2,856	.17	**	2,111	.20	**	1,588	.23	**
5 Financial management and income	2,850	.18	**	2,108	.17	**	1,589	.20	**
6 Relationships with partner, family and relatives	2,855	.08	**	2,111	.12	**	1,591	.12	**
7 Relationship with friends and acquaintances	2,847	.21	**	2,106	.18	**	1,585	.22	**
8 Drug misuse	2,851	.14	**	2,113	.16	**	1,591	.21	**
9 Alcohol misuse	2,844	.08	**	2,109	.12	**	1,586	.19	**
10 Emotional well-being	2,853	.05	*	2,111	.04		1,589	.08	**
11 Thinking and behaviour	2,850	.19	**	2,109	.22	**	1,588	.20	**
12 Attitudes/Orientation	2,833	.22	**	2,094	.22	**	1,574	.15	**
Overall RISc score	2,434	.27	**	1,803	.31	**	1,311	.31	**

Note: * $p < .01$ ** $p < .001$. [a] Sample size differs within age groups for each section due to missing values.

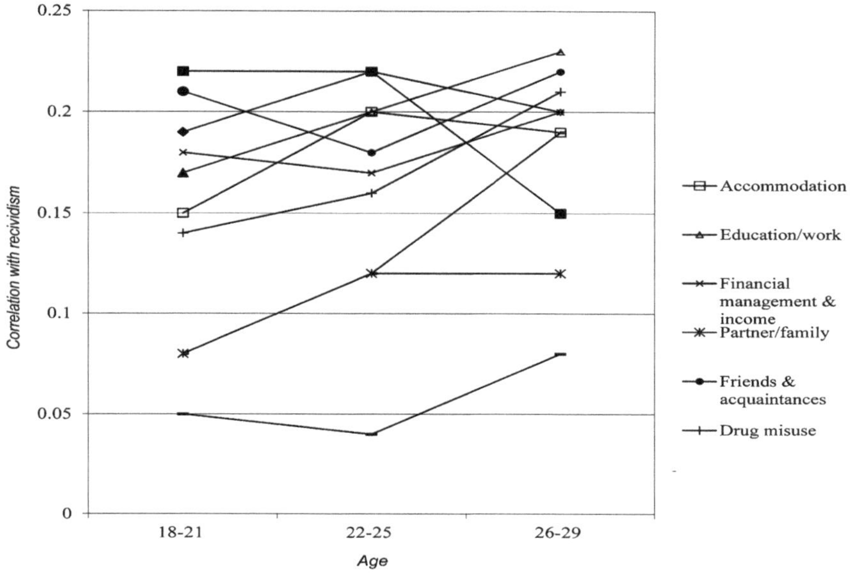

Figure 6.3 Correlation between criminogenic factors and recidivism in different ages in young adulthood

also the number of significant variables and their correlations were higher for the 14 –15 age group compared to the 16–17 age group.

Criminogenic Risk Factors for Young Adults

RISc section scores and the RISc overall scores indicate that each of the criminogenic needs was related to recidivism (see Table 6.7 and Figure 6.3). In every age group the correlations between almost all RISc sections and recidivism were statistically significant, albeit small. In general, correlations were smaller for ages 18–21 as compared to the two older age groups (ages 22–25, and 26–29). Few RISc sections, however, showed a consistent trend with regard to the strength of the relationship with recidivism. Notable exceptions were the sections relating to education and work, drug misuse, and alcohol misuse. With increasing age these criminogenic needs indicated a stronger relationship with recidivism. A significant difference between the youngest and the oldest age groups was observed regarding alcohol misuse ($p = .00$). The other correlations did not differ significantly between age groups, but showed some trends. For example, the difference in correlations for alcohol misuse in ages 22–25 and 26–29 constitutes a trend ($p = .09$). Another trend was found in the correlation of drug misuse and recidivism for the youngest and the oldest age group ($p = .07$).

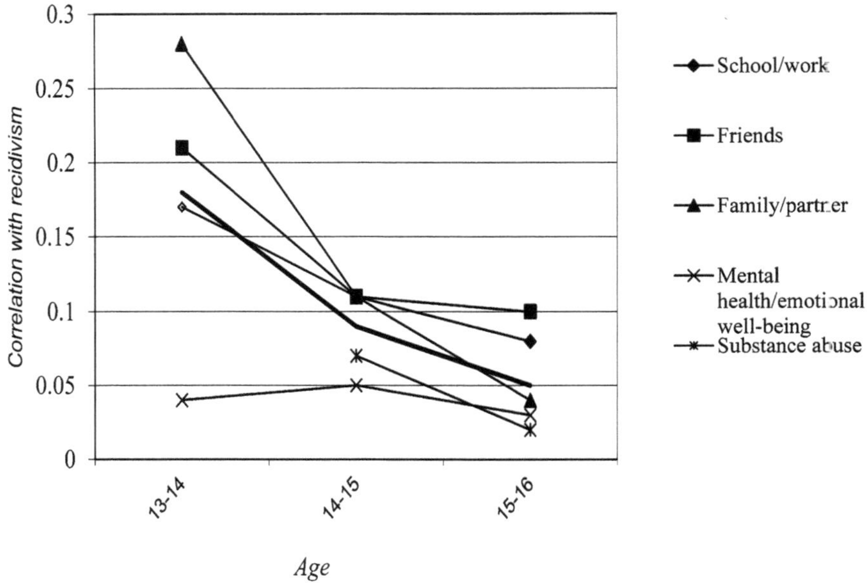

Figure 6.4a Correlation between recidivism and criminogenic factors in adolescence (WSJCPA Dutch)

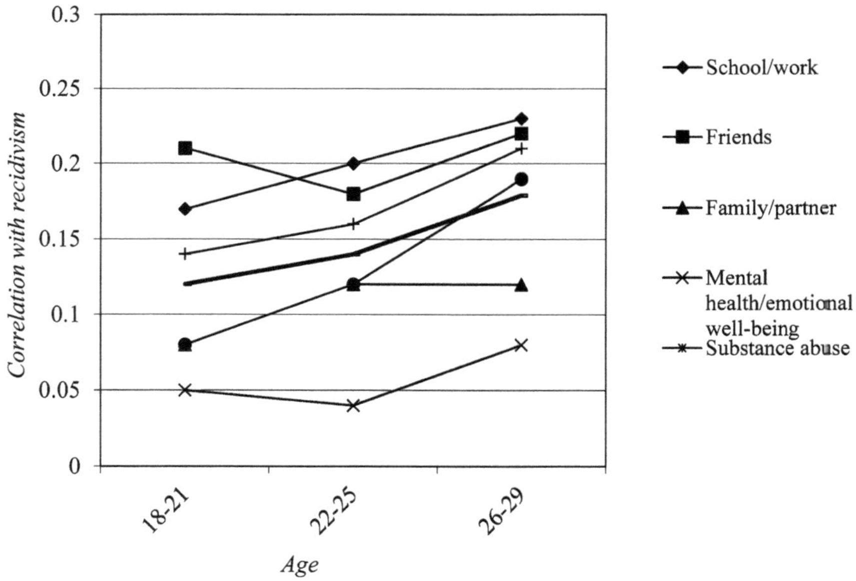

Figure 6.4b Correlation between recidivism and criminogenic factors in young adulthood (RISc)

Criminogenic Needs and Age

When we combine the available information on criminogenic factors, we see an image comparable to an 'age–risk curve': it appeared that criminogenic factors had less impact as young adolescents grew older, but gained slightly more impact during early adulthood (see Figure 6.4). At age 18, we see that the impact of dynamic risk factors as estimated with the RISc was higher than as estimated with the Dutch version of the WSCJ*P*A at age 17. This can be explained by the difference in age or difference in definition of the risk factor in question. Another possible explanation is that the assessment of dynamic factors by the Dutch version of the WSCJ*P*A (limited number of items regarding dynamic factors) was not comprehensive.

During adolescence the influence of all the dynamic factors that were assessed (measures of individual factors such as social and cognitive skills, attitude and self-control were not available) seemed to decrease. The correlations between, on the one hand, family factors, performance and behaviour in school, anti- or prosocial friends, and free-time activity, and on the other hand, recidivism, decreased as adolescents get older. The data on assessment of young adults showed that each of the criminogenic needs was related to recidivism. In general, correlations were a little lower for the youngest age group (18–21) as compared to the two older age groups (22–25 and 26–29). On average, the correlation between dynamic risk factors and recidivism increased in young adulthood, but only the impact of alcohol misuse showed a significant increase. Other criminogenic needs did not show significantly different correlations between age groups.

Conclusions and Discussion

Developing instruments for risk and needs assessment is a considerable challenge. Construction of reliable and valid instruments takes time and concerted effort. Prosecutors, courts, probation officers, and trainers and therapists of interventions need reliable and valid information about the risk of recidivism and how the predicted outcome can be influenced: what supervision and interventions, if any, are needed to prevent recidivism? Therefore both static and dynamic factors are important. To know the risk of general recidivism, a score based on at least static factors is needed. Scores on dynamic factors are needed in order to know which risk factors should be 'tackled' and what kind of protective factors can be used or activated to protect a young person against the influence of risk factors.

In this chapter we presented findings from two Dutch assessment instruments used with delinquents aged 12–30 to examine the impact of static and dynamic factors at different ages. As mentioned, different developmental stages require different risk assessment instruments for adolescents and for young adults. We would like, of course, to be able to confidently predict which young delinquents will continue their offending behaviour into adulthood. However, because most research assessing the predictive validity of assessment instruments has limited follow-up, this is not yet possible. Instead, we compared the results for different age groups assessed with different risk assessment instruments. Although the data presented in this chapter are cohort data instead of longitudinal data, some interesting preliminary conclusions can be drawn.

We examined the recidivism rates at different ages and found evidence for a *recidivism curve*. This curve has the same shape as the age–crime curve, although the peak may be somewhat earlier and the decrease somewhat slower. The accuracy of the prediction of recidivism was somewhat better when the recidivism rate was lower: when juveniles grow older the accuracy of the prediction of recidivism appears to decrease; on the other hand when young adults grow older, the accuracy appears to increase.

Using static risk factors is generally considered an efficient method of predicting outcomes because of the ease of their measurement and the assumed greater measurement reliability that can be obtained when using historical records. This is supported by the data presented in this chapter; only for the 12–13 age group is the prediction of recidivism based on both static and dynamic factors significantly more accurate than the prediction based only on static or dynamic factors.

The data on young adults show that the prediction of the likelihood of recidivism improved as the prevalence of recidivism decreased. Since RISc's assessment of risk of recidivism cannot be split into a static and a dynamic model, these results do not inform us about the relative importance of static versus dynamic risk factors. It can be argued, however, that if the group of offenders decreases, the group will contain relatively more (life-course) persistent offenders (Moffitt, 1993). But even for the life-course persistent offenders in their 20s, dynamic factors can be critical: Roisman, Aguilar and Egeland (2004) showed that positive work and romantic involvement between ages 21 and 23 were significantly associated with fewer externalizing problems for 'early-onset/persistent' offenders. In addition, the data in this chapter suggest that in early adulthood some dynamic factors become more important.

The accuracy of prediction of recidivism based on dynamic factors is also a matter of the quality of the instrument and of the professional who uses the instrument. The validation results of YASI-assessments of 3,249 youth in New York State by probation officers demonstrate that juvenile probation officers when using a semi-structured interview are capable of validly measuring dynamic factors (Orbis Partners, 2007). The predictive accuracy statistics obtained for the dynamic scores was found to slightly exceed the level of predictability associated with the pre-screen measures that combine both static and dynamic risk factors. In the Dutch version of the WSJC*PA* we could not use data gathered with an appropriate semi-structured interview. Future research should give better insights.

When we combined the available data about dynamic factors of adolescents and young adults we found evidence for a second curve: the *dynamic risk curve*. This curve seems to have the opposite shape as the age–crime curve of the prevalence of delinquency and the recidivism curve. During late adolescence dynamic factors appear to become less predictive for recidivism, but during early adulthood the impact of dynamic factors appear to become higher. The decreasing importance of some dynamic risk factors and increasing importance of static risk factors (especially earlier crimes) in adolescence has been found in other research (see for example, Van der Laan et al., 2009a). The declining influence of dynamic risk factors on recidivism in late adolescence illustrates the importance of early intervention. In early adolescence the correlations between dynamic risk factors and recidivism are high. Thus, relatively more success in preventing recidivism can be expected by focusing on these factors.

The measurement of dynamic risk factors with the Dutch version of the WSJC*P*A was neither exhaustive nor fully reliable. Data gathered with another instrument (the BARO) were used to fill the Dutch version of the WSJC*P*A; for some factors, no data were available. Attitude and, especially, skills are not easy to measure – in the pre-screen these factors were not present at all. Furthermore, the so-called 'dose–response' relation between risk factors and outcomes was not measured either ('dose–response' implies a cumulative effect with the higher the number of risk factors, the higher the risk of recidivism: see Van der Laan and Blom, 2006; Loeber, Slot and Stouthamer-Loeber, 2006).

Protective factors should also be taken into account: some risk factors can be buffered by protective factors. This 'balance-model' of risk and protective factors is part of the full-risk screening of the LIJ; unfortunately the protective factors were not present in the available data on juveniles.

Further validation research is needed to find out the relative importance of static and dynamic factors and risk and protective factors at different ages for boys/men and girls/women. What are predictors for recidivism in early and late adolescence and early adulthood? Further research should investigate the impact of dynamic risk and protective factors, broader than the ones discussed above, that link to recidivism at different ages. Such research should find ways to measure individual factors, since a review by Loeber, Slot and Stouthamer-Loeber (2008) shows that individual risk factors tend to increase throughout late childhood to early adulthood. Examples are: poor social skills, cognitive distortions, low capability to reason morally, positive attitude towards antisocial behaviour, impulsive behaviour, lack of remorse, and attention problems (Loeber, Slot and Stouthamer-Loeber, 2008; Deković and Asscher, 2008). It is also necessary to examine whether (some of) these variables improve the capability of assessment instruments to predict recidivism as juveniles grow older. Knowledge of the most important dynamic predictors of recidivism for ages 16–17 especially is needed in order to develop adequate interventions for this age group. It is possible that the influence of individual factors like attitude and skills increases as youth progress through adolescence.

There is also room for the improvement of risk assessment instruments. In general, risk assessment instruments give an overall risk score but generally do not differentiate between general and specific forms of recidivism. This surely is one of the directions in which assessment instruments can be developed further. In predicting recidivism it would be useful to have more specific information about what kind of crime(s) are likely to be committed, their severity and frequency, and how soon.

A second recommendation concerns the kind of factors used in prediction. The full risk assessment of the LIJ takes into account all factors: static and dynamic, risk and protective. The RISc uses static and dynamic risk factors for risk and needs assessment. The RISc may benefit from rethinking its exclusive use of risk factors. Only some dynamic factors known to influence recidivism are covered in its current assessment of risk factors.

Our final recommendation is to differentially weigh items and answer possibilities for different age groups and for boys and girls (Van der Put et al., 2011a, 2011b). Because our studies in this chapter and other studies cited in our literature review show that the impact of static and dynamic factors on recidivism may vary by age and gender, it is particularly important that the criminal justice system uses risk assessment instruments with a predictive validity that is sufficient for different age groups and for males and females.

References

Adviesbureau Van Montfoort and Reclassering Nederland (2004). *RISc versie 1.0. Recidive Inschattings Schalen. Handleiding*. Harderwijk: Flevodruk.

Andrews, D.A. (1982). *The Level of Dupervision Inventory (LSI): The First Follow-up*. Ontario, CN: Ministry of Correctional Services.

Andrews, D.A. and Bonta, J. (1994). *The Psychology of Criminal Conduct*. Cincinnati, OH: Anderson.

Andrews, D.A., Bonta, J., and Wormith, J.S. (2004). *Level of Service/Case Management Inventory: An Offender Assessment System*. Toronto, ON: Multi-Health Systems, Inc.

Andrews, D.A., Bonta, J.L., and Wormith, J.S. (2006). The recent past and near future of risk and/or need assessment. *Crime & Delinquency*, 52, 7–27.

Baglivio, M. (2007). *The Prediction of Risk to Recidivate Among a Juvenile Offending Population*. Gainesville, FL: University of Florida: Department of Criminology, Law and Society.

Barnoski, R. (2004a). *Assessing Risk for Re-offense: Validating the Washington State Juvenile Court Assessment*. Olympia, WA: Washington State Institute for Public Policy, 2004.

Barnoski, R. (2004b). *Washington State Juvenile Court Assessment Manual, Version 2.1*. Olympia, WA: Washington State Institute for Public Policy.

Barnoski, R. and Drake, E. (2007). *Washington's Offender Accountability Act: Department of Corrections' Static Risk Instrument* (Document No. 07-03-1201). Olympia, WA: Washington State Institute for Public Policy.

Bonta, J. (1996). Risk-needs: Assessment and treatment. In A.T. Harland (ed.), *Choosing Correctional Options That Work: Defining the Demand and Evaluating the Supply*. Thousand Oaks, CA: Sage Publications, pp. 18–32.

Borum, R., Bartel, P., and Forht, A. (2002). *SAVRY. Manual for the Structured Assessment of Violence Risk in Youth*. Tampa, FL: University of South Florida.

Brennan, T., Dieterich, W., and Ehret, B. (2009). Evaluating the predictive validity of the COMPAS risk and needs assessment system. *Criminal Justice and Behavior*, 36, 21–40.

Deković, M. and Asscher, J.J. (2008). *Interventies voor jongeren die antisociaal gedrag vertonen: Kenmerken, werkzame mechanismen en moderatoren van effectiviteit*. The Hague: WODC.

Dolan, M. and Doyle, M. (2000). Violence risk prediction: clinical and actuarial measures and the role of the Psychopathy Checklist. *British Journal of Psychiatry*, 177, 303–11.

Doreleijers, Th.A.H., Bijl, B., Van der Veldt, M.C. and Van Loosbroek, E. (1999). *BARO. Standaardisatie en Protocollering Basisonderzoek strafzaken Raad voor de Kinderbescherming*. Amsterdam: VU/NIZW.

Farrington, D.P. (2003). Developmental and life-course criminology: Key theoretical and empirical issues – the 2002 Sutherland Award Address. *Criminology*, 41, 221–56.

Goodman, R. (1997). The Strengths and Difficulties Questionnaire: A research note. *Journal of Child Psychology and Psychiatry*, 38, 581–6.

Grisso, T. and Barnum, R. (2006). MAYSI-2. Massachusetts Youth Screening Instrument: User's manual & technical report. Sarasota, FL: Professional Resource Press.

Hoge, R.D. and Andrews, D.A. (2001). The youth level of service/case management inventory (YLS/CMI): Intake manual and item scoring key. Ottawa, ON: Carleton University Press.

Hoge, R.D., Vincent, G.M., and Guy, L.S. (2012). The prediction and risk and need assessment. In R. Loeber and D.P. Farrington (eds), *From Juvenile Delinquency to Adult Crime: Criminal Careers, Justice Policy and Prevention*. New York: Oxford University Press.

Howard, P., Clark, D., and Garnham, N. (2003). *Evaluation and Validation of the Offender Assessment System (OASys)*. UK: OASys Central Research Unit. Report to HM Prison Service and National Probations Service.

Lipsey, M.W. and Derzon, J.H. (1998). Predictors of violent or serious delinquency in adolescence and early adulthood: A synthesis of longitudinal research. In R. Loeber and D.P. Farrington (eds), S*erious & Violent Juvenile Offenders: Risk Factors and Successful Interventions*. Thousand Oaks, CA: Sage Publications.

Lodewijks, H.P.B. (2008). *Violence Risk Assessment in Adolescents in the Dutch Juvenile Justice System: Studies on the Reliability and Predictive Accuracy of the SAVRY*. Amsterdam: Vrije University.

Lodewijks, H.P.B., Doreleijers, Th., De Ruiter, C., and De Wit-Grouls, H. (2003). *Savry. Handleiding voor de gestructureerde risicotaxatie van gewelddadig gedrag bij jongeren (geautoriseerde vertaling SAVRY)*. Eefde: Rentray.

Loeber, R. and Stouthamer-Loeber, M. (1987). Prediction. In H.C. Quay (ed.), *Handbook of Juvenile Delinquency*. New York: John Wiley, pp. 325–82.

Loeber, R., Slot, W., and Stouthamer-Loeber, M. (2006). A three-dimensional, cumulative developmental model of serious delinquency. In P-O.H. Wikström and R.J. Sampson (eds), *The Explanation of Crime: Context, Mechanisms and Development*. Cambridge: Cambridge University Press, pp. 153–94.

Loeber, R., Slot, W., and Stouthamer-Loeber, M. (2008). A cumulative developmental model of risk and promotive factors. In R. Loeber, H.M. Koot, N.W. Slot, P.H. van der Laan, and M. Hoeve (eds), *Tomorrow's Criminals: The Development of Child Delinquency and Effective Interventions*. Farnham: Ashgate, pp. 133–61.

Moffitt, T.E. (1993). Adolescence-limited and life-course-persistent antisocial behavior: A developmental taxonomy. *Psychological Review*, 100, 674–701.

Orbis Partners (2007). *Long-term Validation of the Youth Assessment and Screening Instrument (YASI) in New York State Juvenile Probation*. New York: New York State Division of Probation and Correctional Alternatives.

Roisman, G.I., Aguilar, B., and Egeland, B. (2004). Antisocial behavior in the transition to adulthood: The independent and interactive roles of developmental history and emerging developmental tasks. *Development and Psychopathology*, 16, 857–71.

Schwalbe, C.S. (2007). Risk assessment for juvenile justice: A meta-analysis. *Law and Human Behavior*, 31, 449–62.

Shapiro, D.E. (1999). The interpretation of diagnostics tests. *Statistical Methods in Medical Research*, 8, 113–34.

Spaander, M. (2003). *Handleiding baro*. Utrecht: Raad voor de Kinderbescherming.

Spanjaard, H., Polak, S., Persoon, A., Vinkenveugel, M., Vogelvang, B., and Sondeijker, F. (2009). *Handleiding Landelijk Instrumentarium Jeugdstrafrechtketen (versie 1.2)*. Amsterdam and Woerden: PI Research/Adviesbureau van Montfoort.

Stouthamer-Loeber, M., Loeber, R., Stallings, R., and Lacourse, E. (2008). Desistance from and persistence in offending. In R. Loeber, D.P. Farrington, M. Stouthamer-Loeber and H.R. White (eds), *Violence and Serious Theft: Development and Prediction from Childhood to Adulthood*. New York: Routledge, pp. 269–306.

Stouthamer-Loeber, M., Loeber, R., Wei, E., Farrington, D.P., and Wikström, P-O. (2002). Risk and promotive effects in the explanation of persistent serious delinquency in boys. *Journal of Consulting and Clinical Psychology*, 70, 11–23.

Thornberry, T.P. and Krohn, M.D. (2003). Taking stock of delinquency: An overview of findings from contemporary longitudinal studies. New York: Kluwer Academic/Plenum.

Van der Knaap, L.M. and Alberda, D.L. (2009). *De predictieve validiteit van de Recidive Inschattingsschalen (RISc)*. The Hague: WODC.

Van der Knaap, L.M., Leenarts, L.E.W., and Nijssen, L.T.J. (2007). *Psychometrische kwaliteiten van de Recidive Inschattingsschalen (RISc). Interbeoordelaarsbetrouwbaarheid, interne consistentie en congruente validiteit*. The Hague: WODC.

Van der Knaap, L.M., Leenarts, L.E.W., Born, M.P., and Oosterveld, P. (2012). Reevaluating interrater reliability in offender risk assessment. *Crime & Delinquency*, 58(1), 147–63.

Van der Laan, A.M., and Blom, M. (2006). *Jeugddelinquentie: Risico's en Bescherming*. The Hague: Boom Juridische Uitgevers/WODC.

Van der Laan, A.M., Van der Schans, C.A., Bogaerts, S., and Doreleijers, Th.A.H. (2009a). *Criminogene en beschermende factoren bij jongeren die een basisraadsonderzoek ondergaan. Een verkennende inventarisatie van de mate van zorg en van risico- en beschermende factoren gesignaleerd door raadsonderzoekers*. Meppel: Boom Juridische Uitgevers.

Van der Laan, A.M., Veenstra, R., Bogaerts, S., Verhulst, F.C., and Ormel, J. (2009b). Serious, minor and non-delinquents in early adolescence: The impact of cumulative risk and promotive factors. The TRAILS study. *Journal of Abnormal Child Psychology*, 38, 339–51.

Van der Put, C.E., Stams, G.J.J.M., Van der Laan, P.H., and Oort, F.J. (2009). *WSJCPA-NL 2009. De Nederlandse versie van de Washington State Juvenile Court Prescreen Assessment*. Amsterdam: University of Amsterdam.

Van der Put, C., Spanjaard, H., Van Domburgh, L., Doreleijers, Th., Lodewijks, H., Ferwerda, H., and Stams, G.J. (2010). *Ontwikkeling van het Landelijk Instrumentarium Jeugdstrafrecht* (LIJ). *Kind & Adolescent Praktijk*, 2, 28–35.

Van der Put, C.E., Deković, M., Hoeve, M., Stams, G.J.J.M., Van der Laan, P.H., and Langewouters, F. (2011a). Risk assessment of girls: Are there any sex differences in risk factors for re-offending and in risk profiles? *Crime & Delinquency*. Advance online publication. DOI: 10.1177/0011128710384776.

Van der Put, C.E., Stams, G.J.J.M., Hoeve, M., Deković, M., Spanjaard, H.J.M., Van der Laan, P.H., and Barnoski, R.P. (2011b). Changes in the relative importance of dynamic risk factors for recidivism during adolescence. *International Journal of Offender Therapy*, 20, 1–21. Published online 21 February 2011, at http://ijo.sagepub.com/content/early/2011/02/18/030662 4X11398462, accessed 27 February 2012.

Wartna, B.S.J. and Tollenaar, N. (2006). *Recidive 1997–2003. Ontwikkelingen in het niveau van de strafrechtelijke recidive van jeugdige en volwassen daders*. Tabellenboek. The Hague: WODC.

Wartna, B.S.J., Tollenaar, N., and Blom, M. (2005). *Recidive 1997. Een cijfermatig overzicht van de strafrechtelijke recidive van volwassen en jeugdige daders*. The Hague: WODC.

Chapter 7

Juveniles in Transition from Juvenile Justice to Adult Criminal Justice

Ton Liefaard

From a legal perspective, a child becomes an adult overnight. According to Dutch law, this happens when he[1] turns 18, the Dutch age of majority. A child's eighteenth birthday marks an important moment: from then on he is entitled to vote and to stand in elections; he is considered to have full legal capacity; and he no longer falls under parental custody. In addition, he is considered to be fully accountable under criminal law. In other words, childhood ends at age 18. Setting age limits, such as the age of majority, is significant in terms of legal certainty and equality. There are several other legal age limits: for example, criminal responsibility begins at age 12 and civil liability starts at age 14.

However, the transition from childhood to adulthood is, *de facto*, a gradual process and is different for each human being. Even though the existence of a sharp dividing line between the juvenile justice and criminal justice system based on age can be justified on legal arguments, it is important not to lose sight of the fact that it can cause a number of questions and challenges with both theoretical (legal) and practical implications. For example, what is to be done with a boy aged 17 who commits a serious crime? And what if this boy can be regarded as more mature than his brother aged 19, with whom he committed the offence?

The main objective of this chapter is to review a human rights-based system that facilitates a responsible and effective judicial response to both juveniles and young adults who are in conflict with the law that serves both the individual's and society's interests. The chapter analyses the upper age limit of the Dutch juvenile justice system and its exceptions in light of historical development and in light of International Human Rights Law. As part of the historical analysis, particular attention will be given to the question of to what extent is felt a need to establish a separate justice system for adolescents between ages 16 and 24. In the analysis of the international legal framework, special attention will be paid to the question of where childhood ends and adulthood commences and what this implies for the treatment of young adults under the justice system. Subsequently, this chapter clarifies the legal and practical implications of the relevant legal provisions concerning the prosecution and sentencing of both juveniles and young adults. It also addresses the challenges in practice, particularly regarding the enforcement of

1 If not stated otherwise, 'he' refers to 'she' as well.

custodial sentences (non-custodial sentences will not be addressed in detail; see for example, Lamet et al., 2010 on young adults and probation services). Finally, the chapter concludes with some observations concerning the treatment of juveniles and young adults in conflict with the law and the resultant challenges confronting both the law and practice of juvenile justice and criminal justice.

Assessment of the Upper Age Limit for Juveniles

The Netherlands was one of the first countries to have a separate criminal law and law of criminal procedure for juveniles (Weijers and Liefaard, 2007; Weijers, 2008; Junger-Tas, 2004). In 1905 three Child Acts entered into Dutch law: the civil law Child Act, the penal law Child Act, and the Child (Framework) Act. All three acts were based on the then revolutionary presumption that intervention in the family should be possible in order to serve the interests of the child and, ultimately, the interests of society as a whole (Weijers and Liefaard, 2007).

The penal law Child Act introduced specific sections in the Criminal Code and the Code of Criminal Procedure, with separate juvenile sanctions and criminal justice proceedings for juveniles. Although the juvenile sanctions have changed in the course of time, the special procedural rules are still applicable today (Weijers and Liefaard, 2007; Doek et al., 2009). These include: the hearing of juvenile cases behind closed doors (*in camera*); the requirement that the child must appear in court and that parents have to be invited to attend the court trial; the requirement that information has to be gathered about the child's personality and personal circumstances; and that each child is entitled to a court-appointed lawyer.

The Children (Framework) Act concerned the enforcement of the measures and sanctions aimed at the protection and correctional education of juveniles, which resulted in separate juvenile penal facilities. The position of the juvenile judge was introduced in 1922, modelled after the Cook County, Illinois, example of the Juvenile Court (Bac, 1998; see also Tanenhaus, 2004; Rosenheim et al., 2002).

Until that time, youth delinquency was considered to be caused by the child's environment and upbringing (Weijers, 2008). The child's own personality and responsibility were not considered relevant. The penal law Child Act was based on the assumption that the court's decision should not be guided by the offence or by the child's guilt or responsibility, but instead by the child's future. As a consequence, retribution was regarded inadequate and the principle of proportionality did not play a role. In addition, the minimum age for criminal responsibility (lower age limit), which had been set at ten years with the introduction of the Criminal Code in 1886, was dropped and stress was placed on the great trust invested in authorities responsible for youth offenders. Classic elements of criminal justice, such as guilt, retribution and proportionality, would regain attention in the second half of the twentieth century, along with others instigated by an increased attention to the personality of the young offender and to the rights of juveniles subject to criminal justice proceedings.

The 1965 revision of laws affecting the juvenile justice system reflected to a certain extent new ideas regarding the causes of and solutions to juvenile delinquency and reintroduced the minimum age of criminal responsibility at 12 (Overwater-Committee, 1951; Bol, 1991). Other changes concerned the position of the juvenile judge as the key figure within the juvenile justice and child protection system, the role of the child care and protection board – which evolved to more of an advisory and supervisory role – and juvenile sanctions (for example, an additional custodial penal measure was introduced – placement in a specialized treatment centre (*plaatsing in een inrichting voor buitengewone behandeling*; *p.i.b.b.*) meant for children with limited development potential or a mental disorder).

The juvenile justice system remained oriented to the re-education of the delinquent child. Classical criminal justice principles had regained some attention but remained marginal. This changed under the influence of increased attention to the rights of individuals and led to the reconsideration of the legal foundation of the juvenile justice system. The recognition of the right of juveniles to a fair trial gained centre stage after the Supreme Court of the United States ruled in *Kent v. United States* (383 U.S. 541, 1966) and *In re Gault* (387 U.S. 1, 1967) that juveniles subject to juvenile justice proceedings must be awarded the same due process rights as adults. These included the right not to incriminate oneself, the right to cross-examine witnesses, and the right to be informed about the charges (Weijers, 2008; Trépanier, 1999). This case law and other rights developments have had a significant influence on many Western European juvenile justice systems, including the Dutch system.

In 1982 the Anneveldt Committee, established by the Dutch government in 1979 to review the juvenile justice system, concluded that juvenile criminal law had to be brought more in conformity with general criminal law. The notion of protection in the law of criminal procedure as applicable to juveniles was, in the view of the committee, the reason why ‘rights guaranteed to adults were denied to juveniles’ (Anneveldt-Committee, 1982, p. 12). At the same time the committee argued that, given the incomplete psychological and social development of minors, there should be a greater focus on socialization and reintegration in the treatment of juveniles than of adults. Consequently, the purposes of punishment (retribution and deterrence) should never be pushed so far that the juvenile’s development would be harmed by it. Special prevention (individual deterrence and re-education of the juvenile) should continue to be the first priority. Among other recommendations, the Anneveldt Committee proposed that juvenile criminal law should be governed by the same general legal rules and should enshrine the same legal safeguards as for adults. The committee stressed the need to take account of the ‘empirical fact’ that young people adopt more mature and independent attitudes at a younger age than they did 20 years earlier. In light of this assumption, the committee also recommended deletion of procedural provisions that were regarded as too paternalistic, such as the compulsory presence of the child and the closed court hearings.

The report of the Anneveldt Committee led to the 1995 revision of the Criminal Code and Code of Criminal Procedure. This revision resulted, as recommended, in a simplified and modernized juvenile justice system with more attention to diversion, alternative sanctions, and the due process rights of the juveniles involved. At the same time – and contrary to the recommendations of the Anneveldt Committee – the legislature found reason to double the maximum duration of the main custodial penalty (youth imprisonment) based on the same 'empirical fact' (that is, the assumption) that young people could be regarded as more mature and independent than before, with which should come increased criminal responsibility. In addition, it loosened the requirements for the application of adult penal law for youths aged 16 or 17 (see below).

Thus the legislature clearly adopted a more repressive approach, which actually characterizes many of the developments in the 1990s and the beginning of the twenty-first century (Weijers, 2008, pp. 28–9, with reference to Van der Laan, 2005). Interestingly enough, the recommendation to abolish the procedural provisions that were regarded as too paternalistic was rejected as well. Meanwhile, the improvement of the rights of juveniles continued and led, for example, to the introduction of the 2001 Youth Custodial Institutions Act (*Beginselenwet justitiële jeugdinrichtingen*), meant to improve the legal status of juveniles in youth institutions (Liefaard, 2008; Boendermaker and Uit Beijerse, 2008).

In these early years of the second decade of the twenty-first century, the repressive approach towards children in conflict with the law is far from gone. However, recent developments show that this approach is, at a minimum, being confronted with interesting alternatives. These developments include an increased attention to 'what works' and evidence-based programmes, together with the introduction of a new penal *non-custodial* measure enabling courts to tailor judicial intervention to the specific needs of the juvenile. In addition, under the recent juvenile justice system there is an actual reduction in the number of children in youth institutions (Liefaard, 2010).

Although classical criminal justice elements of guilt, accountability and proportionality have become relevant and confirm that juvenile justice is part of the criminal justice system, the notion that juvenile justice revolves around young persons who are not fully capable of understanding or influencing their behaviour and who are entitled to be treated in a way that takes into account their age and maturity remains recognizable. Juvenile justice interventions must still be pedagogically oriented and juvenile criminal proceedings still contain special features introduced in 1905. That is what makes juvenile justice essentially different from adult criminal justice (Overwater-Committee, 1951).

Youth and the Upper Age Limit of the Juvenile Justice System

The upper age limit of the juvenile justice system was set at age 18 when the penal Child Law was adopted in 1905. It has remained unchanged ever since, although for a long time it did not correspond to the age of majority (until

1988, age 21). In addition, since 1905 the Criminal Code has left room for the application of criminal penal law for adults to juveniles aged 16 or 17. Under the penal law Child Act this was entirely at the discretion of the court. After the 1965 law revision, however, the Criminal Code provided that two criteria had to be met: the application of adult penal law must be required with consideration for the 'seriousness of the offence' and the 'personality of the offender'. These requirements were deliberately formulated broadly and cumulatively. On the one hand, they would leave sufficient room for the courts to impose an adult sentence on juveniles aged 16 or 17. On the other, they would limit the application of this legal option to serious cases, and only if the juvenile's personality gave reason to do so (Overwater-Committee, 1951; Weijers, 2006).

Since the 1995 law revision, the court has been empowered to sentence a juvenile aged 16 or 17 as an adult if it finds reason to do so due to the seriousness of the offence, the personality of the offender, or the circumstances under which the offence was committed. Article 77b CrimCo, which is still applicable, has been formulated in such a way that any one of these grounds may apply. In addition, it contains another requirement that was introduced to enable the sentencing of a juvenile aged 16 or 17 if, for example, he committed an offence in consort with a young adult offender (Weijers, 2006; Uit Beijerse, 2009b).

The specific position of the young adult and/or the older juvenile in the juvenile criminal justice system has been addressed by the Wiarda and the Anneveldt committees. In 1971 the Wiarda Committee, established to review the child protection system, acknowledged that age limits in essence are arbitrary and that they reflect societal developments and perspectives. Still, it found reason to propose the lowering of the age of majority from 21 to 18 because of the assumed increase in independence of youth from, among others, parents. In general, the committee observed – particularly among older minors – a significantly increased desire to become more involved in all kinds of decisions that affected them (Wiarda Committee, 1971). The committee concluded that, given the fact that, for example, young adults aged 19 and 20 can actually act independently, these young adults should be granted full legal capacity at an earlier age than 21, and they should no longer be held under parental custody or guardianship. The lowering of the age of majority would mean that youth sentences would end at age 18, rather than at age 21, which could have significant consequences for the use of penal measures, such as treatment orders, and the option to impose an adult sentence. The committee also worried that it would no longer be possible to impose a juvenile sentence on a young adult aged 18 or older (although this legal option, introduced in 1965, was hardly used in practice, arguably due to the difficulty of adequately enforcing it). In light of this, the committee recommended creating a separate criminal justice system for young adults ages 18–23 or 25.

Eleven years later, the Anneveldt Committee concurred with the need for a separate justice system for adolescents, defined as young adults from ages 18–23 (Anneveldt-Committee, 1982). The committee stressed that the path towards adulthood is a gradual process and as a consequence there is a need for a transitional legal system that serves as a bridge between the juvenile justice system and the adult criminal justice system. In this regard, the committee paid particular attention to the fact that adolescents were responsible for a significant number of crimes committed and that this percentage was in fact increasing. The Anneveldt Committee argued that the line between juvenile and adult penal law should be drawn at the age at which juveniles are no longer predominantly influenced by the 'youth-subculture', at which point they tend to desist from delinquent behaviour, and they demarcated this at age 24 (Anneveldt-Committee, 1982, p. 17).

Another important question addressed by the committee was how such a separate adolescent criminal justice system should be regulated. The committee wanted to set certain age limits, but it also wanted to leave room for diversion by the court, stressing the need for a specialized and individualized approach in the enforcement of sentences. The recommendation was for one criminal justice system for juveniles aged 12–24. In addition, the courts should have room to impose higher sentences on juveniles older than 16 but younger than 24 who committed serious offences (a maximum of 12 months of imprisonment for ages 16–18 and a maximum of 18 months for ages 18–23). Furthermore, the courts should have the option, clearly as an exception, of sentencing this particular group of juveniles according to adult penal law if the serious offences in question were not caused by the juvenile's immaturity, or in the case of seriously derailed and recidivist juveniles. Unfortunately, the committee did not provide recommendations regarding the enforcement of custodial sentences for juveniles and young adults.

Despite these recommendations of the Anneveldt Committee, the legislature decided to reject them. The Minister of Justice agreed with the committee that young adults ages 18–24 form a specific group, but he regarded a separate justice system, with specific sanctions and separate facilities, as not being feasible. Instead, he elaborated on the fact that these young adults should be dealt with under adult criminal law. In addition, age differentiation within the adult penitentiary should be used in order to address the specific needs of this category of offenders. Juvenile justice should therefore apply to juveniles ages 12–18 only.[2] Where the Anneveldt Committee recommended actions to be taken at both the level of the legislature as well as the level of the competent enforcement authorities, the Minister of Justice primarily refers to the latter in order to address the specific circumstances of juveniles in the transition between adolescence and adulthood.

More recently, the Minister of Justice has reaffirmed this position and referred to the fact that the current juvenile justice and adult criminal justice system provides the courts with 'sufficient possibilities' to tailor the penal response to both juvenile and young adults; and that, moreover, the implementation/fulfilment of sentences leaves room for an individualized and tailored approach.[3] However,

2 *Parliamentary Documents II* 1989/90, 21 327, no. 3, pp. 5–6.

3 *Parliamentary Documents II* 2008/09, Appendix of Proceedings, no. 1211, pp. 2539–41.

as will be addressed later, it can be questioned to what extent age differentiation has really come to be taken into account.

International Human Rights Law for Juveniles and Young Adults in Conflict with the Law

Juvenile Criminal Justice: A Human Rights Issue

Criminal justice principles have been part of the human rights paradigm since the early stages of the development of International Human Rights Law after World War II. International (i.e., at the level of the United Nations [UN]) and regional human rights instruments contain specific provisions regarding the right to a fair trial (see, for example, art. XVIII of the 1948 American Declaration of the Rights and Duties of Man; art. 6 of the 1950 European Convention for the Protection of Human Rights and Fundamental Freedoms (ECHR); art. 14 of the 1966 International Covenant on Civil and Political Rights (ICCPR); and art. 8 of the 1969 American Convention on Human Rights (ACHR)), the principle of legality (see, for example, art. 7 ECHR and art. 15 ICCPR), and the treatment of detainees and prisoners (see, for example, arts 9 and 10 ICCPR; art. 5 ECHR).

During the 1970s and 1980s the position of the individual subject to criminal justice proceedings gained attention, among other reasons through the development of case law of the European Court on Human Rights and the adoption of conventions on specific human rights issues, such as the prohibition of torture and other forms of cruel, inhuman or degrading treatment or punishment, which had important implications for the treatment of detainees and prisoners (Rodley and Pollard, 2009).

The first specific recognition of the human rights of *juveniles* in conflict with the law dates from 1985, the year in which the UN General Assembly adopted the UN Standard Minimum Rules for the Administration of Juvenile Justice (the Beijing Rules).[4] Four years later, the 1989 UN Convention on the Rights of the Child (CRC) that contains legally binding provisions concerning the administration of juvenile justice (arts 40 and 37) was adopted. This meant that juvenile justice was internationally recognized as a human rights issue. In 1990 the UN General Assembly adopted the UN Rules for the Protection of Juveniles Deprived of Their Liberty (unofficially referred to as the Havana Rules)[5] and the UN Guidelines for the Prevention of Juvenile Delinquency (Riyadh Guidelines).[6] The CRC and the three UN resolutions just mentioned provide a comprehensive legal framework concerning the rights of juveniles subject to criminal justice proceedings and dispositions, including rules regarding the objectives of juvenile

4 Adopted by the UN General Assembly by Resolution 40/33 of 29 November 1985.
5 Adopted by the UN General Assembly by Resolution 45/113 of 14 December 1990.
6 Adopted by the UN General Assembly by Resolution 45/112 of 14 December 1990.

justice and strategies for prevention and diversion (i.e., diverting a juvenile away from the criminal justice system, for example, through 'out-of-court settlement').

The relevance of human rights for juvenile criminal justice revolves around the concept of fair trial and the treatment of accused, prosecuted and sentenced individuals with humanity and with respect for their inherent human dignity. Each individual subject of criminal justice proceedings and dispositions is entitled to lawful and non-arbitrary treatment with respect for his fundamental rights and freedom including, for example, his right to life (art. 6 ICCPR; art. 2 ECHR), liberty (art. 9 ICCPR; art. 5 ECHR), and physical integrity (art. 7 ICCPR; art. 3 ECHR). In this regard, International Human Rights Law does not distinguish between adults and children. Both 'shall be equal before the courts and tribunals' (art. 14 (1) ICCPR) and are entitled to the same rights and freedoms.

However, the CRC recognizes the position of the juvenile as an independent, developing human (art. 6 CRC) by providing him with special entitlements and safeguards. This approach of equality and special recognition implies that the transition from childhood to adulthood is relevant under International Human Rights Law. Before looking more closely at the dividing line between childhood and adulthood under international law, it is important to highlight the implications of International Human Rights Law for the justice system for adults and juveniles, respectively.

Criminal Justice under International Human Rights Law

Under International Human Rights Law, all persons accused of having committed a criminal offence are entitled to a fair trial, which first of all means that they are entitled to 'a fair and public hearing by a competent, independent and impartial tribunal established by law' (art. 14 (1) ICCPR; cf. art. 6 (1) ECHR). In addition, a person must be presumed innocent until proved guilty according to the law (art. 14 (2) ICCPR; art. 6 (2) ECHR) and has the right not to incriminate himself (*nemo tenetur* principle; art. 14 (3) (g) ICCPR), which, for example, has implications for police interrogations.

Furthermore, International Human Rights Law provides specific procedural rights that must be guaranteed to all persons without distinction of any kind (art. 2 ICCPR; art. 14 ECHR; see Nowak, 2005; Trechsel, 2005; Human Rights Committee, 2007). These procedural rights include that a person have:

- the right to be informed about the charges, promptly and in a language he understands (art. 14 (3) (a) ICCPR; art. 6 (3)(a) ECHR);
- the right to have adequate time and facilities for the preparation of his defence, including the right to have counsel or legal assistance of his choosing (art. 14 (3) (b) and (d) ICCPR; art. 6 (3) (b) and (c) ECHR);
- the right to a trial 'without undue delay' (art. 10 (3) ICCPR) or 'within a reasonable time' (art. 6 (1) ECHR);
- the right to examine or have examined witnesses *à charge* or *à décharge*

(equality of arms; right to adversarial proceedings; art. 14 (3)(e) ICCPR; art. 6 (3)(d) ECHR);

- the right to have the free assistance of an interpreter if he cannot understand or speak the language used in court proceedings (art. 14 (3)(f) ICCPR; art. 6 (3)(e) ECHR);
- the right to appeal (art. 14 (5) ICCPR; art. 2 Protocol 7 of the ECHR).

The principle of legality is another key principle for everyone subject to criminal justice proceedings, adults and children alike (art. 15 ICCPR; art. 7 ECHR). It means that retroactive justice is prohibited and that no one can be prosecuted or sentenced for acts that were not considered criminal acts by law at the time they were committed.

Furthermore, other human rights have implications for criminal justice proceedings as well. The right to privacy (art. 17 ICCPR; art. 8 ECHR) is, for example, of significance for the use of coercive measures and for the role of the mass media regarding criminal cases. In addition, the right to liberty of the person (art. 9 (1) ICCPR; art. 5 (1) ECHR) has implications for the use of dispositions leading to pre-trial detention and imprisonment.

International Human Rights Law contains various rules and principles regarding dispositions and the enforcement of sentences, of which the following should be mentioned. First, it prohibits torture and cruel, inhuman or degrading treatment or punishment (art. 7 ICCPR; cf. art. 3 ECHR and the UN Convention against Torture and its regional equivalents). Second, the use of capital punishment has been prohibited under Protocol No. 13 to the ECHR; although art. 6 ICCPR leaves room for the imposition of capital punishment, it merely prohibits the imposition of the death penalty for persons under age 18 and the carrying out of such a sentence on pregnant women (art. 6 (5) ICCPR). Third, both the ICCPR and ECHR provide requirements regarding the use of deprivation of liberty (i.e., imprisonment or pre-trial detention). Since imprisonment and pre-trial detention imply a limitation of a person's fundamental right to liberty (art. 9 (1) ICCPR; art. 5 (1) ECHR), International Human Rights Law provides for legal requirements and safeguards. States are not allowed to deprive an individual of his right to personal liberty unlawfully or arbitrarily and everyone who is arrested or detained has the right to challenge the legality of his detention before a competent judicial authority (art. 9 (4) ICCPR; art. 5 (4) ECHR). In addition, article 10 (1) ICCPR stipulates that each person deprived of his liberty must be treated with humanity and with respect for the inherent dignity of the human person. This implies in the first place that States parties refrain from ill treatment, such as torture and other forms of cruel, inhuman or degrading treatment or punishment. Moreover, it places States parties under the positive obligation to recognize the prisoner as a rights holder and to provide good prison conditions that enable him to enjoy his rights (Nowak, 2005). A number of international and regional standards (such as the UN Standard Minimum Rules for the Treatment of Prisoners, the European Prison Rules of the Council of Europe, and the European Committee for the Prevention of Torture (CPT) standards) give substance to this positive obligation and provide detailed rules in this regard. In addition, article 10 of the ICCPR contains particular requirements regarding the accommodation of different groups of prisoners (for example, children must be separated from adults and pre-trial detainees should be housed separately from convicted prisoners; art. 10 (2) and (3) ICCPR). Furthermore, it provides that the penitentiary system should ultimately foster the prisoner's 'reformation and social rehabilitation' (art. 10 (3) ICCPR).

Specific Characteristics of Juvenile Justice under International Human Rights Law: Administration of Juvenile Justice – Fair Trial

Founded on art. 14 (and 15) ICCPR and significantly influenced by the 1985 Beijing Rules, article 40 CRC contains specific standards for the administration of *juvenile justice* (Detrick, 1999). Above all, it stipulates that States parties must 'recognize the right of every child alleged as, accused of, or recognized as having infringed the penal law to be treated in a manner consistent with the promotion of the child's sense of dignity and worth, which reinforces the child's respect for human rights and fundamental freedoms of others and which takes into account the child's age and the desirability of promoting the child's reintegration and the child's assuming a constructive role in society' (para. 1). This should be the overall objective of the juvenile justice system and reflects its assumed pedagogical character. The juvenile justice system aims at responding to the (alleged) criminal act committed by the juvenile, who is considered to be less culpable than an adult on the one hand, and at providing him with guidance for the future on the other hand (CRC Committee, 2007; Doek 2008). In light of this, the proclaimed general principles of the CRC must be taken into account as well: the prohibition of non-discrimination (art. 2 CRC), the best interests of the child (art. 3 (1) CRC), the right to life and development (art. 6 CRC), and the right to be heard (art. 12 CRC).

In addition, article 40 CRC provides juveniles with the right to a fair trial. It contains the fair trial principles addressed earlier and adds a number of child-specific elements. For example, it contains the presumption of innocence (art. 40 (2)(b)(i) CRC) and stipulates that the child is entitled to have the criminal trial determined 'without delay by a competent, independent and impartial authority' (art. 40 (2)(b)(iii) CRC). However, by using the wording 'without delay' rather than 'without undue delay' (see art. 14 ICCPR) it assumes that juveniles are entitled to a more speedy trial (CRC Committee, 2007).

Furthermore, a juvenile must be 'informed promptly and directly of the charges against him or her' (i.e., 'as soon as possible'; CRC Committee, 2007, para. 47). If appropriate this must happen 'through his or her parents or legal guardians'. The parents can also be present during the court hearings. Article 40 CRC thus recognizes the special position of the juvenile's parents, which conforms to the general recognition of the juvenile's family and parents as primary caretakers under the CRC (arts. 18 and 5 CRC; see also arts. 3 (2) CRC).

A child is also entitled to legal or other appropriate assistance (art. 40 (2)(b)(iii) CRC) and his privacy must be 'fully respected at all stages of the proceedings' (art. 40 (2)(b)(vii) CRC; art. 16 CRC). According to the CRC Committee this stretches out over the disposition phase as well and *inter alia* implies that criminal records should not be used in adult proceedings regarding the same offender. Preferably, criminal records should be erased (for example, once the juvenile reaches age 18; CRC Committee, 2007; see also below). Above all, the full respect of privacy implies that a juvenile justice trial should 'as a rule' be held behind closed doors (*in camera*). Article 40 CRC provides in this regard a different approach for juveniles than in the general provisions; article 6 ECHR, for example, stipulates that everyone is entitled to a public hearing, unless the interests of juveniles requires a court session *in camera*. Article 4 CRC implies a closed court session as the point of departure in juvenile justice cases (CRC Committee, 2007; cf. CRC Committee, 2009b).

While bearing in mind the objectives of juvenile justice, the third paragraph of article 40 CRC furthers the creation of a separate and special juvenile justice system: 'the establishment of laws, procedures, authorities and institutions' should be promoted towards this aim. This has implications for the institutions in which juveniles are detained or imprisoned. These should be specifically designed for juveniles and meet their specific requirements, which includes appropriate and adequate staff (cf. rule 10.3 Beijing Rules). The same applies to the establishment of special laws and procedures. One particular aspect of a separate justice system for juveniles is the establishment of a minimum age of criminal responsibility (MACR). States parties must 'seek to promote' the establishment of a MACR, which serves as the minimum age for deprivation of liberty under the juvenile justice system. The CRC does not provide for a minimum age, but the CRC Committee has set age 12 as the absolute minimum age limit (CRC Committee, 2007).

The second specific aspect is the use of diversion, which is an important feature in order to avoid the negative impact of criminal justice proceedings and to enable a quick response to delinquent behaviour (art. 40 (3)(b) CRC; see also Van Bueren, 2006). In addition, paragraph 4 of article 40 provides that States parties have the positive obligation 'to ensure that children are dealt with in a manner appropriate to their wellbeing and proportionate to both their circumstances and the offence', which must be fostered by a 'variety of dispositions, such as care, guidance and supervision orders; counselling; probation; foster care; education and vocational training programmes and other alternatives to institutional care'. States parties must make available a variety of alternatives to institutional care, which is directly linked to the use of deprivation of liberty as a measure of last resort (art. 37 (b) CRC; see below). It is important to note that article 40 (4) CRC also underscores the significance of the principle of proportionality for juvenile justice dispositions.

Finally, in considering a disposition, article 37 (a) CRC should be taken into account as well. It prohibits torture or other forms of cruel, inhuman, and degrading treatment or punishment, which, for example, rules out corporal punishment (CRC Committee, 2006). In addition, it prohibits capital punishment (unconditionally) and life imprisonment without the possibility of release. Much can be said about this life imprisonment clause, which was the result of a political compromise and added in the final stages of the drafting process (Detrick, 1992; see also Van Zyl Smit, 2006). In essence, it has led to an inconsistency with article 37 (b) CRC, which stipulates that imprisonment may only be used as a measure of last resort and for the shortest appropriate period of time (see below) and also with the overall objectives of juvenile justice as enshrined in article 40 (1) CRC (CRC Committee, 2007; Liefaard, 2008).

Deprivation of Liberty

Article 37 CRC is primarily concerned with deprivation of liberty, including custodial sentences under criminal law. It recognizes the impact of deprivation of liberty on children, as well as the need for a child-specific human rights approach for children deprived of their liberty. To this end, article 37 CRC contains legal requirements regarding deprivation of liberty and provisions regarding the quality of treatment of children deprived of liberty and their (procedural and substantive) legal status.

Article 37 (b) CRC prohibits unlawful or arbitrary deprivation of liberty and introduces two additional requirements concerning *juveniles* by stipulating that 'the arrest, detention or imprisonment of a child ... shall be used only as a measure of last resort and for the shortest appropriate period of time'. States parties are under the obligation to use deprivation of liberty regarding juveniles with the utmost restraint and only after careful consideration: that is, based upon an individual assessment regarding the appropriateness and duration of the deprivation of liberty while giving due weight to the best interests of the child, including *inter alia* his age and maturity, and to family environment (Schabas, Sax and Alen, 2006). Among other prohibitions, this rules out minimum or mandatory sentences (Liefaard, 2008). Both child-specific requirements have no precedent in international treaty law (cf. rules 13, 17 and 19 Beijing Rules) and their introduction can be considered as 'among the most notable improvements and innovations which the [CRC] sets out' (Cantwell, 1992, pp. 28–29).

If a child is deprived of his liberty, he must be treated with 'humanity and respect for the inherent dignity of the human person, and in a manner which takes into account the needs of persons of his or her age'. This 'right to be treated with humanity', as stipulated by article 37 (c) CRC (and derived from art. 10 (1) ICCPR; Detrick, 1999), can be considered as the core article regarding the quality of treatment of children deprived of liberty. It embodies a positive obligation for States parties to ensure minimum guarantees for the humane treatment of detained children. In general, it implies that each child deprived of his liberty must be recognized as entitled to all rights under the CRC. At the same time the treatment of a juvenile must be child specific, which also implies that limitations of the enjoyment of the rights of the child must serve the objectives of the deprivation of liberty; in addition, decisions in this regard must be taken individually and the best interests of the child must be taken into account as a primary consideration (art. 3 (1) CRC; Liefaard, 2008). Article 37 (c) CRC stipulates that 'in particular, every child deprived of liberty shall be separated from adults unless it is considered in the child's best interests not to do so and shall have the right to maintain contact with his or her family through correspondence and visits, save in exceptional circumstances'. These elements are aspects of the 'right to be treated with humanity' and, therefore, relevant to the enforcement of custodial sentences. The minimum conditions of detention have been worked out in detail in the 1990 Havana Rules, which should be implemented and incorporated into domestic law (CRC Committee, 2007). In this regard, the 2008 European Rules for juvenile offenders subject to sanctions or measures of the Council of Europe (i.e., the European Havana Rules) should be mentioned as well.[7]

Finally, article 37 (d) CRC provides a number of procedural safeguards for juveniles who are threatened to be deprived of their liberty, such as prompt access to legal *and* other appropriate assistance. This right is not so much related to the criminal justice proceedings (cf. art. 40 (2)(b)(ii) and (iii) CRC as mentioned earlier), but to the status of the juvenile (i.e. deprived of his liberty).

Childhood and Adulthood under International Human Rights Law

Since International Human Rights Law has different implications for the treatment of juveniles ('children') in contrast to young adults, the distinction between these two groups matters from a legal point. It is worthwhile to look briefly at the dividing line(s) between childhood and adulthood under international law.

Both the ICCPR and the ECHR contain some references to juveniles, but they do not define childhood or minority. Under the ECHR, minority is a matter of national law (Bleichrodt, 2006), although the Committee of Ministers of the Council of Europe recommended in 1972 to set the age of majority at 18.[8] The Human Rights Committee under the ICCPR also refers to national law, but in addition has indicated that it 'should not be set unreasonably low' and that 'a States party cannot absolve itself from its obligations [under the ICCPR] regarding persons under the age of eighteen' (Human Rights Committee, 1989). In addition, it states that 'article 6, paragraph 5, suggests that all persons under the age of 18 should be treated as juveniles, at least in matters relating to criminal justice' (Human Rights Committee, 1992).

The CRC does provide for a definition of 'child', which determines 'childhood'. It considers children those 'below the age of eighteen years, unless under the law applicable to the child, majority is attained earlier' (art. 1 CRC). As far as the applicability of the CRC is concerned, this definition is decisive. Obviously, the upper age limit relevant for the applicability of the CRC and all related instruments

7 Rec. (2008) 11 on the European Rules for juvenile offenders subject to sanctions or measures.

8 Res. (72) 29E on the Lowering of the Age of Full Legal Capacity, 19 September 1972.

should be considered. This aims primarily at maximizing the protection of the CRC and making the group that ought to benefit from the rights of the CRC as large as possible (Detrick, 1999 with reference to Alston, 1992). At the same time, it could be seen as an instruction to States parties not to consider young adults as children anymore.

Although there is a clear divide between childhood and adulthood (at least under the CRC) that serves legal certainty, this age limit can be problematic within the context of the criminal justice system. The complicating factor concerns the question of which age is decisive in order to determine the applicability of the juvenile justice system. What is to be done if a child commits an offence at age 17, but the prosecution, conviction and execution of his sentence takes place after his eighteenth birthday? Or what is to be done if a child turns 18 during the enforcement of a custodial sentence? Does this mean that he has to be transferred at once to an adult facility? Assuming that he is currently in a youth facility, does article 37 (c) CRC imply that he can no longer be held there since adults must be separated from children?

There are several points in time in the justice system at which a juvenile's age can be assessed: the point at which the child commits the (alleged) offence, the point at which the child is being prosecuted, the point at which the child is being convicted and sentenced, and the point at which the sentence is being enforced.

It is safe to assume that article 40 CRC is applicable to those juveniles considered to be a child while committing the alleged offence, based on what could be referred to as the 'crime date criterion' (Liefaard, 2008). While the article does not explicitly provide for this criterion, it is directly related to the justification of a separate juvenile justice system based on the assumption that children are less culpable than adults (see among others CRC Committee, 2007). This implies that, even if the child turns 18 during prosecution, he remains entitled to be treated in accordance with article 40 CRC. He therefore also remains entitled to treatment in accordance with article 37 (a) CRC, which *inter alia* provides that 'neither capital punishment nor life imprisonment without the possibility of release shall be imposed for offences committed by persons below 18 years of age'. The requirements concerning deprivation of liberty remain applicable as well. This means in the first place that both children and young adults who turn 18 during trial are entitled to imprisonment or detention that is lawful under article 37 (b) CRC, which includes that imprisonment or detention may only be used as a measure of last resort and for the shortest appropriate period of time. Secondly, this implies that young adults are entitled to be placed in a youth facility or that they can stay there. According to the CRC Committee, 'This rule does not mean that a child placed in a facility for children has to be moved to a facility for adults immediately after he/she turns 18. Continuation of his/her stay in the facility for children should be possible if that is in her/his best interest and not contrary to the best interests of the younger children in the facility' (CRC Committee, 2007, para. 86). In other words, the best interests of younger children should be paramount. This implies that young adults should be transferred if their presence in the child detention centre or child prison is deemed to negatively affect the interests of the other children. In order to avoid transfers, separate units for young adults could be created. This ought to be favoured anyway in recognition of the differences between children according to age, maturity, and vulnerability to violence.

If the approach that young adults who were children when they committed alleged offences and are tried accordingly should not be detained or imprisoned together with children at all is adopted, it means that they should be placed in facilities for adults. This may also be undesirable, but could be made less so by establishing special facilities for young adults (for example, for adults between ages 18 and 24).

In addition to the recommendations of the CRC Committee, the Committee of Ministers of the Council of Europe recommended in 2003 that, 'reflecting the extended transition to adulthood, it should be possible for young adults under the age of 21 to be treated in a way comparable to juveniles and to be subject to the same interventions, when the judge is of the opinion that they are not as mature and responsible for their actions as full adults'.[9] In 2008, the Council of Europe took the concern for young adults further by recommending in the European Rules for juvenile offenders that 'young adult offenders may, where appropriate, be regarded as juveniles and dealt with accordingly' (rule 19). In addition, the Council recommends that 'juveniles shall not be held in institutions for adults, but in institutions specially designed for them', although it leaves room for exceptional circumstances in which a juvenile has to be held in an institution for adults. In such an event, 'they shall be accommodated separately unless in individual cases where it is in their best interest not to do so' (rule 59.1). Furthermore, it recommends that 'juveniles who reach the age of majority and young adults dealt with as if they were juveniles shall normally be held in institutions for juvenile offenders or in specialized institutions for young adults unless their social reintegration can be better effected in an institution for adults' (rule 59.3).

It is interesting that the Council calls upon States parties to pay particular attention to the special position of older juveniles and young adults in order to avoid transitions taking place in a rigid manner. In addition, in the European Prison Rules meant for adult facilities, the Council recommends that young adults be kept separately from older prisoners (rules 18.8 and 18.9).

Related issues concern the practice of transfer or waiver of juveniles (generally ages 16 or 17) to adult criminal courts, and the practice of sentencing them as adults, with subsequent confinement in adult facilities. This can only be defended if prompted by the interests of the child (see art. 37 (c) CRC). Application of such mandatory or discretionary waivers or transfers for other (often retributive) reasons violates article 37 (c) CRC and the prohibition of discrimination (according to the CRC Committee, 2007). In light of this, it is interesting to note that the CRC Committee appreciates 'that some States parties allow for the application of the

9 Rec(2003)20 concerning new ways of dealing with juvenile delinquency and the role of juvenile justice, 24 September 2003, para. 11.

rules and regulation of juvenile justice to persons aged 18 and older, usually till the age of 21, either as a general rule of by way of exception' (CRC Committee, 2007, para. 38).

A question that remains to be answered is to what extent should the actual age of the individual, regarded as a child under the CRC or not, be taken into account. The actual age, for example, is relevant to the question of whether the child's parents or legal guardian should still be involved, since from a legal perspective a young adult no longer falls under parental custody or guardianship. Furthermore, the actual age can be relevant in order to determine the appropriate response to the delinquent behaviour of the juvenile, who may have become a young adult in the meantime. In addition, the actual age is relevant to differentiate between young people within a custodial institution and to tailor the regime and, more importantly, the individual programme in order to achieve the objectives of the (juvenile) criminal justice intervention that, with regard to former children, may not be merely repressive. Young adults who were children when they committed an offence remain entitled to a constructive response to their delinquent behaviour and to treatment, as stipulated by article 40 CRC. Unfortunately, International Human Rights Law provides little further guidance regarding the conditions necessary to realize these objectives for young adults. In light of this, the hard and fast division can be very problematic, since the transition from childhood to adulthood takes place gradually and not necessarily along arbitrary age limits.

Juvenile Justice and Criminal Justice: Key Issues Concerning Juveniles in Transition

Scope and Applicability of the Juvenile Justice System

This section describes the relevant key issues concerning juveniles in transition from childhood to adulthood who are subject to criminal justice proceedings in the Netherlands. As mentioned earlier, the Dutch juvenile justice system is applicable to juveniles between ages 12 and 18 (art. 486 Code of Criminal Procedure [CCP] and art. 77a CrimCo). The age of 18 corresponds with the age of majority. A young person at that specific age will no longer be regarded as a minor under civil law (art. 1:233 of the Civil Code). Likewise under criminal law, he is considered to be fully capable of understanding the consequences of his behaviour and as a consequence he is assumed to be fully accountable for his actions. In other words, the upper age limit draws a sharp distinction between individuals who can or cannot (yet) be held fully accountable for their criminal behaviour. It is important to make two remarks at the outset. The first concerns the question of which specific age norm applies to the juvenile justice system. Currently, the Dutch juvenile justice system is based on the 'crime-date criterion', which, as explained earlier, implies that the age at which the juvenile commits the offence is decisive for the applicability of the juvenile justice system.

The second remark concerns the fact that the relevant juvenile justice provisions refer to the juvenile as ‘the one who, at the time he committed the offence, has not yet reached the age of eighteen’ (art. 77a CrimCo; art. 488 (2) CCP). The legal provisions do not refer to the juvenile as a ‘minor’. This is related to the fact that under Dutch law a juvenile can attain majority at an earlier age than 18 (art. 1:233 Civil Code). For example, a juvenile of age 16 or 17 can be declared of full age by a juvenile judge (*meerderjarigverklaring*) in order to establish custody over a newborn child (art. 1:253ha Civil Code). In addition, a girl aged 16 or 17 who is pregnant can receive special permission to marry the father if he is older than 18 (art. 1:31 (2) Civil Code). This marriage implies that the girl attains majority once the marriage is official (Doek et al., 2009). Given the absence of a reference to minority, the law does not prevent young people who attain majority before they turn 18 from being prosecuted and tried under the juvenile justice system.

Juvenile Criminal Law: Special Provisions as Part of Criminal Law

The Dutch juvenile justice system is regulated by special sections in the general Code of Criminal Procedure (art. 486 ff CCP) and Criminal Code (art. 77a ff CrimCo). As clarified earlier, juvenile justice requires a special, pedagogical approach, without disregarding the right of the juvenile to a fair trial (art. 40 CRC). In light of this, it is important to note that the special sections regarding juveniles in the CCP and the Criminal Code provide exceptions to provisions that are applicable to adults on the one hand, and special provisions applicable to juveniles on the other. This underlines the presumption that juvenile justice is criminal justice – a significant point of departure. It implies that general criminal law principles are equally applicable to adults and juveniles, such as the principle of legality (art. 1 CrimCo; art. 1 CCP), the principle of equality, the presumption of innocence, and the principle of proportionality. In addition, the prosecution in both juvenile and criminal justice is regulated by the CCP, which includes rules regarding coercive measures, such as search and seizure, arrest, police custody and pre-trial detention. Substantive criminal law is primarily regulated by the Criminal Code, which, *inter alia*, means that the same descriptions of offences (*delictsomschrijvingen*) apply to adults and juveniles alike. However, as far as sentencing is concerned, special juvenile justice provisions in the Criminal Code provide a specific set of juvenile sentences. In general, the differences between the juvenile justice system and the adult criminal justice system concern various aspects of both criminal procedure as well as the penal system.

Juvenile Justice Proceedings under the Code of Criminal Procedure

If a juvenile is brought before a court, the court must consist of one specialized juvenile judge or of three professional judges, one of whom is a juvenile judge (art. 495 CCP). The trial will be held behind closed doors unless the court orders a public hearing. This can only be done if the interests of a public hearing outweigh the interests of the protection of the privacy of the juvenile, his co-accused, or his parents or legal guardian (art. 495b CCP). Under the adult criminal justice system the trial will be held in public. Only in specific cases can the court decide to close the doors of the courtroom (art. 269 CCP). In both juvenile and adult cases the court's decision is always delivered in a public court session (art. 121 Dutch Constitution).

Unlike an adult, a juvenile is compelled to be present during his trial (art. 495a CCP) and, since 1 January 2011, his parents or legal guardian have to be present as well (art. 496 CCP; previously they were merely invited to be present; cf. De Jonge and Weijers, 2008). If the juvenile is not present, the court – in principle – postpones the court hearing and issues a warrant to bring the juvenile before the court. The parents have the right to bring forward anything that can contribute to the defence of their child. It is important to note that the participation of parents or legal guardian is provided for as long as a juvenile is a minor (art. 488 (3) CCP). This is one of the few references to the minority of juveniles and since it refers to the actual age of the young person, it is one of the few exceptions to the 'crime-date criterion'.

Another key feature of the juvenile justice system concerns the right to a court-appointed lawyer for every juvenile prosecuted before the district court (art. 489 CCP). In addition, the Netherlands Supreme Court (*Hoge Raad*) recently ruled that a juvenile is entitled to have a lawyer present during initial police interrogations (The Netherlands Supreme Court, 30 June 2009, LJN: BH3079; BH3081; BH3084).

Throughout the criminal procedure (before and during the trial) there is specific regard for the juvenile's personal circumstances. Here the Child Care and Protection Board (*Raad voor de Kinderbescherming*) has a special position and role. As soon as a juvenile is in police custody the Board must be informed in order to provide 'early assistance' (*vroeghulp*) to the juvenile: that is, the Board makes a first assessment, which results in information that the public prosecutor must take into account, if he is considering pre-trial detention (art. 491 CCP). In general, the public prosecutor is compelled to consult the Child Care and Protection Board for additional information on the personal circumstances of the child (art. 494 CCP). The Board can also advise the public prosecutor of its own accord. During the court hearing, the court specifically addresses the personal circumstances of the child and takes these into account when considering the appropriate response to the child's alleged delinquent behaviour. Personal circumstances play a bigger role in juvenile cases than in adult cases.

Another significant juvenile criminal law provision affects pre-trial detention. While pre-trial detention of juveniles is regulated by the same provisions as for adults (in particular arts. 67 and 67a CCP), article 493 CCP contains a few significant special provisions for juveniles. The court (i.e., a special chamber of the court or an examining juvenile judge) has the option to suspend pre-trial detention for adults under special conditions (art. 80 CCP), but where a juvenile is concerned the court is compelled to consider suspension of the pre-trial detention. This provision is particularly important for the requirement that pre-trial detention is used only as a measure of last resort and for the shortest appropriate period of time (art. 37 (b) CRC; see earlier). This instruction to the court also implies that it should clarify why it does not suspend the pre-trial detention, although arguably this hardly happens in practice. It is assumed that in a significant number of juvenile cases the court suspends pre-trial detention immediately or after a few weeks (Bartels, 2007; Berger and Van der Kroon, 2011).

The court can suspend pre-trial detention of juveniles under a number of special conditions, such as intensive probation, youth care, a training order (max. 120 hours), a restraining order, or an order to compensate damages (art. 2 of the Decree Measures meant to influence juveniles' behaviour [hereinafter: Decree *Gedragsbeïnvloeding jeugdigen*]). The pre-trial phase could thus be used to respond relatively quickly to the juvenile's delinquent behaviour. It is, however, vitally important that the juvenile's entitlement to be treated in accordance with the presumption of innocence is respected (see for example, Imkamp, 2006; Uit Beijerse, 2009a). The law stipulates that the juvenile must consent to the suspension under special conditions. In practice, it may be assumed that the juvenile will easily agree, since it prevents him from being detained. This places courts under a special obligation to carefully consider the need for pre-trial detention as well as the arguments for its suspension.

The court can order the enforcement of pre-trial detention of juveniles at any place the court finds suitable that, for example, can include the juvenile's home (art. 493 (3) CCP). Although pre-trial detention of juveniles is generally enforced in a youth institution, this provision can be regarded as significant.

A special form of pre-trial detention called 'night detention' (art. 493 (3) CCP) has also been introduced. In this approach, a juvenile is detained in a youth institution, but during the day he is allowed to attend school, work as an intern or have a job. This form of pre-trial detention has been practised for a number of years, but has not yet been adopted throughout the country (Bos et al., 2006; Bos and Mehciz 2001). Night detention only applies to juveniles and can be regarded as an interesting formula for limiting the negative effects of pre-trial detention (see also Van der Laan et al., 2008).

Current juvenile justice provisions do not affect the maximum duration of police custody and pre-trial detention. As a consequence a juvenile can, like any adult, be held in police custody for three to six days and subsequently in detention for 14 days, followed by a court-ordered period of 90 consecutive days of detention, without judicial review in the interim. Only if the juvenile did not have a hearing can the court order pre-trial detention for a maximum of 30 days. This is the only exception applicable to juveniles (art. 493 (4) CCP).

The terms regarding police custody and pre-trial detention do not meet the recommendations of the CRC Committee, which refers to a periodic judicial review of preferably every two weeks (CRC Committee, 2007; see also Council for the Administration of Criminal Justice and Youth Protection 2011a). Recent research seems to indicate that courts are reluctant to order a juvenile's pre-trial detention for 90 consecutive days (Buruma and Van Toor, 2010). Still, pre-trial detention does not appear to be used as a measure of last resort, particularly in comparison to other Western European countries (Van der Laan, 2006; Van Kalmthout, Knapen and Morgenstern, 2010), which has been criticized by the CRC Committee (CRC Committee, 2009a).

The question as to what extent the Dutch juvenile justice system, so far as criminal procedures are concerned, really represents a child-specific approach is justified. In particular, the regulations regarding pre-trial detention and its duration lack a clear child-specific and rights-based orientation. Nevertheless, a number of special provisions – many preserved from 1905 – can indeed serve the objectives of the juvenile justice system as a whole and highlight a child-rights orientation. Finally, it is important to again stress that all juveniles under age 18 at the time they committed the alleged offence are entitled to be treated within the context of juvenile justice procedures, even if they turn 18 during the pre-trial phase. Those who were already age 18 or older face regular criminal justice proceedings.

Juvenile Justice under the Criminal Code

The special section of the Criminal Code (art. 77a ff CrimCo) that applies to juveniles primarily regulates specific dispositions for juveniles (see art. 77h CrimCo and also Doek et al., 2009). The regular criminal justice sentences, such as imprisonment (potentially for life or for a maximum period of 30 years), do not apply.

Before addressing the principal sentencing guidelines for juveniles, it is important to stress that diversion (by the police and the public prosecutions office) and alternative sentences are key features of the Dutch juvenile justice system. The vast majority of juvenile justice cases are diverted (arts. 77e and 77f CrimCo). In addition, the majority of dispositions by the juvenile court result in a non-custodial sentence, such as community service or a suspended custodial sentence (see also Van der Laan et al., Chapter 8, this volume).

According to article 77h CrimCo there are three principal penalties (*hoofdstraffen*) available to the sentencing judge: youth imprisonment (*jeugddetentie*), community service orders and/or training orders (maximum duration of 240 hours), or fines.

Youth imprisonment can be imposed for felonies (i.e., not for misdemeanours) and the maximum duration is dependent upon the age of the juvenile at the time of the offence. If the juvenile was between ages 12 and 15, the maximum duration is 12 months; if he was aged 16 or 17, the maximum sentence is 24 months (art. 77i CrimCo). Youth imprisonment is the only custodial penalty applicable to juveniles. It replaces the penalty of imprisonment that could have been imposed if the juvenile were aged 18 or older. For example, if an adult is convicted for theft, he can be sentenced to a maximum of four years imprisonment (art. 310 CrimCo), while a juvenile aged 16 can be sentenced to a maximum youth imprisonment of

24 months. Youth imprisonment – in principle – is enforced in a youth institution, and regular imprisonment in a prison.

The court can decide to suspend (part of) the youth imprisonment (art. 77x CrimCo). According to article 3 of the Decree *Gedragsbeïnvloeding jeugdigen*, the court can attach all kinds of special conditions to a suspended youth imprisonment, similar to the conditions regarding suspended pre-trial detention. If the juvenile fails to meet one or more of the conditions, he can be committed to a youth institution. If he turned 18, the custodial sentence can be enforced in an adult facility as if it were an adult sentence (art. 77dd CrimCo).

Juveniles can also be sentenced to a community service order and/or training order. These sentences are similar to the community sentences for adults. However, there are also several differences. First, the programmes for juveniles are different, particularly where training programmes are concerned (see Child Care and Protection Board 2011 and Reclassering Nederland, Leger des Heils and Verslavingsreclassering, 2010). Second, the terms for juveniles are shorter (i.e., max. 240 hours rather than max. 480 hours) and, third, the competent enforcing authorities are different (Child Care and Protection Board for juveniles and probation services (*Reclassering Nederland*) for adults). The community service order or training order can be replaced by youth imprisonment if the juvenile fails to fulfil his tasks (i.e., alternative youth imprisonment); if this replacement takes places after the juvenile turned 18, the alternative youth imprisonment will – in principle – be replaced by a alternative detention in an adult facility (*vervangende hechtenis*; see below).

Despite the differences, the character of the penalty is quite similar. Its use on both sides of the dividing line of the juvenile justice and criminal justice system can result in similar sentences. Consequently, the rather sharp division between the two justice systems in practice is more flexible. However, this requires that special programmes for older juveniles and young adults are available, which does not seem to be currently the case (Lamet et al., 2010). Fines for juveniles are limited to €3,800, while in very serious cases an adult can be fined up to €760,000. If a juvenile does not pay the fine entirely, he can be committed to a youth institution (i.e., alternative youth imprisonment) or a detention centre if he has turned 18.

In addition to these penalties the court can impose several *penal measures*, which are different from penalties. The latter, in essence, serve as retributive sentences linked to the guilt of the offender and the seriousness of the offence. The imposition of a penalty is justified by the crime committed, and the principle of proportionality must be taken into account. Penal measures are meant to positively influence the offenders' behaviour in order to prevent recidivism. The nature of the offence committed is the reason to impose a penal measure, but a link with the guilt of the offender and the seriousness of the crime is not required. Consequently, the principle of proportionality is – in principle – not regarded as relevant (Kelk, 2005). This distinction is also present in the juvenile justice system, although it has been blurred, among others, because all juvenile sentences are intended to serve the pedagogical objectives of juvenile justice, as well as the best interests of the child (Doek et al., 2009; Bruning et al., 2011).

Two of the penal measures will be mentioned here. The first is the measure of placement in a youth facility (*maatregel van plaatsing in een inrichting voor jeugdigen* or *PIJ-maatregel*), which is a custodial treatment order under penal law (art. 77s CrimCo). This treatment order can only be imposed for a serious offence and if required for the safety of society and the interests of the juvenile offender, and only after an assessment based on the reports of two independent behavioural experts from different academic disciplines. Unlike the custodial treatment order under adult penal law, this order is not limited to persons who cannot, or only partly, be held criminally accountable due, for example, to a mental disorder.

A court can order a juvenile's treatment for three years (i.e., a fixed term to start with; art. 77s (6) CrimCo) and can prolong it for up to five or seven years, depending on the nature of the crime and the personality of the juvenile offender (art. 77t CrimCo). After two years (or four or six years after an extension of the order) the treatment order terminates conditionally in order to facilitate compulsory aftercare. Like youth detention, the measure results in the juvenile's placement in a youth custodial institution, although the treatment can be enforced in another facility (art. 77s (5) CrimCo). The extension of the treatment order is limited to seven years and it cannot be converted into a treatment order for adults, which could endure for life.

The second penal measure is called the 'penal measure meant to influence the child's behaviour' or the 'behavioural order' (*gedragsbeïnvloedende maatregel*), and is aimed at the re-education of the juvenile (persistent or first offender) in order to positively influence his behaviour and prevent recidivism (art. 77w ff CrimCo). This is a non-custodial measure that lasts for six to 12 months (which can be extended once). It does not result in the juvenile's deprivation of liberty but in a limitation of his freedom; he can be forced to attend a specific training programme, a non-residential treatment programme, or a youth care programme. In addition, the juvenile can be placed under intensive probation (art. 4 of the Decree *Gedragsbeïnvloeding jeugdigen*; see further Doek et al., 2009). This measure was introduced on 1 February 2008 and can be considered one of the most significant changes in the penal law for juveniles since the 1995 law revision. The court can issue a behavioural order (see below) if the Child Care and Protection Board have advised to do so; the court determines the programme(s) the juvenile has to attend. If he does not meet the court's requirements and instructions, he can be detained instead (i.e., alternative youth imprisonment; see Bartels, 2008). The behavioural order has many resemblances to the suspended sentence, particularly to suspended youth imprisonment.

Since the introduction of the behavioural order, the courts are also allowed to combine all available juvenile sanctions, whereas beforehand the law only allowed for a number of fixed combinations (Volf, 2001; Vlaardingerbroek, 2001). This aims at enabling courts to tailor decisions to the specific circumstances of the case, including the personal circumstances and best interests of the juvenile offender. Such an approach can be welcomed, although there is a risk that as a result sentencing practice becomes more severe. In this regard, it is important to recall that the principle of proportionality should be upheld, even though this new way of sentencing could imply a reduction of the use of deprivation of liberty (cf. art. 40 (4) CRC; see furthermore Drost, Van de Grift and Jongebreur, 2009; Ministry of Justice, 2009; Buysse et al., 2010).

In these ways, the Criminal Code provides a specific set of juvenile sentences. Some of these sentences are completely different from the adult sentences, while others are similar. The court has a significant amount of discretion in determining the appropriate sentence. Here the court is often dependent on the advice and reports from, *inter alia*, the Child Care and Protection Board, and requires sufficient knowledge about the differences between the various sentences and their enforcement (see Bruning et al., 2011; Verberk and Ten Berge, 2010).

Exceptions to the Age Demarcation between Juvenile Justice and Criminal Justice

There are two exceptions to the demarcation point between the juvenile justice system and the adult criminal justice system. As explained earlier, the first exception allows for a 'transfer' of juveniles from the juvenile penal system to the adult penal system (art. 77b CrimCo); the second exception allows for a similar transfer of young adults under age 21 to the juvenile penal system.

Transfer of Juveniles to Adult Penal Law

The juvenile court can sentence a juvenile who was aged 16 or 17 when he committed the offence to an adult sentence (art. 77b CrimCo). This generally occurs upon request of the public prosecutor. The court can do so if it finds reason in the severity of the offence, the personal circumstances of the offender, or the circumstances under which the offence has been committed. As explained earlier, these grounds leave much discretion to the courts.

Under Dutch criminal law this penal transfer means that the juvenile can be sentenced for up to 30 years' imprisonment or to an adult treatment order, which can be indefinitely prolonged by the court. Life imprisonment for juveniles is prohibited (art. 77b (2) CrimCo). The transfer also means that the juvenile will – in principle – be placed in an adult facility (however, see also below). This is on strained terms with article 37 (c) CRC, which stipulates that children should be separated from adults. However, the Dutch government has made a reservation to this CRC provision, specifically meant to enable the application of article 77b CrimCo (art. 2 Kingdom Act of 24 November 1994, *Bulletin of Acts and Decrees* 1994, 862). Strictly speaking Dutch law is not in violation of international law, but the CRC Committee has called upon the Dutch government to withdraw its reservation and abolish the option of transferring juveniles to the adult penal system (CRC Committee, 2009a; see also Hammarberg, 2009). The former Minister of Youth and Family Affairs announced his intention to reassess the added value of article 77b CrimCo.[10]

It is important to reiterate that the application of article 77b CrimCo does not have implications for criminal procedure. All relevant juvenile justice provisions of the CCP remain applicable (i.e., there is no transfer or waiver to adult court).

Research regarding the application of article 77b CrimCo has *inter alia* revealed that it has been used less frequently since the 1995 law revision (Weijers, 2006). The conclusion that the use of this provision is not limited to very serious offences and does not result in higher sentences (i.e., higher than possible under the juvenile penal law) seems to be justified. As a result the main difference in terms of dispositions is that the juvenile is confronted with an adult sentence that will generally be enforced by adult institutions, custodial or non-custodial.

Weijers' research also reveals that little can be divined about how the courts apply article 77b CrimCo. Courts tend to repeat the legal grounds that underpin the provisions, rather than to explicitly clarify reasons for applying them. Courts are supported in this approach by the Netherlands Supreme Court, which has taken the position that the mere repetition of the legal grounds suffices to fulfil the requirements of clarification (The Netherlands Supreme Court, 21 November 2000, NJ 2001, 97). This position has been heavily criticized, among others by Doek, who claims that this approach ignores the relevance of extensive clarification, especially since juveniles are concerned (Doek, 2001). According to Weijers, this limited clarification fosters improper use of article 77b CrimCo (Weijers, 2006; cf. Uit Beijerse, 2009a). In addition, it could be argued that this can lead to legal uncertainty, particularly given the sustained pattern of limited clarification. According to the Ministry of Justice, the potential inequality (for example, between a juvenile sentenced to 15 years' imprisonment and a juvenile sentenced to two years of youth imprisonment) can be justified based on wide diversity in the circumstances of cases, personal circumstances included.[11]

Recent case law provides some examples of very serious cases in which rather high sentences were imposed on juveniles. The District Court of Groningen imposed 15 years' imprisonment on a juvenile who was involved in the brutal murder of a German married couple (District Court of Groningen, 27 April 2007, LJN: BA4035) and the Amsterdam Criminal Court of Appeal sentenced a juvenile to 18 years' imprisonment (after the District Court of Amsterdam imposed 20 years) for the brutal murder of a garage owner in the north of Amsterdam (Amsterdam Criminal Court of Appeal, 2 April 2010, LJN: BL9992; District Court of Amsterdam, 4 February 2009, LJN: BH1795). Both court cases deal with very serious and indeed horrifying cases, which clearly was the primary reason to transfer the juveniles to the adult penal system in order to impose a severe custodial sentence. However, these sentences

10 *Parliamentary Documents II* 2008/09, 31 001, nos. 66 and 69.

11 *Parliamentary Documents II* 2008/09, Appendix of proceedings, no. 1211, pp. 2540–1.

can be regarded as extremely high compared to maximum juvenile sentences and to previous practice (see Weijers, 2006).

Another reason, found in case law, for applying article 77b CrimCo, concerns the fact that under juvenile penal law a treatment order is limited in time. This can be regarded as too short a term for certain serious offenders with serious mental health issues (see for example, The Netherlands Supreme Court, 22 November 2005, NJ 2006, 138). The court then may choose to apply article 77b CrimCo in order to impose a treatment order under adult law, which can be prolonged indefinitely (see Waals, 2005; Janssens, 2005).

Transfer of Young Adults to Juvenile Penal Law

Article 77c CrimCo allows criminal courts to sentence young adults who were aged 18, 19 or 20 when they committed the offence under juvenile penal law if they find reason to do so in either the personality of the offender or in the circumstances under which the offence was committed. Little is known about the application of this legal provision. However, courts rarely use this option to transfer young adults to the juvenile penal system (Van der Laan et al., Chapter 8, this volume; see also Doreleijers and Fokkens, 2010).[12] Application of the article implies that the young adult can be sentenced to all juvenile sentences, including youth detention and a treatment order for juveniles. These sentences can be executed in a youth facility (see the recently revised art. 8 Youth Custodial Institutions Act (YCIA)/*Beginselenwet justitiële jeugdinrichtingen*). It also mandates that the treatment order for juveniles be executed as if it were a treatment order for adults (i.e., in an adult treatment facility). At the same time, article 8 YCIA (new) provides that an adult treatment order imposed on a juvenile aged 16 or 17 (under art. 77b CrimCo) can be executed in a youth institution until the juvenile turns 21 (para. (1)(h)). In addition, the court can order the execution of the entire adult treatment order in a youth institution if this is regarded appropriate given the development of the individual involved, and the Minister of Justice can allow a young adult to stay in a youth institution after he turns 21 if his treatment requires him to do so (art. 8 (6) YCIA).

Article 77c CrimCo is the only legal option to impose a juvenile sentence on a young adult. It seems important to clarify why this provision is hardly used and whether it should be recommended for more frequent use (see Dronkers and Ten Voorde, 2010 about a special project for young adults in the District Court of Almelo called 'Project 18–/18+').

Enforcement of Custodial Sentences

When relevant criminal justice provisions for both juveniles and young adults are considered, it is important to keep an eye on the implementation of the relevant

12 See also *Parliamentary Documents II* 2008/09, Appendix of proceedings, no. 1211, pp. 2539–41.

provisions. As pointed out by the Anneveldt Committee, the actual enforcement of the sentences is rather significant for the appropriateness of general treatment of the individual involved and of the effectiveness of the intervention. More particularly, it suggested that, if the specific needs of adolescents are to be addressed, attention should be paid, *inter alia*, to the diversity of treatment programmes, specifically where custodial sentences are concerned.[13]

The general approach concerning the enforcement of custodial sentences is that juvenile sentences are enforced in youth facilities and adult sentences in adult facilities.[14]

Juvenile Sentences in Youth Institution: Points of Departure and Exceptions

According to article 8 of the YCIA, juveniles sentenced to youth imprisonment or a treatment order can be placed in youth institutions (*justitiële jeugdinrichting*). Alternative youth imprisonment (for example, for not paying a fine or failing to complete a community service order) will be enforced in a youth institution as well. The same is true for enforcing the implementation of a suspended custodial sentence.

Placement in a youth institution means that the juvenile will be accommodated in a specialized (closed or semi-open) facility, with the explicit objective of providing education (i.e. upbringing; art. 2 (2) YCIA) – a pedagogical approach that distinguishes youth facilities from adult facilities. It goes beyond the scope of this chapter to elaborate extensively on the characteristics of youth institutions in the Netherlands, but a few remarks will be made (see also Liefaard, 2010; Boendermaker and Uit Beijerse, 2008; Junger-Tas, 2007).

Juveniles in youth institutions generally stay in groups of eight to ten (boys and girls separated, in principle), supervised by group leaders (i.e., no security staff). There is a compulsory educational programme. This is completely different to adult prisons, treatment centres or remand homes, where the stay is not group based and education is not compulsory. In addition, the programme in youth institutions is based on a method called 'YOUTURN' and the special needs of juveniles are addressed through an individual treatment programme (*perspectiefplan*). A similar approach is recognizable in adult treatment facilities and some other facilities (such as institutions for persistent offenders) but in general not in prisons or in remand homes. Furthermore, the YCIA endows juveniles with a rather strong legal status, which also stems from an international human rights perspective (Liefaard, 2008). It provides rules regarding supervision by an independent supervisory committee (*Commissie van Toezicht*) and rights such as to have contact with the outside world, including family and parents (again

13 As clarified in the introduction, this section primarily focuses on custodial sentences.

14 See also the letter of the State Secretary of Justice of 31 January 2008, *Parliamentary Documents II* 2007/08, 24 587 and 31 215, no. 246.

a specific juvenile feature), and for privacy protection. In addition, limitations of rights and freedoms are rather strictly regulated and the competence to order limitations is generally laid down at the level of the institution administration, not at the level of the group leaders. In order to protect against unlawful and arbitrary treatment, a juvenile has the right to file complaints. The legal status of the juvenile in a youth institution very much corresponds to the rights of the adult prisoner and in that regard can be considered as recognition of the juvenile as a rights holder (art. 37 (c) CRC). At the same time, the appropriateness of some of the options available to the youth institution administration in imposing far-reaching measures such as forced medical treatment and the use of violence can be questioned. Here the laws governing youth institutions are partly too penitentiary and look too much like adult penitentiary laws (although, for example, the maximum duration of disciplinary sanctions is much lower than in adult facilities; see below).

If a juvenile offender turns 18 while in a youth institution there is no legal obligation to transfer him to an adult facility. Despite the general approach that juveniles sentenced to a custodial sentence will be placed in a youth institution and stay there, the Criminal Code does provide a few exceptions in cases where the juvenile has turned 18 and his youth imprisonment was (partly) to be executed after his eighteenth birthday (Doek et al., 2009). In the event of a youth imprisonment (i.e., not an alternative youth imprisonment), article 77k CrimCo provides that the court can replace the youth imprisonment by imprisonment in an adult prison if it finds this appropriate. If art. 77k CrimCo is not applied, the youth imprisonment will take place in a youth facility, even if the enforcement starts after the juvenile turns 18 (see also the letter of the Chair of the Board of Procurators General of 20 December 2009 [PaG/HB/14415]).

Articles 77l (5) and 77p (4) CrimCo provide that, if an alternative youth imprisonment is to be enforced after the juvenile turns 18, it will be enforced as an alternative imprisonment for adults. This will not happen if in advance the court orders that regarding this particular juvenile the sentence is to be implemented as a youth imprisonment. A similar approach is recognizable in the event the court orders the enforcement of a suspended custodial sentence (art. 77dd (3) CrimCo). If the juvenile is age 18 or older when the sentence is to be enforced, it will be done as an adult sentence, unless the court has ordered otherwise.

As far as a penal treatment order for juveniles is concerned, Dutch law does not explicitly provide for a transfer to an adult facility once a juvenile turns 18. However, article 77s (5) CrimCo leaves room for the court to order the enforcement of the treatment order at a place other than a youth institution.[15]

15 See also *Parliamentary Documents II* 2007/08, 24 587 and 31 215, no. 246, p. 2.

Young Adults in Youth Facilities

It is therefore to be expected that young adults who stay in a youth institution will be: (1) sentenced to a treatment order under juvenile law; (2) sentenced to a youth imprisonment that has not been replaced by a regular imprisonment after they turn 18; (3) subjected to an alternative youth detention, regarding which either the court blocked its replacement by a alternative imprisonment or the implementation started before the young person turned 18; or (4) sentenced to a youth imprisonment under article 77c CrimCo.

Due to the recent revision of article 8 YCIA (see above), it can be assumed that young persons sentenced under article 77b CrimCo to an adult treatment order can be allowed to stay in a youth facility until they are age 21, or later if required by their treatment. Another new feature concerns the option of holding young adults, whose pre-trial detentions have been ordered, in a youth institution, if the public prosecutor expects to demand the application of a juvenile sentence under article 77c CrimCo (art. 8 (1)(a) YCIA).

In essence, there is no legal imperative to transfer juveniles to an adult facility as soon as they turn 18 (cf. CRC Committee, 2007). In practice, a substantial part of the population of youth institutions consists of young adults. In former youth treatment facilities housing juveniles under a penal treatment order, more than 50 per cent of the population is older than 18. And in 2009, 21 per cent of the population in former remand homes consisted of young adults (Custodial Institutions Service, 2010a).[16]

At the same time, about four per cent of the population of adult prisons and remand homes consists of young persons under age 19 (Custodial Institutions Service, 2010b). The Custodial Institutions Service reports that there were no young persons under age 19 in adult treatment centres (Custodial Institutions Service, 2010c). Unfortunately, public data of this service do not reveal the number of juveniles under age 18 in adult facilities, but it is known that there are (or at least have been) juveniles in prison or remand homes for adults (Detrick et al., 2008). In light of this, it is important to note that adult penitentiary laws leave room for the placement of juveniles in adult facilities (Liefaard, 2008).

In the YCIA there are hardly any specific references to differentiation according to age and maturity. A distinction is found between juveniles under age 16 and age 16 or older regarding the use of measures of order and disciplinary sanctions. However, there is no explicit guidance regarding differentiation on substantive aspects of a juvenile's stay in a youth institution, such as accommodation, parental involvement, and education. This is remarkable. More guidance by the legislature, particularly concerning parental involvement (since young adults are no longer under parental custody), and regarding compulsory education (since young adults are no longer compelled to attend school), should be expected. In light of article 37 (c) CRC's requirement that children should be separated from adults, guidance

16 See also *Parliamentary Documents II* 2007/08, 24 587 and 31 215, no. 246, p. 2.

regarding the accommodation of young adults and juveniles should also be expected.

The YCIA does allow the director of the institution to differentiate between juveniles according to age or specific needs. He could, for example, designate a specific department for younger juveniles or for young adults (art. 17 YCIA). In addition, the Minister of Justice has the ability to designate certain youth institutions (or departments) for specific groups of juveniles, while taking into account, *inter alia*, age and maturity and individual needs (art. 8 (3) YCIA). In practice, none of the youth institutions is exclusively designated to accommodate young adults. Almost all institutions refer to juveniles as ranging in age from 12–23 (see, for example, their websites accessible through http://www.dji.nl/Organisatie/Locaties/Justitiele-jeugdinrichtingen/, accessed June 2011). It is unclear to what extent institutions actually differentiate between younger and older inhabitants. According to the Ministry of Justice, youth institutions should in future differentiate according to the developmental stage of juveniles but at the time of writing it remains unclear what this implies.[17]

Given the individual plan-based approach (i.e., an individual treatment plan will be drawn up, which significantly determines life in the institution), institutions are able to differentiate substantively according to age and maturity and individual needs. In light of this a tailor-made daily programme, even though education is compulsory for all, may be expected. Regarding young adults, educational programmes may be used to facilitate vocational training or internships. However, this is entirely at the discretion of the institutions. Each juvenile (or young adult) has to be invited to participate in the drawing up and interim evaluation of the individual plan but, due to lack of specific guidance in the law, his legal status and therefore his ability to edit or influence a plan is rather weak.

Young Adults in Adult Facilities

As mentioned, both the Criminal Code and the penitentiary laws governing adult penal facilities (prisons, treatment centres, remand homes, etc.) contain provisions that allow or even foster the transfer of young adults to adult facilities even if they were tried as juveniles under the juvenile justice system. An important question to be asked, however, is to what extent adult facilities address the specific status of young adults (cf., for example, the recommendations of the Council of Europe in this regard, as highlighted earlier).

In general, the answer is that, although the stay in an adult facility can be customized to each individual prisoner, there is hardly any specific reference to young adults and their specific needs, such as (vocational) education, as a prerequisite for their reintegration. Although there is a right to education, its availability is made dependent upon the duration of the detention and the person

17 *Parliamentary Documents II* 2008/09, Appendix of proceedings, no. 1211, p. 2540.

involved (art. 48 Penitentiary Principles Act). In addition, the penitentiary laws do not provide for age differentiation, for example regarding accommodation and designated use. Furthermore, the differences between the YCIA and the penitentiary laws for adult facilities are significant, particularly regarding relevant issues such as upbringing, education and family contact as well as limitations of rights and freedoms. Penitentiary laws regarding adult facilities are more repressive if, for example, the gravity of the disciplinary sanctions is considered (De Groot, 2009). In reality, adult institutions have been subject to severe financial cutbacks for years and daily programmes can be very limited (Kelk, 2008; Muller, 2009; Boone and Moerings, 2007). Consequently, for a young adult a transfer from a youth institution to an adult institution is substantial and problematic given the significant differences between them.

Previously, the special position of young adults ages 18–23 was explicitly recognized by law. However, since the enactment of the 1999 Penitentiary Principles Act (PPA), the law no longer recognizes young adults as a separate category of prisoners (Kelk, 2008; Fiselier, 2009; Verwers and Bogaerts, 2005). Differentiation has been the key word since 1999, which means that the Ministry of Justice can differentiate between departments of institutions according to the level of security or according to gender. In addition, the Ministry can designate certain departments of institutions to accommodate certain prisoners according to their problematic behaviour (for example, drug addiction), the offence committed (for example, sex offenders) or according to their age (art. 14 PPA; see also Fiselier, 2009). As in youth institutions, the director has the power to designate special departments within the institution.

Between 2002 and 2008 prisons had special departments designated for young adults with a JOVO-regime, named after the Dutch word for young adults: *jong-volwassenen*. The main objective of this approach was to limit the potential damage of detention and to avoid 'criminal contamination' by offering a special, protected environment and intensive supervision (Fiselier, 2009). In 2007, the departments started closing down these separate regimes for young adults for a number of reasons (see Fiselier, 2009, p. 188 with reference to the letter of the director of the prison section of the custodial institutions service of 30 October 2007 [5513805/07/DJI]). Evaluation of the JOVO-regimes pointed out that there was no real added value; they did not offer the desired extra protection nor did they offer better prospects in terms of the reintegration of young adult prisoners. In addition, it is legitimate to ask whether the segregation of this group did not have a negative impact on the inmates and stimulated negative behaviour (Council for the Administration of Criminal Justice and Youth Protection, 2004). Of note also is that only 10 per cent of young adult prisoners could be regarded as vulnerable prisoners in need of special care and assistance. Moreover, the closing of the JOVO-regimes fitted in with the new categorization of prisoners provided for by a policy document called 'Tailored detention and treatment for adult detainees' (*Detentie en behandeling op maat voor volwassen gedetineerden*).[18]

The current categorization of prisoners stems from the most recent policy document *Masterplan Gevangeniswezen 2009–2014* (Master plan for Adult Penitentiary Facilities), which argues against drawing up separate departments for young adults.[19] According to the Minister of Justice, the specific needs of these young adults should be dealt with under existing options to individualize and tailor prisoners' accommodation and regimes.[20] However, young adults are not mentioned here as a specific group that may require special accommodation.

Summary

There are significant differences between the custodial regimes for juveniles and adults in law and in practice. For that reason, the rules affecting young people on both sides of the dividing line between juvenile justice and criminal justice are important. It is clear that young adults – particularly when they end up in an adult facility – are at risk of being denied the special care and assistance they may need. This may not be true for everyone, but young adults are fully dependent on the prison administration for their physical, social, psychological and educational welfare, assistance and guidance. It begs the question whether this can be justified, particularly if the legal position of these young adults is compared to that of young adults who are allowed to stay in a youth facility.

In addition, the question needs to be raised as to what extent the law and practice regarding young adults meet with the requirements of International Human Rights Law, in particular the recommendations of the Committee of Ministers of the Council of Europe; although, it was claimed that the European Prison Rules did not block the closing down of the JOVO regimes (Fiselier, 2009, p. 188).

The position of the young adult in a youth facility has received attention during the past few years, as evidenced by regulations regarding automatic transfer of young adults sentenced under the juvenile justice system to adult facilities, which was part of the Ministry of Justice's efforts to address the lack of places in youth facilities.[21] Currently there appears to be sufficient space in youth institutions, but recent suggestions of transforming one institution, which was threatened to be closed, into a special young adult facility was rejected by the Minister of Justice for financial reasons.[22] This supports the assumption that the desire to transfer

18 *Parliamentary Documents II* 2005/06, 30 300 VI, no. 147.

19 *Parliamentary Documents II* 2008/09, 24 587, no. 341.

20 *Parliamentary Documents II* 2008/09, Appendix of proceedings, no. 1211, p. 2540.

21 See the letter of the State Secretary of Justice of 31 January 2008, *Parliamentary Documents II* 2007/08, 24 587 and 31 215, no. 246.

22 See the letter of the Ministry of Justice of 29 April 2010, *Parliamentary Documents II* 2007/08, 24 587, no. 386, p. 3.

young adults to the adult prison system is primarily based on financial motives and not on the wish (and duty) to provide these individuals with the best chances for reintegration into society. This is a perilous situation for young adults within the criminal justice system, but even more perilous for juveniles who become adults while they are subject to juvenile proceedings and dispositions (cf. art. 40 (1) CRC). Moreover, this can be perilous for society as a whole, because this approach may very well have a negative impact on young people's chances to reintegrate into society.

Reintegration and Registration of Judicial Data

A final issue that deserves attention concerns the potential impact of the registration of judicial data on the reintegration of juveniles and adults who have been subject to criminal justice proceedings. Under Dutch law, the 2004 Justice System Data Act (*Wet justitiële en strafvorderlijke gegevens*; *Bulletin of Decrees* 2004, 129) regulates data registration within the criminal justice system. Another act, the DNA Testing (Convicted Persons) Act (*Wet DNA-onderzoek bij veroordeelden*), mandates DNA registration for everyone convicted for a serious offence in order to prevent, investigate, prosecute and adjudicate future criminal offences. This act will not be addressed here, but provides a good example of an increased effort to collect and register data of individuals who have been subject to criminal justice proceedings, juveniles included (see also Netherlands Supreme Court, 13 May 2008, LJN: BC8231 and BC8234).

The Justice System Data Act regulates, first of all, which data can be registered and how long these data can be kept. Judicial data (hereinafter: data) regarding sex offender cases will be kept for 20 years after the death of the accused or convicted person. Data regarding other offences can – in principle – be kept for 30 years after the closure of the case (art. 4). Regarding the registration and removal of data, the act does not distinguish between adults and juveniles. The Justice System Data Act also regulates which organizations and persons have access to the registered data (see also Boone, 2011). Judicial authorities, the Minister of Justice and the Public Prosecutions Office have access to judicial data in order to acquire judicial information regarding suspects or convicted persons to be used in court proceedings or in procedures regarding clemency or out-of-court settlements (art. 8). Other public authorities or persons, such as the administrators of custodial institutions and the Child Care and Protection Board, can be granted access to judicial data for specified purposes, such as the enforcement of sentences (art. 9, 10 and 8a). However, the latter categories of authorities or persons are denied access to judicial data regarding juveniles who were younger than 16 when they (allegedly) committed the offence (art. 12). Access to data regarding juveniles who were 16 or older is furthermore limited to data concerning cases in which the conviction consists of a custodial sentence (youth imprisonment or treatment order), a fine of more than €113, or a community sentence of more than 40 hours. In addition, access in these cases is limited in time, to two or four years, and no access is granted if the sentence was suspended entirely (art. 12). Thus, article 12 of the act provides several examples of access to judicial data of juveniles and adults.

Under the current act, private individuals or organizations do not have access to the registered data. However, employers may find out more about the judicial history of their future employees through the requirement of a certificate of good behaviour (*verklaring omtrent het gedrag*) from the Minister of Justice (art. 28ff). The number of applications for a certificate have increased significantly during the past years, but the proportion of refusals remained low (Boone, 2011). Recent information provided by the State Secretary of Justice confirms the low number of refusals (i.e., 0.4 per cent in 2010).[23] The Minister of Justice can, in order to assess whether he should issue such a certificate, access judicial data, as well as data from police registration systems (art. 36). The limitations regarding juveniles as just mentioned do not apply in this regard, which implies that all data (including data concerning juveniles between ages 12 and 16) can be accessed and used, with the exception of judicial data regarding cases in which the accused was acquitted (art. 35 [3]). Based on current policy, a certificate of good behaviour will be issued if the name of the person involved has not been found in the judicial data register during the previous four years. However, if he has been prosecuted or convicted for a sex offence, or has been incarcerated, the issuing authority will assess whether there is a risk to society (i.e., a risk of recidivism) or whether other circumstances of the case may interfere with the proper functioning of the person involved (art. 35). Consequently, the certificate of good behaviour may be denied (Bruning and Berger, 2008, p. 185 with reference to 'Policy regulations 'VOG NP-RP 2004', *Government Gazette*, 31 March 2004, no. 63). Recently, the State Secretary of Justice underscored that the relatively young age of the juvenile when he committed an offence will be taken into account when assessing the application for a certificate of good conduct, since juveniles have a particular interest in enrolling in specific educational programmes or in finding a job.[24] Despite the significance of these remarks for juveniles, it should be kept in mind that the same applies to young adults.

Thus, the 2004 Justice System Data Act can have significant consequences for the future functioning of juveniles who have been subject to police investigation and/or criminal justice proceedings, regardless of their age at the time they committed the offence. It can particularly affect an individual's prospects in the labour market. It is claimed by legal experts that the act has worsened the legal position of juveniles (Bruning and Berger, 2008). Although there are some exceptions to the general rules for juveniles, it is questionable whether these suffice to fulfil the recommendations of the CRC Committee with regard to the implementation of the right of the juvenile to have his privacy fully respected during all stages of the criminal justice proceedings (article 40 (2)(b)(vii) jo. 16

23 *Parliamentary Documents II* 2010/11, Appendix of Proceedings, No. 1640.

24 *Parliamentary Documents II* 2010/11, 32 500 VI, no. 104.

CRC). This right also serves to protect the juvenile in trouble with the law against undue publicity and the possibility of labelling (see also rule 8 Beijing Rules). According to the CRC Committee, 'no information shall be published that may lead to the identification of a child offender because of its effect of stigmatization, and possible impact on his/her ability to have access to education, work, housing or to be safe' (CRC Committee, 2007, para. 64). The CRC Committee recommends that records of child offenders be kept confidential and should not be used in future adult proceedings and sentencing. Domestic law should furthermore provide for the deletion of criminal records either automatically when the juvenile offender turns 18 or upon request by the juvenile, for example, in the event of a serious offence after he has not reoffended for a certain period of time (CRC Committee, 2007).

Conclusions

The upper age limit of the Dutch juvenile justice system has been set at 18. As soon as someone reaches that age, he is no longer regarded as a juvenile under criminal law and can consequently be tried and sentenced as an adult, and is considered fully accountable for his behaviour. This chapter clarifies that this dividing line based on age serves significant criminal justice principles, such as legal certainty and equality, and corresponds with the distinction between childhood and adulthood under International Human Rights Law, most clearly prompted by the CRC and implying that once a person turns 18 he should no longer be regarded as a child, but as an autonomous and independent human being.

It has also become clear that the differences between the juvenile justice system and the criminal justice system in both law and practice are significant and have become more apparent during the past decade. This is particularly true for custodial sentences, while the distinction between juvenile justice and criminal justice seems to be less prominent as far as non-custodial sentences are concerned.

Even though legally defensible, the distinction between juvenile justice and criminal justice based on age is also problematic, for both legal and practical reasons, and seems *de facto* particularly detrimental to young adults. Young people in youth institutions have received a fair amount of attention. However, attention for young adults in adult facilities has decreased. In the penitentiary legal system young adulthood is no longer recognized as a specific developmental phase requiring special attention, while the regime in adult institutions has become more stultifying over time. Dutch legislators increasingly enacted provisions that facilitate and foster the transfer of young adults from the juvenile penitentiary system to the adult penitentiary system.

The position of young adults should require more attention. In the first place, increased attention for young adults seems to be a matter of better use of existing legal provisions, such as article 77c CrimCo, as well as the (re-)establishment of special enforcement modalities for young adults. As far as custodial sentences are concerned, the empty beds in youth institutions provide a wonderful opportunity. A need for systematic – and thus legislative – change does not seem to have a high priority as long as the *de facto* recognition of young adults as a separate category of offenders has not come to its full potential. Nevertheless, recognition of their specific status in statutory law could foster recognition in practice and it is therefore worthwhile to explore (see also Council for the Administration of Criminal Justice and Youth Protection, 2011a; Doreleijers and Fokkens, 2010; Hoekendijk and Niemeijer, 2010).

It needs no explanation that a strict division between childhood and adulthood does not correspond with the reality that becoming an adult is a gradual process, which arguably continues after age 18 (see also Loeber et al., Chapter 12, this volume). Important issues in this regard revolve around the question of how mature are young adults, and what do scientific insights tell us about the culpability and autonomy of these young people and about their special needs? Two essential legal questions are: *what justifies a special justice approach for young adults (for example, between ages 18 and 24) as a group and what should this approach entail?* While answering these questions, the following observations should be taken into account.

1. Both juvenile justice and criminal justice interventions are linked to and justified by a person's accountability for his behaviour. It is assumed that children are less culpable than adults (i.e., one of the justifications for a separate juvenile justice system). If young adults as a group should be considered less culpable than 'older' adults, separate justice interventions could be justified corresponding with the level of accountability. If a general justification cannot be found, individual cases could be approached on the basis of legal exceptions for the upper age limit of childhood, for example through a provision such as article 77c CrimCo.
2. Justice interventions should aim at realizing the objectives of the justice system as a whole, while taking into account differences between people in terms of age and maturity (and other characteristics such as gender, and special needs such as the level of education or IQ; see for example, Council for the Administration of Criminal Justice and Youth Protection, 2011b). Here it is important to clarify these objectives and translate them into concrete sentences. Juvenile justice interventions are based on the assumption that children should be seen as human beings in development and that they should be treated accordingly while taking into account their best interests as a primary consideration (art. 3 (1) CRC), for example by means of (compulsory) re-education, training orders, parental involvement, etc. Regarding young adults, the common characteristics and needs of this specific group should be clearly defined and clarified as to what extent a special approach is required (for example, through the development of specially adjusted sentences with a separate legal basis) and/or a more tailored approach in individual cases (i.e., under the competence of the judiciary and/or enforcing authorities). The seriousness of the offence

committed, the status of the offender (i.e., first or repetitive offender, and the existence and relevance of criminal justice objectives such as deterrence and protection of society) should be taken into account.

3. The nature and content of legal procedures should be taken into account. Both children and adults of any age are entitled to be treated fairly during all stages of the proceedings. In addition, children are entitled to be treated differently from adults based on the assumption that children are more vulnerable than adults and require special facilities and assistance (see also art. 12 CRC). This requires specialized authorities (judges, prosecutors, police, lawyers, etc.) as well as special safeguards such as legal or other appropriate assistance, trials *in camera* and participation of parents or guardians. It is important to clarify whether young adults as a group require separate facilities and procedures or whether they are fit to stand trial in adult court.
4. There does not seem to be much room for a compulsory, protective approach towards young adults as a group. They, like children, may be in need of care and (re-)education,[25] and this could lead to denial of the rights of young adults to be recognized as autonomous human beings and a paternalistic approach. Consequently, it does not seem to be justifiable to increase the upper age limit of childhood.
5. The discussion regarding criminal justice for juveniles and young adults should by no means lead to the lowering of the current upper age limit of 18. This is not acceptable under International Human Rights Law and would inevitably result in even more public scrutiny by international monitoring bodies, such as the UN Committee on the Rights of the Child.

Defining groups of individuals by setting age limits will always remain problematic. Provided that there is agreement about the definition of young adulthood, setting a new minimum age for adulthood will inevitably raise the issue. Every dividing line based on an objective criterion such as age will create borderline cases. However, the way laws on both sides of the dividing line are designed and enforced can make the divide less problematic and facilitate a more gradual approach for young, maturing people as a group and as individuals. More attention of policymakers to the evidence base concerning young people in this transition period from juvenile justice to adult criminal justice is likely to have long-term benefits to young people themselves and to society.

25 Cf. the problems that youth care agencies encounter while dealing with compulsory protective and educational (and custodial) programmes for young adults; Steketee et al., 2009 and Bruning and Liefaard, 2009; see also The Hague Court of Appeal, 26 March 2009, LJN: BH9207

References

Alston, P. (1992). The legal framework of the convention on the rights of the child. *Bulletin of Human Rights*, 91, 1–15.

Anneveldt-Committee (1982). *Sanctierecht voor jeugdigen.* The Hague: Staatsuitgeverij.

Bac, J.R. (1998). *Kinderrechter in strafzaken: Evolutie en evaluatie.* Deventer: Gouda Quint.

Bartels, J.A.C. (2007). *Jeugdstrafrecht.* Deventer: Kluwer.

Bartels, J.A.C. (2008). Jeugdstrafrecht en een effectieve maatregel tot beïnvloeding van gedrag. *Familie- en Jeugdrecht*, 67, 145–51.

Berger, M. and Van der Kroon, C. (2011). *Een 'paar nachtjes' in de cel. Het VN-Kinderrechtenverdrag en het voorarrest van minderjarigen in politiecellen.* Leiden: Defence for Children International.

Bleichrodt, E. (2006). Right to Liberty and Security of Person (Article 5). In P. van Dijk et al. (eds), *Theory and Practice of the European Convention on Human Rights.* Antwerp and Oxford: Intersentia, pp. 455–509.

Boendermaker, L. and Uit Beijerse, J. (2008). *Opvoeding en bescherming achter 'tralies'. Jeugdinrichtingen tussen juridische beginselen en pedagogische praktijk.* Amsterdam: SWP.

Bol, M. (1991). *Leeftijdsgrenzen in het strafrecht.* Arnhem: Gouda Quint (Ph.D. dissertation).

Boone, M. (2011). Judicial rehabilitation in the Netherlands: Balancing between safety and privacy. *European Journal of Probation*, 1, 63–78.

Boone, M. and Moerings, M. (2007). De cellenexplosie. Voorlopig gehechten, veroordeelden, vreemdelingen, jeugdigen en tbs. *Justitiële Verkenningen*, 33, 9–30.

Bos, J. and Mehciz, M. (2001). *Evaluatie nachtdetentie.* Amsterdam: Regioplan Onderzoek Advies en Informatie B.V.

Bos, J., Hissel, S.C.E.M., Dekkers, S., and Homburg, G.H.J. (2006). *Nachtdetentie voor jeugdigen in de voorlopige hechtenisfase.* Amsterdam: Regioplan Beleidsonderzoek.

Bruning, M.R. and Berger, M.J.F. (2008). Recht op privacy van minderjarige delinquenten over justitiële documentatie en DNA-afname bij jeugdigen. *Strafblad*, 2, 183–94.

Bruning, M.R. and Liefaard, T. (2009). Ontwikkelingen en knelpunten in de gesloten jeugdzorg. *Familie- en Jeugdrecht*, 42, 99–105.

Bruning, M.R., De Jong, M.P., Liefaard, T., and Schuyt, P.M. (2011). *Wegwijs in het jeugdsanctierecht: Onderzoek naar het juridisch kader voor de zwaarste jeugdsancties in theorie en praktijk.* Nijmegen: Wolf Legal.

Buruma, Y. and Van Toor, D. (2010). *Minder beschikken, meer wikken. De invloed van twee wetten op de werklast van gerechten.* Nijmegen: Wolf Legal.

Buysse, W., Maarschalkerweerd, A., Loef, L., and Hilhorst, N. (2010). *Overwegingen voor het adviseren van een gedragsbeinvloedende maatregel.* Amsterdam: DSP-groep.

Cantwell, N. (1992). The origins, development and significance of the United Nations Convention on the Rights of the Child. In S. Detrick (ed.), *The United Nations Convention on the Rights of the Child: A Guide to the 'Travaux Préparatoires'*. Dordrecht: Martinus Nijhoff, pp. 19–30.

Child Care and Protection Board (2011). *Landelijke menukaart leerstraffen en gedragsinterventies 2011*. Utrecht.

Committee on the Rights of the Child ('CRC Committee') (2006). *General Comment No. 8, The Right of the Child to Protection from Corporal Punishment and Other Cruel or Degrading Forms of Punishment (arts. 19; 28, para.2, and 37, inter alia)*. UN Doc. CRC/C/GC/8, 2 March 2007.

Committee on the Rights of the Child ('CRC Committee') (2007). *General Comment No. 10, 'Children's Rights in Juvenile Justice'*. UN Doc. CRC/C/GC/10, 25 April 2007.

Committee on the Rights of the Child ('CRC Committee') (2009a). *Concluding Observations: The Kingdom of the Netherlands*. UN Doc. CRC/C/NLD/CO/3, 30 January 2009.

Committee on the Rights of the Child ('CRC Committee') (2009b). *General Comment No. 12, 'The Right of the Child to be Heard'*. UN Doc. CRC/C/GC/12, 20 July 2009.

Council for the Administration of Criminal Justice and Youth Protection (2004). *Advies JOVO-inrichtingen*. Government Gazette, 1 June 2004, No. 101.

Council for the Administration of Criminal Justice and Youth Protection (2011a). *Advies het jeugdstrafproces: Toekomstbestendig!* Government Gazette 2011, No. 6593.

Council for the Administration of Criminal Justice and Youth Protection (2011b). *Advies zorg voor ingesloten licht verstandelijk beperkte jongeren*. The Hague: 6 June 2011.

Custodial Institutions Service (2010a). *JJI in getal 2005–2009*. The Hague.

Custodial Institutions Service (2010b). *TBS in getal 2005–2009*. The Hague.

Custodial Institutions Service (2010c). *Gevangeniswezen in getal 2005–2009*. The Hague.

De Groot, M.F.M. (2009). *Vrijheidsbeneming en wetgeving*. In E.R. Muller and P.C. Vegter (eds), *Detentie: Gevangen in Nederland*. Alphen aan den Rijn: Kluwer.

Detrick, S. (1992). *The United Nations Convention on the Rights of the Child: A guide to the 'Travaux Préparatoires'*. Dordrecht: Martinus Nijhoff.

Detrick, S. (1999). *A Commentary on the United Nations Convention on the Rights of the Child.* Dordrecht: Kluwer Law International.

Detrick, S., Abel, G., Berger, M., Delon, A., and Meek, R. (2008). *Violence Against Children in Conflict with the Law: A Study on Indicators and Data Collection in Belgium, England and Wales, France and the Netherlands*. Amsterdam: Defence for Children International.

Doek, J.E. (2001). De jeugdige delinquent, de toepassing van het strafrecht voor volwassenen en het IVRK. Enkele beschouwingen n.a.v. HR 21-11-2000, NJ2001, 97. *Familie- en Jeugdrecht*, 5, 144–51.

Doek, J.E. (2008). Juvenile Justice: International rights and standards. In R. Loeber, N.W. Slot, P.H. Van der Laan and M. Hoeve (eds), *Tomorrow's Criminals: The Development of Child Delinquency and Effective Interventions*. Farnham: Ashgate, pp. 229–46.

Doek, J.E., Vlaardingerbroek, P., Bruning, M.R., and Liefaard, T. (2009). *Jeugdrecht en jeugdzorg*. Amsterdam: Elsevier Juridisch.

Doreleijers, T. and Fokkens, J.W. (2010). Minderjarigen en jongvolwassenen: Pleidooi voor een evidence based strafrecht. *Rechtsreeks*, 2, 1–47.

Dronkers, C. and Ten Voorde, J. (2010). OM-gaan met gestoorde ontwikkeling bij jongvolwassenen. De regiefunctie van het Openbaar Ministerie bij strafzaken van jongvolwassenen. In T.A.H. Doreleijers, J. ten Voorde and M. Moerings (eds), *Strafrecht en forensische psychiatrie voor 16-24-jarigen*. The Hague: BJu Legal, pp. 39–50.

Drost, V., Van de Grift, M., and Jongebreur, W. (2010). *Impactanalyse gedragsbeïnvloedende maatregel*. Barneveld: Significant.

Fiselier, J.P.S. (2009). Penitentiaire inrichtingen in soort en maat. In E.R. Muller and P.C. Vegter (eds), *Detentie; Gevangen in Nederland*. Alphen aan den Rijn: Kluwer, pp. 161–98.

Hammarberg, Th. (2009). *Report by the Commissioner for Human Rights on his Visit to the Netherlands* (21–25 September 2008), CommDH(2009)2.

Hoekendijk, G.P. and Niemeijer, E. (2010). Over de betekenis van grenzen in het jeugdstrafrecht. *Sancties*, 5, 233–46.

Human Rights Committee (1989). *General Comment No. 17, Rights of the Child (Art. 24)*, UN Doc. A/44/40, 7 April 1989.

Human Rights Committee (1992). *General Comment No. 21, Replaces General Comment 9 Concerning Humane Treatment of Persons Deprived of Liberty (Art. 10)*, UN Doc. A/47/40(SUPP), 10 April 1992.

Human Rights Committee (2007). General Comment No. 32, Article 14: Right to equality before courts and tribunals and to a fair trial, UN Doc. CCPR/C/GC/32, 23 August 2007.

Imkamp, F.M.J.A. (2006). De wet gedragsbeïnvloeding jeugdigen: een verrijking? *Sancties*, 2, 69–77.

Janssens, A.L.J.M. (2005). Opmerkingen over de motiveringsplicht bij toepassing art. 77b Sr. In A. Harteveld, D.H. de Jong and E. Stamhuis (eds), *Systeem in ontwikkeling, Liber amicorum G. Knigge*. Nijmegen: Wolf Legal, pp. 289–300.

Jonge, G. de, and Weijers, I. (2008). De rol van de ouders in jeugdstrafrechtspleging. In I. Weijers and F. Imkamp (eds), *Jeugdstrafrecht*. The Hague: BJu Legal, pp. 283–95.

Junger-Tas, J. (2004). Youth justice in the Netherlands. In M. Tonry and A. Doob (eds), *Youth Crime and Youth Justice: Comparative and Cross-national Perspectives*. Chicago, IL: University of Chicago Press, pp. 293–347.

Junger-Tas, J. (2007). De behandeling van jongeren in justitiële inrichtingen. *Delikt en Delinkwent*, 10, 1001–19.

Kelk, C. (2005). *Studieboek materieel strafrecht*. Amsterdam: Kluwer.

Kelk, C. (2008). *Nederlands detentierecht*. Deventer: Kluwer.

Lamet, W., James, C., Dirkzwager, A., and Van der Laan, P.H. (2010). Reclasseringstoezicht en jongvolwassenen. *Proces*, 6, 371–83.

Liefaard, T. (2008). *Deprivation of Liberty of Children in Light of International Human Rights Law and Standards*. Antwerp: Intersentia.

Liefaard, T. (2010). De rechtspositie van jeugdigen in justitiële jeugdinrichtingen in het licht van internationale mensenrechten en actuele ontwikkelingen. *Delikt en Delinkwent*, 70, 1115–40.

Ministry of Justice (2009). *De gedragsbeïnvloedende maatregel: Bevindingen van de eerste 25 vonnissen waarin de gedragsmaatregel is opgelegd*. The Hague.

Muller, E.R. (2009). Detentie in perspectief. In E.R. Muller and P.C. Vegter (eds), *Detentie: Gevangen in Nederland*. Alphen aan den Rijn: Kluwer, pp. 643–62.

Nowak, M. (2005). *UN Covenant on Civil and Political Rights. CCPR Commentary*. Kehl, GR: N.P. Engel.

Overwater-Committee (1951). *Rapport van de commissie ingesteld met het doel van advies te dienen over de vraag in welke richting het rijkstucht- en opvoedingswezen en in verband daarmede het kinderstrafrecht zich zullen moeten ontwikkelen*. The Hague: Staatsdrukkerij- en Uitgeverijbedrijf.

Reclassering Nederland, Leger des Heils and Verslavingsreclassering (2010). *Menukaart Gedragstrainingen 2010*. At http://www.reclassering.nl/documents/Menukaarten/100318_menukaart_gedragsinterventies.def.pdf, accessed 22 June 2011.

Rodley, N. and Pollard, M. (2009). *The Treatment of Prisoners under International Law*. Oxford: Oxford University Press.

Rosenheim, M.K., Zimring, F.E., Tanenhaus, D.S., and B. Dohrn (2002). *A Century of Juvenile Justice*. Chicago, IL: University of Chicago Press.

Schabas, W., Sax, H., and Alen, A. (2006). Article 37; Prohibition of torture, death penalty, life imprisonment and deprivation of liberty: A commentary on the United Nations Convention on the Rights of the Child. In A. Alen, J.V. Lanotte, E. Verhellen, F. Ang, E. Berghmans and M. Verheyde (eds), *A Commentary on the Rights of the Child*. Leiden: Martinus Nijhoff, pp. 1–96.

Steketee, M., Vandenbroucke, M., and Rijkschroeff, R. (2009). *(Jeugd)zorg houdt niet op bij 18 jaar*. Utrecht: Verwey-Jonker Instituut.

Tanenhaus, D.S. (2004). *Juvenile Justice in the Making*. New York: Oxford University Press.

Trechsel, S. (2005). *Human Rights in Criminal Proceedings*. New York: Oxford University Press.

Trépanier, J. (1999). Juvenile courts after 100 years: Past and present orientations. *European Journal on Criminal Policy and Research*, 7, 303–27.
Uit Beijerse, J. (2009a). De nieuwe regeling van de schorsing van de voorlopige hechtenis bij jeugdigen in het licht van de onschuldpresumptie. *Proces*, 88, 314–26.
Uit Beijerse, J. (2009b). De toepassing van een volwassenensanctie op 16- en 17-jarigen: pro's, contra's en alternatieven. *Delikt en Delinkwent*, 75, 1067–88.
Van Bueren, G. (2006). Article 40: Child criminal justice. In A. Alen, J.V. Lanotte, E. Verhellen, F. Ang, E. Berghmans and M. Verheyde (eds), *A Commentary on the Rights of the Child*. Leiden: Martinus Nijhoff, pp. 1–41.
Van der Laan, A.M., Vervoorn, L., Van der Schans, C.A., and Bogaerts, S. (2008). *Ik zit vast. Een exploratieve studie naar emotionele verwerking van justitiële vrijheidsbeneming door jongeren*. The Hague: BJu Legal.
Van der Laan, P.H. (2005). Jeugd, criminaliteit, politie en justitie. *Delikt en Delinkwent*, 70, 986–1013.
Van der Laan, P.H. (2006). Just desert and welfare: Juvenile justice in the Netherlands. In J. Junger-Tas and S.H. Decker (eds). *International Handbook of Juvenile Justice*. Dordrecht: Springer, pp. 145–70.
Van Kalmthout, A.M., Knapen, M.M., and Morgenstern, C. (2010). *Pre-trial Detention in the European Union: An Analysis of Minimum Standards in Pre-trial Detention and the Grounds for Regular Review in the Member States of the EU*. Nijmegen: Wolf Legal.
Van Zyl Smit, D. (2006). Life imprisonment: Recent issues in national and international law. *International Journal of Law and Psychiatry*, 29, 405–21.
Verberk, S. and Ten Berge, M. (2010). *Kennis- en informatiepositie van het OM en de ZM met betrekking tot de tenuitvoerlegging en de doelgroep van de PIJ-maatregel*. Rotterdam: Erasmus University.
Verwers, C. and Bogaerts, S. (2005). *Strafrechtelijke aanpak van jongvolwassenen (18–24 jaar). Een verkenning*. The Hague: WODC.
Vlaardingerbroek, P. (2001). Combineren is jongleren. Over combinaties van straffen en maatregelen en het doel van het jeugdstrafrecht. *Familie- en Jeugdrecht*, 1, 12–14.
Volf, L.M.Z. (2001). De combinatie van de vrijheidsstraf en de vrijheidsbenemende maatregel in het jeugdstrafrecht. *Familie- en Jeugdrecht*, 23, 7–12.
Waals, M.R. (2005). Toepassing van volwassenensanctierecht bij jeugdigen. De beperkingen van het sanctierecht voor jeugdigen. *Familie- en Jeugdrecht*, 9, 207–11.
Weijers, I. (2006). *Jeugdige dader, volwassen straf? Artikel 77b Sr*. Deventer: Kluwer.
Weijers, I. (2008). Geschiedenis van het jeugdstrafrecht. In I. Weijers and F. Imkamp (eds), *Jeugdstrafrecht*. The Hague: BJu Legal, pp. 13–30.
Weijers, I. and Liefaard, T. (2007). Youngsters. In M. Boone and M. Moerings (eds), *Dutch Prisons*. The Hague: BJu Legal, pp. 127–66.
Wiarda-Committee (1971). *Jeugdbeschermingsrecht*. The Hague: Staatsuitgeverij.

Chapter 8
Offending and Justice Response at the Juvenile–Adult Interface

Peter H. van der Laan, André M. van der Laan, Machteld Hoeve, Martine Blom, Willemijn H. Lamet and Rolf Loeber

The Netherlands currently is at a crossroads in how best to deal with adolescent offenders (ages 12–17) and with young adult offenders (ages 18–24). On the one hand, there are calls for the justice system to become harsher in response to delinquent acts committed by adolescents and apply longer sanctions, including incarceration. On the other hand, there are calls to extend the more humane and traditional juvenile justice approach to young adult offenders. Among the reasons behind the latter calls is the fact that most young adult offenders tend to overcome immature behaviours that are typical of adolescence and early adulthood, and that maturation – including brain maturation – for many is only completed during early adulthood.

Rarely are findings from empirical studies about this issue brought into the discussions to ensure that decisions, new legislation, and judicial procedures are informed by scientific results and not solely by the understandable desire on the part of legislators and judicial authorities to respond to the general public's request to 'do something'. The stakes are high, not just in the political arena but especially in terms of the life course of thousands of offenders and victims, and the prospects of reducing the impact of the recidivism of offenders on society in general. The financial stakes are also high because some forms of legal sanctions – especially incarceration – are very costly, and the important issue is how the justice system can deal with crime without increasing the prison population and incurring even higher costs in the future.

Several key empirical questions that are relevant to the debates are addressed in this chapter. First, when using police statistics and self-reported delinquency surveys, can we state which age groups of offenders – adolescents, young adults, and adults (the latter defined as ages 25–29) – are most responsible for crime; does this vary by ethnicity and gender, and has this changed over recent decades? Second, given that many young offenders stop offending as they mature, a key question is when does desistance typically occur between ages 12 and 29, and why is this relevant for the administration of justice? However, before dealing with these important questions, we shall present a brief history of Dutch legislative committees and changes in Dutch law that have taken place over the past 60 years that pertain to adolescent and young adult offenders.

A Brief History of Policy and Research

Almost 60 years ago, the Overwater Committee presented a report to the Minister of Justice with suggestions and a model for a new penal law for juveniles.[1] The Committee proposed the reintroduction of a minimum age of criminal responsibility, to be set at 12,[2] and a series of special provisions and sanctions for youths up to age 17. Since the civil age of adulthood was expected to go down from 21 to 18,[3] penal law for adults would soon apply to those aged 18 and older. Young adults aged 18–21 would no longer be treated according to juvenile penal law. Therefore, the Overwater Committee also suggested a separate penal system for young adults aged 18–23 or 25. The proposals resulted in a new law in 1965 that incorporated most of the Overwater Committee ideas, with the exception of separate provisions for young adults. Instead, the Minister of Justice appointed a new committee, the 'Commissie herziening strafrecht voor jeugdigen' (Committee for the reform of penal law for juveniles) under the chairmanship of Mr Anneveldt, president of the court of Assen. The Anneveldt Committee was asked, among other things, to explore the need of special provisions in penal law for young adults.

In 1982, the committee published its final report 'Sanctierecht voor jeugdigen' (Sanction law for juveniles).[4] Recommendations were made to simplify the law for juveniles and also to limit the number of penal sanctions for juveniles. The Committee also suggested extending some of the provisions to young people between ages 18 and 23. From a psychological and developmental point of view, this age period was recognized as a separate category, and while individuals within it could no longer be considered juveniles, neither had they reached full adulthood. Therefore, it was proposed that penal sanctions for young adults should be similar to those for minors – i.e., limited in length, less repressive, and of a more pedagogical nature compared to sanctions for adults. The Committee recommended that the sanction system for minors should thus be extended to ages 18–23, with the possibility of longer sentences for juveniles aged 16 and older (but still shorter than those for adults). However, the idea was not to change penal procedures. The Committee believed that for ages 18 and

---

1 In 1955, a working group of the Ministry of Justice published a study to evaluate prisons for young adults aged 18–23 – 'half-adults', as they were called in the report. The working group also proposed several separate sanctions for young adults (Overwater Committee, 1955)

2 This minimum age had been set at 10 at the beginning of the twentieth century but was skipped in the 1920s. Until the mid-1960s there was no minimum age of criminal responsibility. It was up to the discretion of the court to adjudicate young children who had committed a crime or to divert them to the child protection system.

3 In the end, this was not established before the early 1990s.

4 In 1981, an interim report had been published proposing the idea of launching an experiment with alternative sanctions (community service and training programmes) for juveniles.

older similar procedures to those for adults should be applied since young adults should benefit from the same legal rights as adults.

Most of the Anneveldt proposals were accepted by the Cabinet. Both provisions and procedures were simplified. For example, the relatively large numbers of penal sanctions were reduced to only three: fines, detention ('jeugddetentie'), and a treatment measure in secure accommodation. Penal procedures were made simpler by introducing expanded possibilities to apply adult penal law to youths aged 16 and 17. It was believed that a smoother transition from the juvenile to the adult system should be advanced. This, for instance, should be the case when very serious offences that severely shocked society were committed. Dealing with such cases behind closed doors, as is usually the case within the juvenile court, would limit transparency in court procedures, with the risk of losing legitimacy. As a result, more openness was warranted. Also, cases in which offences were committed by groups of both juvenile and adult offenders should not result in different sanctions for group members simply because of their different ages.

The Committee's suggestion to have the same penal sanctions for young adults as for minors was rejected by the Cabinet, not because of a general disagreement with the proposal but simply for practical and economic reasons. The overall idea was that it made sense to consider young adults a separate age category with its own particularities, characteristics and needs, and more similar to minors. However, in practice it was believed that it would mean a far-reaching reorganization of the system and perhaps rather drastic adjustments and rebuilding of custodial provisions in particular in order to more adequately respond to the needs of that age group. In a new system, adolescents (young adults) could no longer stay in the same facilities as adults. Such an operation would put too much of a burden on already tight budgets. The Cabinet's refusal to do something for offenders aged 18–23 did not receive much attention and was not really criticized, perhaps because most of the proposed changes in juvenile justice for minors were acceptable and were adopted.

After the publication of the Anneveldt report in 1982 and the revision of the penal law for juveniles in 1996, justice issues surrounding young adults did not receive public and judicial attention for many years. Most research and policy papers in the 1980s and 1990s were devoted to juveniles under age 17 rather than young adults. In 1994, the Van Montfrans Committee published a report that gave an overview of trends in juvenile delinquency and recommended a series of measures to more adequately deal with youth crime. The Committee's report had quite an impact and resulted in the Ministry of Justice creating an extensive policy plan fully devoted to juvenile delinquency. Many already-existing policies were intensified and new ones introduced. The Committee also put young children prominently on the political agenda, stating that – from a preventive point of view – children under age 12, who cannot be held responsible for their criminal acts and therefore cannot be prosecuted, deserve special attention. Several policy papers and circular letters were published dedicated to young children and specific interventions for them were recommended.[5] But the Van Montfrans report did not devote a single word to young people over age 17.

The lack of attention to young adults lasted until 2002 when the then State Secretary of Justice issued a new policy plan entitled 'Vasthoudend en effectief' (Persistent and effective). For the first time since the recommendations of the Anneveldt Committee, young adults were mentioned as a group that also required special attention. It was announced that the Raad voor de Kinderbescherming (Council of Child Care and Protection) and the probation services for minors and for adults had been asked to develop ideas on how to deal with this age category of young adults. But not much happened apart from arrangements being made for new clients of probation services aged 17, who would no longer be supervised by the probation service for minors but instead transferred to that for adults. Furthermore, the Dutch prison service introduced a special regime for young adults in order to prevent harm resulting from detention for this vulnerable group of young detainees. This special regime was characterized by a more protective environment and more intensive support. The report did not spark any special interest in the prevalence and crime trends among young adults. Reports on juvenile crime were continuously published, but young adults as a separate age category remained ignored and crime trends were not addressed.

In 2003 the Council of Europe issued Recommendation 2003(20), 'New ways of dealing with juvenile delinquency'. Among the numerous topics addressed was that of the need for paying attention to young adults by means of a separate penal system and/or penal sanctions adapted to the age category 18–23. Germany and Austria were mentioned as examples of countries taking such an approach. Even though the recommendation was signed by the ministers of justice of all member states, including the Dutch Minister of Justice, it did not affect policy and practice in the Netherlands. This is probably due to the fact that Council of Europe recommendations are 'soft law' (Nijboer, 2001) and, consequently, member states are not bound by it.

Matters changed rather dramatically in January 2004 when a 17-year-old boy murdered a vice-principal of a secondary school in The Hague. The young offender was sentenced according to adult penal law by the criminal court, and later by the Court of Appeals. The courts ruled against the advice of three behavioural experts who saw no need to apply adult law and raised serious concerns about the young man's state of mental health and developmental age. But the experts disagreed on whether or not a maximum six-year treatment measure in a closed institution would suffice. Therefore, the courts decided to apply adult law since under adult law there is no fixed maximum for a treatment measure. Treatment measures can be prolonged by court decision every two years.

The case of this 17-year-old offender activated discussions about transfer to adult court and the possible need of a separate penal system for young adults. Lawyers

---

5 See for instance 'Notitie kinderen en criminaliteit' (Memorandum children and crime) (1997) from the State Secretary of Justice and Van den Hoogen-Saleh (2000).

published opinions on the matter, often concluding that perhaps some changes in the law were necessary in order to make it possible in exceptional cases to extend the measure or to convert the treatment measure for juveniles with a maximum of six years into a treatment measure for adults with no maximum. Such an extension or conversion should only be decided by the court after having consulted those responsible for treatment and treatment progress (see, for example, Doek, 2004).

This case also led to renewed interest in the whole issue of young adult offenders. The Research and Documentation Centre (WODC) of the Ministry of Justice explored penal practice regarding young adults in Belgium, Germany, the United Kingdom and the United States, and more marginally in some other Western countries (Verwers and Bogaerts, 2005). In Germany, youths aged 18–21 are considered adults but can be tried according to juvenile law. All cases are handled by the juvenile court even if adult law is applied.

In other countries no such provisions exist but minors can be dealt with by an adult court. In Scotland, adult law is automatically applied to youths aged 16 and older. In a separate development, the WODC widened its periodical monitor of recorded juvenile delinquency from ages 12–17 to ages 12–24 (Van der Laan et al., 2010). The findings of this survey are reported later in this chapter.

Doreleijers and Fokkens (2010) recently approached the issue from a slightly different angle and focused on new insights from developmental psychological and biological studies (see also Loeber et al., Chapter 12, this volume). Young adults are mainly seen as adults for formal or legal reasons, but psychologically and sociologically they are not yet fully grown up. For instance, from a neurobiological point of view young adults are not fully developed before approximately age 25. For these reasons, the authors were not really satisfied with the fact that youths aged 16 and 17 can be transferred to adult court. For the same reasons also they argued that more young adults aged 18–20 should be handled by the juvenile court. They proposed to extend an experiment in the court district of Almelo, where young adult cases were handled more according to juvenile justice than to adult justice principles and where young adults also had access to juvenile justice provisions. If the outcomes of such an experiment are promising, perhaps a further extension to ages 21–23 could be considered at other judicial locations.

The latest addition to the discussion about young adult crime and the application of juvenile versus adult penal law came from the recently installed centre-right Cabinet. In the fall of 2010, the Cabinet announced in its coalition agreement to propose a new penal law for adolescents aged 15–23. More details were given in a letter to Parliament in the summer of 2011 (TK, 2010–2011). The most important changes included increasing the maximum length of detention for youths ages 16 and 17 from two to four years,[6] and extending the option of applying juvenile law to young adults up to age of 23 who are not yet fully mature. Furthermore, an option was created to convert the treatment measures for juveniles that currently have a maximum of six

6 Juveniles aged 15 were no longer mentioned in the letter.

years into treatment measures for adults with no fixed length. Young adults, including those aged 16 and 17, were presented as the most problematic age group since they are responsible for a relatively large proportion of crime committed.[7] The proposals reflect a tougher and more repressive approach, in particular towards minors aged 16 and 17, and did not include a separate penal system for late adolescents and young adults. Thus, the ideas do not seem to follow the recommendations of the Anneveldt Committee in 1982, the Recommendation 2003 (20) of the Council of Europe, or the proposal by Doreleijers and Fokkens (2010).

In summary, several policy documents have focused on lower- and upper age limits for penal procedures. Repeatedly and from various perspectives a case has been made to implement separate or amended sanctions and procedures for young adults. However, hardly any empirical data on crime and crime trends have been introduced in the discussions. Proposals for change have rarely been initiated by information on the prevalence and trends of young adult crime but were usually triggered by considerations regarding psychological and biological development, and the granting or denial of juvenile and adult rights. We shall fill this gap by presenting in the remainder of this chapter police and other data concerning offending during adolescence and early adulthood.

Delinquency by Adolescents, Young Adults and Adults as Seen Through the Prism of Police Reports

In this section we use police records to describe the number and proportion of young adults suspected of a crime in 2007 out of the general population and briefly examine the crime trends for the period 1996–2007. We compare three offender groups: adolescents (ages 12–17), young adults (ages 18–24) and adults (ages 25–29),[8] based on the Herkenningsdienstsysteem (HKS) (Recognition service system) of the Dutch police.[9]

---

7 Apparently the Cabinet did not take into account recent figures indicating a possible decrease of offending by adolescents and young adults (Van der Laan and Blom, 2011).

8 A more extensive report is available from the authors.

9 In the Netherlands several police statistics give insight into the number of crime suspects nationwide. One is the *Herkenningsdienstsysteem* (HKS). This statistic contains nationwide information on reported crimes and unique suspects, including some background characteristics, such as age, gender, ethnic background and place of living. In this chapter we report on the number of persons who were suspected of a crime by the police using the HKS statistic. HKS does not include minor offences or misdemeanors. Some persons can be arrested more than once in a year. In our analyses these persons were counted just once in a year. Therefore, for each year our analyses concern the number or proportion of unique suspects. Another statistic is the *Politiestatistiek* (Police Statistics) of Statistics Netherlands. This statistic shows insight into all juvenile and adult suspects, including those who in the end are no longer considered formal suspects, and include moderate and serious offences. The *Politiestatistiek* contains information on the number of police suspects. It

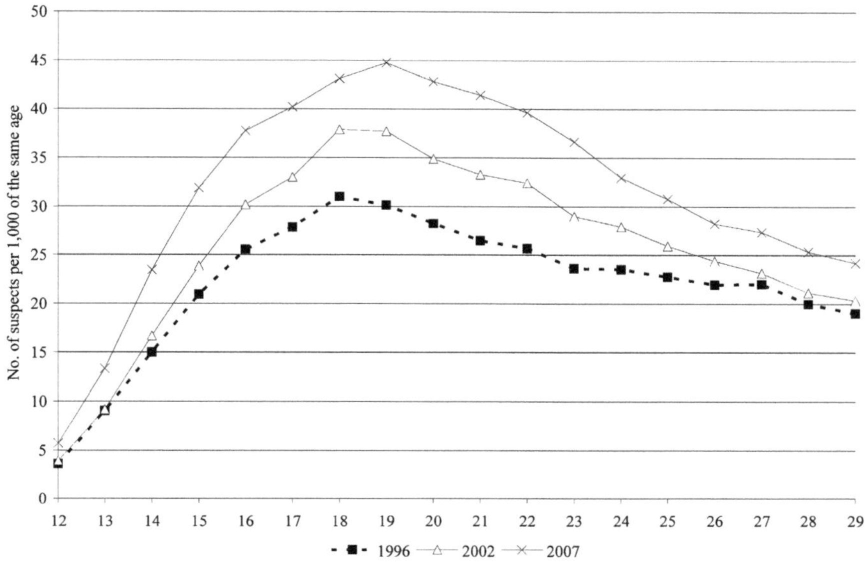

Figure 8.1 The number of suspects per 1,000 in the age group 12–29 for 1996, 2002 and 2007

Trends and Developments

In 2007, 245,000 persons were suspected of one or more moderate to serious crimes. Of these suspects 30,600 were adolescents, 54,700 were young adults, and 26,900 were adults. In the total population of suspects, almost four out of ten were aged 12–24.[10] Relative to the population in the same age groups in 2007, 40 per 1,000 young adults were suspected of a crime compared to 25 per 1,000 adolescents, and 27 per 1,000 adults. The likelihood of being a suspect of a moderate or serious crime among young adults is one-and-a-half times higher than among adolescents and adults (Odds Ratios = 1.6 and 1.5 respectively). We consider this a first indication as to why young adults merit special attention.

Figure 8.1 shows the age–crime curves of suspects aged 12–29 for 1996, 2002 and 2007. The three curves show a similar pattern to the age–crime curve presented by Blokland and Palmen (Chapter 2, this volume): the percentage of suspects increases from age 12, peaks between ages 18–20, and decreases slowly

does not contain information on specific background characteristics such as age (it only includes the categories 12–17 years and 18 years or older) or ethnic origin.

10 Cases in which the Public Prosecutor has decided to dismiss the case for technical reasons (too little evidence) or has come to an acquittal are not included. This means that the proportion of adolescents and young adults that is reported in this paragraph is slightly lower than the proportion of suspects in other reports based on HKS (for example, Van Mantgem, Van Nobelen and Uljee, 2009).

thereafter. The curves also show increased numbers of suspects per 1,000 for each age group over the years, particularly in 2007.

Table 8.1 presents crime rates per 1,000 in 2007 for different types of crime for the three age groups. The three most common crimes among young adults were traffic offences followed by assault and serious property crime. Traffic offences were also the most common offence type among adults, but assault and serious property crime were much less common. Serious property offences were the most common offence type among adolescents, followed by crime against public order and assault. In all three age groups sexual offences were the least common.

Most types of crimes showed an increase in the period 1996–2007 (Figure 8.2),

Table 8.1 Number of suspects per 1,000 persons of the same age group for different types of offences in 2007

	Crime rates per 1,000 of the same age group		
	12–17	18–24	25–29
Sexual offences	0.6	0.5	0.3
Threat	2.2	3.4	2.6
Assault	8.0	11.0	6.6
Robbery	2.1	2.1	1.1
Property crime	4.1	4.5	3.2
Serious property crime	10.8	10.8	5.7
Other property crimes	2.7	4.9	4.2
Crimes against public order	9.3	7.3	2.1
Crimes against public authorities	0.9	2.8	1.7
Vandalism	6.4	5.6	2.6
Traffic offences	1.4	11.7	10.2
Drug offences	0.7	4.4	4.4
Weapon possession	0.9	1.4	0.8
Other crimes	1.7	3.4	2.3

Source: HKS and CBS/WODC.

with the exception of property crime. Young adults had higher crime prevalence rates in this period with regard to most types of crime. However, with regard to crimes against public order, young adults have lower crime rates than adolescents, and with regard to robbery, serious property crime and vandalism the rates for young adults are close to the rates for adolescents. With regard to traffic offences and drug offences, the rates for young adults are close to that for adults.

The increase in the proportion of suspects was not the same for each age group (Figure 8.3). Compared to 2002, the highest increase (40 per cent) was among the youngest age group (12–15), whereas the increase of suspects in the older

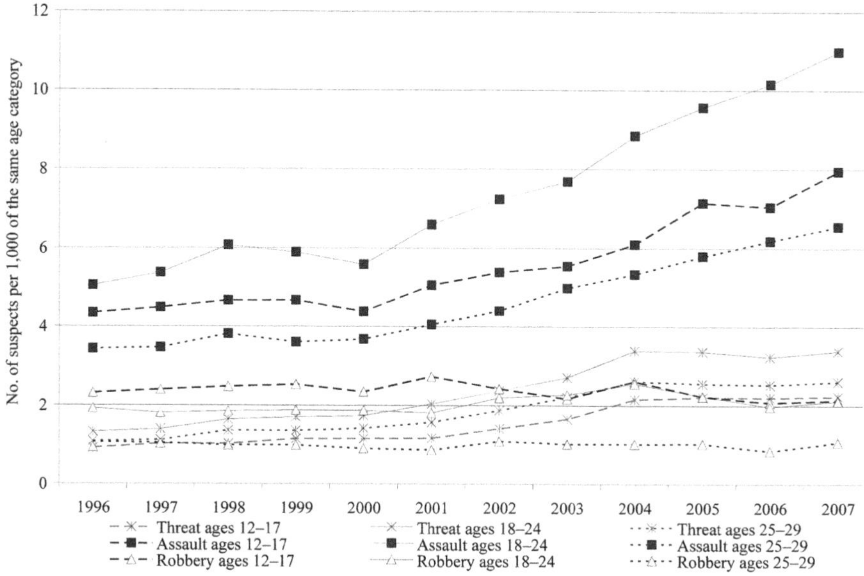

Figure 8.2a Trends in suspects per 1,000 adolescents, young adults and adults for different types of crime – Violence

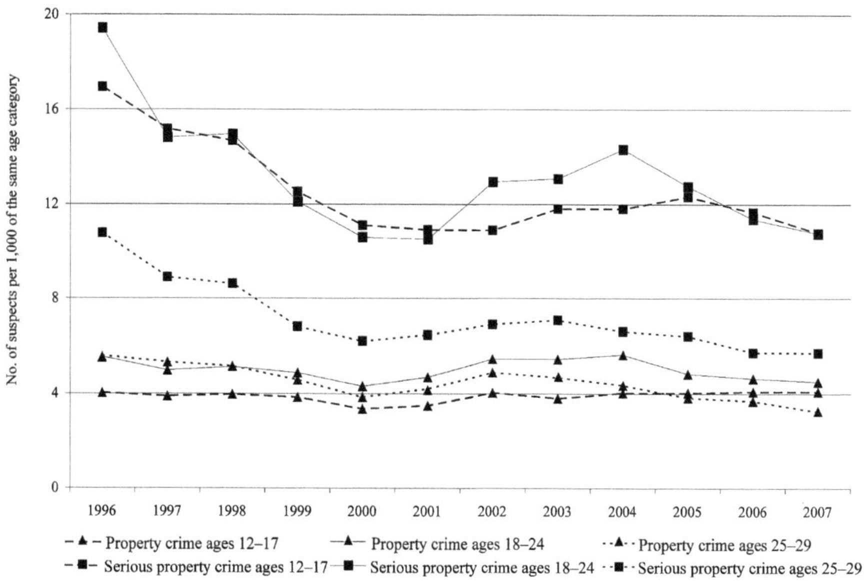

Figure 8.2b Trends in suspects per 1,000 adolescents, young adults and adults for different types of crime – Property crime

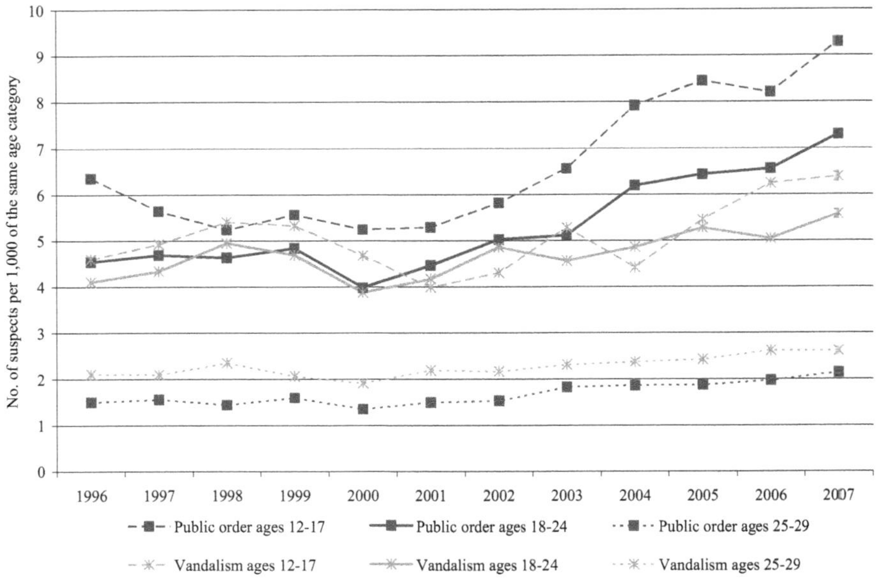

Figure 8.2c Trends in suspects per 1,000 adolescents, young adults and adults for different types of crime – Public order crime

age groups was similar (23 per cent).[11] This difference is difficult to explain. The youngest age category may have become criminally more active, but the increase may also be the result of the police focusing more intensely on younger juveniles since it is commonly known that behavioural problems at a young age are indicative of a longer criminal career. This line of thinking stresses the importance of early interventions.

In summary, although the shape of the age–crime curve would suggest that the transition from adolescence to adulthood is associated with a desistance from crime for many young people, police data show that young adults are more often suspects of delinquent acts than adolescents or adults. Young adults, compared to adolescents and adults, had a higher prevalence of crime during the period 1996–2007 with regard to most types of crime. Particularly for young adults, assault and threatening behaviour was relatively high and increased between 1996 and 2007. However, with regard to crimes against public order, young

11 As mentioned, traffic offences are the most common offence among young adults (see further Table 8.1), whereas among adolescents this offence is rare. In order to examine the impact of traffic offences on the trends in crime among young adults compared to the trends among adolescents, analyses were carried out excluding traffic offences. As a result, trends in suspects among young adults were slightly lower (for example, an increase of 18 per cent in 2007 compared to 2002), but the trend remained the same. Therefore, we decided to include traffic offences in the analysis.

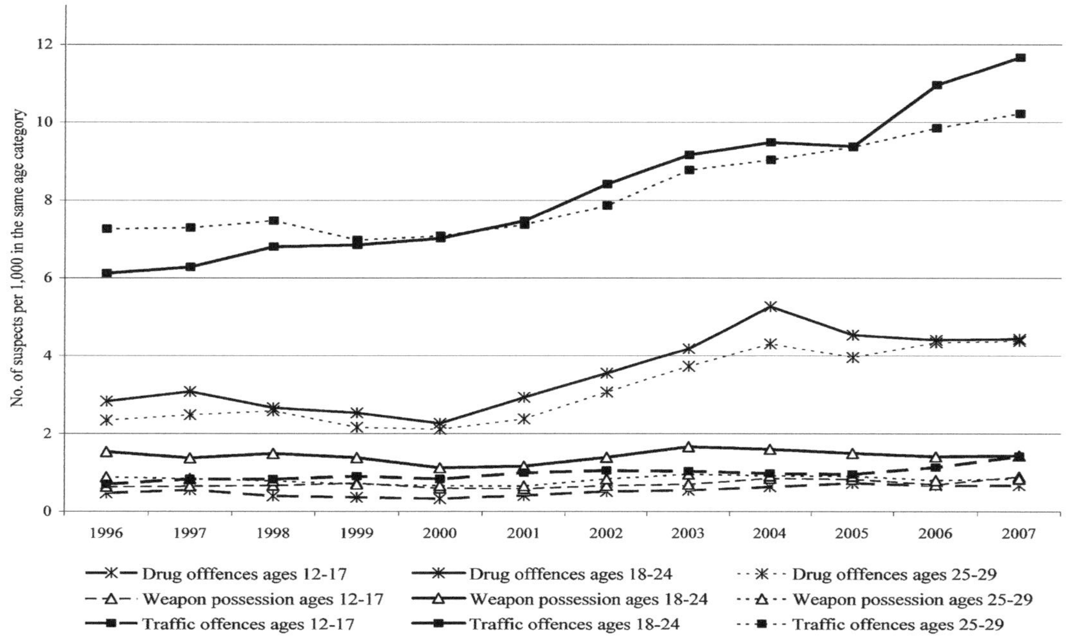

Figure 8.2d Trends in suspects per 1,000 adolescents, young adults and adults for different types of crime – Other types of crime

Source: HKS/WODC.

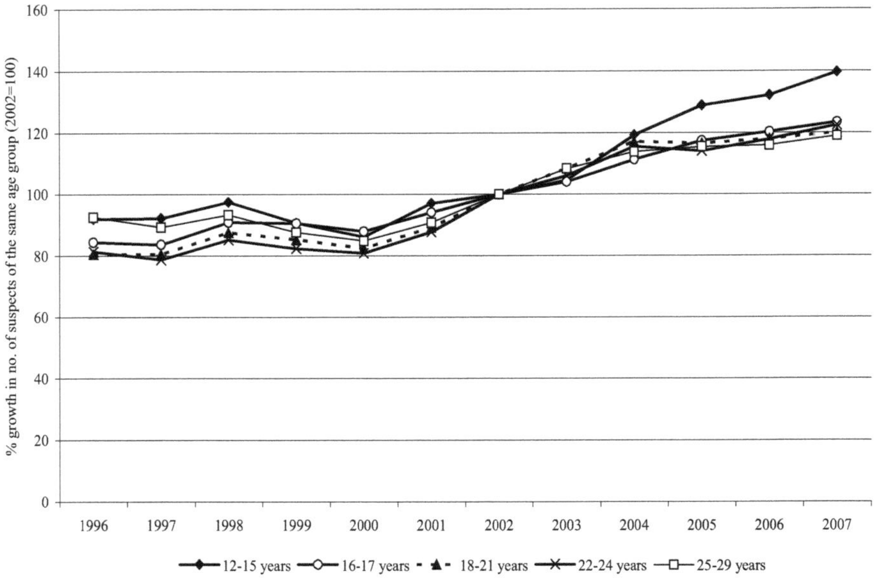

Figure 8.3 Trends in suspects among different age groups in the period 1996–2007 (% growth)

adults had lower crime rates than adolescents, and with regard to other offences the rates were similar to adults and close to those of adolescents.

Gender

Not surprisingly, the number of suspects (absolute and per 1,000) was lower for women than for men. This held for all three age groups, with the highest proportions among young adults. In 2007, 68 per 1,000 young adult males were suspected of a crime compared to 12 per 1,000 females, whereas in the adolescence and adulthood groups these figures were 40 and 46 per 1,000 males and 10 and 8 per 1,000 females. Among young adult males the odds of being a suspect of a crime (versus not being a suspect) were 1.8 times higher than among adolescent and adult males. Among young adult females, the odds of being a suspect were similar to adolescent females (Odds Ratio = 1.1), and slightly higher than adult females (Odds Ratio = 1.4). This indicates a substantially higher age–crime curve pattern among males than females. However, in the period 1996–2007 the number of suspects per 1,000 young adults increased more sharply among females than among males.

Ethnic Origin

Certain minorities were disproportionally overrepresented in the police statistics. In 2007, the number of ethnic suspects per 1,000 was highest among juveniles of

Table 8.2 Probability of being a suspect of crime (versus not being a suspect) across different ethnic groups for Young Adults compared to Adolescents and Adults (Odds Ratio)

	Young Adults versus Adolescents	Young Adults versus Adults
Native Dutch	1.6	1.7
Eastern Europe	1.1	1.6
Other Western origin	1.3	1.6
Dutch Antilles and Aruba	1.2	1.2
Moroccan	1.3	1.6
Turkish	1.3	1.3
Surinamese	1.4	1.3
Other non-Western origin	1.3	1.6

Source: HKS and CBS/WODC.

Moroccan descent (107 per 1,000), followed by juveniles from the Dutch Antilles – including Aruba – (96 per 1,000) and Surinam (82 per 1,000). The percentage of suspects among native Dutch juveniles was the lowest (30 per 1,000). This

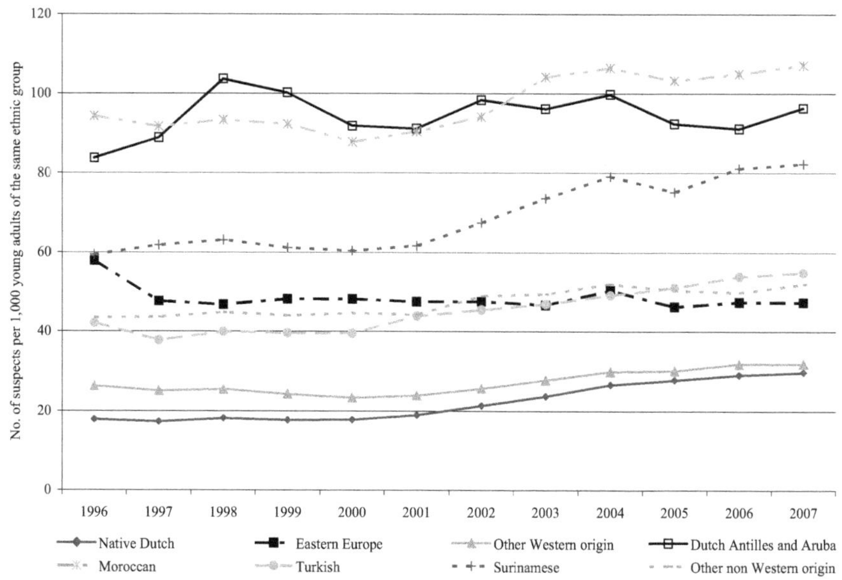

Figure 8.4a Trends in suspects of a crime per 1,000 18–24 years across different ethnic groups in the period 1996–2007 – Number of suspects per 1,000

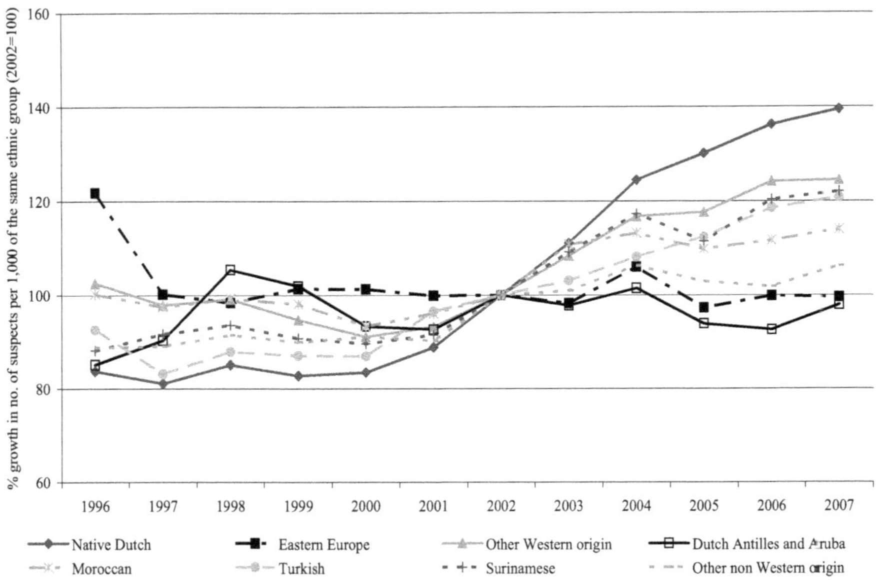

Figure 8.4b Trends in suspects of a crime per 1,000 18–24 years across different ethnic groups in the period 1996–2007 – Percentage growth in the number of suspects per 1,000 young adults in the period 1996–2007 (2002=100)

ranking of suspects of specific ethnic origin groups applies to adolescents, young adults and adults.

The odds of being a crime suspect (versus not being a suspect) for young adults compared to adolescents and adults differ within each ethnic origin group (see Table 8.2), with the largest differences within the native Dutch group. Young adults of native Dutch origin had higher odds of being a crime suspect (versus not being a suspect) than adolescents (Odds Ratio = 1.6) and adults (Odds Ratio = 1.7). Among other ethnic groups, young adults were more similar to adolescents, but the odds for young adults being a crime suspect were higher than among adults of the same ethnic origin. Exceptions were individuals from Dutch Antillean and Aruban, Turkish, and Surinamese origin. In these groups, the odds of being a crime suspect among young adults and adults is quite similar (Odds Ratios = 1.2–1.3), indicating a smaller decrease in life-course offending than among the other ethnic groups.

Jennissen (2009) investigated in more depth the age–crime curve for Moroccans and young persons from the Dutch Antilles and Aruba. Both ethnic groups were disproportionally overrepresented as crime suspects during adolescence and early adulthood. The curve for Moroccan suspects decreased strongly from age 21, following a more normative age–crime curve during the adult period. However, individuals from the Dutch Antilles and Aruba disproportionately remained crime suspects during adulthood. The decrease in suspects among this ethnic group began only at age 40.

The number of suspects per 1,000 increased for all ethnic groups. However, the increase varied among the different groups (Figure 8.4). The percentage of suspects among native Dutch young adults increased more sharply in the most recent years than among young adults of other descent. The percentages of suspects among young adults of Moroccan and Antillean origin showed the lowest increase and were even relatively stable in the period 2003–2007. These trends suggest a ceiling effect among those ethnic groups with the highest proportion of crime suspects.

Table 8.3 Prevalence of self-reported delinquency over the past year

	Age		
Offence	**8–11***	**12–17****	**18–24*****
Fare dodging	2.0	15.7	20.3
Graffiti	1.7	10.1	1.3
Harassment	19.6	14.1	8.3
Vandalism	6.4	9.1	6.4
Shoplifting	1.4	7.0	3.3
Arson	6.4	4.3	1.1
Receiving stolen goods	0.5	4.2	8.7
Bicycle theft	0.9	1.3	5.0
Assault	2.6	2.7	1.9
Burglary	0.8	1.6	0.3
Theft from a phone box or automated machine	0.8	1.1	0.2
Theft at school	3.7	7.2	5.6
Threatening to extort money	0.9	0.3	0.1
1 or more 'original' offences	26.9	37.8	36.1

Note: *n=699; **n=1,096; ***n=1,572

Source: WODC 1994 Self-Reported Delinquency survey.

Delinquency by Adolescents, Young Adults and Adults as Seen through the Prism of Self-reports

Police data can only include crimes reported to or known by the police. Of those crimes reported to the police, the clear-up rate in 2007 was 23 per cent (Eggen, 2009). Self-reported crime can be an important supplement to police data, particularly when dealing with a wide range of delinquent behaviours, many of which remain undetected. But in the Netherlands, as in most other countries,

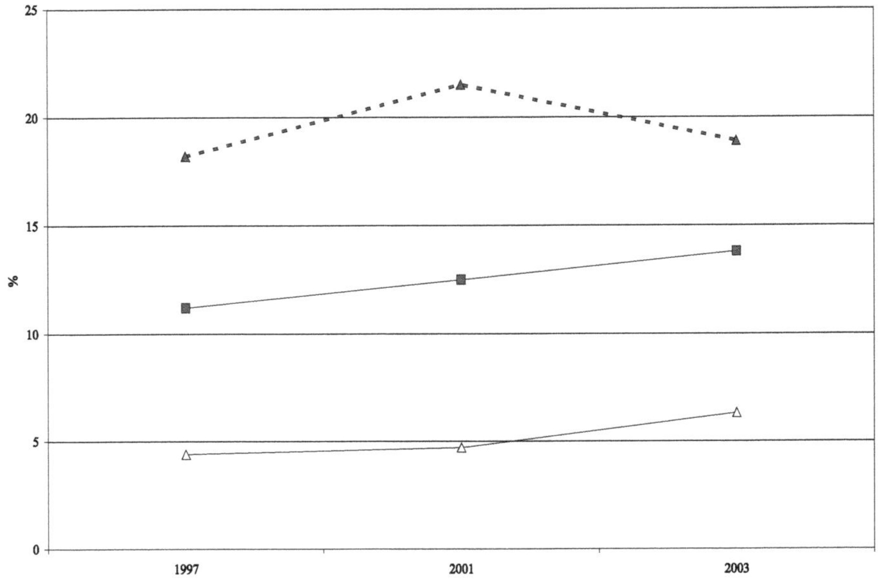

Figure 8.5a Prevalence in self-reported violent and property crime among adolescents, young adults, and adults in 1999, 2001, 2003 – Violent crime

Source: CBS-POLS.

only a few studies have examined self-reported crime and crime trends over the years among young adults in population-based samples (CBS, 1997, 2001, 2003; Donker, 2004; Van der Laan et al., 1997).

In 1994, the first known Dutch self-report survey among young adults aged 18–24 was conducted by the WODC (Van der Laan et al., 1997). This biannual self-report study was originally conducted among ages 12–17, but in 1994 the sample was expanded to include ages 8–11 and 18–24, and consisted of 1,572 young adults. Table 8.3 shows a higher prevalence of self-reported crime during adolescence and early adulthood. Whereas 26.9 per cent of ages 8–11 reported a crime, among adolescents 37.8 per cent reported a crime and among the young adults 36.1 per cent reported having committed a crime in the past year (minor offences such as fare-dodging included). With regard to specific offences, compared to adolescents young adults showed a higher prevalence of fare-dodging, receiving stolen goods, and bicycle theft. In comparison, the prevalence of graffiti, harassment, shoplifting, arson, and theft at school was substantially lower among young adults than among adolescents.

Donker (2004) examined self-reported delinquency in 1997–1998 among 1,547 young Dutch adults aged 18–32 living in the province of South Holland. The overall prevalence of self-reported crime, excluding fare-dodging, among respondents aged 18–32 in the past year was 23.9 per cent. Furthermore, 28.7

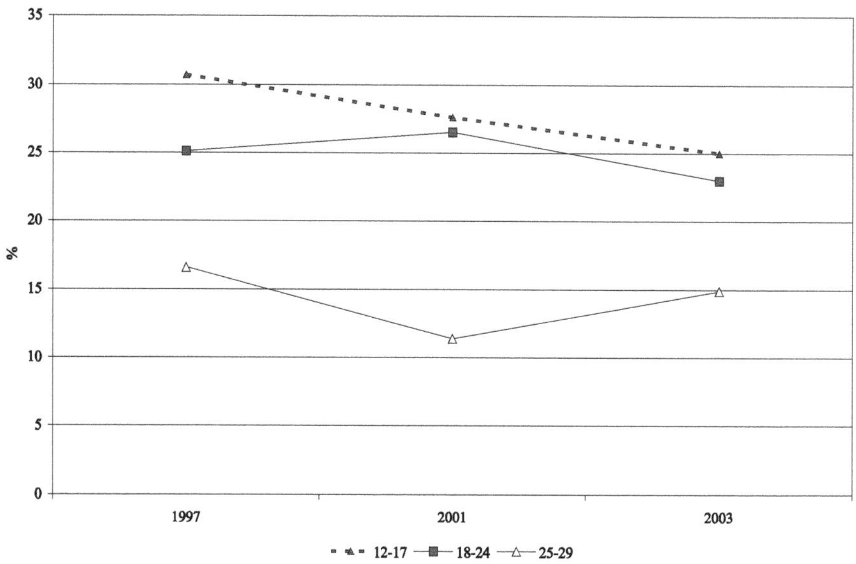

Figure 8.5b Prevalence in self-reported violent and property crime among adolescents, young adults, and adults in 1999, 2001, 2003 – Property crime

Source: CBS-POLS.

per cent of the young adults reported at least one property crime. The highest prevalence for specific forms of delinquency was receiving stolen goods (8.5 per cent) and theft from the workplace (8.4 per cent). Violence-related crimes (including vandalism) were reported by 6.5 per cent of the young adults, with the highest prevalence for carrying a weapon (3.7 per cent), vandalism (2.2 per cent), and group fighting in a public place (1.4 per cent). Selling drugs was reported by 1.4 per cent of the young adults. More males than females reported an offence (respectively 41.1 per cent versus 23.2 per cent). Donker also investigated traffic offences among young adults (unauthorized driving, joy-riding, driving more than 30 km/h too fast, drunk driving, and hit-and-run accidents). Of the young adults, 39.8 per cent reported a traffic offence in the past year, with the highest prevalence for driving too fast (34.7 per cent), followed by drunken driving (5.4 per cent) and unauthorized driving (5.2 per cent). Even though Donker could not compare young adults with adolescents, her results seem to be similar to those reported by Van der Laan et al. (1997). They also show that specific types of crime, such as theft from the workplace and various traffic offences, are typical for young adults.

The only cross-sectional nationwide trend study of self-reported crime in the Netherlands among adolescents, young adults and adults has been conducted by the Central Bureau of Statistics in their study 'Permanent Leefsituatie Onderzoek'

(Permanent Living Situation Survey) (POLS), with waves in 1997, 2001 and 2003 (CBS, 1997, 2001, 2003).[12]

Between 50 per cent (1997) and 55 per cent (2001) of the young adults reported being involved in a crime at least once in the past year, not including traffic offences. In all three years the prevalence of self-reported delinquency among young adults was similar to the rates among adolescents. Adults showed lower prevalence rates. The prevalence of self-reported violent crime was the highest among adolescents and the lowest among adults. It showed an increase among young adults and adults in consecutive years, whereas among adolescents self-reported violent crime peaked in 2001 and since then decreased (Figure 8.5). The prevalence of property crimes was also the highest among adolescents (25 per cent in 2003), followed by young adults (23 per cent) and adults (15 per cent).

In conclusion, studies on self-reported delinquency showed prevalence rates among young adults between 31.5 and 55.4 per cent. However, self-reported delinquency studies have shown contradictory results. Whereas one study showed almost no differences between young adults and adolescents in the overall prevalence rates of self-reported crime (Van der Laan et al., 1997), another study showed lower prevalence rates among young adults than among adolescents (CBS, 1997, 2001, 2003). The higher prevalence of crime among young adults relative to that of adolescents based on police records is not mirrored when based on self-reports.

Penal Sanctions and Judicial Measures for Delinquent Acts Committed by Adolescents, Young Adults and Adults

In this section we focus on adolescents, young adults, and adults with a criminal case that has been settled by the public prosecutor or the court. We define these individuals as offenders and not as suspects since the prosecutor and/or the court considered them guilty of having committed a crime. We are interested in answering the following questions: What is the burden on the prosecutor and courts in terms of the prevalence of referral of offenders including adolescents, young adults, and adults? Second, are there major secular changes in the referral burden during the last decade? And what is the rate of offenders' recidivism after particular actions undertaken by the prosecutor or the court?

To address these questions we used data from the 'Onderzoek- en Beleidsdatabase Justitiële Documentatie' (Research and Policy Database for Judicial Documentation) (OBJD). The OBJD is an encrypted copy of the official judicial documentation system (JDS) that is managed by the 'Justitiële Informatiedienst' (Judicial Information Service) (JustId) and is anonymous – i.e., not bearing any names. The JDS provides an overview of all resident persons who have come into contact with the judicial system for moderate and serious offences in the Netherlands, and of the cases of

12 See also http://statline.cbs.nl/statweb/ ('Zelfgerapporteerde delicten onder jongeren (12–29) jaar naar kenmerken', retrieved 6 November 2009).

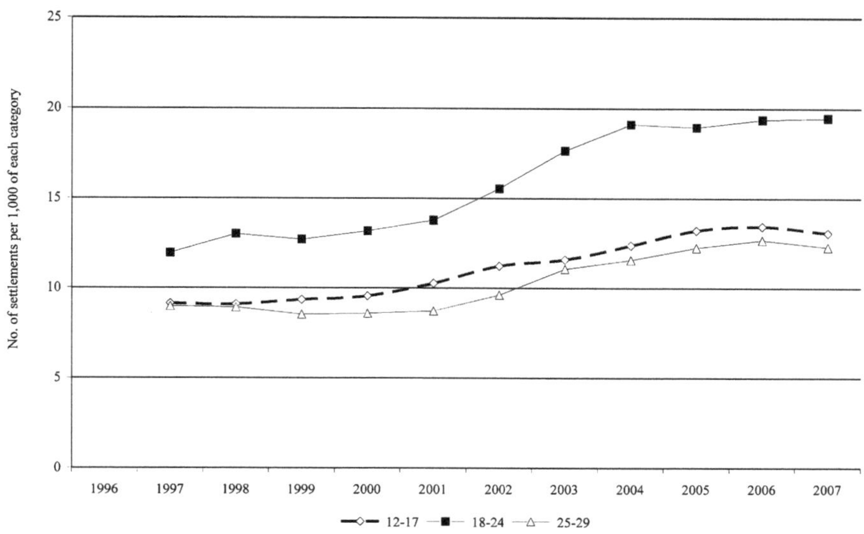

Figure 8.6a Settlements by the Public Prosecutor per 1,000 of each age category – Number of settlements by each age category

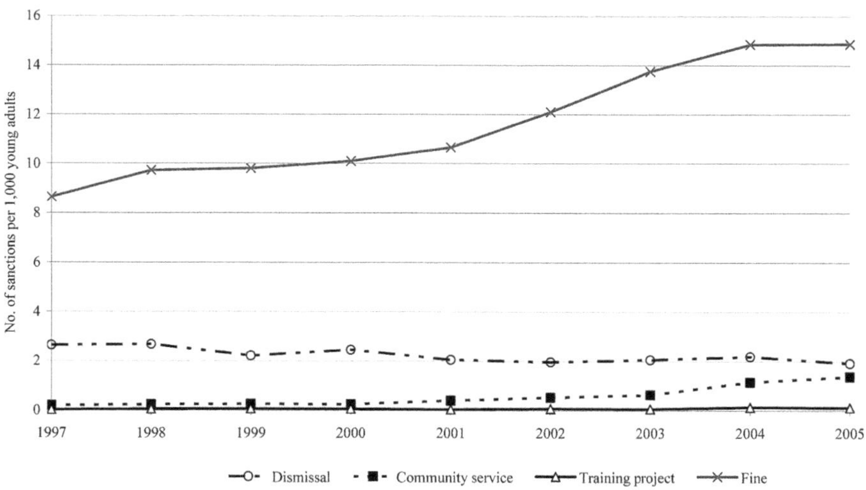

Figure 8.6b Settlements by the Public Prosecutor per 1,000 of each age category – Type of settlements per 1,000 young adults

Source: OBJD.

which they were suspected. We excluded cases ending in an acquittal, dismissal by reason of unlikelihood of conviction, or a technical decision by the court. Only cases in which the court pronounced a finding of guilt, or which were settled by the public prosecutor by means of a discretionary dismissal or a transaction without being referred to the court, are included.

The Prevalence of Criminal Cases Referred to the Public Prosecutor and the Court

In 2007, 46,800 young adults aged 18–24 had a criminal case settled by the public prosecutor or a sanction imposed by the court (34 per 1,000 young adults). In the same year, 23,200 adolescents had at least one criminal case (19 per 1,000 juveniles aged 12–17), as did 23,750 adults (24 per 1,000 adults aged 25–29). Thus the proportion of cases (offenders) dealt with by the judiciary was the highest among young adults.

Rates of offenders reported to the public prosecutor and/or referred to the court per 1,000 young adults increased during the period 1997–2007, but not as sharply as the trends in those suspected of a crime as reported in police statistics (see above). This implies that the police did not file an official report with the prosecutor's office for all suspects known to them. Compared to 2002, in 2007 the rate of offenders among young adults had increased by 20 per cent, from 29–34 per 1,000. Among adolescents the rate of offenders who received a sanction increased by 19 per cent, and among adults aged 25–29 the rate had increased by 15 per cent. Whereas clear age differences in trends were found with regard to *suspects*, there are hardly any age differences in the trends of *offenders*.

Gender

Young females accounted for only a small proportion of youths whose cases were dealt with by the judiciary. In 2007, the rate was 10 offenders per 1,000 young adult females whereas the rates for young adult males were much higher (58 per 1,000). However, the number of offenders per 1,000 increased more sharply among women than among men. Between 2002 and 2007, the rate increased from 7 to 10 offenders per 1,000 young adult females, which amounts to an increase of 48 per cent. For young adult men the increase was from 50–58, an increase of 16 per cent. Among adolescents and adults the rate among females also showed a higher increase than among males. This indicates that the gap between men and women has become somewhat smaller but is still large.

Dismissals and Sanctions Imposed by the Public Prosecutor

In 2007 the public prosecutor settled 15,740 cases of adolescents (13 per 1,000), 26,460 of young adults (19 per 1,000), and 12,150 of adults aged 25–29 (12 per 1,000). Almost half (49 per cent) of all dismissals and sanctions imposed by the

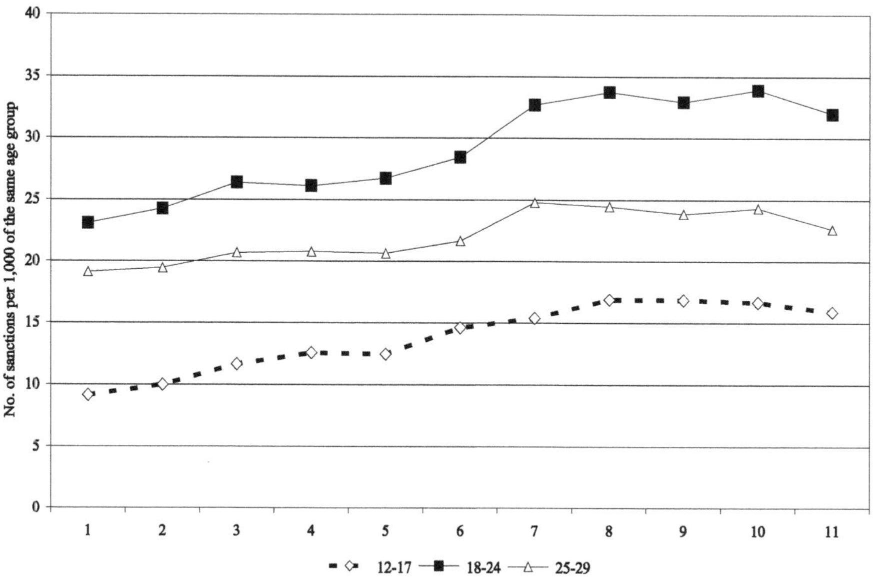

Figure 8.7 Number of sanctions imposed by court per 1,000 of the same age category period 1997–2007

Source: OBJD

public prosecutor concerned young adults. The number of prosecutor settlements of young adults (aged 18–24), was an increase of 25 per cent compared to 2002. In the period 1997–2007, the rate of settlements per 1,000 individuals was lower among adolescents and adults than among young adults. The trends among the age groups differ slightly, but the overall picture shows a flat pattern before 2001, an increase until 2004, followed by a flat pattern until 2007. Figure 8.6a shows the number of settlements by the prosecutor.

With regard to the type of sanctions decided by the public prosecutor, our data contained valid results only for the period 1997–2005. The most common sanction for young adults was a fine. This also applied to adults aged 25–29, whereas for adolescents the most common decision was a community service order. Among all three age groups, the most common decisions showed an increase in the period 1997–2005. For example, the number of fines for young adults increased to 15 per 1,000 in 2005 (Figure 8.6b), an increase of 23 per cent compared to 2002. Community service orders increased as well but were imposed much less frequently. Dismissals remained more or less the same.

Sanctions Imposed by the Court

In 2007 the courts in the Netherlands imposed sanctions on 19,140 adolescents aged 12–17 (16 per 1,000), on 43,440 young adults aged 18–24 (32 per 1,000), and

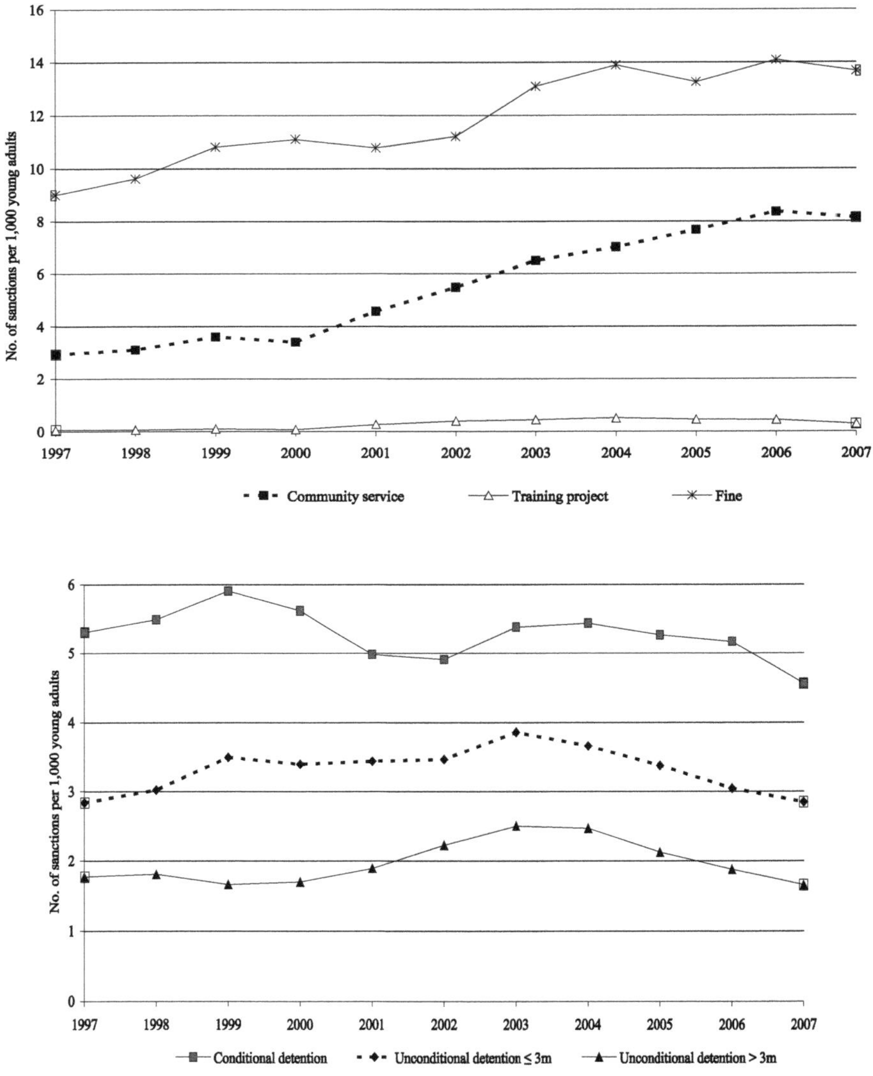

Figure 8.8 Types of sanctions imposed by court, per 1,000 young adults, period 1997–2007

Source: OBJD.

on 22,360 adults aged 25–29 (23 per 1,000). Young adults accounted for 51 per cent of all sanctions imposed by the court in the age group 12–30.

Among the three age groups, the trends of sanctions imposed by the court were comparable. Overall, the trend for young adults showed an increase in the period 1997–2006. Figure 8.7 shows a comparable trend for the rates of sanctions imposed

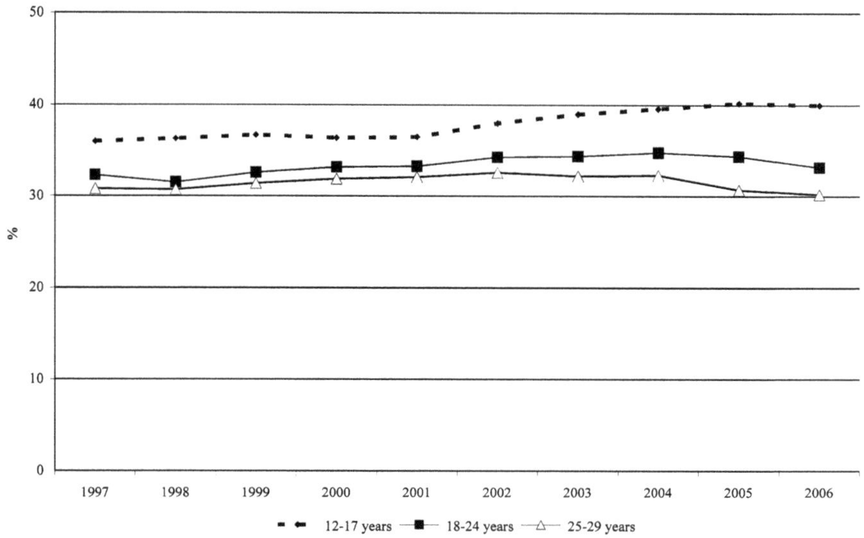

Figure 8.9 Prevalence of general recidivism rates (within two years) of persons with a criminal case in the period 1997–2006

Note: Percentages are shown of offenders who recidivated within 2 years after their initial criminal case had been settled by the Public Prosecutor or a sanction was imposed by the court in the period 1997–2006. This is considered 'general recidivism', meaning that an individual has a renewed contact with the Public Prosecutor or the court because of a criminal offence. Type or frequency of recidivism is not accounted for. The rates are not corrected with regard to population size in a given year; recidivism rates are based on absolute (raw) numbers. These trends are based on the WODC 'Recidive monitor' (Recidivism Monitor), a long-term research project that measures standardised rates of recidivism among various offender groups (Wartna, Blom and Tollenaar, 2011).

Source: OBJD/WODC Recidivism Monitor.

by the court for the other age groups. The numbers indicate that young adults form a much bigger and, therefore, perhaps a more important age group for the judiciary than adolescents and older adults.

Figure 8.8 shows the rate in the type sanctions imposed by the court per 1,000 young adults. Overall, for the young adult group, fines were most common (14 per 1,000), followed by a community service order (eight per 1,000) and a conditional detention sentence (five per 1,000). The rank order of sanctions was the same for adults. However, among adolescents the most common sanctions were community orders followed by a fine and a conditional detention sentence.

Among young adults, fines and community service orders showed an increase since 1997, whereas suspended and non-suspended detention showed a (small) decrease since 2003. This trend can also be observed in dispositions for other age categories but not as strongly as for young adults, which could point to a decrease in more serious crimes and an increase in less serious crimes among convicted offenders. Official crime statistics support this assumption.

Recidivism Rates

Aside from the retribution of justice, actions by the public prosecutor and the court are meant to reduce the likelihood of recidivism of referred offenders. Figure 8.9 shows the trends in recidivism rates for individuals convicted between 1997 and 2006. The two-year recidivism rates of young adults were in between the rates of adolescents and adults. Of those young adults whose cases were settled by the public prosecutor or the court in 2006, 33.2 per cent recidivated within two years. In the period 1997–2006, adolescent offenders showed the highest recidivism rates two years after their criminal cases had been settled.

The trends for two-years reconviction rates for young adults and adults in the period between 1998 and 2004 show more or less the same pattern: the reconviction rates increased, and decreased slightly afterwards. The trends in two-year recidivism rates among adolescents, on the other hand, showed a relatively stable pattern in the period up to 2001, increased between 2001 and 2003, and showed a stable pattern afterwards.

Little is known about recidivism rates as a consequence of specific penal dispositions such as fines, community service orders or detention sentences. However, Wermink et al. (2009) reported mean yearly recidivism rates for those who received either a community service order or a short custodial sentence. Both groups were comparable with regard to personal and criminal background, including offence severity. In general, mean recidivism rates for community service order recipients were half those of detention sentence recipients. For both groups, the recidivism rates were higher for younger than for older offenders. For ages 18–21, the mean yearly recidivism rates for those receiving community service orders versus detention sentences were 0.42 and 0.71, respectively, and for ages 22–25 the rates were 0.28 and 0.61. For older adults the mean rates were lower: for ages 26–30 they were 0.22 and 0.36 respectively. These outcomes indicate a lower recidivism rate following community service orders compared to detention sentences for all age groups.

In summary, compared to other age categories, young adults constituted the highest proportion of offenders dealt with by the judiciary. Rates of young adult offenders reported to the public prosecutor and/or referred to the court increased during the period 1997–2007, but not as sharply as the trends in the number of crime suspects. This indicates an increase in the number of reports that the police do not file with the public prosecutor. Whereas clear age differences in trends were found with regard to *suspects*, there were hardly any age differences in the trends of *offenders*. Furthermore, in recent years courts tended to impose more non-custodial sentences such as fines and community service orders and fewer detention sentences in criminal cases of young adults. These trends in sanctioning

Table 8.4 Probation Service activities (July 2008–June 2009)

	N	%
Supervision orders	7,160	36
Community service orders	33,290	29
Visits at police station	37,989	21
Social enquiry reports	13,824	30
Advisory reports	16,530	26
Behavioural interventions	1,671	34
Risk assessments (RISc)	12,757	31

Source: Probation Service Netherlands.

Table 8.5 Probation supervision (July 2008–June 2009)

	Age	n	% Finished successfully	% Finished prematurely/ revoked	% Not started
Males	17–24	2,368	65	24	11
	25+	4,071	75	17	8
Females	17–24	238	69	23	8
	25+	483	80	14	6
Total	17–24	2,606	66	24	10
	25+	4,554	76	16	8

Source: Probation Service Netherlands.

could point to a decrease in more serious crimes and an increase in less serious crimes among convicted offenders.

Organizations Involved in the Execution of Sanctions of Young Adults

The principal organizations involved in the execution of sanctions of young adults are the Prison Service and the Probation Service. For a long time the Prison Service operated several prisons and remand centres for young adults that provided only additional education and vocational training. These institutions were abolished for financial reasons in the 1990s.

The Probation Service is involved in the execution of several penal sanctions of a non-custodial nature, such as community service orders and supervision

Table 8.6 Probation supervision and ethnic origin (July 2008–June 2009)

Ethnic background	n	% Finished successfully		% Finished prematurely/ revoked		% Not started	
		Age		Age		Age	
		17–24	25+	17–24	25+	17–24	25+
Native Dutch	4,323	73	80	20	15	7	6
Turkish	405	63	78	27	16	10	6
Moroccan	531	52	67	33	25	16	8
Surinamese	595	62	69	33	19	5	12
Dutch Antilles/Aruban	414	55	65	31	21	15	14
Other non-Western	783	58	72	29	20	13	9
Unknown	109	27	22	11	24	62	54
All	7,160	66	76	24	16	10	8

Source: Probation Service Netherlands.

within the framework of conditionally suspended sentences. In terms of absolute numbers, community service orders form an extensive part of the Probation Service's work. From mid-2008 until mid-2009, 33,290 offenders received a community service order, of which 10,000 were imposed on young adults. In the same period, 7,160 offenders were under probation supervision, 2,600 of whom were young adults. The Probation Service also provides immediate support for arrested suspects held at police stations, informs the court about the backgrounds of the alleged offender, and gives advice to the court about the preferred action to be taken or sanction imposed (see Table 8.4). Such reports are often supported by risk assessment, for which a standardized instrument – the RISc – is used (see the paragraph on risk assessment below; see also Spanjaard et al., Chapter 6, this volume). The Probation Service also carries out court-ordered behavioural interventions, which are aimed at reducing recidivism. These interventions are conducted both in prisons for detainees and outside for offenders under probation supervision. Young adults account for 20–36 per cent of Probation Service clients.

Probation Supervision

Supervision within the context of a conditionally suspended sentence is a key activity of the Probation Service since it not only affects large numbers of offenders (see above) but also implies a long-lasting relationship between the Probation Service and the clients under supervision. On average, supervision lasts for two years, during which period there is frequent contact between probation worker and client. Contact often includes behavioural interventions, referrals to specialized care and support agencies, and other support and control activities such as urine testing for drug use. An important indicator for the

Table 8.7 Risk assessment

Level of risk	Age 17–24		Age 25+	
	n	%	n	%
Low	542	23.2	1,478	36.7
Lower middle	633	27.1	1,124	27.9
Upper middle	485	20.8	537	13.3
High	310	13.3	303	7.5

Source: Probation Service Netherlands.

ultimate success and completion of probation supervision is less recidivism. Table 8.5 shows that more adults successfully finished their supervision order and more young adults had their supervision order revoked. Over one third of all young adults' supervision orders had either not started (11 per cent) or had been stopped for negative reasons such as not showing up at appointments, not meeting other engagements, committing a new offence, and/or being arrested (24 per cent). For adults aged 25 and older, the figures were eight per cent and 17 per cent respectively. The average length of a supervision order was almost 18 months for successfully finished orders and about one year for those ended prematurely or revoked. Young adult and adult female clients did slightly better than the average.

Ethnicity and Probation Supervision

Moroccan, Antillean and Aruban offenders had their supervision orders revoked more often than native Dutch offenders. Of the young adult Moroccans, Antilleans and Arubans, almost 50 per cent did not finish their supervision order successfully (see Table 8.6).

Supervision Units for Young Adults

In some regions of the Netherlands, separate supervision units for young adults have been created. Probation Service staff in these regions were convinced that supervision of young adults should be more intensive and more outreaching (Van der Laan et al., 2010). Professionals from other organizations in the so-called 'judicial chain', such as the police, the prosecutor's office, the court and local government, have supported this kind of approach. They, too, believed that more should be done for and with young adults because of the developmental stage of young adulthood and individual differences in the transition to adulthood. However, in practice it was difficult to implement additional supervision. According to the Probation Service's monitoring system of activities (CVS), a higher frequency of client contacts and intensified supervision activities were not accomplished and

Table 8.8 Risk profiles in life domains

RISc scale	Rating of criminogenic factor	Successfully finished supervision			
		Age 17–24		Age 25+	
		n	%	n	%
Delinquency	Not a problem	1,245	62.2	2,582	74.1
	Present	651	32.6	802	23,00
	Seriously present	104	5.2	100	2.9
Accommodation and housing	Not a problem	1,462	71.1	2,563	75.7
	Present	498	24.2	690	20.4
	Seriously present	95	4.6	134	4.0
Education, training and employment	Not a problem	857	38.8	2,050	53.9
	Present	1,013	45.9	1,329	34.9
	Seriously present	336	15.2	426	11.2
Income and budgeting skills	Not a problem	1,601	72.8	2,779	73.0
	Present	559	25.4	974	25.6
	Seriously present	39	1.8	53	1.4
Relationships with partner, relatives and family	Not a problem	1,171	53.4	1,914	50.5
	Present	691	31.5	1,374	36.3
	Seriously present	332	15.1	499	13.2
Relationships with friends and peers	Not a problem	1,092	50.1	2,951	78.3
	Present	883	40.5	733	19.4
	Seriously present	204	9.4	85	2.3
Drug use	Not a problem	1,331	60.7	2,832	74.7
	Present	768	35.0	800	21.1
	Seriously present	93	4.2	161	4.2
Alcohol use	Not a problem	1,533	70.2	2,645	69.9
	Present	342	15.7	566	15.0
	Seriously present	308	14.1	571	15.1
Emotional well-being	Not a problem	1,659	75.5	2,648	69.7
	Present	319	14.5	565	14.9
	Seriously present	218	9.9	588	15.5
Thinking patterns, behaviour and skills	Not a problem	351	16.0	862	22.7
	Present	1,555	70.9	2,493	65.7
	Seriously present	287	13.1	440	11.6
Attitude	Not a problem	1,187	54.9	2,358	62.9
	Present	735	34.0	1,065	28.4
	Seriously present	241	11.1	327	8.7

Source: Probation Service Netherlands.

were similar to the supervision of older clients. This may, however, have been a matter of programme teething troubles.

Risk Assessment

The Probation Service is also involved in risk assessment (see also Spanjaard et al., Chapter 6, this volume). The instrument used – the RISc – is based on the Offender Assessment System (OASys) (Raynor et al., 1999) which was developed and used in the United Kingdom and was adapted for the Netherlands (Vinke et al., 2003). Risk assessment outcomes are used to inform the court and give advice about sanctions to be imposed. Table 8.7, using RISc-based information, shows that relatively more young adults than adults were thought to be medium- to high-risk offenders. Twice as many young adults compared to older adults fell in the category of high risk. This outcome supports the Probation Service's idea that, compared to adults, young adults' unique needs require more and higher intensity supervision.

Risk assessment is based on assessing various life domains, for example, accommodation and housing, education, training and employment, and relationships with peers and friends. Difficulties in one or more life domains are associated with problems in successfully completing probation supervision. Table 8.8 shows that young adults score high on most domains and particularly in terms of relationships with friends, which is more problematic for them than for adult offenders.

Intervention Programmes

Three intervention programmes have focused on young adult offenders: social skills training, probation supervision, and reintegration into the labour market. The probation department of the Salvation Army has organized social skills training programmes for groups of young adult offenders. The evaluation of these training programmes showed that in 2000 and 2001 almost 100 young adults participated (Van der Laan, Van der Knaap and Wartna, 2005a). Almost 50 per cent of the participants reoffended within three years. Recidivism was related to earlier police contact (the more police contacts in the past, the greater the likelihood of recidivism) but not related to age, gender, or completion or non-completion of the training. Recidivism outcomes were compared to those of other offenders of the same age and gender and with similar offences and offence histories but who had received a different penal sanction. The two-year recidivism rate for the controls was higher than for the intervention group. But since both the experimental and control groups could not be fully matched on relevant background characteristics and not all relevant variables could be matched, we cannot draw firm conclusions about the effectiveness of the programme. Similar outcomes were presented in an evaluation of probation supervision of minors and young adults (Van der Laan, Van der Knaap and Wartna, 2005b). Of the 722 clients under probation supervision during the first quarter of 2000, two thirds were under age 17 and one third 17 or older. About 65 per cent reoffended once or more within four years. Recidivism was predominantly related to earlier police contacts but also to gender (higher recidivism rates among boys) and age (more recidivism for the youngest age category: those under 15). Again, comparisons were made to a 'virtual' control group. Even though recidivism rates of the control group were lower, the incomplete match between experimental group (supervision) and control group (other sanctions) made it difficult to draw conclusions about the relative effectiveness of probation supervision.

Another programme that has focused on young adults is *Binnenste Buiten* (Inside Out). It aims at integrating young adult detainees into the labour market after release by means of vocational training and apprenticeships (Van der Knaap, Van der Laan and Wartna, 2005). Between 1997 and 2001 some 300 young adults took part in the programme in a detention centre in the south of the Netherlands. Participants seemed to be better prepared for the labour market. But within six years after the programme almost 70 per cent of the participants had come into contact with the judiciary again. Recidivism rates within three or four years seem similar to those who participated in the social skills training and in probation supervision. Comparisons with a similar 'virtual' control group as mentioned before showed higher recidivism rates among the control group, but, again, it is not possible to draw conclusions about effectiveness.

In summary, the results of the three evaluation studies are promising, but the controls were not very strong and do not exclude the possibility that other, unmeasured factors could have influenced the results. Clearly, replications of the studies are needed before policy implications can be formulated on the basis of evaluation findings.

Transfers to Adult or Juvenile Court

As was mentioned by Liefaard (Chapter 7, this volume), in the Netherlands adolescent offenders aged 16 and 17 can be tried according to adult penal law. It is also possible to try young adult offenders aged 18–21 according to juvenile penal law.[13] Until 1996 the following three conditions all had to be met in order to allow for a transfer to adult court: the seriousness of the offence, the personality of the juvenile offender, and the circumstances under which the offence was committed. With the revision of the penal law for juveniles in 1996, the possibility to transfer youths aged 16 and 17 was widened by the stipulation that only one of the three conditions had to be met. Conversely, considering the same conditions, penal cases of young adults can be dealt with according to juvenile penal law. Assessment of the personality of the young offender has to be ordered by the court and carried out by a forensic behavioural expert.

13 See also Weijers (2006).

Of the 8,342 criminal cases concerning youth ages 16–17 years settled by the court in 2008, only a very small proportion (N=103, 1.2 per cent) was waived to adult court, which was about half of the transfers in 1997 (2.6 per cent). Although it was expected that, since the conditions for transfer were extended in 1996, more young people would be transferred to adult court, the actual practice was different. The number of transfers to adult court decreased slightly since 2002 and has remained between 100–160 cases per year.

A study of 116 case files of juveniles referred to the adult court revealed that in two thirds of the cases the court referred to the seriousness of the offence, the personality of the offender, as well as the circumstances under which the offence was committed as reasons to transfer to adult court. In other cases only two – or one – of these considerations were given (Dijkstra and Van Zuijlen, 2005). Over 80 per cent of the offenders were aged 17 when they committed the offence. By the time they appeared before the court, 65 per cent were aged 18 or older. Almost two thirds of the sanctions (fines, detention) imposed according to adult penal law were higher than the maximum juvenile sentences, and about one third were smaller or shorter sentences. Weijers (2006) analysed 62 files and concluded that in about half of all cases the sanction imposed under adult law was within the maximum of juvenile law. Therefore, transfer to adult court did not automatically imply longer sentences. It should also be noted that youths transferred to adult court were often almost aged 18 – and thus of age – when they committed the offence. Transfers to adult court for youths aged 16 were very exceptional.

Transfer of young adults to juvenile court has never been extensive. In 2008 a total of 15,300 criminal cases were settled against youths aged 18–21. Only 34 were transferred to juvenile court (0.2 per cent). This proportion has remained stable for the period 1997–2007 (0.1–0.2 per cent). Unfortunately, no information is available on the type of sanctions imposed in these cases.

Conclusions

Politicians and policymakers in the Netherlands periodically pay attention to offenders of varying ages, such as children, adolescents and young adults. Few, if any of them, disagree with the basic assumption that separate provisions for minors are justified for reasons of limited culpability, different and not yet finished social, psychological and biological (neurological) development, maturity and autonomy (see also Loeber et al., Chapter 12, this volume). However, specific incidents or new scientific insights have triggered discussions about moving up (or down) the lower- and upper age limits of juvenile and adult penal law. Occasionally these discussions have focused on young adult offenders. Every now and then, legislators and administrators have proposed separate laws and administrative systems for adolescents and young adults, sometimes in order to create a more flexible transfer from the juvenile to the adult penal system, or to facilitate the access for young adults to youth facilities and provisions. With a few exceptions, such proposals have never been approved by the Cabinet and formal proposals to change the law have never been presented to Parliament. However, in June 2011 the State Secretary of the Ministry of Security and Justice proposed to the Parliament a new penal law for adolescents aged 15–23 (TK 2010–2011). This proposal includes: (1) the extension of the possibility for young adult offenders in some cases to be sanctioned under juvenile law, and (2) to raise the age limit for young adults to be eligible for juvenile law from 21–23. The proposal seems in line with the recommendations of the Anneveldt Committee that appeared in 1982. However, the State Secretary also proposed longer maximum detention sentences from two to four years for juveniles aged 15–18.

Young Adult Offenders in Official Crime Data

The first set of key questions in this chapter was which age category – adolescents, young adults or adults – commits most crime; and to what extent are there gender and ethnic differences in offending, and what are the trends? The likelihood of being a suspect of a moderate or serious crime (versus not being a suspect) for young adults is one and a half times higher than for adolescents and adults. Whereas the proportion of suspects among all three age groups showed an increase during the period 1996–2007,[14] the highest increase took place within the youngest age group (12–15), while the increase of suspects in the older age groups was similar.

For young adult males the odds of being a suspect of crime were higher than for adolescent and adult males. For young adult females the odds of being a suspect were similar to that of adolescent females, and slightly higher than for adult females. This indicates a flatter age–crime curve pattern for females than for males (see also Blokland and Palmen, Chapter 2, this volume).

Among all three age categories, persons of Dutch Antillean, Aruban, Moroccan and Surinamese descent were overrepresented in the number of crime suspects, whereas persons of native Dutch origin were underrepresented. The data show a classic age–crime curve for suspects of Dutch origin, but among youth of Dutch Antillean, Aruban, Turkish and Surinamese descent, we found an age–crime curve that extended more into adulthood.

For all age groups, the number of suspects per 1,000 showed an increasing trend in the period 1996–2007, but this varied in magnitude for different ethnic groups. Contrary to popular perceptions about the role of minorities in offending, the percentage of suspects among young adults of a native Dutch background increased more sharply in recent years than among other ethnic groups. The percentages of suspects among young adults of Moroccan and Antillean origin showed the lowest increase over time and remained relatively stable in recent years.

---

14 The most recent report on trends in juvenile and young adult crime (Van der Laan and Blom, 2011) shows a decrease in the number of suspects among most subgroups (gender, age, ethnic origin) in 2008. Compared to 1996, however, the number of suspects is still higher in 2008 among all groups.

The three most common crimes among young adults were the same as among adults: traffic offences, followed by assault and serious property crime. Serious property crimes were most common among adolescents, followed by crime against public order and assault. During the period 1996–2007, young adults compared to adolescents and adults had higher crime rates for most types of crime. However, young adults compared to adolescents were less involved in crimes against public order but similarly involved in robbery, serious property crime, and vandalism. In contrast, the prevalence of young adults who committed drug offences and traffic offences was similar to that of adults, but higher than that of adolescents. Most types of crime increased in the period 1996–2007. The trends in crime prevalence rates were more or less similar for all age groups.

In summary, we found that more young adults than adolescents and adults engaged in recorded crime. This conclusion may be partly affected by lower dismissal rates among young adults by the police than that are typical for adolescents (informal warnings, and referrals to Halt that are not applicable to young adults)[15] and in accord with a more pedagogically oriented juvenile justice system. We believe that the police tend to be less inclined to deal informally with young adults and are filing official reports more often for them than for adolescents. In the end, and compared to adolescents, more cases of young adults end up in court but not as disproportionally as may be suggested by the relatively high number of official police reports filed with the public prosecutor. Crime rates of young adults are also higher than for adults. This may be explained by increasing desistance from crime after age 25. Rates of recidivism also decrease with age, but since crime statistics are cross-sectional in nature it is not possible to determine desistance or persistence within individuals (but see Blokland and Palmen, Chapter 2, this volume).

Self-reported Delinquency by Young Adult Offenders Compared to Official Records

Police and judicial data do not contain information on crimes that are unreported by victims or where the offender has not been identified. For these reasons, self-reported delinquency studies provide information that cannot be found in official records. Studies on self-reported delinquency (including fare-dodging) showed prevalence rates among young adults of between 31 and 55 per cent.

Although official records of offending show major differences between adolescents and young adults, the differences are much less evident in self-reported delinquency studies. This may have to do with the underreporting of more

15 Halt is a diversion programme for young offenders who have committed minor offences such as shoplifting and vandalism. Adolescents are referred to Halt by the police as an alternative to filing an official report with the public prosecutor. The Halt programme comprises various types of community service that are performed for a maximum of 20 hours.

serious crimes and the emphasis on less serious and less controversial types of crime in self-reports (Junger-Tas and Marshall, 1999). Similarities in self-reported prevalence rates of delinquency of young adults and adolescents can also mean that desistance from crime does not generally take place shortly after age 18, as found in police recorded statistics, but instead for some individuals occurs later in their early 20s.

Judicial Sanctions

Our second set of key questions referred to the judicial interventions among the age groups. First, do the age groups differ in number and kind of sanctions they receive from the public prosecutor or the court? The results show that more criminal cases are settled by the public prosecutor or imposed by the court for young adults than for adolescents and adults. This may reflect more diversion for adolescent offenders and lower delinquent involvement by adults.

Young adults hardly differ from adults with regard to the types of sanctions settled by the public prosecutor or imposed by the court. The most common sanction for young adult offenders was a fine, a practice that increased greatly from 1997–2005. This was the same for adults, whereas for adolescents the most common sanction was a community service order. There are several explanations possible for this difference, for instance the relatively high numbers of traffic offences among young adults and adults, which are often settled with a fine. Also, the number of people with a paid job increases during the life course, raising the likelihood of a fine actually being paid.

After fines, the most common sanctions imposed by the court on young adults and adults alike were community service orders and conditional detention sentences. For adolescents, community service orders were followed in ranking by fines and conditional detention orders. For all three groups, the trends in sanctions were comparable. Fines and community service orders showed an increase, whereas detention orders showed a decrease.

The second question is whether there were differences in recidivism of adolescent, young adult and adult offenders identified in the justice system. The trend in two-year recidivism rates of young adults with a criminal case in the period 1997–2006 was in between those of adolescents and adults. Of those young adults with a criminal case in 2006, 33 per cent recidivated within two years after their case was settled. Recidivism rates and other outcomes among young adults were less favourable compared to adults but better in part compared to adolescents. The difference may be explained by a smaller proportion of individuals in the young adult group who started offending early and persisted in their offending pattern (see Blokland and Palmen, Chapter 2, this volume). Late starters – i.e., those who started offending during young adulthood – perhaps desist from crime earlier or at the same age (around 25) as early starters (see Loeber et al., Chapter 12, this volume). Recidivism rates among different age groups have not been linked to specific penal sanctions. We believe, however, that general findings such as lower recidivism rates for community service orders compared to custodial sentences, or for suspended sentences compared to non-suspended sentences, apply to adolescents as well as to young adults and adults.

The third question concerns whether different judicial sanctions result in different recidivism rates? There is no adequate answer as yet in the Netherlands to tell us which judicial interventions result in the lowest recidivism rate. Young adults are referred to a variety of treatment programmes, but information on participation levels, outcomes, and programme efficacy is lacking or difficult to obtain. This is also the case with the three intervention programmes focusing exclusively on young adult offenders described above.

The Risk Assessment of Recidivism

Relevant data on risk assessment of recidivism come from the Probation Service. Risk assessment information from the Probation Service on young adults showed that, in general, they pose a greater risk of recidivism than adult clients because of more serious problems in most life domains. This reinforces the conclusion that young adults form a separate group, not only from adolescents but also from older adults in many respects. This also justifies a separate and more intensified approach and calls for intervention programmes developed particularly for this age group. However, very few – if any –such programmes are available (see Boendermaker, Deković and Asscher, Chapter 10, this volume; see also Welsh et al., 2012). Separate probation supervision units for young adults have recently been set up, but it appears difficult to accomplish higher levels of intensity and frequency of supervision contacts. No information on recidivism rates of participants is available as yet. Several behavioural interventions, such as social skills training programmes, aggression regulation programmes and addiction programmes, are available for adult offenders in general and can be imposed as a special condition to a suspended detention sentence.

Transfer of Juvenile Offenders to Adult Court

This takes place between 100 and 160 times a year. In most cases, transferred juveniles were aged almost 18 when they committed the crime and aged over 18 by the time they had to appear before the court. Compared to current transfer practices in the United States (see Howell et al., 2012), the Dutch transfer practice is certainly much less prominent. Since ample legal options for transfers are available but used in relatively few cases, it is questionable whether a fundamentally new penal law system for adolescents should be created. Transfer of adult offenders to the juvenile court is also possible but occurs in few cases. Unfortunately, too little is known about the characteristics of juvenile offenders transferred to the adult court and vice versa. In order to more adequately respond to young adult offender's needs, either transfer to juvenile court should be enhanced or similar provisions as for adolescent offenders should be introduced in the adult penal system. The

Probation Service has already made a start by setting up separate supervision units for young adults. Ideally such units should also be set up for the execution of community service orders and in the prison system.

Research Priorities

More information from self-report studies is needed to better understand prevalence and trends of young adult offending over time, and also why some youths who have started committing offences at a relatively young age continue to do so, whereas others desist from crime (see Blokland and Palmen, Chapter 2, this volume, and Donker et al., Chapter 4, this volume). Such data may also shed light on late starter offenders among young adults. Self-report studies can provide offence- and offender-related information including risk and protective and promotive factors that are not included in police data. Such information is particularly helpful for exploring relevant explanatory factors that should be targeted by behavioural interventions and for developing specific policies and interventions for young adult offenders in justice settings.

It is well known that young people, including adolescents and young adults, who commit offences are also often victims of crime and that it is not always easy to disentangle the offender from the victim. However, it is not yet known to what extent this is also the case for young adults. Victimization studies focusing on young adults are needed.

Finally, more detailed information is required on the effect of penal sanctions on recidivism, as well as efficacy studies on behavioural interventions and treatment for young adults. Evaluation studies are scarce, and controlled evaluation studies, i.e., with a quasi-experimental or experimental design, are completely absent.[16] The Probation Service has invested in the development of various behavioural interventions, some of which have been accredited by the Dutch Offending Behaviour Programmes Accreditation Panel. Accreditation, however, implies an ex-ante evaluation only. Evidence of the effectiveness of the programmes is required only five years after accreditation. None of the accredited programmes has as yet produced any valid and reliable evidence.

References

Anneveldt Committee (1982). *Sanctierecht voor jeugdigen*. The Hague: Staatsdrukkerij en Uitgeverijbedrijf.

CBS (1997). *Permanent Onderzoek Leefsituatie (POLS). Module Jongeren Jong 1997. Documentatie*. Heerlen/Voorburg: CBS.

16 In 2010, an evaluation of an aftercare programme for young adult detainees was started in several regions in the Netherlands using a design of a randomized controlled trial. Outcomes are not expected before early 2013.

CBS (2001). *Permanent Onderzoek Leefsituatie (POLS). Module Jongeren Jong 2001. Documentatie.* Heerlen/Voorburg: CBS.

CBS (2003). *Permanent Onderzoek Leefsituatie (POLS). Module Jongeren Jong 2003. Documentatie.* Heerlen/Voorburg: CBS.

Dijkstra, M. and Van Zuijlen, Y. (2005). *Jeugdigen in het strafrecht: waar ligt de grens?* Leiden: University of Leiden (Ph.D. dissertation).

Doek, J.E. (2004). Murat D. *Pedagogiek in Prakijk*, 20, 27.

Donker, A. (2004). Self reported delinquency among (young) adults. In A. Donker, *Precursors and Prevalence of Young-Adult and Adult Delinquency.* Leiden: University of Leiden (Ph.D. dissertation), pp. 25–52.

Doreleijers, Th.A.H. and Fokkens, J.W. (2010). Minderjarigen en jongvolwassenen: Pleidooi voor een evidence-based strafrecht. *Rechtstreeks*, 7, 9–46.

Eggen, A.Th.J. (2009). Geregistreerde criminaliteit. In S.N. Kalidien and A.Th.J. Eggen (eds), *Criminaliteit en Rechtshandhaving 2008. Ontwikkelingen en samenhangen.* The Hague/Voorburg: WODC/CBS, pp. 85–100.

Howell, J.C., Feld, B.C., and Mears, D.P. (2012). Young offenders and an effective justice system response: What happens, what should happen, and what we need to know. In R. Loeber and D.P. Farrington (eds), *From Juvenile Delinquency to Adult Crime: Criminal Careers, Justice Policy and Prevention.* New York: Oxford University Press.

Jennissen, R.P.W. (2009). *Criminaliteit, leeftijd en etniciteit. Over de afwijkende leeftijdsspecifieke criminaliteitscijfers van in Nederland verblijvende Antillianen en Marokkanen.* The Hague: WODC.

Junger-Tas, J. and Marshall, H.I. (1999). The self-report methodology in crime research. In M. Tonry (ed.), *Crime and Justice: A Review of Research*, 25. Chicago: University of Chicago Press, pp. 291–367.

Nijboer, J.F. (2001). Recommendations; over het 'zachte' (straf)recht van de Raad van Europa. *Justitiële Verkenningen*, 27, 81–87.

Overwater Committee (1955). *Strafbejegening.* The Hague: Staatsdrukkerij- en Uitgeverijbedrijf.

Raynor, P., Kynch, J., Merrington, S., and Roberts, C. (1999). *Evaluating Risk and Need Assessment in Probation Services: Interim Report to the Home Office.* Swansea: University of Wales and Oxford: Probation Studies Unit.

State Secretary of Justice (1997). *Notitie kinderen en criminaliteit.* The Hague: Ministerie van Justitie.

TK (2010–2011). Jeugdcriminaliteit. Brief van de staatssecretaris van veiligheid en justitie. TK 28 741 nr. 17. The Hague: Ministerie van Veiligheid en Justitie.

Van den Hoogen-Saleh, T. (2000). *Hoe eerder hoe beter: Evaluatierapport van het pilotjaar van het Twaalfmin-project in Haaglanden in 1999.* The Hague: Politie Haaglanden.

Van der Knaap, L.M., Van der Laan, A.M., and Wartna, B.S.J. (2005). *Recidivemeting onder de deelnemers van Binnenste Buiten.* The Hague: WODC.

Van der Laan, A.M., and Blom, M. (2011). *Jeugdcriminaliteit in de periode 1996–2010. Ontwikkelingen in zelfgerapporteerde daders, door de politie*

aangehouden verdachten en strafrechtelijke daders op basis van de Monitor Jeugdcriminaliteit 2010 (Cahier 2011-2). The Hague: WODC.
Van der Laan, A.M., Blom, M., Tollenaar, N., and Kea, R. (2010). *Trends in de geregistreerde jeugdcriminaliteit onder 12- tot en met 24-jarigen in de periode 1996-2007. Bevindingen uit de Monitor Jeugdcriminaliteit 2009*. The Hague: WODC.
Van der Laan, A.M., Van der Knaap, L.M., and Wartna, B.S.J. (2005a). *Recidivemeting onder de deelnemers aan de Sociale Vaardigheidstraining voor groepen van het Leger des Heils*. The Hague: WODC.
Van der Laan, A.M., Van der Knaap, L.M., and Wartna, B.S.J. (2005b). *Recidivemeting onder jeugdreclasseringcliënten*. The Hague: WODC.
Van der Laan, P.H., Spaans, E.C., Essers, A.A.M., and Essers, J.J.A. (1997). *Jeugdcriminaliteit en jeugdbescherming. Ontwikkeling in de periode 1980–1994*. The Hague: WODC.
Van der Laan, P.H., Lamet, W., Grandia, K., James, C., Meijer, T., and Wanschers, L. (2010). *Reclasseringstoezicht en jongvolwassenen*. Amsterdam: NSCR.
Van Mantgem, J., Van Nobelen, D., and Uljee, N. (2009). *Landelijk verdachtenbeeld 2008*. Zoetermeer: KLPD.
Van Montfrans Committee (1994). *Met de neus op de feiten*. The Hague: Staatsdrukkerij.
Verwers, C. and Bogaerts, S. (2005). *Strafrechtelijke aanpak van jongvolwassenen(18–24 jaar). Een verkenning*. The Hague: WODC.
Vinke, A., Erftemeijer, L., Bruggemann-Kluvers, M., and Vogelvang, B. (2003). *Recidive inschattingsschalen*. Woerden: Adviesbureau van Montfoort.
Wartna, B.S.J., Blom, M., and Tollenaar, N. (2011). *The Dutch Recidivism Monitor*. The Hague: WODC.
Weijers, I. (2006). *Jeugdige dader, volwassen straf? Artikel 77b Sr*. Deventer: Kluwer.
Welsh, B.C., Lipsey, M.W., Rivara, F.P., Hawkins, J. D., Aos, S., and Peel, M.E. (2012). Promoting change, changing lives: Effective prevention and intervention to reduce serious offending. In R. Loeber and D.P. Farrington (eds), *From Juvenile Delinquency to Adult Crime: Criminal Careers, Justice Policy and Prevention*. New York: Oxford University Press.
Wermink, H., Blokland, A., Nieuwbeerta, P., and Tollenaar, N. (2009). Recidive na werkstraffen en na gevangenisstraffen. *Tijdschrift voor Criminologie*, 51, 211–27.

Chapter 9
Prevention Programmes in Early and Middle Childhood and Their Effect on Adult Crime

Maja Deković, Jessica J. Asscher, Meike I. Slagt and Leonieke Boendermaker

This chapter focuses on prevention efforts that aim to reduce serious antisocial behaviour and involvement in crime in early adulthood. The main questions addressed are: (1) What are the long-term effects of prevention programmes conducted during early and middle childhood on adult crime? (2) What are the characteristics of effective prevention programmes? In addition to international research literature on the topic, we discuss prevention programmes that are currently implemented in the Netherlands. We conclude with the implications of our findings for research, policy, and clinical practice.

To clarify what we mean by prevention, we distinguish between four types of prevention: *criminal justice prevention* (deterrence, incapacitation and rehabilitation strategies conducted by law enforcement and criminal justice agencies), *situational prevention* (reducing opportunities and increasing obstacles to committing antisocial behaviour), *community prevention* (changing the social conditions and/or community norms and social institutions), and *developmental prevention* (increasing protective factors and decreasing risk factors that influence the development of antisocial behaviour in individuals) (Farrington and Coid, 2003). Another distinction often made in the literature is that between *universal prevention*, which targets a whole population – such as those in classrooms – without selection of specific groups, and *targeted prevention*, which focuses on a specific group of children considered to be at risk. In the present chapter we concentrate on developmental prevention and include both universal and targeted prevention. Targeted children are considered to be at risk for various reasons, some because of early child behaviour problems, such as early disruptive behaviour, non-compliance and aggression; others because of environmental risks, such as living in high-crime neighbourhoods, having parents with low education, low income, etc.

Longitudinal studies on the development of antisocial behaviour consistently indicate that chronic behaviour problems early in life predict serious delinquency and crime during adolescence and adulthood (Dishion and Patterson, 2006; Loeber and Farrington, 2000; Loeber et al., 2008; Piquero, 2008). These findings suggest that early childhood is an important developmental period for the prevention of serious chronic antisocial behaviour. Current early childhood prevention programmes mostly try to alter risk and protective factors within the child or within the child's environment and include facilitating the child's cognitive development, enhancing parents' social support, fostering positive parenting and parent–child interaction, and reducing poverty at the family level and the community level. The beneficial changes in these domains are expected to be helpful in preventing the development of chronic delinquency (Welsh and Farrington, 2001). In contrast to early childhood programmes that attempt to improve functioning of the parents and children in general (with the prevention of child problem behaviour being only one of many objectives), the programmes aimed at middle childhood often specifically target child disruptive/antisocial behaviour.

Several reviews (for example, Olds, Sadler and Kitzman, 2007; Welsh and Farrington, 2006; Yoshikawa, 1995) and meta-analyses (for example, Piquero et al., 2009) have described the long-term effects of early prevention programmes. However, in contrast to the present study, these reviews mostly focused on other outcomes (for example, educational achievement), other developmental periods (for example, adolescence), or described effects of only one specific type of programme (for example, parental training). In the present systematic review we specifically searched for empirical studies that examined the effects of programmes carried out during early and middle childhood (i.e., from infancy until the end of primary school) for which information regarding effectiveness in reducing offending during early adulthood (from 20 years on) was available. Only the studies with a high-quality research design (i.e., experiments or quasi-experiments with an adequate control group) were included. The literature search included all studies published before the end of 2009. Tables 9.1 and 9.2 present a summary of the identified studies examining programmes administered during early childhood and middle childhood, respectively.

In the following two paragraphs we provide an overview of the prevention programmes. In each case we shall discuss the programme model (i.e., the context in which the programme takes place and the risk and protective factors on which it focuses), the research design, the methods, and the major findings regarding crime prevention.

Early Childhood Programmes

We identified three programmes that met the above-described criteria. The summary of these and the studies that examined their effectiveness can be found in Table 9.1. In addition to providing a narrative overview of the study results, for each study we also calculated, following Welsh and Farrington (2006), the percentage differences in offending between experimental and control groups (i.e., the relative difference in the percentage of offenders in experimental and control groups at follow-up). Although we do not want to suggest that other types of outcomes are less relevant, this simple dichotomy (offender versus non-

Table 9.1 Summary of studies examining early childhood programmes' long-term effects

Study	Programme	Design	Age at start	Age at outcome	Outcome
Reynolds et al., 2007	The Chicago Child–Parent Center Program *Programme components*: school-based educational enrichment and comprehensive family services *Length*: 2 years (preschool intervention) to 6 years (additional school intervention) *Participants*: low-income families	quasi-experimental (n_E = 888; n_C = 480) *Comparison*: alternative childhood programmes (full-day kindergarten)	3–4 years	24 years	*Source*: Official records *Results*: Preschool programme group had lower rates of felony arrests, convictions and incarceration than comparison group. No differences between preschool programme group and comparison group were found for violent arrest and violent crime conviction. School-age intervention in itself did not have any effects in late adulthood. *% difference*: −20.6% (preschool intervention) (felony convictions by age 24: E=15, 8%; C=19.9%)
Campbell et al., 2002; Clarke and Campbell, 1998	Abecedarian Project *Programme components*: child-centred, full-day educational childcare *Length*: 5 years *Participants*: impoverished families	RCT (n_E = 53; n_C = 51) *Control*: nutritional supplements for the first 15 months of age, supportive social services as needed	4 months	21 years	*Source*: Self-reports *Results*: No significant differences were found between the programme group and the control group in misdemeanour conviction, felony conviction or incarceration. *% difference*: −36.4% (felony convictions by age 21: E=7.5%; C=11.8%)
Nores et al., 2005; Schweinhart et al., 2005	High/Scope Perry Preschool Program *Programme components*: centre-based programme, home visits by teachers, parent group meetings *Length*: 1 or 2 years *Participants*: low parental education and SES, low child IQ test score	RCT (n_E = 58; n_C = 65) *Control*: no preschool programme	3–4 years	40 years	*Source*: Official records *Results*: The programme group had fewer lifetime arrests, fewer arrests for violent, property and drug crimes than the control group. The programme group was sentenced to fewer months in prison. *% difference*: −46.2% (sentenced to prison or jail by age 40: E=28%; C=52%)

offender) is a very straightforward indication of the programme's effectiveness in the context of the present chapter.

Chicago Child–Parent Center Program

This longitudinal study is a prospective investigation into the effects of the Child–Parent Center Program (CPC) for a large cohort of low-income minority children in the city of Chicago, Illinois, US (Reynolds et al., 2001, 2007).

Programme model The CPC is an early-intervention initiative administered through the Chicago public school system since 1967. Located in or close to elementary schools, the programme offers school-based educational enrichment and comprehensive family services from preschool to third grade. The intervention stresses the acquisition of basic skills in language and math through relatively structured but diverse learning experiences such as teacher-directed whole-class instruction, small-group and individualized activities, and fieldtrips. It also includes an intensive parental programme consisting of parenting education, volunteering in the classroom, attending school events and fieldtrips, advancing educational attainment, and home visitation. Parents are expected to participate in the programme for one half day per week. Additionally, health and nutrition services are offered. The preschool programme has an intensity of three hours per day, five days per week during the school year and usually includes a six-week summer programme. During kindergarten the programme consists of providing school-age services under the direction of a parent-resource teacher. The intervention continues through the first two (at 14 sites) or three (at six sites) years of primary school.

Research design and methods A total of 1,539 low-income minority participants were enrolled in this quasi-experimental study. They either participated in the CPC (n = 989) or constituted a comparison group (n = 550). The intervention and comparison groups were matched on age, eligibility for enrolment in government-funded early childhood interventions, neighbourhood, and family poverty level. For the follow-up at age 24, 1,389 participants were available (91 per cent of the original programme group and 89 per cent of the original comparison group). The attrition sample (n = 150) had background characteristics similar to the follow-up sample regardless of programme status. Educational attainment, adult arrest, incarceration, health status and behaviour, and economic wellbeing were measured at follow-up. Analysis compared those who had received preschool intervention (n = 888), those who had received school-age intervention (n = 778), and those who had received both (n = 522) to the comparison group (n = 487). In addition, those who had received both interventions were compared to preschool-only participants (n = 254).

Major findings With regard to criminal activities, participants who had received preschool intervention were less likely to have had felony arrests (17 per cent vs 21 per cent), felony convictions (16 per cent vs 20 per cent) and incarceration (20 per cent vs 26 per cent) by age 24 than the comparison group. No group differences were found for violence arrests and violence convictions. In general, the same results were found when comparing participants who had received both preschool and school-age intervention to the comparison group. School-age intervention in itself did not have any effects in late adulthood, nor did it add additional value to the preschool intervention.

Abecedarian Project

The Carolina Abecedarian Project was a controlled experiment conducted in 1972 in North Carolina, US, by the Frank Porter Graham Child Development Institute to study the potential benefits of early childhood education for poor children to enhance school readiness. This project evaluated the benefits of intensive early educational intervention for children from low-income, multi-risk families (Campbell et al., 2002; Clarke and Campbell, 1998).

Programme model Treatment was administered in two phases: a preschool intervention initiated at birth and lasting five years, and a school-age intervention during the first three years of public school. The preschool intervention was child-centred, with treated children having full-day childcare year round. Within the childcare setting a systematic curriculum was offered involving educational games focusing on the development of cognition, language, and adaptive behaviour (Sparling and Lewis, 2000). Families treated in the school-age phase were assigned a home–school resource teacher who functioned as a link between the school and the home with the goal of increasing parental involvement in the children's learning. To help parents with this task, individualized curriculum packets were developed for each child based on the child's needs as identified by the classroom teacher. These packets were delivered to the home every other week and parents were encouraged to use them with their child for at least 15 minutes each day. In addition to the educational intervention, families in both the treated and control groups received supportive social services as needed. Infants in the control group did not receive the educational intervention but instead were offered nutritional supplements for the first 15 months of life. The Abecedarian Project derives its conceptual framework from General Systems Theory (Ramey, MacPhee and Yeates, 1982).

Research design and methods The programme targeted low-income, predominantly African–American children (98 per cent). Four cohorts of multi-risk families were enrolled in the study between 1972 and 1977. Random assignment was accomplished in two steps. First, recruited family pairs were matched on high-risk index scores and then assigned to preschool treatment or control status. A total of 111 infants were born to these families during the period of the study, resulting in 57 infants in the experimental (E) group, and 54 infants in the control (C) group. Second, based on their cognitive test score at age 4, pairs of children were matched within the preschool treatment and control groups and allocated to school-age treatment and control groups. This created four treatment groups: children with preschool plus school-age treatment (EE), those with preschool alone (EC), those with school-age treatment alone (CE), and those who were untreated in both phases (CC). At age 21, 104 participants were available for the follow-up of the preschool treatment (n = 53 for E, n = 51 for C). Information was obtained on several domains, including intellectual level and academic skills, educational attainment, skilled employment, self-sufficiency and social adjustment, which included indices of substance abuse and lawbreaking. Because of the small sample sizes, only the cognitive and academic data were analysed using the four-group model, whereas the crime data were analysed for effects of the preschool intervention compared to the control group.

Major findings At age 21, no statistically significant differences were found between the preschool treatment group and the control group in misdemeanour conviction (14 per cent vs 18 per cent), felony conviction (8 per cent vs 12 per cent) or incarceration (14 per cent vs 21 per cent).

HighScope Perry Preschool Program

The HighScope Perry Preschool programme is a preschool intervention administered during the 1960s in Ypsilanti, Michigan, US, to improve the personal and economic opportunities for a small group of children aged 3 and 4 born in poverty and at high risk of failing in school (Schweinhart et al., 2005; Nores et al., 2005).

Programme model The HighScope curriculum model, developed by David Weikart and his associates (Weikart et al., 1971; Hohmann and Weikart, 1995), represents an open-framework approach of teaching and is based on Jean Piaget's constructivist theory of child development. In the open-framework approach, both child and teacher initiate events at their own levels of responsibility. The programme was delivered to successive classes beginning in 1962 and continuing for three years. The first class received only one year of preschool, but the remaining classes received two years of preschool. The programme itself was delivered from October to May of each school year, with three components: (a) a centre-based programme for 2.5 hours each weekday morning (with four teachers trained in special education and early childhood development for 20–25 children) that emphasized children's intellectual and social development; (b) home visits by teachers for 1.5 hours per week; and (c) monthly parent group meetings.

Research design and methods A total of 123 African–American children participated in the programme. The children were selected on the basis of low levels of parental education and socioeconomic status, as well as low Stanford–Binet IQ test scores. From 1962–1967, each school year children age 3 and 4 were randomly assigned to a preschool programme group and a comparison group. This resulted in a total of 58 children receiving the preschool programme and 65 children in the control group not receiving the preschool programme. All participants were available for the follow-up at age 40. The findings of programme effects through age 40 spanned the domains of education, economic performance, crime prevention, family relationships and health.

Major findings At age 40, outcomes for the treatment group were generally superior to those of the control group. Crime-related outcomes revealed that the programme group had fewer lifetime arrests than the control group (36 per cent vs 55 per cent arrested five or more times) and fewer arrests for violent crimes (32 per cent vs 48 per cent ever arrested), property crimes (36 per cent vs 58 per cent ever arrested), and drug crimes (14 per cent vs 34 per cent ever arrested). Moreover, the programme group was sentenced to fewer months in prison by age 40 (28 per cent vs 52 per cent ever sentenced). These findings reflect earlier reported findings on the same sample (Schweinhart, Barnes and Weikart, 1993): By age 27, seven per cent of the programme group vs 35 per cent of the control group had been arrested five or more times.

Commentary on the Early Childhood Programmes

Our review provides mixed evidence regarding the effects of early childhood programmes on adult crime: two of the examined programmes show long-term benefits of participation in such programmes, as indicated by lower rates of arrests, convictions and incarceration for participants in the experimental as compared to those in the control group, but no such positive effects were found for the Abecedarian Project. By age 21, neither preschool intervention nor its school-age extension programme significantly affected criminal behaviour, although positive effects were found for cognitive (IQ) and academic outcomes (years of education). It should be noted that the Abecedarian Project differed from two other early intervention programmes in three ways. First, it placed more emphasis on intellectual development and academic skill development than the other two programmes, which also focused on socioemotional development. Second, the preschool phase of the programme was child centred (i.e., without parental involvement and home visits), whereas both the CPC and the HighScope Perry Preschool programme included parent/family components. Third, in contrast to the two other programmes, the outcomes at adult age in the Abecedarian Project were assessed though self-reports, rather than official records. It is important to note that the Abecedarian Project still led to 36 per cent fewer convictions in programme participants up to age 21 compared to the control group, although this difference – probably due to the small sample – is not statistically significant.

Although the number of available studies is too low for definite conclusions, it is interesting to note that the two programmes that included both preschool and school intervention (the Chicago Child–Parent Program and the Abecedarian Project) both show that preschool interventions affected outcome more than did

Table 9.2 Summary of studies examining middle childhood programmes' long-term effects

Study	Programme	Design	Age at start	Age at outcome	Outcome
McCord, 1978	Cambridge-Somerville Youth Study *Programme components*: individualised, multimodal: counsellors for family problems, tutoring in academic subjects, medical or psychiatric attention, summer camps *Length*: 5 years *Participants*: both 'difficult' and 'average' boys, from densely populated factory-dominated areas	RCT (n_E = 253; n_C = 253) *Control*: no programme	5–13 years	42–50 years	*Source*: Official records *Results*: No differences between the programme group and control groups were found on having a juvenile or adult criminal record. Men in programme group who had criminal records were more likely to have had two or more convictions compared to men in the control group. *% difference*: 0% (criminal record by ages 40–48: E: 66.4%; C: 66.4%)
Boisjoli et al., 2007	Montreal Longitudinal Experimental Study *Programme components*: home-based parent training, school-based social skills training (prosocial skills and self-control), teacher support *Length*: 2 years *Participants*: boys from low socioeconomic backgrounds and according to teachers disruptive behaviours, all French-speaking, with Canadian-born parents	RCT (n_E = 69; n_C = 181) *Control*: no programme	7 years	24 years	*Source*: Official records *Results*: Being in the programme group was marginally (p=.06) associated with a lower rate of having a criminal record. *% difference*: −33.4% (criminal record by age 24: E=21.7%; C=32.6%)

Hawkins et al., 2005	Seattle Social Development Project *Programme components*: teacher training, child social and emotional skill development, and parent training *Length*: about 4 years for full-intervention group, and about 1.5 years for late-intervention group *Participants*: children from high-crime areas in Seattle	quasi-experimental ($n_{E\ full\text{-}intervention}$ = 144; $n_{E\ late\text{-}intervention}$ = 256; n_C = 205) *Control*: no programme	6 years (full-intervention group); 11 years (late-intervention group)	21 years	*Source*: Self-reports and official records *Results*: Full-intervention participants were less likely to be involved in a high variety of crime, have sold illegal drugs in the past year, and have an official lifetime court record than the control group. No differences were found between the intervention group and control groups for past-year crime, past-year arrests, or past-year court charges. *% difference*: −20.8% (full intervention); −9.4% (late intervention) (court charges lifetime by age 21: Efull: 42%; Elate: 48%; C: 53%)
Kellam et al., 2008	The Good Behavior Game *Programme components*: classroom management *Length*: 2 years *Participants*: schoolchildren (classroom-based universal intervention) in poor to lower middle class, mainly African–American urban areas	RCT (Cohort 1: n_E = 238; n_C = 165; Cohort 2: n_E = 208; n_C = 157) *Control*: a reading achievement programme or the standard programme	6 years	19–20 years	*Source*: Official records *Results*: Significant reduction in the rates of violent and criminal behaviour among males in persistent high aggressive, disruptive trajectory. For the other two less aggressive trajectories (stable low and escalating medium group), the impact of the programme was not significant. In the Cohort 2 replication (with lower fidelity in delivering the programme), the effects were in the hypothesised direction, but not significant. *% difference*: −32% (males in persistent high group n=28) (having a record of violent and criminal behaviour at follow up: E: 34%; C: 50%)

school-age interventions. These findings suggest that programme benefits are greater with earlier exposure.

Middle Childhood Programmes

We identified four programmes that fit the above-described criteria, which are summarized in Table 9.2.

Cambridge-Somerville Youth Study

The Cambridge-Somerville Youth Study is a pioneering longitudinal–experimental study of delinquency prevention that followed the development of a group of boys from densely populated factory-dominated areas in eastern Massachusetts into adulthood (McCord, 1978, 1990).

Programme model The programme was developed by a social philosopher and physician, Dr Richard C. Cabot. It started in 1939, when the boys were between ages 5 and 13 (median age = 10.5) and lasted for five years. Each participating family was assigned a counsellor who visited it, on average, twice per month. Through the counsellors, families were offered assistance tailored to their needs and wishes. Support focused on family problems for approximately one-third of the treatment group; over half of the boys received help with academic subjects; more than 100 participants had medical or psychiatric care; one quarter was sent to summer camps, and most of the boys were brought into contact with community programmes, such as Boy Scouts or the YMCA. The control group did not receive such services.

Research design and methods Both 'difficult' and 'average' boys were referred to the programme by schools, welfare agencies, churches and the police. Pairs of boys were matched on age, delinquency prediction scores, delinquency-prone histories, family background and home environments, and were then randomly allocated to a treatment group (n = 325) or a control group (n = 325). Due to a counsellor shortage in 1941, several pairs of boys dropped out of the study, leaving 253 matched pairs who were followed into adulthood. For the 30-year follow-up, 241 men who had received treatment and 239 control men were traced. Of these, 113 from the treatment group and 122 from the control group returned questionnaires that asked for information about marriage, children, occupations, drinking, health and attitudes. Official records provided additional information on all 253 pairs.

Major findings Outcomes of the 30-year follow-up show that treatment was ineffective in preventing offending: 28 per cent of the men who had received treatment and 26 per cent of the control men had official crime records as juveniles, and 66 per cent of both groups were convicted as adults.

Montreal Longitudinal Experimental Study

The aim of the Montreal Longitudinal Experimental Study, which took place from 1985–1987, was to examine the development of a large sample of inner-city Montreal, Canada, kindergarten boys from low socioeconomic backgrounds, with a particular focus on antisocial behaviour and school adjustment (Boisjoli et al., 2007; Tremblay et al., 1992, 1995).

Programme model The prevention programme consisted of three components: social skills training, parent training and teacher support. The social skills training was offered at school in small groups and lasted for two years. During the first year, nine sessions focusing on pro-social skills (for example, 'how to make contact', 'how to help') were given. During the second year, ten sessions were devoted to self-control (for example, 'look and listen', 'what to do when I am angry'). The parent training, based on the Oregon Social Learning Center Model (Patterson et al., 1975), focused on effective childrearing (M = 17.4 sessions). Among other things it involved training parents to monitor their children's behaviour, to give positive reinforcement for prosocial behaviour, and to punish effectively without being abusive. Finally, the teachers received information and support regarding at-risk boys. Due to their limited availability, meetings with teachers were fewer than planned (about 50 per cent of teachers participated in at least one meeting).

Research design and methods A total of 895 boys aged 7 from low socio-economic backgrounds who formerly had attended kindergarten in Montreal were approached for the study. The boys had to have Canadian-born parents and to speak French as their first language to be eligible for participation. From the total sample, 250 boys were considered to be at risk of later antisocial behaviour and school dropout, based on teacher ratings of their disruptive behaviour. These boys were randomly assigned to a prevention group ($n = 69$), an attention control group ($n = 123$) and a control group ($n = 58$). As there were no differences between the latter groups at follow-up they were eventually combined. The other 645 boys comprised a low-risk sample and were kept in the study to test the clinical significance of the prevention programme. At the follow-up at age 24, information on high school diplomas was retrieved for $n = 242$ of the original sample. Criminal record data were collected for the complete 250 original sample.

Major findings When the participants were age 24, a marginal difference (p=.06) was found between the programme group and the control group with regard to criminal records (21.7 per cent for the prevention programme group, and 32.6 per cent for the control group). The clinical significance of the programme is indicated by the fact that the boys in the programme group had similar rates of criminal records as the low-risk group, whereas the control group had significantly higher rates of criminal records than the low-risk group.

Seattle Social Development Project

This project began in 1981 and examined whether a multimodal intervention administered during elementary school promoted positive functioning and prevented mental health problems, crime and substance use in adolescence and adulthood in public elementary school students in high-crime areas of Seattle, Washington, US (Hawkins et al., 2005).

Programme model The Seattle Social Development Project is guided theoretically by the social development model (Hawkins and Weis, 1985; Catalano and Hawkins, 1996), hypothesizing that strong bonds of attachment and commitment to family and school set children on a positive developmental trajectory. The intervention consisted of three components: teacher training, child social and emotional skills development, and parent training. The content of these components differed, depending on whether the participant received an intervention during the full course of elementary school (full intervention) or an intervention delivered for just two years in grades 5 and 6 (late intervention). The teacher training component consisted of five days in-service training in instructional methods, including proactive classroom management, interactive teaching and cooperative learning. To facilitate child social and emotional skill development, grade 1 teachers in the full-intervention group learned to use a cognitive and social skills training curriculum in their classes. The parent training for the full-intervention group entailed a seven-session curriculum in child behaviour management skills and a four-session curriculum in skills for supporting children's academic development. These curricula were offered to parents on a voluntary basis when children were in grades 1 through 3. During grades 5 and 6, parents of children in the full- and late-intervention groups were offered a five-session curriculum aimed at strengthening their skills to reduce their children's risks for drug use and other problem behaviours.

Research design and methods The intervention started among grade 1 students in classrooms in eight public schools serving high-crime areas in Seattle. When these children entered grade 5, the study was expanded to include grade 5 students in ten additional schools. All 18 schools were then assigned non-randomly to the following groups: the full-intervention group ($n = 156$) consisted of students who received at least one semester of intervention in grades 1 through 4 and at least one semester of intervention in grades 5 and 6; the late-intervention group ($n = 267$) consisted of those who received the intervention during grades 5 and 6 only; the control group ($n = 220$) received no intervention. When participants were age 21, 605 of those 643 were interviewed for follow-up ($n = 144$ for the full-intervention group, $n = 256$ for the late-intervention group, and $n = 205$ for the control group).

Outcomes were measured in terms of positive functioning in school or work, emotional and mental health, and crime and substance use.

Major findings Crime and substance use measures revealed that full-intervention group participants were significantly less likely to be involved in a high variety of crime (four per cent vs nine per cent); have sold illegal drugs in the past year (four per cent vs 13 per cent), or have an official lifetime court record at age 21 (42 per cent vs 53 per cent). Only one effect was found for the late-intervention participants: they were less likely to have sold illegal drugs than the control group (six per cent vs 13 per cent). No differences were found between either intervention group and the control group with respect to committing any crime in the past year, having been arrested in the past year, or having a court charge in the past year.

The Good Behavior Game

The Good Behavior Game (GBG) is a classroom behaviour management strategy that teachers can apply to a classroom as a whole, aiming to reduce aggressive and disruptive behaviour and to socialize children to their roles as students (Kellam et al., 2008; Kellam and Rebok, 1992). The original randomized controlled trial of the Classroom Prevention Program was conducted in nine high-poverty Baltimore schools in 1993–2009.

Programme model The GBG was developed as a classroom behaviour management tool, aimed at creating a classroom environment that facilitates learning for all students (Kellam et al., 2008). The intervention is guided by life course/social field theory (Kellam and Rebok, 1992) as well as the early-starter and late-starter models of the development of antisocial behaviour (Patterson, Reid and Dishion, 1992). The GBG attempts to teach children to regulate their own and their classmates' behaviour. This is accomplished by way of interdependent team behaviour-contingent reinforcement.

In 1985 and 1986 the GBG was introduced into 19 classrooms of first- and second-grade students in the public school system of Baltimore, Maryland, US. The intervention was delivered by GBG teachers, who were trained for 40 hours before the start of the programme and received supportive monitoring during the rest of the school year. Children were divided into three heterogeneous teams that were similar in terms of the numbers of boys, and the number of aggressive, disruptive, shy and socially isolated children. To play the game, teachers first stated basic classroom rules of student behaviour and teams were rewarded if the team members committed less than four violations of these classroom rules. During the first weeks of the intervention, the GBG was played three times per week for a period of ten minutes each time. Over the following weeks the duration of the game increased, up to a maximum of three hours. A replication was implemented with a second cohort, using the same teachers, but with diminished mentoring and monitoring.

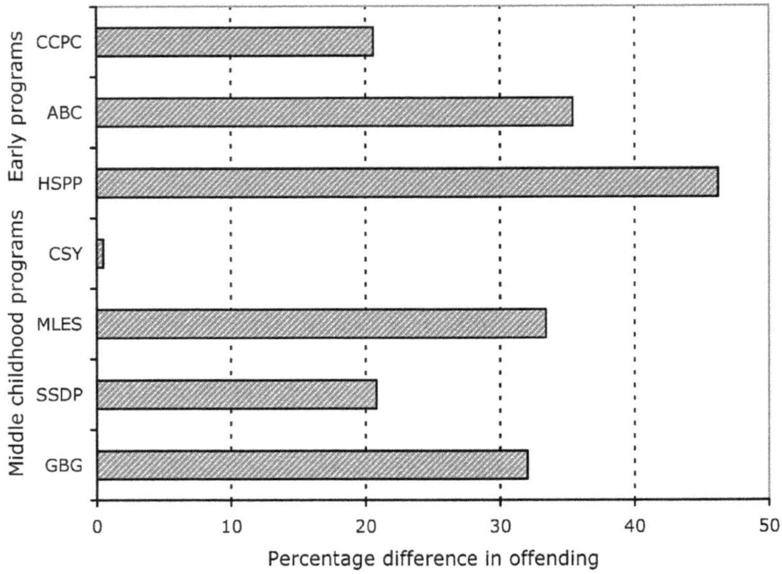

Figure 9.1 The effects of early prevention programmes on adult crime expressed as a difference in the percentage of recidivists in experimental and control groups at follow-up

Research design and methods In the 1985 and 1986 Baltimore study, two cohorts of first-grade students were recruited to take part in the study of the effectiveness of the GBG. They were from schools drawn from five parts of the city that varied in ethnicity, socioeconomic status, violent crime and school dropout rates. These schools were randomly assigned into three groups: (1) schools in which the GBG was tested, (2) schools in which mastery learning (ML) was tested, or (3) external control schools with no intervention. Following the school assignment, first-grade classrooms within the GBG and ML schools were randomly assigned to either the intervention or internal control group. Internal control classrooms were used to rule out school building, family and community differences and as a control group for the follow-up study. Two cohorts (N = 403, n = 238 in the CBG group, n = 165 internal control group, for cohort one; N = 365, n = 208 in the CBG group, n = 157 internal control group, for cohort two) took part in the study. The effectiveness trial involved the first cohort, whereas the second cohort was a replication with less mentoring and monitoring. When participants were ages 19–21, juvenile court and adult incarceration records of violent and criminal behaviour were obtained.

Major findings First, three trajectories of aggressive behaviour during elementary school were identified: a persistently high group, an escalating medium group, and a stable low group. At the time of follow-up, 34 per cent of GBG males in the persistently high group and 50 per cent of control males had a record of violent and criminal behaviour ($p < .001$). Within the other two trajectories the GBG group and the control group did not differ on violent and criminal behaviour (13 per cent vs 20 per cent in the escalating medium group; six per cent vs 0 per cent in the stable low group). For females in the first cohort, no effects of the GBG were found in young adulthood. In the second cohort replication, GBG effects on violent and criminal behaviour were not significant but were in the hypothesized direction.

Commentary on Middle Childhood Programmes

Similar to the early childhood prevention programmes, middle childhood prevention programmes showed mixed effects on crime during adulthood. The oldest programme, the Cambridge-Somerville Youth Study, was ineffective in preventing offending. The Montreal Longitudinal Experimental Study reported a marginal difference between the experimental and control groups in criminal records, probably due to a small sample size at follow-up. There were, however, indications of clinical significance of effects: the criminal records of the experimental group were similar to those of a non-risk group, whereas those of the control group were higher than a non-risk group. The participants in the Seattle Social Development Project full-intervention group (but not those in late-intervention group) were less likely to have an official lifetime court record at age 21 than those in the control group. The Good Behavior Game study reported significant effects, but only for males in the highest initial risk group and only in the first cohort, which was characterized by the better implementation of the intervention.

The results of these studies suggest that programme effectiveness might be dependent on participants' and/or programme characteristics. First, programmes might be more effective for some participants than for others. For example, effects of the Good Behavior Game in cohort one was larger for males with higher initial levels of behaviour problems than for participants with lower levels of behaviour problems and for females. Second, the results of these studies suggest that it is crucially important that the programme is carried out as intended. In the Montreal study it was reported that the teacher component was not implemented as hoped (fewer teachers participated), which might explain the modest effects. The Good Behavior Game study points out the importance of treatment fidelity as well0ffects were smaller and not significant. Finally, a programme's timing and intensity might also influence its effectiveness. In the Seattle Social Development Project, there is suggestive evidence that the 'full intervention' in which the children were treated from first though sixth grade may be more effective than 'late intervention', which took place only in fifth and sixth grade.

Early Prevention Programmes in the Netherlands

The good news in the Netherlands is that there is no shortage of early prevention programmes. There are about 30 different prevention programmes aimed at reducing behaviour problems and preventing antisocial development currently administered in the Netherlands (Jonkman, Van Yperen and Prinsen, 2009). Some of these programmes have been developed in Dutch clinical practice and some are adaptations of programmes developed and tested abroad. The bad news is that Dutch intervention research is still lagging. Until now, there has been very little information regarding the short-term effects of such programmes and virtually no information regarding their long-term effects.

Two early prevention programmes similar to those discussed above, Opstap and Kaleidoscoop, have been implemented in the Netherlands. Opstap, an adaptation of HIPPY (Home Instruction Program for Preschool Youngsters), is a prevention programme aimed at improving academic achievement for children from disadvantaged neighbourhoods It consists of a structured curriculum of play and learning activities for Turkish and Moroccan immigrant children ages four to six. Van Tuijl, Leseman and Rispens (2001) carried out a quasi-experimental evaluation, indicating modest effects on cognitive development and emergent numeracy for Turkish children, and no effects for Moroccan children. Long-term follow-up (six years after the programme ended) indicated positive effects at the end of elementary school as well as improved parent–child interactions for a small Turkish sample (Van Tuijl and Siebes, 2006). It should be noted, however, that this research was carried out with a very small sample size and selective dropout may have taken place.

The second early prevention programme implemented in the Netherlands, Kaleidoscoop, is an adaptation of the HighScope Perry Preschool programme. However, to date no Dutch effectiveness study has been carried out on Kaleidoscoop.

One of the middle childhood prevention programmes that has been implemented and evaluated in the Netherlands is the Good Behaviour Game (*Taakspel* in Dutch). In this game, children ages eight to ten are taught to better follow classroom rules, aiming to decrease early disruptive problems and enhance positive behaviours. The classroom is divided into several teams in which pupils are rewarded if they show positive behaviours. The first effectiveness study, a randomized controlled trial, reported positive results in terms of diminished externalizing behaviour problems and improvements in peer acceptance (Witvliet et al., 2009).

In summary, only two of the foreign programmes that have been evaluated for effectiveness in influencing behaviour during adulthood (the HighScope Perry Preschool programme and the Good Behavior Game) are carried out in the Netherlands, of which only one, the Good Behavior Game, has been studied rigorously in the Dutch context (Van Lier, Methén, Van der Sar and Crijen, 2004). For the other two Dutch programmes aimed at prevention of delinquency, no convincing evidence has been reported on the basis of Dutch research. Moreover, for none of these programmes have the effects during adulthood been examined.

Conclusions

As the present review shows, in the international literature only a small number of well-conducted studies on the long-term effects of early prevention programmes on adult crime is available. In the Netherlands, no such studies yet exist. Therefore, at this moment a definitive statement as to whether early childhood prevention programmes are effective in preventing crime in adulthood is impossible to make. Tentatively, it appears that these programmes have some beneficial effects. When we look at the decrease in recidivism in adulthood, out of eight evaluations, the experimental groups did better than the control groups in seven cases (the exception is the oldest programme, the Cambridge-Somerville Youth Study). The percentage of differences in recidivism between experimental and control groups at follow-up varied from −21 per cent to −46 per cent (see Figure 9.1).

How can these effects be explained? The prevention programmes that we reviewed all focus on risk factors for child maladjustment. It is likely that the programmes set in motion a favourable set of direct and indirect influences on children that improved their long-term outcomes. The child components of early prevention programmes focus mainly on cognitive–scholastic skills. The improvement in these skills is supposed to increase school commitment, decrease school failure, and increase the rate of high school graduation. Better educational achievement and school commitment are expected to offer more opportunities for involvement in conventional activities and to function as protective factors against involvement in delinquency later in life. In middle childhood there is also a focus on social skills and on value education (for example, teaching socially appropriate ways of obtaining desired goals, avoiding health risk behaviour, having respect for others). The family components in early prevention programmes attempt to provide parents with more information and with emotional and instrument support, but often do not include behavioural training for parents that can reduce antisocial behaviour in their children. Such training is more often part of middle childhood programmes that aim to improve parental skills. By improving the childrearing environment, the programmes aim to prevent maladaptive developmental trajectories.

The beneficial effects, however, should not be overestimated. First, some of the programmes provide no evidence that the participants were significantly less likely than control group participants to be involved in crime during adulthood. The clearest example is the Cambridge-Somerville Youth Study, which showed no positive effects and even produced some negative effects (McCord, 1978). These effects may be due to, first, the lower quality of this oldest programme, or to the fact that it involved working with *groups* of deviant youth. Aggregation of antisocial peers in high-risk youth has been shown to have iatrogenic effects (Dishion, McCord and Poulin, 1999; Gatti, Tremblay and Vitaro, 2009). Second, even within the same study, the effects for all assessed crime outcomes were not consistently found. Reynolds et al. (2007), for example, found positive effects for felony arrests, convictions and incarceration, but not for violent arrest and violent crime conviction. Third, the positive effects were often found only for some groups or some programme components: males who showed high levels of disruptive behaviour, but not females or males with lower levels of problems (Kellam et al., 2008); the participants in full-intervention groups, but not those in late-intervention groups (Hawkins et al., 2005); the participants who followed preschool intervention or both preschool- and school intervention, but not those who followed only school intervention (Reynolds et al., 2007), or the participants who were the first cohort to follow the programme (Kellam et al., 2008). Finally, a sizeable percentage (21 per cent to 66 per cent) of participants in the early prevention programmes still had a criminal record later in life.

Building on this systematic review, we recently conducted a meta-analysis of early prevention programmes (Deković et al., 2011). In order to include as many studies as possible, we broadened the criterion 'age at follow-up' to include two additional studies that assessed participants at age 18 (McCormick et al., 2006) and age 19 (Eckenrode et al., 2010). Thus, in this meta-analysis, the results of nine studies that investigated the long-term effects of early prevention programmes on crime (in total 3,611 participants) were synthesized. An additional aim of the meta-analysis was to compare the effect sizes on crime to the effect sizes on positive outcomes such as academic attainment and involvement in productive activities like school or work.

Not surprisingly, the results of the meta-analysis regarding long-term effects of early prevention programmes on crime confirmed the conclusion of the present review. The effect size for adult criminal offending was significant, but small in magnitude (OR = 1.26; *95% CI* = 1.06 – 1.50, $p = .011$). The effects of the programmes on positive outcomes (academic attainment and involvement in productive activity) were somewhat larger and more consistent than effects on crime (OR = 1.36, *95% CI* = 1.20 – 1.55, $p < .001$), indicating that early prevention programmes can help put children on a more positive developmental trajectory that is maintained into adulthood, although no convincing evidence was found that they can prevent adult crime.

An additional advantage of a meta-analysis over a narrative review is that it allows identification of factors that may act as moderators of programme effects. The potential moderators were grouped into the following domains: participant-, programme- and study characteristics. Several of these characteristics indeed moderated the effectiveness of early prevention programmes. Children who were more at risk and those from a lower SES benefited more. Shorter, but more intensive programmes, and programmes that focus on social and behavioural skills rather than on academic skills or family support, tend to produce larger effects. Moderator analysis also showed that an early start might be more beneficial, as indicated by a significant negative relationship between child age at the start of the programmes and programme effectiveness, and that the programme effects attenuate over time, as indicated by a significant relationship between the age at follow-up and effect size.

Implications for Policy, Clinical Practice, and Research

Despite the commonly held belief that early interventions are more effective than interventions with older children, we have seen that only a few empirical studies are available that tested the long-term effects of early prevention programmes. Moreover, only some of these programmes provide convincing evidence that intervening in early or middle childhood produces long-lasting beneficial effects on crime committed in adulthood. Still, there are some valuable lessons to be learned from these pioneering projects. Some of these lessons are relevant to most interventions, regardless of their aims and targeted populations, whereas some of the lessons are especially relevant for prevention of crime during the transition to adulthood. We start with the latter.

The results of both our present review and our meta-analysis show that programmes that explicitly aim to prevent problem behaviour tend to produce better results regarding adult criminal offending than programmes with the more general objectives of improving a wide range of child behaviour outcomes. Moreover, the effects of the programmes on educational achievement and mental health later in life were more consistent and higher than the effects on crime. It is possible that a tighter focus on specific risk factors for antisocial behaviour would improve the effectiveness of these programmes for crime prevention. Hawkins et al. (2005) came to the same conclusion when the results of their own study were evaluated: the relatively modest effect on crime as compared to the effects on other outcomes could be due to the fact that the programme focused largely on strengthening bonds between the family and school rather than on explicitly promoting norms or standards to counter illegal behaviour. Thus, crime prevention research should focus on the effects in adulthood of preventive programmes targeting early disruptiveness, rather than research into the long-term effects of programmes promoting mainly academic achievement, in order to determine whether the effects on crime can be strengthened. However, improved academic achievement may mediate or moderate programme effects on delinquency. This issue deserves further research attention.

Related to this issue is the question of where to intervene. Given that antisocial behaviour emerges from a complex array of risk factors, programmes targeting a single risk factor are unlikely to be effective (Reese et al., 2000). Programmes aiming to change the course of disruptive behaviour must focus on modifying the different sources of influence that affect the development of antisocial behaviour. In other words, the multimodal approach targeting both child and family factors is the most promising. Many of the early prevention programmes focus on proximal risk factors for development of antisocial behaviour either within the child (for example, the lack of academic and social skills) and/or within the child's direct environment (for example, inept parenting, inadequate school climate). In addition to these factors, there is a need to consider the broader environment in which a child grows up: neighbourhood, availability of medical, social, and child care services, etc. Even when early programmes have positive short-term effects, in order to sustain these positive changes, improvement in this larger social context might also be needed to support children and families living in disadvantaged conditions.

The following issues are important not only for programmes that aim to prevent adult crime but for any other early preventive effort. The results of the meta-analysis suggest that positive effects of early prevention programmes fade with time. It is not realistic to expect – especially for children living in difficult circumstances – that a single intervention during early or middle childhood is enough. On the other hand, the results of the meta-analysis also indicate that more lengthy programmes tend to produce a smaller effect size. Possibly the quality of implementation of the programme tends to decrease with the programme's length. The best approach might be to deliver a relatively short, intense programme, followed by regular booster sessions. A booster session at crucial developmental phases (for example, before and immediately after the transition to high school, which is known to be an especially sensitive period for development of a variety of problems) may help consolidate positive initial effects of early prevention programmes (Tolan et al., 2009).

The next issue concerns the selection of programme participants. The findings from the above studies indicate that it might be more beneficial to focus on children who are more at risk and thus in real need of intervention. Several meta-analyses found that targeted programmes, directed at children who are indentified as at higher risk for developing more serious problem behaviours, rather than universal programmes delivered to general populations, were more effective in reducing problem behaviours (Wilson, Gottfredson and Najaka, 2001; Wilson, Lipsey and Derzon, 2003). It is important to carefully consider the selection criteria for participants and it might be more beneficial to use selection criteria that are closely linked to antisocial behaviour, such as high disruptiveness, non-compliance, aggression, rule breaking or inept parenting, rather than more general criteria such as living in a high-crime neighbourhood or low SES.

It is clear from the present review that empirical evidence regarding long-term effects of early prevention programmes on adult crime is quite limited. Obviously much more research is needed. This is especially true for the Netherlands where such studies (well designed and with long follow-up) are unfortunately non-existent. Before early prevention programmes are broadly implemented, they should be tested rigorously on a small scale. After that, large-scale implementation should be accompanied by a long-term (preferably up to adulthood) randomized, controlled trial in order to establish the effectiveness of the programme. In addition to the first important and obvious question in every evaluation study ('What are the effects of the programme?'), more attention should be given to the investigation of moderators, or factors that affect the effectiveness of the programme. In order to do so, a sufficiently large sample should be included. In addition to participant characteristics, such as age, gender, ethnicity, the initial level of disruptive behaviour, etc., programme characteristics, such as programme intensity, duration, timing and specificity, might also be influential moderators of programmes' effectiveness. The moderator analyses should further clarify their importance. Finally, very little is known about the potential mediators of the effectiveness of early prevention programmes. If these programmes are effective, what are the programme components responsible for these effects? Therefore, the hypothesized mediators of change should be assessed. Such research can provide information that is crucial for underpinning more conceptually and empirically informed preventive efforts, and thus can help policymakers to decide which programmes are worth implementing.

References

Boisjoli, R., Vitaro, F., Lacourse, E., Barker, E.D., and Tremblay, R.E. (2007). Impact and clinical significance of a preventive intervention for disruptive boys: 15-year follow-up. *British Journal of Psychiatry*, 191, 415–19.

Campbell, F.A., Ramey, C.T., Pungello, E., Sparling, J., and Miller-Johnson, S. (2002). Early childhood outcomes from the Abecedarian Project. *Applied Developmental Science*, 6, 42–57.

Catalano, R.F. and Hawkins, J.D. (1996). The social development model: A theory of antisocial behavior. In J.D. Hawkins (ed.), *Delinquency and Crime: Current Theories*. New York: Cambridge University Press, pp. 149–97).

Clarke, S.H. and Campbell, F.A. (1998). Can intervention early prevent crime later? The Abecedarian Project compared to other programs. *Early Childhood Research Quarterly*, 13, 319–43.

Deković, M., Slagt, M.I., Asscher, J.J., Boendermaker, L., Eichelsheim, V.I., and Prinzie, P. (2011). Effects of early prevention programs on adult criminal offending: A meta-analysis. *Clinical Psychology Review*, 31, 532–44.

Dishion, T.J. and Patterson, G.R. (2006). The development and ecology of antisocial behavior. In D. Cicchetti and D. Cohen (eds), *Developmental Psychopathology. Vol. 3: Risk, Disorder, and Adaptation* 2nd edn. New York: Wiley & Sons, pp. 503–41.

Dishion, T.J., McCord, J., and Poulin, F. (1999). When interventions harm: Peer group and problem behavior. *American Psychologist*, 9, 755–64.

Eckenrode, J., Campa, M., Luckey, D.W., Henderson Jr, C.R., Cole, R., Kitzman, H., Olds, D. (2010). Long-term effects of prenatal and infancy Nurse Home Visitation on the life course of youths: 19-year follow-up of a randomized trial. *Archives of Pediatrics and Adolescent Medicine*, 164, 9–15.

Farrington, D.P. and Coid, J. (2003). *Early Prevention of Adult Antisocial Behaviour*. Cambridge: Cambridge University Press.

Gatti, U., Tremblay, R.E., and Vitaro, F. (2009). Iatrogenic effect of juvenile justice. *Journal of Child Psychology and Psychiatry*, 50, 991–8.

Hawkins, J.D. and Weis, J.G. (1985). The social development model: An integrated approach to delinquency prevention. *Journal of Primary Prevention*, 6, 73–97.

Hawkins, J.D., Kosterman, R., Catalano, R.F., Hill, K.G., and Abbott, R.D. (2005). Promoting positive adult functioning through social development intervention in childhood. *Archives of Pediatrics and Adolescent Medicine*, 159, 25–31.

Hohmann, M. and Weikart, D.P. (1995). *Educating Young Children: Active Learning Practices for Preschool and Child Cure Programs*. Ypsilanti, MI: High/Scope Press.

Jonkman, H., Van Yperen, T., and Prinsen, B. (2009). Prevention. In R. Loeber, N.W. Slot, P.H. Van der Laan and M. Hoeve (eds), *Tomorrow's Criminals: The Development of Child Delinquency and Effective Interventions*. Farnham: Ashgate, pp. 179–96.

Kellam, S. and Rebok, G. (1992). Building developmental and etiological theory through epidemiological based preventive intervention trials. In J. McCord and R.E. Tremblay (eds), *Preventing Antisocial Behavior: Interventions from Birth through Adolescence*. New York: Neale Watson Academic Publishers, pp. 162–95.

Kellam, S.G., Brown, H.C., Poduska, J.M., Ialongo, N.S., Wang, W., Toyinbo, P., Petros, H., Ford, C., Windham, A., and Wilcox, H.C. (2008). Effects of a universal classroom behavior management program in first and second grades on young adult behavioral, psychiatric and social outcomes. *Drug and Alcohol Dependence*, 95S, S5–S28.

Loeber, R. and Farrington, D.P. (2000). Young children who commit crime: Epidemiology, developmental origins, risk factors, early interventions, and policy implications. *Development and Psychopathology*, 12, 737–62.

Loeber, R., Farrington, D.P., Stouthamer-Loeber, M., and White, H.R. (2008). *Violence and Serious Theft: Development and Prediction from Childhood to Adulthood*. New York: Routledge.

McCord, J. (1978). A thirty-year follow-up of treatment effects. *American Psychologist*, 33, 284–9.

McCord, J. (1990). Crime in moral and social contexts: The American Society of Criminology 1989 Presidential Address. *Criminology*, 28, 1–26.

McCormick, M.C., Brooks-Gunn, J., Buka, S.L., Goldman, J., Yu, J., Salganik, M., and Casey, P. (2006). Early intervention in low birth weight premature infants: Results at 18 years of age for the Infant Health and Development Program. *Journal of Pediatrics*, 117, 771–80.

Nores, M., Belfield, C.R., Barnett, W.S., and Schweinhart, L. (2005). Updating the economic impacts of the High/Scope Perry Preschool Program. *Educational Evaluation and Policy Analysis*, 27, 245–61.

Olds, D.L., Sadler, L., and Kitzman, H. (2007). Program for parents of infants and toddlers: Recent evidence from randomized trials. *Journal of Child Psychology and Psychiatry*, 48, 355–91.

Patterson, G.R., Reid, J.B., and Dishion, T.J. (1992). *Antisocial Boys*. Eugene, OR: Castalia.

Patterson, G.R., Reid, J.B., Jones, R.R., and Conger, R.E. (1975). *A Social Learning Approach to Family Intervention. Vol. 1: Families with Aggressive Children*. Eugene, OR: Castalia Publishing Company.

Piquero, A.R. (2008). Taking stock of developmental trajectories of criminal activity over the life course. In A.M. Liberman (ed.), *The Long View of Crime: A Synthesis of Longitudinal Research*. New York: Springer, pp. 23–78.

Piquero, A.R., Farrington, D.P., Welsh, B.C., Tremblay, R., and Jennings, W.G. (2009). Effects of early family/parent training programs on antisocial behavior and delinquency. *Journal of Experimental Criminology*, 5, 83–120.

Ramey, C.T., MacPhee, D., and Yeates, K.O. (1982). Preventing developmental retardation: A general systems model. In L.A. Bond and J.M. Joffe (eds), *Facilitating Infant and Early Childhood Development*. Hanover, NH: University Press of New England, pp. 343–401.

Reese, L.E., Vera, E.M., Simon, T.R., and Ikeda, R.M. (2000). The role of families and care givers as risk and protective factors in preventing youth violence. *Clinical Child and Family Psychology Review*, 3, 61–77.

Reynolds, A.J., Temple, J.A., Robertson, D.L., and Mann, E.A. (2001). Long-term effects of an early childhood intervention on educational achievement and juvenile arrest: A 15-year follow-up of low-income children in public schools. *Journal of American Medical Association*, 285, 2339–46.

Reynolds, A.J., Temple, J.A., Ou, S., Roberson, D.L., Mersky, J.P., Topitzes, J.W., and Nils, M.D. (2007). Effects of a school-based, early childhood intervention on adult health and well-being. *Archives of Paediatrics and Adolescent Medicine*, 161, 730–9.

Schweinhart, L.J., Barnes, H.V., and Weikart, D.P (1993). *Significant Benefits: The High/Scope Preschool Study through Age 27*, Monographs of the High/Scope Educational Research Foundation, 10. Ypsilanti, MI: High/Scope Press.

Schweinhart, L.J., Montie, J., Xiang, Z., Barnett, W.S., Belfield, C.R., and Nores, M. (2005). *Lifetime Effects: The High/Scope Perry Preschool Study through Age 40*, Monographs of the High/Scope Educational Research Foundation, 14. Ypsilanti, MI: High/Scope Press.

Sparling, J. and Lewis, I. (2000). *Learning Games: The Abecedarian Curriculum*. Tallahassee, FL: Early Learning Press.

Tolan, P.H., Gorman-Smith, D., Henry, D., and Schoeny, M. (2009). The benefits of booster interventions: Evidence from a family-focused prevention program. *Prevention Science*, 10, 287–97.

Tremblay, R.E., Pagani-Kurtz, L., Massé, L.C., Vitaro, F., and Pihl, R.O. (1995). A bimodal preventive intervention for disruptive kindergarten boys: Its impact through mid-adolescence. *Journal of Consulting and Clinical Psychology*, 63, 560–8.

Tremblay, R.E., Vitaro, F., Bertrand, L., LeBlanc, M., Beauchesne, H., Boileau, H., and David, L. (1992). Parent and child training to prevent early onset of delinquency: The Montreal longitudinal experimental study. In J. McCord and R.E. Tremblay (eds), *Preventing Antisocial Behavior: Intervention from Birth through Adolescence*. New York: Guilford Press, pp. 117–38.

Van Lier, P.A.C., Methén, B.O., Van der Sar, R.M., and Crijen, A.A.M. (2004). Preventing disruptive behavior in elementary schoolchildren: Impact of a universal classroom-based intervention. *Journal of Consulting and Clinical Psychology*, 72, 467–78.

Van Tuijl, C. and Siebes, R. (2006). *Het rendement van Opstap in de basisschoolperiode. Een longitudinaal onderzoek naar de effecten van een gezinsgericht stimuleringsprogramma bij Turkse en Marokkaanse gezinnen. Een samenvatting*. Utrecht: Nederlands jeugdinstituut NJI.

Van Tuijl, C., Leseman, P.P.M., and Rispens, J. (2001). Efficacy of an intensive home-based educational intervention programme for 4- to 6-year-old ethnic minority children in the Netherlands. *International Journal of Behavioural Development*, 25, 148–59.

Weikart, D.P., Rogers, L., Adcock, C., and McClelland, D. (1971). *The Cognitively oriented Curriculum: A Framework for Preschool Teachers*. Urbana, IL: University of Illinois.

Welsh, B.C. and Farrington, D.P. (2001). Towards an evidence-based approach to preventing crime. *The Annals of the American Academy of Political and Social Science*, 578, 159–73.

Welsh, B.C. and Farrington, D.P. (2006). Effectiveness of family-based programs to prevent delinquency and later offending. *Psicothema*, 18, 596–602.

Wilson, D.B., Gottfredson, D.C., and Najaka, S.S. (2001). School-based prevention of problem behaviors: A meta-analysis. *Journal of Quantitative Criminology*, 17, 247–72.

Wilson, S.J., Lipsey, M.W., and Derzon, J.H. (2003). The effects of school-based intervention programs on aggressive behaviour: A meta-analysis. *Journal of Consulting and Clinical Psychology*, 71, 136–49.

Witvliet, M., Van Lier, P., Cuijpers, P., and Koot, H.M. (2009). Testing links between childhood positive peer relations and externalizing outcomes through a randomized controlled intervention study. *Journal of Consulting and Clinical Psychology*, 77, 905–15.

Yoshikawa, H. (1995). Long-term effects of early childhood programs on social outcomes and delinquency. *The Future of Children*, 5, 51–75.

Chapter 10
Interventions

Leonieke Boendermaker, Maja Deković and Jessica J. Asscher

Our objective in this chapter is to examine interventions carried out with late adolescents and young adults that aim to reduce serious antisocial behaviour. As the legal response to early adult offending (arrest, prosecution and imprisonment) is discussed by Van der Laan et al. (Chapter 8, this volume), the focus here is limited to psychosocial interventions or programmes applied in young offender institutions and adult prisons, or community approaches especially focused on the age group 18–25.

Although the notion that young people are qualitatively different from adults is widely shared, and accordingly that their crimes should be handled differently, there seems to be less recognition for the fact that there is not one specific, clear-cut age-point when an individual stops being juvenile and becomes an adult (see Blokland and Palmen, Chapter 2, this volume). The Dutch legal system, for example, treats everyone 18 and over as an adult (Tonry, 2007). However, as others in this volume note, the transition to adulthood is a developmental phenomenon that varies widely between individuals and over time has become increasingly prolonged. Young adults have distinct needs and confront different developmental tasks than both adolescents and fully formed adults (see Blokland and Palmen, Chapter 2, this volume). For example, this is a period of change in the family context, with youth leaving the family of origin to live on their own. In addition to gaining more emotional and behavioural autonomy, they also engage in new roles (for example, employment or parenthood) and become economically independent. Some types of relationships become less important (for example, with school friends), whereas other relationships increase in their importance (for example, with a romantic partner) (see Bijleveld, Geest and Hendriks, Chapter 5, this volume). If a programme for young adult offenders is to be successful, it should take into account these specific developmental tasks as well as the factors related to continuation, initiation or desistance of offending during this important developmental period (Mulvey et al., 2004).

Here we pose the following questions: What are the non-specific and specific active ingredients in interventions for young adult offenders? Which interventions for young adult offenders are available in the Netherlands and are these interventions composed of promising active ingredients? In our search for answers, we focus on programmes for young adult offenders themselves, and we leave aside those interventions primarily focusing on young offenders, the parents of young offenders, or on the family of origin.

Active Ingredients for Young Adult Offenders: International Findings

Effective interventions are grounded in a treatment theory that describes the risk and protective factors to be influenced by the intervention, as well as the non-specific and specific active ingredients to achieve the goals of the intervention (Van Yperen and Boendermaker, 2008). General or non-specific intervention ingredients are those elements of an intervention that contribute to the outcome irrespective of the type of intervention, the type of problem, or the group of individuals involved. Specific intervention ingredients are responsible for the effect of interventions that focus on the particular dynamic factors relevant to the target group of the intervention, in this case young adult offenders.

Non-specific Ingredients

Reviews and meta-analyses show the importance of the risk, need and responsivity principles in working with offenders. Interventions should be in tune with the severity and complexity of the offenders' problem behaviour, focusing on the characteristics, risk factors and needs that are directly related to the criminal behaviour. Also, the intervention should consist of different modalities, using different methods that effectively address different risk factors (Andrews et al., 1990; Lipsey, 2009; Lowenkamp, 2004). Other non-specific working ingredients are: a high treatment integrity of treatment staff; a good fit between the intervention and the motivational stage of the client; a proper treatment planning and treatment structure; a working alliance between the worker and the client; and finally, well-trained and educated personnel (for example, Shirk and Karver, 2003; Weisz et al., 1995; Van Yperen et al., 2010).

Specific working Ingredients

International research on interventions aimed at the reduction of serious antisocial behaviour in young offenders shows that interventions with a cognitive or cognitive-behavioural emphasis reduce recidivism of serious (institutionalized as well as non-institutionalized) juvenile offenders. In contrast, interventions that focus on deterrence or discipline without aftercare or without a therapeutic component, or on self-esteem, are not effective and can even produce negative results (Brestan and Eyberg, 1998; Chorpita et al., 2002; Garrido and Moralez, 2007; Lipsey, 1992, 1995, 2009; Lipsey and Wilson, 1998; Wilson, Mackenzie; and Ngo Mitchell, 2008).

The same findings apply to adult offenders (for example, Aos, Miller and Drake, 2006; Milkman and Wanberg, 2007). Welsh et al. (2010) reviewed studies on the effects of cognitive-behavioural therapy for young and adult offenders. They concluded that there is no reason to expect cognitive-behavioural therapy to be any less effective with offenders in the transitional age range. Applications of cognitive-behavioural therapy programmes in secure correctional settings for young offenders also had positive outcomes (Genovés, Morales and Sánchez-Meca, 2006). However, the treatment effects at one-year follow-up in a secure setting were small (Armelius and Andreassen, 2007).

Most cognitive-behavioural therapy programmes consist of distinct training modules that focus on social and problem-solving skills, cognitive restructuring, anger control, and moral reasoning or understanding of the impact of delinquency on victims. Landenberger and Lipsey (2005) showed that a combination of social and problem-solving skills training, anger control and cognitive restructuring, plus the use of group as well as individual training components, was the most effective combination for young offenders.

Many interventions take place in residential (juvenile justice) institutions. Working with the young person's family or social network and offering aftercare support helps to sustain the results of cognitive-behavioural programmes in residential care (Hair, 2005; Lipsey and Wilson, 1998; Whittaker, 2004). Recent meta-analyses have added new outcome information on mentoring interventions. When a young person is supported by an older, experienced adult who functions as a role model and offers emotional support and advice, mentoring for high-risk youth has a modest positive effect for delinquency, aggression, drug use and school achievement (Lipsey, 2009; Tolan et al., 2008).

The specific ingredients discussed so far are the essential components of interventions aimed at the reduction of antisocial and delinquent behaviour. The reduction of antisocial and delinquent behaviour, however, is only one of the goals in the treatment of young offenders. Another important goal, especially for young adult offenders, is a smooth transition to an independent life in society. Studies show that many young offenders leaving care facilities lack the life skills or resources necessary to succeed independently (Stein, 2004). Compared to the normal population, these young people face higher rates of homelessness, unemployment, dependency on public assistance, physical and mental health problems, and involvement in crime (Donkoh, Underhill and Montgomery, 2006; Stein, 2004). Independent living programmes that focus on personal development and offer educational and vocational support and training in independent living skills are one of the strategies to improve outcomes. Unfortunately, there is a lack of experimental or quasi-experimental studies evaluating interventions for young people leaving care (Stein, 2004).

The same conclusion prevails regarding independent living programmes. Donkoh, Underhill and Montgomery (2006) intended to conduct a meta-analysis on independent living programmes but found no studies using adequate methodology on which to base such an analysis. They identified 18 studies using non-randomized or non-comparative designs, which generally reported favourable outcomes for the participants of independent living programmes. Due to the weak design of these studies, however, no reliable conclusions could be drawn.

Research in a related area, on non-custodial employment programmes, faced more or less the same problems. Here studies with a job placement or job training component were included, although other components such as life-skills training, remedial education, or multiple services could be involved. A heterogeneous group of eight studies was identified. The participants ranged from older youth (ages 16–17) to adults in their 40s, and the treatment ingredients differed from job preparation programmes and vocational training to placement assistance. Despite the limitations of these programmes, the authors proceeded in their analysis and found no significant effect of the eight interventions on the likelihood of participants' recidivism. The authors concluded that employment-focused interventions have not yet been adequately evaluated (Visher, Winterfield and Coggeshall, 2006). A similar conclusion was drawn by Welsh et al. (2010), who reviewed research on programmes aiming to increase employment of individuals or populations at risk for serious offending. Experimental research on the nationwide Job Corps programme in the US, with about 15,000 participants, showed a significant reduction in criminal activity, improvements in educational attainment, and greater earnings. Programme participants had an average arrest rate of 29 per cent compared to 33 per cent of their control counterparts. Besides this study, few impact evaluations have been done on other national job training programmes. The available studies indicate that educational, vocational and employment programmes, as a group, are somewhat more effective with adult rather than juvenile offenders, presumably because employment issues are less important for young offenders compared to adult offenders.

Another related area to be reviewed here is the research on rehabilitation programmes for people with mental illness. Although rehabilitation programmes usually do not work with young adult offenders, research on them could spread some light on effective support for independent living. Unfortunately, research in this area is also limited. There is some evidence on the individual Psychiatric Rehabilitation Approach in other countries, which shows that this approach helps clients to reach their goals in the areas of work, independent living, and social relations (Michon and Van Weeghel, 2008).

Interventions for Young Adult Offenders in the Netherlands

In 2005, Verwers and Bogaerts published an inventory of approaches to young adult offenders in different countries. They concluded that no special programmes for this group were available either in or outside the Netherlands. A 2007 report of the Auditor General in the Netherlands also showed that interventions that support young people in the transition to adult life, described above, were scarce. Moreover, aftercare programmes, both in young offender institutions as well as in community settings, were limited. A recent Dutch study (Steketee, Vandenbroucke and Rijkschroeff, 2009) demonstrated that the need for programmes for young adults is not limited to young adult *offenders*. Young people who grow up in residential or foster care, or have specific mental problems, or have a mild mental handicap tend to get lost between the youth and adult care system. The authors stress the need for cooperation between the two systems to prevent young people

Box 10.1 Quality criteria used by the Dutch Accreditation Panel for Behavioural Programmes for offenders

1. A clear model of change backed by research evidence, i.e., the programme has a realistic evidence-based plan for creating change in offenders' future behaviour.
2. Selection of offenders, i.e., the programme chooses participants whose behavior needs changing and whose risk for negative outcomes is likely to be reduced by the programme.
3. Targeting dynamic risk factors, i.e., the programme focuses on risk factors that need to be and can be reduced.
4. Effective methods, i.e., uses interventions with proven efficacy.
5. Skills orientation: the intervention is aimed in part at acquiring practical, cognitive, social and problem-solving skills.
6. Sequencing, intensity and duration, i.e., the frequency and number of programme sessions matches participants' learning styles and abilities.
7. Engagement and motivation: the programme encourages a positive response.
8. Continuity of programmes and services, i.e., coordinates them to maximize the effect of treatment and monitoring.
9. Programme integrity: the programme is being implemented as designed.
10. Ongoing evaluation: a continuous evaluation provides insights into the results of the behavioural programme.

from becoming homeless, unemployed, and involved in crime, and they underline the need for these young adults for coaching and guidance in daily life skills.

Although the above three publications emphasize the lack of special programmes for young adult offenders, some programmes do exist. In the last decade, programmes for young offenders have been developed in the juvenile justice institutions, and programmes for adult offenders have been introduced in adult prisons.

In order to identify available programmes in the Netherlands, we used three sources: a list of programmes that have been approved by the Dutch Accreditation Panel on Behavioural Programmes for Offenders (Erkenningscommissie Gedragsinterventies Justitie), a similar list of programmes approved by the Dutch Accreditation Panel on Interventions (Erkenningscommissie Interventies), and newsletter information on new programmes in the Netherlands (www.nji.nl).

The Accreditation Panel on Behavioural Programmes for offenders was established by the Ministry of Justice in 2005, with the aim of identifying programmes that are promising, i.e., that they could result in reducing recidivism of both adults and minors. The Accreditation Panel on Interventions was established by the Ministry of Youth and Families in 2007 to stimulate effective healthcare for children and young people. This latter panel focused on programmes to reduce problem behaviour in general, rather than solely to reduce recidivism.

Both accreditation panels used similar evaluation criteria (see Box 10.1). Accreditation was based on a programme's proper theoretical foundation in combination with the existence of a protocol for ongoing evaluation. The programme had to be based on a clear model of change based on research evidence, i.e., a realistic evidence-based plan for creating change in offenders' future behaviour. Next, the selection of participants had to be clear and based on the risks likely to be reduced by the programme. A programme had to be focused on skills training, and it should be clear how the treatment integrity was to be guaranteed. Information on the effectiveness of the accredited interventions was not available yet. Research on some of the programmes had started recently. Research on other programmes will be conducted in the coming years.

Screening of the programmes from these sources resulted in a list of 23 interventions geared towards young adult offenders. Programmes that primarily focused on the parents of young offenders or on the family of origin were excluded, as were interventions meant solely for young offenders up to age 18. (See Welsh et al. (2010) for a review on the impact of these programmes on offending in young adults.)

The 23 interventions can be grouped into two categories: interventions that focus on reduction of problem behaviour of the young person (social and problem-solving skills, aggression, alcohol and drug use – Table 10.1), and interventions that focus on skills for independent living, such as the transition to adult life (housing, education and training, health and social relationships – Table 10.2). Nine interventions took place in adult prisons (age 18+ interventions), while the other interventions took place in juvenile justice institutions. All but two of the interventions have been approved by one of the two accreditation panels. We added the interventions 'Teenage Mothers and their Children' and 'Adult Life' (Table 10.2) because they have been described in newsletters on new programmes in the Netherlands as promising independent living programmes.

Interventions Aimed at Reduction of Problem Behaviour

We identified 13 interventions aimed at the reduction of problem behaviour: eight interventions that focused on the reduction of antisocial and delinquent behaviour by enhancing social and problem-solving skills, self-control, and aggression regulation skills, and five interventions that focused on the reduction of the use of drugs and alcohol and on relapse prevention (Table 10.1). Two of these interventions are Dutch applications of well-known and evidence-based interventions developed abroad. ART-Wiltshire-NL is an adaptation of aggression replacement training developed by Goldstein, Glick and Gibbs (1998).

Cognitive Thinking Skills is the Dutch adaptation of Enhanced Thinking Skills (the British application of Reasoning and Rehabilitation, by Ross, Fabiano and Ewles, 1988). The other interventions originated within the Dutch juvenile or adult prison or probation system. As explained earlier, outcome information on these programmes is not yet available.

Individually Tailored Social Skills Training

This intervention is a social and problem-solving skills training programme that combines working individually with young offenders (ages 15–23) and with their parents (Hoogsteder, 2008). The training has a broad theoretical foundation and integrates existing knowledge on risk and protective factors in the development of antisocial and delinquent behaviour (for example, Loeber and Farrington, 1998) with knowledge on social information processing and aggression (Crick and Dodge, 1994), moral development (for example, Kohlberg, 1984), and self-control (Gottfredson and Hirschi, 1990). The programme consists of group training (in a group of seven young people) as well as individual training and can be delivered in as many sessions and combinations as needed in each individual case. The duration and intensity is flexible, between four and 18 months. The programme has five modules: social and problem-solving skills, emotion regulation, self-control, checking consequences, and working with the family. Each module consists of ten sessions. The last module teaches parents about antisocial behaviour and its causes, offers five sessions of parental skills training, and helps parents and young people to solve their problems in a non-aggressive manner.

Individually Tailored Aggression Replacement Training

This intervention is more or less similar to the social skills training, but it is focused on aggression regulation in offenders aged 16–21. It consists primarily of aggression replacement training and can be applied in either a residential or non-residential approach (Hoogsteder, 2007). The training uses research findings on social information processing and aggression (Crick and Dodge, 1994), moral development (for example, Kohlberg, 1984), and self-control (Gottfredson and Hirschi, 1990), and comprises compulsory and optional modules that enable an optimal fit to the problems of each individual young person. The programme is designed as an individual intervention but can be combined with a group intervention, with a maximum of seven young people, for 12 sessions. Duration and intensity is flexible, between five and 18 months. The programme works with modules on motivation, offence analysis, self-control, relapse prevention and cognitive restructuring. In the community version the duration is anywhere between six and 24 months.

In Control

This intervention consists of training in self-control for young adult offenders (ages 16–24) and their parents (Valenkamp, Rutten and Reijntjens, 2008). The training

Table 10.1 Interventions aimed at the reduction of problem behaviour for early adults

Name of the intervention	Dynamic factors addressed	Age group	Dutch outcome information	Specific ingredients	
				(Cognitive) behavioural approach	Group/individual sessions
Individually tailored social skills training	Social and problem solving skills	15–23	-	+	Both
Individually tailored aggression replacement training	Aggression regulation	16–21	-	+	Both
In control	Social and problem solving skills and aggression regulation	17–21	-	+	Both
Learning from one's offence	Social and problem solving skills and reduction of violence	14–23	-	+	Both
Dialectic behavioural therapy with delinquent adolescents	Emotion regulation, self-control and aggression regulation	12–21	-	+	Both
Cognitive thinking skills training	Social and problem solving skills and aggression regulation	18+	-	+	Group training individual start
Cognitive thinking skills training, version for people with a mild mental handicap	Social and problem solving skills and aggression regulation	18+	-	+	Group training individual start

Aggression Replacement Training Whiltshire (ART-Whiltshire)	Social and problem solving skills and aggression regulation	18+	-	+	Both
Brains-4-use	Drug and alcohol use and relapse prevention	12–23	Quasi-exp. (N=60) 60% decrease in drug use (exp) versus base rate (control).	+	Individual
Stay-a-Way	Drug and alcohol use and relapse prevention	12–19	-	+	Both
Lifestyle Drug Abuse Program extended version	Drug and alcohol use and relapse prevention	18+	-	+	Group training
Lifestyle Drug Abuse Program 'lifestyle' short version	Drug and alcohol use and relapse prevention	18+	-	+	Group training
Relapse Prevention Program	Drug and alcohol use and relapse prevention	18+	-	+	Group training

Table 10.2 Interventions aimed at independent living for early adults

Name of the intervention	Central focus	Age group	Dutch outcome information	Specific ingredients	
				(Cognitive) behavioural approach	Group/individual sessions
Moving On (Vertrek Training)	Enhancing independent living skills including going to school, keeping a job, building a social network and having leisure time activities	13+	-	+	Individual
New Prospects by Reintegration (Nieuwe Perspectieven bij Terugkeer)	Enhancing independent living skills including going to school, keeping a job, building a social network and having leisure time activities	16–23		+	Individual
New Prospects by Reintegration for young people with a mild mental handicap (Nieuwe Perspectieven bij Terugkeer LVB)	Enhancing independent living skills including going to school, keeping a job, building a social network and having leisure time activities	16–23	-	+	Individual
Work-Wise Reintegration Programme (Buitenprogramma Workwise)	Enhancing independent living skills focused on going to school and/or keeping a job.	15–23	-	+	Individual

Your Future (Werken aan je toekomst)	Enhancing motivation on going to school and solving problems in school	15–23	-	+	Group training, individual start
Working Skills	Enhancing skills to get and keep a job	18+	-	+	Group training
Housing and Living skills	Enhancing skills to get and keep a house and solve housing-related problems	18+	-	+	Group training
Budgeting Skills	Enhancing budgeting skills.	18+	-	+	Group training
Adult Life	Enhancing independent living skills	16–23	-	+	Individual
Teenage Mothers and their Children	Enhancing parental skill, reduction of problem behaviour of the mother, independent living	14–23	-	+	Individual

focuses on social and problem-solving skills, aggression replacement training, and moral development. The training has a broad theoretical foundation and uses, for example, the research finding on social information processing and aggression (Crick and Dodge, 1994), moral development (for example, Kohlberg, 1984), self-control and anger (Novaco, 1997), and research findings on criminogenic factors. Based on this, promising existing interventions such as Novaco's Anger Management training, self-instruction methods (McGuigan, 1993), biofeedback (Raine, 1996) and cognitive restructuring are combined into a new training programme. Biofeedback, relaxation techniques and physical exercises are an important part of the training, which works with two distinct age groups: boys under and over age 16. The training consists of two individual consultations (one with the parents and one with the personal coach/group worker); 19 group sessions (maximum of six young people) and three individual sessions with parents and the personal coach; three aftercare sessions with parents and the probation officer; and five parallel parental skills groups sessions for parents.

Learning from One's Offence

This intervention is a social and problem-solving skills training programme focusing on violent offenders (Jagers and Lodewijks, 2008). The intervention is aimed especially at young violent offenders (ages 14–23) and consists of a detailed analysis of the crime committed (which takes at least six individual sessions), 12 individual sessions (half of them with a personal coach present and the last session together with parents), and booster sessions at moments of transition (for example, leave outside the institution or transfer to an open setting). The twelve sessions are focused on self-control, cognitive restructuring, problem-solving skills and relapse prevention. The intervention is based on the knowledge of risk factors for violence (for example, Loeber and Farrington, 1998) and of social information processing and aggression (Crick and Dodge, 1994).

Dialectic Behavioural Therapy with Delinquent Adolescents

The title of this intervention is the Dutch translation of a therapy developed by Linahan known as Cognitive Behavioural Treatment of Borderline Personality Disorder (Linahan, 2002). Linahan developed this therapy for adults with severe borderline disorder. The version described here is an adaptation for delinquent adolescents (ages 12–21) in institutions for young Dutch offenders (Backer, 2007). As young offender institutions were confronted with delinquent girls with emotional disorders, the emotion regulation training of Linahan's therapy consisted of teaching girls how to handle their emotions, which was then adapted to the general population of girls and boys in young offender institutions to form Dialectic Behavioural Therapy. The intervention links cognitive-behavioural work (cognitive restructuring) with relaxation techniques, mindfulness and research on the role of parents and the family on behaviour change (the dialectic part of the intervention). The programme consists of an individual pre-treatment phase (aimed at motivation for treatment), a 16-week group training period (maximum of four young people) in combination with individual sessions, and a relapse prevention module. Participants may attend individual and group therapy as long as necessary.

Cognitive Thinking Skills Training (and 'Plus' Version)

This intervention is a Dutch application of Enhanced Thinking Skills, an accredited intervention in England and Wales, that was originally developed as Reasoning and Rehabilitation (Ross, Fabiano and Ewles, 1988). A recent meta-analysis by Tong and Farrington (2006) reported a drop in recidivism of 14 per cent among attendees of R&R programmes. The Dutch application has two versions. The 'plus' version is meant especially for offenders with a mild mental handicap (Valenkamp, Vogelvang and Krooi, 2006). The training focuses on enhancing self-regulation, problem-solving skills, thinking skills and changes in social perspective as the main dynamic risk factors in delinquency. The training is meant for adults (ages 18+) and is rooted in the knowledge of research on social information processing and aggression (Crick and Dodge, 1994), moral development (for example, Kohlberg, 1984), and self-control and anger (Novaco, 1997). In its application for people with a mild mental handicap ('*cognitive thinking skills training plus*'), special attention is paid to generalization of new skills and other special aspects of working with offenders with a mild mental handicap. Self-instruction techniques based on the work of Lindsay (1999) is one of the instruments used for this group of offenders. The training consists of two group sessions of 2.5 hours per week, amounting to 22 sessions in total. In the 'plus' training, sessions of 1.5 hours per week are used, with a total of 36 group sessions. In both versions, two individual sessions are part of the programme at the start and at the end of the training.

ART-Wiltshire-NL

This intervention is a translation and Dutch adaptation of the Aggression Replacement Training as it is used for adults in the Wiltshire region of England (McGuire and Clark, 2006). ART-Wiltshire is based on the work of Goldstein, Glick and Gibbs (1998). Like the preceding intervention, ART-Wiltshire-NL is meant for adults (ages 18+) and is based on research on social information processing and aggression (Crick and Dodge, 1994), moral development (for example, Kohlberg, 1984), and self-control and anger (Novaco, 1997). The training consists of 18 two-hour group sessions and two individual sessions at the start and at the end of the training.

Brains-4-Use

This intervention is based on the prevention and intervention method 'doing by knowing' ('Weet wat je doet'), developed by one of the Dutch alcohol abuse and drug clinics in Assen, and is used as an individual intervention within one of the young offender institutions. All young people in the institution are confronted with a drug use deterrent policy, of which urine analysis and education of both the young people and their parents on the risks of drug and alcohol use are central elements. This individual intervention is applied to young people (ages 12–23) with a medium- or high risk of recidivism, young people who committed a drug-related offence, or young people who committed an offence while under the influence of alcohol or drugs (Rentray, 2008). The intervention is based on the model of motivational phases by Prochaska, DiClemente and Norcross (1992), and consists of 12 individual sessions on the use of alcohol and drugs in which self-control, self-management, cognitive restructuring and relapse prevention are central. In the event of relapse, the individual sessions go on for as long as necessary. A quasi-experimental design was used to evaluate Brains-4-Use in 60 young people in the institution: 40 young people formed the experimental group and 20 the control group. The base rate for drug use was 14 per cent in both groups (due to the deterrent policy of the institution). Urine analysis of both groups showed a 60 per cent decrease in drug use for the experimental group, while drug use in the control group stayed the same. A six-month follow-up showed drug use in seven per cent of the experimental group and 14 per cent of the control group ($p<.01$). It was not possible to investigate the effect on alcohol use because of its very low base rate in this population.

Stay-away

This is an individual training programme for young offenders (ages 12–19) who have problems with alcohol and drug use. The training aims at regulating alcohol and drug use, and preventing risky forms of alcohol and drug use. The intervention focuses on personal characteristics that play a role in susceptibility to addiction and also play a role in delinquency, such as sensation seeking and low self-control. Based on the biopsychosocial model, problem behaviours (delinquency, alcohol and drug use) are best understood in terms of a combination of biological (genetic vulnerability), psychological (cognitions, emotions, behaviours and learning experiences) and socio-cultural factors (Rutter, 2002; Van de Wetering and Czyzewski, 2005). Young people follow a 21-week programme, with sessions on enhancing motivation and separate sessions on self-regulation. Parents attend group sessions on alcohol and drug use in young people and are trained to handle this specific kind of problem behaviour. The three modules can be applied separately if necessary and may be extended with an aftercare module.

Lifestyle Drug Abuse Programme (Short and Extended Version)

The Lifestyle programme is an optional module for offenders (age 18+) who finish the Cognitive Thinking Skills training and have serious problems in the use of alcohol and/or drugs (Buntjer et al., 2008). Addicted offenders with chronic alcohol and drug use follow the extended version; the short version is meant for the less problematic offenders who use alcohol and drugs in a risky manner. During the training offenders apply cognitive thinking skills to their addiction problems. The relapse prevention model by Marlatt and Gordon (1985) and motivational interviewing (Miller and Rollnick, 2005) form the basis of the training. The extended version consists of 16 weekly group sessions of 2.5 hours where the pros and cons of alcohol and drug use are discussed, as are the seemingly irrelevant decisions that lead to the use of alcohol and drugs. Self-control and adequate problem-solving skills are practised. The short version consists of ten sessions. Both versions provide for booster sessions, homework together with one of the group members, and an individual starting and closing session.

Relapse Prevention Programme

This programme is an optional module that can be applied as an extended version of the Lifestyle Drug Abuse Programme (Nieuwenhuys and Smeerdijk, 2006). High-risk offenders (age 18+) with addiction problems may need more than the 22 sessions of cognitive skills training and the 16 Lifestyle Drug Abuse Programme sessions to allow the cognitive thinking skills to take root. For this group, an extra 14 weeks of the Lifestyle programme can be applied with the Relapse Prevention Programme. The programme base and session content are similar to the Cognitive Thinking Skills Training and the Lifestyle Drug Abuse Programme.

Comments on Interventions Aimed at Problem Reduction

The eight interventions focused on the reduction of aggression and antisocial behaviour reviewed above have many similarities. They are rooted in the same theoretical foundations and combine known active working ingredients (see Table 10.1). All interventions use a cognitive-behavioural model of change. The interventions developed in juvenile justice institutions combine group and individual training sessions and can be applied in a very flexible way. The intensity and duration can be adapted around the needs of the individual, which is in line with the needs principle. Most of these interventions allow for special sessions with parents. Five interventions focus on the reduction of drug use. In these interventions, cognitive thinking skills are applied to alcohol and drug use and motivation to change is a central element. With one exception (Brains-4-Use), the effectiveness of the 13 interventions has not been examined yet. However, the characteristics of the programmes (that is, the theoretical background and mode of delivery) appear promising.

Interventions Aimed at Independent Living

We identified ten interventions aimed at independent living (Table 10.2). All ten originated within the Dutch juvenile or adult prison or probation system. Research information is available on some interventions and will be summarized below, but proper outcome information is not yet available.

Moving On

This is an intensive individual training programme for young people over age 13 who are at risk of becoming homeless because they have a limited social network, cannot return home after their stay in an institution, or are runaway youth before they entered the institution. The intervention consists of a ten-week training programme in combination with support in finding a place to live, finding a school or job, arranging for an income and leisure time activities, and activating an informal social network. The programme is based on the social competence model, learning theory, and social network approach (Slot and Spanjaard, 2009). Trainers give individual support and training, using techniques from social and cognitive skills training. They focus on planning, thinking before acting, finding a prosocial network, and positive communication with family members. One post-test only study was published in 1997, which showed that 32 per cent of the graduates had a place to live, school or job, legal income, no cases in court, and a social network (Van Haaster, Van der Veldt and Van den Boogaart, 1997).

New Prospects by Reintegration (and a Version for Young People with Mild Mental Handicaps)

The New Prospects programme consists of three versions for distinct groups: New Prospects offers individual coaching and support to young people aged 12–23 at risk of developing a criminal lifestyle. New Prospects by Reintegration is an adaptation of this programme for offenders leaving a juvenile justice institution or secure child protection institutions. The third version is for offenders with a mild mental handicap and is an adaptation of the programme to the learning style of this specific category of offenders (Vogelvang, 2008).

The re-entry programme has a broad theoretical foundation. As with most other such programmes, it combines knowledge based on research on social information processing and aggression developed by Crick and Dodge (1994) with the coping-relapse model developed by Brown, Amand and Zamble (2009). This model helps programme coaches to predict recidivism by mapping the risk and protective factors on situational factors, individual factors, actual behaviour, and consequences. The trainers offer individual support by using motivational interviewing and, by using a cognitive-behavioural approach, focusing on situational and individual factors. The programme concentrates on social and problem-solving skills (such as getting and keeping a job, going to school, and finding a place to live) and arranges informal social supports. It starts in the young offender institution and continues for nine months after release.

Since young offenders with a mild mental handicap have problems in generalizing acquired skills to life outside the institution, the adaptation of the programme for this group offers 12 months of individual coaching. In addition, special attention is paid to the creation of a social network to continue long-term support after release.

As mentioned, this is an adaptation of the New Prospects programme for young people at risk. A first evaluation (Bürmann et al., 2004) showed that 90 per cent of the participants completed the New Prospects programme. According to the coaches, 71 per cent of the participants had better outcomes at its end. About a third showed progress in all four programme areas (family contacts, attending school or having a job, leisure time activities, and crimes committed). Nauta (2008) published recidivism rates and reported that half of the 2004 and 2005 participants had contact with the prosecutor's office by the end of 2007. Research on the New Prospects by Reintegration programme outcomes started in 2010.

Work-Wise Reintegration Programme

This re-entry programme offers young and young adult offenders aged 15–23 individual coaching on getting and keeping a job. The programme starts in the young offender institution and continues for nine months after release. It helps young people to sustain the skills learned in the institution while living in the community. Having a job is seen as an important bond to society and therefore a protective factor in the prevention of recidivism (Sampson and Laub, 1993). Individual coaches offer support in daily life to get and keep a job. They continue the cognitive-behavioural approach used in individual and group training sessions in the institution. Coaches use motivational interviewing (based on the model of motivational phases by Prochaska, DiClemente and Norcross, 1992) to motivate young people to keep up with all their new responsibilities. They apply social and problem-solving training exercises in individual sessions to enable participants to work on aggression regulation, self-esteem, responsible behaviour, and positive communication with parents or other family members. Overall, the approach is a practical one. The coach practices job interviews with a young person, accompanies him or her to interviews, and offers help when needed. The coaching is intensive at the start of the programme, but gradually becomes less so. Follow-up visits are planned at three, six and nine months after finishing the programme.

Your Future

This is part of the larger family of programmes by Work-Wise Reintegration Programme, which aims to help participants on getting and keeping a job to prevent recidivism. Your Future focuses on the preconditions for work (Work-Wise, 2010). The intervention starts with an individual intake session and consists of an 11-week programme, with two group sessions a week, finishing with a closing session. The programme starts in the institution and consists of two modules: one working on self-knowledge, exploring opinions on work or school in relation to the future, and another on training social and problem-solving skills to successfully attend school or to keep a job. As it is part of a larger family of programmes and precedes the Work-Wise Reintegration Programme, it has the same theoretical foundation as Work-Wise (2010).

Working Skills

This is an optional extension of the Cognitive Thinking Skills training described above for early adults (age 18+) with a medium or high risk for recidivism and little knowledge and skills for how to get and keep a job, and it shares the same theoretical basis. Working Skills consists of three modules of group training. The first module focuses on job motivation, self-knowledge, and job-related beliefs and possibilities. The second module is skills oriented: job interviews, learning to take the perspective of colleagues or employers, responsible behaviour, and self-control and communication skills. In the last module the central element is the search for a job. The first two modules have nine two-hour sessions each; the last module contains four two-hour sessions. Sessions are held once a week and exercises have to be done between sessions to apply the skills in daily life.

Housing and Living Skills

Like Working Skills, this is an extension of the Cognitive Thinking Skills programme and is designed for those who have problems in finding and keeping a place to live. It consists of 14 weekly sessions of about two hours each. As in the Working Skills programme, self-regulation, social and problem-solving skills, responsible behaviour and communication skills are central parts of the training. Participants apply their newly acquired skills to finding and keeping a place to live.

Budgeting Skills

This intervention is the third optional extension of the Cognitive Thinking Skills programme and focuses on the prevention of severe financial problems. The module consists of seven two-hour group sessions held once a week. Here the skills acquired are applied to the financial situation of the participant. Central elements are training in self-efficacy, self-control and responsible behaviour.

Teenage Mothers and their Children

This intervention offers a residential shelter to young mothers or pregnant early-adult women between ages 14 and 23 with severe antisocial behaviour.

The programme focuses on the behavioural problems of the mother and her parenting skills in an effort to prepare mother and child for a responsible, healthy and independent life (Rentray, 2010). This is a skills training programme with a cognitive-behavioural basis, which is combined with the knowledge of early childhood programmes that attempt to improve the functioning of parents as well as children in order to prevent childhood behaviour problems (see Deković et al., Chapter 9, this volume). Skills for independent living, such as budgeting, keeping a daily routine, childcare and parenting, attending school or keeping a job, are all part of the intervention.

Adult Life

This intervention has its roots in a residential setting (De Pluryn Hoenderloogroep, Oosterbeek) for young people with severe conduct disorder. Together with one of the rehabilitation institutes (RIBW Oost-Nederland) and Saxion (the University for Applied Sciences in Enschede), this setting is the start of an intervention trajectory for young people (ages 16–23) leaving residential care (Holsbrink-Engels, 2009). Those who are not returning home move to a special shelter unit of four or five young people where they receive support in living on their own. They are individually coached in eight predefined areas: living circumstances, getting and keeping a job, education, leisure-time activities, finances, social contacts and support, sexuality, and personal care. The coaching is rooted in the Individual Rehabilitation Approach in combination with the Social Competence Model and cognitive skills training. The Individual Rehabilitation approach dates back to the work of Anthony and Liberman (1986) and is aimed at coaching individual adult former psychiatric patients in a lifestyle that is appropriate for themselves and their surrounding social network. Activation of the social network is an important part of the approach. The Social Competence Model (Slot and Spanjaard, 2009) specified social competencies at each developmental stage in children and adolescents. Central to this programme are the competencies that enable young people to live an independent life. Social and problem-solving skills training are applied in individual cases, as are the so-called Liberman modules on social relations, leisure time, and getting and keeping a job.

Comments on Interventions Aimed at Independent Living

The aforementioned ten independent living programmes can be divided into four different types of interventions: (1) three interventions that train skills for finding and keeping a job, going to school, finding housing, and budgeting; (2) an intervention that combines training on these subjects with a short period of coaching after release; (3) three interventions where post-release coaching is available for about a year after release; and (4) two interventions that combine shelter, training and coaching for a longer period of time. The skills-training interventions can be seen as an extension of the cognitive skills-training interventions described previously: participants are trained to apply their cognitive thinking skills and social and problem-solving skills to situations they are confronted with in daily life. Likewise, the other interventions can be seen as advanced training programmes, but in this case the skills training is integrated with daily life. The two interventions that combine shelter, training and coaching are the most intensive. The long-term programmes for adolescents and young adults focus on individual coaching and preparation for an independent life. Due to the lack of research in this area, no conclusions can be drawn about the effectiveness of the programme or its ingredients.

Conclusions

The central questions addressed in this chapter are which interventions for young adult offenders are in use in the Netherlands and whether the interventions consist of known effective active ingredients. Our survey shows that 23 mostly accredited interventions are in use. The interventions are applied in juvenile justice institutions, locked institutions for child protection cases, and in community settings. They can be divided into four different groups.

The first group consists of eight interventions focused on the reduction of antisocial and delinquent behaviour by enhancing social and problem-solving skills. These are: individually tailored social skills training; individually tailored Aggression Replacement Training; In Control; Learning from one's offences; Dialectic Behavioural Therapy with delinquent adolescents; cognitive thinking skills training (including a version for people with a mild mental handicap); and ART-Wiltshire-NL.

These interventions have a common theoretical basis, use a cognitive-behavioural approach, and apply the combination of known active ingredients: social and problem-solving skills training, anger control, and cognitive restructuring. In addition they use group as well as individual training sessions and can be applied as long as needed, which is consistent with the needs principle.

The second group of interventions consists of nine interventions that offer extended training of the same skills but also deal with alcohol and drug use (Brains-4-Use, Stay-away, the Lifestyle Drug Abuse Programme and its short version, and the Relapse Prevention Programme); work (Working Skills); housing (Housing and Living Skills); finances (Budgeting Skills); or a combination of these skills (Your Future).

The third group offers coaching in the application of the same skills in daily life (Moving On, New Prospects on Reintegration and an adaptation for persons with a mild mental handicap, and the Work-Wise Reintegration Programme).

Finally, the fourth group includes two non-accredited interventions that combine training and coaching with shelter (Adult Life and Teenage Mothers and their Children). In these interventions, the application of new skills can be practised in a safe and protected environment.

All interventions, and especially those that work on the reduction of alcohol and drug use and on relapse prevention, take the motivational state of the participants into account. In this respect, all interventions consist of known specific working ingredients. However, the working ingredients of independent living programmes, non-custodial employment programmes and rehabilitation programmes are still unknown. Well-designed studies in this area are rare and research is not yet of the quality to allow reliable conclusions.

We conclude that the package of interventions available in the Netherlands includes known active ingredients on aggression regulation and the reduction of antisocial behaviour. However, much needs to be learned, especially regarding the effectiveness of the interventions designed to help young adults to apply the skills taught to daily life. These interventions use two working ingredients: they offer a careful transition back to society and focus on establishing an informal social network (Lipsey and Wilson, 1998). However, information is not available on their efficacy. This kind of intervention definitely deserves further research attention. Moreover, new information on the effects of mentoring programmes (Lipsey, 2009; Tolan et al., 2008; Jolliffe and Farrington, 2008) shows that coaching by non-professionals has a modest positive effect on recidivism in high-risk cases. Therefore, it would be worthwhile to investigate the effects of mentoring programmes for young people and early adults reintegrating into the community.

Several issues pertaining to interventions warrant attention. A first issue concerns the actual implementation of the interventions in the juvenile justice institutions and adult prisons. Most juvenile justice institutions typically design their own intervention, which is then applied on a small scale in one or two institutions. In adult prisons the first pilot programmes implementing the Cognitive Thinking Skills Training for people with a mild mental handicap and ART-Wiltshire-NL showed the difficulties in the implementation of the intervention. Only a very small group of ten to 15 inmates took part in the interventions, and both interventions faced a high dropout rate (Van Burik and Persoon, 2008; Van Poppel, 2008). In the four independent living interventions, where coaching on the job is the core element, the question of the number of participants is especially important. The Work-Wise Reintegration Programme is said to be available in all juvenile justice institutions. Unfortunately, information on the number of participants is not available. The two variants of the New Prospects intervention are implemented in the Amsterdam region. Recent research shows that a broad implementation of interventions like these is necessary for young people and early adults facing difficulties in living an independent life (Steketee, Vandenbroucke and Rijkschroeff, 2009).

The next issue concerns the skills targeted for training. The available interventions focus on a broad range of skills for independent living, including skills for getting and keeping a job, finding housing, keeping healthy finances, and creating a social network. However, limited attention is paid to parenting skills. Deković et al. (Chapter 9, this volume) extensively discussed the importance of early prevention. The astonishing fact is that almost no attention is paid to the teaching of parenting and parental skills to youth at risk to become parents at a young age. The intervention Teenage Mothers and their Children typically focuses on mothers and runs in locked institutions for child protection cases. Other shelters for teenage mothers exist, but usually they are not equipped to work with antisocial young mothers. The risk of early motherhood in this group is especially high, as approximately 20 per cent of the girls had been pregnant prior to detention, although none had actually given birth (Hamerlynck, 2008). The number of young fathers in juvenile justice institutions and prisons is not known, nor is the number of young fathers and mothers attending the four reintegration interventions. More attention should be paid to these groups and their parenting skills in order to prevent the transmission of antisocial behaviour to the new generation.

Finally, we reviewed a package of interventions, based on a proper theoretical foundation, which has been approved by one of the two Dutch accreditation panels. The model of change in these interventions is usually backed up by research findings from abroad. As argued above, the next step for the development of these interventions lies in information research on the actual implementation of the interventions and their effectiveness in the Netherlands in other European countries.

References

Andrews, D.A., Zinger, I., Hoge, R.I., Bonta, J., Gendreau, P., and Cullen, F.T. (1990). Does correctional treatment work? A clinically relevant and psychologically informed meta-analysis. *Criminology*, 28, 369–417.

Anthony, W.A. and Liberman, R.P. (1986). The practice of psychiatric rehabilitation: historical, conceptual and research base. *Schizophrenia Bulletin*, 12, 542–59.

Aos, S., Miller, M., and Drake, E. (2006). *Evidence-based Public Policy Options to Reduce Future Prison Construction, Criminal Justice Costs and Crime Rates*. Olympia, WA: Washington State Institute for Public Policy.

Armelius, B-Å. and Andreassen, T.H. (2007). *Cognitive-behavioral Treatment for Antisocial Behavior in Youth in Residential Treatment*. Cochrane Database of Systematic Reviews 2007, Issue 4, Art. No. CD005650, DOI: 10.1002/14651858. CD005650.pub2.

Auditor General (2007). Proceedings of the Dutch Lower House of the States General, 2007 2008, 31215, numbers 1–2 & 3 (part II, chapters 4 & 5).

Backer, H. (2007). *Dialectische gedragstherapiebij delinquente adolescenten*. Den Helder: De Doggershoek.

Brestan, E.V. and Eyberg, S.M. (1998). Effective psychosocial treatment of conduct disordered children and adolescents: 29 years, 82 studies and 5272 kids. *Journal of Clinical Child Psychology*, 27, 180–9.

Brown, S., Amand, M., and Zamble, E. (2009). The dynamic prediction of criminal recidivism: A three-wave prospective study. *Law and Human Behavior*, 33, 22–45.

Buntjer, R., Schoemakers, A.E., Smeerdijk, M., and Nieuwenhuys, M. (2008). *Leefstijltraining voor verslaafde justitiabelen*. Amsterdam: JellinekMentrum/AIAR/SVG.

Bürmann, A., Geldrop, M., Groen, H. Hilhorst, N., and Rietveld, M. (2004). *Evaluatie Nieuwe Perspectieven 1998-2003*. Amsterdam: DSP-groep.

Chorpita, B.F., Yim, L.M., Donkervoet, J.C., Arensdorf, A., Amundson, M.J., McGee, C., Serrano, A., Yates, A., Burns, J.A., and Morelli, P. (2002). Towards large-scale implementation of empirically supported treatments for children: A review and observations by the Hawaii Empirical Basis to Services Task Force. *Clinical Psychology: Science and Practice*, 9, 165–90.

Crick, N.R. and Dodge, K.A. (1994). A review and reformulation of social information processing mechanisms in children's social adjustment. *Psychological Bulletin*, 115, 74–101.

Donkoh, C., Underhill, K., and Montgomery, P. (2006). *Independent Living Programmes for Improving Outcomes for Young People Leaving the Care System*. Campbell Systematic Reviews 2006: 8.

Ellis, A. (1962). *Reason and Emotion in Psychotherapy*. New York: Citadel Press.

Garrido, V. and Morales, L.A. (2007). *Serious (Violent or Chronic) Juvenile Offenders: A Systematic Review of Treatment Efectiveness in Secure Corrections*. Campbell Systematic Reviews 2007: 7.

Genovés, V.G., Morales, L.A., and Sánchez-Meca, J. (2006). What works for serious juvenile offenders? A systematic review. *Psicothema*, 18, 611–19.

Goldstein, A.P., Glick, B., and Gibbs, J.C. (1998). *Agression Replacement Training: A Comprehensive Intervention for Aggressive Youth*. Champaign, IL: Research Press.

Gottfredson, M.R. and Hirschi, T. (1990). *A General Theory of Crime*. Stanford, CA: Stanford University Press.

Hair, H.J. (2005). Outcomes for children and adolescents after residential treatment: A review of research from 1993 to 2003. *Journal of Child and Family Studies*, 14, 551–75.

Hamerlynck, S. (2008). *Girls in Juvenile Justice Institutions: Psychopathology and Sexual Risk Behavior*. Amsterdam: Vrije University (Ph.D. dissertation).

Holsbrink-Engels, G. (ed.) (2009). *Hoe(Zo)Volwassen? Een methodiek in het begeleiden van jongeren met probleemgedrag van 16 tot 23 jaar*. Amsterdam: SWP.

Hoogsteder, L.M. (2007). *Agressie regulatie op maat*. Den Helder: RIJ De Doggershoek.

Hoogsteder, L.M. (2008). *Sociale Vaardigheidstraining op maat*. Den Helder: RIJ De Doggershoek.

Jagers, H. and Lodewijks, H. (2008). *Leren van Delict. Gedragstraining voor jongeren die een gewelddadig delict pleegden*. Zutphen, Eefde and Harreveld: De Sprengen, Rentray, Harreveld.

Jolliffe, D. and Farrington, D.P. (2008). *The Influence of Mentoring on Recidivism*. Stockholm, Sweden: National Council for Crime Prevention.

Kohlberg, L. (1984). *Essays on Moral Development: Vol. 2. The Psychology of Moral Development*. San Francisco, CA: Harper & Row.

Landenberger, N.A. and Lipsey, M.W. (2005). The positive effects of cognitive-behavioral programs for offenders: A meta-analysis of factors associated with effective treatment. *Journal of Experimental Criminology*, 1, 451–76.

Linahan, M.M. (2002). *Dialectische gedragstherapie bij borderline persoonlijkheidsstoornissen: theorie en behandeling*. Lisse: Swets & Zeitlinger.

Lindsay, W.R. (1999). Cognitive therapy. *The Psychologist*, 12, 238–41.

Lipsey, M.W. (1992). Juvenile delinquency treatment: A meta-analytic inquiry into the variability of effects. In T. Cook (ed.). *Meta-analysis for Explanation: A Casebook*. New York: Russell Sage Foundation, pp. 83–128.

Lipsey, M.W. (1995). What do we learn from 400 research studies on the effectiveness of treatment with juvenile delinquents? In J. McGuire (ed.), *What Works: Reducing Reoffending, Guidelines from Research and Practice*. Chichester: John Wiley & Sons, pp. 63–78.

Lipsey, M.W. (2009). The primary factors that characterize effective interventions with juvenile offenders: A meta-analytic overview. *Victims and Offenders*, 4, 124–47.

Lipsey, M.W. and Wilson, D. (1998). Effective intervention for serious juvenile offenders: A synthesis of research. In R. Loeber and D.P. Farrington (eds), *Serious and Violent Juvenile Offender: Risk Factors and Successful Interventions*. Newbury Park, CA: Sage, pp. 313–45.

Loeber, R. (1998). Ontwikkelingspaden en risicopatronen voor ernstige jeugddeliquentie en hun relevantie voor interventies: Nooit te vroeg en nooit te laat. In W. Koops and W. Slot (eds), *Van lastig tot misdadig*. Houten: Bohn Stafleu Van Loghum, pp. 15–32.

Loeber, R. and Farrington, D.P. (1998). *Serious and Violent Juvenile Offenders: Risk Factors and Successful Interventions*. Thousand Oaks, CA: Sage.

Lowenkamp, C.T. (2004). *Correctional Program Integrity and Treatment Effectiveness: A Multi Site, Program-level Analysis*. University of Cincinnati, OH Division of Research and Advanced Studies (Ph.D. dissertation).

McGuigan, F.J. (1993). Progressive relaxation: Origins, principles, and clinical applications. In P.M. Lehrer and R.L. Woolfolk (eds), *Principles and Practice of Stress Management*. New York: Guilford, pp. 17–52.

McGuire, J. and Clark, D. (2006). A national dissemination program. In A.P. Goldstein, R. Nensén, B. Daleflod and M. Kalt (eds), *New Perspectives on Aggression Replacement Training: Practice, Research and Application*. Chichester: Wiley, pp. 139–50.

Marlatt, G.A. and Gordon, J.R. (1985). *Relapse Prevention: Maintenance Strategies in the Treatment of Addictive Behaviors*. New York: Guilford.

Michon, H. and Van Weeghel, J. (2008). *Rehabilitatie-onderzoek in Nederland. Overzicht van onderzoek en synthese van bevindingen in de periode 2000-2007*. The Hague/Utrecht: ZonMw/Trimbos-Instituut/Kenniscentrum Rehabilitatie.
Milkman, H. and Wanberg, K. (2007). *Cognitive-behavioral Treatment: A Review and Discussion for Corrections Professionals*. Washington, DC: U.S. Department of Justice, National Institute of Corrections.
Miller, W.R. and Rollnick, S. (2005). *Motiverende gespreksvoering*. Gorinchem: Ekklesia.
Ministerie van Justitie (2008). *Kwaliteitscriteria en vereiste documentatie*. The Hague: Ministerie van Justitie.
Mulvey, E.P, Steinberg, L., Fagan, J., Kauffman, E., Piquero, A.R., Chassin, L., Knight, G.P., Brame, R., Schubert, C.A., Hecker, T., and Losoya, S.H. (2004). Theory and research on desistance from antisocial activity among serious adolescent offenders. *Youth Violence and Juvenile Justice*, 2, 213–36.
Nauta, O. (2008). *Recidivemeting trajecten aanpak en preventie jeugdcriminaliteit. Een recidivemeting onder trajectdeelnemers van zes Amsterdamse jeugdinterventies en jeugdreclassering*. Amsterdam: DSP-groep BV.
Nieuwenhuys, M. and Smeerdijk, M. (2006). *Module Terugvalpreventie Middelen*. Amsterdam: Jellinek Innovatie & Preventie.
Novaco, R.W. (1975). *Anger Control: The Development and Evaluation of an Experimental Treatment*. Lexington, MA: D.C. Heath.
Prochaska, J.O., DiClemente, C.C., and Norcross, J.C. (1992). In search of how people change: Applications to addictive behaviors. *American Psychologist*, 47, 1102–14.
Raine, A. (1996). Autonomic nervous system factors underlying disinhibited, antisocial, and violent behavior: Biosocial perspectives and treatment implications. In C.F. Ferris, T. Grisso, C.F. Ferris and T. Grisso (eds), *Understanding Aggressive Behavior in Children*. New York: New York Academy of Sciences, pp. 46–59.
Rentray (2008). *Individuele interventie Brains4use, een interventie om het alcohol- en druggebruik bij jongeren in een JJI terug te dringen*. Eefde: Rentray.
Rentray (2010). *Het moeder en kind huis*. Eefde: Rentray.
Ross, R.R., Fabiano, E.A., and Ewles, C.D. (1988). Reasoning and rehabilitation. *International Journal of Offender Therapy and Comparative Criminology*, 32, 29–35.
Rutter, M. (2002). The interplay of nature, nurture and developmental influences: The challenge ahead of mental health. *Archives of General Psychiatry*, 59, 96–1000.
Sampson, R. and Laub, J. (1993). *Crime in the Making: Pathways and Turning Points through Life*. Cambridge, MA: Harvard University Press.
Shirk, S.R. and Karver, M. (2003). Prediction of treatment outcome from relationship variables in child and adolescent therapy: A meta-analytic review. *Journal of Consulting and Clinical Psychology*, 71, 452–64.
Stein, M. (2004). *What Works for Young People Leaving Care?* Ilford: Barnardo's.

Steketee, M., Vandenbroucke, M., and Rijkschroeff, R. (2009). *(Jeugd)zorg houdt niet op bij 18 jaar*. Utrecht: Verwey-Jonker Institute.

Slot, N. and Spanjaard, H. (2009). *Competentievergroting in de residentiële jeugdzorg. Hulpverlening voor kinderen en jongeren in tehuizen*. Baarn: HB Uitgevers.

Tolan, P., Henry, D., Schoeny, M., and Bass, A. (2008). *Mentoring Interventions to Affect Juvenile Delinquency and Associated Problems*. The Campbell Collaboration (http://www.campbellcollaboration.org).

Tong, L.S.J. and Farrington, D.P. (2006). How effective is the 'reasoning and rehabilitation' programme in reducing re-offending? A meta-analysis of evaluations in four countries. *Psychology, Crime & Law*, 12, 3–24.

Tonry, M. (2007). Treating juveniles as adult criminals: An iatrogenic violence prevention strategy if ever there was one. *American Journal of Preventive Medicine*, 32, S3–S4.

Valenkamp, M., Rutten, E., and Reijntjens, W. (2008). *In Control! Cadier en Keer*. Woerden: Stichting Jeugdzorg St. Joseph/JJI Het Keerpunt/Adviesbureau Van Montfoort.

Valenkamp, M., Vogelvang, B., and Krooi, H. (2006). *COVA+. Houd je hoofd Cool met de Helpende Hand*. Almere/Woerden: Leger des heils/adviesbureau Van Montfoort.

Van Burik, A.E. and Persoon, A.M. (2008). *Procesevaluatie CoVa+. Een onderzoek naar de implementatie van een nieuwe gedragsinterventie voor volwassen justitiabelen*. Woerden: Adiesbureau Van Montfoort.

Van de Wetering, B. and Czyzewski, E. (2004). Herijking van de grondslagen van de verslavingszorg. *Sociale Psychiatrie*, 24, 39–49.

Van Haaster, A.G.J., Van der Veldt, M.C.A.E., and Van den Bogaart, P.H.M. (1997). *VertrekTraining ter voorkoming van thuisloosheid bij jongeren. De empirische evaluatie van de ontwikkeling van een nieuw trainingsprogramma*. Leiden: University of Leiden (COJ).

Van Poppel, J. (2008). *Procesevaluatie testfase ARVA training*. Tilburg: IVA.

Van Yperen, T. and Boendermaker, L. (2008). Interventions. In R. Loeber, W.N. Slot, P.H. van der Laan and M. Hoeve (eds), *Tomorrow's Criminals: The Development of Child Delinquency and Effective Interventions*. Farnham: Ashgate, pp. 197–213.

Van Yperen, T., Van der Steege, M., Addink, A., and Boendermaker, L. (2010). *Algemeen werkzame factoren: stand van de discussie*. Utrecht: Nji.

Verwers, C. and Bogaerts, S. (2005). *Strafrechtelijke aanpak van jongvolwassenen (18–24 jaar). Een verkenning*. The Hague: WODC.

Visher, C.A., Winterfield, L., and Coggeshall, M.B. (2006). *Systematic Review of Non-custodial Employment Programs: Impact on Recidivism Rates of Ex-offenders*. Campbell Systematic Reviews 2006: 1.

Vogelvang, B.O. (2008). *Nieuwe perspectieven bij terugkeer, hulp voor jongeren na vrijheidsbeneming*. Woerden/Amsterdam: Adviesbureau Van Montfoort/Spirit.

Weisz, J.R., Donenberg, G.R., Han, S.S., and Kauneckis, D. (1995). Child and adolescent psychotherapy outcomes in experiments versus clinics. *Journal of Abnormal Child Psychology*, 23, 83–106.
Welsh, B.C., Lipsey, M.W., Hawkins, J.D., Aos, S., and Peel, M.E. (2012). Promoting change, changing lives: Effective prevention and intervention to reduce serious offending. In R. Loeber and D.P. Farrington (eds), *From Juvenile Delinquency to Adult Crime: Criminal Careers, Justice Policy and Prevention*. New York: Oxford University Press.
Whittaker, J.D. (2004). The re-invention of residential treatment: An agenda for research and practice. *Child and Adolescent Psychiatric Clinics of North America*, 13, 267–78.
Wilson, D.B., Mackenzie, D.L., and Ngo Mitchell, F. (2008). *Effects of Correctional Boot Camps on Offending*. Campbell Systematic Reviews 2003: 1.
Work-Wise (2010). *Werken aan je toekomst*. Eefde: Workwise.

Chapter 11
European Perspectives

Martin Killias, Santiago Redondo and Jerzy Sarnecki

This chapter presents an overview of European research on the transition between juvenile offending and adult crime that is relevant for policymakers, researchers and practitioners. First, we shall review relevant European longitudinal studies. Next, we present some major cross-sectional studies that provide information about important across Europe and the United States. A section on special offenders includes information on homicide, domestic violence, gangs, and the nexus between migration and crime. The next section on the evaluation of interventions emphasizes their effectiveness regarding juvenile offenders. In the final section, we look at Europe's highly heterogeneous policy responses to young offenders, including age limits of juvenile penal laws, sentencing (including the use of custody and other sanctions), and drug and alcohol policies.

Understanding Criminal Behaviour

Longitudinal Studies in Europe

In presenting an overview of European longitudinal studies, we focus on studies that are relevant to the understanding of crime during late adolescence and early adulthood, including studies outside of the field of criminology. In order to facilitate the overview, all European studies are summarized in Table 11.1. Studies based on samples of less than 100, or without results on adolescence including early adulthood (for example, Saar, 2003; Kuppens et al., 2009; Eisner et al., 2007) are not included.

All European longitudinal studies that looked at the influence of family and childhood factors found that later delinquency, persistence of careers and seriousness of offences are largely explained by a dysfunctional family (including lack of orderly and structured activities within the family – Hoeve, 2008), early problems at school (Scotland), and a generally unfavourable surrounding (including parental imprisonment). In this connection, problems arising at mid-childhood (around age 13) have also been found to be important (Mannheim study). Self-control (or regulatory self-efficacy), irritability and impulsivity were further found to influence later offending and violence (Italy, Spain).

Regarding protective factors, the story is more complex. Beyond social isolation (Cambridge Study in Delinquent Development), attachment to a teacher was a protective factor associated with low offending in two studies (Scotland,

Table 11.1 Longitudinal (cohort) studies in Europe

Author(s), year of publication, country	Birth year of cohort, sample	Research questions and methods	Main results	Observations
Sarnecki, 1985 (Sweden)	846 boys born 1943–1951 (including 195 official property offenders by age 15 matched with controls). Sample includes 100 boys from a reformatory and their 222 matched pairs.	Long-term development of deviance (including drug use) as outcomes of early risk factors. Methods: official records, SRD (2000 variables collected at age 11–15).	(1) At age 15, convicted boys were worse off than controls with respect to personality, family, and school variables. (2) By 35, seven per cent of men with one conviction before 15 had died, 11 per cent of those with 2+ convictions, and 13 per cent of those from a reformatory (vs one per cent among remaining sample). For men convicted once before 15, 18 per cent developed drug addiction by 35 and 24 per cent among those with at least 2 convictions (vs two per cent among other men). (3) Adult drug abuse is strongly related to (multiple) risk factors at age 15. But even among high-risk youths, 60 per cent did not develop substance dependency and lived well-adjusted lives.	
Janson, 1975, 1984; Stenberg and Vägerö, 2006; Stenberg et al., 2007; Nilsson and Estrada, 2009 (Sweden)	(1) Project Metropolitan (Janson, 1995) included all individuals born in Stockholm in 1953 who still lived there in 1962 (N=13,852) and who were followed until 1983. (2) A probability-matched sample out of the original sample was followed until subjects were 48.	Four groups were distinguished: (1) subjects without known criminality; (2) subjects who desisted from crime after age 20; (3) subjects known for offending before and after age 20 ('persisters'); (4) later starters, i.e., subjects with first-known offences after age 20 ('late starters'). Methods: (1) up to age 30: surveys, at different times; (2) registers at age 48.	Male 'persisters' make up 11 per cent of the cohort but are responsible for 76 per cent of all youth- and 80 per cent of all adult (known) offences; female 'persisters' make up one per cent of the cohort, but commit about 50 per cent of all (known) offences. 'Persisters' of each gender come from highly problematic childhood conditions. Female persisters live, as adults, under worse conditions than males from similar backgrounds who in their majority live relatively well.	

Author(s), year of publication, country	Birth year of cohort, sample	Research questions and methods	Main results	Observations
Bergman, 2009; Bergman and Andershed, 2009 (Sweden)	Individual Development and Adaptation (IDA): The sample includes all 1,400 children who, in 1965, were aged 10, 13 and 15 years and who attended primary schools in Örebro. Follow-ups were carried out when cohort was aged 13, 15, 16, 17, 18, 21, 23 and 43.	Development of offending in different groups (non-offenders, adolescent-only offenders, adolescent and adult offenders, adult-only offenders). Methods: surveys and official records.	Sixty per cent of men and 91 per cent of females have no criminal record, 16 per cent of men and three per cent of females have known offences before age 21 only, 11 per cent of men and five per cent of women have known offences as adults only, and 13 per cent of men and 1.5 per cent of women are recorded both for juvenile and adult offences. Five per cent of men have criminal records as children, juveniles, and adults, and accounted for two thirds of all known offences committed by the entire cohort. More efficient prevention focused on this small group might, thus, prevent a substantial proportion of crime. Lifelong persisters came from particularly unfavourable milieus and suffered from disproportionate numbers of risk factors. Late starters were more similar to law-abiding cohort members, but were more often known for hyperactivity, broken homes (females), and marijuana smoking (males).	
Pulkkinen and Hämälainen, 1995; Kokko and Pulkkinen, 2000; Pitkänen, Lyyra and Pulkkinen, 2005 (Finland)	A total of 369 subjects attending 12 second-grade school classes in 1968 in the town of Jyväskylä. They were re-interviewed at ages 14, 20, 27, 36 and 42 (in 2001). Retention rate was 90 per cent at 42.	The study is of a wide array of issues, ranging from violence to alcohol abuse and unemployment. Methods: interviews and teacher ratings.	Teacher-rated aggression at age 8 is related to school maladjustment at age 14 that predicts, directly and through problem drinking and lack of occupational alternatives, unemployment at age 27. Drinking problems are best predicted by early-onset alcohol consumption. Low self-control in childhood and adolescence was a precursor to crime and accidents by age 32, but only among subjects with other adverse life circumstances.	

Table 11.1 ***Continued***

Author(s), year of publication, country	Birth year of cohort, sample	Research questions and methods	Main results	Observations
Kyvsgaard, 2003 (Denmark)	Official Danish databases, with information regarding offence dates, charges, dispositions, confinement records, but also basic demographics and the workforce registers. The sample comprises 1/15 of the Danish population from 1979–1991 aged 15 and above (>333,000 persons). Of these, nearly 45,000 have a criminal record. Trajectories of the criminal careers are followed over 13 years.	Characteristics of criminal careers – prevalence, individual crime frequency, criminal onset, duration of and desistance from criminal careers, specialisation and escalation in crime seriousness. Methods: official data on police records, prosecutorial dispositions and court decisions (convictions).	The study shows a relationship between patterns of prevalence and frequency of offences and duration of careers and desistance. Furthermore, the study shows that criminal careers of high frequency offenders are characterised both by specialisation and by versatility. Finally, crime seriousness is related to individual offending frequency. Careers do not follow the expected pattern of escalating in seriousness with increasing numbers of offences.	
Olweus, 2011 (Sweden)	A total of 780 Stockholm boys, first data collected 1950s–1960s.	The relation between bullying at ages 13–16 and offending at ages 16–24.	A total of 73 bullies have more convictions (55 per cent vs 26 per cent) and move violent convictions (26 per cent vs five per cent) than 707 boys not involved with bullying.	

Author(s), year of publication, country	Birth year of cohort, sample	Research questions and methods	Main results	Observations
(1) Kazemian and Farrington, 2006; (2) Farrington, Ttofi and Coid, 2009; (3) Murray and Farrington, 2005; (4) Kazemian, Farrington and Le Blanc, 2009; (5) Zara and Farrington, 2009 (England)	Cambridge Study in Delinquent Development (CSDD): 411 London boys followed from age 8 to 48 (i.e., from 1961–2001).	Do age of onset and type of offences predict career length and number of offences over the lifespan? Methods: interviews and official records.	(1) Residual career length and number of offences declined with age, but it is not clear whether this is predicted by age of onset or type of offence. (2) All subjects become more successful with age, but persistent offenders show the most unsuccessful lives at 32 and 48. (3) Boys separated from their parents due to parental imprisonment had the highest score of antisocial outcomes at age 32. (4) Social bonds, cognitive predispositions and behavioural variables (such as drug use) at age 17–18 predict seriousness of offending and de-escalation by age 32. (5) Personal factors such as isolation, nervousness, anxiety and neuroticism protect against offending under age 21, but not later.	Lack in accuracy of official records may distort findings.
(1) Wikström, 2009; (2) Wikström et al., 2010 (England)	Peterborough Adolescent and Young Adult Development Study (PADS+): 700 young people followed from the age of 7.	Explores the impact of crime propensity and criminogenic exposure on individual crime involvement during early to mid-adolescence. Methods: PADS+ questionnaire and data from the small-area community survey (PCS) and the space–time budget.	(1) A person's criminal involvement depends on his propensity to crime and his exposure. Changes in a person's crime involvement are dependent on changes in his propensity and exposure. (2) Youths' activity fields and exposure to criminogenic settings predict criminal involvement.	

Table 11.1 *Continued*

Author(s), year of publication, country	Birth year of cohort, sample	Research questions and methods	Main results	Observations
(1) Smith and Ecob, 2007; Smith, 2004a; (2) Smith, 2004b; (3) McAra, 2004; Smith, 2006a; (4) Smith, 2006b (Scotland)	Edinburgh Study of Youth Transition and Crime	Nexus between delinquency and victimisation. Methods: interviews.	(1) Offending and victimisation are interrelated and predict each other three years later. The nexus is largely explained by being in risky situations and having antisocial friends. (2) Parenting and family functioning at age 13 are good predictors of delinquency at age 15. (3) Attachment to and behaviour at school at age 13 predict offending at 15. (4) Desistance was important by 17, but boys from disadvantaged neighbourhoods and those caught by the police were more likely to remain delinquents. (5) Typical age of first conviction was 17. Best predictors were exclusion from school (or dropping out), being male, living in a deprived neighbourhood, serious and persistent offending, and early contacts with the police/criminal justice system.	
Verhulst Akkerhuis and Althaus, 1985; Bongers et al., 2006; Donker et al., 2003 (Netherlands)	South Holland Study: 2,600 children of Dutch nationality from 13 birth cohorts aged 4 to 16, selected in 1983 from municipal registers. Consent from parents was obtained for 2,076 children. Follow-up every 2 years until 1991 and again in 1997. A total of 1,149 remained in the sample until 1997.	What is the trajectory of externalising behaviour (opposition, property, violent and status offences) across childhood and adolescence? Methods: interviews (Child-Behavior Checklist) with parents; teacher reports and SRD.	Follow-up of 1991 (Bongers et al., 2006): contrary to expectation, aggression did not peak at age 13, but was most prevalent among younger children. Physical aggression decreases and is largely resolved by the beginning of adulthood. Gender differences are considerable during childhood, but level off by late adolescence. Property offences decreased, whereas status violations increased. Follow-up of 1997 (Donker et al., 2003): aggressive behaviour is more stable than non-aggressive antisocial behaviour.	Parents may not be aware of many of their (older) children's norm violations (follow-up until 1991).

Author(s), year of publication, country	Birth year of cohort, sample	Research questions and methods	Main results	Observations
Gerris et al., 1993; Hoeve et al., 2006 (Netherlands)	Child-rearing and Family in the Netherlands Study: population sample of 788 families, children followed from age 9 to 27 (original study in 1990, follow-ups in 1995 and 2000).	The impact of family factors and parenting styles on delinquency in adulthood (comparison with the Pittsburgh Youth Study): self-reports.	The lack of orderly and structured activities within the family during adolescence was a strong predictor of delinquency in young adulthood after controlling for prior aggression and demographic variables. Authoritarian and authoritative parenting styles, family SES, supervision, punishment, and attachment were not related to delinquent behaviour in young adulthood.	The attrition rate in the Hoeve et al. study (2006) was 62 per cent.
Meeus and 't Hart, 1993; Meeus et al., 2004 (Netherlands)	Utrecht Study of Adolescent Development: representative sample of 3,392 Dutch adolescents aged 12–23 was drawn from a panel of 10,000 households. Out of this sample, 1,300 subjects were randomly selected for the longitudinal study.	How does having an intimate partner influence delinquency? How does this moderate parental influence on delinquency? Methods: interviews (SRD) at homes – first wave in 1991, waves 2 and 3 in 1994 and 1997.	If an adolescent finds a partner, that partner takes over the role of parents in reducing criminality. For subjects without a partner, parents remain important.	

Table 11.1 ***Continued***

Author(s), year of publication, country	Birth year of cohort, sample	Research questions and methods	Main results	Observations
Gavray, 1997 (Belgium)	In 1992, 444 subjects aged 16–21 were sampled for ISRD-1 in the region of Liège (Belgium). Among these, 139 (who agreed to leave their address in 1992) were re-interviewed in 1996 (when they were between ages 21 and 25).	Development of offending across adolescence. Methods: interviews (SRD).	Delinquency (including seriousness of offences and versatility) in 1996 was strongly predicted by abuse of substances in 1992. Leaving school did prevent later offending only if subjects succeeded with integration on the labour market.	
Born, 2002 (Belgium)	A total of 363 children placed in institutions were followed over time, along with the sample used by Gavray (1997).	The process of desistance from delinquency at late adolescence. Methods: interviews and official records.	In both samples, delinquency is not adolescence limited but often continues into adulthood, particularly among adolescents with early substance abuse, victimisation in their biography and high versatility. The end of a delinquent career comes about with entering social and emotional responsibilities.	
Göppinger, 1985; Bock, 2000 (Germany)	'Tübingen' study: influenced by the Glueck study (1950), 200 prison inmates were matched with 200 men from the same region without known history of offending. The study started in the 1960s.	Understanding differences in trajectories over life between known serious offenders and 'normal' men. Methods: official records and retrospective interviews; recently, prospective SRD and official records were collected.	Offending is embedded in a long biographic continuity. Early deviance starts during leisure time and later spreads to the professional (educational) sphere.	Originally retrospective, the study became gradually prospective in nature.

Author(s), year of publication, country	Birth year of cohort, sample	Research questions and methods	Main results	Observations
Remschmidt and Walter, 2009 (Germany)	'Marburg Study': the sample included 1,009 boys aged 14 in 1971 who were known offenders in the Marburg district between 1962 and 1971. A total of 347 matched pairs without records had been selected from population registers. Between 1975 and 1977 (when boys were around age 22), 263 were interviewed (61 refused).	Six groups were distinguished: (1) boys with at least one known offence prior to age 14 and none prior to age 18; (2) boys with at least one known offence prior to age 14 and at least two offences by age 18; (3) boys with at least two offences prior to age 14 and none by age 18; (4) boys with at least two offences before age 14 and before age 18; (5) boys without known offences at age 14 and at least two offences prior to age 18; (6) boys without known offences by age 14 and between ages 14 and 18. Methods: interviews (lasting 2–4 hours) with intelligence and personality tests, a questionnaire on parental style of education, biographic data, and SRD. After age 22, criminal records were collected until subjects were age 42.	Important risk factors for offending later in life are (in combination) family and social risk factors, personality characteristics and undiscovered property offences committed during childhood.	The study has a 'catch-up prospective' design.

Table 11.1 ***Continued***

Author(s), year of publication, country	Birth year of cohort, sample	Research questions and methods	Main results	Observations
Albrecht and Grundies, 2009 (Germany)	'Freiburg cohort study': all juveniles born in 1970, 1973, 1975, 1978, 1985 and 1988 in Baden-Württemberg having at least once been known as suspects or convicted were considered for follow-up.	Development of official offending over adolescence and young adulthood. Methods: criminal records concerning all members of the cohort are registered in a database.	Convictions reach a maximum between ages 18 and 22 (7 per cent of cohort members being convicted every year at this age). The rate decreases to three per cent after age 33. The results do not support the view of adolescence-limited and life-course persistent career patterns, but suggest that, at any given age, some subjects without previous criminal history are convicted for the first time. The proportion of career offenders decreases with age, but is independent of age of onset.	The results support the 'life-course desistance' model (by Sampson and Laub).
Schmidt et al., 2009 (Germany)	'Mannheim longitudinal study': The sample includes 1,444 children born in Mannheim in 1970 who still lived there in 1978.A total of 216 children were randomly selected for regular follow-up interviews (one third refused). To this reduced sample, 183 children with psychiatric symptoms were added. These 399 subjects were interviewed at ages 8, 13, 18 and 25. A total of 321 were retained until age 25.	Development of offending (among other problems) over adolescence and young adulthood. Methods: intensive interviews. SRD when subjects were aged 18 and 25.	Family dysfunctions are particularly important at mid-childhood (age 8–13), especially for later chronic offending.	

Author(s), year of publication, country	Birth year of cohort, sample	Research questions and methods	Main results	Observations
Schumann et al., 2009 (Germany)	'Bremen study': all students born between 1971 and 1974 in their final year of two lower tracks schools in Bremen were first interviewed in 1989 (of these, 90 per cent entered an apprenticeship). At wave 2 (1992), 426 former students accepted to be re-interviewed, and at wave 5 (2000), 333. The study was designed as a comparative study to the Denver Youth Survey.	Development of offending during the transition from school to apprenticeship and the labour market. Methods: SRD (waves 2–5).	Delinquency was similar in the Bremen and Denver samples at age 14. It dropped more during the following years in the American sample, despite less institutionalised transitions from school to the labour market. Vocational training and having a stable job requiring job qualifications does not reduce delinquency. Possibly including drug use (cannabis) and shoplifting may have reduced differences over time and across countries. Only two per cent among the Bremen sample experienced pre-trial detention by wave 5, but 20 per cent among the Denver sample were arrested. No deterrent effect was discovered.	Authors wonder whether vocational training may have delayed effects (by age 25?). Custody (D) and arrest (US) are not the same!
Boers, Seddig and Reinecke, 2009 (Germany)	'Duisburg study': 3,411 seventh-grade students from Duisburg were recruited for a longitudinal SRD-study to start in 2002. The sample was re-interviewed every year until 2006. A total of 1,552 remained in the sample until the last wave.	Development of delinquency through the ages 14–18. Methods: Annual SRD.	Delinquency also affects social bonds and may jeopardise successful integration. (Results are preliminary as yet.) The study having covered, at every wave, the entire school population and not only those remaining in the panel (i.e., those remembering their personal codes), it is possible assessing to what extent rigid data protection laws affect sample composition. Retention was better among female students in higher tracks with low delinquency scores.	Rigid data protection laws reduced the retention rate. Students had to note, on their questionnaire, a personal code (instead of their names) they had to remember during the following waves.

Table 11.1 *Continued*

Author(s), year of publication, country	Birth year of cohort, sample	Research questions and methods	Main results	Observations
Laubacher et al. (in press) (Switzerland)	In 1971, 6,315 Army conscripts were interviewed during the day of conscription. Sample covered all Swiss males aged 19 living in the Canton of Zurich. Randomly, for half of the sample (3,155) criminal records were checked. A total of 123 had a record at that time (54 per cent property, 28 per cent violent and 30 per cent drug offences). Records continued to be checked for these 123 men until they were aged 52 (in 2004).	Development of psychiatric symptoms (and delinquency) over the life-span. Methods: interviews (for psychiatric symptoms). Criminal records for delinquency.	(1) Adolescent delinquency is not necessarily episodic (68 per cent had been reconvicted by age 52, of which about one in four for a violent offence); (2) socio-demographic variables and psychiatric diagnosis (at age 19) are only weakly related to later violent criminality; (3) type of offences committed during adolescence have high predictive validity, especially for violent offences; (4) number and seriousness of offences including versatility at age 19 are important predictors of serious adult offending.	
Haas, 2001, Haas et al., 2004; Haas and Killias, 2003, Staubli and Killias (2011) (Switzerland)	Cross-sectional, retrospective study of 21,300 Swiss Army recruits and a random sample of Swiss men aged 20 not drafted (born 1997).	Explanations of very serious offences committed at age 20 through past biographic experiences (before age 6, between ages 6 and 11, and after age 12). Methods: written interviews (questionnaires to be dropped into a ballot box). SRD and victimisation over the lifespan.	Results match (including for very serious offences, such as serious assault, offences committed with guns, rape, and child abuse) many findings from longitudinal studies on the role of family and socialisation variables, protective factors (for example, a positive relationship with teachers), and versatility vs specialisation. Serious offenders are committing a wide range of offences. Certain victimisations (including bullying and sexual abuse) have far-reaching consequences (including suicide attempts and violent offending) at age 19.	

Author(s), year of publication, country	Birth year of cohort, sample	Research questions and methods	Main results	Observations
Caprara, Regalia and Bandura, 2002; Caprara et al., 2007; Paciello et al., 2008 (Italy)	During the school year 1989/90, approximately 400 third-grade students (aged about 9) from Genzano (suburban town near Rome) were assessed. Three additional cohorts were assessed during the following three years. Each cohort was assessed annually until it reached age 14–15 and every second year afterwards until 2008 (when the oldest subjects were age 27).	Development of aggression from mid-childhood into young adulthood in relation to self-efficacy by age 20 (366 subjects retained). Methods: measures of aggressive traits and delinquency from ages 12– 23. SRD (violence) at waves 3–5.	Irritability and perceived self-regulatory efficacy (measured from age 14 through the item: 'How well can you resist peer pressure to drink beer, wine or liquor?') were important predictors of violence at age 20. There was also a high continuity of irritability and offending across adolescence.	The study was originally designed in collaboration with Albert Bandura and Jerry Patterson.
Luengo et al., 1994 (Spain)	1,226 adolescents aged 12–17 interviewed in 1989 and one year later.	How do different forms of impulsivity influence antisocial behaviour? Methods: SRD and several impulsivity scales.	Non-planning impulsivity (i.e., not caring about consequences of actions) best explains anti-social behaviour one year later, and best distinguishes stable non-delinquents from persistent offenders.	

Switzerland). Ironically, successful vocational training did not reduce offending in one German study (Bremen), although this may be due to a small sample that did not allow isolating more serious offences. Two studies (Finland, and Duisburg in Germany) looked at the ways a child's behaviour affects social bonds and found the relationship to be far from unidirectional. This should be kept in mind in interpreting findings showing higher odds of later offending for those who were excluded from school or caught by the police and, eventually, sanctioned by the criminal justice system (Scotland).

Some European studies have found a significant impact of various opportunities on later offending (Scotland), leisure-time activities (including drug use, Belgium), having an intimate partner (the Utrecht study), unemployment (Finland), and neighbourhood disadvantage. Lifestyles may influence delinquency, but also create the risk for victimization (Scotland).

Some European studies have found career patterns that do not necessarily match the distinction between adolescence-limited and persistent offenders and late starters. According to some studies, late adolescent offenders continue offending long beyond age 30 (Mannheim, Freiburg, Switzerland), particularly among some minorities (Netherlands – Jennissen, 2009). Substantial numbers of people are later convicted without having had a record by age 20 (England – Soothill et al., 2003). Two Swedish studies found that the proportion of offences committed by persistent criminals is beyond 60 per cent for the most 'productive' five per cent, and 50 per cent for the 'top' one per cent. Similar results are reported from the Netherlands where only 1.6 per cent of the offenders were versatile serious delinquents, who were responsible for 20–30 per cent of all offences committed by the entire cohort (Meeus et al., 2001).

The often invoked 'normalization' of delinquent youths during adolescence seems to refer to mostly trivial offenders and offences (Timmermans, 2009) but not necessarily to persistent and serious offending. Blokland and Palmen (Chapter 2, this volume) found that, among their 1984 birth cohort whose criminal record could be followed up to 2007 (N=170,891), offending was more prevalent between ages 18 and 23 than before or in the later 20s when desistance from offending became more common. At the same time, however, a substantial proportion of offenders started during early adulthood, and others continued offending, especially among those who were chronic offenders between ages 12 and 23.

Using data on the same cohort (born in 1984), Averdijk, Elffers and Ruiter (Chapter 3, this volume) have combined data on recidivism after age 12 and mobility across neighbourhoods over time to assess, for the first time in Europe, such effects in a longitudinal perspective. Controlling for a certain number of background variables (such as employment, marriage, and leaving parental households), they found a weak but consistent (positive) effect of neighbourhood disadvantage (as measured by the proportion of non-Western residents) on offending, but – paradoxically – a small negative effect of mobility on re-arrest. They argue that mobility may isolate young offenders from delinquent peers.

Given the costs of longitudinal studies, it should be recognized that retrospective studies (such as the Tübingen (Germany) study comparing prison inmates with non-convicted matched pairs, or the Swiss army recruits study using an unusually large sample) offer opportunities to look at very serious offences in a (retrospective) biographic perspective. The Bremen (Germany) and the Child-rearing and the Family in the Netherlands Study illustrate how much might be gained from combining longitudinal studies across countries. Unfortunately, no longitudinal studies (either in the fields of criminology or in other related fields, such as psychiatry) could be located in Norway, Ireland, Austria, Portugal, Greece, or in former communist countries (with the exception of Estonia). Rather surprising is the absence of any longitudinal study in France. Such a study was prepared by a panel of international experts (including Richard Tremblay) in 2006 ('Troubles des conduites chez l'enfant et l'adolescent'), but it was contested on ethical grounds and abandoned.[1]

International (European) Studies

Studies on offending during adolescence and young adulthood are dominated by longitudinal research. Macro-level and contextual variables, traditionally, have found more attention in international studies. Cross-national differences in crime rates are considerable and reflect to a large extent crime among young males. Given Europe's diversity in macro-level variables and the highly fragmented policy responses across the continent, a few notes on international trends may be of interest to scholars and policymakers.

The International Crime Victimization Survey (ICVS) This survey was conducted in 1989, 1992, 1996, 2000 and 2005 in a significant number of European countries (Van Dijk, Van Kestern and Smit, 2007). According to these data, robbery increased compared to 1989 (or the earliest available year) in about half of European countries and remained stable (i.e., within a margin of +/− 20%) or decreased in the other half of the countries. Assault increased in the vast majority of European countries. Police-recorded assault and robbery, as measured by the *European Sourcebook of Crime and Criminal Justice Statistics* (ESB, 2010), by and large matched ICVS trends. On the other hand, survey-measured and police-recorded property crime decreased after 1995 (Tavares and Thomas, 2008). This was true especially for domestic burglary and motor vehicle thefts. Drug offences including drug trafficking increased more substantially. So far, Europe has not seen a general drop in violent crime.

How can these changes be explained? Unfortunately, ICVS lifestyle measures were too crude to grasp the relevant changes. Outdoor activities (particularly in inner-city areas) increased dramatically in many countries, often way beyond

1 See http://www.vie-publique.fr/actualite/alaune/delinquance-depistage-enfance-critique.html, accessed 3 February 2012.

midnight, and combined with high consumption of alcohol and other substances. However, the 'revolution' of leisure-time activities following the extension of hours of operation of public transportation, the abolition of closing hours for pubs, and the 'liberalization' of policies regulating the sale of alcoholic beverages was not universal across Europe but limited to certain countries and cities. The surprisingly different trends in rates of assault and robbery across Europe may well be attributable to the highly variable development of 'routine activities' and risky lifestyles. Cross-national comparative research, for example, based on data from Peterborough (England) and Eskilstuna (Sweden), has shown that differences in lifestyle predict differences in delinquency levels (Wikström and Svensson, 2008).

In many European countries, however, increases in violence, especially among juveniles, is subject to debate, particularly in Scandinavia (Sarnecki, 2009b; Balvig, 2006; Kivivuori and Salmi, 2006; BRÅ, 2010), in Germany (Baier et al., 2009) and in the Netherlands (Wittebrood and Nieuwbeerta, 2006). While the rate of young violent offenders known to the police is increasing, self-report and victimization studies (focusing on young people as victims of crime) suggest more stable trends. The favourite explanation for these discrepancies is generally the presumed increase in propensity to report violence to the police and/or more complete recording of violent offences by the police. According to ICVS data (see ESB, 2010, Table 5.2.3), reporting to the police increased on average in all European countries from 30–33 per cent for assault, and from 45–49 per cent for robbery. However, surveys may be less suitable to monitor trends in serious injuries that are more regularly reported to and recorded by the police and other services, such as medical emergency centres (Exadaktylos, Häuselmann and Zimmermann, 2007; BRÅ, 2008, p. 100) and insurance companies (Lanfranconi, 2009). Sources of this kind often match trends with police-recorded offences.

The International Survey on Violence Against Women (IVAWS) According to the results of this survey, conducted in 2004 on samples of 2,000 women in nine countries (including Poland, Switzerland, Denmark and the Czech Republic), the strongest single correlate of partner violence is the male partner's history of non-domestic violence. Men described by female respondents as being sometimes violent outside the home are between two and 12 times more likely to assault their female partner. This finding underlines the importance of general criminal violence in the causation of domestic violence (Lussier, Farrington and Moffitt, 2009) and the priority its prevention deserves in the context of domestic violence. Next in importance came frequent binge drinking, which varies considerably across Europe (Johnson, Ollus and Nevala, 2008).

The International Self-Reported Delinquency Survey (ISRD-2) The first ISRD survey was conducted in 1992 in 12 countries (Junger-Tas, Terlouw and Klein, 1994). In 2006, a second survey of this kind was conducted in 30 countries (Junger-Tas et al., 2010). It provides comparative data on most of continental Europe including countries in Central and Eastern Europe. The results show that juvenile delinquency, as assessed by the ISRD-2 self-report instrument, is substantially correlated with national rates of minor offenders known to the police, according to the ESB 2010 (Enzmann et al., 2010).

Further, the national rates of self-reported delinquency are also quite strongly correlated with several features of school systems. For example, countries having a high standard deviation of their ninth-grade students' PISA (the international tests of students' intellectual abilities) performance scores face higher rates of serious (rare) violent offences, suggesting that low integration of the weakest students (and, thus, a high standard deviation) has a significant impact on students' behaviour. This correlation holds in multilevel analyses even when gender, age, migrant status and several school variables (such as school disorganization, attachment to school, school climate and students' performance at school) were taken into account (Lucia and Killias, 2011).

Beyond schools, the ISRD-2 shows that delinquency – and particularly serious violence – is highly correlated with lifestyles and going out (and hanging around) during late night hours, as well as neighbourhood characteristics (Junger-Tas et al., 2012). These are among the strongest explanatory variables among the wide array of independent variables that were collected through the ISRD-2. As far as the neighbourhood is concerned, this could be related to the possibility of observing deviant situations (including littering, graffiti, and other signs of disorder) that, as a remarkable Dutch experiment revealed, produce not only 'imitation' but offences that are different in nature from those that are observed, such as theft (Keizer, Lindenberg and Steg, 2008).

Special Offenders

Homicide

The rate of completed homicide in Western Europe is generally low, i.e., it nowhere exceeds 2 per 100,000 (with the exception of Finland and Scotland) according to police statistics. In Eastern Europe, however, rates are far higher, namely between 6 and 10 per 100,000 during the years 2003–2007 (ESB, 2010, Table 1.1). However, these global rates never tell the full story. Homicide constellations vary greatly across space and time, since homicide includes family killings, murder in connection with robbery or black markets, and terrorist and political homicide. Looking at varying constellations is, therefore, far more helpful to an understanding of the dynamics of this crime. In this respect, research has benefited from national databases on homicide established during the last decade in the Netherlands (Nieuwbeerta and Leistra, 2007), Finland (Kivivuori and Lehti, 2003), and Switzerland (Killias et al., 2009). These data include many details on victims, offenders and events that allow international comparisons. If street homicide rates are very high in the US, American rates of domestic homicide are not out of range of other countries, as Table 11.2 illustrates.

Table 11.2 Prevalence of completed intentional homicide (total, within the family including intimate partners, and homicides followed by suicide) in seven countries (several recent years)

Country	Total	Within the family		Homicide followed by suicide	
	per 1 million population	per 1 million population	in % of all homicides	per 1 million population	in % of all homicides
US	56	7.9	14	2.2	3.9
Finland	24	6.9	29	1.6	5.8
Canada	20	5.7	29	2.0	10
Australia	20	7.0	35	1.2	6
Netherlands	15	4.3	29	0.5	3.3
Switzerland	10	4.1	43	0.9	14
Spain	10	1.8	18	n.a.	n.a.

Sources for total and family homicides: US: Supplementary Homicide Reports, years 1976–2003; Finland: Kivivuori (2001); Canada: Statistics Canada, years 2000–2004; Australia: Mouzos and Rushforth (2003); Netherlands: Leistra and Nieuwbeerta (2003); Switzerland: Killias et al. (2009); Spain: Instituto Nacional de estadística (INE) and Centro Reina Sofía para el Estudio de la Violencia

Sources for homicide followed by suicide: Liem et al. (2011); Finland: Kivivuori and Lehti (2003); Canada: Statistics Canada (2005); Australia: http://www.aic.gov.au/publications/current%20series/cfi/161-180/cfi176.aspx (accessed 3 February 2012); Spain: Instituto Nacional de estadística (INE) and Centro Reina Sofía para el Estudio de la Violencia.

In view of these data, it is inappropriate to consider levels of homicide as an expression of a society's 'intrinsic violence' and to call the US a 'violent country'. Similarly, differences in homicide rates over time and space may be related to variations in homicide constellations including, in the case of Scandinavia, drinking patterns (Lenke, 1990; Sarnecki, 2009b, p. 96). In America, guns are far more often used in street-level murder, whereas the use of guns is less common among European criminal networks, with the exception of the Italian mafias. This is true even in countries with substantial gun ownership rates, such as Finland and Switzerland. Rarely used in the streets, guns are, however, very often used in domestic homicide in these two countries. Data from the International Survey on Violence against Women (IVAWS) further suggest that the extent of domestic violence is not related to domestic homicide rates. Rather, the presence of deadly instruments at home increases the likelihood of fatal outcomes in cases of family and partner disputes, as well as risks of multi-person killings and homicide followed by the offender's suicide (Liem et al., 2001).

According to mortality as well as police statistics, homicides in Europe have levelled off after 1997 and the average number of police-recorded homicides dropped from four to two per 100,000 by 2007 (ESB, 2003, 2006, 2010, Tables

1.2.1.4 and 1.2.1.5). Since non-lethal violence did not decrease (see the preceding section), the question remains whether trends in murder rates are influenced by improved medical services, as suggested by American research (Harris et al., 2002; Doerner, 1988).

Domestic Violence

Partner violence is a prominent issue in many European countries, including Greece (Papadakaki et al., 2009) and Spain. Although the rates of women battered by their partner in Spain (four per cent last year) was not out of range of other countries (Instituto de la Mujer, 2006), cases of partner violence are far more often recorded by the police in Spain than in other countries. In 2007, the rate per 100,000 was roughly three times the European median (of about 50) and substantially higher than in neighbouring Portugal or in Finland (ESB, 2010, Table 1.1). Much more debated than probably in any other country is the nexus between partner violence and partner killing, although Spain's homicide rate is among the lowest in Europe (Table 11.2).

Gangs

Beyond the 'revolution' of the leisure-time industry and decreasing parental control over children, the last decades have brought about a switch from *vertical social control* (parents, other adults and superiors) to *horizontal social control* (peers, schoolmates) on the behaviour of young people. In two studies in Stockholm (Sarnecki, 2001) and Copenhagen (Sarnecki, 2009a), youth co-offending networks have been studied through official records over several years. The results show that young offenders (up to age 20) often acted in loose and short-lived networks. Co-offending of two or more individuals over a period of more than one year is, according to crime records, extremely uncommon. This research suggests that there may be differences between American and European gangs.

On the other hand, many European cities reported significant gang activity over the last decade (Klein, 1995). Research on this topic has been intensified by the 'Eurogang Network' (Esbensen and Lynskey, 2001), an informal group of American and European scholars whose work has influenced the construction of the questionnaire of the International Self-report Study (ISRD-2). Work on gangs in Europe has identified some common features with American models, in particular far higher incidence rates for particularly serious and violent offences for gang members compared to juveniles who say they do not belong to any group, or who admit to belonging only to an informal group sharing leisure-time activities (Esbensen and Weerman, 2005). This is true for girls as well as boys (Haymoz and Gatti, 2010).

Migration and Crime

An issue with a high degree of relevance in Europe is crime by immigrants, and in particular by young minority males who grow up in Western Europe. In most European countries – and contrary to the American experience (where migrants are underrepresented in crime) – this group is overrepresented in police and court statistics, especially for violent crime (see, for example, for the Netherlands: Junger, Wittebrood and Timman, 2001). This situation has existed over several decades and has apparently worsened over time (Tonry, 1997). Three reasons for this overrepresentation have been proposed: (1) discrimination by the victims (when they decide to report a crime), by the police, and at the following steps within the criminal justice system, (2) disproportionate exposure to problems (such as politically and ethnically motivated violence) in the country of origin, and (3) integration problems these groups face in Western Europe. Results of international self-report studies (Junger-Tas et al., 2012) and victims' accounts of offender characteristics, as measured through victimization surveys in England and Wales (Shah and Pease, 1992) and in Switzerland (Killias, 2009), show, however, that the overrepresentation of minorities is present also in victimization surveys and self-report measures of crime. Validity problems of self-report measures seem even to underestimate the size of this problem (Junger, 1989). Further studies on how the criminal justice system operates lend only limited support to the discrimination hypothesis (Hood, 1992). One way of assessing possible discrimination within the criminal justice system is to compare the proportion of alien suspects at the police level with the proportion of alien defendants convicted. As Table 11.3 shows, for the countries collecting such data, there is no systematic increase in the proportion of aliens across different stages of justice processing.

The question arises as to what produces these differences. For example, immigrants may be more likely to suffer from lack of *social capital* (Bakker, Walberg and Bloom, 2005) including school failure, unemployment, social isolation, and concentration in poor and socially disorganized areas of major cites (Junger-Tas et al., 2012). The role of social problems is further underlined by self-report surveys showing that delinquency is far less prevalent in some countries of origin (such as Bosnia-Herzegovina – Killias, Maljevic and Lucia, 2010) than among juveniles from those countries who have grown up in Western Europe. This suggests that violence is not 'imported' from the regions of origin, as suggested by culture conflict theories, but produced locally by difficulties of integration. According to a Swedish study (Hällsten, Sarnecki and Szulkin, 2010), up to 80 per cent of differences between young native Swedes and young immigrants can be explained by differences in life circumstances.

It has often been observed (and first noted by Dorothy Krall) that children of migrants may have higher crime rates than their parents. A recent Swedish study lends supports to the notion of higher criminal engagement of the so-called second generation of immigrants (Kardell and Carlsson, 2009). Results of the international self-report project, however, find rather little difference

Table 11.3 Per cent alien suspects (known to the police) and convicted alien defendants across Europe in 2006

Country	Bodily injury (assault)		Rape		Robbery	
	% Alien suspects known to the police	% Alien defendants convicted	% Alien suspects known to the police	% Alien defendants convicted	% Alien suspects known to the police	% Alien defendants convicted
Austria	23	24	36	36	42	40
Czech Republic	7	5	16	16	n.a.	n.a.
Finland	8	6	22	24	11	18
France	14	12	14	8	14	n.a.
Germany	21	24	30	35	29	31
Switzerland	49	58	64	68	60	61

Source: ESB 2010, Tables 1.2.2 and 3.1.2.

between first- and second-generation immigrants in most countries (Junger-Tas et al., 2010). A further controversial issue is whether young migrants are disproportionately victimized. Again, the international self-report project (Junger-Tas et al., 2010) shows that victimization rates were similar or lower for migrant youths in most countries.

In several parts of Europe, illegal migrants – mainly from overseas countries who are living from shadow economy jobs and sometimes episodic crime – are a particularly difficult problem. Many of them are men around the age of 20. So far, this issue has not been systematically addressed in European research.

Evaluations of Interventions

Throughout European countries, several treatment programmes have been implemented and evaluated. Many programmes have been adapted from models developed in Anglo-Saxon countries. Most prominent are cognitive-behavioural programmes, including '*reasoning and rehabilitation*', and several variants of STOP (*Sex Offender Treatment Program*), the main objectives of which are the confrontation and cognitive restructuring of justifications and excuses commonly used by sex offenders (Hollin and Palmer, 2006). In the following section, we shall focus on European reviews of studies on the effectiveness of treatment programmes, particularly with respect to adolescent and young adult offenders.

Reasoning and Rehabilitation (R&R) is a pioneering programme in the cognitive treatment of offenders. It was developed by Ross and Fabiano (1985) and applied to both juveniles and adults offenders in many countries, including Spain (Alba et al., 2007; Redondo et al., 2008) and Switzerland (Eisner et al.,

2007). The main objective of R&R is to improve the thinking skills of offenders. To that end, the subjects are trained to be more reflective (rather than reactive), to anticipate and plan their responses to problems, and to think more about alternative solutions to interpersonal problems.

There have been numerous evaluative studies of this programme with both juveniles and adults. Tong and Farrington (2006) carried out a meta-analysis of the effectiveness of the Reasoning & Rehabilitation programme for reducing criminal recidivism, based on 26 comparisons between treated and control groups. On average, treated groups showed a significant recidivism reduction of 14 points. Effectiveness was observed both in community and institutional applications, and for both high-risk and low-risk offenders. One notable exception to the generally positive results of the R&R programme is a Home Office evaluation of Prison programmes (Falshaw et al., 2004). In this study, no significant effects were found on reconviction rates. The authors attributed this outcome to problems of implementation related to the programme's rapid expansion.

Redondo and Sánchez-Meca (2003) conducted a meta-analysis of 17 European programmes developed between 1980 and 2001 that included 2,775 juvenile offenders. This study distinguished between three categories of juveniles: adolescents (age <16), young adults (age 16–21) and mixed groups (youths and adults, with an average age under 29). An overall effect size of $r = 0.18$ was obtained, i.e., treated groups had a recidivism rate of 18 points below control groups. The analysis of variance detected a progressive decrease of effectiveness with subjects' age: six programmes implemented with adolescents obtained an average effect size of $r = 0.49$, eight programmes with young adults an effect size of $r = 0.15$, and three programmes with mixed groups (juveniles and adults) of $r = 0.11$. Concerning the type of interventions, the best results were achieved by the three educational programmes ($r = 0.42$), followed by the five diversion programmes ($r = 0.29$), the three community-based treatments ($r = 0.14$), and the four cognitive-behavioural programmes ($r = 0.12$). Nevertheless, the results of the effectiveness of the different categories of programmes should be taken with caution because of the small number of studies included in each category, and because the original theoretical foundations are not necessarily reflected in the programme's actual contents (Lösel, 1995, 2000).

Garrido, Anyela Morales and Sánchez-Meca (2006) conducted a meta-analysis on treatment programmes with young delinquents (ages 12–21) serving sentences in closed institutions or youths prisons. It included 30 experimental or quasi-experimental studies involving control group comparison or pre-/post-assessments. The overall sample consisted of 2,831 juveniles in the treatment groups and 3,002 subjects in the comparison groups. The programmes included psychological treatments (in the categories non-behavioural, behavioural and cognitive), social and educational interventions, and interventions in therapeutic communities. An overall effect size of $d = 0.14$ was obtained, which can be translated into an average recidivism reduction of seven points. Although almost all the interventions achieved favourable results, higher effect sizes were obtained by cognitive-behavioural (d = 0.21) and cognitive-psychological treatments (d = 0.12).

Lösel and Köferl (1989) published a review on the effectiveness of the socio-therapeutic prisons in Germany where young and adult recidivists with serious personality disorders were treated. These treatments were conducted in accordance with a broad concept of 'social therapy' that includes changes in living and institutional conditions, group processes, strengthening contacts and promoting jobs in the community, use of prison permissions, and preparation for release. This review incorporated 16 primary studies with partially overlapping samples. It found that socio-therapeutic prisons reduced recidivism on an average by 11 points in comparison to the expected recidivism following discharge from ordinary prisons. The success of the interventions was modestly associated to a smaller size of the prisons. In the province of Westphalia, the same programmes were evaluated through a randomized controlled trial – again with positive, though weaker, effects (Ortmann, 2000).

Endrass et al. (2008) presented a systematic review of studies of the effectiveness of treatment approaches with sex and violent offenders. They concluded that results of meta-analyses in this field must be interpreted with caution, studies being difficult to compare because of the heterogeneity in design of the original studies.

Grietens and Hellinckx (2004) summarized five previous meta-analyses, three from North America (Garrett, 1985; Dowden and Andrews, 2000; Lipsey and Wilson, 1998) and two from Europe (Lösel and Köferl, 1989; Redondo, Garrido and Sánchez-Meca, 1997; Redondo, Sánchez-Meca and Garrido, 1999) regarding the effectiveness of treatment with institutionalized juvenile delinquents. They concluded that effect sizes, or average effectiveness, is equivalent to a recidivism reduction of nine per cent (with a range of nine per cent to 31 per cent).

In sum, European reviews on juvenile offender treatments, similar to American reviews, have highlighted that treatments have a modest but significant effect in reducing delinquency (Hollin, 2001; McGuire, 2004). The interventions achieved an average recidivism reduction of about ten points, based on recidivism rates ranging between 50 per cent and 65 per cent (Cooke and Philip, 2001; Cullen and Gendreau, 2006; Lösel, 1996, 1998; McGuire, 2004). The best treatment programmes may even achieve reductions of recidivism between 15 and 25 points. In other words, treatment can decrease the expected recidivism rate between a quarter and one half, depending on the quality of the programme. In this way, treatments can help to reduce criminal careers (Israel and Hong, 2006). However, high-quality evaluations including randomized controlled trials are almost nonexistent in Europe in this domain, despite a myriad of projects implemented in many countries. This is true even for the Netherlands where such studies are still lacking (Boendermaker, Deković and Asscher, Chapter 10, this volume; Deković et al., Chapter 9, this volume).

Criminal Justice Responses

The *European Sourcebook of Crime and Criminal Justice Statistics* (ESB) contains data from about 40 countries on police-recorded offences and offenders (back to 1990) on prosecutorial decisions, on convictions, sentences (including length of custodial sentences and alternative sanctions), corrections and surveys. It documents Europe's wide variation in justice responses and serves as the basis for this report.

Incarceration Rates

Incarceration rates vary widely across Europe. The highest rates are found in Russia, with about 700 prisoners per 100,000, and the lowest in Denmark, Finland, Sweden and Switzerland with roughly about 70. Since prisoners are predominantly young men below age 30, using data for all age groups is relevant for young adult offenders. In the following section we will look more specifically at incarceration of minors.

In the international literature, the view prevails that the number of prisoners per population reflects sentencing styles rather than crime rates. With ESB offence-specific data on (1) convicted offenders, and (2) length of custodial sentences, it is possible to show that the rate of defendants convicted of murder is a major driving factor, given that everywhere in Europe this group is likely to serve very long sentences. The correlation (r), when outliers are eliminated, is substantial (between .52 and .62). Homicide is particularly frequent in Russia and a few other countries in Eastern Europe where incarceration rates are also very high. Earlier analyses (Aebi and Kuhn, 2000) showed that the average length of custodial sentences for offences such as robbery, domestic burglary, aggravated assault, rape and drug trafficking is the next important variable in explaining incarceration rates. Sentences for less serious offences are far shorter than for murder, but the number of defendants is far higher. Again, variety in sentencing practices across Europe is considerable.

However, the use of alternative sanctions (such as community service, electronic monitoring and fines) explains less than expected of the variation in incarceration rates. Such sanctions are widely used throughout Europe but tend to replace short prison sentences rather than reducing prison time. In a comparative perspective, it is less the number of persons sent to prison than the length of stay that affects overall incarceration rates. Using ESB data and excluding outliers, the correlation between the number of persons entering prisons ('flow') and the incarceration rate ('stock') is weak (r=.17). In conclusion, there may not be much to gain, in terms of controlling or even reducing incarceration rates, by sending fewer people to prison through replacing short custodial sanctions by other punishments.

The preventive potential of Western Europe's policy of using custody only for serious crimes and for limited periods is hard to assess. Systematic reviews suggest that custodial and non-custodial sanctions differ little in recidivism rates (Villettaz,

Killias and Zoder, 2006). The same has been found for systematic reviews based on studies comparing custodial sentences of different length (Gendreau, Goggin and Cullen, 1999). Given this knowledge, and taking the direct (economic) and indirect (human) costs of incarceration into account, Europe's moderate use of prison sentences may be wise and humane, particularly for juvenile and young adult offenders.

Juvenile Justice

One of the peculiarities of the American juvenile justice system is the extent to which it allows juvenile justice waivers (Liefaard, Chapter 7, this volume). In Europe, systems vary widely, and some countries (such as the Netherlands, Belgium, Portugal and Poland) also allow juvenile defendants (above ages 15 or 16) to be treated as adults. Other countries, such as Germany and Austria, do not allow bringing juveniles below age 18 before an adult court to be sentenced under adult law; they even allow young adults (between ages 18 and 20) to be treated under juvenile law and to be tried under the juvenile criminal justice system, although authorities have some discretion in this regard. These countries, however, have very long maximum custodial sentences for juveniles below age 18: ten years in Germany, 15 years in Austria. These sentences are in the range of what other countries allow (Table 11.5). Even if defendants aged between 18 and 21 are put on trial before a juvenile court, the sentence they receive may not be different from what defendants of that age might receive under the adult system in other countries. It is true that young adult defendants in Germany, Switzerland and Sweden can be sent to special institutions for the treatment of young offenders, but that would also be possible under the adult system in many other countries. An extreme case is Switzerland, where the age limit is strictly 18, but where the maximum sentence for juveniles is one year (only in exceptional cases is this four years). Thus, countries either have low maximum penalties for juveniles (below age 18) and apply, in certain circumstances, adult criminal sanctions to juvenile defendants, or they have sanctions for juveniles that are not all too different from what their law provides for adults (Stump, 2003). These policies make it easier to stick to the age limit of 18 and even to apply juvenile law to young adults (aged 18–20).

The case of Scandinavian countries is particularly interesting since they do not allow juveniles below ages 14 or 15 to be held responsible for their offences in court. Until the end of 2009, the age of legal responsibility, in all Scandinavian countries, was 15. In Denmark, this age has now been lowered to 14. Juveniles below the age of criminal responsibility are regarded as children and cannot be punished regardless of the seriousness and other circumstances related to their crimes. Police investigations of crimes committed by children are reported to the local social welfare committee that has to take adequate action, including various types of support and treatment for the young offender and his/hers parents. In severe cases, compulsory institutional treatment can be ordered. The decision may be appealed to an administrative court.

Table 11.4 The minimum age of criminal responsibility in European countries

Country	Age of criminality responsibility	Full criminal responsibility (adult law can/must be applied)
Albania	14	18
Armenia	14	18
Austria	14	18/21
Belgium	16	16/18
Bulgaria	14	18
Bosnia-Herzegovina	14	18
Croatia	14	18/21
Cyprus	10	16/21
Czech Republic	15	18
Denmark	14	14/18
Estonia	13	18
Finland	15	15/18
France	10/13	18
Georgia	12	18
Germany	14	18/21
Greece	8/13	18/21
Hungary	14	18
Iceland	15	15
Ireland	10	18
Italy	14	18/21
Latvia	14	18/21
Lithuania	14	14/21
Malta	18	18
Moldova	14	18
Netherlands	12	16/21
Norway	15	15
Poland	13	15/18
Portugal	12/16	16/21
Romania	14	18
Russia	14	18/21
Slovakia	14	18/21
Slovenia	14	18/21
Spain	14	18
Sweden	15	15/21
Switzerland	10	18
Turkey	12	15/18
Ukraine	14	18/21
UK: England and Wales	10	10/21
UK: Northern Ireland	10	17/21
UK: Scotland	8/16	16/21

Source: Junger-Tas and Dünkel, 2009. Table 13.1.

Table 11.4 shows that the lowest limits of criminal responsibility are ages 8 and 10, whereas most countries have opted for age 14. Countries with higher age limits often directly apply the adult criminal law to persons that reach the age of criminal responsibility. This is, for example, the case in Scandinavia where persons who are between ages 15 and 17 are treated by and large as adults, but more leniently. Custodial sentences are very uncommon for young people in this age group and are, when imposed, much shorter than for adults who commit similar crimes. Swedish legislation allows sentencing individuals in this age group to treatment in special youth institutions (special approved homes) where the treatment's duration (up to a maximum four years) is determined by the seriousness of the offence, while its form is determined by the nature of the problems that are associated with the offence. The most common reaction to more serious delinquency in the age group ranging from 15 (14) to 17 in Scandinavia is, however, diversion from the justice system under the form of various types of treatment interventions provided by social services. Community service and fines are also common for less serious offences.

Offenders aged 18–20 are treated more leniently than adults not only in Scandinavia, but also in 18 other European countries (including Austria, Germany and the Netherlands), as indicated in Table 11.4. A practical, important consequence of having young adults dealt with under juvenile law is that, for example, in Germany (Heinz, 1994) they may benefit from more lenient procedural rules, such as the wide use of diversion. On the practical effects of such interventions, there is either no systematic research or the results are conflicting. Whereas Heinz (2005), for example, considered diversion as a very effective measure, Entorf and Spengler (2008) conclude that its extension undermined the certainty of punishment and increased particularly violent offences, such as robbery.

Beyond the age of criminal responsibility, custodial sanctions are available to a greatly variable extent in various countries. As Table 11.5 shows, countries differ as to what age they allow custodial sanctions to be imposed upon minors. The variety is just as great regarding the legally allowable maximum custodial sentences. It should be noted that the definition of custody is ambiguous and may include, in some countries, secure accommodation of juveniles under child protection legislation.

As Table 11.5 illustrates, only five among 31 countries allow custodial sanctions against minors for acts committed before their fourteenth birthday. After that age (or eventually the fifteenth birthday), only six countries do not allow custodial sanctions. Thus, two competing systems coexist in Europe. Some countries allow very long custodial sentences for defendants aged 16 or older, or they allow – usually from that same age – the use of adult criminal law. The only cases where neither alternative exists are Switzerland and Iceland, where the age limit of age 18 is absolutely rigid and where the maximum penalties greatly differ between the juvenile and the adult systems (four years compared to three months for minors, versus life for adults).

Table 11.5 Maximum custodial sentence (in months) available under juvenile criminal law

Country	Prior to age 14	age 14–15	age 16–17
Albania	Custody not available	150 months	150 months
Armenia	Custody not available	84 months	120 months
Austria	Custody not available	120 months	180 months
Belgium	Custody not available	custody not available	Detention for life
Bulgaria	Custody not available	120 months	120 months
Croatia	Custody not available	custody not available	120 months
Czech Republic	Custody not available	120 months (15 yrs)	120 months
Denmark	custody not available	96 months (15 yrs)	96 months
Estonia	custody not available	120 months	120 months
Finland	custody not available	144 months (15 yrs)	144 months
France	240 months	240 months	Detention for life
Georgia	120 months	120 months	180 months
Germany	custody not available	120 months	120 months
Greece	custody not available	240 months	240 months
Hungary	custody not available	180 months	240 months
Iceland	custody not available	3 months	3 months
Italy	custody not available	360 months	360 months
Netherlands	12 months	12 months	24 months
Poland	custody not available	300 months	300 months
Portugal	custody not available	custody not available	36 months
Russia	custody not available	120 months	120 months
Slovakia	custody not available	72 months	132 months
Slovenia	custody not available	custody not available	360 months
Spain	custody not available	108 months	216 months
Sweden	custody not available	48 months	48 months
Switzerland	custody not available	12 months	48 months
Turkey	144 months	360 months	360 months
Ukraine	custody not available	180 months	180 months
UK: England and Wales	Detention for life	Detention for life	Detention for life
UK: Northern Ireland	custody not available	custody not available	48 months
UK: Scotland	custody not available	custody not available	Detention for life

Note: In the Czech Republic, Denmark, Iceland, Finland, Sweden, Switzerland, and Poland, the maximum applies to juveniles aged 15 (not 14).

Source: Survey conducted for this report among ESB correspondents.

A different question is to what extent sanctions that are legally available are actually applied. Table 11.6 gives an overview on how many minors are sentenced to immediate custodial sanctions (as a percentage of all sentenced juvenile defendants), minus those placed in institutions for treatment under a child protection order. Unfortunately, data on young adults are not available.

As Table 11.6 illustrates, European countries vary widely as to the extent to which they use imprisonment as a sanction against minors below age 18. Not surprisingly, this produces wide variations also in the numbers of juveniles actually incarcerated. European countries differ greatly as to the extent that they use prison not only for adults but also for juveniles. Figure 11.1 presents the rate of minors (below age 18) actually imprisoned per 100,000 inhabitants. The highest rates (Netherlands 11 and Russia 9) are far below the American rate of 31 minors incarcerated. Such differences are unlikely to be caused by definitional problems, such as the statistical treatment of institutions that are, legally speaking, not penal institutions, or juveniles placed in pre-trial detention (as a rule, such cases are

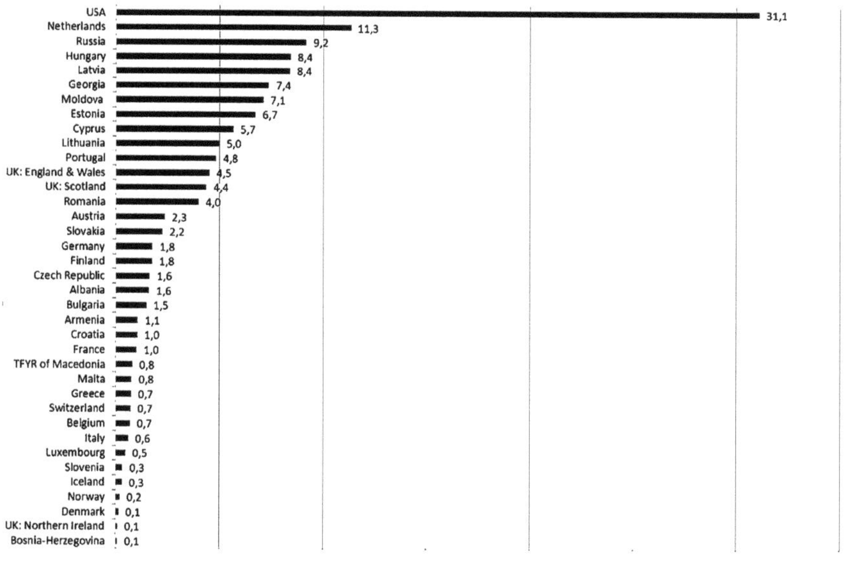

Figure 11.1 Minors (below 18) incarcerated in Europe (convicted or awaiting trial/sentencing), per 100,000 of the general population in 2006

Note: The percentage of Dutch incarcerated juveniles under civil law is about 30%.
Source: ESB 2010; U.S. data: Sourcebook of criminal justice statistics.

Table 11.6 Defendants aged below 18 sentenced to immediate custodial sanctions in 2006 (in percentage of all sanctions imposed), by offence

	Criminal offences: Total	Intentional homicide: Total	Bodily injury (Assault): Total	Rape	Sexual abuse of minors	Robbery	Theft: Total
Armenia	20.8						
Austria	14.5	100	5.3	30.0		51.9	13.7
Belgium	3.3					23.5	44.9
Finland	0.6		0.8	25.0	8.3	15.2	0.0
France	9.1	92.6	8.3	37.3			10.7
Georgia	33.9	100	25.0	100		38.5	30.4
Germany	6.3	90.3	6.3	31.6	13.1	23.6	6.9
Hungary	4.2	87.5	2.8	37.5		26.5	2.9
Latvia	25.6	100	32.1	50.0		27.2	29.6
Netherlands	12.0	33.5	7.7	32.2	19.4	31.6	11.8
Portugal	5.5					21.0	
Romania	26.7	93.8	7.4	80.6	11.1	43.9	25.3
Slovakia	7.2	100	3.8		7.4	27.5	8.5
Slovenia	2.2		3.3	50.0		12.0	2.1
Switzerland	1.5		1.1		1.4	3.8	0.5
UK: England and Wales	6.6	75.0	13.5	61.2	15.9	32.0	8.4
UK: Northern Ireland	7.0		15.5	100		45.5	10.0
UK: Scotland	22.8	100	34.8			40.0	19.2

Source: ESB 2010, Tables 3.2.2.

included here). The high percentage of juveniles in the Netherlands is related to the counting rules applied in that country, which includes all juveniles being the object of a civil or penal measure.

Surprisingly, very little research is available on the effects of Europe's highly variable systems of juvenile justice. The same is true for interventions and particularly for treatment institutions designed for juveniles and young adults.

Welfare Policies

European and American welfare policies differ substantially and children from poor families may, overall, receive more support in Europe. Unfortunately, little research has been conducted on the effects of welfare policies on crime. The very limited evidence from Germany (Rabold and Baier, 2007) and from Switzerland (Haas and Killias, 2001) suggests that poverty, if its effects are ameliorated by welfare, is not accompanied by increased levels of violent and other serious offences. In Europe, poverty and welfare are not necessarily concentrated in 'social housing' or other disadvantaged areas, as is often the case in America (Wikström, 1998).

An intervention programme including increased controls and training of unemployed subjects has been evaluated in Denmark through a randomized trial with 5,180 subjects (Andersen, 2010). The treated group committed significantly fewer offences than the control group that received the standard programme for unemployed persons. Since the intervention was not accompanied by increased welfare benefits, the success of the programme may be due to increased controls and reduced opportunities to offend (through reduced leisure time) rather than to improved 'welfare' in a traditional sense.

Drug and Alcohol Policies

Drug and alcohol policies vary considerably across Europe. On the continent, and particularly in wine-producing countries, alcohol policies are traditionally tolerant, whereas in Scandinavia these were traditionally much more repressive. A lot can be learned from data on change over time. Sweden, for example, is one of the countries where policies have changed several times (Lenke, 1990). There, the homicide rate increased substantially during the period of increasing alcohol consumption in the early nineteenth century, and decreased after severe restrictions were enacted (Von Hofer, 2011). When restrictions were gradually repealed during the second half of the twentieth century, violent crime increased again. Following Sweden's admittance to the European Union in 1995, more restrictions on alcohol sales were lifted, but violent crime did not increase as expected. A possible explanation might be that the 'continental' drinking style, characterized by less concentrated but more recreational use, became increasingly popular in Sweden.

With respect to cannabis use, the Netherlands is usually identified as the most liberal country. The Czech Republic, Estonia, Spain and Switzerland are other countries that liberalized cannabis policies during the 1990s (though in practice more than in law). According to a European survey on drug use (Hibell et al., 2009) and data from the ISRD surveys of 1992 (Junger-Tas, Terlouw and Klein, 1994) and of 2006 (Junger-Tas et al., 2010), cannabis use among teenagers increased in all these countries by more than 100 per cent and parallel to the liberalization of cannabis policies. In recent years, however, there are also countries that have experienced a drop in cannabis use, such as Austria, Belgium, France, Germany, Ireland, Italy, Slovenia, Switzerland, the United Kingdom and Portugal. The top scorers for cannabis use in 2007 were the Czech Republic, Switzerland and the Netherlands (Hibell et al., 2009).

So far, it is not clear to what extent cannabis use is influenced by policies aimed at restricting availability. In the Netherlands, lifetime prevalence of cannabis use among students aged 12–18 increased since 1988 (when cannabis policies started to be liberalized) from less than 10 to over 20 per cent and subsequently levelled off (Nationale Drug Monitor, 2010, p. 39). A similar natural experiment with important policy shifts was monitored in Switzerland over the last seven years (Chabloz et al., 2010). Population surveys, observation studies and extensive interviews with police, school and public health professionals as well as with coffee shop owners and street-level dealers showed that a less tolerant approach, including closing shops where the sale of cannabis was allowed, decreased the availability of cannabis, increased prices, and deeply affected market structures including lines of distribution (Killias et al., 2011). Consumption (particularly among those aged 15–19 years) decreased substantially. It is not clear, however, whether similar changes in other countries were the result of parallel shifts in policies – or whether other factors reduced the attraction of a product that might have gone out of fashion.

Plagued by high rates of street crime among many heroin addicts during the 1990s, several European countries have established programmes to administer opiates to long-term users. Such programmes have been in operation over several years in Switzerland, Denmark, Germany and the Netherlands. A recent Campbell review (Egli et al., 2009) addressed the effects on crime among addicts of administering different opiates, including methadone and heroin. Based on randomized trials, the meta-analysis suggests that opiate substitution reduced crime committed by addicts more than the administration of methadone, or therapies based on abstinence. In contrast to these results, Norway, Finland and Sweden continue to apply very restrictive policies towards narcotics, and there is substantial opposition even to needle exchange programmes. From an American point of view, the highly divergent European policies may be as interesting as the fact that substitution therapy seems basically effective in reducing crime committed by addicts.

Conclusions

We found a substantial number of longitudinal studies in 11 European countries. Many of the studies were unpublished or available only in national languages other than English. Most of these studies have found a strong impact of family malfunctioning and other problems during childhood on later offending. Less consistent are the findings regarding the causes of desistance from offending. Some studies have included social correlates of delinquency, such as unemployment, neighbourhood, and leisure-time activities, but little is known from European research about criminal career features between ages 15 and 29, and in particular to what extent the results are similar to or different from North America. Further, very little research has addressed adult-onset offending, or continuity versus discontinuity in offending from juvenile to young adult years. Finally, influences of national and legal contexts remain largely unknown.

We also found that European research is often comparative and international. This brings about (and corresponds) to a strong interest in macro-sociological factors. It supports the view that situational changes affect, to a large extent, the volume of crime across space and over time. European data collection initiatives indicate considerable differences (both within Europe and compared to the United States) in rates of homicide and types of responses to crime.

Evaluations of interventions show encouraging results for treatment, but have rarely used sound experimental methods. Research on optimal preventive interventions is largely absent but very much needed. The same is true for prediction methods. Despite their wide use, little is known to what extent predictions turn out to be accurate.

Responses to crime differ greatly across Europe, but generally are more 'soft', especially with respect to young offenders. Some of the differences in incarceration rates can be attributed to low homicide rates in Western Europe. Juvenile laws, even in Eastern Europe, are considerably more lenient, compared to the United States. It is hard to argue to what extent different 'harsh' or 'lenient' policies are effective in controlling crime rates. Again, current research does not provide answers about the effects of different age limits, sanctions and procedural arrangements for juveniles, young adults and adults on recidivism, and financial benefits (or costs) of competing approaches.

Research has focused on either juveniles (mainly minors) or crime across all age groups, but rarely on young people between the ages of 15 and 29. Much of current general knowledge applies directly to young adults, however, since most offenders known to the police, processed through the criminal justice system or imprisoned, fall into this broad age of transition from adolescence to young adulthood.

Acknowledgements

The authors express their deep thanks to Peter H. van der Laan for his valuable suggestions and support during the meetings of the study group. They also wish to thank Ana Martínez Catena (University of Barcelona), Lorenz Biberstein and Nora Markwalder (University of Zurich) for their excellent support during data collection and the preparation of this report. N. Wim Slot has offered invaluable help in locating appropriate Dutch studies.

References

Aebi, M.F. and Kuhn, A. (2000). Influences on the prisoner rate: Number of entries into prison, length of sentences and crime rates. *European Journal on Criminal Policy and Research*, 8, 65–75.

AIC National Homicide Monitoring Program, years 1989–90 to 2006–07. Found under http://www.aic.gov.au/publications/current%20series/cfi/161-180/cfi176.aspx, accessed 27 February 2012.

Alba, J.L., Burgués, M., López, J., Alcázar, M., Baró, V., Garrido, V., and López, M.J. (2007). El Programa del Pensamiento Prosocial. Versión corta para jóvenes. Tercera aplicación en medio abierto. *Boletín Criminológico*, 98, 1–4.

Albrecht, H.J. and Grundies, V. (2009). Justizielle Registrierungen in Abhängigkeit vom Alter. *Monatsschrift für Kriminologie und Strafrechtsreform*, 92, 326–43.

Andersen, S.H. (2010). Unemployment and crime: On the causal effects of intensified welfare state interventions on unemployed persons' crime rates. Paper presented at the annual meeting of the European Society of Criminology.

Baier, D., Pfeiffer, C., Simonson, J., and Rabold S. (2009). *Jugendliche in Deutschland als Opfer und Täter von Gewalt*. Hannover, GER: Kriminologisches Institut Niedersachsen.

Bakker, B.F.M., Walberg, A., and Blom, M. (2005). Jeugdige verdachten. In M. Blom, J. Oudhof, R. V. Bijl and B.F.M. Bakker (eds), *Verdacht van criminaliteit. Allochtonen en autochtonen nader bekeken. Cahier 2005-2*. The Hague: Ministerie van Justitie, Wetenschappelijk Onderzoek- en Documentatie Centrum, pp. 45–58.

Balvig, F. (2006). *Den ungdom! Om den stadigt mere omsiggribende lovlydhed blandt Unge i Danmark* (The youth! About the ever-increasing low-obedience among young people in Denmark). Copenhagen: Det Kriminalpreventive Råd.

Bergman, L.R. (2009). IDA: Individual Development and Adaptation, at http://www.oru.se/English/Research/Research-projects/project/School-of-Law-Psycology-and-Social-work/IDA-Individual-Development-and-Adaptation, accessed 6 February 2012.

Bergman, L.R. and Andershed, A. (2009). Predictors and outcomes of persistent or age-limited registered criminal behavior: A 30-year longitudinal study of a Swedish urban population. *Aggressive Behavior*, 35, 164–78.

Bock, M. (2000). *Kriminologie*. Munich: Vahlen.

Boers, K., Seddig, D., and Reinecke, J. (2009). Sozialstrukturelle Bedingungen und Delinquenz im Verlauf des Jugendalters. Analysen mit einem kombinierten Markov- und Wachstumsmodell. *Monatsschrift für Kriminologie und Strafrechtsreform*, 92, 267–88.

Bongers, I.L., Koot, H.M., Van der Ende, J., and Verhulst, F.C. (2006). Developmental trajectories of externalizing behaviors in childhood and adolescence. In A. Blokland and P. Nieuwbeerta (eds), *Developmental and Life Course Studies in Delinquency and Crime*. The Hague: Boom Juridische Uitgevers, pp. 35–52.

Born, M. (2002). Continuité de la délinquance entre l'adolescence et l'âge adulte. *Criminologie*, 35, 53–67.

BRÅ (2008). *Brottsutveckling i Sverige fram till år 2007* (Crime development in Sweden until 2007). Stockholm: Swedish National Council for Crime Prevention (Report 2008.23).

BRÅ (2010). *Brott bland ungdomar i årskurs nio. Resultat från Skolundersökningen om brott åren 1995–2008* (Crime among young people in grade nine. Results from the school survey on crime years 1995–2008). Stockholm: Swedish National Council for Crime Prevention (Report 2010: 6).

Caprara, G.V., Regalia, C., and Bandura, A. (2002). Longitudinal impact of perceived self regulatory efficacy on violent conduct. *European Psychologist*, 7, 63–69.

Caprara, G.V., Paciello, M., Gerbino, M., and Cugini, C. (2007). Individual differences conducive to aggression and violence: Trajectories and correlates of irritability and hostile rumination through adolescence. *Aggressive Behavior*, 33, 1–16.

Chabloz, J-M., Gervasoni, J-P., Arnaud, S., Dubois-Arber F., Vuille, J., and Killias M. (2010). *Monitoring de la problématique du cannabis en Suisse: Etude sentinelle 2004–2008*. Lausanne: Raisons de Santé.

Cooke, D.J. and Philip, L. (2001). To treat or not to treat? An empirical perspective. In C.R. Hollin (ed.), *Handbook of Offenders Assessement and Treatment*. Chichester: Wiley, pp. 17–34.

Cullen, F.T. and Gendreau, P. (2006). Evaluación de la rehabilitación correccional: política, práctica y perspectivas. In R. Barberet and J. Barquín (eds), *Justicia penal siglo XXI: Una selección de Criminal Justice 2000*. Granada: Editorial Comares, pp. 275–348.

Doerner, W.G. (1988). The impact of medical resources on criminally induced lethality. *Criminology*, 26, 171–9.

Donker, A.G., Smeenk, W.H., Van der Laan, P.H., and Verhulst, F.C. (2003). Individual stability of antisocial behavior from childhood to adulthood: Testing the stability postulate of Moffitt's developmental theory. *Criminology*, 41, 593–609.

Dowden, C. and Andrews, D.A. (2000). Effective correctional treatment and violent reoffending: A meta-analysis, *Canadian Journal of Criminology*, 42, 449–67.

Egli, N., Pina, M., Skovbo Christensen, P., Aebi, M.F. and Killias M. (2009). Effects of drug substitution programs on offending among drug-addicts: The Campbell Collaboration. At http://www.campbellcollaboration.org, accessed 6 February 2012.

Eisner, M., Ribeaud, D., Jünger, R. and Meidert, U. (2007). *Frühprävention von Gewalt und Aggression; Ergebnisse des Zürcher Interventions- und Präventionsprojektes an Schulen*. Zürich: Rüegger Verlag.

Endrass, J., Rossegger, A., Noll, T. and Urbaniok, F. (2008). Wirksamkeit von Therapien bei Gewalt- und Sexualstraftätern. *Psychiatrische Praxis*, 35, 8–14.

Entorf, H. and Spengler, H. (2008). Is being soft on crime the solution to rising crime rates? Evidence from Germany, IZA Discussion Paper No 3710 (University of Frankfurt, Department of Economics).

Enzmann, D., Marshall I., Killias. M., Junger-Tas, J., Steketee, M. and Grusczynska, B. (2010). Self-reported youth delinquency in Europe and

beyond: First results of the second international self-report delinquency study in the context of police and victimization data. *European Journal of Criminology*, 7, 159–83.
ESB (2003). European sourcebook of crime and criminal justice statistics – 2003 (2nd edn). The Hague: Boom Juridische Uitgevers. At www.europeansourcebook.org, accessed 6 February 2012.
ESB (2006). European sourcebook of crime and criminal justice statistics – 2006 (3rd edn). The Hague: Boom Juridische Uitgevers. At www.europeansourcebook.org, accessed 6 February 2012.
ESB (2010). European Sourcebook of Crime and Criminal Justice Statistics (4th edn). The Hague: Boom Juridische Uitgevers. At www.europeansourcebook.org, accessed 6 February 2012.
Esbensen, F.A. and Lynskey, D.P. (2001). Young gang members in a school survey. In M.W. Klein, H-J. Kerner, C.L. Maxson and E.G.M. Weitekamp (eds), *The Eurogang Paradox*. Amsterdam: Kluwer Academic, pp. 93–114.
Esbensen, F.A. and Weerman, F. (2005). Youth gangs and troublesome youth groups in the United States and the Netherlands: A cross-national comparison. *European Journal of Criminology*, 2, 5–37.
Exadaktylos, A.K., Häuselmann, S., and Zimmermann, H. (2007). Are times getting tougher? A six-year survey of urban violence-related injuries in a Swiss university hospital. *Swiss Medical Weekly*, 37, 525–30.
Falshaw, L., Friendship, C., Travers, R., and Nugent, F. (2004). Searching for 'What Works': HM Prison Service accredited cognitive skills programmes. *The British Journal of Forensic Practice*, 6, 3–13.
Farrington, D.P., Ttofi, M.M., and Coid, J.W. (2009). Development of adolescence-limited, late onset, and persistent offenders from age 8 to age 48. *Aggressive Behavior*, 35, 150–63.
Garrett, P. (1985). Effects of residential treatment of adjudicated delinquents: A meta-analysis. *Journal of Research in Crime & Delinquency*, 22, 287–308.
Garrido, V., Anyela Morales, L., and Sháncez-Meca, J. (2006). What works for serious juvenile offenders? A systematic review. *Psicothema*, 18, 611–19.
Gavray, C. (1997). Trajectoire déviante à la lisière entre adolescence et âge adulte. *Déviance et Société*, 21, 273–88.
Gendreau, P., Goggin, C., and Cullen, F.T. (1999). *The Effects of Prison Sentences on Recidivism*. Ottawa: Solicitor General of Canada.
Gerris, J.R.M, Vermulst, A.A., Van Boxtel, D.A.A.M., Janssens, J.M.A.M., Van Zutphen, R.A.H., and Felling, A.J.A. (1993). *Parenting in Dutch Families: A Representative Description of Dutch Family Life in Terms of Validated Concepts Representing Characteristics of Parents, Children, the Family as a System and Parental Socio-cultural Value Orientations*. Nijmegen: Institute of Family Studies, University of Nijmegen.
Glueck, S. and Glueck, E. (1950). *Unraveling Juvenile Delinquency*. New York: Commonwealth Fund.

Göppinger, H. (1985). *Angewandte Kriminologie. Ein Leitfaden für die Praxis*. Berlin: Springer.

Grietens, H. and Hellinckx, W. (2004). Evaluating effects of residential treatment for juvenile offenders by statistical metaanalysis: A review. *Aggression and Violent Behavior*, 9, 401–15.

Haas, H. (2001). *Agressions et victimisations: Une enquête sur les délinquants violents et sexuels non détectés*. Aarau: Sauerländer.

Haas, H. and Killias, M. (2001). L'assistance sociale – un moyen pour prévenir la délinquance? In G. Étienne, J-L. Chaléard and A. Dubresson (eds), *Mélanges en l'honneur de Jean-Louis Duc*. Lausanne: IRAL-UNIL, pp. 157–70.

Haas, H. and Killias, M. (2003). The versatility vs specialization debate: Different theories of crime in the light of a Swiss birth cohort. In C. Britt and M. Gottfredson (eds), *Control Theories of Crime and Delinquency*. New Brunswick, NJ: Transaction, pp. 249–73.

Haas, H., Farrington, D.P., Killias, M., and Sattar, G. (2004). The impact of different family configurations on delinquency. *British Journal of Criminology*, 44, 520–32.

Hällsten, M., Sarnecki, J., and Szulkin, R. (2010). *Crime as a Price for Inequality? The Delinquency Gap between Children of Immigrants and Children to Native Swedes*. Stockholm: SULCIS, Stockholm University.

Harris, A.R., Thomas, S.H., Fisher, G.A., and Hirsch D.J. (2002). Murder and medicine: The lethality of criminal assault 1960–1999. *Homicide Studies*, 6, 128–66.

Haymoz, S. and Gatti, U. (2010). Girl members of deviant youth groups, offending behavior and victimization: Results from the ISRD2 in Italy and Switzerland. *European Journal on Criminal Policy and Research*, 16, 167–82.

Heinz, W. (1994). Verfahrensrechtliche Entkriminalisierung (Diversion) im Jugendstrafrecht: Zielsetzungen, Implementation und Evaluation. *Neue Kriminalpolitik*, 6, 29–36.

Heinz, W. (2005). Zahlt sich Milde wirklich aus? Diversion und ihre Bedeutung für die Sanktionspraxis, Teil 1, *Zeitschrift für Jugendkriminalrecht und Jugendhilfe*, 16, 166–78, 302–12.

Hibell B., Guttormsson U., Ahlström S., Balakireva O., Bjarnason T., Kokkevi, A., and Kraus, L. (2009). *The 2007 ESPAD Report: Substance Use Among Students in 35 European Countries*. Council of Europe (Pompidou Group).

Hoeve, M. (2008). *Parenting and Juvenile Delinquency*. Nijmegen: Radboud University (Ph.D. dissertation).

Hoeve, M., Smeenk, W.H., Loeber, R., Stouthamer-Loeber, M., Van der Laan, P.H., Gerris, J.R.M., and Dubas, J.S. (2006). Long-term effects of parenting and family characteristics on delinquency of male young adults. In A. Blokland and P. Nieuwbeerta (eds), *Developmental and Life Course Studies in Delinquency and Crime*. The Hague: Boom Juridische Uitgevers, pp. 209–32.

Hollin, C.R. (2001). To treat or not to treat? An historical perspective. In C.R. Hollin (ed.), *Handbook of Offender Assessment and Treatment*. Chichester: Wiley, pp. 3–15.

Hollin, C.R. and Palmer, E.J. (2006). Offending behavior programmes: History and development. In C.R. Hollin and E.J. Palmer (eds), *Offending Behavior Programmes*. Chichester: Wiley, pp. 1–32.

Hood, R. (1992). *Race and Sentencing: A Study in the Crown Court*. Oxford: Clarendon.

ICVS. International Crime Victimization Survey. At http://rechten.uvt.nl/icvs/, accessed 6 February 2012.

Instituto de la Mujer (2006). Macroencuesta 'Violencia contra las mujeres' (Violence against women) (2002–2006). At www.inmujer.es, accessed 6 February 2012.

Israel, M. and Hong, W. (2006). If 'something works' is the answer, what is the question? Supporting pluralist evaluation in community corrections in the United Kingdom. *European Journal of Criminology*, 3, 181–200.

Janson, C-G. (1975). *Project Metropolitan: A Presentation*. Project Metropolitan Research Report No. 1. Stockholm.

Janson, C-G. (1984). *Project Metropolitan: A Presentation and Progress Report*. Stockholm: University of Stockholm, Department of Sociology.

Janson, C-G. (1995). *On Project Metropolitan and the Longitudinal Perspective*. Project Metropolitan Research Report No. 40. Stockholm.

Jennissen, R. (2009). *Criminaliteit, leeftijd en etniciteit* (Crime, age and ethnicity). The Hague: WODC (Onderzoek en Beleid 277).

Johnson, H., Ollus, N. and Nevala, S. (2008). *Violence against Women: An International Perspective*. New York: Springer.

Junger, M. (1989). Discrepancies between police and self-report data for Dutch racial minorities. *British Journal of Criminology*, 29, 273–83.

Junger, M., Wittebrood, K. and Timman, R. (2001). Etniciteit en ernstig en gewelddadig crimineel gedrag. In R. Loeber, N.W. Slot and J.A. Sergeant (eds), *Ernstige en gewelddadige jeugddelinquentie: Omvang, oorzaken, en interventies*. Houten: Bohn Stafleu en Van Loghum, pp. 97–129.

Junger-Tas, J. and Dünkel, F. (eds) (2009). *Reforming Juvenile Justice*. New York: Springer.

Junger-Tas, J., Terlouw G-J. and Klein, M. (eds) (1994). *Delinquent Behavior of Young People in the Western World*. Amsterdam: Kugler.

Junger-Tas, J., Marshall, I., Enzmann, D., Killias, M., Gruszczynska, B. and Steketee, M. (2010). *Juvenile Delinquency in Europe and Beyond: Results of the Second International Self-report Delinquency Study*. New York: Springer.

Junger-Tas, J., Marshall, I.H., Enzmann, D., Killias, M., Gruszczynska, B. and Stekeete, M. (2012). *The Many Faces of Youth Crime*. New York: Springer.

Kardell, J. and Carlsson, K.M. (2009). Lagföringar av invandrare och invandrares barn i de olika nordiska länderna. *Nordisk tidskrift for kriminalvidenskab*, 96, 237–61.

Kazemian, L. and Farrington, D.P. (2006). Exploring residual career length and residual number of offenses for two generations of repeat offenders. *Journal of Research in Crime and Delinquency*, 43, 89–113.

Kazemian, L., Farrington, D.P. and Le Blanc, M. (2009). Can we make accurate long-term predictions about patterns of de-escalation in offending behavior? *Journal of Youth and Adolescence*, 38, 384–400.

Keizer, K., Lindenberg, S., and Steg, L. (2008). The spreading of disorder. *Science*, 322, 1681–85.

Killias, M. (2009). Paradise lost? New trends in crime and migration in Switzerland. In W.F. McDonald (ed.), *Immigration, Crime and Justice*. Bingley: Emerald, pp. 33–45.

Killias, M., Maljevic, A. and Lucia, S. (2010). Imported violence? Juvenile delinquency among Balkan youths in Switzerland and in Bosnia-Herzegovina. *European Journal of Criminal Policy and Research*, 16, 183–9.

Killias, M., Isenring, G., Gilliéron, G. and Vuille, J. (2011). Do changing policies have an impact on cannabis markets? A natural experiment in Switzerland 2000–2010. *European Journal of Criminology*, 8, 171–86.

Killias, M., Markwalder, N., Walser, S., and Dilitz, C. (2009). *Homicide and Suicide in Switzerland over Twenty Years (1980–2004): A Study Based on Forensic Medicine, Police and Court Files*. Report to the Swiss National Science Foundation n°101312–104167/1.

Kivivuori, J. (2001). Patterns of criminal homicide in Finland 1960–1997. In T. Lappi-Seppälä (ed.), *Homicide in Finland: Trends and Patterns in Historical and Comparative Perspective*. National Research Institute of Legal Policy, Publication 181, Helsinki. National Violent Death Reporting System (NVDRS).

Kivivuori, J. and Lehti, M. (2003). Homicide followed by suicide in Finland: Trend and social locus. *Journal of Scandinavian Studies in Criminology and Crime Prevention*, 4, 223–36.

Kivivuori, J. and Salmi, V. (2006). Trends of self-reported juvenile delinquency in Finland, 1995–2004. In E. Mykkänen (ed.), *Research Report Summaries 2005*. Helsinki: National Research Institute of Legal Policy, pp. 9–16.

Klein, M.W. (1995). *The American Street Gang: Its Nature, Prevalence, and Control*. New York: Oxford University Press.

Kokko, K. and Pulkkinen, L. (2000). Aggression in childhood and long-term unemployment in adulthood: A cycle of maladaptation and some protective factors. *Developmental Psychology*, 36, 463–72.

Kuppens, S., Grietens, H., Onghena, P. and Michiels, D. (2009). Relations between parental psychological control and childhood relational aggression: Reciprocal in Nature? *Journal of Clinical Child and Adolescent Psychology*, 38, 117–31.

Kyvsgaard, B. (2003). *The Criminal Career: The Danish Longitudinal Study*. Cambridge: Cambridge University Press.

Lanfranconi, B. (2009). *Gewalt unter jungen Menschen. Diskussionsbeitrag auf Basis der Daten der Unfallversicherung nach UVG*. Luzern: SUVA. At http://www.unfallstatistik.ch/d/publik/artikel/pdf/Gewalt_d.pdf, accessed 27 February 2012.

Laubacher, A., Rossegger, A., Endrass, J., Angst, J., Urbaniok, F. and Vetter, S. (in press). Adolescent delinquency and antisocial tendencies as precursors to adult violent offending: A prospective study of a representative sample of Swiss men. *Journal of Offender Therapy and Comparative Criminology*.

Leistra, G. and Nieuwbeerta, P. (2003). *Moord en doodslag in Nederland 1992–2001*. Amsterdam: Elsevier/NCSR.

Lenke, L. (1990). Alcohol and criminal violence: Time series analyses in a comparative perspective. Stockholm: Almqvist & Wiksell International.

Liem, M., Barber, C., Markwalder, N., Killias, M. and Nieuwbeerta, P. (2011). Homicide-suicide and other violent deaths in three countries. *Forensic Science International*, 207, 70–76.

Lipsey, M.W. and Wilson, D.B. (1998). Effective intervention for serious juvenile offenders: A synthesis of research. In R. Loeber and D.P. Farrington (eds), *Serious and Violent Juvenile Offenders: Risk Factors and Successful Interventions*. Thousand Oaks, CA: Sage, pp. 313–45.

Lösel, F. (1995). The efficacy of correctional treatment: A review and synthesis of metaevaluations. In J. McGuire (ed.), *What Works: Reducing Reoffending*. Chichester: Wiley, 79–111.

Lösel, F. (1996). What recent meta-evaluations tell us about the effectiveness of correctional treatment. In G. Davies, S. Lloyd-Bostock, M. MacMurran and C. Wilson (eds), *Psychology, Law, and Criminal Justice: International Developments in Research and Practice*. Berlin: De Gruyter, pp. 537–56.

Lösel, F. (1998). Treatment and management of psychopaths. In D.J. Cooke, A.E. Forth and R.D. Hare (eds), *Psychopathy: Theory, Research and Implications for Society*. Dordrecht: Kluwer, pp. 303–54.

Lösel, F. (2000). The efficacy of sexual offender treatment: A brief review of German and international evaluations. In P.J. van Koppen and N. Roos (eds), *Rationality, Information and Progress in Law and Psychology*. Maastricht: Metajuridica, 145–70.

Lösel, F. and Köferl, P. (1989). Evaluation research on correctional treatment in West Germany: A meta-analysis. In H. Wegener, F. Lösel and J. Haisch (eds), *Criminal Behavior and the Justice System*. New York: Springer, 334–55.

Lucia, S. and Killias, M. (2011). Gewalt und belastende Kindheitserlebnisse. Neue Aspekte anhand der internationalen Self-report-Studie (ISRD-2). *Trauma und Gewalt*, 5(1), 36–43.

Lucia, S. and Killias, M. (2012). School systems and their effects on delinquency. In J. Junger-Tas, I.H. Marshall, D. Enzmann, M. Killias, B. Gruszczynska and M. Stekeete (eds), *The Many Faces of Youth Crime*. New York: Springer.

Luengo, M.A., Carrillo-de-la-Peña, M.T., Otero, J.M. and Romero, E. (1994). A short-term longitudinal study of impulsivity and antisocial behavior. *Journal of Personality and Social Psychology*, 66, 542–48.

Lussier, P., Farrington, D.P. and Moffitt, T.E. (2009). Is the antisocial child father of the abusive man? A 40-year prospective longitudinal study on the developmental antecedents of intimate partner violence. *Criminology*, 47, 741–79.

McAra, L. (2004). Truancy, school exclusion and substance misuse. *Edinburgh Study of Youth Transitions and Crime Research Digest*, 4.

McGuire, J. (2004). Commentary: Promising answers and the next generation of questions. *Psychology, Crime & Law*, 10, 335–45.

Meeus, W. and 't Hart, H. (1993). *Jongeren in Nederland*. Amersfoort: Academische Uitgeverij.

Meeus, W., Branje, S. and Overbeek, G. (2004). Parents and partners in crime: A six-year longitudinal study on changes in supportive relationships and delinquency in adolescence and young adulthood. In A. Blokland and P. Nieuwbeerta (eds), *Developmental and Life Course Studies in Delinquency and Crime*. The Hague: Boom Juridische Uitgevers, pp. 307–21.

Meeus, W., Rie, S. de la, Luijpers, E., and Wilde, E. (2001). De harde kern; ernstige gewelddadige en persistente jeugdcriminaliteit in Nederland. In R. Loeber, N.W. Slot and J.A. Sergeant (eds), *Ernstig gewelddadige jeugddelinquentie: Omvang, oorzaken en interventies*. Houten: Bohn, Stafleu, Van Loghum, pp. 51–73.

Mouzos, J. and Rushforth, C. (2003). Family homicide in Australia. *Trends and Issues in Crime and Criminal Justice*, 255. Canberra: Australian Institute of Criminology.

Murray, J. and Farrington, D.P. (2005). Parental imprisonment: Effects on boys' antisocial behavior and delinquency through the life-course. *Journal of Child Psychology and Psychiatry*, 46, 1269–78.

Nationale Drug Monitor (2010). *Jaarbericht 2009*. Utrecht: Trimbos-Instituut/The Hague: WODC.

Nieuwbeerta, P. and Leistra, G. (2007). *Lethal Violence: Homicide in the Netherlands 1992–2006*. Amsterdam: Prometheus.

Nilsson, A. and Estrada, F. (2009). *Criminality and Life-chances: A Longitudinal Study of Crime, Childhood Circumstances and Living Conditions*. Department of Criminology, Report series 2009: 3. Stockholm: Stockholm University.

Olweus, D. (2011). Bullying at school and later criminality: Findings from three Swedish community samples of males. *Criminal Behaviour and Mental Health*, 21, 151–6.

Ortmann, R. (2000). The effectiveness of social therapy in prison: A randomized experiment. *Crime and Delinquency*, 46, 214–32.

Paciello, M., Fida, R., Tramontano, C., Lupinetti, C., and Caprara, G.V. (2008). Stability and change of moral disengagement and its impact on aggression and violence over the course of adolescence. *Child Development*, 79, 1288–309.

Papadakaki, M., Tzamalouka, G., Chatzifotiou, S., and Chlioutakis, J. (2009). Seeking for risk factors of intimate partner violence (IPV) in a Greek national sample. *Journal of Interpersonal Violence*, 24, 732–50.

Pitkänen, T., Lyyra A-L., and Pulkkinen, L. (2005). Age of onset of drinking and the use of alcohol in adulthood: A follow-up study from age 8–42 for females and males. *Addiction*, 100, 652–61.

Pulkkinen, L. and Hämäläinen, M. (1995). Low self-control as a precursor to crime and accidents in a Finnish longitudinal study. *Criminal Behaviour and Mental Health*, 5, 424–38.

Rabold, S. and Baier, D. (2007). Delinquentes Verhalten von Jugendlichen. Zur differentiellen Bedeutsamkeit verschiedener Bedingungsfaktoren. *Kriminalsoziologie + Rechtssoziologie*, 2, 9–42.

Redondo, S. and Sánchez Meca, J. (2003). Guía de tratamientos psicológicos eficaces para la delincuencia juvenil. In M. Pérez, J.R. Fernández Hermida, C. Fernández Rodríguez and I. Amigo Vázquez (eds), *Guía de tratamientos psicológicos eficaces III. Infancia y adolescencia*. Madrid: Pirámide, pp. 183–21.

Redondo, S., Garrido, V. and Sánchez-Meca, J. (1997). What works in correctional rehabilitation in Europe: A meta-analytic review. In S. Redondo, V. Garrido, J. Pérez and R. Barberet (eds), *Advances in Psychology and Law: International Contributions*. Berlin: De Gruyter, pp. 499–523.

Redondo, S., Sánchez-Meca J. and Garrido, V. (1999). Tratamiento de los delincuentes y reincidencia: Una evaluación de la efectividad de los programas aplicados en Europa. *Anuario de Psicología Jurídica*, 9, 11–37.

Redondo, S., Cano, A., Álvarez, M. and Antequera, M. (2008). Estudio de eficacia del Programa de Intervención para la Mejora del Autocontrol y la Assertivitat en Jóvenes con Medidas Judiciales en Medio Abierto. Memoria de investigación no publicada, Departamento de Personalidad, Evaluación y Tratamientos Psicológicos.

Remschmidt, H. and Walter, R. (2009). *Kinderdelinquenz: Gesetzesverstösse Strafmündiger und ihre Folgen*. Heidelberg: Springer.

Ross, R. and Fabiano, E.A. (1985). *Time to Think: A Cognitive Model of Delinquency Prevention and Offender Rehabilitation*. Johnson City, TN: Institute of Social Sciences and Arts.

Saar, J. (2003). Later criminal careers of occupants of juvenile reformatory and penal institutions. *Juridica International*, 8, 100–9.

Sarnecki, J. (1985). *Predicting Social Maladjustment: Stockholm Boys Grown up*. Stockholm: Brottsförebyggande rådet (National Council for Crime Prevention).

Sarnecki, J. (2001). *Delinquent Networks: Youth co-offending in Stockholm*. Cambridge: Cambridge University Press.

Sarnecki, J. (2009a). Delinquent networks: Youth co-offending. In H.J. Schneider (ed.), *Internationales Handbuch der Kriminologie* (vol. 2, pp. 995–1023). Berlin: De Gruyter Recht.

Sarnecki, J. (2009b). *Introduktion till kriminologi (Introduction to Criminology)*. Lund: Studentlitteratur.

Schmidt, M.H., Esser, G., Ihle, W. and Lay, B. (2009). Die Bedeutung psychischer und familiärer Faktoren für die Delinquenzentwicklung bis ins

Erwachsenenalter. *Monatsschrift für Kriminologie und Strafrechtsreform*, 92, 174–84.
Schumann, K.F., Huizinga, D., Ehret, B. and Elliott, A. (2009). Cross-national findings about the effect of job training, gangs and juvenile justice reactions on delinquent behavior and desistance. *Monatsschrift für Kriminologie und Strafrechtsreform*, 92, 308–25.
Shah, R. and Pease, K. (1992). Crime, race and reporting to the police. *The Howard Journal*, 31, 192–99.
Smith, D.J. (2004a). Parenting and delinquency at ages 12 to 15. *Edinburgh Study of Youth Transitions and Crime Research Digest*, 3.
Smith, D.J. (2004b). The links between victimization and offending. *Edinburgh Study of Youth Transitions and Crime Research Digest*, 5.
Smith, D.J. (2006a). School experience and delinquency at ages 13 to 16. *Edinburgh Study of Youth Transitions and Crime Research Digest*, 13.
Smith, D.J. (2006b). Social inclusion and early desistance from crime. *Edinburgh Study of Youth Transitions and Crime Research Digest*, 12.
Smith, D.J. and Ecob, R. (2007). An investigation of causal links between victimization and offending in adolescents. *British Journal of Sociology*, 58, 633–59.
Soothill, K., Ackerley, E. and Francis, B. (2003). The persistent offenders debate: A focus on temporal changes. *Criminal Justice*, 3, 389–412.
Statistics Canada (2000–2004). At http://www.statcan.ca, accessed 6 February 2012.
Statistics Canada (2005). Family violence in Canada: A statistical profile. *Canadian Centre for Justice Statistics*, years 1961–2003, 60.
Staubli, S. and Killias, M. (2011). Long-term outcomes of passive bullying during childhood: Suicide attempts, victimization and offending. *European Journal of Criminology*, 8(5), 377–85.
Stenberg, S. and Vagerö, D. (2006). Cohort profile: The Stockholm birth cohort of 1953. *International Journal of Epidemiology*, 35, 546–48.
Stenberg, S., Vagerö, D., Österman, R., Von Otter, C. and Janson, C. (2007). Stockholm Birth Cohort Study 1953–2003: A new tool for life-course studies. *Scandinavian Journal of Public Health*, 35, 104–10.
Stump, B. (2003). *Adult Tme for Adult Crime*. Mönchengladbach: Forum Bad Godesberg.
Supplementary Homicide Reports (1976–2003). U.S. Department of Justice. Office of Justice Programs. Bureau of Justice Statistics.
Tavares C. and Thomas, G. (2008). Crime and criminal justice. *Statistics in Focus*, 19, *Eurostat*.
Timmermans, M. (2009). Antisocial behaviors: Courses and consequences from toddlerhood to late adolescence. Amsterdam: Vrije University (Ph.D. dissertation).
Tong, L.S. and Farrington, D.P. (2006). How effective is the 'Reasoning and Rehabilitation' programme in reducing reoffending? A meta-analysis of evaluations in four countries. *Psychology, Crime & Law*, 12, 3–24.

Tonry, M. (1997). *Ethnicity, Crime, and Immigration: Comparative and Cross-national Perspectives* (vol. 21, pp. 1–29). Chicago, IL: University of Chicago Press.

Van Dijk, J., Van Kestern, J. and Smit P. (2007). Criminal victimization in international perspective: Key findings from the 2004–2005 ICVS and EU ICS. The Hague: Boom.

Verhulst, F.C., Akkerhuis, G.W., and Althaus, M. (1985). Mental health in Dutch children: (1) A cross-cultural comparison. *Acta Psychiatrica Scandinavica*, 323, 1–108.

Villettaz, P., Killias, M., and Zoder, I. (2006). The effects of custodial vs non-custodial sanctions on re-offending: A systematic review of the state of knowledge. The Campbell Collaboration. At http://www.campbellcollaboration.org, accessed 6 February 2012.

Von Hofer, H. (2011). Punishment and crime in Scandinavia 1750–2008. In M. Tonry and T. Lappi-Seppala (eds), *Crime and Justice in Scandanavia* (vol. 40, pp. 33–107). Chicago, IL: Chicago University Press.

Wikström, P-O. (1998). Communities and crime. In M. Tonry (ed.), *The Handbook of Crime and Punishment*. Oxford: Oxford University Press.

Wikström, P-O. (2009). Crime propensity, criminogenic exposure and crime involvement in early to mid adolescence. *Monatsschrift fur Kriminologie und Strafrechtsreform*, 92, 253–66.

Wikström, P-O. and Svensson, R. (2008). Why are English youths more violent than Swedish youths? *European Journal of Criminology*, 5, 309–30.

Wikström, P-O., Ceccato, V., Hardie, B., and Treiber, K. (2010). Activity fields and the dynamics of crime: Advancing knowledge about the role of the environment in crime causation. *Journal of Quantitative Criminology*, 26, 55–87.

Wittebrood, K. and Nieuwbeerta, P. (2006). Een kwart eeuw stijging in geregistreerde criminaliteit. Vooral meer registratie, nauwelijks meer criminaliteit. *Tijdschrift voor Criminologie*, 48, 227–42.

Zara, G. and Farrington, D.P. (2009). Childhood and adolescent predictors of late onset criminal careers. *Journal of Youth and Adolescence*, 38, 287–300.

Chapter 12
Overview, Conclusions, and Policy and Research Recommendations

Rolf Loeber, Machteld Hoeve, David P. Farrington,
James C. Howell, N. Wim Slot and Peter H. van der Laan

The preceding chapters by members of the Dutch Study Group on Transitions between Juvenile Delinquency and Adult Crime have advanced the field in many different ways. The following summaries of the chapters also include additional information from the US Study Group report on the transition between juvenile delinquency and adult crime (Loeber and Farrington, 2012). Because the following text is integrative and overarching, it occasionally contains new information that is not to be found in the preceding chapters.

Section I summarizes the most important points of Chapters 2 to 5 and relevant portions of Chapter 11 (which concerns European issues) by addressing key findings that are relevant for juveniles' transition of offending from adolescence (up to age 18) into adulthood. Section I focuses also on: (1) criminal careers including criminal careers of special categories of offenders (for example, drug dealers, homicide offenders); (2) explanations of persistence and desistance across adolescence and early adulthood; and (3) vulnerable populations.

Section II deals with practical issues and covers Chapters 6 to 10 and relevant portions of Chapter 11. The section focuses on six topics: (1) prediction and risk assessments to ascertain the risk of recidivism during the transition period between adolescence and adulthood; (2) legal boundaries between adolescence and adulthood and whether they need to be changed; (3) justice systems responses for juveniles and young adults; (4) preventive and remedial interventions outside of the justice system; (5) gender issues; and (6) ethnic minorities. Finally, Section III of this chapter contains the headlines, conclusions, and policy and research recommendations.

Section I: Criminal Careers, Explanatory Processes and Vulnerable Populations

The first set of overarching questions in Section I concerns criminal careers: How common is persistence in and desistance from offending between adolescence and early adulthood, and how common is the onset of offending during early adulthood? The second set of major questions asks: What explains persistence in and desistance from offending during the transition between adolescence and early adulthood, and what explains the onset of offending during early adulthood? The third question poses: How well does persistence in and desistance from offending during the transition between adolescence and adulthood map onto the minimum legal age of adulthood (i.e., age 18 in most countries)?

The three sets of questions, in conjunction with assessment, legal and intervention questions addressed in Section II, are essential for establishing whether a period called 'emerging adulthood' should be designated (Arnett, 2000), in which the judicial rules should apply more as they do in adolescence than as in adulthood. Particularly relevant to the discussion around 'emerging adulthood' is whether most offending in late adolescence is of short duration and naturally declines; whether legislation should be changed as a result of growing knowledge about adolescent maturation; whether long judicial sentences overreach the natural occurring decline in offending and consequently are unnecessary and are wasting scarce prison resources and taxes (discussed in Section II); and which vulnerable groups are cognitively less competent and take a longer time than others to cognitively mature and outgrow delinquency.

I.1 Criminal Career Patterns, the Age–Crime Curve, and Persistence/Desistance During the Transition between Adolescence and Early Adulthood

We shall first review findings on criminal careers between adolescence and early adulthood based on several major longitudinal data sets on the development of offending between ages 15 and 29 (the review is based on Blokland and Palmen, Chapter 2, this volume; Bijleveld, Van der Geest and Hendriks, Chapter 5, this volume; Piquero, Hawkins and Kazemian, 2012; and Rosenfeld, White and Esbensen, 2012). The criminal career parameters that are most relevant are prevalence and frequency, persistence and desistance, escalation and specialization, and types of criminal careers from adolescence to early adulthood.

How does the Prevalence of Offending Change between Adolescence and Early Adulthood?

Blokland and Palmen (Chapter 2, this volume) showed that the prevalence of delinquency increases from late childhood, peaks in the teenage years (around ages 15–19), and then declines in the early 20s, which is consistent with the international literature. This age trend is called the *age–crime curve* (Farrington, 1986; Piquero, Farrington and Blumstein, 2007, Fig. 8.1), which is universal in known populations of youth.

However, age–crime curves may vary in significant ways. For example, the age–crime curve for violence tends to peak later than that for property crime (Blokland and Palmen, Chapter 2, this volume; Piquero, Hawkins and Kazemian, 2012). Studies also show that the age–crime curve for girls peaks earlier than for boys (Blokland and Palmen, Chapter 2, this volume; Farrington, 1986; Elliott, Pampel and Huizinga, 2005). The curve is also higher and wider for young males (especially minorities) growing up in the most disadvantaged than in advantaged neighbourhoods (Fabio, Cohen and Loeber, 2011; Elliott, Pampel and Huizinga, 2004).

Important for our understanding of the transition between adolescence and adulthood is the right-hand tail of the age–crime curve. The higher and longer that tail, the more this indicates that there is a population of youth who may not have outgrown delinquency or who may have started offending during adulthood (see below). In the Netherlands, the prevalence of offending – as evident from official records – is higher in early adulthood than in adolescence or later adulthood (see Blokland and Palmen, Chapter 2, this volume; Van der Laan et al., Chapter 8, this volume). It should be understood, however, that the typical age–crime curve is a cross-sectional prevalence curve and not an indicator of individuals' persistence or desistance in offending. Information about persistence and desistance derives from longitudinal follow-up data and is the key to understanding age-normative vs delayed outgrowing of delinquency (see below).

There are several other caveats about the age–crime curve that may influence conclusions drawn from it. For example, self-reported delinquency shows an earlier peak than official records (Blokland and Palmen, Chapter 2, this volume; Piquero, Hawkins and Kazemian, 2012). This may reflect the fact that juvenile offending at a young age (as evident from self-reports) may not be identified by the police or there may be a delay in arrest; and as a consequence, these offences remain undetected in official records until a later age (Piquero, Hawkins and Kazemian, 2012). Another important methodological caveat is that most published age–crime curves based on official records consist of aggregate data from different age cohorts. Only the follow-up of the same participants in longitudinal data can provide us with an estimation of the age–crime curve independent of cohort effects (see for example, Loeber et al., 2008).

In summary, the down-slope of the age–crime curve varies between different populations of young people, but it often extends from adolescence to adulthood. It is important to realize that the majority of serious forms of crime – including violence – take place in the period of the down-slope of the age–crime curve. Since most of the violence is directed at same-age victims, it is not surprising that the age period 16–24 is also a high-risk period for violent victimization (for example, Kershaw, Nicholas and Walker, 2008; Truman and Rand, 2010).

All available age–crime curves show that the legal age of adulthood at 18 (or for that matter ages 16 or 17) is not characterized by a sharp change (or decrease) in offending at exactly that age and has no specific relevance to the down-slope of the age–crime curve. Instead, research shows a steady increase in the number of active offenders between ages 12 and 23 (Blokland and Palmen, Chapter 2, this volume; Piquero, Hawkins and Kazemian, 2012).

What is the Typical Age of Onset of Specific Categories of Offences?

It is important to establish which types of delinquent acts on average emerge during the transition between adolescence and early adulthood. Unfortunately, in the Netherlands data on the onset of delinquency careers of special categories of offenders is very scarce. Bijleveld, Van der Geest and Hendriks (Chapter 5, this volume) found that the peak age of offending for sex offenders was age 14, which was also the average age at which sex offences were committed.

Findings from the US Study Group reported by Rosenfeld, White and Esbensen (2012) on special categories of offenders (homicide offenders, gang members, drug dealers, and those carrying weapons) revealed that on average the age of onset of gang membership, drug use, weapon carrying and drug dealing occurred during adolescence (ages 13–17). They also summarized the sequences of the average ages of onset among major categories of offences. The average age of onset sequence was first gang membership (15.9), followed by marijuana use (16.5), drug dealing (17.0), gun carrying (17.3) and hard drug use (17.5). Other studies also support the finding that the onset of gang membership mostly occurs early rather than late in adolescence. A large majority of youths who join gangs do so typically between ages 11–15, and ages 14–16 are the peak ages for gang involvement (Howell, 2011). In contrast, most homicides are single events and are committed in the 19–24 age window. It should be noted, however, that the age of onset of homicide and other serious delinquent acts may cover a wide range. For instance, about one quarter of the onset of drug dealing recorded in the Pittsburgh Youth Study (PYS) took place during early adulthood (ages 18–25).

How does the Frequency of Offending (by Active Offenders) Vary from Adolescence to Early Adulthood?

Piquero et al. (2012) concluded that the annual frequency of offending is higher for non-violent rather than violent forms of delinquency. The frequency of offending usually peaks round ages 17–19, and remains stable only among a small number of offenders over time (this is because most criminal careers are only 5 to 10 years in duration). However, Blokland and Palmen (Chapter 2, this volume) found that the average frequency of offending was stable over time, as Blumstein et al. (1986) have argued.

How does Co-offending Vary from Adolescence to Early Adulthood?

Criminologists rightly have stressed that much offending during the juvenile years occurs in the company of others (Reiss and Farrington, 1991). At the same time, it is clear that changes in co-offending occur, particularly during the transition years between adolescence and adulthood. Piquero, Hawkins and Kazemian (2012) reviewed the literature and concluded that there were few empirical studies for that period, especially studies based on self-reported delinquency. Using official data from the Cambridge Study in Delinquent Development in South London, Piquero, Farrington and Blumstein (2007) found that, like the age–crime curve, the age–co-offending curve peaked in the late teenage years. The results also showed that the frequency of co-offending decreased with age primarily because individual offenders changed and became less likely to offend with others (not because group offenders dropped out). Just over half of the total crimes committed by persistent offenders (those males who had each committed at least ten offences by age 40) were committed alone. Thus, co-offending is typical during the adolescent to early adult years, but tends to decrease subsequently and change to solo offending.

To What Extent is there Adult-onset of Offending Between Ages 18 and 29?

Blokland and Palmen (Chapter 2, this volume) found, at least judging from official data, that a large proportion of offenders showed an adult-onset offending pattern. Of the total group of offenders in their 1984 cohort 65 per cent were adult-onset offenders. Piquero, Hawkins and Kazemian (2012) reviewed several studies on the adult onset of offending and concluded that there is a substantial number of adult-onset offenders (amounting to 40–50 per cent of all officially recorded offenders). For example, McGee and Farrington (2010) in the Cambridge Study found that 23 per cent of all convicted offenders were first convicted at age 21 or 24. However, there are wide variations in the estimates. Findings indicate that an adult onset of offending is more common among females than males. Fontaine et al.'s review of antisocial trajectories (2009) reported that a proportion of women start their delinquent or criminal career in adulthood. They noted that it is unclear to what extent adult-onset females are 'truly problem free earlier in life' (p. 375).

Killias, Redondo and Sarnecki (Chapter 11, this volume) emphasize that some longitudinal studies in Europe have reported that a proportion of adult-onset offenders continue offending beyond age 30. However, precise numbers of adult-onset offenders depended on the nature of measurement (for example, self-reports vs official records). One study (Stouthamer-Loeber, 2010) used a combination of self-report and official records of moderate and serious delinquency in the PYS and found that, by age 25, only 3.5 per cent of a school-based sample of young males became moderate to serious adult offenders between ages 20 and 25, and another 5.4 per cent became moderate to serious offenders between ages 17 and 19. However, these percentages depend considerably on the criterion of what is considered delinquency. If less serious offences are included, this has an impact on the percentage of early-onset offenders found. Blokland and Palmen (Chapter 2, this volume) reported on subjects detained by the police, thus not convicted for delinquency. The authors found that nearly half of the young adult offenders did not have a criminal record, a finding that is concordant with Blumstein et al.'s (1986) report. However, Zara and Farrington (2010) found that 23 per cent of offenders up to age 50 were first convicted at age 21 or later.

What is Known about the Continuity in Offending (Persistence as Opposed to Desistance) from Childhood to Adulthood?

Much has been written about life-course persistent offenders (Moffitt, 1993), but there are actually few longitudinal datasets that can address this issue. Blokland

and Palmen (Chapter 2, this volume) found that about one third of the officially registered juvenile delinquents are also arrested as adults. Le Blanc and Fréchette (1989) concluded that 'from 30 to 60 percent of adolescents arrested by the police or convicted by a court will have a criminal record as adults' (p. 83). They also warned that criminal activity during adolescence does not contain 'the seeds of an assured stability' of offending into adulthood (p. 85). However, a study of 1,354 adolescents adjudicated for serious offence in Philadelphia (Philadelphia County) and in Phoenix (Maricopa County, AZ) found that 'the general trend among these offenders is to reduce their level of involvement in antisocial activities' (Mulvey et al., p. 470). Almost six out of ten members of this sample evidenced very low levels of involvement in antisocial activities during the *entire* three-year follow-up period, and less than nine per cent of the sample consistently reported high levels of offending.

There are large individual differences in the likelihood of juvenile offenders persisting in offending into adulthood. In general, those juveniles who start offending prior to age 12, compared to those who start at a later age, are more likely to persist into early adulthood (Loeber and Farrington, 2001). In those individuals who do persist, Donker et al. (2003) found particularly higher levels of stability for overt antisocial behaviour. Using best-estimate methods of self-report and official records, Stouthamer-Loeber et al. (2010) found that only 2.8 per cent of young males in the PYS's youngest cohort continued to offend from late childhood (ages 10–12) to early adulthood, and only a slightly higher percentage (3.6) continued to offend (defined as moderate to serious forms of delinquency) from early adolescence (ages 13–15) to early adulthood. Relatively few young males were childhood-onset delinquents who persisted in their offending into adulthood, and about the same percentage became adolescent-onset offenders who also persisted into adulthood. Thus, small numbers of young males could be characterized as 'life-course' persisters, at least into early adulthood.

Not all offence types have the same years of persistence. P.H. van der Laan et al. (Chapter 8, this volume) concluded in their review of Dutch findings that suspects of drug offences were more often (young) adults (ages 12–17) and comprised only 16 per cent of the number of young adult suspects (ages 18–24) and adult suspects (ages 25–29). These findings are in line with Le Blanc and Fréchette's report (1989) that the median age of termination of offending was the highest (age 21.6) for drug trafficking. They also found that minor offences (such as vandalism, shoplifting and motor vehicle theft) tended to cease before age 18. Findings reported by Rosenfeld, White and Esbensen (2012) show that drug dealing and possession of weapons have the highest likelihood of duration/persistence into early adulthood, while gang membership has a shorter duration. Among drug offences, marijuana use has the longest duration – continuing two to four times longer than serious theft and violence.

Bijleveld, Van der Geest and Hendriks (Chapter 5, this volume) distinguished between 'hands-on' young sex offenders (thus, excluding exhibitionists) who abused children and those who abused peers. The authors concluded that child abusers offend less often and less frequently than peer abusers. The authors reported that sex offenders also committed many non-sex offences. Their delinquent activity followed a pattern similar to the age–crime curve, with a peak at age 15. After this age, general offending tended to decrease, while at an older age the offence pattern became unstable, but this may be a result of the smaller sample size at the end of the observation period. Rosenfeld, White and Esbensen (2012), using US data, found that child abusers start at an older age compared to peer and adult abusers, but this group persisted for a longer period in adulthood.

In summary, against the backdrop of continuity, there is also evidence that (according to official records of convictions) the probability of recidivism decreases from the teenage years to the twenties (Prime, Farrington and Blumstein, 2001; Farrington et al., 2006; Piquero et al., 2007). However, does this also mean that the average residual length (in years) of a criminal career (up to the age of desistance) or the average residual number of offences in a criminal career would decline similarly? Kazemian and Farrington (2006) investigated these quantities in the Cambridge Study, based on official records of convictions, and found that the average residual length of a criminal career and the average residual number of offenses *also* decreased steadily with age. The average residual career length decreased from 8.8 years for offenders at age 18 to 6.1 years for offenders at age 25, and the average residual number of offences decreased from 5.4 at age 18 to 3.8 at age 25. These quantities should be taken into account by judges who sentence young offenders, because these quantities could be predicted by the age of the offender, the serial number of the conviction, the time since the last conviction, and the age of onset of offending.

What is Known about Escalation Versus De-escalation in the Seriousness of Offending During this Age Range?

In general, studies show that serious offences accelerate during late adolescence and early adulthood, reflecting the fact that the transition between adolescence and adulthood denotes a period of increasing severity of offences and an increase in lethal violence (for example, Farrington, 2003; Le Blanc and Fréchette, 1989; Loeber and Farrington, 1998). The serious offences include violence and homicide, drug dealing, and gun or weapon carrying (Loeber and Farrington, 2011).

However, the prevalence of these serious outcomes in early adulthood varies greatly between cities and rural areas. It is also typical that individuals in the process of desistance during late adolescence and early adulthood de-escalate the severity of their offending. For example, Blokland and Palmen (Chapter 2, this volume) found that one in seven offenders persists from adolescence to adulthood. Another seven per cent showed a stable pattern of chronic offending and had at least three convictions in either period. Another seven per cent were young adult offenders with prior juvenile convictions who showed a pattern of stable sporadic offending, while the category of de-escalators was the least common (less than one per cent).

In summary, the period between late adolescence and early adulthood is characterized by an increasing severity of offending in a minority of delinquents, and a decreasing severity of offending in others whose delinquency decreases during that period. This process of escalation for some young males and de-escalation for others is usually not complete for all juvenile delinquents by age 18 but extends to early adulthood.

To what Extent is there Specialization as Opposed to Versatility in Offending During this Age Range?

The review by Piquero, Hawkins and Kazemian (2012) stated that it is premature to draw conclusions about specialization in offending during the period of late adolescence to early adulthood. The field is plagued by different definitions of offence categories, the use of official records, and developmental aspects of specialization. One of the better measures, a standardized variety score used by Blokland and Palmen (Chapter 2, this volume), shows a decrease in the variety score of official records between ages 18 and 36 (which may reflects a general decrease in offending with age). The authors reported that the variety of public order offences decreased first, followed by violent offences, which in turn was followed by property offences. Thus, the findings support the notion of some specialization in the late adolescent to early adult period.

What Types of Criminal Careers Can Most Usefully be Distinguished between Ages 15 and 29?

Criminal career types are defined as classes of individuals who share a specific pattern of development of offending over time. Individual-level criminal trajectories tend to have varied shapes compared to the aggregate age/crime curve (see also Piquero, 2008). Moffitt's notion that there are two types of criminal careers, early-onset life-course delinquents and adolescent-limited delinquents, has been qualified by recent research (Moffitt, 2006) and reviews (for example, Piquero, 2008). For example, Moffitt (2006) formulated additional types of low-level chronic offenders and adult-onset antisocial individuals. Actually, it has become clear that several subgroups of offenders are identifiable, and new research in Rochester, New York, shows that there may be as many as eight trajectory groups (Thornberry, 2005), although most research has revealed four to six distinguishable groups (Loeber et al., 2008).

Blokland and Palmen (Chapter 2, this volume) identified several categories of offenders on the basis of their officially recorded pattern, including juvenile-only offenders, adult-onset offenders, escalators and de-escalators, and stable (sporadic, recidivist or chronic) offenders. Likewise, Piquero, Hawkins and Kazemian, in a review of developmental trajectories, indicated that the offending career for one category of offenders showed a steep decrease in offending after a peak in adolescence, while desistance for another category of offenders was far more gradual and extended into early adulthood. In contrast, a third category of offenders showed a low level of offending during adolescence and a flat rate for much of adulthood. A fourth category showed an onset and increase in offending during early adulthood. Thus, different types of offender patterns exist and these patterns intersect age 18 at different phases of the delinquency career; and for some individuals that career extends into or starts in adulthood.

When is the Peak Period of Desistance?

It is not often recognized that desistence processes operate throughout the period of the age–crime curve. For example, a proportion of youth in the PYS with onset of delinquency in middle childhood (ages 7–9) desisted soon after and the same was true for those whose onset was during late childhood (10–12), early adolescence (13–16), and so on. However, this raises the question: *Do youth with different ages of onset share a period in which desistance becomes more common?* Analyses based on the PYS data indicate that, although there is an inverse relationship between age of onset and persistence (Loeber and Farrington, 2002), most of the desistance of different age-at-onset groups takes place during late adolescence and early adulthood (Stouthamer-Loeber, Pardini and Loeber, 2010). This reinforces the fact that what is most needed now is to explain this massive desistance during the transition period between adolescence and early adulthood (reviewed in Section II.2).

The findings by Le Blanc and Fréchette (1989, Table 5.2) concur. The authors followed up two samples of male adolescents: one based on a representative sample, the other based on an adjudicated sample. Juveniles whose self-reported offending started at ages seven or eight tended to be active offenders for a median of 12 years (thus, continued to offend up to ages 19–20), whereas those who began offending between ages nine and ten had a delinquency career of a median of nine years (thus ending also around the same age), while those who started offending between ages 11 and 16 had an active delinquency career with a median of five to eight years, thus also ending at ages 16–23. When official records of offending were the criterion, the results were basically replicated but with slightly shorter offending durations than for self-reported delinquency. Thus, desistance processes for 50 per cent of the youth in the two samples occurred a few years after the youth turned age 18.

The results of the Stouthamer-Loeber, Pardini and Loeber (2010) and the Le Blanc and Fréchette (1989) studies indicate the irrelevance for desistance processes of the legal age of adulthood at 18. The findings imply that many youthful offenders, including those already in contact with the court, cease offending soon after age 18. Thus, many young people who offend at ages 18–20 and who are now fed into the adult justice system, and are therefore more likely to receive longer sentences than in the juvenile justice system, would have been likely to desist in the next few years.

In summary, delinquency career research has informed the field about onset, persistence and desistance patterns relevant for understanding the transition between juvenile delinquency and adult crime. This period is a watershed in terms of distinctive pathways for some juvenile delinquents to become adult criminals and for other youth to desist from offending. A third, less studied group, becomes adult-onset offenders without a significant juvenile delinquency career (often these include individuals engaging in fraud). The key questions that future research on desistance can clarify are: How much desistance occurs during the young adult period (for example, ages 18–25), and how does the probability of desistance vary with age? If desistance is very high during the 18–25 age period, this would be a good argument for delaying severe punishment until after age 25.

I.2 Explanatory Processes

In Chapter 1, we distinguished between ten possible processes that are thought to explain offending between adolescence and early adulthood (see Figure 1.3) and particularly explain differences among young people in the age–crime curve. Almost all of these processes have been reviewed in the preceding chapters, but overviews are presented here in more details. The processes are:

1. Early individual differences in self-control.
2. Brain maturation.
3. Cognitive changes (for example, decision making to change behaviour).
4. Behavioural risk factors (disruptive behaviour and delinquency) and behavioural protective factors (nervousness and social isolation).
5. Social risk and protective factors (family, peers, school).
6. Mental illnesses and substance use/abuse.
7. Life circumstances, such as getting married, becoming employed, moving to another neighbourhood.
8. Situational context of specific criminal events, including crime places and routine activities.
9. Neighbourhood (for example, living in a disadvantaged neighbourhood, and the concentration of impulsive and delinquent individuals in disadvantaged neighbourhoods).
10. Justice response (for example, transfer to adult court, longer sentences).

The putative explanatory factors will be evaluated by addressing three empirical questions: (a) *Does each process explain persistence in offending from adolescence to adulthood?* (b) Does *each process also explain desistance during that period?* and (c) *Does each process explain the onset of offending during early adulthood?*

It should be noted that the aforementioned processes map to some degree onto the four theoretical orientations presented by Donker et al. (Chapter 4, this volume): static or population heterogeneity models (early individual differences in self-control), dynamic or state dependence models (behavioural risk and protective factors), dual developmental models, and the biosocial perspective (brain development and change in impulsivity). Thornberry et al. (2012) present two additional models: social psychological theories (cognitive changes) and the developmental psychopathology perspective (including mental illness and exposure to risk and protective factors), which we also review in Sections I.3, I.4 and I.6.

1. Early Individual Differences in Self-control

Individual differences in self-control are presumed to emerge relatively early in life and are thought to be stable over much of the life course. The individual difference framework can also be conceptualized as a population heterogeneity model because subsets of individuals differ in self-control, and associated with that is their probability of becoming serious offenders between adolescence and early adulthood (Donker et al., Chapter 4; Thornberry et al., 2012).

Although popular in criminology (for example, Gottfredson and Hirschi, 1990; Jolliffe and Farrington, 2010), the early individual differences framework lacks agreement among scholars about the exact nature of the underlying construct. Loeber and Pardini's review (2008) has shown that many scholars have pursued different paths as to the defining characteristics of these individual differences. There is little agreement on whether poor self-control, reckless behaviour, impulsivity, poor executive functioning or sensation seeking are the important constructs (see also Jolliffe and Farrington, 2009), and there is even less agreement on how best to quantify them independent of disruptive child behaviour and delinquency. Also, the assumed stability of the underlying constructs across the life course is often untested and is rarely based on a follow-up of the same individuals over time (but see Piquero, Jennings and Farrington, 2009, 2010a). Another possible flaw is the fact that individual differences in, for example, self-control, do not easily map onto the age–crime curve, especially on the up-slope of the curve representing the increase of offending from childhood (ages 7–12) to middle adolescence (ages 13–16) *and* the down-slope of the age–crime curve representing the decrease of criminal activities from late adolescence (ages 17–19) to early adulthood (ages 20–25). Further, the individual differences approach usually pays lip-service to brain maturation from childhood to early adulthood (but see Moffitt, 1993).

The conceptualization of individual differences has been applied but not empirically tested in relation to adult-onset offending. For example, one plausible explanation by Megargee (1966) of late-onset violence without antecedent patterns of aggression rests on the concept of 'overcontrol'. Blackburn (1993) summarized the concept and stated that 'overcontrolled offenders … have strong inhibitions, and aggress only when instigation (anger arousal) is sufficiently intense to overcome inhibitions' (p. 238). In support of the notion of over-control, Pulkkinen (1982) found that highly submissive girls were at risk for developing conduct problems later in life. However, several uncertainties remain. First, it is unclear to what extent adult-onset offenders are truly problem free earlier in life. Second, we are not aware of effective screening devices that identify adult-onset offenders.

In summary, the individual differences approach is much better at explaining persistence in offending than desistance from offending on the basis of 'stable' individual differences. Further, the individual differences approach usually does not attempt to explain adult-onset offending. And moreover, the traditional individual differences approach assumes stability of key underlying factors, and does not take into account that an underlying construct such as self-control is malleable and that it can change as a result of social interactions and systematic interventions (Piquero, Jennings and Farrington, 2009, 2010b). In addition, Lewis et al. (2008) have shown that changes in self-regulation resulting from treatment of boys aged 8 to 12 for their behaviour problems are accompanied by changes in specific areas of the brain. Thus, self-control and impulsivity processes are far from immutable, and changes in these processes can be related to changes in brain functioning. Below we shall review the evidence for brain maturation and developmental changes in impulsivity from adolescence to early adulthood and the relevance of that evidence for persistence in and desistance from offending.

2. Brain Maturation

The critical issue is whether mental maturation and the associated emergence of internal controls are related to brain maturation and whether both correspond to the down-slope of the age–crime curve. In brief, an improved understanding of individual differences would suggest something like the following. Young people differ in the speed of brain maturation (see Donker et al., Chapter 4, this volume; Thornberry et al., 2012), and this brain maturation, accompanied by learning, causes improved internal controls. These improved controls become evident through a decrease in risk-taking behaviours, reckless behaviour and sensation seeking, and advances in problem solving, future orientation and decision making. Improved controls are thought to reduce deviant behaviour, including the commission of delinquent acts, and increase prosocial behaviours.

Prior et al. (2011) carried out a very useful literature review in their book entitled *Maturity, Young Adults and Criminal Justice*. They found that physical maturity (the completion of puberty) usually occurred by age 12 or 13, while intellectual maturity was usually complete by age 18. However, the higher executive functions of the brain, such as planning, verbal memory and impulse control, were not usually fully developed until age 25. They concluded that 'the human brain is not mature until the early to mid-twenties' (p. 8).

There are several pieces of research that fit these conclusions. There is increasing evidence that the brain continues to develop during childhood to early adolescence, including ongoing myelination (for example, Giedd et al., 1996; Sowell et al., 2001), and into adulthood when white matter increases and synapses are pruned. Research also shows that 'the dorsal lateral prefrontal cortex, important for controlling impulses, is among the latest brain regions to mature without reaching adult dimensions until the early 20s' (Giedd, 2004, p. 77). The importance of white matter is underscored by the finding that decreased white

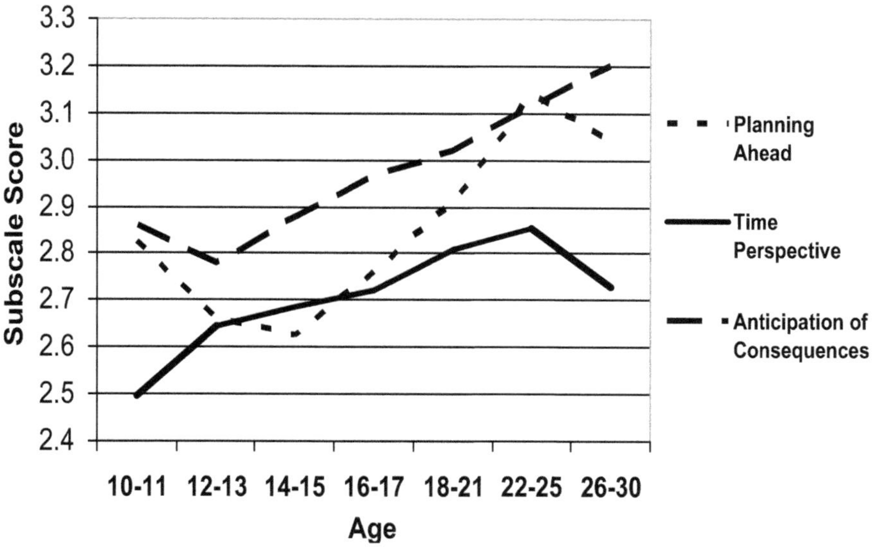

Figure 12.1 Planning ahead, time perspective, and anticipation of future consequences improves between ages 10 and 30 (Steinberg et al., 2009)

matter is significantly more common among boys with psychopathic tendencies compared to controls (De Brito et al., 2009). Biological changes in the prefrontal cortex during adolescence and the early 20s lead to improvements in executive functioning, including reasoning, abstract thinking, planning, anticipating consequences, and impulse control (Sowell et al., 2001).

The data on brain development, although mostly cross-sectional, is much in line with behavioural evidence that reckless behaviours tend to decrease as late as early adulthood, as is evident from data on the number of car accidents even when controlling for the number of miles travelled (Foss, 2002). This is widely recognized by insurance companies whose premiums for car insurance for young drivers up to about age 25 are dramatically higher than for older drivers. It is also recognized by car rental companies who either do not rent cars to young people under age 25 or levy a surcharge for young drivers under that age.

The idea of improved behavioural controls that emerge between late adolescence and early adulthood is also evident from psychological research. For example, Steinberg et al. (2009) investigated time perspective, planning ahead, and anticipation of consequences among individuals between the ages of 10 and 30 (Figure 12.1). Although this was a cross-sectional study, the results suggest that the ability to plan ahead improves dramatically between early adolescence and the early 20s, while time perspective improves slightly less in that same period, and the anticipation of consequences substantially improves as well. In addition, a recent meta-analysis concluded that children's and adolescents' coping repertoires increase with age, including planful problem solving, more diverse distraction techniques, positive self-talk, and intentional self-regulation of emotions (Zimmer-Gembeck and Skinner, 2011).

In addition, a key piece of evidence derives from longitudinal research in which the same individuals are followed up over time. In general, research shows that childhood impulsivity measured by ratings by adults (as early as age five) is significantly predictive of violence (Jolliffe and Farrington, 2009). Corresponding to the thesis that young individuals differ not just in their stable traits over time but also in their developmental maturation, research based on the PYS (Loeber et al., 2011) shows that individual differences in cognitive impulsivity, as measured by young males' performance on several psychometric tasks at age 12, map onto individual differences in the age–crime curve. Individuals tested at age 13 were divided into those scoring one standard deviant above or below the mean on the index of cognitive impulsivity. Particularly relevant outcome parameters are the height and width of the curve for convictions for delinquent acts, with the width indicating a delayed outgrowing of delinquency. Figure 12.2 shows that individuals scoring worst on cognitive impulsivity on average had the highest prevalence of arrest for delinquent acts throughout adolescence to early adulthood (ages 12–26).

Second, those scoring high and those scoring low on cognitive impulsivity showed a decline in arrest. This is contrary to the notion that highly impulsive individuals or individuals with little self-control, on average, remain highly delinquent over time (for example, Gottfredson and Hirschi, 1990). Instead, the results show that, on average, even highly impulsive individuals decreased their level of delinquency with age, although they took longer to outgrow delinquency than less impulsive individuals. Yet another piece of evidence contradicts the assumed stability of underlying traits with the development of offending. Piquero, Jennings and Farrington (2009) reviewed the evidence that several intervention programmes both improve self-control and reduce delinquency in young people. The reviewed programmes targeted those up to age 10 and showed that juveniles' self-control is malleable as a result of systematic interventions. Less well documented is how well interventions promoting self-control apply to older populations.

In summary, the central issue is not whether there are stable individual differences between individuals in their cognitive control and their delinquent acts. Instead, the key question is: *To what extent do individual differences balloon over time and then deflate?* Thus, the age–crime curve with its increase, peak, and then decrease in prevalence *and*, possibly, severity over time should be related to within-individual differences in brain and cognitive development. However, brain and cognitive development have not been related to adult-onset offending.

3. Cognitive Changes

Cognitions, such as particular ways of thinking, are implicated in the prediction of delinquency and desistance from offending (see also Kazemian and Farrington,

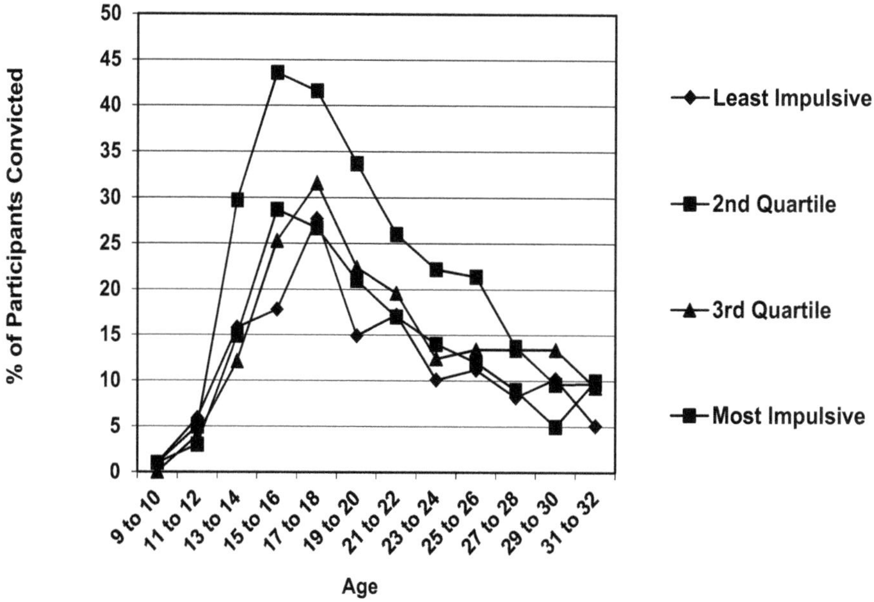

Figure 12.2 Cognitive impulsivity measured at age 12 and the age–crime curve for arrest for delinquency (Loeber et al., 2011)

2010). For example, research shows that cognitions such as deviant attitudes predict later delinquency during adolescence (Zhang, Loeber and Stouthamer-Loeber, 1997). Further, a positive attitude to delinquency is negatively predictive of desistance (meaning is predictive of persistence) (Stouthamer-Loeber et al., 2008). In the Cambridge Study in Delinquent Development, Farrington and Hawkins (1991) found that anti-establishment attitudes at age 18 predicted persistence rather than desistance of offending between ages 21 and 32.

Often, individuals who stop offending report changes in their thinking, including an increased emphasis on the negative effects of a delinquent lifestyle. Whereas some argue that brain maturation causes behavioural change, including a decrease or cessation of offending, others posit that cognitive changes are necessary requirements for desistance (see Donker et al., Chapter 4, this volume; Thornberry et al., 2012). For example, Sampson and Laub (1990) in their age-graded conceptualization of desistance postulated that individuals' investment in conventional (adult) roles reduces offending and encourages desistance. In a different vein, Giordano, Cernkovich and Rudolph (2002) hypothesized that offenders need to make a cognitive shift to accept the view that their deviant lifestyle is undesirable and involves too high a cost, and in the process they adopt a different self-image and adjust their life accordingly. Although these cognitive changes sound plausible, we are still far away from integrating brain changes with cognitive changes, establishing their temporal order, and demonstrating that both lead to desistance from offending.

In summary, some cognitive factors, such as positive attitudes to delinquency, are predictive of delinquency and are presumed to be correlated with persistent offending. The research on cognitions predictive of desistance from offending is scarce. As mentioned, some scholars propose that positive changes in cognitions are necessary elements in criminals' decision making to change course and desist from crime (see Donker et al., Chapter 4, this volume; Thornberry et al., 2012). Although plausible, it is far from clear to what extent such cognitive changes relate to brain maturation and what comes first. It is also unclear to what extent cognitive changes may underlie adult-onset offending.

4. Behavioural Risk and Protective Factors

It is well known that the best predictor of future behaviour is past behaviour (Farrington, 2003; Loeber and Dishion, 1983). This also applies to disruptive behaviour during childhood and adolescence, including oppositional behaviour and conduct problems, which tend to predict later delinquency (Loeber et al., 2000). It is also well established that earlier forms of delinquency predict later offending (see studies reviewed by Blokland and Palmen, Chapter 2, this volume; Piquero, Hawkins and Kazemian, 2012). For example, Donker et al. (2003) found that overt problem behaviour measured at ages 6 to 11 predicted overt behavioural problems at ages 20–25. In the Cambridge Study in Delinquent Development, the odds that a young person with officially recorded delinquency between ages 10–15 would become an officially recorded delinquent during ages 16–20 were 9.7 (Piquero, Farrington and Blumstein, 2007). Piquero, Hawkins and Kazemian (2012), using data from the US, concluded that early arrest for juvenile offences, frequent arrests, and arrests over several years during adolescence were significantly associated with criminal activity during adulthood, and this applied to males and females.

The notion that earlier behaviour helps to explain the persistence of offending has received much support in the empirical literature (Farrington, 2003). At the same time, the empirical studies have attempted to explain why many youth do not commit serious crime. There is good support for the notion that children and adolescents who score higher on nervousness (or qualify for an anxiety disorder) are less likely to commit delinquent acts than those who score low on that factor (for example, Zara and Farrington, 2009, 2010; O'Brien and Frick, 1996; Joyal et al. 2007). Analyses based on conviction data from the Cambridge Study in Delinquent Development showed that adult-onset offenders (i.e., those who were first convicted from age 21 onwards), compared to early-onset offenders and non-offenders, were significantly more neurotic at ages eight to ten, and were more characterized by social isolation and withdrawal (Zara and Farrington, 2009, 2010). Parent-rated nervousness of the boys and self-reported neuroticism functioned as protective factors in the first two decades, but these factors lost their protective power subsequently (i.e., for adult convictions).

Turning to desistance by juvenile offenders, there is far less support for deviant behaviours (or nervous behaviours) predicting desistance from offending. Those who have not escalated to the most serious offences are more likely to desist and more likely to do so early than those who have escalated to serious levels of offending. In the Cambridge Study in Delinquent Development, Farrington and Hawkins (1991) found that high nervousness at ages 8 to 10 was negatively related to offending, but among the offenders high nervousness predicted persistence rather than desistance between ages 21 and 32 (see also Hodgins et al., 2010). Further, there is very limited evidence that earlier behavioural risk factors explain the *onset* of offending during the early adult years (Zara and Farrington, 2009, 2010).

5. Social Risk and Protective Factors

Studies generally agree that a multitude of explanatory risk and protective factors in the social and physical environment (thus, excluding the person's prior conduct problems and delinquency) predict later offending (Thornberry et al., 2012). Scholars often categorize the explanatory risk and protective factors in terms of domains: individual, family, peers, school and neighbourhoods, with some distinction within the family domain between parents' childrearing practices and family demographics. The reviews by Donker et al. (Chapter 4) and Thornberry et al. (2012) show that juveniles' exposure to these risk domains tends to change with age and development, with peer and school influences following the influences of family factors, and with neighbourhood factors becoming more important with juveniles' increased freedom from adult supervision to roam the streets (Loeber, Slot and Stouthamer-Loeber, 2006).

Generally, the higher the number of different risk factors, the higher the probability of later offending, even when earlier disruptive behaviour and delinquency are not taken into account (Farrington, 1997; Loeber et al., 2008). This supports the notion that individuals' exposure to risk factors is predictive of persistence in offending from adolescence to adulthood.

Findings reported by Rosenfeld, White and Esbensen (2012) revealed that most risk factors for violent and general delinquency have also been found in relation to special categories of offences, including homicide. Research shows that more homicide offenders compared to violent offenders are exposed to known risk factors and thus, that risk factors explaining homicide are quantitatively rather than qualitatively different from risk factors explaining violence (Loeber and Farrington, 2011; Loeber et al., 2005). In addition, a comparison between juvenile rapists and violent offenders showed that risk factors for rape are similar to those for other violent offences (Van Wijk et al., 2005).

Increasingly, studies show that protective factors are associated with desistance by known delinquents (Stouthamer-Loeber et al., 2008). However, the power of protective factors to explain desistance from offending during the adolescence/early adulthood period, at least in the PYS, does not appear to be very good. Stouthamer-Loeber et al. (2008) examined a large array of protective factors measured either in early adolescence (ages 13–16) or late adolescence (ages 17–

19) and found that *none* of the promotive factors predicted desistance in early adulthood (ages 20–25).[1]

In contrast, several 'explanatory' risk factors (for example, family on welfare) and several deviant behaviours (for example, high alcohol use, drug dealing, gang membership and gun carrying) measured during early or late adolescence impeded the probability of desistance in early adulthood. That earlier deviant behaviours are negatively associated with later desistance is not that surprising and may reflect the persistence of individual differences over time. The fact that none of the protective factors predicted desistance during early adulthood gives us pause. Is this an odd finding or is this concordant with the overriding influence of brain maturation on desistance during this period of life?

6. Mental Illness and Substance Use

There is a popular perception that mental illnesses have causal effects on recidivism (Cuellar, McReynolds and Wasserman, 2006; Doreleijers and Fokkens, 2010). This is supported by survey studies showing that mental illnesses are more common among delinquents, especially those in juvenile institutions (for example, Teplin et al., 2005). This may not mean, however, that mental illnesses cause offending in the majority of offenders or that they predict persistence of offending between adolescence and early adulthood. Even if there is a causal link, it remains to be seen whether mental illnesses explain more than a minority of those who persist in their delinquency between adolescence and early adulthood. For example, Odgers et al. (2007) found that by age 32 a higher percentage of life-course persistent conduct disordered males in the Dunedin Multidisciplinary Health and Development Studies, compared to those with childhood-limited conduct disorder, qualified for one or more psychiatric disorders including major depressive disorder, cannabis dependence, other drug dependence, and post-traumatic stress disorder.

Our understanding of mental illnesses as causes of offending is also important from a legal and a court processing point of view. Impulsivity combined with mental illness is thought to deprive an individual 'of the ability to understand the [delinquent] act … or causes the individual to lose the ability to control his or her actions' (Ogloff, 1997, p. 67).

The aforementioned finding by Odgers et al. (2007) of a high prevalence of mental illnesses among life-course persistent offenders is in line with results from mental health survey studies showing that mental illnesses are more common among delinquent inmate populations, including those incarcerated in jails and prisons. Further, the studies show a higher rate of comorbid psychiatric disorders among incarcerated populations (for example, McReynolds, Schwalbe

1 In contrast, several promotive factors measured at middle childhood (ages 7–9), late childhood (ages 10–12) or early adolescence (ages 13–16) predicted desistance during early adolescence (ages 13–16) and/or late adolescence (ages 17–19) (Stouthamer et al., 2008, Table 9.7).

and Wasserman, 2010; Teplin et al., 2002; Vreugdenhil, 2003; Wasserman et al., 2010; see also Hoge, Vincent and Guy, 2012). On the other hand, the percentage of juveniles or young adults who are certified mentally incompetent to stand trial because of a psychiatric condition is small, but the proportion with impairments in understanding and reasoning is larger for juveniles than for adults (Grisso et al., 2003). The key questions for this volume are whether persistent offending between adolescence and early adulthood is 'caused' by single or multiple psychiatric disorders, whether there are psychiatric disorders that can explain desistance from offending, and whether any psychiatric disorder predicts adult-onset offending.

Which Psychiatric Disorders are Common among Delinquent Youth, and which of the Disorders involve Deficits in Behavioural, Cognitive and Emotional Controls?

Since Conduct Disorder (CD) symptoms (such as bullying, physical cruelty, or theft) largely overlap with delinquency and often precede delinquent offending, it goes without saying that many delinquents qualify for a diagnosis of Conduct Disorder. Therefore, the explanation for persistence in offending because of CD is largely tautological and does not do us much service. However, some evidence suggests that CD increases the risk for precocious transitions to adulthood (for example, early home leaving or full-time employment) either via high school-dropout (Capaldi and Stoolmiller, 1999) or early initiation of sexual intercourse. Although accelerated transition to adulthood is itself linked to adverse mental health consequences (Ge et al., 2001), the role of CD in these transitions has not been well documented.

Other disorders with cognitive control problems include Attention Deficit Hyperactivity Disorder (ADHD), and in adulthood Antisocial Personality Disorder, possibly Borderline Personality Disorder (American Psychiatric Association, 2005), and those who qualify for Impulse Control Disorder, not otherwise specified (Hucker, 1997). ADHD in early studies was seen as an important precursor to CD and Antisocial Personality Disorder, but research findings tend to agree that ADHD does not predict the other two disorders once earlier CD is taken into account (see review by Loeber et al., 2000). Although there is some research on ADHD and the prediction of delinquency (for example, Satterfield et al., 2007), we do not know of studies that have examined the extent to which ADHD explains persistence or the lack of desistance in offending among juvenile delinquents. Yet, as mentioned, one ADHD symptom – impulsivity – appears relevant for the prediction of the age–crime curve.

Other major disorders that are common among delinquents, especially among female offenders, are depression (Wasserman et al., 2010) and Post-traumatic Stress Syndrome (PTSS: Kerig and Becker, 2010; Wasserman and McReynolds, 2011). Hamerlynck et al. (2008) in a Dutch study of detained young females found that especially the severely aggressive females had high levels of PTSS symptoms and suicidality. Depression tends to follow rather than precede the onset of conduct problems and delinquency, and whereas delinquency predicts depression, depression did not predict delinquency in early adulthood (for example, Siennick, 2007). For these reasons, it is not plausible that depression is a causal factor for the persistence of offending between adolescence and adulthood. In addition, the absence of depression is not known to be associated with desistance from offending. In the same vein, the presence of PTSD is not known to account for individuals' persistence in or desistance from offending between adolescence and early adulthood.

It has been hypothesized that psychoses are more common among delinquents than non-delinquents. For example, a Dutch survey by Vreugdenhil (2003) showed that in juvenile institutions 32 per cent of the offenders showed psychotic symptoms (but did not necessarily qualify for a diagnosis of psychosis). Schizophrenia and particularly paranoia have been linked to offending and violence (American Psychiatric Association, 1994; Joyal et al., 2007). However, the prevalence of schizophrenia is very low and typically schizophrenia develops between the late teens and the mid-30s (American Psychiatric Association, 1994). We have not identified studies showing that schizophrenia prior to age 18 is associated with persistence in offending from adolescence to adulthood, or that it predicts the onset of violence in adulthood. Bipolar disorder (sometimes called manic–depressive disorder), which is rare and usually has an onset in early adulthood, has been linked to violence in adulthood (Fazel et al., 2010). However, it is unclear whether this disorder in adolescence predicts persistent offending into adulthood or adult-onset offending.

Turning to substance use, research findings are consistent in showing that criminal offenders report higher rates of substance use, and substance users and abusers report higher rates of offending compared to non-users (Rosenfeld, White, and Esbensen, 2012). Of all substances, alcohol use especially is known to disinhibit and predict violence (White, Jackson, and Loeber, 2009). However, at least one study failed to show that frequent alcohol use, marijuana use or any hard drug use distinguished persisters from desisters of serious delinquency in early adulthood (Stouthamer-Loeber et al., 2004). On the other hand, McReynolds et al. (2010) found that the combination of substance use and affective disorders were especially predictive of recidivism among adolescent females in the care of probation authorities. Importantly, Chassin et al. (2010) reported that frequent alcohol and marijuana use by serious juvenile offenders predicted lower psychosocial maturity six months later. For boys, those with the highest level of marijuana use showed the smallest increase in psychosocial maturity.

In summary, a range of psychiatric disorders are common among arrested and incarcerated populations of young offenders, and frequent alcohol and drug use are implicated in delay in psychosocial maturity. Mental illnesses, however, do *not* constitute a common explanation, for example, for violence. Joyal and colleagues in their review of studies concluded that between 85 per cent and 95 per cent of violence in communities is not related to major mental disorders (Joyal et al., 2007).

However, the fact is that the majority of young offenders have mental health problems. This has major implications for justice processing, including the need to screen for psychiatric disorders, including substance use disorders and dependence. Thus, there is an urgent need to eliminate the possibility that young people with mental illnesses are fed into those areas of the justice system that do not assess or deal with their mental health needs (McReynolds, Schwalbe and Wasserman, 2010; Wasserman et al., 2003). Several programmes in and outside of the justice system (for example, MST) for juveniles and young adults are known to reduce psychiatric symptoms and recidivism (Cuellar, McReynolds and Wasserman, 2006; Henggeler et al., 1996).

In addition, the justice system is in a strong position to divert alcohol or drug abusing youth to undergo treatment for their dependence or addiction, particularly when such treatment can speed up psychosocial maturation and improve self-control processes. Evaluation studies in this area are much needed (Cuellar, McReynolds and Wasserman, 2006; Wasserman et al., 2003).

The above issues are important, independent of the question of whether mental disorders have causal effects on offending and are implicated in the persistence of offending from adolescence to early adulthood. Our review indicates that, despite popular perceptions of a causal connection between psychiatric illnesses in young people and their risk of recidivism (Cuellar, McReynolds and Wasserman, 2006), there is a lack of evidence for a significant numbers of juvenile offenders that common mental illnesses have causal effects on the persistence in offending from adolescence to adulthood. On the other hand, certain combinations of psychiatric disorders appear particularly important for recidivism. More plausible is that cognitive impairments, including cognitive impulsivity, are germane to a range of psychiatric disorders and that these impairments are somehow responsible for the variations in offending in a subgroup of young delinquents.

We did not find evidence that the cessation of mental illnesses explained desistance from juvenile offending in adolescence. Further, there is a scarcity of findings explaining adult-onset offending by means of earlier mental illness. However, it is plausible that there are subgroups of offenders for whom the preceding conclusions do not apply. Sherman et al. (1998) concluded that factors such as a safe place to live, a job that pays and a social network have a better predictability for desistance than does the degree of psychopathology. A multi-state study in the US of returning inmates (Baer et al., 2006) found that their most immediate needs are finding and maintaining legitimate job opportunities, treatment of serious mental and physical illness, stable housing arrangements, and restoring and rebuilding non-criminal family and social networks. In addition, returning inmates need to overcome the effects of the economic deprivation that often characterizes the communities to which they return, which may compound their personal challenges and burdens.

Irrespective of the question whether substance use or psychiatric disorders have a causal impact on offending during the transition between adolescence and early adulthood, there is much agreement that screening for mental illness is necessary in the justice system to ensure that alternative measures to long sentences and incarceration are meted out to young people who are mentally ill (see further Section II.1).

7. Life Circumstances

There is a tradition in the criminological literature to emphasize individuals' changes in life circumstances, such as marriage, parenthood and moving to a different neighbourhood, as critical factors for the reduction of offending during the transition from adolescence to adulthood, and that these changes in life circumstances can help to explain the down-slope of the age–crime curve. Averdijk, Elffers and Ruiter (Chapter 3, this volume) focused especially on the effect on offending of moving from one neighbourhood to another. The review by Horney, Tolan and Weisburd (2012) concentrated on the short-term effects on offending of marriage and romantic relationships, parenthood, employment, and leisure activities.

Marriage and cohabitation Donker and colleagues (Chapter 4, this volume) discussed dynamic explanatory frameworks including Sampson and Laub's (1993) social control theory, indicating that bonds such as marital bonds can enhance desistence. A Dutch longitudinal study on a convicted sample revealed that marriage is important in accounting for a decrease in recidivism and desistence (Blokland and Nieuwbeerta, 2005; Bersani, Laub and Nieuwbeerta, 2009). Horney, Tolan and Weisburd (2012) showed that, for males, marriage on average is linked to a reduction in criminal behaviour and substance use, but the evidence for females is less clear. The effect of formalized relationships on offending appears greater than that of non-marital relationships. Why marriage is associated with a reduction of delinquency seems to depend partly on spending less time with friends and partly on social bonding with a partner inhibiting offending. However, the favourable potential of marriage does not appear to operate when individuals chose an antisocial partner. Many of the most serious delinquents have children by different partners and are not permanently involved with former partners or their joint offspring (Wei, Loeber and Stouthamer-Loeber, 2002). It may well be that the critical factors are not the presence of children in a relationship, but whether the parents are living with their children – some delinquent parents are separated from their offspring by their incarceration (Murray and Murray, 2010). Horney, Tolan and Weisburd (2012) concluded that overall the effects of parenthood are not as robust as those of marriage, and appear stronger for a reduction in substance use than for a reduction in offending.

Employment In a longitudinal study, Blokland and Nieuwbeerta (2005) found that employment can increase desistence from offending. This is consistent with the review of Horney, Tolan and Weisburd (2012), which found that studies generally indicate that employment is associated with a reduction of crime and substance use during adulthood. However, studies on employment during adolescence, which is a time when delinquency peaks, have found either a deleterious effect or a beneficial effect of work. It may well be that job stability, job characteristics and job satisfaction are playing mediating roles, but the results of studies are mixed in these respects.

Several well-designed studies have examined the negative effects of the criminal justice system on adult employment outcomes (see Bushway and Reuter, 2002), but high-quality studies on juvenile offenders are lacking, leaving unresolved questions such as the temporal sequence among dropout, criminal activity, juvenile justice system involvement, and unemployment (for example, Bernburg and Krohn, 2003). Using a national sample of adolescents, Sweeten (2006) established a suggested temporal order and concluded that, 'aside from mediating mechanisms, it is evident that court appearance hinders educational attainment, increasing the probability of dropout'. High school dropout, in turn, may set in motion a number of negative outcomes including unemployment and increased criminal involvement' (p. 478). We are very concerned about increasing unemployment among young people and what effect that may have on broadening the age–crime curve for successive cohorts with high unemployment in their early 20s. We shall return to employment in Section II.4 when discussing the effectiveness of job training programmes on offending.

In summary, findings on employment and its possible impact on offending are less consistent than those of marriage. Specifically, not all studies support the notion that employment fosters desistance from offending and/or substance use. More consistent is the finding that periods of unemployment are associated with higher delinquency in juveniles and adults alike (for example, Farrington et al., 1986).

Leisure activities During the transition between adolescence and early adulthood, major changes usually take place in the pattern of leisure activities, including less involvement with peers, which involves a decline in the time spent riding in a car for fun, visiting with friends, going to parties, spending evenings out for fun and recreation, and other joint peer activities. One of the best studies conducted by Osgood, Gold and Miller (1986) concluded that adults' decreased control over juveniles' behaviour outside of the home is accompanied by juveniles' increased spending of leisure time with deviant peers. Horney, Tolan and Weisburd (2012) in their review of the empirical literature concluded that there are consistent findings that a change in leisure activities reduces offending during the transition between adolescence and early adulthood. However, more needs to be known about which specific activities are most critical in this respect.

Conclusions In summary, there is reasonably consistent evidence that marriage and employment on average are associated with a reduction in offending, but that there are gender differences in the effects. Some studies have examined youth's precocious transitions through several types of life circumstances, including early school leaving. For example, Bosick (2009) found that 'juvenile offenders are especially likely to transition precariously by exiting school early and becoming early parents, and with the notion that those who do not couple these precarious transitions with early entry into steady employment, independent residence and marriage will be particularly likely to continue offending into adulthood' (p. 132).

Unfortunately, the study of the impact of life circumstances on reducing delinquency is plagued by methodological limitations that have been addressed only in a minority of studies. Key limitations are the relative lack of within-individual (as opposed to between-group) analyses to show how individuals' rate of offending changes from before to after a change in a life circumstance. Further, life circumstances research is limited by selection effects in that those who marry may already differ from those who do not marry in terms of delinquency propensity and/or exposure to known criminogenic risk factors. Several researchers (for example, King, Massoglia and Macmillan, 2007; Theobald and Farrington, 2009) have used propensity score matching to deal with selection effects in within-individual analyses of the effects of marriage.

Moreover, effect sizes of changes in life circumstances, such as marriage, often are small (for example, Theobald and Farrington, 2009). Siennick and Osgood (2008) in their review of the impact of life circumstances on crime concluded that 'they have little direct bearing on whether role transitions can explain the age–crime curve' (p. 161). In fact, many of the life circumstances, such as marriage or full-time employment, often occur late into the down-slope of the age–crime curve, where they could still cause a decrease in offending.

8. Situational Contexts

Most of the studies on putative explanations of offending have focused on factors that are somewhat distal to the criminal events. For that reason it is important to consider the impact of more proximal and situational effects on offending and whether situational contexts change from adolescence to early adulthood. Examples of such situational effects are the presence of bystanders in high-risk criminal situations (peers vs others) and the carrying of weapons. Horney, Tolan and Weisburd (2012) concluded that in the absence of studies covering the transition between juvenile delinquency and adult crime there is little known as to which situational context changes are associated with desistance in offending during that period.

Crime hot spots Horney, Tolan and Weisburd (2011) summarized studies showing that crime is concentrated in certain hot spots in cities (for example, bars), and this applies to juvenile and adult crime. However, government rules regulating the minimum age of allowable alcohol consumption are likely to affect the presence of crime hot spots around bars. Juveniles are known to hang out at other spaces, and it is reasonable to speculate that there is a shift in hot spots that takes place from adolescence to early adulthood. How shifts in hotspots in the community affect individuals' persistence or desistance between juvenile delinquency and adult crime is far from clear.

9. Neighbourhood

Averdijk, Elffers and Ruiter (Chapter 3, this volume) and Horney, Tolan and Weisburd (2012) summarized the large literature on neighbourhood effects on offending. Studies agree that the highest level of crime occurs in the worst neighbourhoods. Persistent offending is more common in disadvantaged- than in advantaged neighbourhoods. Scholars postulated that structural factors (such as concentrations of poverty) and social processes (including social disorganization) of neighbourhoods are among the possible causes of neighbourhood differences in crime levels. Thus, it is probable that neighbourhood contexts are important in the explanation for young people's persistence in and lack of desistance from offending both at an individual and at an aggregate level. This notion is reinforced by analyses executed by Averdijk, Elffers and Ruiter (Chapter 3, this volume), showing that moving to another neighbourhood is associated with a decrease in individuals' offending. However, in an American experiment that moved families out of poverty-stricken neighbourhoods, girls benefited but boys did not (Popkin, Leventhal and Weismann, 2010).

As mentioned, cognitive impulsivity can be noted at a relatively young age, and certainly prior to the peak in the age–crime curve. Lynam et al. (2000) documented that impulsive individuals (including cognitively impulsive individuals) are concentrated in the most disadvantaged neighbourhood (Lynam et al., 2000). This finding corresponds to another, important finding, namely that the age–crime curve is higher and broader for youth living in disadvantaged than for those in more advantaged neighbourhoods (Fabio, Cohen and Loeber, 2011).

We mentioned previously that cognitively impulsive individuals, compared to more controlled individuals, tend to have a higher and broader age–crime curve and that they show a delayed outgrowing of delinquency. We posit that the concentration of impulsive and delinquent individuals in disadvantaged neighbourhoods stimulates co-offending and also victimization of both delinquents and non-delinquents. In that contagion process crime and particularly violence is fuelled over and above the effect caused by each individual, and at a higher aggregate level than for impulsive and delinquent individuals living in more advantaged neighbourhoods.

The concentration of impulsive and delinquent individuals in the most disadvantaged neighbourhoods means that there are larger numbers of young people who show delayed outgrowing of delinquency. This delayed outgrowing occurs in environments with high exposure to known criminogenic risk factors, which tend to be concentrated in disadvantaged neighbourhoods as well (Horney, Tolan and Weisburd, 2012) and which are likely to support offending and impair desistance from crime.

10. Justice Response

It can be argued that the down-slope of the age–crime curve is at least partially influenced by ways that the justice system – both for juveniles and young adults – is assumed to reduce offending. Interventions through the justice system such as sanctions including lengthy sentences, incarceration, and transfer of juveniles to the adult court all influence delinquency careers and recidivism. Some of these measures are known to increase rather than decrease recidivism. These aspects are discussed in Section II.

Summary of the Explanatory Factors

As set out in Chapter 1, it should be understood that the explanatory frameworks that we reviewed typically cover different age periods in the childhood/early adult time window (see Figure 1.3) and, consequently, may deal with slightly different but interrelated outcomes. Thus, early individual differences are thought to become manifest after birth and consolidate during the first eight to ten years (for example, Gottfredson and Hirschi, 1990), whereas direct exposure to risk factors increases but also changes during childhood and adolescence (Donker et al., Chapter 4, this volume; Thornberry et al., 2012; Childs, Sullivan and Culledge, 2010; Loeber, Slot and Stouthamer-Loeber, 2006), and changes in life circumstances – such as marriage – typically accelerate from late adolescence and early adulthood onwards. There are secular changes in many countries showing that more young people than in the past postpone leaving the family home, marriage, and bearing children. However, Hanford and Furstenberg (2008) concluded that there is little evidence for deviant behaviours typical of adolescence to become manifest later.

As mentioned in Section II.2, early individual differences appear related to self-control and brain development, and normal maturational processes often are not yet complete by age 18. Yet age 18 currently serves in most European countries and in most states in the US as the dividing line between adolescence and adulthood (Griffin, 2012; Killias, Redondo and Sarnecki, Chapter 11, this volume). Research indicates that individuals with early cognitive impulsivity tend to have a higher and wider age–crime curve, which may help to explain the fact that desistance from delinquency is delayed in these youth. Whereas risk factors tend to explain a lower probability of desistance from offending during the period between adolescence and early adulthood, the evidence for protective factors explaining desistance is far from clear. Very few of the ten processes reviewed are buttressed by data to explain adult-onset offending.

Which of the Ten Processes are Implicated in Juveniles' Persistence in or Desistance from Offending into Adulthood?

We conclude that there is evidence that the following processes are implicated in persistence: early individual differences, behavioural risk factors, individuals' exposure to risk factors, delayed maturation in impulsivity, justice response in the form of incarceration, and possibly, the concentration of impulsive and delinquent individuals in disadvantaged neighbourhoods. Thus, persistence processes can be explained by risk and protective factors, with the understanding that protective factors have their own significant contributions and that the protective factors are not necessarily the inverse or the absence of risk factors.

In contrast, desistance from offending between adolescence and adulthood can be facilitated by favourable individual differences early in life and exposure to few behavioural risk factors. But evidence for exposure to protective factors is less clear. Also, early brain maturation, the presence of cognitive changes and several contextual changes (including marriage) are associated with desistance. Unfortunately, the sparse research on adult-onset offending provides little guidance on which factors explain why some individuals who were non-delinquent during adolescence become adult offenders.

In the absence of meta-analyses documenting effect sizes, it remains unclear which of the different processes associated with persistence (or desistance) are the most important across studies. Further, none of the published longitudinal studies has ascertained the relative contribution of each of the ten processes from childhood through early adulthood. Kazemian and Farrington (2010) have pointed out the important need to integrate objective and subjective types of explanation for desistance from crime.

In those instances in which the explanatory processes of desistance are malleable, we do not know which explanatory factors, once changed, will produce the highest yield in lowering the persistence of juveniles' offending into adulthood. We will return to this when reviewing the effectiveness of preventive and remedial interventions (Section II.4).

What are the Legal Implications of Knowledge of Explanatory Processes?

Importantly, *none* of the aforementioned processes for which we have some evidence that they may operate during the transition between adolescence and early adulthood (such as early individual differences in self-control, behavioural risk factors, brain maturation, cognitive changes, contextual influences and justice response) clearly map onto the age 18 dividing line, which is the most widely accepted distinction between adolescence and adulthood, and between the operation of the juvenile and the adult justice system. Instead, age 18 appears irrelevant with respect to most of the above processes that are ongoing around that age, including incomplete brain maturation. This leaves open the question whether it is a deterrent for juveniles to know that adult laws with their typically heavy sanctions will eventually apply to them. This apparent disregard or lack of awareness is not surprising given that the cognitive and behavioural maturation of the majority of juveniles is far from complete until they reach an early adulthood.

I.3 Vulnerable Populations

Youths reach adulthood at different ages (for example, Foster et al., 2005) and differ particularly in their rates of cognitive maturation. *Which categories of youth are likely to mature more slowly in their cognitive ability to control their behaviour and take longer than others to desist from delinquency?* Bijleveld, Van der Geest and Hendriks (Chapter 5, this volume) reviewed new research findings on vulnerable groups, including youth formerly in juvenile institutions and low intelligence youth. The authors showed that both groups had longer criminal careers and were convicted more often than comparison youth.

Low intelligence youth require special attention, not just because they often are less competent to understand court proceedings, but also because they, compared to more intelligent youth, tend to score higher on cognitive impulsivity and are more often charged with delinquent offences (Koolhof et al., 2007).

The following questions pertain to vulnerable youth populations:

Do Vulnerable Populations have Different and Longer Delinquency Careers?

Bijleveld, Van der Geest and Hendriks (Chapter 5, this volume) found that men with low intelligence (IQ below 85) continue to have high conviction rates until in at least their 30s (see also Rutter, Quinton and Hill, 1990). Differences between women with low intelligence and women with average or high intelligence are smaller. Zara and Farrington (2009) showed that adult-onset offenders, compared to non-offenders, had a lower IQ.

Do Vulnerable Groups Experience More Atypical Life Transitions between Adolescence and Early Adulthood?

Bijleveld, Van der Geest and Hendriks (Chapter 5, this volume) also found that men and women who were placed in residential care in their childhood were, on average, less successful in making the transition to adulthood, but some of them compared to non-vulnerable youth make transitions at an atypical early age. For example, motherhood happens relatively early for such females, as does marriage. Whereas marriage, as well as parenthood, reduces offending for the vulnerable men, no effect was found for the vulnerable females. In addition, researchers found that males with a low intelligence tended to marry less often than males with normal intelligence. On the other hand, more females than males with low intelligence tended to marry.

While vulnerable males performed less well in the labour market compared to males in the general population, vulnerable females were similar to other low-educated Dutch females: both groups on average did not participate at high rates in the labour market but instead often chose to be housewives or mothers. Compared to controls, the vulnerable groups, especially those of low intelligence, made late transitions into employment and were less likely to be employed. Thus, key adult life transitions were often experienced differently by populations of vulnerable young people. It is less clear whether changes in life circumstances reduce offending and have a reforming effect in the same way as for less vulnerable populations.

Examples of other vulnerable groups that need to be investigated are those formerly in foster care (Courtney, 2009), early school dropouts, youth from disadvantaged neighbourhoods (for the latter, see Fabio, Cohen and Loeber, 2011; Lynam et al., 2000), and homeless youth (Hagan and McCarthy, 2005). There is evidence of vulnerable groups for whom the outgrowing of delinquency takes longer than for more advantaged groups (see also Foster et al., 2005). We shall return to the important issue of vulnerable populations when reviewing the role of justice systems during the transition between adolescence and early adulthood.

Section II: Practical Issues

This section focuses on six practical topics: (1) Prediction and risk assessments to ascertain the risk of recidivism during the transition period between adolescence and adulthood; (2) Legal boundaries between adolescence and early adulthood and whether these need to be changed; (3) Responses of the justice system; (4) Prevention and intervention; (5) Gender issues; and (6) Ethnicity issues.

II.1. Prediction and Risk Assessments to Ascertain the Risk of Recidivism during the Transition Period between Adolescence and Adulthood

Which Risk Assessment Should Be Used with Young Offenders?

Spanjaard et al. (Chapter 6, this volume) reviewed risk assessment instruments used in the Netherlands. Hoge, Vincent and Guy (2012) reviewed the international literature on risk assessments used to inform the sentencing of juveniles. Risk assessments often are carried out by mental health professionals or by others such as probation officers, intake officers or youth workers, and the results are taken into consideration by judges. This is consistent with the more individualized, rehabilitative approach of the juvenile court. Risk assessments are rarely used to inform the sentencing of adults (including young adults), because of the more punitive retributive approach of the adult criminal court, even when the probability of recidivism is low due to a decrease in offending as part of the down-slope of the age–crime curve. We argue that risk assessment instruments could be used to inform the sentencing of young adult offenders.

Risk assessment instruments are also used with juveniles and adults in institutional settings (including mental health settings) to inform release decisions.

Consequently, the main aim of many instruments is to predict the probability of recidivism.

Four types of risk assessment can be distinguished (Hoge, Vincent and Guy, 2012; Spanjaard et al., Chapter 6, this volume). First, unstructured clinical assessments depend on the unguided collection of information and the formulation of a judgement about levels of risk through subjective interpretation of the information. Research has shown that unstructured clinical assessments have poor reliability and validity. Second, static actuarial measures are based on static (unchanging) historical risk factors such as aspects of a person's previous criminal record. Actuarial measures are often superior to unstructured clinical assessments in predicting recidivism and violence (for example, Quinsey et al., 1998), but actuarial instruments are not useful for intervention planning or for assessing individual progress (Hoge and Andrews, 2010). Third, static/dynamic actuarial measures (risk/need assessments) include both static and dynamic risk factors and are both theoretically and empirically grounded. They are better than static actuarial measures because they can be used for intervention planning and for assessing individual progress. Fourth, structured professional judgement (SPJ) tools are based on static and dynamic risk factors (and strengths and protective factors), but the evaluator can use discretion in generating a final risk estimate. Often, a summary risk rating (SRR) is given (Low, Moderate or High). The idea is to improve clinical judgement by adding structure, and to improve actuarial decision making by adding a rater's discretion. Generally, the SPJ instruments are considered to be the most useful, and they are at least as accurate as actuarial measures.

What are the Best Risk Assessment Instruments That are Currently Used in the Netherlands with Young Offenders?

In the Netherlands 26 risk assessment instruments are used for assessing adolescents and (young) adults (Harte and Breukink, 2010). About half of these instruments have been subjected to research on the quality of the instruments. Dutch research has concentrated on the HCR-20 (Historical Clinical Risk; five studies), the HKT-30 (Historical Clinical Future; four studies) and the SVR-20 (Sexual Violence Risk; three studies). A recent review by Harte and Breukink (2010) concluded that the predictive validity of risk assessment instruments in Dutch studies was poor to satisfactory. Studies focusing on the HCR-20 showed higher predictive validity with AUC-values (Area under the ROC curve) ranging between .62–.91. It seems that items related to violations of conditions or disregard of supervision are best in the prediction of recidivism (Harte and Breukink, 2010). From previous research it can be concluded that risk assessment instruments should include both static and dynamic factors, which is in line with findings in this volume showing that criminogenic needs as well as criminogenic risk are related to recidivism (Spanjaard et al., Chapter 6, this volume).

What are the Most Useful Instruments with Juveniles?

Hoge, Vincent and Guy (2012) reviewed the major juvenile assessment tools, including the Youth Level of Service/Care Management Inventory (YLS/CMI), the Structured Assessment of Violence Risk in Youth (SAVRY), the Washington State Juvenile Court Assessment (WSJCA), the North Carolina Assessment of Risk (NCAR), and the Psychopathy Checklist: Youth Version (PCL:YV).

Comparisons of the most commonly used tools (YLS/CMI; SAVRY; PCL:YV) suggest that they have rather similar predictive accuracy. The main measure of predictive accuracy is the AUC, which roughly measures the probability of a prediction being correct (for example, the probability that a reoffender will score higher than a non-reoffender). AUC measures are typically of the order of .65–.70. It would also be useful to focus on false positives and false negatives and their relative prediction costs (see for example, Kraemer, 1992).

Other categories of vulnerable youth that stand out in their slower or impaired maturation concern youth with one or more mental illnesses involving deficits in cognitive, behavioural and emotional controls. Examples are youth who qualify for a diagnosis of ADHD, depression, drug addiction or dependence (Hussong et al., 2004), or Antisocial Personality Disorder. The reader is referred to these and other disorders discussed in more detail in Section I.6.

What are the Most Useful Instruments with Adults?

Hoge, Vincent and Guy (2012) also reviewed the major adult assessment tools, including the Classification of Violence Risk (COVR), the Historical, Clinical, Risk Management-20 (HCR-20), the Violence Risk Appraisal Guide (VRAG), the Level of Service Inventory-Revised (LSI-R), and the Psychopathy Checklist-Revised (PCL-R). As with the juvenile tools, comparisons of these assessment devices suggest that they have similar predictive accuracy. However, SPJ tools such as the HCR-20 seem to be the best option because of their usefulness in intervention planning and assessing individual progress.

Which Instruments can be Used with Young Adults?

No risk assessment instrument has been specifically designed to be used with young adults, although adult tools are used with young adults as well. Hoge, Vincent and Guy (2012) carried out a reanalysis of existing risk assessment evaluation data to investigate predictive accuracy during early adulthood (defined as ages 18–25). The most impressive result was that the HCR-20 was a good predictor of both general recidivism (AUC = .73) and violence (AUC = .82) during this age range. In survival analyses focusing on time to recidivism, the Hazard ratios were of the order of 1.14–1.15, showing that a 1-point increase in the total score predicted a 14–15 per cent increase in the likelihood of recidivism. Hoge and his colleagues concluded that their results indicated that both juvenile and adult assessment tools predicted recidivism during early adulthood.

What Items should be Included in Risk Assessment Instruments?

Hoge, Vincent and Guy (2012) usefully summarized the items included in ten major risk assessment instruments (five for juveniles and five for adults). Many static factors were commonly included, such as an early age of onset of offending, a history of violence, a history of joblessness, a history of school suspensions/expulsions (personal factors) and criminality in the family, parental conflict, mental illness in the family, low family income and high-crime neighbourhood (contextual factors). Dynamic factors included impulsivity, hostility, drug abuse, alcohol abuse, mental illness (personal factors) and poor parenting, parent–youth conflicts, lack of family supports and negative peer associations (contextual factors). Strengths/protective factors were often included in the juvenile instruments, including a prosocial attitude, good social skills, job stability, educational achievement, positive attitude towards authority/treatment (personal factors), stable/cohesive family, supportive parents and positive peer associations (contextual factors). All of these kinds of items could be considered for inclusion in a risk assessment instrument for young adults.

Hoge, Vincent and Guy (2012) pointed out that about two thirds of juvenile offenders met the criteria for one or more psychiatric disorders, even after excluding conduct disorder. Spanjaard et al. (Chapter 6, this volume) concluded that mental health problems and low emotional wellbeing had a relatively low impact on recidivism compared to problems in other domains. Nevertheless, the impact of mental health problems on recidivism was significant, with the largest impact for the oldest age group (26–29). Hoge, Vincent and Guy (2012) especially emphasized ADHD and psychopathic features (callous/unemotional traits) as important factors associated with recidivism. They concluded that risk assessment instruments should include items on impulsivity, attention problems, sensation seeking, low empathy, low remorse and callousness, all of which were strongly related to chronic offending.

Earlier we mentioned the role that cognitive impulsivity may play in forecasting the age–crime curve (see Section I.2). However, we are not aware of assessment instruments that have incorporated psychometric test results on cognitive impulsivity together with information on other known predictors of delinquency. In general, there is a need to have assessments of psychosocial maturity (Helyar-Cardwell, 2009a) that are sensitive to change as a result of naturally occurring maturation or as a result of interventions aimed at improving self-control and decreasing cognitive and behavioural impulsivity.

How does the Predictive Accuracy of Risk Assessment Instruments Vary With Age?

Hoge, Vincent and Guy (2012) agreed about the importance of risk factors that varied with age (Odgers, Vincent and Corrado, 2002; see also Donker et al., Chapter 4, this volume, and Thornberry et al., 2012). Spanjaard et al. (Chapter 6, this volume) investigated temporal differences in the impact of risk factors on recidivism in two Dutch cohorts of adolescents and young adults. The impact of dynamic factors decreased during adolescence, but increased during early adulthood. Dynamic factors were least prevalent in the youngest age group (12–13), but the impact of dynamic risk factors concerning free time, friends and school was relatively strong for this age group and weaker for older age groups. However, for young adults the reverse pattern was found: on average the impact of criminogenic factors was relatively small in the youngest age group (18–21), but the impact on recidivism increased for the older groups with the highest impact for the group aged 26–29. In particular, the impact of criminogenic factors increased, including problems with regard to school and work, and the use of alcohol and drugs. Possible explanations for this pattern are that: (1) there may be fewer late starters before age 16 and after age 18; (2) the groups aged 12–13 and 26–29 contain relatively more early-onset and life-course persistent offenders; (3) even for early starters at a later age dynamic factors can reduce recidivism and improve their lives.

It seems likely that many risk factors that are important in the later juvenile years (15–17) would still be important in the early adult years. Hoge, Vincent and Guy also reported that several instruments (for example, YLS/CMI, HCR-20, VRAG and LSI-R) have high predictive accuracy across gender, race and countries. However, the predictive validity of the WSJCA was higher for boys and Caucasians than for girls and minorities; the NCAR was not predictive for Caucasian girls, and the association between PCL-R scores and recidivism likely was moderated by several factors (for example race, gender, institutional setting, and country).

Summary of Screening Instruments

Well-researched screening instruments are available to assess juveniles' competence to stand trial, and for sentencing and release. However, there are no screening devices available that discriminate between offenders with different developmental trajectories of offending during the period between adolescence and early adulthood. New initiatives are required to generate and validate assessment devices to ascertain cognitive maturity so that this can be measured at an earlier age than entry into the justice system.

In addition, since little is known about the prediction of young adult onset, or about continuation of offending from the juvenile to the young adult years, Hoge, Vincent and Guy call for longitudinal studies to investigate these topics.

They also call for post-hoc re-analyses of existing longitudinal studies to score risk assessment tools (retrospectively) using variables measured in the data set. The authors also suggest that a new risk assessment instrument, based on the SPJ approach, should be devised for the young adult years, and to investigate its predictive accuracy using self-reports as well as official records, focusing on numbers, seriousness and cost of offences in a five-year follow-up period rather than merely the probability of recidivism in a short follow-up period. In any new instrument, strengths and protective factors should be measured as well as static and dynamic risk factors.

For the present, we believe that many current risk assessment instruments that are used with juveniles or adults (especially those based on the structured professional judgement approach, such as the HCR-20) can be used with young adults. We suggest that these instruments should be used to inform the sentencing of young adults' probability of recidivism and their allocation to intervention programmes. Cost-benefit analyses should be carried out to investigate whether the use of these instruments saves money, for example by reducing recidivism and/or the prison population.

II.2. Legal Boundaries between Adulthood and Whether These Need to be Changed

What are the Legal Age Boundaries between Juvenile and Adult Justice Systems?

Currently the upper age of delinquency jurisdiction of the juvenile court in most European countries is 17 (Liefaard, Chapter 7, this volume), and thus adult justice system jurisdiction begins at age 18. In the Netherlands, juveniles aged 16 and 17 can be sentenced under adult penal law if the juvenile court finds reason in the severity of the offence, the personal circumstances of the offender, or the circumstances under which the offence has been committed. Conversely, in special circumstances young offenders aged 18–20 can be sentenced under juvenile penal law.

Changes in Legislation

It can be argued that changes in legislation are warranted to deal with the large numbers of juvenile offenders who persist into adult criminal careers. To address this issue, four strategies have been proposed by politicians and researchers: (1) lowering the legal age at which adult justice becomes applicable; (2) raising the legal age for juveniles at which the adulthood justice system becomes applicable; (3) increasing sanctions, particularly by means of legislative offence exclusion, minimal length of sentences, and longer incarceration; and (4) the creation of special courts for young adult offenders. It should be understood that whereas the first two options can be advanced in unison, the third option is inherently the opposite of the first two options. Three key questions in discussions about legal changes are: *Are legal boundaries related to young people's development of cognitive control (or lowered impulsivity)? Is the legal system relevant to improving young people's cognitive control or does young people's cognitive development take place independently from the juvenile and adult justice system? What would be the usefulness of legislation stipulating minimum or longer sentences for young offenders?* This last question is particularly acute because of the long delays common between arrest, sentencing and incarceration during the time that many young offenders are likely have completed the brunt of their delinquent activity and be on the down-slope of the age–crime curve.

(a) Raising the legal age for juveniles at which the adult justice system becomes applicable It can be argued that raising the age of juvenile jurisdiction will have benefits, even if these benefits are limited to misdemeanours and low-level felonies. In the Netherlands cost–benefit studies of this strategy have not been conducted, but in the US the costs and benefits of raising the age of juvenile jurisdiction from 16–18 are chronicled in a report commissioned by the North Carolina General Assembly (Henrichson and Levshin, 2011). The motivation for the report was based on research findings showing cognitive and behavioural differences between adolescents and adults, a national consensus to treat juveniles in the justice system differently than adults, and an improved awareness about the lifelong negative consequences of juveniles' criminal conviction in the adult court. Some of the highlights of the report are:

- Recidivism rates among youth ages 16–17 under the juvenile justice system are expected to be 10 per cent lower than the rates of similar youth currently handled by the criminal justice system.
- Raising the adult jurisdiction age from age 16–18 for misdemeanants and low-level felons is anticipated to accrue $97.9 million in long-term benefits over the cost for each successive annual cohort of youths aged 16–17.
- From the viewpoint of taxpayers and the government, the policy change will have a net annual cost of $49.2 (that is, a cost of $70.9 million to justice agencies minus $21.7 million in benefits to the criminal justice system).

In summary, there are considerable benefits but also costs to raising the legal age of adulthood.[2] The report does not include cost–benefit assessments of first-time more serious felony offenders. It can be expected that raising the age of adulthood will have greater benefits than those reported here. An English report concluded that 'diversion from trial under adult law to trial under juvenile law following maturity assessment is likely to produce cost saving to society' of £420 per offender (Barrow Cadbury Trust, 2009, p. 3). More cost–benefit analyses are needed to quantify the yields of raising the legal age of juvenile jurisdiction to 21 or 23 or even 25, which is our favoured recommendation.

2 As of 17 March 2011, the recommended change died in the NC finance committee, due to the high price tag that would come with the proposed change.

(b) Lowering the legal age at which adult justice becomes applicable Would lowering the age of adulthood, for example to 16, decrease young people's offending and lower the crime rate of young individuals? The watershed between juvenile and adult justice has major implications about how young people are dealt with in the court and in institutions. Compared to the juvenile justice system, the adult system is more punitive and more focused on retribution (Liefaard, Chapter 7, this volume). Typically, diversion from judicial proceedings is available to juveniles but not to adults. Rehabilitation services during incarceration (such as education and job training) often are not available in adult prisons, and to a degree are more common in juvenile institutions. Further, in the Netherlands, juvenile convictions are not erased from justice records at the age of majority, and such a record (or a record received as an adult) remains attached to a person for the remainder of his/her life and usually imposes limits on employability in a range of professions.

There are precedents for lowering the age of adulthood by law. Until 1988, the age of adulthood in the Netherlands was 21, which was then lowered to age 18 (Doreleijers and Fokkens, 2010). It can be argued that further legislative action lowering the age of jurisdiction when adult justice becomes applicable (for example, from 18 to 16) may have distinct advantages. Among the putative advantages are possible deterrent effects by means of communicating to juveniles that there are more serious consequences to their offending than those that are applied by the juvenile court. However, we are not aware of any evidence that such an attempt at deterrence reduces young people's rate of offending or contributes to their desistance from delinquency. Another putative advantage of absorbing more youth into the adult justice system is to provide a release valve for juvenile court judges in handling the toughest cases.

However, from a legal perspective the lowering of the current upper-age limit would not be acceptable under International Human Rights Law and would inevitably result in even more public scrutiny by authoritative international bodies, such as the UN Committee on the Rights of the Child (Liefaard, Chapter 7, this volume).

Moreover, there are distinct disadvantages to lowering the legal age of adulthood. Mention has been made of the restrictions in rehabilitative programmes in the adult- compared to the juvenile justice system, the increased exposure of juveniles to adult criminals in the criminal justice system, and the disadvantages of having an adult conviction over a juvenile one in terms of re-entry into society and engagement in the work force. In addition, lowering the age of adult jurisdiction increases costs for the adult justice system, particularly since here longer sentences than are common in the juvenile court are applied.

Although we have identified only one cost–benefit study of lowering the age of adult jurisdiction (Henrichson and Levshin, 2011), we anticipate that such a move can have major negative cost effects. While the juvenile system has more assessment and treatment, the adult justice compared to the juvenile justice system is characterized by longer sentences. A new influx of young people into the adult justice system is likely to cause major cost increases associated with longer incarceration periods, the need to increase the capacity of prisons, new construction of prisons, and higher long-term staffing costs.

The other critical question is whether legislative change to an earlier threshold of adult justice will lead to both a reduction of individuals' persistence in offending and in offending volume for populations of young people. The answer is that there is no empirical evidence for either outcome. Also, it can be argued that the lowering of the adulthood threshold is counter to what we know about adolescent development, particularly brain maturation and improved cognitive control over behaviour. The evidence that we reviewed above (Section I.2) indicates that lowering the threshold for the application of adult court proceedings restricts options for rehabilitation and does not map at all on what is known about age-normative developments in brain maturation during the transition between adolescence and adulthood.

Moreover, the fact that brain maturation is delayed in some categories of vulnerable youth (for example, boys and girls of low intelligence) implies that these groups disproportionally will be the recipients of more serious sanctions in the adult compared to the juvenile court. Further, such implementation will do injustice to the principle of competency to stand trial, understand court proceedings, and benefit from the positive counsel from court officials. Finally, lengthier sanctions administered in the adult court aimed at offenders of a younger age will have no bearing on the age–crime curve and our understanding of normative outgrowing of delinquency in young populations. In summary, if lowering the age of adulthood is advocated, legislative change needs to be informed about the age–crime curve, cost and benefits, and the need to screen vulnerable populations who take longer than others in their brain maturation and their outgrowing of the age–crime curve.

(c) Increasing sanctions, particularly by means of legislative offence exclusion, transfer of juveniles to the adult court, longer sentences, and longer incarceration In their attempts to deal with crime, legislators often respond to (or generate themselves) calls for increasing sanctions, including higher minimum and longer sentences, and legislation to exclude certain offence categories from the jurisdiction of the juvenile court and transfer juvenile delinquents who committed such offences to the adult court, effectively placing juveniles under the jurisdiction of courts for adult offenders (see Howell, Feld and Mears, 2012). Legislators' motivations for such changes are often driven by citizen's cries for action and by notions of retribution rather than by beliefs in rehabilitation or by empirical findings on recidivism and the age–crime curve.

Most research shows that there is no evidence that lengthening the period of incarceration provides practical benefits in terms of reducing recidivism for serious offenders (Lipsey and Cullen, 2007; Loughran et al., 2009; Mulvey, 2011). A mistaken but common assumption by advocates of longer sentences is that the rate of offenders is constant and, therefore, locking the person up will reduce 'street' crime and make communities safer. However, the assumption of a constant rate of offending is mistaken for offenders in the transition between adolescence and adulthood when typically their rate of offending declines (see Piquero, Hawkins and Kazemian, 2012). The findings by Loughran et al. (2009) imply that lengthening sentences, for example, by legislative exclusion of certain offence categories from the jurisdiction of the juvenile court into the hands of the adult court, is unlikely to reduce recidivism among young serious offenders.

(d) The creation of special courts for young adult offenders as a separate entity between the juvenile and the adult court As Dunkel and Pruin (2012) point out, the International Association of Penal Law in 2004 passed a final resolution stating that the applicability of the special provisions for offending by juveniles could be extended up to the age of 25. In Germany since 1953, all young adults aged 18–21 have been transferred to the jurisdiction of the juvenile courts, which allows the needs of the young adult to be taken into account and allows rehabilitative measures to be used. Whether the young adult receives a juvenile or adult sanction depends on such factors as whether the moral and psychological development of a young adult is like a juvenile and whether the offence is like a juvenile crime (for example, spontaneous, unplanned, motivated by anger). Thus, practice in Germany conforms to the 2003 Council of Europe recommendation that young adult offenders under 21 should be treated in a way comparable to juveniles when the judge is of the opinion that they are not as mature and responsible for their actions as full adults (Dunkel and Pruin, 2012).

Some other European countries, including Sweden and Austria, have separate young adult sentencing provisions and separate institutions for 18- to 21-year-olds (see Transition to Adulthood Alliance, 2010). The Netherlands, the Scandinavian countries, and the countries of the former Yugoslavia have special provisions for young adults within the general criminal law or provide for the possibility of avoiding the requirements of the adult law or reducing adult sentences. In Switzerland, young adults can be treated as juveniles until they are aged 25. In Sweden, there is 'youth mitigation' up to age 21. In Finland, all those who committed their crime under age 21 are regarded by the prison service as juveniles.

Offenders aged 18–20 are dealt with more leniently than older adults not only in Scandinavia but also in 18 other European countries (including Austria, Germany and the Netherlands). On the effects of such interventions, there is either no systematic research or the results are conflicting.

In England and Wales, as in the US, the legal treatment of offenders changes dramatically when they reach their eighteenth birthday. Instead of being dealt with in the youth justice system, which focuses more on rehabilitation, they start being dealt with in the adult criminal justice system, which focuses more on punishment. However, there are some special provisions for young adult offenders, defined as those between ages 18 and 20 inclusive. In particular, these offenders are not sent to a prison but to a young offender institution, and their incarceration sentences must be followed by statutory supervision. At age 21 offenders are considered to be fully adult and fully responsible for their actions.

Because of concern about the legal treatment of young adult offenders in England and Wales, the Barrow Cadbury Trust established an independent Commission on Young Adults and the Criminal Justice System in 2004, and this produced the report *Lost in Transition* (Barrow Cadbury Trust, 2005). The Commission highlighted the problems that every offender aged 18 or over was regarded as an adult and that judges applying sentences were under no obligation to take account of the immaturity of offenders aged 21 or older. The Commission argued against using birthdays as an arbitrary indicator of adulthood, and considered that, ideally, there should be only one English criminal justice system for offenders of all ages that took account of the needs and maturity of offenders of different ages.

More realistically, the Commission argued for special provisions for young adult offenders that took account of their immaturity and malleability. It recommended that Transition to Adulthood (T2A) teams should be established in each local criminal justice area to oversee the treatment of young adult offenders and ease their transition between the youth and adult justice systems. It argued that most young adult offenders would naturally desist from crime in their 20s as they matured. Because criminal justice system treatment allegedly made them more likely to offend, there should be presumptions in favour of diversion and against custody for young adult offenders. The Commission pointed out that nearly 70 per cent of incarcerated 18- to 20-year-olds were reconvicted within two years of release, although (in the absence of some comparison condition) this statistic in itself does not necessarily prove that young offender institutions are ineffective or damaging. The Commission also recommended that judges applying sentences should be required to take account of the emotional maturity of young adult offenders, and that specialists in the National Offender Management Service should submit an assessment of an offender's maturity to the court.

In 2009, the Transition to Adulthood Alliance (www.t2a.org.uk) published *A New Start* (Helyar-Cardwell, 2009a) and the *Young Adult Manifesto* (Helyar-Cardwell, 2009b). The *Manifesto* recommended that young adult offenders aged 18–24 should be recognized as a distinct category. It advocated that the government should consider how maturity and developmental stage could be taken into consideration in the sentencing of young adults, and should pilot a maturity assessment instrument for use by the criminal justice system. The *Manifesto* also recommended more diversion of young adults from the courts, increased use of restorative justice, the abolition of short sentences for non-violent offenders, and more support in the community to deal with drug, alcohol, mental health and employment problems of young adult offenders (see Allen, 2012).

In the Netherlands, two committees, the Wiarda Committee in 1971 and the Anneveldt Committee in 1982, proposed a separate criminal justice system for older juveniles and young adults. The latter stressed that the development towards adulthood is a gradual process and as a consequence there is a need for a transitional legal system that serves as a bridge between the juvenile justice system and the adult criminal justice system (Liefaard, Chapter 7, this volume). Despite this recommendation, the legislature decided to reject it. Recently, several scholars have argued for a new Dutch juvenile justice system for adolescents and young adults (Doreleijers and Fokkens, 2010), but others are sceptical and point to the current punitive climate in Dutch politics (Hoekendijk and Niemeijer, 2010), which may allow for harsher sentences for juveniles in this new justice system. Two sets of reasons, discussed below, support creating such special courts: (i) immaturity as a mitigating factor; and (ii) the developmental needs of young people.

(i) Immaturity as a mitigating factor We have stressed the unique diminished capacities of juvenile and young adult offenders. We offer three reasons why states should not punish youths they find to be criminally responsible as severely as adults:

1. First, juveniles' immature judgement and lesser self-control cause them to act impulsively and without full appreciation of consequences and thus reduce their culpability.
2. Second, juveniles are more susceptible than adults to negative peer influence, which further diminishes their criminal responsibility.
3. Third, juveniles' personalities are less well formed than those of adults and their crimes provide less reliable evidence of 'depraved character'.

For these reasons, youths' diminished responsibility requires mitigated sanctions to avoid disfiguring penalties and provide room for reform. Research suggests that these diminished capacities are present in juvenile and young adult offenders up to approximately age 25 (Feld, 2008; Loeber et al., 2008; Mears and Travis, 2004).

Many European countries, including Sweden, Germany, Austria and several others, have long had separate young adult sentencing options and separate institutions for ages 18–21 (see Killias, Redondo and Sarnecki, Chapter 11, this volume). For example, in Germany since 1953, all young adult offenders ages 18–21 have been transferred to the jurisdiction of the juvenile courts, which can sentence according to juvenile law if the young adult has the maturity of a juvenile or if his/her personality is still developing. Austria and Lithuania introduced a similar system in 2001. The Netherlands, Scandinavian countries, and countries of the former Yugoslavia have special provisions for young adults. In Switzerland, young adults can be treated as juveniles until they are over age 25. In Sweden, there is 'young mitigation' up to age 21. In Finland, those who committed their crime under age 21 are treated as juveniles by the prison service (T2A – International Norms & Practices).

(ii) Developmental needs of young people Developmental needs undergird the second set of factors that support the creation of Young Offender Courts. Persons in late adolescence (ages 16–19), and early adulthood (ages 20–25) have special developmental needs (Loeber and Farrington, 1998, 2001; Loeber et al., 2008) that cannot be met in criminal courts. These include (Mears and Travis, 2004, p. 16):

- Programmes that focus on developing capabilities associated with successful transitions to adulthood, such as life skills, education, and vocational and educational training. Programmes in these areas should build on the resiliency and strengths unique to each youth.
- This effort to tailor programmes to the unique circumstances of each young person should also take into account age, gender, race/ethnicity, and the distinctive racial, ethnic and cultural dimensions of the communities to which they will return if confined. They also should take account of any mental or substance abuse disorders or disabilities that might impede a successful transition to the community.
- One of the key strategies in promoting positive youth development is to engage, early in the incarceration period, community groups, family members and service providers who can begin to build the positive connections that will support the young person following release. These strategies should focus on providing a continuum of care and must be consistently implemented and, where appropriate, sustained for at least six months to a year, a period when the risk of recidivism and return to prison is highest.

In summary, a variety of legal and practical strategies have been proposed, each of which varies in advantages and disadvantages, and known or unknown costs and benefits. In reality, however, officials in the juvenile and the adult legal systems have considerable leeway, and vary in their practices from jurisdiction to jurisdiction.

II.3 Responses of the Justice System

There are many uncertainties attached to the ways that the justice system for young people, whether in the juvenile or adult justice system, is thought to reduce recidivism in known offenders. We address here some key questions.

What is Known about Justice System Responses to Juvenile and Young Adult Offending in the Netherlands?

Van der Laan et al. (Chapter 8, this volume) analysed data from judicial and police records and self-reported data of adolescents and young adults. They found that for young adults the odds of being a suspect was higher than for adolescents and adults. Thus, contrary to previous research that found evidence that crime rates are highest among late adolescents, it seems that young adults' prevalence rates of official crime are higher than those of adolescents. Van der Laan et al. (Chapter 8, this volume) suggest that this may be a result of higher dismissal rates for adolescents, which are relatively common in the Netherlands as police officers have the authority to refer minors to Halt (community service) or give an informal warning. Offences of young adults are similar to those of adults, the most common of which are traffic offences, assault and serious property crime. In addition, sanctions settled by the Public Prosecutor or imposed by the court on young adults were found to be similar to adults. While fines are most common for young adults and adults, community service is most common for adolescents.

What is Known About the Relative Effectiveness of the Juvenile and Criminal Justice Systems in Reducing Recidivism?

Howell, Feld and Mears (2012) reviewed the evidence on this topic from US studies. First, they pointed out that arrests, convictions and imprisonment of youth and adults often lead to an increase in offending (see for example, Huizinga and Henry, 2008; Killias, Aebi and Ribeau, 2000; Nieuwbeerta, Nagin and Blokland, 2009). Sending youth to adult prisons usually increases rather than decreases recidivism (see for example, Kupchik, 2006), possibly because only 10 per cent of adult prisons provide any kind of counselling or treatment programmes. Second, Howell and colleagues concluded that juveniles transferred to the adult court are more likely to reoffend, reoffend more quickly and at higher rates, and commit more serious offences than juveniles retained in the juvenile justice system (see for example, Bishop and Frazier, 2000). Third, they cited a finding by the U.S. Centers for Disease Control Task Force (McGowan et al., 2007) that juveniles who experience the adult justice system commit more violent crimes following release than juveniles retained in the juvenile justice system. Fourth, they concluded that changes in transfer laws and practices do not produce a specific or a general deterrent effect (see for example, Redding, 2008).

In summary, it seems clear that the rehabilitative approach of the juvenile justice system is more successful with youth than the retributive approach of the adult criminal justice system. Therefore, it seems likely that a more rehabilitative approach might also be more successful with young adult offenders.

What is the Justification for Special Treatment of Young Compared to Adult Persons?

The main justification for the special treatment of juvenile offenders is that youths have diminished responsibility and culpability because they are immature, have greater impulsivity, lower self-control, poorer cognitive abilities, less appreciation of the consequences of their actions, and a generally poorer ability to make decisions. Furthermore, youths are more susceptible to influences by peers and their offending is less likely to indicate ingrained criminal habits. Howell, Feld and Mears (2012; see also Section I.2) point out that psychosocial capacities that improve decision making and risk taking – such as impulse control, emotion regulation, delay of gratification and resistance to peer influence – continue to mature well into early adulthood (see Steinberg, 2004).

Howell, Feld and Mears (2012) also point out that the same developmental characteristics that diminish youths' criminal responsibility also reduce their adjudicative competence, or ability to understand legal proceedings. Adjudicative competence is especially problematic for those with low intelligence, mental impairment or mental illness.

Many of the arguments about diminished responsibility and adjudicative competence can apply to young adult offenders. It would be important for any special sentencing and treatment programmes for young adult offenders to be based on an assessment of competency and responsibility, and to be rigorously evaluated using randomized experiments.

In light of all the empirical evidence reviewed by Howell and his colleagues, we recommend that experiments be mounted to assess the likely effectiveness of special sentencing and treatment provisions for young adult offenders. There may be resistance to this from legislators who are worried about being seen as 'soft on crime'. However, if a more juvenile-like rehabilitative approach proves to be more effective than the adult retributive approach in reducing the recidivism of young offenders, that would be in the interest of taxpayers (lower cost), young persons (constructive futures), and a safer society at large.

II.4 Prevention and Intervention Outside of the Justice System

One of the advances in criminology and public health is the advent and evaluation of programmes to prevent conduct problems and delinquency or intervene once conduct problems become apparent. The major advantage of such programmes tends to be that they are often implemented earlier than the implementation of justice programmes. The crucial question is whether programmes outside of the justice system reduce the probability of delinquency and particularly persistence of offending between adolescence and early adulthood (see Boendermaker, Deković and Asscher, Chapter 10, this volume; Deković et al., Chapter 9, this volume; Welsh et al., 2012). Deković et al. (Chapter 9, this volume) conducted a systematic review focusing on studies that examined the effects of early and middle childhood programmes on offending during (young) adulthood. Only eight high-quality studies on long-term effects were available, which were all conducted outside the Netherlands. In general, the programmes had positive effects: offending rates were lower in the experimental group than in the control group in seven out of eight studies.

How Effective are Family-based Programmes during Childhood in Reducing Offending during the Young Adult Years?

Deković et al. (Chapter 9, this volume) reviewed the Cambridge-Somerville Youth Study, which is a longitudinal-experimental study that aimed to prevent delinquency in boys in eastern Massachusetts (for example, McCord, 1978). Although the programme did not exclusively focus on the family, it had a family component, which consisted of assistance tailored to families' needs by counsellors. In addition, boys received academic help and medical or psychiatric care, and one quarter of the boys were sent to summer camp. This programme was found to be ineffective.

Welsh et al. (2012) examined early childhood education, in the context of home visits during pregnancy and infancy as part of a randomized experiment by Olds and colleagues to evaluate the Elmira (NY) Nurse Family Partnership programme. At age 15, children of the higher-risk mothers who received home visits incurred significantly fewer arrests than controls. A further follow-up at age 19 found that the daughters of mothers (but not their sons) who had received home visits incurred fewer arrests and convictions. In summary, there is tentative evidence of benefits of early interventions in childhood for preventing delinquency. However, a meta-analysis showed that the effects of programmes that focused on family support were smaller compared to programmes that focused on social and behavioural skills (Deković et al., Chapter 9, this volume).

How Effective are Individually Based Programmes during Childhood in Reducing Offending during the Young Adult Years?

The Perry Preschool Program in Ypsilanti, Michigan, shows that an early cognitively based intellectual enrichment programme can have long-term beneficial effects. Children were randomly assigned either to receive the programme at ages three and four or to be in a control group. A long-term follow-up showed that, at age 19, the experimental group was less likely to have been arrested and more likely to be employed and to have graduated from high school (Berrueta-Clement et al., 1984). By age 27, the experimental group had only half as many arrests as the controls (Schweinhart and Weikart, 1993). The programme has been implemented in the Netherlands, but no Dutch effectiveness study has been carried out yet.

Similarly, the Child-Parent Center (CPC) in Chicago provides disadvantaged children aged 3 to 4 with a high-quality, active learning preschool supplemented by family support. A controlled evaluation of the programme showed that up to age 18 the CPC children were significantly less likely to be arrested, both for any offence and for violence (Reynolds et al., 2001). Up to age 24, the CPC children had significantly lower rates of felony arrest and incarceration, both of which are likely to have occurred in the young adult years (Reynolds et al., 2007).

In the Carolina Abecedarian Project, children aged three were randomly assigned either to receive full-time preschool childcare (focusing on the development of cognitive and language skills) or to be in a control group. Up to age 21, significantly fewer of the experimental children were convicted, and fewer were regular marijuana users.

In summary, the best programmes of early interventions during childhood that included non-treatment controls have yielded reductions in offending that extended into adulthood (Deković et al., Chapter 9, this volume; Welsh et al., 2012).

How Effective are School-based interventions in reducing young adult offending?

Deković et al. (Chapter 9, this volume) and Welsh et al. (2012) highlighted results from the Seattle Social Development Project (SSDP), which combined parent training, teacher training and skills training for children, beginning at age 6. At age 27, the intervention group scored significantly better on educational and economic attainment, mental health and sexual health, but not on substance abuse or offending (Hawkins et al., 2008).

In the Montreal Longitudinal-Experimental Study, aggressive/hyperactive boys aged 6 were randomly assigned either to receive social skills training with their parents receiving child management training or to be in a control group. In a follow-up to age 24, Boisjoli et al. (2007) found that the experimental boys were somewhat less likely to have a criminal record than the control boys (28 per cent compared to 33 per cent).

Deković et al. (Chapter 9, this volume) and Welsh et al. (2012) also cited evidence that the Good Behavior Game (GBG) has long-term desirable effects on offending. This uses a classroom behaviour management strategy that is designed to foster learning by teaching children to regulate their own and their classmates' behaviour. In an experiment in Baltimore, Maryland, first-grade students were randomly assigned either to the GBG or to a control condition. A long-term follow-up to ages 19–21 showed that GBG participants had less violent and criminal behaviour and fewer drug abuse/dependence disorders (Petras et al., 2008). The programme has been implemented and tested in the Netherlands under the name *Taakspel*. The first effectiveness study, a randomized controlled trial, indicates positive results in terms of diminished externalizing behaviour problems and improvements in peer acceptance (Witvliet et al., 2009). Some but not all of the school-based interventions have led to a reduction in offending even during the transition between adolescence and early adulthood. Deković et al. in a meta-analysis, found that effects of academic skills programmes were lower than programmes focusing on social and behavioural skills. Replication of the best programmes is much needed.

In summary, with the exception of the Good Behaviour Game, Deković et al. (Chapter 9 of this volume) have been unable to identify Dutch prevention programmes in early and middle childhood that effectively reduced offending during late adolescence and adulthood. The Dutch programmes in early childhood used a far too universal approach and thus did not sufficiently take into account the specific risks and protective factors that affect children's development. Nor did they specify the intervention targets for parents. Instead of a universal approach, selection criteria should be used that are more closely linked to antisocial behaviour. The lack of good evaluation studies and the low number of subjects involved in these studies leave us with the question of at what age a prevention programme should be applied, which behaviours and circumstances call for prevention, which components should be incorporated, and which children are most likely to benefit.

What are the Most Effective Interventions with Offenders Aged 15–23?

Research of interventions in (late) adolescence and young adulthood is important for two reasons. First, it can be expected that interventions that are effective for (older) juveniles can also be valuable in reducing adult offending. That means that salient ingredients of these programmes could be 'transformed' for adult interventions. Second, to determine which interventions for juveniles result in desistance, Deković et al. (Chapter 9, this volume) presented a comprehensive description of various programmes and their results. Compared to early childhood and school programmes, there are a number of differences. Many programmes target juveniles who, in contrast to schoolchildren, have been adjudicated. Often this means that the process or characteristics of juvenile justice interferes with the intervention. Clear examples are the programmes in custodial care that are limited in the possibilities for family interventions, and vocational training. The restrictions of living in an institution, for instance, reduce the possibilities for learning life skills for autonomous living or romance. A second difference stems from the fact that individual risk factors become more salient during puberty and adolescence. As a result the programmes for juveniles pay more attention to these factors. For some youth the growing weight of individual risk factors as they get older implies a proliferation of mental health problems. A large proportion of delinquent youths suffer from comorbid conditions (see section I.2.6) and it comes as no surprise that some programmes seek to rehabilitate these youngsters by focusing on the reduction of mental health problems. A combination of medication and cognitive-behaviour therapy, for example, has shown to be effective in reducing ADHD symptoms. But less is known about results in terms of improvement of academic skills in reducing offending.

A third difference is related to the fact that acquiring skills for independent living and economic autonomy is a crucial task in adolescence (Van der Knaap et al., 2009; Masten, Obradović and Burt, 2006). As Donker et al. (Chapter 4, this volume) show, having a job, even on an irregular level, is a protective factor that may interrupt a pathway to adult offending. A fourth difference pertains to problems that typically start in puberty or adolescence. Examples are drug use and teenage pregnancy.

In summary, despite extensive information on the various programmes, little is known about their effectiveness in terms of promoting desistance in late adolescence and early adulthood. Recidivism rates in juvenile justice approaches vary from 30–40 per cent (Van der Laan et al., Chapter 8, this volume). Even the most extensive meta-analytic studies (for example, Lipsey and Derzon, 1998) do not include studies with long-term desistance data.

In an effort to improve the quality of Dutch programmes, the Ministry of Justice established an Accreditation Panel that allows the use of a treatment intervention if the programme has a good quality on the basis of several criteria and if the programme will be evaluated using an appropriate experimental research design. Among those programmes are two family-based programmes that have been thoroughly studied in the US: Multisystemic Therapy (MST) and Functional Family Therapy (FFT).Within a few years more information on the effectiveness of these programmes will be available (Boendermaker, Deković and Asscher, Chapter 10, this volume).

How effective are interventions with Older Juvenile Delinquents (ages 14–17) in Preventing Continuation into Young Adult Offending?

Welsh et al. (2012) pointed out that there is good evidence that Multisystemic Therapy (MST) as reported in North American studies is effective in preventing later offending. In a long-term follow-up between ages 14 and 28 of a randomized experiment, Schaeffer and Borduin (2005) found that MST participants had lower recidivism rates (50 per cent versus 81 per cent), including lower rates of re-arrest for violent offences (14 per cent versus 30 per cent). MST participants also had 57 per cent fewer days of confinement in adult detention facilities.

Similarly, a long-term follow-up between ages 15 and 22 of an experiment on FFT showed that it was effective in preventing continuation into young adult offending (Gordon, Graves and Arbuthnot, 1995). Only nine per cent of FFT participants were re-arrested compared to 41 per cent of controls (who received probation services). Also, there is evidence from shorter-term follow-ups (from approximately ages 15–17) that Multidimensional Treatment Foster Care (MTFC) is effective in preventing recidivism (Eddy, Whaley and Chamberlain, 2004; Chamberlain, Leve and DeGarmo, 2007).

Killias, Redondo and Sarnecki (Chapter 11, this volume) review several meta-analyses of the effectiveness of European programmes with juvenile and young adult offenders. They concluded that 'reasoning and rehabilitation' is generally effective in decreasing recidivism by about 14 per cent (Tong and Farrington, 2008). Further, a meta-analysis of 17 European programmes by Redondo, Sánchez-Meca and Garrido (2003) found that recidivism decreased by 18 per cent, that educational and diversion programmes were the most effective, and that the programmes worked better with juveniles than with young adult offenders. A later meta-analysis of treatment programmes for serious delinquents by Garrido, Anyela Morales and Sánchez-Meca (2006) concluded that recidivism was decreased by seven per cent, and that cognitive-behavioural programmes were the most effective.

Do Early Interventions Lower the Age–Crime Curve?

One of the limitations of evaluation studies is the absence of yearly follow-ups of treated and non-treated individuals during adolescence and early adulthood. For that reason, published evaluation studies have not been able to show the degree to which interventions lowered the age–crime curve. To resolve this, Loeber and Stallings (2011) used longitudinal data from the PYS to simulate the impact of an intervention on the offending by at-risk youths. Simulation can be compared with

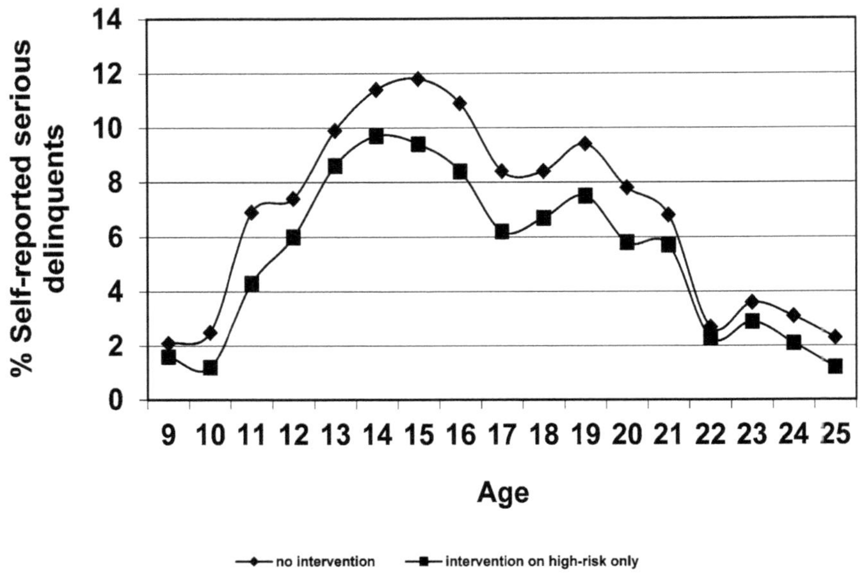

Figure 12.3 Age–crime curve of self-reported delinquency before and after simulated intervention on high-risk participants (PYS; youngest and oldest cohorts) (Loeber and Stallings, 2011)

asking the question, 'What if…' one aspect of the data set were changed, what impact would that have on future offending? To address this, the authors modelled first the efficacy to screen for high-risk individuals and then to apply a treatment that 'knocked out' youth who otherwise would have been at risk of committing serious delinquency. To identify high-risk boys, a screening risk score was computed from data collected at the first assessment for each of the three cohorts at ages 7, 10 and 13, for the youngest, middle and oldest cohorts, respectively (Loeber et al., 2008). This screening score included conduct problems and delinquency as reported by the boys and their parents and teachers. The intervention modelled was inspired by the best intervention programmes available (Lipsey and Wilson, 1998), evaluated by the comparison of an experimental sample receiving the intervention versus a control sample not receiving the programme (or receiving an alternative programme). Loeber and Stallings (2011) took as a conservative criterion a success rate of 30 per cent.

Figure 12.3 shows the comparison between the age–crime curve for serious delinquency without the 'intervention' and the curve with the 'intervention'. The intervention was associated with a substantial reduction in serious delinquents by one fifth to one quarter (21.5 per cent and 27.6 per cent for the youngest and oldest cohort, respectively), especially from ages 11–21. Other results (not shown in Figure 12.3) indicate that the intervention was also associated with a decrease of

20 per cent in the prevalence of arrest by the police, a 35 per cent lower prevalence of homicide offenders and homicide victims, and a 29 per cent reduction in the weeks of incarceration. Thus, the modelled intervention had a substantial benefit of lowering the age–crime curve by reducing the prevalence of self-reported serious offenders, officially recorded homicide offenders and homicide victims during adolescence and early adulthood, and had benefits for the justice system by greatly reducing arrests and convictions.

Summary of the Interventions Outside of the Justice System

There are many intervention programmes available outside of the justice system that reduce recidivism and prevent persistence of offending from adolescence to early adulthood. Preliminary results indicate that interventions may lower the age–crime curve. In particular, multimodal programmes that target both child and family risk factors appear promising (Deković et al., Chapter 9, this volume). A recent meta-analysis by Deković and colleagues (Chapter 9) revealed that some children benefited more from early programmes than others in terms of reduced rates of offending during early adulthood, including at-risk children and children from a lower SES. Furthermore, shorter and more intensive programmes have stronger effects and programmes focusing on social and behavioural skills outperform those focusing on academic skills or family support. Much needed are programmes for low intelligence youth to reduce their impulsivity (Koolhof et al., 2007). Given that empirical studies on long-term effects are scarce or non-existent in the Netherlands, further extended follow-up studies are clearly needed (Deković et al., Chapter 9, this volume).

How Effective are Labour Market Interventions in Reducing Young Adult Offending?

Welsh et al. (2012) concluded that the nationwide US Job Corps programme, which is designed to improve the employability of at-risk youth aged 16–24, is effective in reducing offending and in improving educational attainment (Schochet, Burghardt and McConnell, 2008). Similarly, the supported work programme was effective in reducing offending and improving employment for ex-offenders over the age of 26 (Uggen, 2000). Killias, Redondo and Sarnecki (Chapter 11, this volume) reported a recent large-scale employment experiment in Denmark that showed that increased training of unemployed persons caused a significant decrease in offending. Thus, there is substantial evidence that labour market interventions reduce offending during the transition between adolescence and early adulthood.

How Effective is Restorative Justice in Reducing Young Adult Offending?

Welsh et al. (2012) found one evaluation of restorative justice with a measure of offending in early adulthood. Bergseth and Bouffard (2007) compared restorative justice with traditional court processing. In a follow-up between ages 15 and 19 on average, referral to restorative justice predicted a slightly lower rate of recidivism.

Do Programmes have Similar Effects on Juveniles and Adults?

If a programme has similar effects on juveniles and adults, it is likely to have the same effect on young adults, even if it has not been evaluated with young adults specifically. Welsh et al. (2012) concluded that, generally, programmes do have similar effects on juveniles and adults. This was true for cognitive-behavioural therapy (Landenberger and Lipsey, 2005), drug treatment programmes (Mitchell, Wilson and MacKenzie, 2006) and sex offender treatment programmes (Hanson et al., 2002). However, educational, vocational and employment programmes seemed to be more effective with adults than with juveniles, according to Welsh and his colleagues; and the review of European programmes by Redondo, Sánchez-Meca and Garrido (2003) concluded that they were more effective with juveniles than with young adults. Boendermaker, Deković and Asscher (Chapter 10, this volume) reviewed existing interventions for adolescents and young adults in the Netherlands. They found several interventions for young adults targeting a broad range of relevant skills, such as social and problem-solving skills, anger control, working, housing and living skills, and budgeting skills, but the effectiveness of the programmes has not been evaluated yet.

What is Known about the Financial Benefits and Costs of Different Interventions that Might Reduce Offending in the Young Adult Years?

Based on research conducted by the Washington State Institute for Public Policy (WSIPP), Welsh et al. (2012) concluded that the financial benefits of programmes often outweigh their financial costs. This was true, for example, of MTFC ($8 saved per $1 expended), FFT ($10 saved per $1 expended), MST ($3 saved per $1 expended), vocational education in prison ($12 saved per $1 expended), cognitive-behavioural therapy in prison ($22 saved per $1 expended), drug treatment in prison ($6 saved per $1 expended) and employment training in the community ($12 saved per $1 expended). Thus, it seems clear that many programmes not only reduce offending in the young adult years but also save a lot of money in the long run.

What Can be Learned about Scale Enlargement of Programmes?

Key to the introduction of effective programmes is scale enlargement in which a proven programme is adopted at a regional, state or national scale. Welsh, Sullivan and Olds (2010) have discussed this in great detail, and they point out that some of the greatest challenges concern insufficient service infrastructure, greater population heterogeneity and loss of programme fidelity (see also Dodge, 2009). As Ogden and Amlund Hagen (Appendix, this volume) show, the experiences of introducing nationwide programmes for young people to reduce recidivism in

Norway may 'serve as a model and inspiration for large-scale implementation of evidence-based practice combining "top-down" and "bottom-up" initiatives both in the child and adolescent services and in the correctional system' (p. 000). Implementation was facilitated by the perception of decision makers that therapeutic approaches to the process of change appeared more effective than correctional sanctions administered by the justice system.

II.5 Gender Issues

A substantial proportion of offenders are girls and women with problems and needs that often are different from those of boys and men. In addition, it is debatable to what extent delinquency careers and causes of delinquency are the same for each gender, and whether programmes are equally effective for males and females. This section addresses several key questions on gender-related issues.

How do Criminal Career Features vary with gender?

It is widely known that crime rates in males are higher than in females (confirmed by Blokland and Palmen, Chapter 2, this volume). It is less well known, however, to what extent trajectories of criminal behaviour in females are different from those in males. Piquero, Hawkins and Kazemian (2012) concluded that usually the age–crime curve for girls peaks earlier than for boys. However, gender differences in adolescent offending are relatively small at ages 14 and 15 (Moffitt et al., 2001; Van der Laan and Blom, 2006). Persistence in crime is less likely in females compared to males. Blokland and Palmen (Chapter 2, this volume) also found that, although the group of persistent female offenders is small, it seems that they are as criminally active as their male peers during late adolescence. Kempf-Leonard, Tracy and Howell (2001) reported that, similar to males, a small proportion of life-course female offenders account for a large proportion of adult crimes. Little is known about adult-onset female offenders and whether there are any markers of late onset that are present earlier in life.

How do Trends in Official Crime Vary with Gender?

Van der Laan et al. (Chapter 8, this volume) analysed secular trends in the Netherlands of suspects (police data) and offenders (court data), and found that the number of young adult female offenders has increased more sharply than young adult males. This trend was also found with regard to suspects. Furthermore, among young adult females offender rates showed the sharpest increase over time between 2002 and 2007: 48 per cent for young adult females, 33 per cent for adolescent females and 38 per cent for adult females.

Are Different Theories of Criminal Behaviour Needed for Each Gender?

Thornberry et al. (2012) summarized the main theories about offending in the transition between adolescence and early adulthood. It was not until feminist criminologists began to criticize mainstream theories for focusing exclusively on the criminal behaviour of males (Daly and Chesney-Lind, 1999) that scholars began to investigate potential explanations of gender differences in delinquency, referred to as the gender gap, and potential explanations of female delinquency. These feminist scholars argued for gender sensitive theories of crime (Miller and Mullins, 2009). However, others have stated that explanations of criminal behaviour in males can be applied to females as well. For example, control theory argues that some females are more likely to engage in delinquency because they have weaker bonds to society and, according to labelling theory, they have been informally labelled as delinquents by parents or teachers (Agnew, 2009). Unquestionably, there are gender differences in the prevalence of risk factors, but the key issue is whether there are gender differences in the strength of associations with offending. Moffitt et al. (2001) did the most extensive study of this by far and concluded that generally there are few gender differences in strength of associations.

Research on gender differences in risk factors for delinquency has been inconsistent. Several studies revealed that the same risk factors apply to boys as to girls (Junger-Tas, Ribeaud and Cruyff, 2004; Moffitt et al., 2001), while others found gender differences in risk factors for delinquency (Hay, 2003; Kroneman et al., 2009; Van de Rakt, Weerman and Need, 2005). A recent European review of risk factors for female adolescents and young adults shows many shared risk factors that explain delinquency in both males and females, but many unique factors that explain female delinquency have also been found (Wong, Slotboom and Bijleveld, 2010). Furthermore, females were found to have a higher prevalence of internalizing problems. Females were also more at risk for criminal behaviour if they were affected by negative life events and physical abuse by parents. Moffitt et al. (2001) reported that boys are more exposed to neurobiological risk factors that increase the risk of persistent offending. Moffitt et al. also concluded that females mature slightly earlier than males and as a consequence girls may associate with older male peers. Peer influence may therefore explain the relatively early peak in delinquency in girls.

Comparing findings on risk factors of female delinquency in the US and Europe, Wong, Slotboom and Bijleveld (2010) concluded that some findings from the US could not be generalized to Europe. For example, a single-parent family appeared to be a risk factor for female offending in the US, but less consistently in Europe. It should be noted that the vast majority of European studies were cross-sectional and therefore further research is necessary to establish unique risk factors in females. Moreover, researchers have not compared female adolescents with female young adults and therefore it is unclear whether unique female risk factors exist during the transition from adolescence to early adulthood.

Are Genetic and Biological Influences the Same for Each Gender?

Hodgins et al. (2009) in their review of neurological factors noted that the impact of explanatory factors in a person's environment on stable antisocial behaviour differed by gender with genetic factors being more important for girls, while antisocial behaviour in boys was largely mediated by explanatory factors (D'Onofrio et al., 2007). However, the genetic and neurological transmission is far from clear. Whereas the MAOA gene has consistently been implicated in persistent male antisocial behaviour and aggression, the results are inconsistent for females, and the same applies to the serotonin transporter (5-HTTPLR) and low cortisol levels (Hodgins et al., 2009).

Do Life Events, Life Transitions, Situational Factor, and Neighbourhood Factors have Different Effects on Each Gender?

There is some evidence to suggest that life events and situational factors have different effects for males and females. For example, Bijleveld, Van der Geest and Hendriks (Chapter 5, this volume) focused on vulnerable groups and found that motherhood happened relatively early for high-risk females, as did marriage. For some high-risk men marriage and parenthood started earlier but not as early as for high-risk women. It should be noted that data with regard to parenthood of males are not always known or reliable. With regard to marriage, studies show that males with a lower intelligence tend to marry less often than intellectually normally functioning males. Females with a lower intelligence, on the other hand, tend to marry more often. Whereas marriage as well as parenthood reduced offending for high-risk men, no effect was found for high-risk females. Horney, Tolan and Weisburd's review (2012) shows that marriage has been associated with lower levels of crime in males. However, the link between marriage and criminal behaviour is less clear for females. Some studies found that the link between marriage and crime was weaker for females than for males. An explanation could be that women, more than men, are more likely to get married to a criminal partner (Bersani, Laub and Nieuwbeerta, 2009), because there are more criminal men than criminal women (Farrington, Barnes and Lambert, 1996). This is consistent with findings that stronger associations have been found between a deviant romantic partner and criminal behaviour for females than for males (Horney, Tolan and Weisburd, 2012). Furthermore, stronger links have been found between parenthood and desistance from crime in females than in males. With regard to employment, there is some evidence to suggest that job satisfaction is more strongly associated with lower levels of criminal behaviour in males than in females. However, findings on the relationship between employment and crime are not very consistent (Horney, Tolan and Weisburd, 2012). Finally, neighbourhood factors may affect girls differently than boys (Popkin, Leventhal and Weismann, 2010). Clearly, further investigation on gender differences in effects of contextual factors is needed, since prior research suggests that context changes may affect males and females differently (Horney, Leventhal and Weismann, 2012).

Are Psychiatric Disorders More Common Among Young Female than Male Offenders?

The prevalence of mental illnesses among young females in the juvenile and adult justice system is higher than for males. This also applies to the prevalence of comorbid (co-occurring) conditions, which is higher among incarcerated females than males (see summary in, for example, Hipwell and Loeber, 2006). Female delinquents generally show higher levels of comorbid problems than delinquent males, including sexual/physical trauma, depression, dissociation and substance use (Bijleveld, Hendriks and Vinke, 2003; Hamerlynck et al., 2008; Hipwell et al., 2002; Slotboom and Bijleveld, 2007). This observation is often referred to as the gender paradox. However, studies are rare on the differential recidivism rates of males and females with one or more mental disorders. An exception is the study by McReynolds, Schwalbe and Wasserman (2010), which found a four-time higher recidivism rate for girls compared to boys with comorbid substance use and affective disorder who were referred to the Texas probation authorities.

How does the Predictive Accuracy of Risk Factors, Needs, and Protective Factors Vary with Gender?

Hoge, Vincent and Guy (2012) and Spanjaard et al. (Chapter 6, this volume) reviewed a range of screening devices to guide sentences, alternative referrals or placements, and release from institutions. They noted that screening devices often differ in their validity for each gender. Van der Put et al. (2010) analysed potential gender differences in risk factors in adolescents (up to age 18) on recidivism within two years (up to age 20). They found that most static and dynamic risk factors were predictive of recidivism for both boys and girls. However, female-specific factors were found to be particularly prevalent in the family domain and concerned the following dynamic risk factors: parents with judicial contact, alcohol and/or drug abuse by parents, being a victim of abuse, and alcohol and/or drug abuse by the adolescent herself. Furthermore, the number of problems in the family domain was found to accumulate more for girls. Family-related problems were serious and concerned abuse and court custody cases (Van der Put et al., 2010). To what extent gender differences exist in risk factors, needs and protective factors during the transition to early adulthood is unknown. Hoge, Vincent and Guy (2012) concluded that, in general, more information about risk, need and protective factors associated with criminal activity during this transition period is needed for both males and females. This also raises the question to what extent instruments are accurate in assessing the risk of recidivism in females.

How Effective is Juvenile Versus Adult Court Treatment for Each Gender?

Once girls are placed on probation – typically for status offences, such as running away or liquor law violations – subsequent probation violations and minor misbehaviours tend to propel them towards confinement (Acoca, 1998; Chesney-Lind, 1997). Girls are far more likely than boys to be held in detention centres for minor offences. When girls are placed in confinement, they are often subjected to further victimization in the form of emotional abuse, emotional distress from isolation, and physical and sexual abuse, threats and intimidation from staff.

Slotboom and Bijleveld (2007) interviewed women who were imprisoned and had children. The women reported many problems in relationships with other detainees, prison employees, loneliness, psychological problems, health problems, and problems with healthcare. In addition, they were dissatisfied with their daily activities in prison and they had troubles with parenthood. Also, children of female detainees had problems including low levels of general wellbeing, internalizing and externalizing problem behaviour, and a disturbed family life and neglect (Ezinga and Hissel, 2010). Thus, it appears that young mothers have many problems when they are imprisoned. Despite the existence of a few special facilities for this group, conditions for these women do not seem to show improvement over the years. In conclusion, much evaluation research remains to be done to show which interventions are effective for females in juvenile jails and institutions and in adult prisons.

Are Interventions Outside of the Justice System Differentially Effective with Each Gender?

Research has shown that gender-specific interventions are rare and that studies on the effectiveness of regular interventions with females are scarce (Hipwell and Loeber, 2006; Zahn et al., 2009). However, a recent meta-analysis concluded that generic types of programme services (for example, cognitive behaviour therapy, individual counselling, and the like) are about equally effective with males and females (Lipsey, 2009). Hipwell and Loeber (2006) showed that there is some evidence to suggest that interventions specifically designed to address female delinquency and multi-modal interventions can be effective for female adolescents. Boendermaker, Deković and Asscher (Chapter 10, this volume) reviewed the interventions in the Netherlands that target young adults and concluded that the effects of these programmes are unknown for both males and females. Deković and colleagues (Chapter 9, this volume) and Welsh et al. (2012) found a few differences in effects between males and females. Deković et al.'s review of the international literature showed that long-term effects of early- and middle childhood prevention programmes on young adults depend among other things on the characteristics of participants. The effects of the Good Behavior Game programme were significantly larger for males than for females. Piquero, Jennings and Farrington (2009) found that early intervention programmes to improve self-control had on average a larger effect size for females than males. They also found that the average effect size for the reduction of delinquency was larger for females than males.

Boendermaker et al. (Chapter 10, this volume) stressed the importance of parenting skills in interventions for young adults. They observed that there are many interventions that focus on relevant skills for young adults, including getting and keeping a job, taking care of housing, financial resources, and a social network, but programmes on parenting skills are often lacking. Given that about 20 per cent of the adolescent girls in juvenile justice institutions have been pregnant (Hamerlynck, 2008) and that the age at which vulnerable females become a parent is relatively early (Bijleveld, Van der Geest and Hendriks, Chapter 5, this volume), the risk on early motherhood is high. In summary, there are inconsistent findings on the effects of treatment programmes for each gender, and much research in this area is needed to ensure that interventions become more predictably applicable to each gender.

II.6 Ethnic minorities

Young adults from minority backgrounds are overrepresented in officially registered crime in the Netherlands (for example, Blokland and Palmen, Chapter 2, this volume; Bijleveld, Van der Geest and Hendriks, Chapter 5, this volume; Spanjaard et al., Chapter 6, this volume). Boys of Moroccan descent especially stand out in terms of the early onset, frequency and persistence of their offending. Police registrations are also more common among Surinam, Moroccan and Dutch Antillean girls compared to Dutch girls. It is important to bear in mind that minority youths are overrepresented relative to their share in the total population. Given that non-Western minorities in the Netherlands constitute only around 10 per cent of the population, in absolute numbers, native Dutch offenders account for the lion's share of all crime.

In 2007, the number of suspects per 1,000 was the highest among juveniles of Moroccan descent, followed by juveniles from the Dutch Antilles (including Aruba) and Surinam. The figure for crime suspects among young adults of Moroccan descent was 107 per 1,000, for Dutch Antilleans this figure was 96, for Surinamese young adults 82, and for young adults of native Dutch origin it was 30. The age–crime curve of Moroccans tended to rise steeply to a peak during the late teens much higher than for the native Dutch population but then showed a steep decline through the 20s and 30s much like the curve for the Dutch population. Thus the overrepresentation of Moroccans in registered crime was highest for juveniles and declined steadily with age. For Dutch Antilleans, on the other hand, the age–crime curve did not show a continued decline beyond age 20, but instead seemed to reach a plateau that lasted well into the 40s. As a result, the overrepresentation of Dutch Antilleans – relative to native Dutch – is especially large during the 20s, 30s and 40s.

Differences in the nature of the offences committed by these minorities typically did not entirely explain variations in the age–crime curves (Blokland

and Palmen, Chapter 2, this volume; Jennissen, 2009; Van der Laan et al., Chapter 8, this volume). For example, Blokland and Palmen (Chapter 2, this volume) found that participation in offending was higher during the young adult age period compared to the juvenile period. In males participation was highest among those of Moroccan background. In females participation was especially high for girls from Surinamese, Moroccan and Dutch Antillean backgrounds.

There are many questions about the impact of ethnicity in the transition between adolescence and early adulthood. Research from the US on this topic is applicable only to a limited extent since European minorities are not in all aspects comparable to minorities in the US. Studies in the Netherlands show that non-indigenous males show an earlier and higher peak in the age–crime curve than either indigenous females or indigenous males and females.

Race/ethnicity differences in offending might be explained by race/ethnicity differences in risk factors. Loeber et al. (2011) showed that in the US African–American boys were more deprived than Caucasian boys on socioeconomic/demographic factors, such as a broken home, a family on welfare, a bad neighbourhood, and a young mother. Other analyses of the PYS data have shown that, once other social and structural factors are taken into account, African–American race does not predict violence (Loeber et al., 2011; see also Huizinga et al., 2006) or homicide offending (Loeber and Farrington, 2011).

Even though the prevalence of violence is much higher among non-indigenous compared to indigenous young males, screening instruments to assess the risk of recidivism are equally effective for various groups (see Hoge, Vincent and Guy, 2012; Van der Put, 2011). Studies in the US show that the same applies to prevention and intervention programmes (Welsh et al., 2012). However, in a Dutch study (Jennissen, 2009), a broken home appeared to be a stronger risk factor for non-ethnic Dutch youths compared to ethnic youths, with the exception of youth from the Dutch Antilles for whom a broken home was a risk factor as well. When focusing on so-called second generation ethnic youths, the difference with their non-ethnic peers in this respect appeared to be less noticeable since broken homes are more common in second-generation families.

Cultural differences and opinions on what is considered the appropriate timing of transitions or the obligations and expectations associated with different adult roles might influence the way crime develops when adolescents transition into adulthood in these different minority populations. Bijleveld et al. (Chapter 5, this volume) found that young men as well as women from ethnic minorities were consistently employed less than their ethnic Dutch counterparts. Fewer of non-ethnic than ethnic Dutch females married. It is also possible that other barriers, such as cultural conflict or dissonance, or discrimination on the labour and marriage market, make it more difficult for minority youths to successfully make the transition to adulthood.

Bakker, Walberg and Blom (2005) sought to explain the overrepresentation of ethnic youths in crime figures as a shortage of social capital. These youths suffer from the fact that social bonds within their own ethnic group are weak or nonexistent. They lack 'social bridges' to other social groups and institutions and therefore are unfamiliar with norms and expectations and thus do not possess adequate social skills. Interventions based on these insights could be promising (Slot, 2010) since the building of social capital implies the use of positive procedures focusing on skill training and enlargement of knowledge that are better tools for reducing crime than repression.

Section III: The Headlines

We started out with Arnett's thesis that there is a period called 'emerging adulthood' (Arnett, 2000) between adolescence and adulthood. We do not think that such a term is useful for future legal purposes because it will be difficult if not impossible to create a new terminology in law statutes. On the other hand, the period between adolescence and early adulthood is unique in two ways. First, because the proportion of juvenile and young adult offenders in populations decreases with time as is evident from the down-slope of the age–crime curve, which usually does not flatten out until early adulthood. Second, the period between adolescence and early adulthood is unique in that, on average, juveniles' cognitive and behavioural maturation, as shown by their impulsivity and sensation seeking, is not complete at age 18, which is the age at which most European countries stipulate that adulthood starts. Thus, two major indicators of adulthood, that is, lowered offending and lowered impulsivity, do not map at all on current definitions of the minimum age of adulthood.

We posit that there is nothing magical about a legal calendar age of adulthood and that it is based on assumptions rather than on evidence. That young people tend to be more impulsive and that the majority grow out of it during early adulthood is well recognized by many commercial organizations, including car insurance and rental companies. It is perplexing why many politicians appear to ignore adolescents' naturally declining propensity to commit crime and naturally improving cognitive maturity. It is also remarkable that, whereas many legislators promote changes in evidence-based and cost-effective policies in multiple areas of government, scientific findings about the intersection between the age–crime curve and juveniles' maturational development often are ignored in legislation and the practice of juvenile and adult law (Doreleijers and Fokkens, 2010).

Legislators and policymakers can learn from research findings showing normative decreases in impulsivity and offending during adolescence and early adulthood, and that these changes do not map well on current legal statutes governing when juvenile justice ends and adult justice starts. This means that many young persons who engage in impulsive forms of offending are directed away from juvenile justice with its rehabilitative programmes to adult justice with its more punitive and longer sentences, resulting in longer periods of incarceration usually without rehabilitative programmes. The situation is especially dire for vulnerable young men and women, such as those with low intelligence who, compared to youth with higher intelligence, often take longer to mature cognitively and behaviourally. Another vulnerable category is offenders with serious mental health disorders. Keeping vulnerable and less vulnerable young offenders in adult prisons beyond their propensity to offend is comparable to keeping patients with physical ailments in hospital beyond their time of recovery. Both examples are economically wasteful, and unjust from a human rights point of view.

There are two other reasons why more legislators and researchers should focus on early adulthood. First, this is a period in which a minority of the juvenile offenders will persist in their delinquency and become adult offenders. Second, another group will experience adult-onset offending. During this time some individuals may become violent, while others start engaging in 'new' forms of crime such as fraud, trafficking in humans, identify theft, cyber criminality, electronic forms of economic crimes, and prostitution.

There is no single 'silver bullet' solution to the problems addressed in this volume. We have the following recommendations for a strategic plan for legislators, policymakers, judiciary, and other individuals working with juveniles in and outside of the juvenile and adult courts:

- All sentencing decisions should incorporate consideration of both reduced competence to understand court proceedings and reduced culpability because of poor maturation. Thus, a 'reduced competency' and a 'reduced maturity' discount should be applied when sentencing young adults under current law.
- We are not in favour of transferring juveniles to the adult court. There are two major reasons: transfer is contrary to article 31 of the United Nation Convention on the Right of the Child. The second reason is that transfer of juveniles to the adult court should not occur for youths of low intelligence and youths who are cognitively immature.
- Four types of screening devices need to be routinely used in the court to optimize fair decision making, including decision making for vulnerable populations of youth:
  - Screening devices to ascertain juvenile offenders' risk of recidivism and to inform on the sentencing need to be used for young adults as well.
  - Screening instruments to assess young people's competence to stand trial.
  - Screening instruments to assess young people's mental health.
  - Screening instruments to assess young people's cognitive immaturity (this category of assessment tools is currently in the greatest need of being validated).
- Drug- and alcohol-using juvenile offenders should be routinely referred to drug treatment.
- Serious consideration should be given to establish Young Offender Courts for offenders between the ages of 18 and 25, modelled after the British examples. Once the most practical and effective models are identified, these should be established in every major European city and thus obviate the need for transfer laws.

- It is not widely recognized that self-control (as the opposite of impulsivity) is malleable (see for example, Piquero, Jennings and Farrington, 2010b). Along that line, intervention programmes in and outside of the justice system show that maturational processes can be accelerated so that youth with delayed maturation can 'catch up'. We recommend that such programmes should be implemented, preferably prior to the minimum age of criminal responsibility (average age 12, but this varies from country to country; Loeber and Farrington, 2002).
- Thus, the adult justice system should be a last rather than a first call to rehabilitate impulsive and immature juveniles and young adults, who constitute a special category of developing youth.

Based on what has been documented in this volume, we advocate a three-pronged approach to achieve key necessary improvements as outlined in part in our recommendations above. First, we advocate interventions with impulsive youth at a young age, well before a contact with the justice system. We believe that the benefits of reduced impulsivity and improved self-control by young people go way beyond offending and include many other positive outcomes as well (for example, enhanced academic achievements, contacts with peers and parents, intimate relations).

Second, we call for justice programmes to use the knowledge amassed by scholars in this volume and elsewhere to investigate how justice can be applied more fairly on the basis of what is known about youngsters' maturational development, and reduce unnecessary severe and long sanctions for those whose offending is likely to soon diminish or cease.

Third, we advocate a forward-looking administrative model in both the juvenile and adult criminal justice systems that bases programme placements and supervision levels upon objective risk and needs assessments, and supports individualized case management plans focused on improving future behaviour rather than punishing past behaviour. Use of this forward-looking administrative framework and advanced management tools should increase the capacity of state juvenile justice systems to more effectively control and rehabilitate adolescents on the verge or at high risk of becoming transition offenders (Howell, Feld and Mears, 2012).

We conclude that young adult offenders aged 18–24 are more similar to juveniles than to adults with respect to features such as their executive functioning, impulse control, malleability, responsibility, susceptibility to peer influence, and adjudicative competence. Therefore, we make the following policy recommendations (some of which are alternatives):

1. Changes in legislation are warranted to prevent large numbers of juvenile offenders becoming adult criminals. We recommend raising the minimum age for referral of young people to the adult court to age 21 or 24 so that fewer young offenders are dealt with in the adult criminal justice system. There are several advantages: fewer young offenders will be incarcerated, fewer of them will be exposed to the criminogenic influences of incarceration,

and more of them can receive alternative, non-custodial, rehabilitative sanctions. We expect that, consequently, the number of adult prisoners will decrease and considerable savings for taxpayers will accrue. To prompt legislative change, we recommend cost–benefit analyses to quantify the benefits of legally raising the minimum age of adult jurisdiction to 21 or 24. There have been cost–benefit analyses in the US of the effects of raising the minimum age from 16–18 (Henrichson and Levshin, 2011). An English report concluded that 'diversion from trial under adult law to trial under juvenile law following maturity assessment is likely to produce cost saving to society' of £420 per offender (Barrow Cadbury Trust, 2009, p. 3). More analyses are needed to quantify the monetary costs and benefits of legally raising the age of juvenile jurisdiction to age 21–24, which is our favoured recommendation.

2. Alternatively, special courts for young adult offenders aged 18–24 could be established on an experimental basis in a small number of areas (building on the experience of the UK Transition to Adulthood Alliance; see www.t2a.org.uk). Three reasons support creating special courts for young adult offenders: (i) preventing excessive punishment of young people who land in the adult justice system; (ii) youthfulness as a mitigating factor; and (iii) the developmental needs of young people. The focus should be on rehabilitation rather than retribution. Since juveniles who are transferred to adult courts tend to receive more severe sentences and tend to have higher recidivism rates than those in juvenile courts, we expect that these special courts would decrease recidivism and decrease incarceration, and consequently save taxpayer money. In addition, they should be designed to have fewer ongoing stigmatizing effects than the adult criminal courts.
3. A third option is to set up special correctional facilities for young adult offenders and include programmes such as cognitive-behavioural therapy, drug treatment, restorative justice, mentoring, education and vocational training, and work release. Most research shows that there is no evidence that either longer sentences or lengthening the period of incarceration provides benefits in terms of reducing the recidivism of serious offenders.
4. There could be a 'reduced maturity consideration' for young adult offenders: a decrease in the severity of penalties that takes account of young persons' lesser culpability and diminished responsibility. Along that line, death sentences and life without parole sentences should be abolished for young adult offenders.
5. There should be risk/needs assessments and screening of young adult offenders to guide the selection of appropriate dispositions and interventions. This screening should assess topics such as executive functioning and impulse control, in addition to risk factors such as low intelligence. Young adult offenders with substance use problems should be diverted to drug courts, and those with mental health problems should be dealt with by mental health professionals.

6. There should be evidence-based programmes for young adult offenders in the community and after release, including multisystemic therapy, cognitive-behavioural therapy, drug treatment, restorative justice, mentoring, educational and vocational training programmes, and programmes such as Communities That Care (see Farrington and Welsh, 2007). Employment and relationship programmes should be offered to encourage desistance, as well as other programmes aimed at reducing disorderly transitions such as not graduating from high school and single teenage parenthood. Other useful programmes are those aiming to reduce opportunities for offending, such as 'hot spots policing' and situational crime prevention, and reducing gang membership and drug dealing (especially targeted at high-crime neighbourhoods). In addition, in light of the long-term positive effects of early nurse home visiting, parent training, and family-based programmes, these also should be more widely implemented and followed up to assess their effects on young adult offending.

In summary, all of these initiatives should be rigorously evaluated, in randomized experiments or high quality quasi-experimental studies, and cost-benefit analyses should be carried out. Age, gender, and racial/ethnic differences in the effectiveness of programs should be studied.

We urge governments in Europe and elsewhere to develop an action plan to implement the key recommendations in this volume to assist institutions in changing their statutes and practices so that justice is applied more fairly and with more knowledge of how youth develop into mature adults. We believe that, in efforts to effect improvements in the safety of citizens and communities, our three-pronged approach offers more hope and more benefits than does the implementation of longer sentencing of young people in the adult justice system. The litmus test will be whether concerted preventive and remedial interventions in and outside of the justice system can lower and shrink the age–crime curve for future generations of young people.

References

Acoca, L. (1998). Outside/inside: The violation of American girls at home, on the streets, and in the juvenile justice system. *Crime and Delinquency*, 44, 561–89.

Agnew, R. (2009). The contribution of mainstream theories to the explanation of female delinquency. In M. Zahn (ed.), *The Delinquent Girl*. Philadelphia, PA: Temple University Press, pp. 7–29.

American Psychiatric Association (1994). *Diagnostic and Statistical Manual of Mental Disorders* (4th edn). Washington, DC: American Psychiatric Association.

Allen, R. (2012). Young adults and the English criminal justice system: The policy challenges. In A.E. Bottoms, F. Lösel and D.P. Farrington (eds), *Young Adult Offenders: Lost in Transition?* London: Routledge.

American Psychiatric Association (2005). *Diagnostic and Statistical Manual of Mental Disorders* (4th edn, text revision). Washington, DC: American Psychiatric Association.

Arnett, J.J. (2000). Emerging adulthood: A theory of development from the late teens through the twenties. *American Psychologist*, 55, 469–80.

Baer, D., Bhati, A., Brooks, L., Castro, J., La Vigne, N., Mallik-Kane, K., Naser, R. Osborne, J., Roman, C., Roman, J., Rossman, S., Solomon, A., Visher, C., and Winterfield, L. (2006). *Understanding the Challenges of Prisoner Reentry: Research Findings from the Urban Institute's Prisoner Reentry Portfolio.* Washington, DC: Justice Policy Center.

Bakker, B.F.M., Walberg, A., and Blom, M (2005). Jeugdige verdachten. In M. Blom, J. Oudhof, R.V. Bijl and B.F.M. Bakker (eds), *Verdacht van criminaliteit. Allochtonen en autochtonen nader bekeken* (Cahier 2005-2, pp. 45–58). The Hague: Ministerie van Justitie, Wetenschappelijk Onderzoek- en Documentatie Centrum.

Barrow Cadbury Trust (2005). *Lost in Transition.* London: Author.

Barrow Cadbury Trust (2009). *Economic Analysis of Interventions for Young Adult offenders.* London: Author.

Barrow Cadbury Trust and International Centre for Prison Studies (2011). *Young Adults and Criminal Justice: International Norms and Practices.* London: Barrow Cadbury Trust.

Bergseth, K.J. and Bouffard, J.A. (2007). The long-term impact of restorative justice programming for juvenile offenders. *Journal of Criminal Justice*, 35, 433–51.

Bernburg, J.G. and Krohn, M.D. (2003). Labeling, life chances, and adult crime: The direct and indirect effects of official intervention in adolescence on crime in early adulthood. *Criminology*, 41, 1287–318.

Berrueta-Clement, J.R., Schweinhart, L.J., Barnett, W.S., Epstein, A.S., and Weikart, D.P. (1984). *Changed Lives: The Effects of the Perry Preschool Program on Youths through Age 19.* Ypsilanti, MI: High/Scope Educational Research Foundation.

Bersani, B.E., Laub, J.H., and Nieuwbeerta, P. (2009). Marriage and desistance from crime in the Netherlands: Do gender and socio-historical context matter? *Journal of Quantitative Criminology*, 25, 3–24.

Bijleveld, C., Hendriks, J., and Vinke, M. (2003). Moeilijke meisjes: Een exploratieve studie naar de relatie tussen delict- en persoon(lijkhei)skenmerken in een groep delinquente meisjes [Problematic girls: An explorative study to the link between offence and personality characteristics in a group of delinquent girls]. *Tijdschrift voor Criminologie*, 45, 53–70.

Bishop, D.M. and Frazier, C.E. (2000). Consequences of transfer. In J. Fagan and F.E. Zimring (eds), *The Changing Borders of Juvenile Justice: Transfer of*

Adolescents to the Criminal Court. Chicago, IL: University of Chicago Press, pp. 227–76.

Blackburn, R. (1993). *The Psychology of Criminal Conduct: Theory, Research and Practice*. Chichester: Wiley.

Blokland, A.A.J. and Nieuwbeerta, P. (2005). The effects of life circumstances on longitudinal trajectories of offending. *Criminology*, 43, 1203–40.

Blumstein, A., Cohen, J., Roth, J.A., and Visher, C.A. (1986). *Criminal Careers and 'Career Criminals'*. Washington, DC: National Academy Press.

Boisjoli, R., Vitaro, F., LaCourse, E., Barker, E.D., and Tremblay, R.E. (2007). Impact and clinical significance of a preventive intervention for disruptive boys: A 15-year follow-up. *British Journal of Psychiatry*, 191, 415–19.

Bosick, J. S. (2009). Crime and the transition to adulthood: A person-centered analysis of at-risk boys coming of age in 1940s Boston, 1970s London, and 1990s Pittsburgh. Unpublished Ph.D. dissertation, Harvard University, Cambridge, MA.

Burnett, R. and Santos, G.H. (2011) Found in transition? Local inter-agency systems for guiding young adults into better lives: Final Report of the Formative Evaluation of the T2A Pilots.

Bushway, S. and Reuter, P. (2002). Labor markets and crime risk factors. In L. Sherman, D. Farrington, B. Welsh and D. MacKenzie (eds), *Evidence-based Crime Prevention*. New York: Routledge, pp. 198–240.

Capaldi, D.M. and Stoolmiller, M. (1999). Co-occurrence of conduct problems and depressive symptoms in early adolescent boys: III. Prediction to young-adult adjustment. *Development and Psychopathology*, 11, 59–84.

Chamberlain, P., Leve, L.D., and DeGarmo, D.S. (2007). Multidimensional treatment foster care for girls in the juvenile justice system: 2-year follow-up of a randomized clinical trial. *Journal of Consulting and Clinical Psychology*, 75, 187–93.

Chassin, L., Dmitrieva, J., Modecki, K., Steinberg, L., Cauffman, E., Piquero, A.R., Knight, G.P., and Losoya, S.H. (2010). Does adolescent alcohol and marijuana use predict suppressed growth psychosocial maturity among male juvenile offenders? *Psychology of Addictive Behaviors*, 24, 48–60.

Chesney-Lind, M. (1997). *The Female Offender: Girls, Women, and Crime*. Thousand Oaks, CA: Sage.

Childs, K.K., Sullivan, C.J., and Culledge, L.M. (2010). Delinquent behavior across adolescence: Investigating the shifting salience of key criminological predictors. *Deviant Behavior*, 32, 64–100.

Courtney, M.E. (2009). The difficult transition to adulthood for foster youth in the U.S.: Implications for the state as corporate parent. *Social Policy Report*, 23, 3–18.

Cuellar, A.E., McReynolds, L.S., and Wasserman, G.A. (2006). A cure for crime: Can mental health treatment diversion reduce crime among youth? *Journal of Policy Analysis and Management*, 25, 197–214.

D'Onfrio, B.M., Slutske, W.S., Turkheimer, E., Emery, R.E., Harden, K.P., Heath, A.C., Madden, P.A.F., and Martin, N.G. (2007). Intergenerational transmission of childhood conduct problems: A children of twins study. *Archives of General Psychiatry*, 64, 820–29.

Daly, K. and Chesney-Lind, M. (1988). Feminism and criminology. *Justice Quarterly*, 5, 497–538.

De Brito, S.A., Mechelli, A., Wilke, M., Laurens, K.R., Jones, A.P., Barker, G.J., Hodgins, S., and Viding, E. (2009). Size matters: Increased grey matter in boys with conduct problems and callous–unemotional traits. *Brain: A Journal of Neurology*, 132, 843–52.

Dodge, K.A. (2009). Community intervention and public policy in the prevention of antisocial behavior. *Journal of Child Psychology and Psychiatry*, 50, 194–200.

Donker, A.G., Smeenk, W.H., Van der Laan, P.H., and Verhulst, F.C. (2003). Individual stability of antisocial behavior from childhood to adulthood: Testing the stability postulate of Moffitt's developmental theory. *Criminology*, 41, 593–610.

Doreleijers, T. and Fokkens, J.W. (2010). Minderjarigen en jongvolwassenen: Pleidooi voor een evidence based strafrecht. *Rechtsreeks*, 2, 1–47.

Dunkel, F. and Pruin, I. (2012). Young adult offenders in juvenile and criminal justice systems in Europe. In A.E. Bottoms, F. Lösel, and D.P. Farrington (eds), *Young Adult Offenders: Lost in Transition?* London: Routledge.

Eddy, J.M., Whaley, R.B., and Chamberlain, P. (2004). The prevention of violent behavior by chronic and serious male juvenile offenders: A 2-year follow-up of a randomized clinical trial. *Journal of Emotional and Behavioral Disorders*, 12, 2–8.

Elliott, D.S., Pampel, F., and Huizinga, D. (2004). *Youth Violence: Continuity and Desistance. A Supplemental Report to Youth Violence: A Report of the Surgeon General*. Boulder, CO: Center for the Study and Prevention of Violence, Institute of Behavior Science, University of Colorado.

Ezinga, M. and Hissel, S. (2010). *Wellbeing and Behavior of the Children of Incarcerated Mothers*. Paper presented at the annual meeting of the American Society of Criminology, San Francisco, CA.

Fabio, A., Cohen, J., and Loeber, R. (2011). Neighborhood socioeconomic disadvantage and the shape of the age–crime curve. *American Journal of Public Health*, 101(1), S325–32.

Farrington, D.P. (1986). Age and crime. In M. Tonry and N. Morris (eds), *Crime and Justice: An Annual Review of Research* (vol. 7, pp. 189–250). Chicago, IL: University of Chicago Press.

Farrington, D.P. (1997). A critical analysis of research on the development of antisocial behavior from birth to adulthood. In D.M. Stoff, J. Breiling and J.D. Maser (eds), *Handbook of Antisocial Behavior*. New York: Wiley, pp. 234–40.

Farrington, D.P. (2003). Key results from the first 40 years of the Cambridge Study in Delinquent Development. In T.P. Thornberry and M.D. Krohn (eds),

Taking Stock of Delinquency: An Overview of Findings from Contemporary Longitudinal Studies. New York: Kluwer-Plenum, pp. 137–83.

Farrington, D.P., Barnes, G.C., and Lambert, S. (1996). The concentration of offending in families. *Legal and Criminological Psychology*, 1, 47–63.

Farrington, D.P., Coid, J.W., Harnett, L.M., Jolliffe, D., Soteriou, N., Turner, R.E., and West, D.J. (2006). *Criminal Careers up to Age 50 and Life Success up to Age 48: New Findings from the Cambridge Study in Delinquent Development*. London: Home Office (Research Study No. 299).

Farrington, D.P., Gallagher, B., Morley, L., St Ledger, R.J., and West, D.J. (1986). Unemployment, school leaving and crime. *British Journal of Criminology*, 26, 335–56.

Farrington, D.P. and Hawkins, J.D. (1991). Predicting participation, early onset and later persistence in officially recorded offending. *Criminal Behaviour and Mental Health*, 1, 1–33.

Farrington, D.P. and Welsh, B.C. (2007). *Saving Children from a Life of Crime: Early Risk Factors and Effective Interventions*. New York: Oxford University Press.

Fazel, S., Lichtenstein, P., Grann, M., Goodwin, G.M., and Långström, N. (2010). Bipolar disorder and violent crime: New evidence from population-based longitudinal studies and systematic review. *Archives of General Psychiatry*, 67, 931–8.

Feld, B. (2008). A slower form of death: Implications of Roper v. Simmons for juveniles sentenced to life without parole. *Notre Dame Journal of Law Ethics and Public Policy*, 9, 26–40.

Fontaine, N., Carbonneau, R., Vitaro, F., and Barker, E.D. (2009). Research review: A critical review of studies on the development trajectories of antisocial behavior in females. *Journal of Child Psychology and Psychiatry*, 50, 363–85.

Foss, R. (2002). Graduated driver licensing. Translating injury prevention research into action: A strategic workshop, Dallas, Texas, 2 January 2002.

Foster, M.E., Flanagan, C., Osgood, D.W. and Ruth, G.R. (2005). The transition to adulthood for vulnerable youths and families: Common themes and future directions. In D.W. Osgood, M.E. Foster, C. Flanagan and G.R. Ruth (eds), *On your Own Without a Net: The Transition to Adulthood for Vulnerable Populations*. Chicago, IL: University of Chicago Press, pp. 375–409.

Garrido, V., Anyela Morales, L., and Sánchez-Meca, J. (2006). What works for serious juvenile offenders? A systematic review. *Psicothema*, 18, 611–19.

Ge, X., Conger, R.D., and Elder, G.H. (2001). Pubertal transition, stressful life events, and the emergence of gender differences in adolescent depressive symptoms. *Developmental Psychology*, 37, 404–17.

Giedd, J.N. (2004). Structural magnetic resonance imaging of the adolescent brain. *Annals of the New York Academy of Sciences*, 1021, 77–85.

Giedd, J.N., Rumsey, J.M., Castellanos, F.X., Rajapakse, J.C., Kaysen, D., Vaituzis, A.C., Vauss, Y.C., Hamburger, S.D., and Rapoport, J.L. (1996). A quantitative

MRI study of the corpus callosum in children and adolescents. *Developmental Brain Research*, 91, 274–80.
Giordano, P.C., Cernkovich, S.A., and Rudolph, J.L. (2002). Gender, crime, and desistance: Toward a theory of cognitive transformation. *American Journal of Sociology*, 107, 990–1064.
Gordon, D.A., Graves, K., and Arbuthnot, J. (1995). The effect of functional family therapy for delinquents on adult criminal behavior. *Criminal Justice and Behavior*, 22, 60–73.
Gottfredson, M.R. and Hirschi, T. (1990). *A General Theory of Crime*. Stanford, CA: Stanford University Press.
Griffin, P. (2012). Legal boundaries between the juvenile and criminal justice systems in the United States. In R. Loeber and D.P. Farrington (eds), *From Juvenile Delinquency to Adult Crime: Criminal Careers, Justice Policy and Prevention*. New York: Oxford University Press.
Grisso, T., Steinberg, L., Woolard, J., Cauffman, E., Scott, E., Graham, S., Lexcan, F., Reppucci, N.D., and Schwartz, R. (2003). Juveniles' competence to stand trial: A comparison of adolescents' and adults' capacities as trial defendants. *Law and Human Behavior*, 27, 333–63.
Hagan, J. and McCarthy, B. (2005). Homeless youth and the perilous passage to adulthood. In D.W. Osgood, E.M. Foster, C. Flanagan and G.R. Ruth (eds), *On your own without a Net: The Transition to Adulthood for Vulnerable Populations*. Chicago, IL: University of Chicago Press, pp. 178–201.
Hamerlynck, S.M.J.J. (2008). Girls in juvenile justice institutions: Psychopathology and sexual risk behavior. Unpublished doctoral dissertation, VU University Amsterdam, Amsterdam.
Hamerlynck, S.M.J.J., Doreleijers, T.A.H., Vermeiren, R., Jansen, L.M.C., and Cohen-Kettenis, P.T. (2008). Aggression and psychopathology in detained adolescent females. *Psychiatry Research*, 159, 77–85.
Hanson, R.K., Gordon, A., Marques, J.K., Murphy, W., Quinsey, V.L., and Seto, M.C. (2002). First report of the collaborative outcome data project on the effectiveness of psychological treatment for sex offenders. *Sexual Abuse*, 14, 169–94.
Harte, J. and Breukink, M. (2010). Objectiviteit of schijnzekerheid? Kwaliteit, mogelijkheden en beperkingen van instrumenten voor risicotaxatie. *Tijdschrift voor Criminologie*, 52, 52–72.
Hawkins, J.D., Brown, E.C., Oesterle, S., Arthur, M.W., Abbott, R.D., and Catalano, R.F. (2008). Early effects of communities that care on targeted risks and initiation of delinquent behavior and substance abuse. *Journal of Adolescent Health*, 43, 15–22.
Hay, C. (2003). Family strain, gender, and delinquency. *Sociological Perspectives*, 46, 107–35.
Helyar-Cardwell, V. (2009a). *A New Start: Young Adults in the Criminal Justice System*. London: Transition to Adulthood Alliance.
Helyar-Cardwell, V. (2009b). *Young Adult Manifesto*. London: Transition to Adulthood Alliance.

Henggeler, S.W., Cunningham, P.B., Pickrel, S.G., Schoenwald, S.K., and Brondino, M.J. (1996). Multisystemic therapy: An effective violence prevention approach for serious juvenile offenders. *Journal of Adolescence*, 19, 47–61.

Henrichson, C. and Levshin, V. (2011). *Cost–benefit Analysis of Raising the Age of Juvenile Court Jurisdiction in North Carolina*. New York: Vera Institute of Justice.

Hipwell, A.E. and Loeber, R. (2006). Do we know which interventions are effective for disruptive and delinquent girls? *Clinical Child and Family Psychology Review*, 9, 221–55.

Hipwell, A.E., Loeber, R., Stouthamer-Loeber, M., Keenan, K., White, H.R., and Kroneman, L. (2002). Characteristics of girls with early onset disruptive and antisocial behaviour. *Criminal Behaviour and Mental Health*, 12, 99–118.

Hodgins, S., De Brito, S.A., Chhabra, P., and Coté, G. (2010). Anxiety disorders among offenders with antisocial personality disorders: A distinct subtype? *Canadian Journal of Psychiatry*, 55, 784–91.

Hodgins, S., De Brito, S., Simonoff, E., Vloet, T., and Viding, E. (2009). Getting the phenotypes right: An essential ingredient for understanding aetiological mechanisms underlying persistent violence and developing effective treatments. *Frontiers of Behavioral Neuroscience*, 3. DOI: 10.3389/neuro.08.044.2009.

Hoekendijk, G.P. and Niemeijer, E. (2010). Over de betekenis van grenzen in het jeugdstrafrecht. *Sancties*, 5, 233–46.

Hoge, R., and Andrews, D. (2010). *Evaluation for Risk of Violence in Juveniles*. New York: Oxford University Press.

Hoge, R.D., Vincent, G., and Guy, L. (2012). Prediction and risk/needs assessments. In R. Loeber and D.P. Farrington (eds), *From Juvenile Delinquency to Adult Crime: Criminal Careers, Justice Policy and Prevention*. New York: Oxford University Press.

Horney, J., Tolan, P., and Weisburd, D. (2012). Contextual influences. In R. Loeber and D.P. Farrington (eds), *From Juvenile Delinquency to Adult Crime: Criminal Careers, Justice Policy and Prevention*. New York: Oxford University Press.

Howell, J.C. (2011). *Understanding and Combating Gangs in America*. Thousand Oaks, CA: Sage.

Howell, J.C., Feld, B.C., and Mears, D.P. (2012). Young offenders and an effective justice system response: What happens, what should happen, and what we need to know. In R. Loeber and D.P. Farrington (eds), *From Juvenile Delinquency to Adult Crime: Criminal Careers, Justice Policy and Prevention*. New York: Oxford University Press.

Hucker, S.J. (1997). Impulsivity in DSM-IV impulse-control disorders. In C.D. Webster and M.A. Jackson (eds), *Impulsivity: Theory, Assessment, and Treatment*. New York: Guilford Press, pp. 195–311.

Huizinga, D. and Henry, K.L. (2008). The effect of arrest and justice system sanctions on subsequent behavior: Findings from longitudinal and other studies.

In A. Liberman (ed.), *The Long View of Crime: A Synthesis of Longitudinal Research*. New York: Springer, pp. 220–54.

Huizinga, D., Thornberry, T.P., Knight, K.E., Lovegrove, P.J., Loeber, R., Hill, K., and Farrington, D.P. (2006). *Disproportionate Minority Contact in the Juvenile Justice System: A Study of Differential Minority Arrest/Referral to Court in Three Cities*. Report to the Office of Juvenile Justice and Delinquency Prevention, at http://www.ncjrs.gov/pdffiles1/ojjdp/grants/219743.pdf, accessed 8 February 2012.

Hussong, A.M., Curran, P.J., Moffitt, T.E., Caspi, A., and Carrig, M.M. (2004). Substance abuse hinders desistance in young adults' antisocial behavior. *Development and Psychopathology*, 16, 1029–46.

Jennissen, R. (2009). *Criminaliteit, leeftijd en etniciteit: Over de afwijkende leeftijdsspecifieke criminaliteitscijfers van Antillianen en Marokkanen*. The Hague: WODC.

Jolliffe, D. and Farrington, D.P. (2009). A systematic review of the relationship between childhood impulsiveness and later violence. In M. McMurran and R. Howard (eds), *Personality, Personality Disorder, and Violence*. New York: Wiley, pp. 41–62.

Jolliffe, D. and Farrington, D.P. (2010). Individual differences and offending. In E. McLaughlin and T. Newburn (eds), *The Sage Handbook of Criminological Theory*. Thousand Oaks, CA: Sage, pp. 40–55.

Joyal, C.C., Dubreucq, J-L., Gendron, C. and Millaud, F. (2007). Major mental disorders and violence: A critical update. *Current Psychiatry Reviews*, 3, 33–50.

Junger-Tas, J., Ribeaud, D., and Cruyff, M.J.L.F. (2004). Juvenile delinquency and gender. *European Journal of Criminology*, 1, 333–75.

Kazemian, L., and Farrington. D.P. (2006). Exploring residual career length and residual number of offenses for two generations of repeat offenders. *Journal of Research in Crime and Delinquency*, 43, 89–113.

Kazemian, L. and Farrington, D.P. (2010). The developmental evidence base: Desistance. In G.J. Towl and D.A. Crighton (eds), *Forensic Psychology*. Hoboken, NJ: Wiley Blackwell, pp. 133–47.

Kempf-Leonard, K., Tracy, P.E., and Howell, J.C. (2001). Serious, violent, and chronic juvenile offenders: The relationship of delinquency career types to adult criminality. *Justice Quarterly*, 18, 449–78.

Kerig, P.K., and Becker, S.P. (2010). From internalizing to externalizing: Theoretical models of the processes linking PTSD to juvenile delinquency. In S.J. Egan (ed.), *Post-traumatic Stress Disorder (PTSD): Causes, Symptoms, and Treatment*. Hauppauge, NY: Nova Science, pp. 33–78.

Kershaw, C., Nicholas, S., and Walker, A. (2008). *Crime in England and Wales 2007/08*. London: Home Office. At www.homeoffice.gov.uk/rds/pdfs08/hosb0708.pdf, accessed 8 February 2012.

Killias, M., Aebi, M., and Ribeaud, D. (2000). Does community service rehabilitate better than short-term imprisonment? Results of a controlled experiment. *Howard Journal of Criminal Justice*, 39, 40–57.

King, R.D., Massoglia, M., and Macmillan, R. (2007). The context of marriage and crime: Gender, the propensity to marry, and offending in early adulthood. *Criminology*, 45, 33–65.

Koolhof, R., Loeber, R., Wei, E.H., Pardini, D., and Collot d'Escury, A. (2007). Inhibition deficits of serious delinquent boys of low intelligence. *Criminal Behaviour and Mental Health*, 17, 274–92.

Kraemer, H.C. (1992). Measurement of reliability for categorical data in medical research. *Statistical Methods in Medical Research*, 1, 183–99.

Kroneman, L.M., Loeber, R., Hipwell, A.E., and Koot, H.M. (2009). Girls' disruptive behavior and its relationship to family functioning: A review. *Journal of Child and Family Studies*, 18, 259–73.

Kupchik, A. (2006). *Prosecuting Adolescents in Adult and Juvenile Courts*. New York: New York University Press.

Le Blanc, M. and Fréchette, M. (1989). *Male Criminal Activity from Childhood through Youth: Multilevel and Developmental Perspectives*. New York: Springer.

Landenberger, N.A. and Lipsey, M.W. (2005). The positive effects of cognitive-behavioral programs for offenders: A meta-analysis of factors associated with effective treatment. *Journal of Experimental Criminology*, 1, 451–76.

Lewis, M.D., Granic, I., Lamm, C., Zelazo, P.D., Stieben, J., Todd, R.M., Moadab, I., and Pepler, D. (2008). Changes in the neural bases of emotion regulation associated with clinical improvement in children with behavior problems. *Development and Psychopathology*, 20, 913–39.

Lipsey, M.W. (2009). The primary factors that characterize effective interventions with juvenile offenders: A meta-analytic overview. *Victims and Offenders*, 4, 124–47.

Lipsey, M.W. and Cullen, F.T. (2007). The effectiveness of correctional rehabilitation: A review of systematic reviews. *Annual Review of Law and Social Science*, 3, 297–20.

Lipsey, M.W. and Derzon, J.H. (1998). Predictors of violent or serious delinquency in adolescence and early adulthood: A synthesis of longitudinal research. In R. Loeber and D.P. Farrington (eds), *Serious and Violent Juvenile Offenders: Risk Factors and Successful Interventions*. Thousand Oaks, CA: Sage Publications, pp. 86–105.

Lipsey, M.W. and Wilson, D.B. (1998). Effective intervention for serious and violent juvenile offenders: A synthesis of research. In R. Loeber and D.P. Farrington (eds), *Serious and Violent Juvenile Offenders: Risk Factors and Effective interventions*. Thousand Oaks, CA: Sage, pp. 313–45.

Loeber, R. and Dishion, T. (1983). Early predictors of male delinquency: A review. *Psychological Bulletin*, 94, 68–99.

Loeber, R. and Farrington, D.P. (eds) (1998). *Serious and Violent Juvenile offenders: Risk Factors and Successful Interventions*. Thousand Oaks, CA: Sage.

Loeber, R. and Farrington, D.P. (eds) (2001). *Child Delinquents: Development, Intervention and Service Needs*. Thousand Oaks, CA: Sage.

Loeber, R. and Farrington, D.P. (2011). *Young Homicide Offenders and Victims: Development, Risk Factors and Prediction from Childhood.* New York: Springer.

Loeber, R. and Farrington, D.P. (eds) (2012), *From Juvenile Delinquency to Adult Crime: Criminal Careers, Justice Policy and Prevention*. New York: Oxford University Press.

Loeber, R., Menting, B., Lynam, D., Moffitt, T.E., Stouthamer-Loeber, M., Stallings, R., Farrington, D.P., Pardini, D. (2011). Findings from the Pittsburgh Youth Study: Cognitive impulsivity and intelligence as predictors of the age–crime curve. Paper submitted for publication.

Loeber, R. and Pardini, D. (2008). Neurobiology and the development of violence: Common assumptions and controversies. *Philosophical Transactions of the Royal Society of Biological Sciences*, 363, 2491–503.

Loeber, R. and Stallings, R. (2011). Modeling the impact of interventions on local indicators of offending, victimization, and incarceration. In R. Loeber and D.P. Farrington (eds), *Young Homicide Offenders and Victims: Development, Risk Factors, and Prediction from Childhood.* New York: Springer, pp. 137–52.

Loeber, R., Slot, W., and Stouthamer-Loeber, M. (2006). A three-dimensional, cumulative developmental model of serious delinquency. In P-O.H. Wikström and R.J. Sampson (eds), *The Explanation of Crime: Context, Mechanisms, and Development*. Cambridge: Cambridge University Press, pp. 153–94.

Loeber, R., Farrington, D.P., Stouthamer-Loeber, M., and White, H.R. (2008). *Violence and Serious Theft: Development and Prediction from Childhood to Adulthood.* Mahwah, NJ: Lawrence Erlbaum.

Loeber, R., Burke, J.D., Lahey, B.B., Winters, A., and Zera, M. (2000). Oppositional defiant disorder and conduct disorder: A review of the past 10 years, part I. *Journal of the American Academy of Child & Adolescent Psychiatry*, 39, 1468–84.

Loeber, R., Menting, B., Lynam, D., Moffitt, T.E., Stouthamer-Loeber, M., Stallings, R., Farrington, D.P., and Pardini, D. (2011). Findings from the Pittsburgh Youth Study: Cognitive impulsivity and intelligence as predictors of the age–crime curve. Paper submitted for publication.

Loeber, R., Pardini, D., Homish, D.L., Wei, E.H., Crawford, A.M., Farrington, D.P., Stouthamer-Loeber, M., Creemers, J., Koehler, S.A., and Rosenfeld, R. (2005). The prediction of violence and homicide in young men. *Journal of Consulting and Clinical Psychology*, 73, 1074–88.

Loughran, T.A., Piquero, A.R., Fagan, J., and Mulvey, E.P. (2009). Differential deterrence: Studying heterogeneity and changes in perceptual deterrence among serious youthful offenders. *Crime & Delinquency*. Advance online publication. DOI: 10.1177/0011128709345971.

Lynam, D.R., Caspi, A., Moffitt, T.E., Wikström, P-O., Loeber, R., and Novak, S. (2000). The interaction between impulsivity and neighborhood context on offending: The effects of impulsivity are stronger in poorer neighborhoods. *Journal of Abnormal Psychology*, 109, 563–74.

Masten, A.S., Obradović, J., and Burt, K. (2006). Resilience in emerging adulthood: Developmental perspectives on continuity and transformation. In J.J. Arnett and J.L. Tanner (eds), *Emerging Adults in America: Coming of Age in the 21st Century*. Washington, DC: American Psychological Association, pp. 173–90.

McCord, J. (1978). A thirty-year follow-up of treatment effects. *American Psychologist*, 2, 284–89.

McGee, T.R. and Farrington, D.P. (2010). Are there any true adult onset offenders? *British Journal of Criminology*, 50, 530–49.

McGowan, A., Hahn, R., Liberman, A., Crosby, A., Fullilove, M., Johnson, R., Moscicki, E., Price, L., Snyder, S., Tuma, F., Lowy, J., Briss, P., Cory, S., Stone, G., and Task Force on Community Preventive Services (2007). Effects on violence of laws and policies facilitating the transfer of juveniles from the juvenile justice system to the adult justice system: A systematic review. *American Journal of Preventive Medicine*, 32, 7–28.

McReynolds, L.S., Schwalbe, C.S., and Wasserman, G.A. (2010). The contribution of psychiatric disorder to juvenile recidivism. *Criminal Justice and Behavior*, 37, 204–16.

Mears, D.P. and Travis, J. (2004). Youth development and reentry. *Youth Violence and Juvenile Justice*, 2, 3–20.

Megargee, E.I. (1966). Undercontrolled and overcontrolled personality types in extreme antisocial aggression. *Psychological Monographs*, 80, 1–29.

Miller, J. and Mullins, C.W. (2009). Feminist theories of juvenile delinquency. In M. Zahn (ed.), *The Delinquent Girl*. Philadelphia, PA: Temple University Press, pp. 30–49.

Mitchell, O., Wilson, D.B., and MacKenzie, D.L. (2006). *The Effectiveness of Incarceration Based Drug Treatment on Criminal Behavior*. The Campbell Collaboration. At http://www.campbellcollaboration.org, accessed 8 February 2012.

Moffitt, T.E. (1993). Adolescence-limited and life-course-persistent antisocial behavior: A developmental taxonomy. *Psychological Review*, 100, 674–701.

Moffitt, T.E. (2006). Life-course-persistent and adolescent limited antisocial behavior. In D. Cicchetti and D.J. Cohen (eds), *Developmental psychopathology: Risk, disorder, and adaptation* (vol. 3, pp. 570–98). New York: Wiley.

Moffitt, T.E., Caspi, A., Rutter, M., and Silva, P.A. (2001). *Sex Differences in Antisocial Behaviour: Conduct Disorder, Delinquency, and Violence in the Dunedin Longitudinal Study*. Cambridge: Cambridge University Press.

Mulvey, E.P. (2011). Highlights from pathways to desistance: A longitudinal study of serious adolescent offenders. *OJJDP Juvenile Justice Fact Sheet*, March.

Mulvey, E.P., Schubert, C.A., and Chung, H.L. (2007). Service use after court involvement in a sample of serious adolescent offenders. *Children and Youth Services Review*, 29, 518–44.

Mulvey, E.P., Steinberg, L., Piquero, A.R., Besana, M., Fagan, J., Schubert, C., and Cauffman, E. (2010). Trajectories of desistance and continuity in antisocial behavior following court adjudication among serious adolescent offenders. *Development and Psychopathology*, 22, 453–75.

Murray, J. and Murray, L. (2010). Parental incarceration, attachment and child psychopathology. *Attachment and Human Development*, 12, 289–309.

Nieuwbeerta, P., Nagin, D.S., and Blokland, A.A.J. (2009). Assessing the impact of first-time imprisonment on offenders' subsequent criminal career development: A matched samples comparison. *Journal of Quantitative Criminology*, 25, 227–57.

O'Brien, B.S. and Frick, P.J. (1996). Reward dominance: Associations with anxiety, conduct problems, and psychopathy in children. *Journal of Abnormal Child Psychology*, 24, 223–40.

Odgers, C., Vincent, G.M., and Corrado, R.R. (2002). A preliminary conceptual framework for the prevention and management of multi-problem youth. In R.R. Corrado, R. Roesch, S.D. Hart and J. Gierowski (eds), *Multi-problem Violent Youth: A Foundation for Comparative Research on Needs, Interventions, and Outcomes*. Amsterdam: IOS Press, pp. 116–29.

Odgers, C.L., Caspi, A., Broadbent, J.M., Dickson, N., Hancox, R.J., Harrington, H., et al. (2007). Prediction of differential adult health burden by conduct problem subtypes in males. *Archives of General Psychiatry*, 64, 476–84.

Ogloff, J.R.P. (1997). A legal perspective on the concept of 'impulsivity'. In C.D. Webster and M.A. Jackson (eds), *Impulsivity: Theory, Assessment, and Treatment*. New York: Guilford, pp. 63–81.

Osgood, D.W., Gold, M., and Miller, C. (1986). *For Better or for Worse? Peer Attachments and Peer Influence among Incarcerated Adolescents*. Paper presented at the annual meeting of the American Society of Criminology, Atlanta, GA.

Petras, H., Kellam, S.G., Brown, C.H., Muthén, B.O., Ialongo, N.S., and Poduska, J.M. (2008). Developmental epidemiological courses leading to antisocial personality disorder and violent and criminal behavior: Effects by young adulthood of a universal preventive intervention in first- and second-grade classrooms. *Drug and Alcohol Dependence*, 1, S45–S59.

Piquero, A.R. (2008). Taking stock of developmental trajectories of criminal activity over the life course. In A. Liberman (ed.), *The Long View of Crime: A Synthesis of Longitudinal Research*. New York: Springer, pp. 23–78.

Piquero, A.R., Farrington, D.P., and Blumstein, A. (2007). *Key Issues in Criminal Career Research: New Analyses of the Cambridge Study in Delinquent Development*. Cambridge: Cambridge University Press.

Piquero, A.R., Hawkins, J.D., and Kazemian, L. (2012). Criminal career patterns. In R. Loeber and D.P. Farrington (eds), *From Juvenile Delinquency to Adult*

Crime: Criminal Careers, Justice Policy and Prevention. New York: Oxford University Press.

Piquero, A.R., Jennings, W.G., and Farrington, D.P. (2009). *Effectiveness of Programs Designed to Improve Self-control*. Stockholm: National Council for Crime Prevention. Via www.bra.se, accessed 8 February 2012.

Piquero, A.R., Jennings, W.G., and Farrington, D.P. (2010a). *Self-control Interventions for Children under Age 10 for Improving Self-control and Delinquency and Problem Behaviours*. Via http://www.campbellcollaboration.org, accessed 8 February 2012.

Piquero, A.R., Jennings, W.G., and Farrington, D.P. (2010b). On the malleability of self-control: Theoretical and policy implications regarding a general theory of crime. *Justice Quarterly*, 27, 803–34.

Popkin, S.J., Leventhal, T., and Weismann, G. (2010). Girls in the 'hood: How safety affects the life chances of low-income girls. *Urban Affairs Review*, 45, 715–44.

Prime, J., White, S., Liriano, S., and Patel, K. (2001). *Criminal Careers of those born between 1953 and 1978*. London: Home Office (Statistical Bulletin 4/01).

Prior, D., Farrow, K., Hughes, N., Kelly, G., Manders, G., White, S., and Wilkinson, B. (2011). *Maturity, Young Adults and Criminal Justice*. Birmingham: Institute of Applied Social Studies, School of Social Policy, University of Birmingham.

Pulkkinen, L. (1982). Self-control and continuity from childhood to late adolescence. In P. Baltes and O. Brim (eds), *Life Span Development and Behavior* (vol. 4, pp. 64–102). San Diego, CA: Academic Press.

Quinsey, V.L., Harris, G.T., Rice, M.E., and Cormier, C.A. (1998). *Violent Offenders: Appraising and Managing Risk*. Washington, DC: American Psychological Association.

Redding, R.E. (2008). *Juvenile Transfer Laws: An Effective Deterrent to Delinquency?* Office of Justice Programs, U.S. Department of Justice.

Redondo, S., Sánchez-Meca, J., and Garrido, V. (2003). Crime treatment in Europe: A review of outcome studies. In J. McGuire (ed.), *Offender Rehabilitation and Treatment: Effective Programs and Policies to Reduce Re-offending*. Chichester: Wiley, pp. 113–42.

Reiss, A.J. and Farrington, D.P. (1991). Advancing knowledge about co-offending: Results from a prospective longitudinal survey of London males. *Journal of Criminal Law and Criminology*, 82, 360–95.

Reynolds, A.J., Temple, J.A., Robertson, D.L., and Mann, E.A. (2001). Long-term effects of an early childhood intervention on educational achievement and juvenile arrest: A 15-year follow-up of low-income children in public schools. *Journal of the American Medical Association*, 285, 2339–46.

Reynolds, A.J., Temple, J.A., Ou, S-R., Robertson, D.L., Mersky, J.P., Topitzes, J.W., and Niles, M.D. (2007). Effects of a school-based, early childhood intervention on adult health and well-being: A 19-year follow-up of low-income families. *Archives of Pediatrics and Adolescent Medicine*, 161, 730–9.

Rosenfeld, R., White, H.R., and Esbensen, F-A. (2012). Special categories of serious and violent offenders: Drug dealers, gang members, homicide offenders, and sex offenders. In R. Loeber and D.P. Farrington (eds), *From Juvenile Delinquency to Adult Crime: Criminal Careers, Justice Policy and Prevention*. New York: Oxford University Press.

Rutter, M., Quinton, D., and Hill, J. (1990). Adult outcomes of institution-reared children: Males and females compared. In L.N. Robins and M. Rutter (eds), *Straight and Devious Pathways from Childhood to Adulthood*. Cambridge: Cambridge University Press, pp. 135–57.

Sampson, R.J. and Laub, J.H. (1990). Crime and deviance over the life course: The salience of adult social bonds. *American Sociological Review*, 55, 609–27.

Satterfield, J.H., Faller, K.J., Crinella, F.M., Schell, A.M., Swanson, J.M., and Homer, L.D. (2007). A 30-year prospective follow-up study of hyperactive boys with conduct problems: Adult criminality. *Journal of the American Academy of Child and Adolescent Psychiatry*, 46, 601–10.

Schaeffer, C.M. and Borduin, C.M. (2005). Long-term follow-up to a randomized clinical trial of multisystemic therapy with serious and violent juvenile offenders. *Journal of Consulting and Clinical Psychology*, 73, 445–53.

Schochet, P.Z., Burghardt, J., and McConnell, S. (2008). Does Job Corps work? Impact findings from the National Job Corps Study. *American Economic Review*, 98, 1864–1886.

Schweinhart, L.J. and Weikart, D.P. (1993). Success by empowerment: The High/Scope Perry Preschool Study through age 27. *Young Children*, 49, 54–58.

Secret, M. (2011). States prosecute fewer teenagers in adult court. *New York Times*, 5 March.

Sherman, L., Gottfredson, D., MacKenzie, D., Eck, J., Reuter, P., and Bushway, S. (1998). *Preventing Crime: What Works, What Doesn't, What's Promising*. Washington, DC: National Institute of Justice.

Siennick, S.E. (2007). The timing and mechanisms of the offending-depression link. *Criminology*, 45, 583–615.

Siennick, S.E. and Osgood, D.W. (2008). A review of research on the impact on crime of transitions to adult roles. In A.M. Liberman (ed.), *The Long View of Crime: A Synthesis of Longitudinal Research*. New York: Springer.

Slot, N.W. (2010). Externaliserende problemen. In N.W. Slot and M.A.G. van Aken (eds), *Psychologie van de adolescentie*. Utrecht: Thieme-Meulenhoff.

Slotboom, A. and Bijleveld, C. (2007). Wat er in je hoofd en je hart zit weet niemand: Gedetineerde vrouwen in Nederland. *Justitiële Verkenningen*, 4, 72–88.

Sowell, E.R., Delis, D., Stiles, J., and Jernigan, T.L. (2001). Improved memory functioning and frontal lobe maturation between childhood and adolescence: A structural MRI study. *Journal of the International Neuropsychological Society*, 7, 312–22.

Steinberg, L. (2004). Risk taking in adolescence: What changes, and why? *Annals of the New York Academy of Sciences*, 1021, 51–58.

Steinberg, L., Cauffman, E., Woolard, J., Graham, S., and Banich, M. (2009). Are adolescents less mature than adults? Minors' access to abortion, the juvenile death penalty, and the alleged APA 'flip-flop'. *American Psychologist*, 64, 583–94.

Stouthamer-Loeber, M. (2010). *Persistence and Desistance in Offending*. Unpublished report. Life History Research Program, University of Pittsburgh, Pittsburgh, PA.

Stouthamer-Loeber, M., Loeber, R., Stallings, R., and Lacourse, E. (2008). Desistance from and persistence in offending. In R. Loeber, D.P. Farrington, M. Stouthamer-Loeber and H.R. White, *Violence and Serious Theft: Risk and Promotive Factors from Childhood to Early Adulthood*. Mahwah, NJ: Erlbaum, pp. 269–308.

Stouthamer-Loeber, M., Wei, E., Loeber, R., and Masten, A.S. (2004). Desistance from persistent serious delinquency in the transition to adulthood. *Development and Psychopathology*, 16, 897–918.

Sweeten, G. (2006). Who will graduate? Disruption of high school education by arrest and court involvement. *Justice Quarterly*, 23, 462–80.

Teplin, L.A., McClelland, G.M., Abram, K.M., and Weiner, D.A. (2005). Crime victimization in adults with severe mental illness: Comparison with the National Crime Victimization Survey. *Archives of General Psychiatry*, 62, 911–21.

Teplin, L.A., Abram, K.M., McClelland, G.M., Dulcan, M.K., and Mericle, A.A. (2002). Psychiatric disorders in youth in juvenile detention. *Archives of General Psychiatry*, 59, 1133–43.

Theobald, D., and Farrington, D.P. (2009). Effects of getting married on offending: Results from a prospective longitudinal survey of males. *European Journal of Criminology*, 6, 496–516.

Theobald, D. and Farrington, D.P. (2010). Should policy implications be drawn from the effects of getting married on offending? *European Journal of Criminology*, 7, 239–47.

Thornberry, T.P. (2005). Explaining multiple patterns of offending across the life course and across generations. *Annals of the American Academy of Political and Social Science*, 602, 156–95.

Thornberry, T.P., Giordano, P.C., Uggen, C., Matsuda, M., Masten, A.S., Bulten, E. and Donker, A.G. (2012). Explanations for offending. In R. Loeber and D.P. Farrington (eds), *From Juvenile Delinquency to Adult Crime: Criminal Careers, Justice Policy and Prevention*. New York: Oxford University Press.

Tong, J. and Farrington, D.P. (2008). Effectiveness of 'reasoning and rehabilitation' in reducing reoffending. *Psicothema*, 20, 20–8.

Transition to Adulthood Alliance (2010). *Young Adults and Criminal Justice: International Norms and Practices*. London: Author.

Truman, J.L. and Rand, M.R. (2010). *Crime Victimization, 2008* (NCJ 231327). Washington, DC: U.S. Department of Justice.

Uggen, C. (2000). Work as a turning point in the life course of criminals: A duration model of age, employment, and recidivism. *American Sociological Review*, 65, 529–46.

Van der Knaap, L.M., Schulze, H-J., Slot, N.W., and Feij, J.A. (2009). Tasks and skills in youth with problem behaviour: Development of a questionnaire. *Vulnerable Children and Youth Studies*, 4, 264–76.

Van der Laan, A.M., and Blom, M. (2006). *Jeugddelinquentie: Risico's en bescherming (Juvenile Delinquency: Risks and Protection)*. The Hague: WODC.

Van der Put, C.E. (2011). Risk and needs assessment for juvenile delinquents. Unpublished doctoral dissertation, Universiteit van Amsterdam, Amsterdam.

Van der Put, C.E., Deković, M., Hoeve, M., Stams, G.J.J.M., Van der Laan, P.H., and Langewouters, F.E.M. (2010). Risk assessment of girls: Are there any sex differences in risk factors for re-offending and in risk profiles? *Crime and Delinquency*. Advance online publication. DOI: 10.1177/0011128710384776.

Van der Rakt, M., Weerman, F., and Need, A. (2005). Delinquent gedrag van jongens en meisjes: Het (anti) sociale kapitaal van vriendschapsrelaties. *Mens en Maatschappij*, 80, 329–54.

Van Wijk, A., Loeber, R., Vermeiren, R., Pardini, D., Bullens, R., and Doreleijers, T. (2005). Violent juvenile offenders compared with violent juvenile nonsex offenders: Explorative findings from the Pittsburgh Youth Study. *Sexual Abuse: A Journal of Research and Treatment*, 17, 333–52.

Vreugdenhil, C. (2003). *Psychiatric Disorders among Incarcerated Male Adolescents in the Netherlands*. Amsterdam: Vrije University (Ph.D. dissertation).

Wasserman, G.A. and McReynolds, L.S. (2011). Contributions to traumatic exposure and posttraumatic stress disorder in juvenile justice youths. *Journal of Traumatic Stress*.

Wasserman, G.A., McReynolds, L.S., Schwalbe, C.S., Keating, J.M., and Jones, S.A. (2010). Psychiatric disorder, comorbidity, and suicidal behavior in juvenile justice youth. *Criminal Justice and Behavior*, 37, 1361–1376.

Wasserman, G.A., Jensen, P.S., Ko, S.J., Cocozza, J., Trupin, E., Angold, A., Cauffman, E., and Grisso, T. (2003). Mental health assessments in juvenile justice: Report on the consensus conference. *Journal of the American Academy of Child and Adolescent Psychiatry*, 42, 752–761.

Wei, E.H., Loeber, R., and Stouthamer-Loeber, M. (2002). How many of the offspring born to teenage fathers are produced by repeat serious delinquents? *Criminal Behaviour and Mental Health*, 12, 83–98.

Welsh, B.C., Lipsey, M.W., Rivara, F.P., Hawkins, J.D., Aos, S., and Peel, M.E. (2012). Promoting change, changing lives: Effective prevention and intervention to reduce serious offending. In R. Loeber and D.P. Farrington (eds), *From Juvenile Delinquency to Adult Crime: Criminal Careers, Justice Policy and Prevention*. New York: Oxford University Press.

Welsh, B.C., Sullivan, C.J., and Olds, D.L. (2010). When early crime prevention goes to scale: A new look at the evidence. *Prevention Science*, 11, 115–125.

White, H.R., Jackson, K.M., and Loeber, R. (2009). Developmental sequences and comorbidity of substance use and violence. In M.D. Krohn and A.J. Lizotte (eds), *Handbook on Crime and Deviance*. Dordrecht: Springer, pp. 434–68.

Witvliet, M., Van Lier, P., Cuijpers, P., and Koot, H.M. (2009). Testing links between childhood positive peer relations and externalizing outcomes through a randomized controlled intervention study. *Journal of Consulting and Clinical Psychology*, 77, 905–915.

Wong, T.M.L., Slotboom, A-M., and Bijleveld, C.C.J.H. (2010). Risk factors for delinquency in adolescent and young adult females: A European review. *European Journal of Criminology*, 7, 266–84.

Zahn, M.A., Day, J.C., Mihalic, S.F., and Tichavsky, L. (2009). Determining what works for girls in the juvenile justice system. *Crime and Delinquency*, 55, 266–93.

Zara, G. and Farrington, D.P. (2009). Childhood and adolescent predictors of late onset criminal careers. *Journal of Youth and Adolescence*, 38, 287–300.

Zara, G. and Farrington, D.P. (2010). A longitudinal analysis of early risk factors for adult-onset offending: What predicts a delayed criminal career. *Criminal Behaviour and Mental Health*, 20, 257–73.

Zhang, Q., Loeber, R., and Stouthamer-Loeber, M. (1997). Developmental trends of delinquent attitudes and behaviors: Replications and synthesis across domains, time, and samples. *Journal of Quantitative Criminology*, 13, 181–215.

Zimmer-Gembeck, M.J. and Skinner, E.A. (2011). Review: The development of coping across childhood and adolescence: An integrative review and critique of research. *International Journal of Behavioral Development*, 35, 1–17.

Appendix: Systems-oriented Interventions in Europe

Terje Ogden and Kristine Amlund Hagen

We propose that intervention programmes and principles that have proven effectiveness in the psychosocial treatment of young delinquents might also be good candidates for the prevention of recidivism in older offenders. Most of the interventions that have turned out to be effective in the treatment of youth delinquency have been developed and tested in the US and later implemented in several European countries (Ferrer-Wreder et al., 2004; see also Deković et al., Chapter 9, this volume; Boendermaker, Deković and Asscher, Chapter 10, this volume). The Norwegian replication studies of Parent Management Training (Ogden and Amlund Hagen, 2008) and Multisystemic Therapy (MST) (Ogden and Amlund Hagen, 2006) illustrate the potential transatlantic relevance of such programmes for European countries. Even if family- and systems-oriented treatment programmes typically serve young delinquents in the family and community context, they may also be of relevance to older offenders.

Meta-analyses of interventions for older adolescents and young adults in the US indicate that rehabilitation treatment is more effective than correctional intervention in preventing recidivism, and effective rehabilitative interventions seem to have much in common with systemic programmes with proven effectiveness for younger persons (Lipsey, 2009; Lipsey and Cullen, 2007). The ecological and systemic approach described in this chapter also emphasizes the importance of securing programme sustainability and avoiding programme drift by encompassing systems for large-scale implementation, and for routine monitoring of treatment integrity and outcomes (Ogden et al., 2009).

Theoretical Basis of the Systems Perspective

During recent decades, Bronfenbrenner's (1979) conceptualization of the ecology of human development has contributed to the understanding of the development of antisocial behaviour. His ecological model states that the social environment consists of different levels or systems of influences, each varying in the proximity to the individual (for example, micro-, meso-, and exo- and macro-systems). His taxonomy of the social environment has contributed to the successful linking of psychological and sociological perspectives on the development and desistance of crime and delinquency. Along with the social ecological perspective, the transactional model also has influenced the development of systems-oriented interventions. The transactional model posits that interactions between individuals and context over time develop into patterns. These patterns or transactions can be either adaptive and constructive or maladaptive and dysfunctional. What maintains stability or persistence is neither the individual nor the context alone, but rather the relationship between the two. As such, psychopathology or dysfunction can be said to reside in *the relationship* between a person and his or her environment. The systems perspective takes into account the many ecologies in which an individual is embedded and the transactional nature of the relationship between these. It has thus been highly influential in the treatment of serious antisocial behaviour in adolescents and young adults. The systems perspective embodies a holistic approach to the understanding of individual development and of the social context in which development unfolds. A systems perspective facilitates the identification of risk and protective factors present within and between the individual, the relationships, and the local ecology, and as such helps direct intervention efforts (Ferrer-Wreder et al., 2004). Several of the theories on the development of criminal behaviour and drug use recognize that both distal factors, such as the values and functions of the wider community and society at large, and proximal factors, such as parents and peers, affect individual development, directly or indirectly. This widening of the focus on behavioural development is a natural consequence of research findings suggesting that, as children become adolescents and young adults, influences from peers, school, and other parts of their social network, increase (Capaldi et al., 2002). Many studies have examined and analysed the family system and other social networks in which adolescents and their families are embedded in order to identify how risk and protective factors work together in the development of antisocial behaviour (Swenson et al., 2005). Results from these investigations have laid the basis for the development of several programmes aimed at ameliorating antisocial or criminal behaviour that have been implemented in Norway.

The Norwegian Nationwide Implementation of Empirically Supported Treatments

In 1998, a governmental initiative was launched in Norway with the goal of increasing the treatment competence of Norwegian practitioners in the reduction of antisocial or delinquent behaviour. The initiative also aimed at increasing the capacity of the service system to address the challenges of violent and criminal behaviour, including drug-related crime and delinquency. Moreover, the government wanted to decrease the use of incarcerations and placements out of home due to serious behaviour problems. Influenced by the recent developments in research on antisocial behaviour, empirically supported family and community treatment programmes were selected. The rationale was that empirically supported therapies (EST) are efficacious with a delineated population (Chambless and Hollon, 1998).

Part of the initiative was devoted to early intervention and prevention by adopting and implementing the Oregon model of Parent Management Training (Ogden et al., 2005) and part of the initiative targeted adolescents by implementing Multisystemic Therapy (MST) (Ogden et al., 2008). The project initiative resulted in the establishment of the Norwegian Centre for Child Behavioural Development (NCCBD). The centre has separate departments for child and youth development, both of which are responsible for the training, supervision and ongoing support to respective local sites. The research department is conducting research on the outcomes and processes of the interventions, as well as carrying out longitudinal studies on child development in general.

The implementation of the adopted ESTs in Norway has now been going on for more than a decade, which has allowed for the study of transatlantic replication and investigation of the application of the programmes. Norway was probably the first European country to adopt, implement and evaluate ESTs on a large scale, and the transportation of EST across geographical and linguistic borders has been a source of inspiration to researchers, scholars and practitioners in other European countries, many of whom have turned to the NCCBD for guidance and training.

In 1999, representatives of all 19 county health directors in Norway accepted an invitation from the government to participate in the nationwide implementation of MST (Henggeler et al., 1998) and Parent Management Training–Oregon model (PMTO) (Reid, Patterson and Snyder, 2002). MST targeted antisocial behaviour in adolescents aged 13–17 and PMTO represented an early family intervention approach for children aged 12 or younger.

The Implementation and Dissemination of PMTO in Norway

The Oregon model of Parent Management Training (PMTO) was developed by Gerald Patterson, Marion Forgatch and their colleagues at the Oregon Social Learning Center (OSLC) in order to train parents to change their preadolescent child's antisocial behaviour in the home (Patterson, 1982; Patterson, Reid and Dishion, 1992; Forgatch, 1994). When the approach was introduced in Norway there were few training opportunities for practitioners to learn the intervention. The first regular practitioner training programme of PMTO was therefore developed in Norway as a collaborative enterprise between the programme developers, Forgatch and Patterson, and the national implementation team for children led by Elisabeth Askeland from the NCCBD (Ogden et al., 2005). Included in the training programme was a PMTO handbook based on Patterson's (1982) social interaction and coercion model and on protocols from previous OSLC clinical trials (Forgatch, 1994). This handbook outlined the principles, procedures and core programme components of the PMTO (Askeland, Christiansen and Solholm, 2005). Forgatch and her colleagues at the OSLC provided an extensive 18-month training programme for Norwegian trainees, resulting in the certification of 30 candidates from all health regions of Norway. This first generation of certified PMTO therapists was central to the process of training, coaching and supervising succeeding generations of therapists. For each new generation of certified PMTO therapists, expertise in the training, supervision and certification of therapists has gradually been anchored in Norway, so that today all aspects of PMTO in Norway are handled completely by the national implementation team at the NCCBD, which provides training, regular supervision, training protocols and additional materials and technical support. By 2008, 208 therapists had been trained and certified in Norway; and on a yearly basis, approximately 1,500 families are currently receiving PMTO.

A randomized controlled trial of PMTO in Norway was conducted with 112 children aged 12 or younger and their parents recruited for this effectiveness study through regular child welfare and child mental health services (Ogden and Amlund Hagen, 2008). The families were randomly assigned to PMTO or to regular services, and were treated individually in a mean number of 26 sessions. Parents who received PMTO reported fewer externalizing behaviour problems in their children, and the children's teachers reported a higher level of social competence at post assessment compared to the children who had received regular services. Parents in the PMTO group were also more competent in setting limits or disciplining their children according to coded observations of video recordings performed by trained coders. PMTO was particularly effective in the treatment of problem behaviour in children who were aged eight or younger at intake to treatment, evidenced by teacher ratings of externalizing and total problem behaviour and by daily parent observational reports over three successive days. In a path model, the indirect effect of treatment condition was found to be that competent limit setting by parents predicted more compliance, fewer negative interactions initiated by the children, and less externalizing problem behaviour. The evaluation of the families' satisfaction with the treatment showed that 77 per cent of the parents in the PMTO group would recommend the treatment to others who might be in need of it, compared to 38 per cent of the comparison families (Ogden and Amlund Hagen, 2008).

The Implementation of Multisystemic Therapy

In the period 1999–2003, 25 MST teams were established in all regions of Norway. Today, 23 teams are still operating and have become a standard part of the specialized national Child Welfare Services. The Norwegian national development team for adolescents has now taken over most of the training, supervision and consultation of the MST teams, and has acquired the status of 'network partner' of MST services, indicating an independent role in the process of maintaining MST competence and fidelity.

Randomized controlled trials (RCT) of MST in Norway have been conducted at post treatment (Ogden and Halliday-Boykins, 2004) and at a two-year follow-up (Ogden and Amlund Hagen, 2006). As was the case with the RCT of PMTO, these studies tested the *effectiveness* of MST, as treatment was delivered via existing child and family services. Moreover, the sustainability of MST has been investigated

(Ogden, Amlund Hagen and Andersen, 2007), as well as gender differences in treatment response (Ogden and Amlund Hagen, 2009). Finally, a study on the effect of MST on drug-abusing adolescents (Holth et al., 2011) is underway.

The effectiveness study of MST was conducted during the first year of implementation and included 100 adolescents aged 13–17 and their families who were randomly assigned to MST or regular Child Welfare Services. This RCT was one of the first independent RCTs of MST not conducted by the developers of MST. In order to make it an independent study, the Norwegian researchers were not involved in the training or supervision of the MST therapists nor were they in any way directly involved with the treatment of families. The results suggested that the positive clinical outcomes in the US were replicated in Norway (Ogden and Halliday-Boykins, 2004): MST prevented placement out of home to a greater extent than regular services, and was associated with a decrease in externalizing and internalizing problems and an increase in social competence. Additionally, MST families gave significantly more positive evaluations of the treatment than did the families receiving regular services. The follow-up study conducted two years after intake showed that MST was still more effective than regular services in reducing out-of-home placement and externalizing and internalizing problems at three of the four sites included in the study (Ogden and Amlund Hagen, 2006).

The sustainability of the effectiveness of MST across participant groups in the second year of operation was examined in a group of adolescents who were referred to MST in the second year of programme operation (Ogden, Amlund Hagen and Andersen, 2007). The aim of the study was to investigate whether the effects of MST on this second group of adolescents would be equivalent to those reported in the earlier RCT. Pre- and post-treatment assessments were conducted at two sites with a group of 105 youths, of whom 55 received MST in the programme's second year of operation. MST clinical outcomes in the second year of programme operation matched and – for key indices of antisocial behaviour – surpassed those achieved during the first year.

Gender as a moderator of clinical outcomes of MST and whether girls and boys differed in referral symptoms (including co-morbidity) and background characteristics were examined in a recent study (Ogden and Amlund Hagen, 2009). Participants were 117 Norwegian adolescent girls (35 per cent) and boys (65 per cent), ranging in age from 13–17, referred to MST treatment in the first and second year of the programme's operation. Results suggested that boys were significantly more likely than girls to be referred because of criminal offences and domestic violence. Girls, on the other hand, were more likely to be referred because of statutory offences and drug use. As far as benefiting from the programme, MST appeared flexible enough to be equally effective for girls and boys. In line with the recommendations from the programme developers, the adolescents who were referred to MST in Norway were aged 17 or younger in order to be eligible for treatment (Henggeler et al., 1998). In the next section we address the question of how to intervene with individuals older than age 17.

Multisystemic Treatment Beyond Age 17

Most of the clinical outcome studies of MST, including the Norwegian trials, are limited to adolescents who were aged 17 or younger at intake to treatment. This age limitation is in some ways arbitrary. Loeber and Farrington (2012) stated that the formal distinction between the juvenile and the adult at age 18 is not reflected in a similar distinction in human development. For some youths, the transition from adolescence to adulthood is characterized by important life changes (for example, entering the work force or having children of their own). For others, this youth–adult divide may be experienced inconsequentially in their daily lives. In other words, age alone is not a good indicator of maturity. For example, many young people well into their 20s continue to live with their parents. In Norway, about 53 per cent of young adults in the age range 20–24 have the same address as their parents (Statistics Norway, 2010). For older delinquent youths, the transition to young adulthood will result in their 'case' being transferred from the responsibility of Child Welfare to the jurisdiction of the Social Services or the legal system. With increasing age criminal offending is more often handled by the adult justice system rather than by child welfare services. Because developmental needs and challenges do not change abruptly or become qualitatively different after age 18, some of the systemic intervention programmes for adolescents presented in this chapter are likely to be effective for this older age group as well. According to Statistics Norway, the cohorts ranging in age from 18–20 and 20–25 have the greatest proportion of lawbreakers than any other age group. Intervening with this group of young adults may therefore yield substantial public gains. But no formal evaluations have so far been undertaken in Norway of MST or parent training programmes for adolescents older than age 17.

Model Programmes Translated to Generic Programmes

In a meta-analysis, Lipsey (2009) set out to identify the types of interventions associated with the greatest reductions in recidivism and from this investigation help articulate the general principles of 'what works'. The meta-analysis included 361 primary research reports (90 per cent from the US) on interventions intended to reduce subsequent delinquency of adolescents aged 12–21 both within and outside of the juvenile correctional system. Few empirically supported model programmes are used and studied in the correctional system, and so very few of these programmes were included and studied in this analysis. Lipsey (2009) defined a therapeutic programme approach as an attempt at engaging youth in a supportive, constructive process of change. Among the therapeutic approaches, counselling and skills training were more effective than control-oriented models. In accordance with previous findings of Andrews and colleagues (Andrews and Bonta, 2006), Lipsey's analysis showed that cognitive-behavioural treatment, social learning, and skill-building interventions were effective, with cognitive-behavioural therapy having the largest mean effect size. Generic programmes included counselling interventions, skill building, restorative programmes and multiple services. Although generic programmes were effective in some cases, their effectiveness depended on the degree of implementation quality and whether they were directed towards high-risk offenders. It also turned out that the interventions, regardless of their status as model or generic programmes, were equally effective for younger and older juveniles, males and females, and for populations of different ethnic backgrounds.

Even if generic programmes are proven effective, there is the problem of getting them ready for large-scale implementation. The advantages of model programmes such as MST are that these programmes are well structured and predefined: they have well-developed systems for training and supervision of practitioners; routines for pre-evaluation of treatment sites, including guidelines for local implementation; standardized routines for the measurement of treatment adherence and for monitoring treatment outcomes; as well as regular site evaluation of programme operation. The Norwegian study of MST highlighted the importance of treatment fidelity for model programmes as well, as treatment adherence varied across sites. The site with the lowest treatment adherence level had the least positive outcomes and the site with the highest scores demonstrated the best results.

Combining 'Top-down' and 'Bottom-up' Implementation Strategies

A case study of the national implementation strategy in Norway suggested that well-established treatment programmes, such as PMTO and MST, were implemented with a high degree of programme sustainability over a period of ten years (Ogden et al., 2009). The implementation strategy used can be described as a combination of a 'top-down' and a 'bottom-up' approach (see Figure A1).

Ferrer-Wreder et al. (2004) emphasize that top-down strategies place a great deal of confidence in research-based methods and competence. This linear model of dissemination of knowledge from researchers to practitioners has an expert orientation that might discourage involvement and create counterforces at the local level. Practitioners seem to tire of top-down initiatives that disappear as soon as the official implementation phase is over. Practitioners' lack of enthusiasm and feelings of ownership may impair the programme's utility and institutionalization beyond the official demonstrations phase. For this reason, Ferrer-Wreder et al. suggest that sustainability should be a principle concern throughout the implementation process (see also Glasgow, Vogt and Boles, 1999; Glasgow, Lichtenstein and Marcus, 2003). This is exactly what bottom-up strategies are taking care of. A bottom-up approach characterizes local initiatives that tend to create sustained engagement and ownership among practitioners. By including local stakeholders from the beginning of the implementation process, this approach seems to increase the practitioners' programme investment and to promote a sense of mastery and commitment. But the approach also has its shortcomings, which become evident

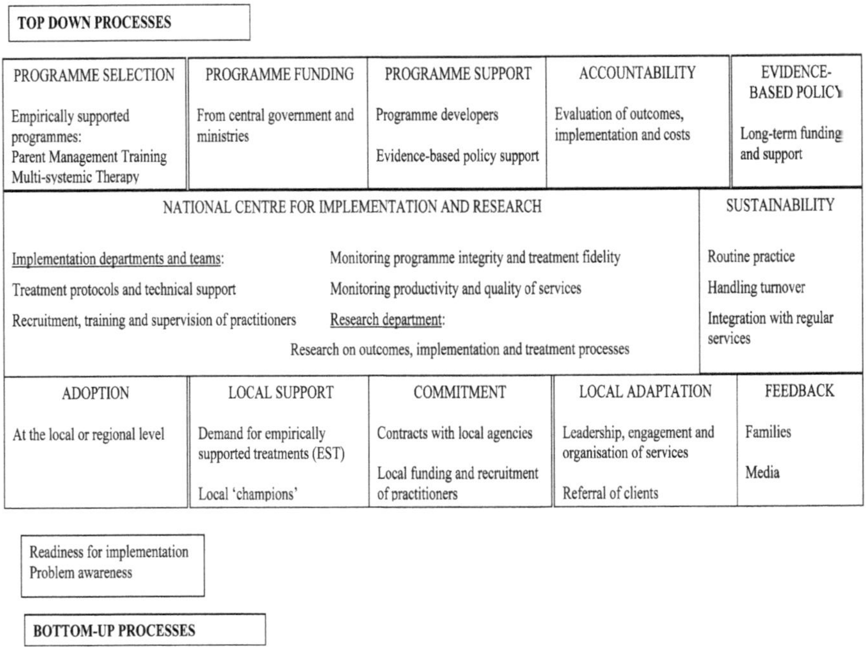

Figure A.1 National implementation as a combination of top-down and bottom-up processes

when local decisions or priorities go against research-based knowledge. This might result in programme drift and reduced programme effectiveness.

The tension between the top-down and bottom-up strategies can be handled by combining them in a hybrid approach that includes aspects of both models (Ferrer-Wreder et al., 2004). Top-down initiatives tend to place programme control in the hands of experts, while bottom-up initiatives are based on shared control between programme implementers and local stakeholders. In this combined approach local groups and organizations take part in the decisions about programme adoption and implementation that match their problem awareness and readiness for change.

In the Norwegian project, the services at the regional and county municipal level were invited to participate in the collaborative process in which the selection of programmes was made by experts at the national level, but the decision to adopt the programmes was made by local stakeholders. Interventions might draw on a large body of research knowledge, and several well-validated treatment programmes are available. In the Norwegian implementation project this knowledge base seemed to be acknowledged by both implementers and practitioners as a common basis of their mutual efforts to improve practice. In addition, before the implementation of new programmes and the training of candidates were started, site assessments were carried out in the municipalities and contracts stating the mutual responsibility of the development teams from the NCCBD and the local authorities were signed. The

Norwegian experience also highlighted the importance of establishing a national self-sustaining implementation unit in order to secure sustainability of programme operations and treatment fidelity at the regional, county, and municipal level.

Challenges in the Dissemination and Implementation of Model Programmes

Several challenges were overcome during the implementation of the MST and PMTO programmes in Norway, particularly in the initial phases. The first was related to controversy concerning evidence-based programmes and there was a general discussion about the actual contribution of the programmes to the improvement of practice. Some of the most prevalent objections were reflected in a report from a conference on the development of evidence-based practice in the Child Welfare Services (Fossestøl and Enehaug, 2008). According to this report, evidence-based practice created new forms of knowledge that reduced the value of clinical reflection and competence based on experience and practice. Critics claimed that the 'relationship' was more important than the 'evidence' and that the practitioners had to be more important than the programmes. Some practitioners opposed the new manual-driven programmes, stating that they were a threat to professional autonomy and the principle of freedom to choose methods of treatment. Although the opponents of evidence-based practice have dominated the debate in Norway, as in other countries, their objections and counterarguments seem to have had little impact on the development of evidence-based practice. And even if there still are differences of opinion about the relevance and value of evidence-based programmes, the positive experiences and feedback from practitioners and families seem to balance the opposition and criticism.

Second, at the system level, funding often represents a major obstacle to the implementation and maintenance of programmes. The financial support from the Ministry of Child and Family Affairs was crucial for the programme training, supervision, and research of MST and PMTO in Norway. Only to a very small extent did local services have to make a shift in funding from existing resources (Ogden et al., 2008). A permanent training programme and supervision network was necessary in order to handle turnover of therapists and to maintain both competence and treatment fidelity. This was secured by long-term funding from several ministries and the establishment of the Norwegian Centre for Child Behavioural Development, a permanent link coordinating research, policy and practice.

Third, at the organizational level, some of the local leaders were not prepared for the new demands that were put on them and their agencies with regard to practical routines for recruiting, training and supporting evidence-based treatment programmes. And there are still great variations in how much leaders of local agencies and regional services have adapted their leadership style to the needs and demands of evidence-based practice.

Fourth, the new programmes also challenged the traditional long-term strategy of placing children and youth out of home in institutions or foster homes for long periods of time. According to the principle of social inclusion, children and youth should to a great extent be treated within their family and local environment. This increased the pressure on their social networks, including families, schools and neighbourhoods, to be supportive and caring, and some still claimed that it would be better to incarcerate the young offenders (Ogden et al., 2008).

Fifth, at the clinical level, the lack of explicit therapeutic skills also turned out to be a challenge. The new programmes expected practitioners to learn clinical skills through role play and apply them to training situations and therapy sessions. The focus on social learning theory, particularly in the PMTO programme, did not match the theoretical orientation and training of several of the candidates. They also had to accept supervision based on video recordings of their therapies (PMTO) and in MST feedback from families on the therapists' treatment adherence was collected on a regular basis. Most therapists gradually adapted to the skills-oriented approach and the increased transparency of the therapy process, but they also enjoyed the advantages of learning how to analyse micro-social processes in the families during training and treatment.

Among the factors that have contributed to the long-term sustainability and effectiveness of MST and PMTO in Norway, the following seem to be most important: (a) a genuine interest and commitment at the political and administrative level for the national implementation of evidence-based programmes; (b) increased interest among practitioners for evidence-based practice; (c) establishing a self-sustaining national centre for implementation and research; (d) ability of the programme developers to support the implementation and research efforts; and (e) positive feedback from families and positive media feedback (Ogden et al., 2009).

Translation of Model Programmes to Europe and Across North America

Most of the model treatment programmes targeting antisocial behaviour in adolescence have been developed and tested in North America and many of them have been successfully transported to Europe (overviews in Ferrer-Wreder et al., 2004; Van Yperen and Boendermaker, 2008). Multisystemic Therapy (MST) is perhaps the programme most widely disseminated in Europe, including in Norway, Sweden, Denmark, the United Kingdom and the Netherlands. European replication studies have thus shed some light on the transportability of a systemic programme and its effectiveness outside the US. The encouraging results obtained in the Norwegian clinical outcome study attested to the ability of the MST programme to be generalized across cultures and demonstrated that the treatment model's success was not unique to American clients. Still, the validity of generalized US findings has been questioned due to differences between the US and European countries in social, political, cultural and economic contexts, and in the organization and availability of mental health and welfare services (Asscher et al., 2007). Differences may also exist in the type and amount of risk factors to which young delinquents are exposed, such as differences in poverty, violence, crime rates, and the availability of drugs and guns. Norway and Sweden have no juvenile justice system and the age of criminal responsibility is higher than in the US (age 15 in Norway). The services targeting children who commit crimes and abuse drugs are more treatment oriented than punitive, and most young delinquents are kept out of the justice system and taken into the care of the Child Welfare Services. In randomized controlled trials, treatment-as-usual (TAU) groups in the US are often exposed to risk factors that are both more severe and numerous than the TAU groups in Scandinavian countries. Compared to Norway and Sweden, the prevalence of stressors such as neighbourhoods with high crime rates and substance abuse are more common in the US, which might stimulate pro-violent attitudes and increase the availability of illegal guns and exposure to antisocial role models (Löfholm et al., 2009). The regular services to which MST was compared in Norway were likely more comprehensive and treatment oriented than the regular services offered to comparison groups in previous MST trials in the US. In the US, TAU often consists of probation office visits with referral to social services when deemed necessary. In Norway, 'usual' services involve a broad array of social services and mental health treatment, including placement in institutions, and in-home services.

The clinical outcome study of MST in Sweden showed fewer encouraging results than the Norwegian trial both at post treatment and at follow-up two years after intake. The Swedish results suggested that MST was equally effective but not more effective than the services already being provided (Löfholm et al., 2009). The authors speculated that this lack of increased effectiveness was attributable to the differences in the effectiveness of regular services. They found the positive changes in the MST group to be comparable in Sweden and in the US, but also that the Swedish regular services group improved considerably during the intervention period. The results also indicated that the transport of MST to Norway had been more successful than to Sweden. The fact that MST was implemented nationally in Norway, with economic and administrative support from the Ministry of Child and Family Affairs (the top-down part of the strategy), is probably the chief explanation for this difference in implementation success. In addition, the implementation was supported by the NCCBD, which also carried out research and installed a comprehensive quality assurance system. In Sweden, however, each of the municipalities was separately responsible for the installation and quality assurance, and was as such more reliant on transatlantic support and supervision from MST services.

The lessons learned from these studies are that it is the relative effectiveness of interventions that is measured in clinical trials, and that these differences are likely somewhat dependent on the level and quality of services already provided. Even if alternative interventions have been developed in European countries to some extent (for example, in the Netherlands), few are based on an articulated treatment theory and few have been properly evaluated (Van Yperen and Boendermaker, 2008). In several of the European countries it might be necessary to evaluate the effectiveness of established services before they are compared to new interventions such as MST. This requires that the contents and procedures of regular services and treatments are more clearly defined and described as regards core intervention components, length and intensity of treatment, and indicators of treatment integrity. In some cases, testing for equivalency (that is, equal effectiveness of interventions) may be more relevant than testing for superiority, particularly if ordinary services are considered to be well established and effective (Chambless and Hollon, 1998).

There are still several obstacles to conducting randomized controlled trials in European countries, particularly within the juvenile justice system. This topic was elaborated on by Asscher et al. (2007), who described some of the general challenges in securing the collaboration of service delivery organizations, practitioners, and families. Legal issues and the complexity of the juvenile justice system, for example, make it difficult to establish the randomization procedure, and resistance towards both the RCT procedure and ESTs in the field may diminish the number of referrals, increase staff turnover, and reduce the ability of the institutions and the participating families involved to cooperate (Asscher et al., 2007).

The Service System Level

Systems-oriented programmes, strategies and methods are mainly developed at the clinical or practical level within adolescent mental health and social welfare services. Systems-oriented interventions developed in the US seem to hold promise for European samples as well, and research has indicated that age is not an important moderator within the range of adolescence and young adulthood. As can be seen from the meta-analyses of Lipsey and colleagues (Lipsey and Cullen, 2007; Lipsey, 2009), the US has been less successful in implementing ESTs within the correctional system than within the mental health or child welfare systems. When programmes have been shown to be effective, the next challenge is to implement them into routine practice while maintaining a high level of programme integrity and treatment adherence. In this process, intervention research has increasingly focused on the change mechanisms that operate within programmes (LaGreca, Silverman and Lochman, 2009). Important mediators and change mechanisms across programmes include informal social support and control in social networks, improved family communication and cohesion, decreased contact with deviant peers, increased contact with pro-social peers, schooling or steady work, and a stable place of living in the least restrictive environment (Weersing and Weisz, 2002). What needs to be done next is to develop implementation teams or organizations that have the support of regional or national stakeholders. These can support the implementation process by offering training and supervision and manage the monitoring of treatment adherence and outcomes on a routine basis. This kind of centralized support for local implementation can help mitigate problems related to maintaining programmes with high fidelity and turnover of staff. Finally, a centralized research unit will likely help secure empirically based improvements and integration of interventions.

At the service system level, the challenge is to establish and maintain interventions that are likely to reach a heterogeneous target group, that will be adopted by widely different organizations, and that will be delivered by staffs that vary greatly in training and expertise. Moreover, the interventions should result in replicable and long-term results at a reasonable cost. A solution to this challenge is offered by Glasgow and co-authors (Glasgow et al., 1999, 2003). These authors address how interventions are adopted and how they function depending on the organizations and practitioners who are going to apply the intervention in their regular practice. Their acronym, RE-AIM, stands for reach, efficacy/effectiveness, adoption, implementation, and maintenance and cost. The target population should be defined, and the number of eligible persons actually receiving the intervention (the participant rate) should be registered. Even a highly efficacious intervention will have a small public health impact if it only reaches a few individuals (Biglan and Ogden, 2008). In addition to information about the participant rate, Glasgow et al. (2003) emphasize the importance of keeping track of the extent to which the intervention is adopted and maintained by relevant practice organizations. They also stress the value of registering the characteristics and participant rate of those who eventually will be delivering services to the clients. Sustainability of programmes is both a question of maintenance of behavioural change in the target group and maintenance of the programme activities in the relevant practice environments. Glasgow et al. (2003) therefore require reports on continuities and discontinuities at the organizational level and how the intervention is adapted or modified when the effectiveness study is terminated. Too little is known about what influences organizations as a whole to adopt and implement new interventions. Therefore, the question remains as to how agencies and organizations are motivated to adopt, implement and maintain new intervention programmes. Increased focus on large-scale implementation of interventions also means increased focus on how many of the adolescents eligible for treatment are actually being served, and on the prevalence of juvenile delinquency from one age cohort to the next. Even if programmes are implemented with fidelity, they may still, over time, be subject to programme drift that can lead to a reduction of treatment adherence and loss of effectiveness. Therefore, there is also a need for a surveillance system for monitoring the prevalence of target problems in the defined populations (Biglan and Ogden, 2008).

Conclusions

When comparing Europe to the US, Bullock (1992) states that continental Europe traditionally applies a philosophical and logical rather than empirical approach to youth problems. However, Britain is an exception in that it has a long history of linking empirical findings and policy. In the US, demonstration projects and outcome studies that sell programmes fit in well with its enterprise culture. This may explain why most evidence-based programmes are developed and tested in efficacy studies in the US before they are transported to other countries such as Norway or the Netherlands. There are also some indications suggesting that randomized controlled trials are more accepted and less controversial among practitioners and researchers in the US than in European countries. The obstacles and resistance toward RCTs reported from the Netherlands (Asscher et al., 2007) are also experienced in other European countries (Ferrer-Wreder et al., 2004; Nutley, Walter and Davis, 2007; Ogden et al., 2008), which might make this kind of research sparse and appear less attractive. Generally, it seems that it is far more difficult to carry out the operations of implementing and evaluating new model programmes than to succeed in the actual treatment of adolescents and families. At the same time, structural forces seem to be at work across both continents that make juvenile crime and delinquency a major challenge on both sides of the Atlantic. To some extent this also indicates that the risk and protective factors targeted in several of the evidence-based treatment programmes operate similarly in most Western countries.

The experiences from Norway could serve as a model and inspiration for large-scale implementation of evidence-based practice combining 'top-down' and 'bottom-up' initiatives both in the child and adolescent services and in the correctional system. The message from research is that systems-oriented intervention programmes such as MST might be applicable in efforts to prevent recidivism among both adolescents and young adults. Potentially effective interventions should be based on sound theory and extensive research and simultaneously target multiple social systems including family, peers, school and workplace. Moreover, therapeutic approaches that motivate, engage and support the young person in the process of change seem to be more effective than correctional sanctions based on external control and coercion.

In summary, the challenge that we face today is the large-scale implementation of theory- and research-based programmes for the psychosocial treatment of young delinquents to reduce their recidivism. The goal is to have high fidelity programmes available nationwide, evaluate the programmes in field trials, and monitor them as they are implemented in regular practice to prevent recidivism of young people and reduce the need for sanctions by the justice system.

References

Andrews, D.A., and Bonta, J. (2006). *The Psychology of Criminal Conduct* (4th edn). Newark, NJ: Lexis/Nexis.

Askeland, E., Christiansen, T., and Solholm, R. (2005). *PMTO Handbook.* Oslo, Norwegian Centre for Child Behavioural Development.

Asscher, J.J., Dekovic, M., Van der Laan, P.H., Prins, P.J.M., and Van Arum, S. (2007). Implementing randomized experiments in criminal justice settings: An evaluation of multi-systemic therapy in the Netherland. *Journal of Experimental Criminology*, 3, 113–29.

Biglan, T., and Ogden, T. (2008). The evolution of the evidence based movement. *European Journal of Behavior Analysis*, 9, 81–95.
Bronfenbrenner, U. (1979). Contexts of child rearing: Problems and prospects. *American Psychologist*, 34, 844–50.
Bullock, R. (1992). A framework for making international comparisons of services for adolescents. In R. Bullock (ed.), *Problem Adolescents: An International View.* London: Whiting and Birch, pp. 1–10.
Capaldi, D., DeGarmo, D., Patterson, G.R., and Forgatch, M. (2002). Contextual risk across the early life span and association with antisocial behavior. In J.B. Reid, G.R. Patterson and J. Snyder (eds), *Antisocial Behavior in Children and Adolescents: A Developmental Analysis and Model for Intervention.* Washington, DC: American Psychological Association, pp. 123–45.
Chambless, D.L., and Hollon, S.D. (1998). Defining empirically supported therapies. *Journal of Consulting and Clinical Psychology*, 66, 7–18.
Ferrer-Wreder, L., Stattin, H., Lorente, C.C., Tubman, J.G., and Adamson, L. (2004). *Successful Prevention and Youth Development Programs across Borders*. New York: Kluwer Academic.
Forgatch, M.S. (1994). *Parenting through Change: A Programmed Intervention Curriculum for Groups of Single Mothers*. Eugene, OR: Oregon Social Learning Center.
Fossestøl, K., and Enehaug, H. (2008). *Konservative byråkrater eller avantgardistiske byråkrater (Conservative practitioners or avantgarde bureaucrats)*. Unpublished report. Oslo, Work Research Institute.
Glasgow, R.E., Lichtenstein, E., and Marcus, A.C. (2003). Why don't we see more translation of health promotion research to practice? Rethinking the efficacy-to-effectiveness transition. *American Journal of Public Health*, 93, 1261–7.
Glasgow, R.E., Vogt, T.M., and Boles, S.M. (1999). Evaluating the public health impact of health promotion interventions: The RE-AIM framework. *American Journal of Public Health*, 89, 1322–7.
Henggeler, S.W., Schoenwald, S.K., Borduin, C.M., Rowland, M.D., and Cunningham, P.B. (1998). *Multisystemic Treatment of Antisocial Behaviour in Children and Adolescents*. New York: The Guilford Press.
Holth, P., Torsheim, T., Sheidow, A.J., Ogden, T., and Henggeler, S.W. (2011). Intensive quality assurance of therapist adherence to contingency management for adolescent substance use problems. *Journal of Child and Adolescent Substance Abuse*, 20, 1–6.
La Greca, A.M., Silverman, W.K., and Lochman J.E. (2009). Moving beyond efficacy and effectiveness in child and adolescent intervention research. *Journal of Consulting and Clinical Psychology*, 77, 373–82.
Lipsey, M.W. (2009). The primary factors that characterize effective interventions with juvenile offenders: A meta-analytic overview. *Victims and Offenders*, 4, 124–47.

Lipsey, M.W., and Cullen, F.T. (2007). The effectiveness of correctional rehabilitation: A review of systematic reviews. *The Annual Review of Law and Social Science*. 3, 297–320.

Loeber, R., and Farrington, D.P. (2012). *From Juvenile Delinquency to Adult Crime: Criminal Careers, Justice Policy and Prevention*. New York: Oxford University Press.

Löfholm, C.A., Olsson, T., Sundell, K., and Hansson, K. (2009). Multisystemic therapy with conduct-disordered young people: Stability of treatment outcomes two years after intake. *Evidence and Policy*, 5, 373–97.

Nutley, S., Walter, I., and Davis, H. (2007). *Using evidence: How Research can Inform Public Services*. Bristol: The Policy Press.

Ogden, T., and Amlund Hagen, K. (2006). Multisystemic Treatment of serious behaviour problems in youth: Sustainability of effectiveness two years after intake. *Child and Adolescent Mental Health*, 11, 142–9.

Ogden, T., and Amlund Hagen, K. (2008). Treatment effectiveness of Parent Management Training in Norway: A randomized controlled trial of children with conduct problems. *Journal of Consulting and Clinical Psychology*, 76, 607–21.

Ogden, T., and Amlund Hagen, K. (2009). What works for whom? Gender differences in intake characteristics and treatment benefit of Multisystemic Therapy. *Journal of Adolescence*, 32, 1425–35.

Ogden, T., Amlund Hagen, K., and Andersen, O. (2007). Sustainability of the effectiveness of a programme of multisystemic treatment (MST) across participant groups in the second year of operation. *Journal of Children's Services*, 2, 4–14.

Ogden, T., Amlund Hagen, K., Askeland, E., and Christensen, B. (2009). Implementing and evaluating evidence-based treatments of conduct problems in children and youth in Norway. *Research on Social Work Practice*, 19, 582–91.

Ogden, T., Christensen, B., Sheidow, A., and Holth, P. (2008). Bridging the gap between science and practice: The effective nationwide transport of MST programs in Norway. *Journal of Children and Adolescence Substance Abuse*, 17, 93–109.

Ogden, T., Forgatch, M., Askeland, E., Patterson, G.R., and Bullock, B. (2005). Implementation of Parent Management Training at the national level: The case of Norway. *Journal of Social Work Practice*, 19, 317–29.

Ogden, T., and Halliday-Boykins, C.A. (2004). Multisystemic treatment of antisocial adolescents in Norway: Replication of clinical outcomes outside of the US. *Child and Adolescent Mental Health*, 9, 76–82.

Patterson, G.R. (1982). *A social learning approach*. Vol. 3. *Coercive Family Process*. Eugene, OR: Castalia Publishing Company.

Patterson, G.R., Reid, J., and Dishion, T. (1992). *Antisocial Boys: A Social Interactional Approach*, Vol. 4. Eugene, OR: Castalia Publishing Company.

Reid, J.B., Patterson, G.R., and Snyder, J.J. (2002). *Antisocial Behavior in Children and Adolescents: A Developmental Analysis and a Model for Intervention*. Washington, DC: American Psychological Association.

Statistics Norway, 2010, at www.sssb.no, accessed 9 February 2012.
Swenson, C.C., Henggeler, S.W., Taylor, I.S., and Addison, O.W. (2005). *Multisystemic Therapy and Neighborhood Partnerships: Reducing Adolescent Violence and Substance Abuse.* New York: The Guilford Press.
Van Yperen, T., and Boendermaker, L. (2008). Interventions. In R. Loeber, N.W. Slot, P.H. van der Laan and M. Hoeve (eds), *Tomorrow's Criminals: The Development of Child Delinquency and Effective Interventions.* Farnham: Ashgate.
Weersing, V.R., and Weisz, J.R. (2002). Mechanisms of action in youth psychotherapy. *Journal of Child Psychology and Psychiatry*, 43, 3–29.

Index

For Product Safety Concerns and Information please contact our EU
representative GPSR@taylorandfrancis.com
Taylor & Francis Verlag GmbH, Kaufingerstraße 24, 80331 München, Germany

www.ingramcontent.com/pod-product-compliance
Ingram Content Group UK Ltd.
Pitfield, Milton Keynes, MK11 3LW, UK
UKHW020024200926
475702UK00014B/2052
* 9 7 8 1 1 3 8 2 7 4 4 5 7 *